A Regimental History
of the
Covenanting Armies
1639 - 1651

EDWARD M FURGOL

JOHN DONALD PUBLISHERS LTD
EDINBURGH

For my parents

ISBN 0 85976 194 0

Phototypeset by Burns & Harris Ltd., Dundee
Printed and bound in Great Britain by Billings & Sons Ltd., Worcester

Acknowledgements

In the course of work on my thesis I discovered that little was known in detail about the armies of the early Covenanters. As a result I undertook to produce this work of reference, which I hope will be of use to those interested in the subject.

The aid of numerous institutions has proved helpful. The staff of the Bodleian Library; the British Library; the Public Record Office; Cambridge University Library; Trinity College Library, Dublin; Strathclyde Regional Archives; the University of St Andrews Library; New Register House; the National Library of Scotland; the University of Edinburgh Library, and the Scottish Record Office, receive my deep gratitude for the help they rendered when I consulted their collections. I would especially like to express my thanks to the Scottish Arts Council for a bursary granted in 1981 at the commencement of this project. Equally, I wish to thank the Twenty Seven Foundation for a grant provided for the preparation of the manuscript for submission to the publisher. I am grateful for the information Major Nicholas Maclean-Bristol was willing to share with me concerning the Maclean regiment of 1651. Throughout I have been inspired by and drawn heavily upon the works of Dr David Stevenson — the principal scholar of the early Covenanting movement. My parents have rendered invaluable assistance and encouragement, and I regret that my father has not lived to see the completion of this book. My wife, Mary, and my three children have provided comfort and support while patiently waiting for me to finish. Mr R. Harris, my map maker, receives my (and hopefully) the readers' thanks for making the subject more understandable. I must also thank my typist, Mrs D. Williamson, for her patience and willingness to interpret my manuscript corrections over these several years. Nevertheless, all errors, omissions or faults in this work should be laid solely at my feet.

Washington, D.C.   E.M.F.

Contents

Abbreviations

Aberdeen Letters	*Aberdeen Council Letters*, vols. ii-iii, ed. Taylor, L. B. (London, 1950).
Acts of the General Assembly	*Acts of the General Assembly of the Church of Scotland, 1638-1842*, ed. Pitcairn, T. (Edinburgh, 1843).
Adair, *Narrative*	Adair, P., *A True Narrative of the Rise and Progress of the Presbyterian Church in Ireland*, ed. Killen, W. D. (Belfast, 1866).
APS	*The Acts of the Parliament of Scotland*, 12 vols., eds. Thomson, T. and Innes, C. (Edinburgh, 1814-75).
Argyll	*Minutes of the Synod of Argyll, i, 1639-1651*, ed. MacTavish, D. C. (Scot. His. Soc., 3rd Ser., xxxvii, 1943).
Army of the Covenant	*The Army of the Covenant*, 2 vols., ed. Terry, C. S. (Scot. His. Soc., 2nd Ser., xvi-vii, 1917).
Balfour, *Works*	Balfour, J., *Works*, 4 vols. (Edinburgh, 1823-5).
Baillie	*The Letters and Journals of Robert Baillie, Principal of the University of Glasgow, 1637-1662*, 3 vols., ed. Laing, D. (Bannatyne Club, lxxii, parts i-ii, lxxvii, 1841-2).
B.L.	British Library, London.
Bod. Lib.	Bodleian Library, Oxford.
C.J.	*Journals of the House of Commons.*
Correspondence of Lothian	*Correspondence of Sir Robert Kerr, First Earl of Ancram and his son William, Third Earl of Lothian*, 2 vols., ed. Laing, D. (Bannatyne Club, xcvi, 1875).
Council of Aberdeen	*Extracts from the Council Register of the Burgh of Aberdeen, 1625-1747*, 2 vols., ed. Stuart, J. (Scot. Burgh Rec. Soc., viii-ix, 1881-2).
Cowan, *Montrose*	Cowan, E. J., *Montrose: for Covenant and King* (London, 1977).

CSPD	*Calendar of State Papers, Domestic, 1639-1651*, 11 vols., eds. Hamilton, W. D. and Green, M. (London, 1873-93).
CSPI	*Calendar of State Papers, Ireland, 1633-1647*, ed. Mahaffy, R. P. (London, 1901).
Edinburgh	*Extracts from the Records of the Burgh of Edinburgh, 1642-55*, ed. Wood, M. (Edinburgh, 1938).
Fasti	*Fasti Ecclesiae Scoticanae: The Succession of the ministers in the Church of Scotland from the Reformation*, 8 vols., ed. Scott, H. (Edinburgh, 1915-50).
Foster, *Members*	Foster, J., *Members of Parliament, Scotland, 1357-1882* (2nd edn., London, 1882).
Furgol, 'Religious Aspects'	Furgol, E. M., 'Religious Aspects of the Scottish Covenanting Armies, 1639-1651' (Oxford Univ., D.Phil. thesis 1983).
Glasgow	*Extracts from the Records of the Burgh of Glasgow, ii, 1630-1662*, ed. Marwick, J. (Scot. Burgh Rec. Soc., xii, 1885).
Gordon, *History*	Gordon, J., *History of Scottish Affairs from 1637-1641*, 3 vols., eds. Robertson, R. and Grub, G. (Spalding Club, i, iii, v, 1841).
HMC Report	*Historical Manuscript Commission Report.*
Kirkcaldie	*The Presbytery Book of Kirkcaldie*, ed. Stevenson, W. (Kirkcaldy, 1900).
KSR	Kirk Session Record.
Lanark	*Selections from the Registers of the Presbytery of Lanark, 1623-1709*, ed. Robertson, J. (Abbotsford Club, xvi, 1839).
List of Regiments	*A List of the Several Regiments and Chief Officers of the Scottish Army quartered near Newcastle* (London, 1644), s.s.
L.J.	*Journals of the House of Lords.*
Lothian and Tweeddale	*The Records of the Synod of Lothian and Tweeddale, 1589-1596, 1640-1649*, ed. Kirk, J. (Stair Soc., xxx, 1977).
Memoirs of Guthry	*The Memoirs of Henry Guthry, late bishop of Dunkeld*, ed. Crawfurd, G. (Glasgow, 1748).

NLS   National Library of Scotland, Edinburgh.

NRH   New Register House, Edinburgh.

OPR   Old Parish Register.

PR   Presbytery Record.

Privy Council   *Register of the Privy Council of Scotland, 1603-1643*, vols., eds. *et al.* (Edinburgh,   ).

PRO   Public Record Office, London.

RCGA   *General Assembly Commission Records, 1646-1652*, 3 vols., eds. Mitchell, A. F. and Christie, J. (Scot. His. Soc., 1st Ser., xi, xxv, lviii, 1892-1909).

Records of the Kirk   *Records of the Kirk of Scotland, containing the acts and proceedings of the General Assemblies, from the year 1638 downwards*, ed. Peterkin, A. (Edinburgh, 1838).

SAUL   St Andrews University Library.

Somerville, *Memorie*   Somerville, J., *Memorie of the Somervilles*, 2 vols. (Edinburgh, 1715).

Spalding, *Memorialls*   Spalding, J., *Memorialls of the Trubles in Scotland and England, 1624-1645*, 2 vols., ed. Stuart, J. (Spalding Club, xxi-ii, 1850-1).

SR   Synod Records.

SRO   Scottish Record Office, Edinburgh.

Stevenson, *Alasdair*   Stevenson, D. *Alasdair MacColla and the Highland Problem in the 17th Century* (Edinburgh, 1980).

Stevenson, *Covenanters*   Stevenson, D., *Scottish Covenanters and Irish Confederates* (Belfast, 1981).

TCLD   Trinity College Library, Dublin.

Terry, *Leslie*   Terry, C. S., *The Life and Campaigns of Alexander Leslie, first earl of Leven* (London, 1899).

Turner, *Memoirs*   Turner, J. *Memoirs of his own Life and Times, 1632-1670*, ed. Thomson, T. (Bannatyne Club, xxviii, 1829).

Wilson, *History*   Wilson, J., *The History of Scottish affairs, particularly during the reign of Charles I* (Trans. Literary Antiq. Soc. Perth, i, 1827).

WRH   West Register House, Edinburgh.

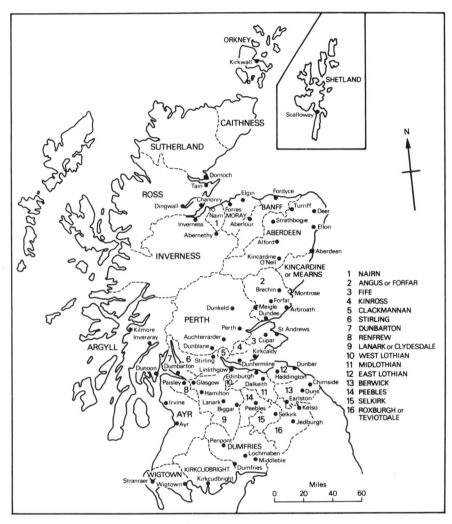

Map 1. Scotland: the recruiting grounds.

xi

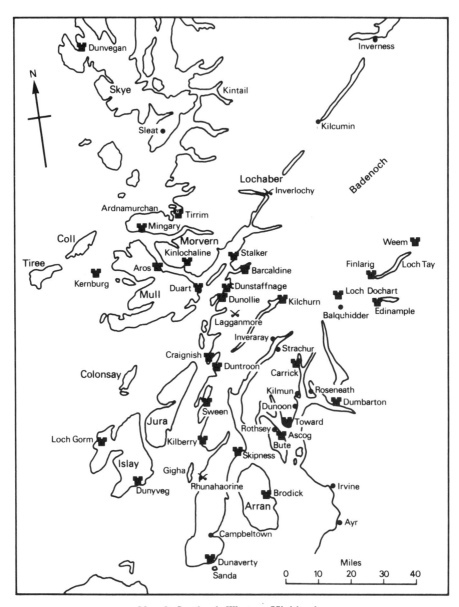

Map 2. Scotland: Western Highlands.

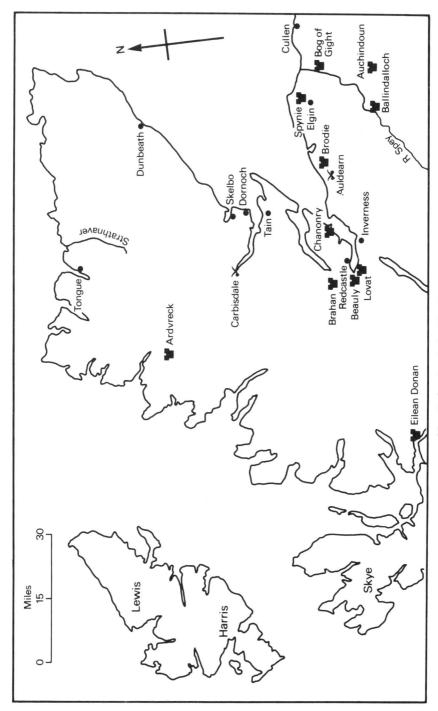

Map 3. Scotland: the North.

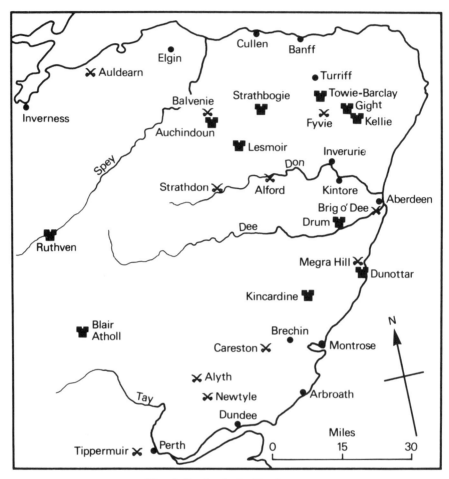

Map 4. Scotland: the Northeast.

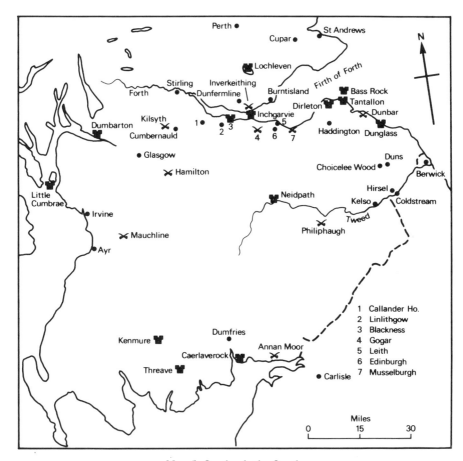

Map 5. Scotland: the South.

Legend on map:
1 Callander Ho.
2 Linlithgow
3 Blackness
4 Gogar
5 Leith
6 Edinburgh
7 Musselburgh

Place names visible on map:
Perth, Cupar, St Andrews, Lochleven, Firth of Forth, Inverkeithing, Stirling, Dunfermline, Burntisland, Bass Rock, Dirleton, Tantallon, Forth, Inchgarvie, Dunbar, Kilsyth, Dumbarton, Cumbernauld, Haddington, Dunglass, Glasgow, Duns, Choicelee Wood, Hamilton, Berwick, Little Cumbrae, Hirsel, Neidpath, Kelso, Coldstream, Irvine, Tweed, Mauchline, Philiphaugh, Ayr, Kenmure, Dumfries, Annan Moor, Caerlaverock, Threave, Carlisle

Miles
0   15   30

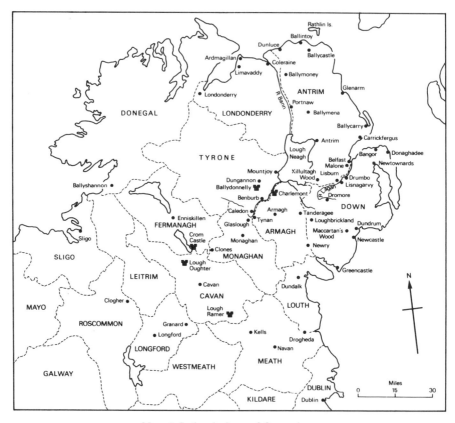

Map 6. Ireland: Area of Operations.

xvi

1 Newburn
2 Boldon Hills
3 Hilton
4 Newcastle
5 Gateshead
6 N. Shields
7 S. Shields

Map 7. England: Area of Operations.

xvii

1
Introduction

When the Covenanters decided in mid-1638 that resistance to Charles I must change from the presentation of petitions to the raising of troops they showed great faith in their cause. Scotland was a country singularly unsuited for embarking on defiance of the king of Great Britain and Ireland who possessed a fleet capable of blockading its ports, friends within it who could tie down large numbers of Covenanting soldiers and the potential of invading with armies from England and Ireland. The last actual war in Scotland had occurred over sixty years previously. With what foundations had the Jacobean and Carolean regimes provided the Covenanters to embark on military endeavours? Was the Scotland of 1638-39 an armed camp long prepared for war or a nation possessing few attributes of military power of an early modern European state?

In the past, Scotland's first line of defence had been its reserves of large numbers of men trained for war. That situation had altered in the period of James VI's personal reign. After the union of crowns the old enemy had become a new friend and the necessity of training men for imminent war vanished. Between 1603 and 1638 the Privy Council authorised few musters or weapon-showings (Wapinschaws) for the shires. When Charles had been at war with France and Spain the council had ordered one national muster by shires and burghs in 1625 and two further ones in 1627.[1] While Edinburgh held annual musters from 1607 to 1637 (and some other burghs may have followed suit), the majority of the population which lived in rural areas of the shires and the landwards of the burghs probably had little or no regular training. Even the Edinburgh musters were of little military significance, which is proved by the lack of reference to Edinburgh trained bands or militia as an important element in the Covenanting war machine. One can therefore dispense with the idea that the Covenanters had an abundance of trained military forces to call out.

Men may also gain military discipline by actual service in the field and it is necessary to see whether the Scots had a large pool of manpower with this experience. Within Scotland the Privy Council had authorised a number of expeditions for pacifying parts of the kingdom after 1603. The Western Isles had witnessed expeditions in 1605-8, 1612-16, 1622 and 1626.[2] There had been official incursions into the western Highlands in 1613-14, 1615-16, 1618, 1621-22, and 1625.[3] Expeditions had also been mounted against the Northern Isles (1614-15), the clan Macgregor (1611-13), Caithness (1622-23), the central Highlands (1624) and the northeastern Highlands (1634).[4] These campaigns, however, were of little use in providing Scotland with large military reserves,

1

because the numbers involved consisted of hundreds of men not thousands. Three further points must be made about these officially authorised campaigns. They were not annual events which would have allowed many different men to receive military experience. Their occurrence was sporadic with none occurring in 1610, 1617, 1619-20, 1626-33 and 1635-38. This meant by 1639 that those Lowlanders who had served on them probably had only vague memories of military discipline. Only the Campbells and their allies the MacAulays, Lamonts, Malcolms, MacDougalls, Macleans and Camerons who had served on the expeditions were supporters of the Covenanters. They also possessed reserves of trained manpower for military training of a sort which remained an essential part of a Highlandman's upbringing. Consequently the importance of the 8th earl of Argyll's (chief of the Campbells) decision to join the Covenanters can be appreciated in a military perspective. Nevertheless these Gaelic-speaking supporters of the Covenant could have done little to impart their military knowledge (which in any case may have been antiquated and unsuitable for resisting men trained in the Swedish and Dutch models), to the rural and burghal residents of the Lowlands.

For training men to be soldiers the Covenanters by necessity relied upon Scottish mercenary veterans of the continental wars. The poverty of Scotland combined with the political activities of James and Charles had provided the Covenanters with vast numbers of these men. From 1620 to 1637 the kings had permitted a large exportation of surplus Scottish manpower to serve in the armies of France, Sweden, the Netherlands, Denmark and Russia. In the years 1624, 1626-29, 1631-33 and 1637 royal warrants had permitted the levying of 41,400 Scots for continental armies.[5] It would have been remarkable and unlikely if all of these troops had been raised; nevertheless thousands had departed from Scotland and had gained military training and experience by 1638-39. To ensure that their armies in the First Bishops' War had some chance of success the Covenanting government required that the lieutenant colonels and majors of each regiment, and the ensign and two sergeants of each company, be veteran Scottish soldiers. The recall of these men occurred in late 1638. They came in sufficient numbers to provide the Covenanting forces with enough military training to convince Charles that 1639 was not the year in which to fight and to conquer Northumberland and Durham. Initially, however, the Covenanting forces were really unprepared for a Lutzen or Rocroi; the military neglect of the previous thirty-six years had seen to that.

Other than the provision of trained men the post-union state could have provided the Covenanters with stockpiles of arms and ammunition and with fortresses from which to defy the king. Unfortunately, the Covenanters received no legacies in these commodities. The last massive importation and manufacture of muskets, pikes, swords, pistols, armour, gunpowder, cannon, projectiles and match had occurred in the invasion scare of 1625-27.[6] Most of these items were subject to decay over time and the evidence does not suggest that they were imported in sufficient numbers to arm a force of thousands such as was required in 1639. Instead the Covenanters relied almost entirely upon the massive importation of armaments from the Netherlands in the autumn of 1638 and the ensuing months before taking the field in spring 1639. Turning to fortifications, one can again see that Scotland was in a sorry condition. In 1608 the border castle of Annan had been transformed into a kirk. While the Privy Council had taken measures to ensure defensibility of Edinburgh and Dumbarton castles after 1603, they were outwith Covenanter control because of their garrisons of royal troops. The burghs which were ideological bastions of the movement could hardly be considered capable of withstanding a siege. In 1627 Anstruther had actually been fortified against naval attack, but it was of little significance. The fortification of Montrose (1622), Leith, Burntisland, Inchgarvie and Aberdeen (all 1627)[7] had been proposed but it is uncertain whether anything had been done and, if so, whether the works had been maintained after the invasion scare. The Covenanters certainly fortified Leith and Burntisland in 1639 and they could have used the earlier plans, but that may have been their sole inheritance from previous efforts. Thus one must conclude that in 1638-39 Scotland was not militarily prepared, lacking as it did established reserves of men trained in the latest military techniques, deficient in the materials of warfare and without any citadels or burghs capable of withstanding an early modern siege.

Having determined that the Covenanters had to commence their creation of a war machine capable of resisting Charles' potential forces *ex nihil*, we may now turn to their achievements in the military sphere in the 1639-1651 period. The matters of recruitment, source of officers, the size of armies, the size of weapons of different types of units, uniforms, banners, strategy and tactics will receive treatment below. This information serves as a general background for the regimental entries.

The mechanism for the levying of a Covenanter army was established in 1639 and adhered to with only a few exceptions until 1651. Although the Covenanters did not control the *de jure* central government in 1638-39, they had established an alternative *de facto* body called The Tables which proposed and implemented policies at the national level. In later years the Covenanters would utilise the Privy Council and Parliament (when they had gained control of them) and would create the Committee of Estates through which they preferred to control the country. From 1639 to 1651, with the exception of the Whiggamore Raid, all armies levied by the Covenanters had their origins at the national level. Whatever the institution, it nominated the colonels, authorised the levying of troops and established the quotas each shire would provide. Following the 1644-45 plague visitations the national executive granted remissions to certain shires and burghs in the levies of 1648-50. Generally, it was the shire government which dealt with burghs. Effective shire-national co-ordination was another innovation and achievement of the Covenanters. The Covenanters created the committee of war or the committee of the shire which had the task of carrying out the commands received from the national government. These committees, which consisted of men nominated by the parliament, were extremely competent. In military matters they arranged the quarterings of regiments and determined the numbers of soldiers that each burgh or rural parish would raise to meet the shire's quotas. In the burghs the traditional council functioned as the recruiting agency.[8] In the rural parishes the clergy and church elders had the responsibility of listing the fencible men (eligible recruits) and selecting them with the assistance of local landowners. The clergy played a vital role in both rural and urban areas by publicising the levies and by encouraging men to join the regiments.[9] Another factor vital to the success of a levy by the Covenanters was the support of the landowners who could bring out their kinsmen, tenantry and servants. On certain occasions, principally in the Highlands and the northeast lowlands, heads of families and their cadets raised forces for the Covenants without recourse to the three-tiered system outlined above.[10] Almost always these retinues served for a short time and usually only within the region in which they were raised. On certain occasions the system failed to work as it ought to have. In 1648 the Kirk opposed the Engagement and did all in its power to disrupt the levy. In addition to massive resistance to the levy from the clergy, most of the burghs and the shire committees in East Lothian, Fife, Ayr, Kirkcudbright, Wigtown, Lanark and Renfrew baulked at raising men. As a consequence army officers resorted to quartering troops on resisters and to kidnapping. The strong support for the Engagement from the landed classes brought out troops in 1648, but probably only two-thirds of the established quota were levied.[11] Following the Act of Classes in 1649 and subsequent acts for preparing the army, these landed supporters of the Engagers found themselves forbidden public employment and the functioning of the shire committees suffered from the absence of their support and experience. The levy of 1651 for the Army of the Kingdom suffered opposition from the south-western Lowland clergy and minor lairds and from a general war weariness. Before the summer campaign commenced several units of the army quartered on those who had not provided their quotas.[12] The forces of the Whiggamores (1648) and Western Association (1650) differ from the normal pattern in that the local clergy played a primary role in bringing men out. However, some members of the landed classes (principally minor lairds) seconded their efforts.[13] For the successful levy of a regiment the co-operation of all three levels of the recruiting system was essential, as was the wholehearted support of the clergy and the landowners.

The Covenanters adopted a sensible policy for providing officers for their armies. In 1639 few of the nobles in Scotland had had military experience, but their social position and kinship ties meant that they could not be overlooked as officers. Consequently The Tables selected Alexander Leslie, a Swedish field marshal, to command the army because his professional status placed him above the jealousies of the nobility. Nobles assumed command of about sixty percent of the units levied that year. However, The Tables ensured the military discipline of its forces by ordering that each regiment's lieutenant colonel and major and each company's ensign and sergeants all be professional soldiers. This arrangement permitted colonels to nominate family members to the ranks of captain and lieutenant. In the Second Bishops' War a similar situation existed.

However, in the Ulster Army the nobles and lairds who commanded regiments selected family and followers for any rank much to the disgruntlement of the professionals. In the Army of the Solemn League and Covenant the nobles continued to predominate as colonels, but some were replaced by professionals. In the Home Army lairds held the majority of command posts, because most of the units were only temporary levies of retainers. In the New Model Army the professionals held a large number of colonelcies and routmastercies. The Engager Army restored the balance to the nobility to such a degree that the duke of Hamilton, a non-professional noble, served as commander. (Usually Leslie, ennobled in 1641 as earl of Leven, was at least titular commander and all staff officers were professionals.) The forces of the Whiggamore Raid were led by a combination of nobles and kirk party professionals. Following the establishment of the kirk party government the number of noble colonels declined due to the exclusion from public office of most of the nobility. Instead the lairds predominated; nevertheless the new regime was desperate to appoint nobles or their sons. The Western Association Army was officered by professional colonels and minor lairds as routmasters. The conservative nature of the Army of the Kingdom was reflected in the predominance of nobles and lairds as colonels (they commanded seven-tenths of the regiments). This was the only Covenanter army that was top heavy, possessing four lieutenant generals and six major generals in an effort to satisfy both the kirk party and the most conservative elements in the government.[14] Usually, the Covenanters sought to utilise the traditional leaders of society as colonels, buttressing them with professional Scottish soldiers.

Between 1639 and 1651 the Covenanters raised over a dozen armies which ranged in size from 2,000 men to 24,000 men. One of the largest armies was the Army of the Kingdom raised when Scotland was in danger of conquest, but following heavy losses of manpower through warfare, plague and famine. In 1639 the Covenanters occupied Aberdeen on four occasions; the first army consisted of 9,000-11,000 men, the second had 4,000 men, the third possessed 7,000 men and the fourth was 4,000 strong. Meanwhile in the eastern borders General Leslie commanded between 12,000 and 20,000 men. An unknown number served in the defence of the Forth coastline against Hamilton's 5,000 royal troops and in the subjugation of the royalists in the southwest borders. In 1640 Leslie invaded England with an army of 17,775 foot and horse; while Argyll devastated the lands of royalist nobles and clans with 4,000 men. In the southwest a regiment was sufficient to capture Caerlaverock and Threave castles. A slightly stronger force was necessary to subdue the royalist Gordons and their allies in the northeast lowlands. Following the Irish rebellion of October 1641 the Covenanters arranged with the English parliament to send an army of 10,000 men to Ulster to help crush the Irish. However, by autumn 1642 they had sent over 11,371 men and officers. Due to wastage from military activity, lack of supplies, disease and evacuation to Scotland this army had shrunk to about 4,000 soldiers in 1647. In the following year the shipment of 2,100 to Scotland to aid the Engagers halved this number. The Army of the Solemn League and Covenant which entered England in January 1644 contained 18,000 foot, 3,000 horse and 500-600 dragoons. In June a second army under the earl of Callander crossed the border to recover strongholds recaptured by the royalists; it had between 6,800 and 8,000 men. By summer 1645 the army's forces in the field were down to 9,000 foot and 5,500 horse, casualties, the plague, evacuation to Scotland and garrisons in northern England having reduced its effectiveness substantially. In January 1646 at the siege of Newark the army mustered only 6,943 men, the retention of men in garrisons and evacuation of regiments to Scotland contributing to this low figure. Meanwhile in Scotland the Covenanters mustered several armies against Montrose, which ranged in size from 2,000 men to 7,000 men. Following the cessation of hostilities at home and the return of the Army of the Solemn League and Covenant in February 1647 a New Model Army of 6,000 foot and 1,200 horse and dragoons was created from elements of old regiments. This army served as the nucleus of the Engager Army of 14,000-15,000 troops which crossed into England in July 1648. The Engagers also kept troops in Scotland to suppress the kirk party. In September this force of New Model units, new levies, Ulster Army men, and refugees from Preston consisted of about 8,000 men. It was opposed by 700-1,000 men under Argyll, 6,500 men from the southwest lowlands and unknown numbers of men from Fife and Scotts under the earl of Buccleuch. The Army of the Covenant was for most of its existence a small force. In July 1649 it mustered only 3,107 foot and 2,231 horse. On the eve of the English invasion in 1650 there had been no increase in numbers. At Dunbar Lieutenant General David Leslie commanded 16,000 foot and 7,000 horse. However, between 2,000 and 5,000 men had been purged from the army before then for failing to meet the requirements of the Act of Classes. After Dunbar Leslie led 4,000-5,000 men. In autumn 1650 the radical officers commanded 2,000 horse and dragoons. The basis of this Western Association Army was four of Leslie's former regiments, so not all were new recruits. The Army of the Kingdom managed to field 15,000 foot and 4,000-5,000 horse by May 1651. In mid-July it contained 19,943 foot alone, but by late July when the army headed south towards England it consisted of no more than 21,000 men and possibly as few as 11,000.[15] The lack of reliable population figures for Scotland in the 1639-1651 period prevents an accurate assessment of the magnitude of Covenanters' success in creating armies. Even assuming that Scotland possessed a large surplus male population in 1639 it could no longer have remained following the large number of war casualties, the plague attack of 1644-45 and the famine of 1648-49. Thus, one can suggest that the Covenanters were good at raising armies particularly when one realises that Scotland had not engaged in prolonged military activity since 1573 and had no established system of levying large numbers of troops.

Turning to the type of units which made up the Covenanting armies, one finds much that is familiar to the early modern army. The backbone of all Covenanting armies, save that of the Western Association, was the foot or infantry regiment. These units were commanded by a colonel, who possessed a staff of a lieutenant colonel, major, scribe, quartermaster, drum major, surgeon, provost marshall and chaplain (the latter appointed by the Kirk on a temporary basis). In 1640 each foot company had a captain (or in the case of the colonel's company a captain lieutenant), who might also be a lieutenant colonel or major, a lieutenant, an ensign, two sergeants and two corporals. In 1647 the company officers remained the same, but only two sergeants are mentioned. This arrangement of regimental, company and non-commissioned officers probably remained the same throughout the period. For signals each regiment possessed drummers. Pipers were found in both Highland and Lowland regiments.[16] The size of infantry units varied enormously, so much so that regimental strengths will be dealt with below in the main body of the work. However, foot companies did run to standard sizes. The Ulster Army in 1642 had companies varying in strength from 93 men to 121 men and officers. In 1643 the same army's average company contained 100 men and officers. But in 1644 that number had slipped to 90 men and officers. One of the regiments evacuated to Scotland possessed only 40 men per company in 1646. On 9 December 1646 parliament set the minimum size of a company at 80 soldiers. At the creation of the New Model Army the strength of a company was made 125 foot. On 21 June 1650 the estates placed the size of a company at 108 men. Following Dunbar many companies had fallen below this level, because in 1651 a company to maintain its status had to field only 70 foot. Simultaneously the minimum strength for regiments under lieutenant colonels was fixed at 300 foot and 150 foot were necessary for a major to serve as commander.[17]

The weapons of foot regiments were subject to less variation than the standard sizes. All men carried swords regardless of their primary weapon. It is difficult to establish the ratio of muskets to pikes in the Bishops' Wars armies. However, Leslie's Life Guard of Foot in 1640 consisted of just over three musketeers to two pikemen. This ratio was probably general throughout the army, because in latter years the Covenanters seem to have preferred it. The Ulster Army contained 6,000 musketeers and 4,000 pikemen, fitting the 3:2 ratio perfectly. Arms shipments to Scotland from the Netherlands provided 10,000 muskets and 4,000 pikes (5:2), but this probably does not reflect the actual ratio in the regiments. In April 1644 the estates provided arms for two new regiments at a ratio of two muskets for each pike. The predominance in firepower over shock was preserved by the Covenanting forces until December 1650. The act of levy of the 23rd authorised the raising of infantry regiments with only two musketeers for every three pikemen.[18] This probably arose from the difficulty of obtaining muskets and powder through the English blockade as well as the high cost of these weapons for the impoverished regime. Some other infantry weapons are also mentioned in the records. In 1644 the estates allowed Argyll's Life Guard firelocks, and his family also provided the men with swords and targes. Firelocks (which used a flint instead of a match to ignite the gunpowder) were usually reserved for artillery and wagon guards due to the danger of fire from the burning match. The only mention of armour for infantry occurred on 25 February 1647, when the estates authorised that the six Lowland regiments would contain seventy-two halberdiers with back, breast and head pieces.[19] The

Covenanter foot regiment relied principally upon its musket fire to decide the issue. This was sound tactics except against the Highland charge where counter shock was the only suitable response.

Regiments of horse in the Covenanting armies come to the fore only in the raising of the Army of the Solemn League and Covenant. Previously the units of horse were brigaded with the foot and not formed into anything larger than troops. The staff officers of horse regiments were similar to foot ones: colonel, lieutenant colonel, major, quartermaster, chaplain, surgeon and possible trumpet major. In 1647 the officers of a horse troop were to be the routmaster (who might be a staff officer), a lieutenant, cornet, quartermaster and three corporals. Each possessed at least one trumpeter. This arrangement may have been standard for all Covenanting horse troops. In addition the regiment would have had a smith and several saddlers. The variations in strength of horse regiments and troops was greater than that of the foot. The Army of the Solemn League and Covenant's standard horse regiment would have contained eight troops of seventy-five men each. But many lacked all eight troops, being deficient by one or two. In 1644 troop strength varied from fifty-four men and officers to sixty-seven of both. In 1646 one regiment contained seven troops which had an average of only twenty-four men each. On 9 December 1646 the estates fixed the minimum troop size within Scotland at fifty horse. On 29 January 1647 the standard size of a New Model troop was set at eighty men, which was later reduced to seventy-five in order to provide another troop. The Engager Army's standard cavalry regiment was to contain 180 horse, of which only 80 would be raised by the shires while the colonels levied the other 100 men privately. In 1650 the estates contrived to establish a standard regiment, but proceeded to deviate from the standard immediately. Each regiment was to contain six troops of seventy-five men each. However, two regiments were to have nine troops each and one was to have five. Troop strength varied from as few as thirty-four horse to as many as ninety-five. In winter 1650-51 the average size of seven horse regiments was 330 horse, suggesting that the levies of 1650 had been deficient because there were few casualties among horse units at Dunbar. In spring 1651 ten horse regiments averaged a strength of 439 horse, indicating that recruiting had increased the size of some older regiments. Nevertheless, some regiments were very weak as indicated by an order that a horse regiment must muster 200 men to have a lieutenant colonel as commander.[20] Usually, horse regiments were devoid of dragoons but in the mid-1640s at least two regiments had companies of dragoons.[21]

The arms and armour of horsemen remained nearly constant throughout the period. In 1640 horsemen were to be protected by a jack and armed either with a lance, carbine or pair of pistols. Later the jacks were replaced by buff coats with breast and back armour worn over them, and helmets. Broadswords were standard weapons but they do not appear to have been the only weapon of attack. At Marston Moor Leven's horse charged the English royalists with lances and in Ulster the lance was the primary weapon against the Irish. The last mention of Covenanting horse using the lance is at Dunbar where the front rank of the

Ministers' horse was armed with lances. As late as December 1650 the government authorised cavalry regiments to be armed either with the lance or pistols in addition to swords. However, in 1651 the only offensive weapons referred to in official documents were swords, pistols and carbines.[22] Despite the frequent mentions of pistols as a cavalry weapon of the period, there is no reference which I have discovered suggesting that the Covenanter horse utilised the caracolle (a type of attack relying solely on massed ranks of pistol-firing horsemen). It is possible that the cavalrymen fired their pistols before the initial impact of the charge, but this would have limited the number of men to those in the two front ranks. Unfortunately the depth of Covenanting cavalry or its more precise tactical arrangements is unknown.

We turn now to a related branch of the army, the dragoons who fought in partnership with the horse. (For details of how this co-operation functioned in combat please see Fraser's dragoons in the Army of the Solemn League and Covenant.) In 1643 the Covenanters raised their first regiment of dragoons. It consisted of seven companies with about sixty-four men each for a total of 448 men. In 1645 Lord Coupar's dragoons had seven companies of about sixty-eight men each or 480 men for the entire regiment. The New Model Army initially possessed only two companies of 100 men each, but the complement was expanded to three companies with seventy men each. The two dragoon regiments raised in autumn 1650 numbered 350 and 272 men respectively, but the number of companies in them is unknown. In addition to possessing the usual staff officers and auxiliaries each company of dragoons possessed a captain (who might be on the staff), a lieutenant, an ensign, two sergeants, three corporals and a drummer. The dragoons usually only rode to the battlefield, thus they had smaller horses than the main cavalry units. In action the dragoons worked in sub-units of ten men, nine of whom fought while the tenth man guarded the horses. The dragoons were armed with short matchlock muskets, swords and pistols, but it was the first which was their chief tool of war.[23] Although the Covenanters possessed dragoon units from late 1643, only at Marston Moor is a unit in action described, therefore it is impossible to make any judgement about the overall quality of these troops.

The last type of unit in the regular armies to be considered is the artillery. Almost all of the Covenanter armies possessed cannon. These were manned by regular officers and gunners, not civilian contractors as was a common practice in early modern armies. The chief officer of the train of artillery was the General of Artillery, who was seconded by a lieutenant colonel. The Covenanters purchased their heavy guns from the continent, but they possessed a cannon foundry for three pounders in Potter Row, Edinburgh until September 1650. The three pounder was the main field gun of all the major Covenanter armies; each regiment was probably assigned two for formal battles. In addition the armies possessed twenty-four, eighteen, twelve, nine and six pounders. There was no standard number of guns for an army. For instance the armies of the Second Bishops' War and Solemn League and Covenant had trains of over sixty pieces; while the army at Duns in 1639 had forty cannon and that at

Dunbar in 1650 possessed between thirty-two and twenty-two. The Engager Army under the duke of Hamilton lacked artillery, because the General of Artillery was too disorganised to make up a train. Certain forces such as the Ulster Army and David Leslie's army in Argyll (1647) found that the terrain rendered the cannon immobile. In 1641-4, 1647-8 and 1648-50 Edinburgh Castle served as a depot for storing cannon not required by the armies. The number of men serving the train of artillery fluctuated with the army; the highest known being 120 in 1651, while in 1647-8 there were only thirty-five. The Covenanters frequently relied upon cannon during sieges, but also relied on them in some battles. Many of the garrisons, whether temporary like Strathbogie or permanent such as Stirling, had artillery pieces for defensive fire. The Covenanter artillery is best remembered for its exotic use of leather guns and frames. Nevertheless for performance in the field these units relied on the traditional brass and iron pieces.[24] Perhaps the difficulty in acquiring cannon may explain the failure of the Covenanters to create a navy.

The clan forces and family retinues fielded by the Covenanters present only an image in silhouette in the sources. Rarely is any mention made of the numbers serving under a particular clan leader or noble or laird. In the cases of units consisting of several hundred men one may assume that there was some sort of company organisation. In clan regiments for instance the chief or his close relatives served as staff officers and the cadets probably acted as captains of the men from their districts. But in either a clan or retinue it is impossible to state how many officers a company may have been expected to have had. It is probably a safe assumption that Highland units (whether a whole clan or part of one) were infantry. However, the retinues fielded from the northeast lowlands probably contained a few horsemen, but the number would have been so small that these mounted men could have acted only as scouts or sentinels. A well-armed clansman would have possessed a musket, sword, dirk, skean dhu and targe. Some might have only had polearms (a pike, Lochaber axe or halberd) and others, probably officers, would have had pistols. The arms possessed by members of retinues are a matter of conjecture. It is possible that the mounted leaders had some armour, a sword and pistols. The better-armed infantry in retinues would have had muskets or pikes, but some certainly appeared in the field with only sharpened agricultural tools. The military qualities of clansmen, members of retinues or of men in mass levies such as those at Kilsyth from Fife or in the Whiggamore Raid from the southwest lowlands would have varied tremendously. The military education of the Highlanders remained part of the process of maturation for males, thus these men could be expected to use their weapons with proficiency. However, not all of them would have had knowledge of how to participate in a 'Highland charge' (which was not created until 1642 and developed in Montrose's army from 1644-45). Those who came out in the northeastern retinues might have had military training or experience, but it would be safe to say that as a whole such units were only a step removed from raw levies from Fife or the southwest lowlands. These lowlanders possessed a great dedication to the cause, but lacked military training, experience or the attributes which would have served as their replacement. The non-regular units of the Covenanters were a mixed lot indeed, varying from men who fought to the last gasp to those who ran at the first sign of serious action.

To state that the Covenanters possessed standard uniforms would probably be making too great a claim. The retinues and mass levies, for instance, appeared in the field with their everyday clothing. Indeed it is possible that until several regiments were retained on foot after August 1641 that the troops previously raised had worn their normal clothing. However, from the raising of the Ulster Army it appears that clothing was issued to the men. The regular lowland infantry units possessed suits of woollen clothing hodden grey in colour. On their feet they wore socks and shoes. Hodden grey was not the only colour of coat worn by the foot regiments, because in 1651 Lord Lorne requested that his regiment be provided with coats of one colour only. The characteristic headgear of both lowland and highland foot was the flat round blue bonnet. Highland infantry wore either a belted plaid (kilt) or in the case of Ross of Balnagowan's foot tartan trews in the red Ross pattern. The Highlanders certainly wore shirts and some had cravats; those not barefoot had pumps and hose. Among cavalry units the buff coats may have been universal either as an undercoat beneath armour or as a substitute for armour. The dragoons wore grey, wool coats. The lack of a standard uniform presented an immediate problem for the Covenanters, one of identification with its important influence on *esprit de corps*. On 30 March 1639 the earl of Montrose devised the solution to the problem of telling his men from the similarly dressed royalists by issuing blue ribbons. The infantry sash was worn from the neck to under the left arm. The blue ribbons were also attached to the infantry bonnets and to the spanners of the cavalry pistols. Blue ribbons as scarves were also utilised as a symbol of the rank of captain.[25] Therefore it was blue bonnets or blue ribbons that served as the identifying badge for the regular forces.

The banner of the Covenanter infantry regiment was the Saltire (that is, the national flag of Scotland — a white St. Andrews cross on a blue field). The armies of the 1639-51 period possessed a variety of mottos on their banners. In 1639 Montrose's army had 'For Religion, the Covenant and the Countrie', while Leslie's used 'For Christ's Croun and Covenant'. The motto from 1640 until the alliance with the English parliamentarians in summer 1643 was 'Covenant For Relligion Crowne and Country'. Leven's army in 1644 used 'Covenant for Religion, Crowne and Kingdomes'. In May 1644 Argyll's regimental banners had 'For the Covenant, Religioun, the Crown and Kingdom', but in September their banners read 'For Religion, Country, Crown and Covenant'. The New Model Army's banners dropped the word 'Covenant' and read 'For Religion, Crown, and Kingdome'. The Engager Army had flags with four different mottos. In addition to using flags of the 1640-43 armies and of the Army of the Solemn League and Covenant, the Engagers utilised two new mottos — 'Covenant for Religion, King and Kingdoms' and 'For Covenant Religion, King and Kingdoms'. The Army of the Covenants adopted a variation of this last motto, changing the wording to 'For Covenant Religion, King and Kingdom'. The Army of the Kingdom retained a number of regiments from its predecessor and they presumably kept their old banners due to the regime's poverty. However, new infantry regiments had banners with the motto 'For Religion, King, and Kingdome' emblazoned on them. The design of dragoon and horse colours is not known, but they probably possessed some variation of the foot's flags. As seen from this description of Covenanting banners religion, the king and kingdom were the chief concerns of the Covenanters, which is an accurate reflection of their priorities.[26]

Before concluding, a brief account of the strategy and tactics of the Covenanting armies remains. Unfortunately, there is no surviving material which links the theory and practice of war in its Scottish context during the 1639-1651 period. Therefore, my conclusions may read more into the events in an attempt to analyse them than was true at the time. The strategy of the Covenanters does tend to reflect the continental preoccupation with fortresses and garrisons, but local variations exist alongside that. The strategy of 'fire and sword', that is the burning of crops, food stocks and houses and the killing of any supporters of the enemy (often without regard to sex or age), had a long tradition in Scottish history, particularly as an instrument of policy against royal opponents. Thus, it should not surprise one that Covenanters claimed this policy as their own as early as 1639. Its use was limited to the Scottish lowland and highland royalists and to the Irish rebels. In Ulster from the beginning the policy of fire and sword (to destroy the basis of the rebels' subsistence and their will to resist) was immediately allied with the establishment of garrisons to protect the friendly Protestant population and to serve as bases for expeditions against the Irish. In Scotland the devastation of the royalists' home bases was not united with a garrisoning policy until 1644. (Before then the garrisons were limited to traditional locations such as Dumbarton, Edinburgh and Stirling Castles and to Leith, Burntisland and Aberdeen.) From 1644 until 1651, however, the Covenanters established a large number of garrisons both within friendly and enemy areas. These were instrumental in the protection of various Covenanter families and in the pacification of royalists. In 1650 Lieutenant General David Leslie practised a variation of the previously outlined policy. He established a number of garrisons in Berwickshire and East Lothian to harass Cromwell's line of supply and created a massive fortified line stretching from Edinburgh Castle to Holyroodhouse to Leith (on the present line of Leith Walk). In addition his men purposefully stripped the abandoned shires of food and fodder, forcing the English to rely on imported supplies, which involved considerable effort even for a regime as rich as the Commonwealth. Finally he employed fabian tactics in the field and by 2 September 1650 had won the campaign. The key policy of Covenanting intervention in England was the capture and garrisoning of important towns. In 1640 Leslie took and held Newcastle which supplied London's coal, and Durham, which was an important symbol of Laudian religious policy. In 1644 his sights were again on Newcastle and Durham, but York was the key to the north and he willingly co-operated in its capture. That December the siege of Carlisle began; its capture would provide the southwest Scottish lowlands with security from royalist incursions and would hinder the linking of an English royal army with Montrose's forces. The other activities of the Army of the Solemn League and Covenant were dictated by the conflicting demands of the Committee of Both Kingdoms, which required the army to serve south of the Trent, and by Leven's fears about a juncture between Montrose and the English royalists, which meant the retention of the army north of the Tyne. In 1648 the strategy of the duke of Hamilton is hard to fathom, however he appears to have desired the capture of two important towns: Manchester and London. The 1651 campaign into England was aimed at London as the ultimate target, however the garrisoning of Worcester was seen as necessary to provide a secure place of muster for western English and Welsh recruits.

The tactics of the Covenanters are an equally murky topic. The ideal formation for an army equipped with the weapons of the time was as follows: two lines one regiment each in depth with the second line covering the gaps between regiments in the first line (a reserve was also permitted which acted as a third line). The flanks of the first and second lines were held by the cavalry and in the case of the first line the dragoons protected the front or flanks of the cavalry. The infantry formed the centre and in front or beside each regiment would have been (ideally) at least two three pounders. An individual infantry regiment was arranged with the pikemen in the centre and the musketeers equally divided on their flanks. It was usual to post a forlorn hope several hundred feet in advance of the infantry to soften up the opposing enemy forces. This was an ideal situation that the Covenanters did not always try to achieve, often because the terrain prohibited it and it was common for either artillery or dragoons to be lacking. The Covenanters were not timid about initiating action against their opponents as the actions at the Brig of Dee, Newburn, Aberdeen, Auldearn, Alford, Kilsyth, Philiphaugh, Balvenie, Carbisdale, Marston Moor, Mussel-burgh, Hamilton and Inverkeithing attest. However, they also stood to receive the enemy attack as at Tippermuir and Inverlochy. The defensive pose at Benburb and Winwick was due more to exhaustion of the troops than any advanced tactical consideration, and the same posture at Dunbar arose from unpreparedness of the units. At Boldon Hills and Hilton in 1644 Leven stood on the defensive against Newcastle, because the cautious approach was the safest for an army deep in enemy territory and far from either a friendly army or garrison. Thus one can conclude that the Covenanters were not militarily ignorant in their campaigns and battles. Defeat arose more often from the exceptional skill of the opposition, the lack of trained men and leaders and sheer bad luck than from any intrinsic flaws in the Covenanting war machine.

The preceding has provided, hopefully, some initiation into the military world of the Covenanters which allows the individual entries to be seen as trees in a vaster forest.

Guide to Users

There are certain things which a reader consulting this work should always remember. Usually a regiment is listed only under the army for which it was raised without cross-referencing. For example, Lawers' foot was raised in 1642 for the Ulster Army and continued in service until 1651 in the Home Army, the Engager Army, the Army of the Covenants and the Army of the Kingdom, but its history is found only under the Ulster Army. However, in the cases of Cochrane's/Home's, Munro's and Lord Sinclair's foot (all first levied for the army of the Second Bishops' War), they are cross-referenced under the Ulster Army, because they have become commonly identified with the latter army. In addition to being known under a territorial designation units were also known by the name of their colonel (or lieutenant colonel, if he was actively commanding). Regiments which were raised by one colonel who was subsequently replaced are only listed under the name of the first colonel if they lack a territorial designation. Garrisons are usually not treated unless the regiment which provided the men has been identifiable. All currency is rendered in value of pounds Scots. In the seventeenth century £1 Scots was exchangeable for 1s. 8d. English.

NOTES

1. *APS*, V. 177, 180-1; *Privy Council*, 2nd Ser. I. 158-9, 180-1, 185-6, 197-8, 213-5, 379, 418-20, 502-5, 591; *Ibid.*, II. 30-1, 61-2, 88-90, 93-5, 114, 168-71.

2. *Ibid.*, 1st Ser. VII. 68-70, 74, 76, 87-8, 91-2, 115, 255, 435; *Ibid.*, VIII. 60, 72-3, 79, 94-5, 106, 113, 126-7, 173-5, 281, 521-4, 738, 740; *Ibid.*, IX. 380-1; *Ibid.*, X. 279-80, 303, 346-8, 350, 389, 488-9, 513, 561, 577, 609-11, 692, 697, 738-40, 742-70; *Ibid.*, XIII. 83-6; *Ibid.*, 2nd Ser. I. 403-5, 450-1.

3. *Ibid.*, 1st Ser. X. 185-6, 189-91, 270-1; *Ibid.*, XI. 403; *Ibid.*, XII. 539-43, 742-5; *Ibid.*, 2nd Ser. I. 18-24, 26-7, 31-6, 38-40, 43-4, 97, 100-110, 188-9.

4. *Ibid.*, 1st Ser. IX. 124-6, 129, 134, 166-70, 178-80, 211, 255, 281, 462, 626; *Ibid.*, X. 47, 289-91, 695, 697, 700-15; *Ibid.*, XIII. 124-8, 280-4, 332-3, 351, 391, 394-5, 477, 591, 609, 657-8; *Ibid.*, 2nd Ser. V. 362-4, 465, 507-9, 522.

5. *Ibid.*, 1st Ser. XII. 257-60, 272-3, 431, 453, 730-1, 739, 781; *Ibid.*, XIII. 137, 146, 478; *Ibid.*, 2nd Ser. I. 49, 67, 83-4, 244-5, 247, 295, 310-1, 313, 315-6, 320-1, 329-30, 347-8, 354-5, 363-4, 381-2, 385, 389, 523, 531-2, 539-40, 542-3, 546, 550-2, 556-7, 561-3, 565-7, 580, 585, 603-4, 608-9, 611-13, 627-8; *Ibid.*, II. 7-8, 31-7, 40, 55-6, 71, 77-8, 84, 97, 105-6, 113-4, 147-8, 162, 241, 295-7, 303-4, 308-9, 325-6, 332-3, 397-8, 405-6, 456-7, 472, 600, 608; *Ibid.*, III. 48, 99, 120-1, 124, 136-8, 142-3, 147, 152, 167, 169, 197, 208, 214-5, 282, 288-9, 313; *Ibid.*, IV. 193-4, 219, 318-20, 342-3, 349-51, 360-1, 482-4, 525, 531-2; *Ibid.*, V. 65-6, 79-81; *Ibid.*, VI. 28-9, 65-6, 140-1, 157, 225-6, 401-2, 458-9, 484-5, 526-7, 533; *Ibid.*, VII. 84-5, 103-4, 106-7.

6. *Ibid.*, 1st Ser. XII. 191-2, 308, 377, 379, 627, 639.

7. *APS*, IV. 441; *Privy Council*, 1st Ser. X. 261, 328, 477-8, 612-5; *Ibid.*, XII. 646, 721; *Ibid.*, 2nd Ser. I. 337; *Ibid.*, II. 44, 52-3, 57-8, 67-8, 70, 74-5, 125-8, 131-2, 159-61, 174-5, 184-8; *Ibid.*, III. 125, *Ibid.*, V. 27.

8. Furgol, 'Religious Aspects', 6, 13, 23-5, 31-2, 51.

9. *Ibid.*, 6, 13, 25, 32.
10. *Ibid.*, 7, 14, 50, 53, 59.
11. *Ibid.*, 40-1.
12. *Ibid.*, 50, 53, 59-60.
13. *Ibid.*, 56.
14. *Ibid.*, 10-11, 15-7, 19-20, 26-9, 33-4, 36, 43-4, 53-4, 59, 61-2.
15. *Ibid.*, 8-9, 14-5, 19, 25-6, 35, 41, 46-7, 49-50, 56, 60-1.
16. *APS*, VI.i. 708-9.
17. *APS*, VI.i. 631, 672; *Ibid.*, VI.ii. 587; SRO, P.A. 11.11, f. 6; see below, chapter four, Ulster Army.
18. *APS*, VI.ii. 599, 625; *The Journal of Thomas Cunningham of Campvere*, ed. E. J. Courthope (Scottish History Society, 3rd Ser. XI, 1928), 65, 95; see below, 149, 154.
19. *APS*, VI.i. 708-9; see below, 112.
20. SRO, P.A. 11.11, f. 6; *APS*, VI.i. 631, 672; *Ibid.*, VI.ii. 587, 590; see below, 108, 114-26, 129-30, 145-8, 150-2, 154-60, 167-8, 171-2, 177-8, 183-7.
21. See below, 134-5, 158.
22. SRO, P.A. 11.11, f. 19; Committee of Parliament, *Act Anent the out comming of Horses* (Edinburgh, 1640), s.s.; *APS*, VI.ii. 599, 625; C. C. P. Lawson, *A history of the uniforms of the British Army*, 2 vols. (London, 1940), i. 83-4; see below, 159, 341.
23. *APS*, VI.i. 708-9; Lawson, *Uniforms*, i. 106; see below, 138-40, 304, 339-40.
24. *Baillie*, i. 211-12; Stevenson, *Covenanters*, 72, 109; see below, 42, 83, 112-3, 248, 297-8, 360-1.
25. Spalding, *History*, i. 108; Gordon, *History*, iii. 260-1; Cowan, *Montrose*, 68; J. Aiton, *The Life and Times of Alexander Henderson* (Edinburgh, 1836), 387; J. Buchan, *Montrose* (London, 1928), 119; Lawson, *Uniforms*, i. 57, 67, 69, 136; see below, 17, 32, 298-9, 319.
26. Spalding, *History*, i. 107; *Ibid.*, ii. 220, 271; *Baillie*, i. 212; Gordon, *History*, iii. 260; Bod Lib. MS Carte 77, f. 601; Brit. Lib. MS Harleian 1460, ff. 2, 8, 34; *APS*, VI.ii. 605; W. Wheatly, *A Declaration of the Scottish Armie concerning their immediate marching towards the Borders of England* (London, 1647), 4; *A great Fight in Scotland between the Lord Gen. Cromwell's forces and the Scots upon the advance of Lieutenant General Lesley, and Col. Massie from Sterling towards Glasgow* (London, 1651), 2.

2
Army of the First Bishops' War, 1639

Ardnamurchan's Retinue

Colonel: Sir Donald Campbell of Ardnamurchan

Ardnamurchan led a force of Campbells from Argyll to raid Colonsay, the stronghold of Coll MacGillesbuig MacDonald (the father of Alastair MacColla MacDonald). The raiders succeeded in capturing Coll and returned to mainland Argyll by 25 June. Ardnamurchan's force was then sent to Islay to prevent landings either by Lord Wentworth's Irish army or the MacDonnells of Antrim (who were allies of the Clan Ian Mor or Clan Donald South).[1] This force probably disbanded when news of the Treaty of Birks reached the area.

Earl of Argyll's Regiments

Colonel: Archibald, 8th earl of Argyll

Ministers: Dugald Campbell; Archibald MacCallum[2]

Although the Tables only authorised Argyll to protect the west coast and the Firth of Clyde, and to watch the MacDonalds, Lord Wentworth's army and the Highland royalists in 1639, the earl had begun to prepare for war in 1638. On 2 August 1638 a muster of the Campbells occurred at Inveraray at which Sir Colin Campbell of Glenorchy (Perthshire) produced information on 124 of his men. In early 1639 Argyll purchased a frigate and arms from the Dutch. By April a regiment of at least 900 foot had been levied from Argyll, Dunbartonshire and the Campbell lands in Perthshire. At the initial muster the first and only difficulty in this regiment's history manifested itself. Glenorchy's men resisted signing the National Covenant and other clansmen seemed ready to mutiny in support of them. However, Argyll coerced his followers into signing by promising to heavily punish those who held back. In April the regiment had its first success when Archibald MacDonald of Sanda, his son and two of the earl of Antrim's agents were arrested. At the same time 500 men under Sir Duncan Campbell of Auchinbreck were despatched to Kintyre to construct and defend a fort at Lochhead. Argyll, himself, landed on Arran and seized Brodick Castle. He forced the islanders to take the Covenant and supply his men. To the north the inhabitants of Dumbarton had captured the castle by a ruse. Argyll claimed the title of governor and garrisoned the castle with 40 men under MacAulay of Ardincaple. Meanwhile in Argyll the regiment had forced Sir James MacDonald of Sleat and about 300 MacDonalds from Kintyre and Islay to flee to Antrim. By April a force under Mungo Campbell of Lawers had reached Aberdeenshire to watch the royalists there. On 6 April the earl of Montrose ordered these 500 men to quarter in the lands attached to Drum and Pitfoddels houses. Lawers' force occupied Aberdeen on 11 April. The detachment retained its discipline during the occupation, for which it received a payment of £333 6s. 8d. upon departing on 13 April. On 10 June the regiment was ordered to rendezvous at Stirling to watch for Irish and English invaders. From there, the men, clad in red trousers, marched towards the Border, which they failed to reach by the signing of the treaty. By 4 July Argyll had begun to disband parts of the regiment; the Lochhead garrison was reduced to 200 men at this time.[3]

Earl of Atholl's Retinue

Colonel: John, 1st Earl of Atholl

Little is known about this force led by a crypto-royalist. During Montrose's May occupation of Aberdeen 300 men served under his command. On 7 June Montrose instructed Menzies of Weem to place his men under Atholl's command for the campaign against the Gordons, which culminated in the battle of the Brig of Dee.[4] Consequently, it may be assumed that this force disbanded on 21 June when Montrose broke up his army.

Auldbarr's Retinue

Colonel: James Lyon of Auldbarr

Auldbarr was a son of the 1st earl of Kinghorn, and a Forfarshire M.P. In 1638 he had persuaded his brother, the 2nd earl, to join the Covenanters. In March 1639 Auldbarr raised a force from his lands and joined Montrose on his first campaign against Aberdeen. On 4 April Auldbarr took up quarters in New Aberdeen. On the same day he seized the magazine in Old Aberdeen. Contrary to his wishes some of his men vandalised the palace of the bishop of Aberdeen. On the 5th Auldbarr, accompanied by his men, went to hear a sermon in Old Aberdeen. He was forced to intervene to protect the palace from further ravaging by his troops.[5] Afterwards he restored the magazine to the inhabitants. This unit evacuated Aberdeen on 12 April with Montrose's army and is not mentioned again; however, it is probable that it served under Montrose in his May and June campaigns.

Lord Balcarres' Horse

Colonel: Sir David, 1st Lord Balcarres

Lord Balcarres was one of the Covenanters responsible for organising the defence of Fife against the marquis of Hamilton's fleet in May 1639. Later in the month he led the Fife contingent of horse to General Leslie's camp at Duns Law.[6] This force disbanded on 20 June following the Treaty of Birks.

Balgillo's Retinue

Colonel: Sir William Blair of Balgillo

The only evidence for the existence of this regiment is found in a kirk session record in Dundee presbytery. On 2 June Monifieth kirk session reported that a soldier in the regiment had returned and that he had previously promised to repent or be banished.[7] From the date it appears that the regiment was part of Montrose's army in the May occupation of Aberdeen.

Lord Balmerino's Horse

Colonel: John, 2nd Lord Balmerino

Balmerino was a leading opponent of Charles I's policies. The king had him tried for treason in 1633 for presenting a petition against a royal policy. He had taken a leading role in protesting against the Prayer Book and in favour of the National Covenant. On Saturday 22 March Balmerino with the earls of Home, Lothian, and Rothes, and Lords Sinclair and Yester, led 1,000 commanded musketeers (probably the same men who had been used against Edinburgh Castle on the previous day) against Dalkeith House. The earl of Traquair immediately surrendered this royal manor, which contained not only the regalia, but also arms and ammunition needed by the Covenanters. After passing the Sabbath in Dalkeith, this force returned to Edinburgh Castle with its prizes. The only mention we have of Balmerino's horse is that it departed from Edinburgh in late March with Colonel Robert Munro's foot and the horse of the earls of Dalhousie, Lothian, Home and Lord Cranston. There were approximately 600 troopers in this unit,[8] which remained on the border until Leslie's army disbanded on 20 June.

Lord Boyd's Regiment

Colonel: Robert, 8th Lord Boyd

Minister: Robert Blair[9]

Like Balmerino, Boyd was an early supporter of the anti-Prayer Book party. On 13 April he and four other lords were ordered to provide a force of 200-300 horse armed with pistols and carbines from Renfrewshire and Lanarkshire for Lord Johnstone's force. By mid-May Boyd had raised his own full or half regiment from the Hamilton and Monkland section of Lanarkshire. It formed part of Leslie's army at Duns Law, disbanding on 20 June.[10]

Buchanan's Foot

Colonel: Sir George Buchanan of Buchanan

This regiment was raised from western Stirlingshire and was one of the few units to contain Highlanders in Leslie's army. The regiment numbered approximately 1,000 foot. Being part of Leslie's army, it saw no action and disbanded with the others on 20 June.[11]

Tutor of Calder's Retinue

Colonel: Colin Campbell, Tutor of Calder and laird of Ardersier

Due to his father's advanced years and his brother John's madness, command of this Campbell force devolved on to Ardersier. By June he had 700 men under his command on Islay. Leaving a Roman Catholic relative (William Campbell) in command of Islay, Ardersier led a plundering expedition against Colonsay. During his absence Richard Owen, the master of one of Lord Wentworth's ships, had lured William aboard his ship by a ruse. On the day of Ardersier's return he too fell into Owen's hands. Before returning to Dublin with the two prisoners, Owen attempted to intercept the boats bringing the plunder of Colonsay to Islay. However, they kept close to the shore and the Campbells on Islay fired on his ship, preventing Owen from gaining any further success against the Campbells. Following the peace treaty Argyll requested that Wentworth return the prisoners. Consequently Ardersier was released by 12 August.[12]

Earl of Cassillis' Foot

Colonel: John, 6th earl of Cassillis

In May Cassillis and the earl of Eglinton were appointed joint commanders of the defence of Galloway and Ayrshire against an Irish invasion. As the attack did not materialise Cassillis led his men (who were probably recruited from the Kyle and Carrick sections of Ayrshire) to join Leslie's army at Duns Law. It is unclear whether this regiment was fully or only partially recruited.[13] It departed from Berwickshire on 20 June, when the army broke up.

Lord Carnegie's Foot

Colonel: James, Lord Carnegie

Lord Carnegie raised his regiment in Angus, probably from among the kinsmen, tenants, servants and workers on his father's (the earl of Southesk) estates. The regiment marched with Montrose to the Tullo Hill rendezvous (29 March). After departing from Aberdeen on 30 March and participating in the campaign against Huntly, Carnegie's men returned to the burgh on 6 April. The regiment marched out of Aberdeen on 12 April with the rest of the infantry under General Leslie's command.[14] As there is no further mention of the regiment in 1639, it may be assumed that it disbanded in mid-April.

Lord Coupar's Foot

Colonel: James, 1st Lord Coupar

This regiment was raised in Perthshire, probably from Strathearn. It served under Montrose in his March-April, May and June campaigns against Aberdeen. The regiment was engaged at the battle of the Bridge of Dee and shared in the occupation of Aberdeen afterwards. On 21 June it disbanded with the rest of Montrose's army following the withdrawal from Aberdeen.[15]

Craigievar's Retinue

Colonel: Sir William Forbes of Craigievar

This force, like others of the northeast lairds, was motivated not only by support of the National Covenant, but just as importantly by a well-established hatred of the Gordon power (which upheld the cause of Charles I). Craigievar's estates were in Aberdeenshire and it was from them that he raised his retinue. Although there is no evidence that Craigievar was one of the lairds who rendezvoused at Kintore on 28 March before joining Montrose at Tullo Hill on the 29th, his subsequent actions suggest that he would not miss an opportunity to be out in the field for the Covenant. Craigievar was one of the Covenanters who fled from Turriff after the royalist attack on 14 May. His retinue formed part of the northeast contingent of 1,000 men which joined Marischal in occupying

Aberdeen on 24 May. This force quartered in Old Aberdeen with other Forbeses. The burgh suffered from their occupation, as did the bishop's palace which they greatly vandalised. Three days after arriving, Craigievar seized the weapons of the Old Aberdonians. On 30 May Montrose's and Marischal's army left Aberdeen and marched to Gight House. They returned to the burgh on 3 June. Craigievar's retinue may have been at the Bridge of Dee and the subsequent occupation of Aberdeen which ended on 21 June.[16]

Lord Cranston's Horse

Colonel: John, 2nd Lord Cranston

Cranston may have raised his cavalry from Midlothian. They formed part of the force that secured the eastern Borders with Balmerino's horse and Munro's foot. There were approximately 600 troopers in the regiment.[17] It is uncertain whether this force served at Duns, but due to Leslie's demands for men Cranston's horse probably remained there until 20 June.

Dalgety's Retinue

Colonel: James Hay of Dalgety and Kinninmonth

Dalgety led the earl of Erroll's men on two occasions for the Covenanters in 1639. On 28 March his retinue formed part of the force of about 500 men under the northeast lairds who had rendezvoused at Kintore. On the next day they advanced to join Montrose's army at Tullo Hill (across the Dee from Aberdeen), where they encamped for the night. On 30 March the retinue entered Aberdeen and remained until Montrose's departure on 12 April. Dalgety and his men were part of the Covenanter force at the Trot of Turriff. On 24 May Dalgety participated in the occupation of Aberdeen by Marischal and Montrose. Three days later Dalgety in company with Ludquharn's retinue took the houses of Foveran and Knockhall, the homes of Sir John Turing and John Udny of Udny respectively. Dalgety's men accompanied Montrose on the remainder of the second campaign and they may have been at the Bridge of Dee.[18]

Earl of Dalhousie's Regiment

Colonel: William, 1st earl of Dalhousie

By late March the earl had raised a force of approximately 600 horse from Midlothian. This regiment accompanied by Balmerino's horse and Munro's foot went from Edinburgh to secure the eastern Borders before April. At Duns it is recorded that the earl led a whole or half regiment.[19] As with the other forces in Leslie's army Dalhousie's would have disbanded on 20 June.

Lord Drummond's Foot

Colonel: James, Lord Drummond

Lord Drummond raised his force from the Perthshire estates of his father, the 2nd earl of Perth. In late May these men accompanied Montrose on his second campaign into the northeast. Drummond's foot occupied Aberdeen for four days, leaving with the rest of the army on 30 May.[20] There is no evidence that it served again until the following year.

Burgh of Dundee Foot

The burgh raised two companies of foot (about 200 men) to serve in Montrose's armies in May and June. As it is unknown under whose command the Dundee contingent served they are treated separately here. Between 24 and 30 May the Dundee men formed part of the occupying army in Aberdeen. On the evening of the first day of the Battle of the Brig of Dee the two Dundee companies tried to seize the southern end of the bridge. However, they were repulsed.[21] On 19 June the men entered Aberdeen and remained there until the 21st when the army disbanded.

Earl of Dunfermline's Retinue

Colonel: Charles, 2nd earl of Dunfermline

The earl raised a force of Fifemen which joined Montrose during his May campaign against Aberdeen. Dunfermline's men remained in the burgh for four days at the end of May, then proceeded to Gight House. Returning to Aberdeen on 3 June, the unit departed from the burgh on the 5th.[22] Although they did not join Montrose for his June campaign, Dunfermline's men may have been involved in the defence of Fife against Hamilton's fleet.

Echt's Retinue

Colonel: Arthur Forbes of Echt

At Turriff on 14 May Echt was one of the Covenanters taken prisoner, but he escaped shortly afterwards. The laird raised a body from his estate in Aberdeenshire which served under Montrose in late May. This retinue was part of a force of northeastern Covenanters which occupied Aberdeen under Montrose's and Marischal's command 24-30 May and served in the field until 3 June. The appearance of the Gordons in the field in June probably kept Echt at home in an attempt to defend his lands against plundering. However, he could have been one of the Covenanters who joined Marischal on 18 June to fight Aboyne.[23]

Earl of Eglinton's Regiment

Colonel: Alexander, 6th earl of Eglinton

Minister: Robert Baillie[24]

In May 1639 Eglinton and Cassillis were placed in charge of the defence of Galloway and Ayrshire against the Irish army of Lord Wentworth. When there was no sign of the Irish Eglinton led his troops to Leith and from there to Duns Law. The regiment reportedly had 1,000 foot, 100 gentry and 200 tenants.[25] Eglinton's force disbanded on 20 June with the rest of Leslie's army.

Lord Elcho's Retinue

Colonel: David, Lord Elcho

Lord Elcho raised his force in Fife in time to join Montrose's first expedition against Aberdeen. The retinue took part in the first occupation of the burgh, after which nothing is heard of them.[26] However, it is possible that Elcho's men formed part of the Fife coastal defence force in the spring of 1639.

Lord Erskine's Foot

Colonel: John, Lord Erskine

Erskine was the heir of the earl of Mar. The earl as hereditary constable of Stirling Castle had delivered that fortress into the Covenanters' hands in early 1639. Lord Erskine raised a force of Perthshire men who had served under Montrose during the first campaign in the northeast. While quartered in the countryside the regiment plundered 120 bolls of grain from Mr. Alexander Reid's lands in Kildrummy. Following the evacuation of Aberdeen on 12 April this regiment marched to the Borders, where it formed part of the army at Duns Law. It was one of the few regiments in that army which contained Highlanders.[27] As with the other regiments in Leslie's army it disbanded on 20 June.

Ferny's Musketeers

Colonel: Sir James Arnot of Ferny

Lieutenant Colonel: Sinclair

Ferny commanded 60 musketeers who were probably raised in Fife. On Sunday 30 March under orders from the earl of Rothes the musketeers marched from Cupar to the Archbishop of St. Andrews' house at Dairsie. Their mission was to search for weapons; however, there were none.[28] It is unknown whether this company formed part of Rothes' regiment or served in the defence of the Fife coast.

Lord Fleming's Regiment

Colonel: John, 8th Lord Fleming

Ministers: George Bennet, Richard Inglis[29]

On 13 April Fleming was one of five nobles ordered to provide 200-300 horsemen from Renfrewshire and Lanarkshire to Lord Johnstone. By May Fleming had raised his own whole or half regiment from Lanark and the Upper Clyde (the parishes of Lesmahagow, Evansdale, Douglas, Carmichael, Carluke, Crawford, Crawford John, Lamington, Culter, Symington, Biggar, Walston, Dolphinton, Dunsyre, Liberton, Covington, Pittenain, Carstairs, Carnwath and Roberton). The regiment served at Duns Law and disbanded on 20 June.[30]

Master of Forbes' Retinue

Colonel: William Forbes, Master of Forbes

The Master of Forbes led the men of his own and his father's estates in Aberdeenshire. This retinue was part of the force of northeastern Covenanters which gathered at Kintore on 28 March. On the next day it marched to join Montrose at Tullo Hill. It then formed part of the army which campaigned in Aberdeenshire from 30 March to 12 April. On 14 May the Master attended the meeting of Forbeses, Frasers and Crichtons at Turriff which a force of Gordons dispersed. However, the Master's military activities were not yet over. On 24 May he led his force into Aberdeen with other Forbeses and the Frasers. Some of his men may have been involved in the vandalisation of the bishop's palace in Old Aberdeen (see above, Craigievar). After Montrose's army dispersed for a second time on 3 June, the Master probably concerned himself with defending the family estates against the royalists. However, on 18 June, he joined the

Covenanting army and fought at the Bridge of Dee. His retinue disbanded on 21 June after sharing in the occupation of Aberdeen.[31]

Lord Fraser's Retinue

Colonel: Andrew, 2nd Lord Fraser

Lord Fraser's seat was at Muchalls Castle in Aberdeenshire and it was from there that he gathered his force of kinsmen, tenants, and followers. On 28 March Fraser with the other northeastern Covenanters rendezvoused at Kintore. The following day they united with Montrose's main army at Tullo Hill. On the 30th his men entered Aberdeen, remaining until the army withdrew on 12 April. Fraser aided the Master of Forbes in defending a house against a band of royalists and accounted for the first blood of the civil wars by killing a servant of Sir George Gordon of Gight. Lord Fraser led his retinue to Turriff for a meeting with the Forbeses and Crichtons on 14 May. However, the sudden appearance of the Gordons caused the Covenanters to flee to their homes. Just ten days later Fraser aided Marischal and Montrose in occupying Aberdeen. During his men's four-day stay in the burgh they supported themselves by foraging in the countryside. Fraser's men accompanied Montrose on his short campaign in Aberdeenshire, which ended by 5 June. Following Aboyne's reappearance Fraser fled from Muchalls Castle, leaving it garrisoned. On 18 June he and his men joined Montrose's army and took part in the battle of the Bridge of Dee and the occupation of Aberdeen. Fraser's retinue disbanded on 21 June with the rest of the army.[32]

Frendraught's Retinue

Colonel: James Crichton of Frendraught

The laird of Frendraught drew his men from the name of Crichton (another Aberdeenshire family). His men were with the Forbeses and Frasers at the Trot of Turriff on 14 May.[33] While it is unknown whether Frendraught had taken the field before that débâcle, it is probable that his men were involved in Montrose's second occupation of Aberdeen (24-30 May), in which so many of the northeast Covenanters took part.

Glenkindie's Retinue

Colonel: Alexander Strachan of Glenkindie

Glenkindie's force originated in Aberdeenshire. In 1639 it participated only in Montrose's second occupation of Aberdeen.[34] Glenkindie may have remained at home when the royalists under Aboyne took the field in June.

Marchioness of Hamilton's Horse

Colonel: Anna, marchioness of Hamilton

Lady Hamilton was a firm Covenanter and one of the chief inspirers of the people in Lothian to resist the royal forces under her son the marquis of Hamilton:

> . . . This lady came forth armed with a pistol, which she vowed to discharge upon her own son, if he offered to come ashore — a notable virago.

By early May she had raised a troop of horse (probably from the Hamiltons' Lanarkshire estates, an area of strong Covenanting sympathies). Lady Hamilton is the only woman known to have taken personal command of Covenanter troops in the field during the 1640s. Her actions worked to inspire the women of eastern Scotland to curse their husbands into resisting the king's forces. Some time in June the horse troop joined Leslie's army at Duns Law. On its banner was a hand repelling a book and the motto 'For God, the King, Religion and the Covenant'. It disbanded on 20 June.[35]

Earl of Home's Horse

Colonel: James, 3rd earl of Home

Home was one of the leading supplicants and Covenanters in Chirnside pres- bytery. In November 1638 he served as an elder at the Glasgow Assembly. On 22 March 1639 he was one of the Covenanter noblemen involved in the seizure of Dalkeith House. By late March he had raised a force of about 600 horse (probably from Berwickshire). These horse were part of the cavalry contingent which accompanied Munro's foot to guard the eastern border.[36] The earl is not mentioned as being at Duns Law, so it is probable that his horse either moved to protect Lothian or disbanded by late May.

Innes' Retinue

Colonel: Sir Robert Innes of Innes

In early April Innes was one of the Moray men who went to Aberdeen to pay his respects to the Covenanters. The laird raised his force from his estates in Nairn- shire. Due to the distance from Aberdeen Innes played a small role in 1639. However, he did take the field after the first royalist resurgence in mid-May. His men were part of the great northern host which reached the Spey near Elgin and then retired after negotiating with the royalists.[37] By late May Innes' force had returned home and disbanded.

Lord Johnstone's Retinue

Colonel: James, 1st Lord Johnstone

Lord Johnstone joined the Covenanting movement in 1637; in the following year he attended the General Assembly at Glasgow. In early spring 1639 he assumed command of a border guard which included the gentry of Annandale. On 13 April Johnstone received orders from the Tables to go where he would to encourage friends and dishearten enemies of the cause. To facilitate his efforts viscount Montgomery and Lords Boyd, Drumlanrig, Fleming and Kirkcudbright were to raise 200-300 horsemen armed with pistols and carbines.[38] Johnstone's force probably disbanded upon learning of the Treaty of Birks.

Earl of Kinghorn's Regiment

Colonel: John, 2nd earl of Kinghorn

Kinghorn was influenced by his brother Auldbarr to join the Covenanters. In 1639 he took part in all three of Montrose's expeditions to Aberdeen. His troops came from both Angus and Fife. In March he was made governor of Aberdeen while Montrose and Leslie marched through the countryside. At that time he commanded a regiment of 1,800 men. On 30 March he ordered the Aberdonians to fill in the trenches that they had dug to protect the burgh or to face the plundering and burning of the town. Three days later he demanded that the burgh provide 6s. 8d. per man per day for eight days as quartering charges. Although this presented the burgh with the unwanted burden of £4,800 in expenses, the earl promised it would be repaid. After remaining in Aberdeen for fifteen days Kinghorn and his men departed from there on 12 April with the rest of the army. Again in late May Kinghorn's regiment occupied Aberdeen for four days. In June the regiment was engaged at the battle of the Bridge of Dee, consequently occupying Aberdeen for a third time. On 21 June the regiment left the burgh and disbanded.[39]

Lord Kirkcudbright's Regiment

Colonel: Thomas, 2nd Lord Kirkcudbright

Kirkcudbright was one of the Covenanting nobles required to provide Lord Johnstone with armed horsemen in April. By mid-May he raised his own whole or half regiment from the Stewartry of Kirkcudbright. This formed part of Leslie's army at Duns Law and disbanded on 20 June with the rest of the army.[40]

Leslie's Retinue

Colonel: John Forbes of Leslie

Forbes of Leslie was the second son of Forbes of Monymusk and yet another of the Aberdeenshire Covenanters. Leslie's retinue formed part of the force of 1,000 northeast Covenanters which joined Montrose in the May occupation of Aberdeen and the subsequent campaign. It is possible that Leslie joined Montrose on his third campaign against Aberdeen in mid-June.[41]

Alexander Leslie's Foot

Colonel: General Alexander Leslie

General Leslie was the commander-in-chief of the Covenanter armies almost continually from 1639 to 1651. In 1605 he entered the Dutch army, where he remained for three years. He then joined the Swedish army, in which he served for thirty years. He gained his fame as defender of Stralsund against Wallenstein. Leslie was with Gustavus Adolphus's army at Lutzen. In 1635 he became a Field Marshall in the Swedish army; two years later that country granted him a pension for his services. His feudal superior, the earl of Rothes, requested that Leslie return to help his country in the following year. In October 1638 Leslie reached Scotland with 'many other' officers who had been in the Swedish service. On 21 March he led a commanded party of 1,000 musketeers in a successful attack against Edinburgh Castle. Besides these men the only troops he is known to have led directly were some Fifemen in Montrose's first occupation of Aberdeen. He served as co-leader of that expedition with Montrose, whom he persuaded to seize the marquis of Huntly in violation of the rules of hospitality. On 12 April he led the army's infantry (save Argyll's men) to the south. During the remainder of the First Bishops' War Leslie was in command of the army on the eastern borders encamped at Duns Law. On 20 June after the Treaty of Birks he disbanded the army and returned to his estate in Fife.[42]

Leslie's Lifeguard of Foot

Joint colonels: Sir Alexander Gibson of Durie, Sir Thomas Hope of Kerse

This unit was also known as the College of Justice regiment, after the institution which raised it. The regiment consisted of 270 musketeers and 160 pikemen. The Lifeguard was in existence by 26 March, so it may have accompanied Leslie on the expedition to Aberdeen. It is certain that it accompanied the General to the eastern border during his stay there. Thus, with the rest of Leslie's army it disbanded on 20 June.[43]

Lord Lindsay's Regiment

Colonel: John, 10th Lord Lindsay

Unlike most of the other regiments Lindsay did not possess sole control of his men. There were two regiments raised from Fife at Duns Law; the earl of Rothes and Lords Lindsay and Sinclair shared their command. This unit disbanded on 20 June following the Treaty of Birks.[44]

Earl of Lothian's Horse

Colonel: William, 3rd earl of Lothian

Ministers: Robert Cunningham, Robert Brownlie, James Ker, Andrew Blackhall, John Makghie/Maghie[45]

Lothian was one of the few Scottish nobles to attend an English university (Cambridge) and to go on a tour of the continent. He served as a captain in the earl of Morton's regiment (1627-8) and as an officer in the Dutch army in 1629. He signed a petition against the Prayer Book in September 1637, and in 1638 he took the National Covenant. The earl also attended the General Assembly of 1638. In March 1639 he was one of the noblemen leading a Covenanter force against Dalkeith House. From the origins of his regimental ministers it appears that his horsemen were raised from the presbyteries of Haddington and Jedburgh. Lothian was one of the five nobles to accompany Munro's foot to the eastern border in late March. At that time his regiment consisted of approximately 600 horsemen.[46] It is unknown whether Lothian's regiment was part of Leslie's army or if it aided in the defence of the Lothian coast against Hamilton.

Lord Loudoun's Regiment

Colonel: Sir John, 2nd Lord Loudoun

Minister: David Dickson

Loudoun had been educated in Scotland and Europe. Although he was knighted by James VI, he had no great love of the Stewarts. Charles I created him an earl and then suspended the charter in 1633. Loudoun had gained his peerage through marriage to the 1st Lord's heiress and probably wished to strengthen his title. In 1639 he was appointed a commissioner to the army; as such he was involved in the negotiations leading to the Treaty of Birks. Loudoun probably raised his regiment from Ayrshire. At Duns Law he commanded 1,200 foot and horse. The regiment disbanded on 20 June after the treaty went into effect.[47]

Lord Lovat's Retinue

Colonel: Hugh, 7th Lord Lovat

Lovat was the chief of the Frasers and held sway over a large part of eastern Inverness-shire. In February his men in alliance with the Mackenzies seized Inverness castle and burgh to prevent it from falling into Huntly's control. In April Lovat's heir attended Montrose's army at Aberdeen. After the first appearance of Aboyne in the field Lovat joined other northern nobles in marching towards Aberdeen. This force numbered 4,000 men, more than a match for the Gordons. However, near Elgin they were persuaded to return home after negotiations with the royalists. It has been suggested that this army was more concerned with keeping outsiders away from the north than in supporting the Covenant.[48]

Ludquharn's Retinue

Colonel: Alexander Keith of Ludquharn

Ludquharn raised his force from amongst Marischal's tenants in Buchan. He was at Turriff when the royalists broke up the meeting there on 14 May. Ludquharn's retinue was out again a few days later when it joined the other northeastern Covenanters in occupying Aberdeen on 24 May. Three days later Ludquharn and Dalgety captured the houses of Foveran and Knockhall, the homes of Sir John Turing and John Udny of Udny respectively. Ludquharn's unit continued to serve with Montrose until 5 June, when the earl marched south.[49] This retinue may have been at the Bridge of Dee and the subsequent occupation of Aberdeen. In which case it would have disbanded on 21 June when the army withdrew.

Earl Marischal's Foot

Colonel: William, 7th earl Marischal

Marischal — a leading Covenanter noble — was the unofficial head of the movement in the shires of Kincardine, Aberdeen and Banff. He raised his regiment from among his tenants in Kincardineshire. On 29 March it was at the Tullo Hill rendezvous of Montrose's army. The regiment withdrew from Aberdeen on 12 April, but Marischal returned to reoccupy the burgh on the 25th. During that occasion his men were not well paid and may have been a burden on the burgesses. On 24 May Marischal entered Aberdeen for a third time. His regiment then numbered 900-1,000 men. Marischal's foot left with the rest of Montrose's army on 30 May on his march to Gight House. On 3 June the regiment was back in Aberdeen and it left the burgh on the 5th with the rest of the army. With the sudden return of Aboyne and his raising of a royalist army Marischal began to feel his position was insecure. He desperately appealed to Montrose to return north with his men. By 14 June Marischal was in the field with 1,200 men against Aboyne. On the 15th at Megra Hill near Stonehaven Marischal routed Aboyne's Highlanders by cannon fire. Two days later Marischal mustered his men, probably inspecting the additional levies. Marischal's men were with Montrose at the battle of the Bridge of Dee. Following the battle the regiment entered Aberdeen and remained for three days when it disbanded on 21 June.[50]

Viscount Montgomery's Regiment

Colonel: Hugh, viscount Montgomery

Ministers: Matthew Brisbane, John Hamilton[51]

Viscount Montgomery was the eldest son of the earl of Eglinton. In 1634 he had served in the French army. The viscount was one of the five nobles instructed to provide Lord Johnstone with armed horsemen on 13 April 1639. Montgomery raised his regiment from Renfrewshire, Cunningham, Paisley and Glasgow, which

> made my Lord Montgomery's regiment among the strongest; both the pietie and militar discipline of his people were commended above all the rest; yea none did doubt bot in all our camp [Dunslaw] those of the West were most-worthie. They came out readilie and in the greatest numbers; they made most conscience of the cause and their behaviour; the feare of them made others stand in awe, who else were near whyles to mutinous insolencies.

The regiment disbanded on 20 June after the Treaty of Birks.[52]

Earl of Montrose's Regiment

Colonel: James, 5th earl of Montrose

Montrose was one of the first to oppose the Prayer Book and support the National Covenant. The Tables appointed him colonel of Perthshire and Angus, from which this regiment was raised. On 1 February Montrose assessed the county of Angus. On the 14th he occupied Turriff with 200 of his own men and 600 northeastern Covenanters. He was there to stent the area. Huntly advanced from Aberdeen with his sons, the Gordon lairds and Lord Reay. On this occasion Huntly withdrew and Montrose completed the stent before heading south. In late March Montrose with Leslie marched north leading 4,000-8,000 men to subdue Huntly. By 29 March the army had reached Tullo Hill, where the northeastern Covenanters joined him. It was at that encampment that Montrose designed the blue cavalry sash, and blue bonnet ribbons for the infantry, which became the symbols of the Covenanter armies. His goal was to instill raw recruits with the feeling of esprit de corps. The regimental colours of his army sported the motto 'For Religion, The Covenant and the Countrie' on a saltire. At 10 a.m. on 30 March the army entered Aberdeen at the Overgate and proceeded out the Justice Gate for a muster on Queen's Links. The army stood at 11,000 men, a sufficient force to overawe the burgh. On 1 April Montrose established a camp at Inverurie. On the 4th Huntly dined with the earl and accepted an altered version of the Covenant. Nine days later Huntly again dined with Montrose, who had been persuaded by Leslie to seize the marquis. Huntly was given the choice of being arrested or journeying to Edinburgh with Montrose at his own free will; he chose the latter. Montrose departed from Aberdeen with the army's horse and Argyll's men on the 13th, going to Edinburgh. Following Aboyne's first appearance in the field Montrose marched north with 3,000-4,000 men of Angus and Strathearn to join Marischal. The latter had already occupied Aberdeen when Montrose re-entered the burgh on 25 May. For its acceptance of Aboyne, Montrose forced the burgh to pay £6,666 13s. 4d. During his stay he received orders from The Tables to proceed south to the Borders with the northern levies. However, on 30 May Montrose commenced a short campaign in Aberdeenshire. He marched to Gight House via Udny and Kellie House. By 3 June his army was back in Aberdeen and he headed south on the 5th, leaving Marischal in charge of securing the northeast. However, Montrose only stayed in the south for a few days. On 18 June he was at the south end of the Bridge of Dee, which had been fortified by Aboyne. If numbers alone had mattered, Montrose would have had little problem. He commanded 4,000-4,600 men from Angus and Mearns (including 1,500 men in his own regiment). Aboyne had only 2,000 foot and 300 horse, but he was secure behind the River Dee. On the first day of the battle Montrose's two twenty-three pounders and light artillery fired too high to be of any effect. During the night he moved his guns up to point-blank range and devised a plan to weaken the royalist position. Although the Dee was too swollen to cross at the nearest fords, Montrose believed he could frighten Aboyne into shadowing a movement inland to protect his flank. On the 19th Montrose marched westwards along the river; Aboyne quickly followed. One of Montrose's officers, John Middleton, led a successful charge across the bridge after the artillery had softened up the defenders. The royalist army fled back to its recruiting areas; Montrose entered Aberdeen. Retribution was swift: forty-eight leading royalists were arrested and the burgh was fined £4,000. In the three days of Montrose's third occupation of Aberdeen his men were estimated to have caused £133,000 of damage and quartering charges. (The city fathers may have been grossly exaggerating to gain tax relief or parliamentary subsidies, for the quartering charge would have been £4,600 at most.) On 21 June Montrose disbanded his army and returned south.[53] His campaigns in 1639 were entirely successful and contributed greatly to the Covenanters' victory in that year.

Monymusk's Retinue

Colonel: Sir William Forbes of Monymusk

Monymusk raised a retinue from his kinsmen, tenants and servants on his Aberdeenshire estate. It formed part of the 1,000 men fielded by the northeast Covenanters in late May. Monymusk's men quartered in Aberdeen (24-30 May), but they supported themselves by foraging in the countryside. While it is unknown whether Monymusk was present at the Trot of Turriff, it is quite possible he attended the meeting there as one of the Forbes lairds. The royalist recovery in June forced him to keep to his house to protect it from plundering. However, he may have brought his retinue out to join Montrose in the earl's third campaign against Aberdeen, which ended on 21 June.[54]

Sheriff of Moray's Retinue

Colonel: Alexander Dunbar of Westfield, Sheriff of Moray

The sheriff led his men of Moray or Elginshire in the northern Covenanting host in May. It is uncertain whether the Moraymen took to the field to prevent the troubles from spreading into their region or to show their solidarity with the Covenanting movement. This unit, like others in the northern army, returned home after negotiating with the royalists near Elgin in late May.[55]

Sir Robert Munro's Foot

Colonel: Sir Robert Munro

Lieutenant Colonel: Colin Pitscottie

Munro came from a military family and served on the continent from 1628-1636. He retired from the Swedish army with the rank of colonel to raise pensions for old mercenaries and to build a hospital for them, as well as to write his memoirs. He was a firm believer in book learning for soldiers. In addition he thought soldiers should be pious. Psychologically, he was prone to bouts of melancholy.[56] His lieutenant colonel was also a veteran of the European wars. Munro's was the first unit raised by the Covenanters. One writer claims that each parish was to provide him with six-eight men, who were adulterers, fornicators, thieves, murderers, drunkards, and sabbath-breakers. However, the evidence which survives connects only one case of fornication with the regiment. Munro's regiment was raised from the lands south of the Tay for the purposes of guarding the border, suppressing the royalists and training soldiers. There were 2,000 foot in the regiment, which must have made it a rather unwieldy unit. On 21 March Munro and some of his regiment took part in the successful attack on Edinburgh Castle. The Tables commissioned him a major general and sent him to guard the eastern border in late March with a force of 3,000 horse. On 13 April Munro received orders to detach 300 foot to garrison Dumfries. Eventually the remainder of the regiment marched to the western border to subdue the Roman Catholic earl of Nithsdale and Lord Herries and to guard the frontier against the English. During the occupation Munro's men took £3,333 13s. 8d. worth of plate from Herries' House of Terregles. By 1 June the regiment had departed from the area, leaving the local Covenanters liable to attack from Caerlaverock Castle or Carlisle. The burgh of Dumfries informed General Leslie that '. . . all honest men were disheartened . . .' when Munro's regiment were ordered out of the region in its request for the return of the men.[57] It is unknown if Munro joined Leslie's army at Duns Law, or marched into Ayrshire or Lothian to defend those areas against expected invasion. In any case Munro's unit disbanded after the Treaty of Birks.

Philorth's Retinue

Colonel: Sir Alexander Fraser of Philorth

Philorth was noted as being a pious and civil man. He attended the General Assembly of 1638 as an elder. In May 1639 he raised a force from his estates, which were located in the Buchan area of Aberdeenshire. On 28 May Philorth's retinue entered Old Aberdeen accompanied by the Tutor of Pitsligo's force. The two units numbered 200 men in all and they stayed in King's College (the only quarters in the area). However, both units drew their subsistence from the countryside. Philorth's retinue accompanied Montrose on his march to and from Gight House. This unit disbanded on 5 June, but it may have been at the Bridge of Dee and reoccupation of Aberdeen.[58]

Tutor of Pitsligo's Retinue

Colonel: Alexander Forbes of Boyndlie, Tutor of Pitsligo

In March Boyndlie raised Lord Pitsligo's men in Aberdeenshire. They formed part of the force which rendezvoused at Kintore on 28 March. The next day they marched on to join Montrose at Tullo Hill whence they served under him until 12-13 April when the army dispersed. They were involved in the Trot of Turriff. However, they joined Montrose in reoccupying Aberdeen between 28 and 30 May. During that time they quartered with Philorth's retinue in Old Aberdeen and lived off the countryside. Tutor's men served on the campaign against Gight House (30 May - 3 June) and returned to its recruiting grounds in

Buchan on the 5th. It is uncertain whether this unit served again on Montrose's last campaign against Aberdeen, 18-21 June.[59]

Pluscardine's Retinue

Colonel: Thomas Mackenzie of Pluscardine

Pluscardine raised this force from his estate in Moray. It joined the other northern Lords who were heading towards Aberdeen in May after Aboyne's first period in the field.[60] This unit also returned homewards after negotiations with the royalists. From Pluscardine's later behaviour it may be reasonably assumed that he was one of the northern Lords more concerned with preventing the troubles from spreading into his bailiwick than upholding the cause of the National Covenant. Following the First Bishops' War he avoided public life until rebelling against the kirk party regime in 1649.

Lord Reay's Retinue

Colonel: Sir Donald, 1st Lord Reay

Lord Reay was the chief of Clan Mackay. As such he was the leading power in the Strathnaver part of Sutherland. In the 1620s and 1630s he had been heavily employed in recruiting Scottish soldiers for the kings of Denmark and Sweden. Although he had signed the National Covenant in 1638, he was a royalist at heart. (For instance in 1644, the marquis of Huntly fled to Strathnaver, where he was protected by the Mackays for nearly two years.) The fact that his enemy Sutherland was a strong Covenanter could only have led him to align himself with the royalist camp. However, in May 1639 Reay led his clansmen in the force of 4,000 northerners who took the field after Aboyne's first rising. For the Mackays this campaign (which ended with a negotiated settlement near Elgin) must have been particularly galling as they had the furthest to march and neither glory nor booty was gained by their exertion.[61] After May 1639 Reay played little part in the public affairs of Scotland.

Earl of Rothes' Regiment

Colonel: John, 6th earl of Rothes

The earl was one of the oldest opponents of the policies of James VI and Charles I. He had opposed the Five Articles of Perth, the Act of Revocation and the introduction of vestments (in 1633). Rothes was the political leader of the

Covenanting movement. On 22 March 1639 he was one of the nobles involved in the taking of Dalkeith House. At Duns Law Rothes was one of the three co-colonels of the two Fife regiments with Lords Lindsay and Sinclair.[62] The regiments disbanded on 20 June. However, Rothes was more of a political animal than his compatriot Montrose and he was probably relieved that politicising could once more return to the fore.

Earl of Seaforth's Retinue

Colonel: George, 2nd earl of Seaforth

Seaforth was the most deceitful and unscrupulous man of his time in Scotland. Although he had signed the National Covenant, this act was nothing more than a way of insuring himself against attacks by the seemingly all-powerful Covenanters. In February 1639 he permitted his clansmen to participate with the Lovat Frasers in seizing Inverness burgh and castle. This act again was probably motivated more by a sense of self-preservation than out of zeal for the Covenant. If Inverness had fallen to Huntly, the earl would have had to answer for his support of the National Covenant. On the other hand, if the Covenanters had installed their own garrison in the most important burgh near his territories Seaforth's local influence could have been curtailed. During the first occupation of Aberdeen Seaforth paid court to the Covenanters by visiting the burgh for a few days. In May he was probably an instigator in raising the northern Lords to march towards Aberdeen. It is likely that the Mackenzies provided the bulk of the 4,000 men in that force. The outcome of the campaign — the northerners returning home after negotiations with a smaller royalist force — casts further doubt on Seaforth's loyalties.[63] There is a good possibility that this force took to the field to prevent the far north from becoming embroiled in the difficulties of the rest of the country. Certainly from Seaforth's future history one would have to be very generous to think that his actions at this time were done out of love for the Covenant.

Lord Sinclair's Regiment

Colonel: John, 9th Lord Sinclair

In March Sinclair was one of the nobles who led the force against Dalkeith House. By mid-May he was one of the co-commanders of the two Fife regiments; the other two nobles were Lindsay and Rothes. The regiments disbanded on 20 June.[64]

Master of Yester's Regiment

Colonel: John, Master of Yester

In 1638 Yester represented the presbytery of Haddington at Glasgow. Like Sinclair, he was involved in the capture of Dalkeith House on 22 March. By mid-May he had raised a whole or half regiment from Peeblesshire. He joined Leslie's army on the eastern border and was in the camp at Duns Law. The regiment disbanded with the rest of the army on 20 June.[65]

NOTES

1. Stevenson, *Alasdair*, 69-70.
2. *Argyll*, i. 36.
3. SRO, GD. 112/39, 754, 772, 774, 777; *The Black Book of Taymouth*, ed. C. Innes (Bannatyne Club, 100, 1855), 398-404; *Council of Aberdeen*, i. 159; *Dumbarton Burgh Records, 1627-1746*, ed. J. Young (Dumbarton, 1860), 57-60; Gordon, *History*, ii. 204-5, 252; Spalding, *Memorialls*, i. 166-7, 171; Cowan, *Montrose*, 71; Stevenson, *Covenanters*, 31; Stevenson, *Alasdair*, 68; C. V. Wedgwood, *The King's Peace 1637-1641* (paperback edn., London, 1973), 235.
4. *Aberdeen Letters*, ii. 130; Spalding, *Memorialls*, i. 193; Cowan, *Montrose*, 77.
5. Spalding, *Memorialls*, i. 159-60; Foster, *Members*, 221; *Scots Peerage*, viii. 294.
6. *Baillie*, i. 211; J. N. Buchanan, 'Charles I and the Scots, 1637-49' (Toronto Univ., Ph.d. thesis 1965), 241.
7. NRH, OPR Monifieth, 2 June 1639.
8. SRO, GD. 112/39, 389; Balfour, *Works*, ii. 321-2.
9. *The Life of Mr. Robert Blair, Minister of St. Andrews*, ed. T. McCrie (Woodrow Society, xiii, 1848), 589.
10. NLS, Acc. 6026, 524; *Baillie*, i. 200.
11. *Baillie*, i. 212; 'The Journal of John Aston, 1639', *North Country Diaries*, i, ed. J. C. Hodgson (Surtees Soc., cxviii, 1910), 28.
12. Stevenson, *Alasdair*, 69-70.
13. *Baillie*, i. 201, 211; Gordon, *History*, ii. 253.
14. *Aberdeen Letters*, ii. 130-1; J. Row, *The History of the Kirk of Scotland from the Year 1558 to August 1637 with a Continuation by his son John Row* (Woodrow Soc., xxii, 1842), 513.
15. *Aberdeen Letters*, ii. 130-1.
16. Spalding, *Memorialls*, i. 185, 192, 196, 209.
17. SRO, GD. 112/39, 389.
18. Spalding, *Memorialls*, i. 154, 185, 193, 196, 209.
19. SRO, GD. 112/39, 389; *Baillie*, i. 211.
20. *Aberdeen Letters*, ii. 130.
21. Gordon, *History*, ii. 253, 276.
22. Spalding, *Memorialls*, i. 193.
23. *Ibid.*, i. 185, 193, 209.
24. *Baillie*, i. 200.
25. *Baillie*, i. 200-1, 211; Gordon, *History*, ii. 253; W. M. Metcalf, *A History of the county of Renfrew from the earliest times* (New Club, xiii, 1905), 257.

26. Row, *History*, 513; Spalding, *Memorialls*, i. 154, 167-8.

27. *Baillie*, i. 211-2; Spalding, *Memorialls*, i. 154, 162.

28. Balfour, *Works*, ii. 323.

29. SRO, PR Lanark, 9 May, 6 June 1639.

30. NLS, Acc. 6026, 524; *Baillie*, i. 200-1, 211.

31. *Aberdeen Letters*, ii. 130-1; Gordon, *History*, ii. 255; Spalding, *Memorialls*, i. 154, 185, 192, 209.

32. *Aberdeen Letters*, ii. 130-1; Gordon, *History*, ii. 255; Spalding, *Memorialls*, i. 154, 198-9, 206-7, 209.

33. Gordon, *History*, ii. 255.

34. Spalding, *Memorialls*, i. 193.

35. *CSPD 1639*, 146, 163, 231, 282.

36. SRO, GD. 112/39, 389; Balfour, *Works*, ii. 321.

37. Spalding, *Memorialls*, i. 157, 194.

38. NLS, Acc. 6026, 524; W. Makey, *The Church of the Covenants 1637-1651* (Edinburgh, 1979), 39; *Scots Peerage*, i. 255-6.

39. *Aberdeen Letters*, ii. 130-1; *Council of Aberdeen*, i. 155; Spalding, *Memorialls*, i. 154, 167-8; *Scots Peerage*, viii. 297.

40. NLS Acc. 6026, 524; *Baillie*, i. 211.

41. Spalding, *Memorialls*, i. 198-9, 209.

42. *Army of the Covenant*, i. x; Balfour, *Works*, ii. 321; Row, *History*, 511, 513; Spalding, *Memorialls*, i. 154, 167-8; *Scots Peerage*, v. 373-4.

43. *Baillie*, i. 212; T. Hope, *A diary of the public correspondence . . . 1633-45* (Bannatyne Club, lxxx, 1843), 88.

44. *Baillie*, i. 211.

45. SRO, PR Haddington, 12 June 1639; PR Jedburgh, 29 May 1639.

46. SRO, GD. 112/39, 389; Balfour, *Works*, ii. 321; *Scots Peerage*, v. 469-71.

47. *Baillie*, i. 200, 211; *Scots Peerage*, v. 506.

48. Spalding, *Memorialls*, i. 164, 194; Cowan, *Montrose*, 64.

49. Spalding, *Memorialls*, i. 185, 192, 195, 198-9, 202.

50. *Aberdeen Letters*, ii. 130-1; G. Burnet, *The Memoirs of the Lives and actions of James and William, dukes of Hamilton and Castle Herald* (2nd edn., Oxford, 1852), 150; Row, *History*, 511, 513; Spalding, *Memorialls*, i. 154, 192, 198-9, 208-9; *Scots Peerage*, vii. 57.

51. SRO, PR Paisley, 11 April, 23 May 1639; W. M. Metcalfe, *A History of Paisley 600-1908* (Paisley, 1909), 257-8.

52. *Baillie*, i. 201; Metcalfe, *Paisley*, 257-8; *Scots Peerage*, iii. 450.

53. *Aberdeen Letters*, ii. 130-1; *Baillie*, i. 196, 211; Burnet, *Memoirs*, 150, 181; *Memoirs of Guthry*, 53, 57; Row, *History*, 511, 513; Spalding, *Memorialls*, i. 154, 192-3, 198-203, 211-12; Wishart, *The Memoirs of James, Marquis of Montrose, 1639-1650*, eds. A. D. Murdoch and H. F. M. Simpson (London, 1893), 18; Cowan, *Montrose*, 63, 65, 70, 72-9.

54. Spalding, *Memorialls*, i. 193, 209.

55. *Ibid.*, i. 194.

56. Stevenson, *Covenanters*, 80-3.

57. NLS, Acc. 6026, 524; Woodrow Analecta Folio 63, 76; SRO, GD. 112/39, 389; KSR Kilconquhar, i. 21; *Baillie*, i. 192; Balfour, *Works*, ii. 321; *The Book of Caerlaverock: memoirs of the Maxwells, earls of Nithsdale, lords Maxwell and Herries*, 2 vols., ed. W. Fraser (Edinburgh, 1873), i. 384; Gordon, *History*, ii. 204; *Historical Notices of St. Anthony's Monastery, Leith and Rehearsal of Events . . . in the North of Scotland from 1635 to 1645 in relation to the National Covenant*, ed. C. Rodgers (Grampian Club, xiv, 1877), 53.

58. Spalding, *Memorialls*, i. 196, 198-9, 209; *Scots Peerage*, vii. 441-3.

59. Spalding, *Memorialls*, i. 154, 185, 196, 198-9, 209.

60. *Ibid.*, i. 194.
61. *Ibid.*
62. *Baillie*, i. 211; Balfour, *Works*, ii. 321; *Scots Peerage*, vii. 297-8.
63. Spalding, *Memorialls*, i. 164, 194; Cowan, *Montrose*, 64.
64. *Baillie*, i. 211; Balfour, *Works*, ii. 321.
65. *Baillie*, ii. 211; Balfour, *Works*, ii. 321; Makey, *Church*, 41.

3
Army of the Second Bishops' War, 1640-1641

Amisfield's Foot

Colonel: Sir John Charteris of Amisfield

Amisfield served as an M.P. for Dumfriesshire and the Stewartry of Annandale in 1639 and in 1641. His regiment was probably raised from eastern and central Dumfriesshire. It was on foot by 2 September 1640 when General Leslie ordered it south from the western Border with the deserters from that region's regiments in tow. Upon the regiment's arrival in Newcastle Amisfield was appointed a commissioner to the negotiations at Ripon. On 15 October the regiment received orders to worship in St. John's church, Newcastle with Lords Loudoun's and Lindsay's regiments. There is no other mention of this regiment, but it may be assumed that it remained in Newcastle until the army withdrew and that it disbanded on 27 August 1641.[1]

Ardnamurchan's Regiment

Colonel: Sir Donald Campbell of Ardnamurchan

Sir Donald raised this unit from among the Campbells, their allies, tenants and servants near his own estates. The earl of Argyll commissioned Ardnamurchan and Glenorchy to raise regiments on 1 October 1640. They were to act against the MacDonalds in Lochaber and Glengarry, Donald Robertson, Tutor of Struan, and their allies. These clans were resisting Argyll's attempts to claim feudal superiority over Lochaber and Badenoch as well as opposing the Covenanters. Even in 1641 the MacDonalds were not fully pacified. Indeed, Ardnamurchan's and Glenorchy's campaigns, which consisted of cattle raiding, plundering and burning, may have incited the MacDonalds to join Alastair MacColla MacDonald in 1644. Ardnamurchan's regiment disbanded sometime in 1641 (by the end of August at the latest).[2]

Earl of Argyll's Foot Regiments

Colonel: Archibald, 8th earl of Argyll

Ministers: Donald Campbell, Duncan McCalman, John MacLachlan[3]

In spring 1640 the Committee of Estates granted Argyll two commissions. One authorised him to defend the western coast against the Irish threat. The other was a commission of fire and sword against the royalists in central Scotland. The latter order was very satisfying to Argyll. On the one hand he was able to pursue hereditary feuds, on the other hand he was enabled to do some empire-building — yet he served the Covenant by doing both. In 1639 Argyll had taken Lochaber and Badenoch as pledges for debts owed to him by the marquis of Huntly. Argyll desired to establish himself as feudal superior over those lands, and a campaign in them against those who opposed him was suitable to his own desires. On 18 June 1640 Argyll held rendezvouses at Inveraray and Clachandysert (in Glenorchy). Between 4,000 and 5,000 of his kinsmen, allies, tenants and servants appeared. They were formed into three regiments, two under the earl and the third under Sir Robert Campbell of Glenorchy. Before taking action Argyll gained the Camerons as allies. After that his forces ravaged the lands of the MacDonalds of Keppoch in Lochaber, which included the burning of Keppoch's house as punishment for his opinions. From there Argyll's army proceeded to pillage and burn in Badenoch, and the Braes of Mar, where the royalist Farquharsons lived. Argyll then entered Atholl where he encountered a force under the earl of Atholl and the local gentry. Under the pretence of negotiating Argyll lured the leaders to his camp and then captured them. Argyll ordered the leaders to disband their men, which they did. Subsequently Argyll forced the Athollmen to pay £10,000 for his army's quartering charges. He also compelled the earl to provide a regiment for Leslie's army. From Atholl Argyll proceeded against the royalist Ogilvies in the Braes of Angus. In the most famous incident of the campaign he had the house of Airlie razed to the ground. Argyll also had Forter House (another home of the earl of Airlie), destroyed. On 13 July after ravaging the Ogilvy lands for a week Argyll marched into Rannoch, home of the royalist Robertsons, which was plundered and wasted. Throughout the campaign Argyll was a strict disciplinarian. He allowed his men to steal food only from non-Covenanters. On 26 July five soldiers, who had stolen goods, were executed. Seldom were Covenanting soldiers dealt with so harshly. On 2 August the campaign ended after six weeks of devastating the lands of enemies of the Campbells and the Covenant.

Argyll's military activities were not finished. The earl laid siege to Dumbarton Castle, which fell on 27 August. This success deprived Lord Wentworth's Irish army of a secure landing spot in Scotland. Mention of Argyll's regiments disappears until 3 October when the Synod of Argyll made provision for ministers with a regiment in England. It is doubtful that any of Argyll's men were in England, because General Leslie did not request Argyll's regiments until 17 October. One week later Argyll countermanded the orders for bringing his men south, believing that the current peace talks would be fruitful. Apparently, Argyll's regiments (save the Dumbarton Castle garrison), disbanded sometime in autumn 1640 after being in existence for less than six months.[4]

Train of Artillery

Commander: Sir Alexander Hamilton, General of Artillery

Ministers: James Ker, Thomas Wilkie[5]

Hamilton was a brother to the 1st earl of Haddington. He had served in the Swedish army until 1635. Hamilton returned to Scotland in 1638, and was made General of Artillery in the next year. During 1639 and 1640 Hamilton supervised the production of light field guns at Potter Row, Edinburgh. These light guns could be drawn by a horse and possessed a barrel not more than a yard long. In 1640 Hamilton made up the train for General Leslie's invasion of England. The constituents of the train are open to debate. One source claims there were eight large brass guns, many smaller pieces and thirty wagons of ammunition. Another, concentrating solely on the artillery, states that the Covenanters possessed eleven nine pounders, fifty-four field pieces (probably three or four pounders), and eighty frames (little more than groups of large muskets mounted upon a box). These guns were only used at the battle of Newburn, where they made a large contribution to the victory over the English royal army.[6] The train returned to Scotland from Newcastle in late August 1641 and was probably sent to Edinburgh Castle after the army disbanded on the 27th.

Earl of Atholl's Foot

Colonel: John, 1st earl of Atholl

Minister: Patrick Omey[7]

As part of the conditions for his release from Argyll, Atholl promised to raise a regiment from the area of his earldom in Perthshire. At least 500, but possibly 800 men made up this regiment. It was part of the Duns contingent of the army and crossed the border under General Leslie on 20 August. As a sign of his dissatisfaction with events in Scotland the earl signed the Cumbernauld Bond. There is no evidence that the earl's views caused disaffection in the regiment. After Newburn the men were quartered near Newcastle, as their assignment to worship in the Castle Hall (with Lords Carnegie's and Drummond's regiments), indicates. Only one minister is known to have served with the regiment. After November 1640 nothing more is heard of Atholl's Foot. However, it returned north with the army in August 1641, dispersing homewards after the disbanding on the 27th.[8]

Auchmedden's Retinue

Colonel: George Baird of Auchmedden

Auchmedden's estate was in Aberdeenshire near its border with Banffshire on the north coast. It was from his tenants and servants, as well as from others of the name of Baird that this retinue was raised. Auchmedden's men aided the earl Marischal in his occupation of Aberdeen (5-8 May 1640). The unit took part in no engagements and served only to overawe the principal royalist burgh.[9]

Blair's Foot

Colonel: (?) Blair

There is very little information on this unit. It was in existence by 3 April 1640 when a Lieutenant Andrew Wood was mentioned in a case of fornication with a resident of North Leith parish. The lieutenant subsequently confessed and was ordered to satisfy both the civil and ecclesiastical magistrates. The regiment was engaged in the siege of Edinburgh Castle (late May – 19 September 1640). However, its position in the line of circumvallation is unknown.[10] After the fall of the castle there is no further mention of Blair's regiment. However, it may have formed the whole or part of the Covenanting garrison of the castle.

Lord Boyd's Foot

Colonel: Robert, 8th Lord Boyd

Major: (?) Hogg

Ministers: David Dickson, Matthew McKail, Matthew Mowat.[11]

Lord Boyd raised his regiment of 500 foot from amongst his Ayrshire tenants, who were strong Covenanters. Boyd, himself, had his doubts and in August 1640 he was one of the signers of the Cumbernauld Bond. Later Boyd was with Montrose when the latter began corresponding with Charles I. It was Boyd who on 19 November 1640 revealed the existence of the Bond while he lay dying. His men were not affected by his anti-Covenanter activities.[12]

The regiment crossed the Tweed at Coldstream in Leslie's division of the army on 20 August. Subsequently the regiment quartered near Newcastle and was assigned All Hallows, Newcastle (with Dalhousie's and Dundas's men) as a place of worship. This is one of the few units whose regimental elder at the presbytery of the army is known — a Captain Crawford.[13] The major frequented a notorious whore — Abigail Wemyss — and aided her to escape prosecution by the army presbytery. For this the presbytery began proceedings against Hogg.

Information on the regiment after Boyd's death is non-existent. Possibly, James, 9th Lord Boyd received the colonelcy. In any case the regiment departed from Newcastle and disbanded in August 1641 with the rest of Leslie's army.

Lord Burleigh's Regiment

Colonel: Robert, 2nd Lord Burleigh

Minister: Robert Bruce[14]

Lord Burleigh served as the president of the Scottish Estates on five occasions in 1640-41 and as a Commissioner to the treaty negotiations in England during the same period. His power base was in Fife and it was there that he was outfitting a regiment for service with Leslie's army in autumn 1640.[15] If the regiment was indeed levied and sent south it would have returned to disband in August 1641.

Clan Cameron

Colonel: Allan Cameron of Lochiel

By playing on this clan's hatred of the marquis of Huntly's feudal pretensions in Lochiel Argyll gained it for his host in June 1640.[16] The Camerons probably took part in all of Argyll's campaign, due to the great opportunities for plundering. However, it is extremely doubtful that they would have attended the siege of Dumbarton Castle. That type of warfare had no appeal to Highlanders as it offered little in the way of glory or booty. The Camerons probably reached their homes sometime after 2 August 1640.

Lord Carnegie's Foot

Colonel: James, Lord Carnegie

Minister: David Campbell[17]

Carnegie had some difficulties in levying his regiment from Angus. General Leslie had chosen him to serve as a colonel for that shire, however, the shire committee desired its men to serve only under Montrose. After receiving a strong letter from the General and Committee of Estates, the shire backed down. Even then William, Master of Gray and John, grandson of Sir John Scrimgeour, obstructed the mustering. Nevertheless, Carnegie managed to raise

800 foot. He marched in company with Rothes and his regiment from Haddington into England. During the occupation of England the regiment was quartered near Newcastle. It shared the Castle Hall as a place of worship with Atholl's and Drummond's regiments.[18] Like other regiments in Leslie's army this one evacuated Newcastle on 21 August 1641 and disbanded at Leith six days later.

Earl of Cassillis' Foot

Colonel: John, 6th earl of Cassillis

Ministers: John Livingstone, George Dick[19]

On 22 June 1640 the Committee of Estates issued a commission to Cassillis to raise a force of horse and foot to suppress enemies of the Covenant and to defend the people from the Borders to Carrick. Cassillis probably raised his 1,000 foot from southern Ayrshire and Wigtonshire. The regiment joined the army at Duns Law and crossed the Tweed under Leslie. This unit was quartered in or near Newcastle. For purposes of worship Cassillis' joined Lothian's regiment in the chapel at the bridge in the town. One of its chaplains, Mr. Livingstone, commented on the piety of the army at night 'but through the process of time we declined more and more!' It is interesting to note that Livingstone left the army in November, a little less than four months into its existence.[20] Cassillis' returned to Scotland in August 1641, disbanding there.

Cochrane's Foot

Colonels: Sir John Cochrane of that Ilk (1640-41), Robert Home of Heugh (1641-45, 1645-48), John Maxwell (1645)[21]

Lieutenant Colonels: Robert Home of Heugh, John Maxwell (1642-48)

Major: William Cochrane

Ministers: John Aird (?), Robert Cunningham[22]

This regiment (later known as Home's Foot), was mustered into service on 14 and 18 April 1640 and remained on foot until autumn 1648. The origin of the regiment is unknown, but it may have been recruited from various parts of Scotland. One company was definitely raised in Galloway.[23]

After mustering on the Links of Leith the regiment marched to Haddington, where it quartered until sometime in May 1640. From there Cochrane's Foot marched to Dumfriesshire to campaign against the earl of Nithsdale's garrisons in Caerlaverock and Threave Castles. Both strongholds fell in September; the former in an assault which caused the deaths of forty Maxwells. Despite a treaty clause protecting it, Caerlaverock was slighted. Lieutenant Colonel Home, who commanded the operation, also uplifted the earl of Nithsdale's rents for the Covenanters and delivered the goods in the castle to a representative of the Committee of Estates, all contrary to the treaty. By October desertion had become a problem, but the Stewartry of Kirkcudbright Committee of War apprehended and returned some of the men. The regiment remained in Dumfries until 16 September 1641 when it removed to quarters near Edinburgh. There were then 1,000 men and officers in the regiment, which was being retained with Munro's and Sinclair's.[24]

The plot in autumn 1641 known as The Incident brought a change in the commander of the regiment. Cochrane backed the plan to seize Argyll and Hamilton. However, Home refused to join him. Instead, he gave evidence against the plot and was rewarded with command of the regiment. Baillie commented following Cochrane's dismissal (after October 1641):

> ... there never was a sojour of his years of so great credite and expectation universallie in all our land, and now none universallie fallen in such disgrace. . . .[25]

With the outbreak of the Ulster Rising by the native Irish in late October 1641 the fortunes of the regiment underwent a great change. Home's men were immediately earmarked to serve as part of the Scottish expeditionary force to quell the rising. Desertions rose when the men learned of this; they increased more after the soldiers were informed they would not receive the higher English pay rate until the regiment reached Ireland. In an effort to rectify the situation the Privy Council issued a proclamation against soldiers who deserted and those who aided them. Yet the best way to combat the problem was to send the regiment to Ireland as quickly as possible. In March 1642 the men embarked at Ayr. Contrary winds forced the transports of Home's and the other two Scottish regiments bound for Carrickfergus into Lamlash Bay, Arran. There they remained until the winds changed two weeks later. On 3 April the regiments reached Carrickfergus and disembarked that evening.[26]

Home's Foot had a rôle in several of the operations in 1642. At its muster on 7 April there was a total of 856 men and officers; the plague of desertions had not made the regiment unfit for campaigning. During the May campaign to Newry Home led a force of 500 commanded musketeers, one horse troop, two companies of dragoons, several cannon and the baggage train. In the campaign to clear the River Bann from Lough Neagh to the sea Home had 800 men in the field. At the end of the campaigning season Home's Foot (now 980 strong) went into winter quarters in Carrickfergus.[27]

The regiment was active again in the following year. On 4 April 1643 Home furnished men for a two-day expedition to burn the Irish out of Clandeboy's woods near McCartan's lands. On 13 May Home led 600 of his men to besiege

Newcastle in County Down. He managed to steal the garrison's cattle and take their outer works. However, the assault on the castle failed. Upon Major General Munro's appearance with reinforcements the castle surrendered on terms.[28] On 28 August Home was one of the signers of a letter asking the Committee of Estates about the Cessation and requesting supplies. The regiment again took up winter quarters in Carrickfergus. Its first action in 1644 was the surprising of the Ormondist garrison in Belfast. Home was allowed to place 400 of his men in the town, which they cessed for food, money, boats and baggage horses. On 27 June Home's men rendezvoused with Munro at Lisnegarvey as part of the original force for the campaign into Leinster. Apparently only seven of the ten companies participated in this most ambitious of the Ulster Army's expeditions. On 25 July Home's was again part of Munro's core force for the summer campaign against Lord Castlehaven's Irish army. Home's men only returned to their quarters in Belfast and Carrickfergus some-time in September.[29]

The new year brought several changes to the regiment. In April Home led a force of 1,400 commanded foot to Scotland, of which 200 men were from this regiment. The lieutenant colonel was made colonel in Home's absence. In July the Scottish parliament passed an act in favour of the regiment's pay arrears and authorised the apprehension of deserters in Scotland and Ireland. Whatever the advantages gained by that act (there may have been none), the regiment never regained the men who had left under Home. The colonel returned to Belfast by 24 December just in time to oppose the English demands for surrender of the town.[30]

In 1646 the fortunes of the regiment declined further. Home led 500-560 men in the Benburb campaign; there are no exact casualty lists for the battle. A reasonable estimate for Home's regiment would be the loss of between one half and two-thirds of the men engaged. It is little wonder that neither this regiment nor the Ulster Army partook of any more campaigns until 1648. Home and his men almost unanimously accepted the Engagement. Approximately 300 men went across the Irish Sea with George Munro as reinforcements for Hamilton's army. They never returned to Ulster (at least not as soldiers, some may have come back as settlers). In September Colonel George Monck captured the Scottish garrisons. Some of the regiment may have joined him. Captain Patrick Bruce, who had been cashiered as an anti-Engager, was made a lieutenant colonel in Monck's army in 1649.[31] At the time of Monck's dissolution of the regiment there could not have been much more than 200 men left due to evacuations (500), casualties (250-370+), disease (unknown) and starvation (unknown). Home's contained the weirdest Covenanting officer, Captain Lieutenant Thomas Weir, who was executed in 1670 for bestiality and incest.[32] The regiment as a whole had an honourable history. And if the successes of the first years turned into failure in the end (1646-48), that was due more to forces outside the regiment's control than to its men or colonel.

Craigievar's Retinue

Colonel: Sir William Forbes of Craigievar

Craigievar's importance as a northeastern Covenanter increased after the end of the First Bishops' War. In 1639 and again in 1640-41 he served as an Aberdeen-shire M.P. On 5 May 1640 his retinue entered Aberdeen as part of Marischal's force. It departed from the burgh on the 8th. In late June Craigievar possibly instigated the plundering of George Gordon's house at Newtown of Culsalmond.[33] There is no other record of Craigievar's men or his own rôle in the military activities of the Second Bishops' War.

Lord Cranston's Regiment

Colonel: John, 2nd Lord Cranston

The history of this unit is so shadowy as to suggest that it did not exist. On 15 July 1640 an English source in Northumberland repeated the rumour that the earl of Lothian, Lords Cranston and Johnston and Sir William Douglas (sheriff of Teviotdale) were planning to enter England with 2,400 men. They would then split into four or five bodies to plunder. This reeks of an attempt to slur the Covenanters as descendants of the Border reivers. A twentieth-century local history claimed that Lothian, Cranston and Douglas were joint colonels of a Teviotdale regiment of 1,600 men which served under Leslie and disbanded in August 1641.[34] There is no reliable primary evidence that Cranston commanded a regiment on his own or with the support of others.

Earl of Dalhousie's Foot

Colonel: William, 1st earl of Dalhousie

Lieutenant Colonel: George, Lord Ramsay

Ministers: Robert Douglas, Archibald Newtoun[35]

The earl raised his men from Lothian. An English source reported the regiment's strength at 800 foot. The unit was in Leslie's army at Duns, which crossed the border on 20 August. Following Newburn the regiment quartered near Newcastle. It shared All Hallows church, Newcastle with Boyd's and Dundas's regiments. Captain Windram was the regimental elder who attended the presbytery of the army.[36] The regiment withdrew from Newcastle on 21 August 1641 and disbanded six days later.

Lord Drummond's Foot

Colonel: James, Lord Drummond

Minister: James Row[37]

Lord Drummond was certainly a questionable noble to commission as a colonel. In 1639 he married a daughter of the marquis of Huntly, which augured ill for Covenanters hoping of strong support from Drummond. According to Baillie Montrose encouraged Drummond to linger over levying his regiment. Drummond's men were raised in Perthshire, probably on or near the estates of his father, the earl of Perth. In August Drummond signed the Cumbernauld Bond. At Duns this regiment numbered 700 men; it proceeded across the Border under Leslie's command. Following the occupation of Newcastle Drummond was one of three nobles who formed a royalist faction with Montrose. During the occupation of England this unit was quartered near Newcastle. It shared the Castle Hall (Newcastle), with Atholl's and Carnegie's regiments as a place of worship. In August 1641 the regiment left Newcastle as part of Leslie's army and disbanded in Scotland.[38]

Dundas' Foot

Colonel: George Dundas of Dundas

Ministers: Andrew Kerr, James Forbes, James Simson[39]

Dundas was an important shire politician in addition to being a colonel. He served as an M.P. for Linlithgowshire in the Estates of 1639-1641. During that time he was a member of the committees for debts and the plantation of kirks, and of the commission to negotiate the Ripon treaty. Dundas raised his regiment from Linlithgowshire, principally from Linlithgow presbytery. The 400 foot formed part of the Duns contingent which Leslie led across the Border. The regiment quartered in or near Newcastle during the occupation of England. Dundas' shared All Hallows, Newcastle with Boyd's and Dalhousie's regiments. As with the other regiments in Leslie's army this one departed from England in August 1641. It disbanded at Leith on 27 August. The colonel then served on the parliamentary commission for trying a fellow colonel — Montrose — and other royalists.[40]

Earl of Dunfermline's Foot

Colonel: Charles, 2nd earl of Dunfermline

Minister: William Marshall[41]

Dunfermline probably raised his regiment from western Fife. The regiment joined the army at Duns and crossed the border on 20 August 1640. Dunfermline was ordered to Durham with a brigade of foot and some troops of horse after the occupation of Newcastle. He served as governor of Durham and as a commissioner for the Ripon negotiations. During the regiment's stay at Durham there was a mutiny on 19 August 1641, but the details are lacking. However, at 6 p.m. on 25 August at Hirslaw Leslie had one of the mutineers shot at the post. The regiment left the army on the 27th and disbanded in Fife several days later.[42]

Edinburgh Foot

Colonel: Sir Alexander Gibson of Durie

This regiment was also known as the Lord Register's regiment of Edinburgh because Durie became Lord Register in November 1641. The town of Edinburgh apparently provided the men. They were in arms on 12 October 1640 and served until October 1641. The regiment consisted of three field officers, twelve other officers, twenty-eight non-commissioned officers, four scribes, twelve drummers and pipers, a quartermaster, a regimental scribe and 506 privates in four companies. The monthly pay was £6,400 6s. 8d. and on 25 August 1641 the arrears stood at £67,203 10s. or ten and a half months' pay. The regiment probably served in England and quartered near Newcastle. Its colonel was also commander of Leslie's Life Guard of Foot. After 27 August it was decided to maintain this regiment with Cochrane's and Munro's as part of a home guard. However, it appears that this regiment disbanded by mid October as it was not nominated to go to Ulster. Instead Sinclair's regiment was retained as part of the Covenanter army.[43]

Lord Elcho's Foot

Colonel: David, Lord Elcho

Ministers: George Gillespie, George Gibson, John Moncreiffe, Thomas Melville[44]

Elcho raised his regiment from the presbytery of Kirkcaldy in June-July 1640. This unit joined Leslie's force at Duns on 28 July. There is some question as to its size; an English source gives the total of 350, while family papers mention the strength as being 700 men. After the occupation of Newcastle Elcho's men were brigaded with Rothes' Foot for ecclesiastical activities, if not quartering. The two regiments were to share a minister and worshipped together in the Spittall or St. Andrews, Newcastle. In November George Gillespie, one of the chaplains, went to London after the Committee of Estates selected him to serve as a chaplain with the Scottish Commissioners for the treaty. Due to the difficulties in receiving adequate supplies the Kirk raised money for the regiments in England. As part of the presbytery of Kirkcaldy's contributions Elcho's men received £288 13s. 4d. This regiment withdrew from the Newcastle area on 21 August 1641 and left the army at Leith Links on the 27th. Upon reaching Fife it disbanded.[45]

Lord Erskine's Foot

Colonel: John, Lord Erskine

Lieutenant Colonel: (?) Bruce

Minister: John Haysdaill[46]

Lord Erskine levied his men from Stirlingshire. Before joining the army at Duns Erskine committed himself to the Cumbernauld Bond. The estimates of the regiment's strength varied from 600 to 1,000 infantry in ten companies. The unit's location during the occupation of England is unknown. However, negative evidence suggests that it may have been located either to the north or south of the Newcastle area, either guarding the supply line to Scotland or watching the English royal army's movement. In any case it evacuated England in August 1641 and disbanded after 27 August.[47]

Lord Fleming's Foot

Colonel: John, 8th Lord Fleming

Ministers: George Bennet, Alexander Livingston, John Weir, John Currie, John Veitch[48]

The recruits for this regiment rendezvoused at Biggar in early July 1640. The 500 men in the regiment came from the presbytery of Lanark, a strong Covenanter area. Fleming was out of sympathy with his men as he was quick to demonstrate. In August he signed the Cumbernauld Bond then joined the army at Duns. After the occupation of Newcastle he became one of the three nobles in Montrose's royalist faction. His activities had probably no repercussions among his men. Following Newburn the regiment quartered in or near Newcastle, sharing Trinity Chapel there as a place of worship with Maitland's regiment. Fleming's unit left Newcastle on 21 August 1641, departing from the army on the 25th and disbanded upon reaching Lanarkshire.[49]

Master of Forbes' Foot

Colonel: William, Master of Forbes

This was one of the few notorious regiments in the Second Bishops' War army. The Master led the men of his family's Aberdeenshire estates during the 5-8 May 1640 occupation of Aberdeen by Marischal. In the summer one of the regiment's captains commanded 500 foot and two troops of horse on Munro's expedition into Strathbogie and to Banff. The men took part in the destruction of Lord Banff's fine town house. In August Captain John Forbes quartered in Old Aberdeen with the 80 men of his company; they did little damage on that occasion. Simultaneously, the colonel was busy extorting a tenth of the heritor's free rent from the people in the parishes of Old and New St. Machar's and the barony of Balgownie with the aid of a party of musketeers. The Master recruited, armed and paid his regiment by impressing men, forcing heritors to give arms and a forty-days loan, otherwise soldiers would have quartered in their homes. Heritors refusing to outfit his men also faced a fine of £10 13s. 4d. Despite all of his efforts the Master never succeeded in fully recruiting his regiment during his governorship of Aberdeen.

The behaviour of the regiment deteriorated in September 1640. On the 8th Captain John Forbes and his wife occupied the house of a Thomas Lillie in Old Aberdeen where they spent their time drinking. Forbes' company quartered in the area for six days without paying before moving to New Aberdeen. On 20 October the provost and baillies learned that Captain Patrick Murray had assaulted three men and had been contumacious to his colonel, Craigievar and the provost. A fellow officer, Ensign Robert Lumsden had also attacked a man. Captain Forbes was cashiered for shooting a poor man's horse; he was later arrested in Edinburgh for highway robbery. The soldiers were guilty of forcing entry into houses and of kissing or abusing the burgesses' wives in their presence. It is not surprising that the town commissioner to the Estates received orders to submit a grievance against the behaviour of this regiment. On 9 February 1641 the Estates had the regiment disbanded (one of the few times this occurred).[50]

Forbes' Horse Troop

Commander: Captain Arthur Forbes

In May 1640 Captain Forbes received command of a troop raised in Aberdeenshire. The troop formed part of Munro's force which marched from Aberdeen to Strathbogie via Drum and Spynie. During the occupation of the Gordon lands in Strathbogie this unit plundered heavily. Munro became incensed and had the troop disbanded immediately (sometime in July).[51]

Lord Fraser's Retinue

Colonel: Andrew, 2nd Lord Fraser

Lord Fraser and possibly other lairds of the name raised a retinue of kin, tenants and servants in spring 1640 from Aberdeenshire. This force took part in Marischal's occupation of Aberdeen (5-8 May). There is no sign that it took part in Munro's campaign or any other actions in the northeast.[52]

Glenorchy's Foot

Colonel: Sir Robert Campbell of Glenorchy

As early as mid April 1640 Argyll was organising his forces for a campaign against the royalist clans. However, it was not until 18 June that this regiment mustered from Glenorchy's lands in Perthshire and Argyll at Clachandysert. No accurate estimate of the unit's strength can be made. The regiment took part in Argyll's summer campaign. In mid August Glenorchy's vassals and tenants from Argyll were to muster at Tarbert, possibly to besiege Dumbarton Castle or to guard Kintyre against the Irish. On 1 October Argyll commissioned Glenorchy with Ardnamurchan to act against the Keppoch and Glengarry MacDonalds, Donald Robertson, Tutor of Struan and their allies. These groups were resisting Argyll's attempts to claim feudal superiority in Lochaber and Badenoch. However, even in 1641 the MacDonalds remained untamed. On 23 October Argyll informed Glenorchy that his men would not be needed as reinforcements for the army in England as negotiations had already commenced. However, in mid November Glenorchy received news that the negotiations were going slowly and that his men might be needed in England. There is no sign that they ever marched south. The last mention of Glenorchy's men is a notice by Argyll in April 1641 to the laird that he should have his men ready with ten days' supply of bread at twenty-four hours notice. This may have been part of a design for another campaign against the Highland royalists. If Glenorchy had any men still in arms after 27 August 1641, they must have disbanded upon hearing of the army's return accompanied by the king.[53]

Earl of Haddington's Brigade

Commander: Major General Thomas, 2nd earl of Haddington

The earl took over command of the forces in the Merse and Lothian, whose purpose was to watch the English royal garrison in Berwick. The choice was peculiar. Haddington had been appointed to the privy council in 1635. As a councillor he had signed the King's Covenant. In 1640 the earl married a daughter of the marquis of Huntly. On the face of it Haddington should have been the last noble given command over such a sensitive area. On 29 August the earl undertook his only military mission. The governor of Berwick, upon learning that Leslie had left a force of 160 foot to guard some guns left at Duns, launched an immediate attack. The artillery guard put up such strong resistance that Haddington was able to bring reinforcements. The English withdrew to Berwick and Haddington returned to his headquarters at Dunglass Castle. That next afternoon the earl and several of his officers were dead, killed by an explosion of the powder magazine ignited by an English servant.[54] While Haddington was removed from the scene his troops probably remained in the area or proceeded south to reinforce Leslie's army. However, by October Major General Munro had arrived with his regiment in the area, replacing Haddington as the area commander.

Earl of Home's Foot

Colonel: James, 3rd earl of Home

Ministers: John Home, James Home[55]

The earl raised his regiment of 900 infantry from Berwickshire, probably from amongst those of his name, his tenants, and servants. Home was one of the signatories of the Cumbernauld Bond in August, which was a foreshadowing of his change of allegiance to the royalist camp. The regiment did not leave Scotland for Newcastle until September.[56] It is uncertain whether Home's men were allocated to protection of the supply line or for watching the English royal army on the Durhamshire-Yorkshire boundary. The regiment withdrew from England in August 1641 and disbanded on the 25th.

Invercauld's Retinue

Colonel: Robert Farquharson of Invercauld

On 14 August 1641 the Committee of Estates commissioned Invercauld to raise 100 men to secure Angus, Mearns, Mar and Banff. The commission was to run for two months and the laird's men would receive their pay from the Estates. Invercauld would have raised his men from the Braes of Mar in which his castle was situated.[57] There is no further evidence as to whether these men were ever in arms.

Lord Johnstone's Foot

Colonel: James, Lord Johnstone

Lord Johnstone levied his regiment of 1,000 infantry from Annandale and other parts of Dumfriesshire. In July it was rumoured that Johnstone and other Covenanters from the Borders were planning a large raid into England. Although Johnstone signed the Cumbernauld Bond, he repudiated it in 1641. This unit was part of Leslie's army at Duns. However, it is uncertain whether the regiment entered England, or if it did where it quartered.[58] The regiment disbanded in August 1641.

Lord Ker's Foot

Colonel: Harry, Lord Ker

Lieutenant Colonel: James Cockburn

Minister: Robert Knox[59]

The colonel of this regiment was a crypto-royalist, although he did not sign the Cumbernauld Bond. Ker raised seven companies from Teviotdale and the remaining three from the earl of Traquair's estates. In July Ker's men plundered Lochtour and Graemhead. The regiment entered England in August from Kelso as part of Lieutenant General Lord Almond's command. After the occupation of Newcastle this regiment went south to Durham under Dunfermline, where it remained until August 1641. During the occupation Ker was sent back to Scotland to gather all the deserters that had been rounded up. He returned leading 1,500 men, not an inconsiderable reinforcement, but also indicative of how severe the problem of desertion was for this army. While in Durham this regiment mutinied, on 19 August 1641, with Dunfermline's for reasons unknown. Upon reaching Hirslaw Leslie had one of the mutineers executed on 25 August at 6 p.m. Later in the evening the army disbanded; the men of this regiment reached home shortly thereafter.[60]

Earl of Kinghorn's Foot

Colonel: John, 2nd earl of Kinghorn

Minister: Alexander Symmer[61]

Kinghorn raised his regiment from Angus. In August he signed the Cumbernauld Bond, being a friend of Montrose. His regiment served in

England and was possibly quartered near Newcastle. In August 1641 Kinghorn's men departed from England. The regiment presumably left the army at the disbanding of the army on Leith Links on 27 August. From there it would have proceeded north to disband.[62]

Lord Kirkcudbright's Regiments

Colonel: Thomas, 2nd Lord Kirkcudbright

Ministers: Samuel Row, John MacClellan, Samuel Bell[63]

On 6 July 1640 Lord Kirkcudbright's Foot was allotted its levy proportion from the Stewartry of Kirkcudbright. Kirkcudbright also raised men from Galloway for his units. It appears that he commanded two units at least, a foot regiment and a cavalry one. As of mid December 1640 the full complement of infantry had been provided by the Stewartry, although nine horsemen were still outstanding. In August Kirkcudbright signed the Cumbernauld Bond, yet he remained a loyal Covenanter. By September the horse regiment was quartered in or near Newcastle, where they remained until August 1641. They disbanded after 25 August. The infantry regiment (also known as the Regiment of the South) quartered in Dumfries burgh. On 10 December 1640 the Committee of Estates instructed Kirkcudbright to widen the regiment's quartering zone into Dumfriesshire and the Stewartry on the 20th, if money was not forthcoming from the rural areas. The regiment remained a burden on Dumfries until the month it disbanded. On 6 August 1641 the provost and baillies of the burgh wrote parliament requesting the payment of arrears to the regiment and either its removal from the area or dispersal into villages and towns in the shire as it was causing food shortages. It is doubtful the regiment moved before it disbanded in late August.[64]

Leslie's Horse

Colonel: General Alexander Leslie

Ministers: Frederick Carmichael, Walter Greig, Thomas Melville, William Bell[65]

General Leslie was again the commander-in-chief of the Covenanter forces in 1640-41. During the Second Bishops' War he commanded a force of Fife Horse raised principally from the presbyteries of Kirkcaldy and Cupar. The campaign of 20-30 August 1640 was undoubtedly the most successful in Leslie's career. In just ten days he penetrated deep into enemy territory, gained a victory over the only enemy forces in his vicinity, and occupied a town which was the principal purveyor of coal to London. However, due to the pace of diplomatic negotiations Leslie's army remained in England for over a year. The general (and the army's ministers), were chiefly responsible for containing and destroying the malcontent which Montrose's faction spread through the officer corps. On 25 and 27 August 1641 Leslie disbanded his army. In a few months he would receive a signal honour of being created the earl of Leven by his foe and sovereign.[66]

Leslie's Life Guard of Foot

Colonel: Sir Alexander Gibson of Durie

This regiment was raised by the College of Justice to act as Leslie's bodyguard. It was made up entirely of volunteers. Due to that reason the Life Guards refused to swear the soldier's oath in the *Articles and Ordinances of War* until the invasion of England. This unit was mustered into existence on 15 July 1640. The Lifeguards quartered in Newcastle during the army's sojourn in England. In late October the presbytery of the army noted a rumour that this unit and the Life Guards of Horse had visited bawdy houses, where they had 'spoyled their bodies'. One of the ministers was appointed to speak with the general about this problem. Unfortunately the record ends soon after this meeting and the results of the conference with the general are unknown. This unit departed from Newcastle on 21 August 1641 and was disbanded on the 25th. At that time there were in the unit three officers, ten non-commissioned officers, five others, and 194 privates, who were owed £1,332 17s. 4d.[67]

Leslie's Life Guard of Horse

Routmaster: Sir Thomas Hope of Kerse

Minister: George Belfrage[68]

This unit was also known as the College of Justice Horse troop. It may be inferred that the men came from Edinburgh, possibly from the lower ranks of the legal profession. At least fifty-five of the troopers were volunteers, who may have been lawyers. An accurate estimate of the size of this unit is difficult to make. An English source puts the strength at 300 horsemen. One Scottish source placed the number at 160 men. The two surviving muster rolls pose even more problems in this matter. The one of 17 August 1641 places the Life Guards' strength at 103 men and officers; the other of 17 September 1641 places the Life Guards at 88 men of all ranks plus eleven servants.[69] If we take the volunteers as not being owed pay then their number with the first muster produces a total very close to that of the Scottish source.

The history of this unit is rather interesting. In August it joined Leslie's army at Duns. At the crossing of the Tweed Hope's men rode into the river and broke the current by standing to the west of the infantry, which eased their progress. At the battle of Newburn 26 men of the troop crossed the Tyne to scout the English breastwork. Then Sir Thomas brought over the remainder of his men supported by two regiments of foot. Sir Thomas gained praise for his rôle in the attacks on the English, which eventually led to a total Scottish victory. After Newburn the Life Guards formed part of the Newcastle town garrison. With the Life Guards of Foot the horse were accused of becoming infected with venereal disease. Hope's men departed from Newcastle on 21 August 1641 and disbanded at Leith Links on the 27th.[70]

Lindsay's Foot

Colonel: Harry Lindsay

Major: James Somerville of Drum

Colonel Lindsay was one of the Scottish mercenaries who returned from the Swedish army to serve the Covenanters. The origins of his regiment are unknown. It was on foot by late May 1640 when it formed part of the force besieging Edinburgh Castle. Major Somerville commanded the Castlehill battery, which was only sixty paces from the Spur. The battery consisted of eight 36-40 pounders and was reckoned the most effective of the four siege batteries. In July Major Somerville led an assault of 250 infantry on the Spur, which had been damaged by a mine. Unfortunately for the Covenanters the attack failed and they had to rely upon starvation forcing the castle's surrender. On 19 September Ruthven's men marched out of the castle and the Covenanters gained control.[71] There is no further mention of this regiment after that date. It may have disbanded, or formed part of the castle's garrison, or marched into England as a reinforcement for Leslie's army.

Earl of Lindsay's Foot

Colonel: John, 1st earl of Lindsay

Ministers: George Hamilton, Robert Traill[72]

Lindsay raised his regiment from eastern Fife, particularly from the presbytery of St. Andrews. The regimental strength was 1,000 men. Lindsay united his regiment with Waughton's in Dunbar, marching from there to Duns. On 8 August 1640 they had united with the main army. On 28 August Lindsay's men in company with the Life Guards of Horse and Loudoun's Foot stormed the

English positions at Newburn. The whereabouts of the regiment becomes vague for some time after the battle. One source states that it was heading for Newcastle in September; another informs us that the regiment quartered outside of that town during part of the occupation. By mid October Lindsay's men were in or near Newcastle. They were then assigned to share St. John's, Newcastle with Loudoun's men. The regiment's connection with Loudoun's appears to have been for more than ecclesiastical purposes. Not only had the two units fought together at Newburn, but Baillie also informs us that they and Queensberry's men were brigaded together for military purposes. Lindsay's regiment departed from Newcastle in August 1641 and disbanded after the 27th.[73]

Lockhart's Horse

Colonel: George Lockhart

Little is known about this unit, which probably served with Leslie's army in England. In July 1640 the ministers of the presbytery of Lanark announced the rendezvous on Lanark Moor of the gentry, troopers and horsemen from whom the regiment (or troop) would be selected. In October the presbytery gave notice that the unit's troopers and deserters should appear on Lanark Moor and in Lanark respectively.[74] There are no further mentions of the unit nor of its commander.

Lothian Horse

Colonel: (Sir James?) Ramsay

Minister: Robert Row[75]

This unit was raised from the three shires composing the region of Lothian. It was at Duns as part of Leslie's army in August 1640. The Lothian Horse crossed into England and quartered outside of the Newcastle area during the occupation. In December one of the troop captains returned to Scotland to gather up deserters. In mid January he held a rendezvous of the deserters in Linlithgow before heading back to England with them.[76] It may be inferred that this regiment returned with the rest of the army and disbanded on Leith Links in August 1641.

Earl of Lothian's Foot

Colonel: William, 3rd earl of Lothian

Lieutenant Colonel: Walter Scott

Ministers: James Ker, Thomas Wilkie, Robert Leighton, Robert Cunningham, William Jamieson[77]

This regiment was raised from Teviotdale, the centre of Lothian's power. It consisted of 1,200 men in ten or twelve companies (depending on whether Lothian or Scott possessed companies). In July an English source believed that Lothian was about to embark on a massive raid of Northumberland with Lord Cranston. The regiment marched from Jedburgh under the command of Lord Almond, the lieutenant general. Lothian's men quartered in Newcastle, where they shared the chapel at the bridge with Cassillis' men. In mid February 1641 Lothian informed his father, the earl of Ancram, that he could not provide him with a fiddler from the regiment, because the only one was an alcoholic. However, the colonel noted that each company possessed a piper instead of a drummer to provide music. Lothian also stated that 'We [the army] are sadder and graver than ordinarie soldiers . . .'[78] His regiment departed from Newcastle on 21 and disbanded in the evening of 25 August 1641.

Lord Loudoun's Foot

Colonel: John, 2nd Lord Loudoun

Lieutenant Colonel: (?) Scott

Minister: John Nevay[79]

Loudoun raised his regiment of 1,200 men from Ayrshire and Lanarkshire. This unit formed part of Leslie's army at Duns, crossing the border on 20 August 1640. With Lindsay's Foot and the Life Guards of Horse it drove the English from their breastworks at the battle of Newburn. Loudoun's men were brigaded with Lindsay's and Queensberry's during the occupation of England. The regiment quartered in or near Newcastle, sharing St. John's with Amisfield's and Lindsay's men. Loudoun served as one of the commissioners for the treaties at Ripon and London.[80] The regiment withdrew from England with the rest of the army, disbanding on 25 August 1641.

Viscount Maitland's Foot

Colonel: John, viscount Maitland

Ministers: John Oswald, Robert Ker[81]

Maitland raised his men from East Lothian (principally from the presbytery of Haddington), and possibly from Midlothian. The regiment formed part of Leslie's army at Duns, serving on the campaign against Newcastle. In mid October it was assigned Trinity Chapel, Newcastle as a place of worship with Fleming's men. However, by January 1641, Maitland's regiment may have moved to quarters in Sunderland.[82] Regardless of its location the regiment evacuated England with the army, disbanding on 25 August 1641.

Earl Marischal's Forces

Colonel: William, 7th earl Marischal

During the Second Bishops' War the earl Marischal led three different units. Between 5 and 8 May 1640 he occupied Aberdeen with 160 horsemen and a force of Forbeses. The burgh paid Marischal a ransom of £4,000 to keep his force from plundering. On 28 May Marischal and Munro occupied Aberdeen. The former was now commanding a regiment of foot. Six hundred of these men quartered in New Aberdeen periodically between 28 May and 18 June, when they disbanded. On 28 May the two Covenanter commanders imposed the Articles of Bon Accord on the burgh. The Articles provided the basis for the suppression of anti-Covenanter activity, the quartering of Munro's and Marischal's men, and the supply of shoes and canvas in exchange for protection from plundering.[83]

In July 1640 Marischal received a commission to raise the fourth man from Aberdeenshire to provide him with a regiment of foot. His success in recruiting the regiment was due to the fear of plundering by the Covenanters. Aberdeen put up stiff resistance to providing Marischal with 110 men (or possibly two companies). Old Aberdeen supplied twenty men under duress; the number provided by New Aberdeen is unknown. In late August a meeting of the barons of the Mearns authorised Marischal to raise 108 men. Eventually the regiment numbered 2,000 men.[84]

Although the regiment failed to reach Leslie's army at Duns, Marischal was already in the south. Sometime in August he signed the Cumbernauld Bond. On 2 September Leslie wrote the Committee of Estates asking it to send Marischal's regiment south to Newcastle with the deserters of his army in tow. By October desertion had become a problem in Marischal's regiment itself. The incredible number of 1,200 men fled from Marischal's regiment, suggesting that he had recruited many anti-Covenanters from the area assigned to him. In October and again in December there were searches for deserters in Aberdeen. Gordon of Tillieangus raised 100 men for Marischal's regiment as a reinforcement in early 1641. After spending a night in Old Aberdeen, they marched south to Edinburgh. However, the Estates refused to accept them as part of the army and Tillieangus' men had to beg their way homewards.[85] Marischal's men probably returned and disbanded in late August/early September 1641. The location of their quarters in England is unknown.

Viscount Montgomery's Foot

Colonel: Hugh, viscount Montgomery

Ministers: John Hamilton, James Ker, Thomas Wilkie[86]

Montgomery raised a force of 300 infantry from Renfrewshire by August 1640. The regiment joined Leslie's army at Duns and took part in the Newcastle campaign. Apparently at this time Montgomery gained command of a brigade of 1,800 men. Other than this regiment the constituent elements are unknown. The brigade shared its chaplains with the train of artillery. During the occupation Montgomery's men quartered near Newcastle, departing from there on 21 August 1641. The regiment disbanded on 28 August.[87]

Earl of Montrose's Foot Regiments

Colonel: James, 5th earl of Montrose

Perthshire ministers: William Row, John Graham, John Cruikshank[88]

Montrose received commissions to raise regiments of infantry from both Perthshire and Angus. On 27 June 1640 the earl began recruiting his regiments. Three days later he seized and garrisoned Airlie Castle (for the fate of that place see above, Argyll). Baillie charges that Montrose 'became somewhat capricious for his own fancies' and made Lord Drummond linger from the rendezvous. However, by 13 July Montrose had 1,600 men at Duns. Sometime in August the earl signed the Cumbernauld Bond, which he was instrumental in drafting. On 13 August the presbytery of the army learned that the Perthshire regiment had not sworn the oath required by the *Articles and Ordinances of War*; this was rectified within two weeks. There is no sign of Montrose's doubts having effect on his actions during the campaign or his men. On 20 August the earl led the army across the Tweed. The two regiments quartered in or near Newcastle after the battle of Newburn. They shared the Novacastrian church of St. Nicholas as a place of worship. The regiments remained in England until the departure of the army in August 1641. They disbanded in late August, but it is not known who replaced Montrose as their colonel.[89]

The reason for Montrose's dismissal from his military duties lay with political developments following the taking of Newcastle. Montrose began to correspond with the king, and recruited Lords Boyd, Fleming and Drummond as his allies. They attempted to subvert the officer corps; however, Leslie and the ministers blocked these efforts. After Boyd revealed the existence of the Cumbernauld Bond, the list of signators so impressed Argyll that he forebore from prosecuting Montrose. However, the sentiments of the Bond lost Montrose allies. By Christmas 1640 he was backed only by a small group of supporters with whom he held meetings in Edinburgh. In February 1641 Montrose left the army for the last time. He became involved with the John Stewart of Ladywell's charges against Argyll in May. On 11 June the earl of Lothian arrested Montrose and committed him to Edinburgh. The execution of Ladywell on 28 July placed Montrose in an unenviable position, because he had lost his only reliable witness against Argyll. During Charles I's stay in Edinburgh a parliamentary commission investigated Montrose's behaviour. However, he was able to gain his release on 16 November by the payment of security money.[90] By maintaining ideological conformity the Covenanters had lost the most original military commander they possessed.

Monymusk's Retinue

Colonel: Sir William Forbes of Monymusk

Monymusk raised his forces from amongst his kinsmen, friends, servants and tenants in Aberdeenshire. They took the field only once in the Second Bishops' War. From 5 to 8 May 1640 they shared in Marischal's occupation of Aberdeen.[91]

Munro's Foot

Colonel: Major General Sir Robert Munro

Lieutenant Colonel: Hew Fraser

Majors: George Barclay (?-1642-44), Thomas Dalyell (1644-48)

Ministers: John Livingstone, William Nairn[92]

Munro received a commission to raise this regiment in March 1640 and it remained on foot until the autumn of 1648. The regiment was raised from a widespread area in eastern Scotland. On 28 May Munro and Marischal arrived in Aberdeen on which they imposed the Articles of Bon Accord. Munro kept his men under strict discipline, although one house was pillaged and another suffered broken windows. On 2 June a party of the regiment brought the Rev. John Gregory of Drumoak to Aberdeen, having taken him naked from his bed. Munro fined him £666 13s. 4d. for being an anti-Covenanter. On the same day Munro besieged and took Sir Alexander Irvine's house of Drum. Munro sent Irvine, his son, and twenty-six Aberdonian anti-Covenanters to Edinburgh to be imprisoned. On 7 June the regiment's strength stood at 966 men and officers. Munro strove to increase its numbers by pressing men in Aberdeen. On 10 June a party of men under Captain Beaton arrested Sir George Gordon of Gight, a Roman Catholic and anti-Covenanter, and pillaged his house of Ardessie. Three days later Aberdeen agreed to provide Munro with £10,000, shoes and supplies for his men. On 27 June an expedition plundered the houses of Lethenty and Newtown of Culsalmond, homes of Patrick Urquhart and George Gordon respectively. During the occupation of Aberdeen the houses of Pitfoddels, Kemnay, Fiddes, Udny, Foveran, Knockhall, Westhall and Fetterneir were also visited by Munro's men. They were searched for arms, at least, if not pillaged.[93] The preliminaries for exerting Covenanter control of the northeast were complete, the time had come to extend that suzereignty.

On 5 July the 1,142 men and officers of Munro's Foot marched out of Aberdeen for a month long campaign in the royalist northeast. They made their base camp at Strathbogie (which is now called Huntly). The men cut down the marquis of Huntly's bushes and trees to make huts; they also plundered his granaries in order to avoid oppressing the common people. Munro had his men gather up all the sheep, horses, and cattle in the area which he then ransomed back to the owners. Throughout the occupation of Strathbogie there were no deaths or injuries sustained by either soldiers or civilians. However, the soldiers became unruly and mutinied because Munro refused to pay them from the animal ransom money and fines on royalists. Munro personally stopped the revolt by slaying one of the leaders. During the sojourn at Strathbogie Munro led a force to Spynie Castle, home of Bishop John Guthry of Moray. The force took the castle, ousted the bishop, and handed it over to the Moray Covenanters. On 10 August Munro now commanding a regiment of 1,438 men, broke camp and headed towards Banff. On the way his men destroyed the orchard of Sir George Ogilvy of Banff at Dowhaugh. Once in Banff Munro's men looted and vandalised the laird's mansion with the help of local Covenanters; the walls alone were left. Before returning to Aberdeen the regiment damaged and pillaged Banff's houses of Forglen and Inchdrewer. The officers' pay was then three months in arrears and that of the privates was a month behind. By 4 September Munro's mission in the northeast was completed and he returned to Aberdeen.[94]

Aberdeen suffered again from Munro, albeit for a short time. On 9 September Munro demanded uniforms and £6,666 13s. 4d. as a loan to be paid back from the tax of a tenth. The burgh had already spent £5,000 to £9,507 1s. 4d. on the regiment, of which it claimed over £2,400 as being owed by the Estates. On 12 September Munro's men departed from Aberdeen for southern Scotland.[95]

The regiment remained in the south for eighteen months. For the rest of September and for half of October Munro's troops quartered in Leith, and Musselburgh. They then moved to within three miles of Berwick to watch the English royal garrison there. Munro replaced the late earl of Haddington as commander of Lothian and the Merse. Within ten days of arriving there the regiment had stolen £2,366 worth of crops, tools, and furnishings from Lord Mordington's estates, as well as 800 sheep from three of his tenants. Munro had taken all of this since the Treaty of Ripon and had disposed of the goods 'at his pleasure . . .'. Lord Mordington later complained that his personal losses were £1,766 excluding the losses of his tenants. In his opinion nothing outside cannon range of Berwick was safe from Munro. There is no mention of the regiment again till 29 July 1641 when Munro sent a letter to the Committee of Estates from Mordington. He claimed that his men were suffering greatly from arrears in pay and requested that some of the money from England be sent to them. He was also reducing the regiment in accordance with the Committee's order, removing two officers per company.[96]

When the Covenanters disbanded their forces in August 1641, Munro's was one of four regiments kept to maintain internal order. In late September the regiment was quartered in Merse and Teviotdale. The regiment then stood at 1,400 men and officers. Sometime before 1642 the regiment moved to the environs of Edinburgh. On 21 October 1641 the native Irish of Ulster revolted. Almost immediately the Scots offered Charles I an army to suppress the rising. From the first Munro's regiment was to serve in this army. Munro, himself, became the army's major general. Desertion from the regiment suddenly increased when the men learned first of their destination and then that they would be under the Scottish pay rate until they reached Ireland. On 10 February 1642 the Privy Council issued a proclamation against soldiers deserting from the regiments bound for Ireland. The deserters faced death if they did not return to the regiment within six days of the proclamation. In the case of Munro's regiment the ordinance may have had a positive effect. The first muster of the regiment in Ireland (on 7 April 1642) revealed a force of 1,405 men and 149 officers. Munro's men embarked for passage to Carrickfergus in mid March from Largs. However, due to the contrary winds they remained in Lamlash Bay, Arran with Home's and Sinclair's regiments. Eventually, when the winds changed, the advance elements of Ulster Army reached their main base within a day.[97]

This regiment with some important exceptions served in Ulster from 1642 to 1648, having its quarters in Carrickfergus. Munro was the effective commander of the Ulster Army for all but a few months in mid to late 1642 when the earl of Leven came over and took up his post as General. (The earl of Lothian, the lieutenant general, never visited Ulster during the army's stay there). It is likely that Munro's regiment participated to some degree in every expedition which he led. However, detailed information on the regiment's activities exists only for a few of the campaigns. (For details of the other expeditions please see the Chronology).[98]

The history of the regiment as part of the Ulster Army is not without interest. In May–June 1642 ten companies of the regiment participated in the campaign to clear the Bann valley of Irish rebels. Munro with 400 of his men captured the earl of Antrim in Dunluce Castle. This was an important success, for the earl, although not a rebel, was an enemy of the Covenanters. Lieutenant Colonel Fraser received command of the castle, which he possessed only for a short time before Argyll's regiment garrisoned the place. After taking Dunluce Munro advanced with 1,000 infantry, two troops of horse and two guns and occupied Antrim. That county had now been pacified. The next mention of the regiment is a muster list which put the unit at 149 officers and 1,411 men with 78 sick.[99]

After October 1642 Munro became the de facto commander of the Ulster Army. Munro initially broke the Cessation between the Irish rebels and 'royal' forces, however, in late August 1643 he had doubts about whether that was the correct policy. In October the major general decided to keep the truce, which he observed until June 1644. While there were no military expeditions during that period, it was not a time of inactivity. In April 1644 Captain James Wallace went to Scotland as one of the three petitioners of the army to the Estates. His mission lasted until 4 May; it produced more promises than improvements in the army's deplorable condition. In early April the entire regiment including Munro and his officers took the Solemn League and Covenant with the exception of Major Dalyell. (The major has the distinction of being one of the only soldiers in Ulster to refuse the Covenant). In May the regiment probably took part in the capture of Belfast from the Ormondist garrison. Later in the year Munro received an English parliamentary commission to command all the forces in Ulster. He used his position not only to pursue military ends, but he also supported the presbytery of Carrickfergus by extending its jurisdiction over the entire Protestant-occupied zone of Ulster.[100]

The remainder of the regiment's history is tied up generally with military matters. On 27 June 1644 eight companies formed part of Munro's force which rendezvoused at Linsnegarvy for the campaign into Leinster. The regiment marched out again on 25 July to serve as part of the force Munro mustered and kept in the field until 21 September against Lord Castlehaven's Irish army. In 1645 the regiment sent 200 men to Scotland as part of Colonel Home's regiment. These men never returned to Ulster. In June 1646 500-600 men of the regiment were at the battle of Benburb. Between 250 and 360 of the men fell in battle, further weakening the regiment which had suffered losses from starvation, disease, and previous campaigns. The position of the Ulster Army had eroded so much that Colonel George Monck usurped Munro's position as commander-in-chief in Ulster in July 1647 with little opposition. Both the Scottish army and Munro's regiment were on the wane.[101]

The year 1648 witnessed the end of the regiment, although some of its officers continued to play important rôles in subsequent events. Munro accepted the Engagement as being ordained by parliament. His previous actions in favour of presbyterianism retained the affection of the ministers and country people, although they opposed the Engagement. The regiment contributed about three hundred men, under Dalyell, to Colonel George Munro's force. There remained between 400 and 560 men, who garrisoned Carrickfergus with little vigilance. On the morning of 13 September Monck in league with some of Glencairn's officers surprised Munro and his lady in bed. The major general was sent as a prisoner to the Tower, where he remained for five years. The regiment was disarmed, although some of the men may have joined Monck's army. However, the involvement of the regiment's officers in Ulster affairs continued. In 1649 Major Dalyell returned to Ulster after the breaking up of George Munro's force. Lord Montgomery of the Ards made Dalyell the governor of Carrickfergus. In November 1648 the Committee of Estates dispatched Major James Wallace (a former captain in the regiment) to Ulster to find anti-Engager soldiers and arrange passage for them to Scotland. On 10 August 1649 the Estates commissioned Wallace lieutenant colonel of the Irish Foot (which became His Majesties Life Guard of Foot in 1650). Wallace returned again to Ulster, where Lord Montgomery appointed him governor of Belfast. Montgomery, after becoming an open royalist, later dismissed Wallace who was a strong supporter of the kirk party. With that the epilogue of the regiment's history ends. It is only necessary to add that some of the soldiers probably settled in Ulster.[102]

Philorth's Retinue

Colonel: Sir Alexander Fraser of Philorth

Philorth raised his men from the Buchan area of Aberdeenshire in late April or early May 1640. They joined in Marischal's occupation of Aberdeen, 5-8 May. After that there is no further mention of the retinue in the Second Bishops' War.[103]

Queensberry's Horse

Colonel: James, 2nd earl of Queensberry

Queensberry probably raised his cavalry unit from amongst his kinsmen and estates in Dumfriesshire. On 13 April 1640 this unit was serving as part of the border guard. It may have entered England with Leslie's army, for it is later found brigaded with Lindsay's and Loudoun's infantry. Those two regiments were quartered in the vicinity of Newcastle; however, Queensberry's men would have stayed in the countryside where fodder for the horses was more easily available. This unit departed from England with Leslie's army and disbanded in late August 1641.[104]

Earl of Rothes' Foot

Colonel: John, 6th earl of Rothes

Ministers: William Bennet, Mungo Law, John Chalmers, John Moncreiffe[105]

Rothes raised his men from central Fife, particularly from the presbytery of Kirkcaldy. The regiment rendezvoused with Carnegie's at Haddington, marching from there into England in August 1640. There were then 1,000 men and officers in the regiment. The regiment quartered in or near Newcastle. For ecclesiastical, if not military purposes, Rothes' men were brigaded with Elcho's Foot. They shared either The Spittall or St. Andrews, Newcastle as a place of worship. A Captain Beaton served as the presbyterial elder of the regiment. In September four parishes of Kirkcaldy presbytery raised £426 13s. 4d. as a voluntary contribution to the regiment to ameliorate its supply problems. Rothes served as a commissioner to London, where he died in 1641. The regiment returned to Scotland on 25 August 1641 and disbanded after the 27th.[106]

Lord Sinclair's Foot

Colonel: John, 9th Lord Sinclair

Lieutenant Colonels: Henry Sinclair (1640-1647), David Sinclair (1640-1642)

Major: James Turner (1642-1648)

Minister: James Simpson[107]

Lord Sinclair's regiment of Foot was one of the noxious weeds in the garden of godliness in which the Covenanters tried to maintain their armies. Sinclair's regiment was on foot from 1640 to 1647; during that time it managed to self-destruct twice. In September 1640 Sinclair began raising men from Caithness and Orkney. By mid October he had levied 438 men plus officers in six companies. On 22 October the regiment occupied Aberdeen, which accepted the garrison because Robert Farquhar, regimental commissar, promised to pay for the billetting charges. The men quickly ran out of money and became an especial burden on the Roman Catholics of Old and New Aberdeen. On 29 October the burgh council instructed the burgh's commissioner to the Committee of Estates to submit a grievance against the regiment for impoverishing the inhabitants. The regiment remained in Aberdeen through the winter of 1640-41. On 19 March 1641 Sinclair sent out a party of men to the laird of Lethenty's lands, where they were to remain until the laird paid over £800 to the regiment. Farquhar paid the regiment's quartering charges after this expedition. On 9 July Sinclair and Farquhar commenced negotiations over billetting with the town. They requested a loan of £5,000 for quartering for which they promised the soldiers would not remain more than a week; he guaranteed to pay the quartering charges. Two days later Sinclair requested billetting for twenty days, beginning on the 14th, which Farquhar would pay. The town accepted these arrangements. However, on 17 November the commissioner of Aberdeen presented a petition to the king and Committee of Estates. He claimed that the regiment had remained a long time in the burgh and was unnecessary. He suggested that it be paid off and disbanded or removed to the south. The petition was without impact. As of 8 December the regiment was still in Aberdeen. On that day the accounts for the previous fourteen months were reckoned. From 8 October 1640 until 8 December 1641 the charges for the men and non-commissioned officers amounted to £93,029 19s. 4d. The regiment had been strongest between June and August 1641, when it had contained 505 enlisted men. On 8 December it consisted of 477 privates, and 84 officers and others.[108]

After the Irish rising in October 1641 Sinclair received orders to reduce his regiment to four companies, which would accompany Munro to Ireland. Sinclair was to raise six more companies to complete the regiment. At this time the officers changed. James Turner, a Scots mercenary, who had served in the Swedish army, became the major. One of the captains, Patrick/Peter Leslie, received the appointment as Adjutant General of the Ulster Army, retaining his captaincy. The regiment departed from Aberdeen in February 1642, but not before some remarkable transformations. Of the 561 men and officers in the regiment in December only 260 had not deserted by its departure. The regiment had impregnated at least sixty-five 'honest women servandis' of Aberdeen. (Some of them followed the regiment, others were tried for whoredom and banished or fled from the burgh.) The men of Sinclair's regiment also debauched, drank heavily, swaggered at night, fought and swore. An Aberdonian commented on their departure:

> Thus, this ribald regiment heaped up sin to our owne numberles sinis, and did no more good, bot lying idle, consuming honest menis viveris.[109]

For Sinclair's regiment the prospect of service in Ulster was a chance for recovery of discipline and integrity. In mid March 1642 the regiment embarked at Irvine. Due to the strong contrary winds (that forced Home's and Munro's regiments to shelter in Lamlash Bay, Arran for two weeks), Sinclair's transport ships also took refuge there. Sinclair's men landed at Carrickfergus on 3 April with the men of the other two regiments. Four days later a muster of the regiment revealed that recruiting had brought its strength up to 486 men and officers. Lieutenant Colonel Sinclair led 200 men of the regiment on the campaign which seized Newry in May. Munro established them as the garrison and provided 200 additional commanded infantry to serve there until more of the regiment arrived. The lieutenant colonel received an order from Munro to banish all the native Irish from the town once the army's expeditionary force had left. On 13 May Munro wrote to Scotland pleading that the regiment required reinforcements to enlarge its foraging zone or it would be out of supplies in ten days. Apparently there was a positive response to this plea. When Major Turner returned to Carrickfergus hoping to collect more men of the regiment, he discovered 500 infantry which he embarked on transports for Carlingford. Due to the lack of houses in Newry only half of the regiment had permanent shelter. Nor could the men spend their time on building barracks. Construction of fortifications was the first priority. Throughout 1642 and 1643 the lieutenant colonel and major led out forays of 300-400 infantry against Irish creaghts and their herds to seize labourers for fortifying the town and food for their garrison. In 1642 Munro required Sinclair to lead 300 infantry and Turner to command the same numbers on two different campaigns. Meanwhile in Scotland Captain William Innes murdered a private John Steill (from Major Borthwick's company of Lindsay's regiment), for refusing to hand him a stick. Leven was asked to judge the case; the outcome is not known. Also in Scotland, on 6 July, Lord Sinclair attended the ordination of the regimental chaplain at Dalkeith. Lord Sinclair arrived in Ireland on 4 August with Leven. The regiment now stood at 1,032 men and 109 officers in ten companies. In September Turner joined Leven with 800 men on his first expedition. The regiment then settled into winter quarters at Newry, except for its attacks on the Irish cattle herds.[110]

The winter of 1642-43 and the 1643 campaigning season are not without interest in the history of the regiment. During the winter many of the regiment became ill, including the colonel. Of the senior officers the lieutenant colonel alone appears to have escaped from the diseases which wracked the garrison. After his recovery Lord Sinclair returned to Scotland, leaving the lieutenant colonel in charge again. In March 1643 the supply situation had deteriorated so much that one of the lieutenants went to Dublin to purchase supplies. On 14 May 1643 in the afternoon Turner with 300 musketeers joined Munro's expedition at Armagh. Turner led the van with Leven's Life Guard of Horse. Turner advanced four miles to Anachshamry in the barony of Loughgall. Sir Phelim O'Neill awaited him with 1,500 musketeers arranged behind the enclosures of Anachshamry House. To begin with the Irish succeeded in driving back the Covenanter horse. However, Turner's men did better. Battling for an hour without support they killed two and wounded three of the Irish. Then Captain William Drummond of Munro's regiment brought up 100 men as reinforcements. Meanwhile Munro was manoeuvering to outflank the Irish; however, after three and a half hours of fighting they withdrew to Charlemont fort followed by the country people. The Covenanters burnt O'Neill's house and those of other Irish gentry. At the end of the day Turner's men had lost one sergeant and thirteen men killed, with an additional eighteen wounded. The Irish had lost sixty men killed. The next day, having returned to Armagh, Turner marched to Tandergee and then to Newry. During the summer Sinclair's had men serving at the Armagh camp and during the siege of Charlemont. Turner appears to have been in command on both occasions. He

signed a letter of 28 August from the army to the Committee of Estates requesting advice concerning the Cessation, but more importantly asking for supplies.
In late 1643 Turner and Colonel Turlagh O'Neill concluded a truce between the
Newry garrison and the Irish rebels. With that the active service of the regiment
in Ulster ended.[111]

The arrangement for the evacuation of Newry required several months to
complete and were done without the authorisation of either the Committee of
Estates or Major General Munro. On 6 December 1643 Lieutenant Colonel
Sinclair offered to sell Newry to the marquis of Ormond for £960. This sum was
to recoup Sinclair and Turner for the money they had spent on fortifying the
town. On 22 January 1644 Sinclair wrote Lord Moore offering him Newry, as
he intended to evacuate Newry. Sinclair assured Moore of his loyalty to the king
and protestantism. A few days later Moore accepted the offer. The lieutenant
colonel led his men out of Newry by 17 February. (Between April 1642 and
February 1644 they had received only three months pay for their service in
Ulster.) Colonel Arthur Chichester's Ormondist regiment provided a detachment to garrison the town. Sinclair and Turner probably received their money
for turning the town over to the Ormondists. The regiment proceeded to
Groomsport, county Down, where they embarked for Scotland, landing on 26
February.[112]

Sinclair's regiment remained in Great Britain from 1644 until its disbanding
in 1647. The regiment arrived at Irvine with Lothian's infantry. The two
regiments then marched to Paisley, where they were met by a force of 700 foot
and 200 cavalry under the leadership of Sir William Ross of Muriston, the earl
of Glencairn and the bailies. This body of Covenanters had turned out to
prevent the regiments from quartering in Paisley. Lord Sinclair demanded
entry, but it was refused. In the end the burgh accepted several companies of
Lothian's. Sinclair's men proceeded on to Glasgow, where they quartered on
23 March at the cost of £782 16s. 4d. The regiment continued on to Stirling,
where it took up quarters.[113]

The integration of the regiment into the other Covenanter forces required
some effort. At first Turner and some captains of Lothian's regiment desired to
enter the earl of Newcastle's service out of loyalty to the king. The Committee of
Estates granted a six-week grace period for those who had not sworn the Solemn
League and Covenant. During that time Lord Sinclair and Turner met with the
royalists — Lords Erskine and Napier, the Masters of Napier and Madderty,
and Stirling of Keir. Two of the latter were to be sent to Montrose promising
him Stirling and Perth. Turner claimed that except for Montrose's failure to
march north of Dumfries, Sinclair's and Lothian's regiments would have joined
him. However, this claim may be an attempt by Turner to gild his past rôle as a
Covenanter officer. On 14 April Sinclair's regiment received orders from the
parliament to move from Stirling to Dumfries on the 16th in order to oppose
Montrose. The government supplied the men with 200 muskets, 300 bandeliers
and 100 pikes, suggesting that the regiment contained a minimum of 300
musketeers and 100 pikemen. On the 25th the regiment was on the march south

to Dumfries via Douglas. Sinclair's men reached the Borders sometime in late April or early May. They quartered at various places, including Kelso for four days, before marching into England on 25 June as part of the earl of Callendar's army. During the sojourn on the Borders each soldier received £6. Lord Sinclair raised £1,200 of this money by means of a personal bond with the treasurer of Stirling. The loan was only repaid on 24 September 1655.[114] For the moment the regiment was loyal and in the active service of the Covenanters.

　　Sinclair's regiment served in England from mid 1644 until early 1647. Lord Sinclair was initially absent from this regiment commanding the College of Justice regiment (of which he was also colonel), at Marston Moor. Both units served at the siege of Newcastle. Sinclair's older regiment was the first Covenanter unit inside Newcastle. Lieutenant Colonel Sinclair and Major Turner led their men in clearing part of the wall. Sinclair's men captured twenty mounted gentlemen and 200 foot soldiers, but they killed no one. The regiment lost one captain and three others in the assault. As a result of its success the entry of the other regiments was eased. After the storming of Newcastle Sinclair's regiment slips from sight for over a year. It is not known where it quartered in winter 1644-45 or whether it served on the Hereford campaign. On 14 November 1645 the Scottish Commissioners in London informed the House of Lords that Lord Sinclair and two other noblemen-colonels had been summoned to appear before the Estates for corresponding with royalists. The Lords were requested to send any of their captured letters to Scotland as evidence. Apparently the regiment took part in the siege of Newark (late November 1645–6 May 1646) because the king wrote to Lord Sinclair asking him to arrange his reception in the army. Sinclair was also working in collusion with Sir Robert Moray, a Scottish mercenary and an agent of Montereuil, preparing the way for Charles I's arrival in the Scottish camp. Their efforts were a failure, the earl of Lothian placing the king under virtual arrest from the moment of his arrival on 5 May. Sometime during the month Major Turner offered the king aid in escaping. However, Charles did not see his situation as being desperate and he refused. The regiment marched north into Durham or Northumberland, where it quartered until leaving England in early January 1647. At least one soldier deserted during that period; he received 6s. from Dron parish, presbytery of Perth. Equally interesting, Turner fought a drunken duel with a Colonel Wren, whom he had known on the continent. Meanwhile Lord Sinclair continued his royalist intrigues. In January 1647 Leven specifically banned him from having access to the king.[115] The regiment's attempts to aid the king had been in vain. In late January the regiment withdrew with the rest of the Army of the Solemn League and Covenant from England.

　　The last painful chapter of the regimental history remains. On 11 February 1647 the Estates placed Lord Sinclair in command of both his own and Lothian's 'Irish' regiments. Sinclair's men were to march from Peebles to Portpartrick via Moffat, Dumfries, Carlingwark, Ferry of Cree, Monigaff and Glenluce. The two regiments were to complete the march in only ten days. The quartering allowance was established at 4s. per man per day. The regiments now numbered only 500 men together, a considerable decline from their previous strengths. However, those figures are questioned by the details of the mutiny at Peebles. As of 11 February 500 infantrymen (in nine companies) with their officers, women, and children were quartered in Peebles. The regiment remained in the burgh from the 11th to the morning of the 13th. That day the soldiers mutinied for their arrears, which they forced the officers to pay. Two hundred of the men departed from the burgh by that evening. The 300 remaining soldiers lived on free quarter until the 16th. The sergeants, corporals, and privates forced the townspeople to provide them with a double quartering allowance and money. These soldiers stole swords, cloaks and other necessities, and destroyed the grain in the barnyards. Only Turner and Captain Lawrence Lundie paid for their quarters. The others did not even provide receipts. The burgh officials requested that the Estates force Sinclair to pay or provide them money from the monthly maintenance to make up the losses. They also requested that no more regiments bound for Ireland be marched through the burgh. The reaction of the Estates to the petition is not known. However, on 6 March they ordered the two regiments to depart immediately from Wigtonshire, which they had presumably reached, as soon as the weather and arrival of transport ships permitted. That was not to be. Turner went over to Ulster to arrange quarters for the regiments. However, the officers there declared the return of the regiments was impossible due to the inadequacy of supplies and quartering areas in Ulster. The regiments then disbanded on the orders of the Committee of Estates. Turner, writing years later, pronounced the verdict that the regiment was 'composed of prettie men, stout and loyall, both officers and sojors. . . .'.[116] One must question this assertion. While the combat record of the regiment was sound, its political loyalties were dubious; its morality was below the standards of most regiments; its discipline was abysmally low.

Sheriff of Teviotdale's Retinue

Colonel: Sir William Douglas, sheriff of Teviotdale

Sir William raised a force of 160 foot and 60 horse from Teviotdale in 1640. He was based at Gerat. This force may have served only as a border guard before Leslie's army began to congregate along the frontier. The sheriff was linked with Lord Cranston as being one of a party of raiders. He was also named with Cranston as being one of the joint colonels of the Teviotdale regiment.[117] It is doubtful whether the sheriff would have left his area of jurisdiction when the possibility of royalist insurrection there could embarrass the Covenanting regime.

Waughton's Foot

Colonel: Sir Patrick Hepburn of Waughton

Lieutenant Colonel: Patrick Hepburn the younger of Waughton

Ministers: John Lauder, John Maghie/Makghie, John Dalyell, John Home[118]

Waughton senior was a member of the Estates for Haddingtonshire in 1639-1641. He and his son raised the regiment from that shire, principally from the presbyteries of Dunbar and Haddington. The regiment numbered 400 men in 1640. The unit camped at Dunbar from 31 July 1640 to 7 August, when it marched with Lindsay's regiment to Dunglass and then to Choicelee. On the 9th the regiment participated in the fast held throughout the camp. Mr. Lauder preached on Psm. 102: 13-18 in the morning, while Mr. Maghie/Makghie used Jeremiah 15: 33-34 as his text. The regiment entered England with Leslie's army, after Newburn it quartered in the vicinity of Newcastle. The colonel served as a commissioner to the negotiations at Ripon. Captain Mathew Hepburn served as the regimental elder at the presbytery meetings. By July 1641 the regiment had moved to Durham, where it quartered until 20 August. By 25 August Waughton's men had returned to Scotland. That day Mr. Lauder (again with the regiment) preached a sermon of thanksgiving on Psm. 126: 1-3. On Thursday the 26th the regiment marched to Dunbar. There on 27 August at 11 a.m. Mr. Lauder preached an exhortation of thanksgiving in Dunbar kirkyard and the regiment disbanded.[119]

Wedderburn's Foot

Colonel: Sir David Home of Wedderburn

The only evidence for the existence of this regiment is a mention in Terry's biography of Leven that Wedderburn's regiment was at Duns in August 1640. Wedderburn was a Berwickshire M.P. in 1639-1641. There is no other reference to the laird having a regiment until late 1643, when he was colonel of the Merse infantry.[120]

Lord Yester's Horse

Colonel: John, 8th Lord Hay of Yester

The family history claims that Lord Yester was at Newcastle without a regiment. However, in early September 1640 an Englishman reported that Yester had begun to plunder in Durham. He reportedly led four troops of horse at 12 a.m. into Sunderland, where he seized £840 of the king's money.[121] There is no other mention of the regiment and this unit may have been an ad hoc force.

NOTES

1. NLS, Wodrow Analecta Folio 31, 33; *Baillie*, ii. 470; Foster, *Members*, 68.
2. Stevenson, *Alasdair*, 72-3.
3. *Argyll*, i. 19.
4. SRO, RH. 13/18; *Argyll*, i. 19; Balfour, *Works*, ii. 380-1; Gordon, *History*, iii. 163-5; *Memoirs of Guthry*, 74-7; *Memorials of Montrose and his Times*, 2 vols., ed. M. Napier (Maitland Club, lxvi, part i, 1848), i. 259; Spalding, *Memorialls*, i. 271, 291-2; J. N. Buchanan, 'Charles I and the Scots, 1637-49' (Toronto Univ., PH.D. thesis 1965), 309; J. K. Hewison, *The Covenanters* (Glasgow, 1913), i. 346; Stevenson, *Covenanters*, 36-7.
5. NLS, Wodrow Analecta Folio 31, 28, 33v.
6. *Army of the Covenant*, i. lxxxix; Balfour, *Works*, iii. 353, 434; *CSPD 1640*, 629; Cowan, *Montrose*, 103; *Scots Peerage*, iv. 309.
7. NLS, Wodrow Analecta Folio 31, 28, 34v.
8. NLS, Wodrow Analecta Folio 31, 33; PRO, SP. 16/464/59II, 134; Balfour, *Works*, ii. 380; Spalding, *Memorialls*, ii. 65; Cowan, *Montrose*, 98.
9. Spalding, *Memorialls*, i. 267-8.
10. SRO, KSR North Leith, 3 April, 22 May 1640; Gordon, *History*, iii. 128; *Memoirs of Guthry*, 85.
11. NLS, Wodrow Analecta Folio 31, 27v, 29, 30, 32, 33, 34-v.
12. PRO, SP. 16/464/59II, 134; *Baillie*, i. 262; Cowan, *Montrose*, 97, 108.
13. NLS, Wodrow Analecta Folio 31, 30, 33; Terry, *Leslie*, 108.
14. SRO, SR Fife, i. 19v.
15. *Ibid.*; R. A. Bensen, 'South-West Fife and the Scottish Revolution: the presbytery of Dunfermline, 1633-52' (Edinburgh Univ., M.Litt. 1978), 44.
16. Gordon, *History*, ii. 164.
17. NLS, Wodrow Analecta Folio 31, 29, 33; SRO, PR Biggar, 18 June, 3 and 17 December 1640.
18. NLS, Wodrow Analecta Folio 31, 33; PRO, SP. 16/464/59II, 134; 'Unpublished papers of John, Seventh Lord Sinclair, Covenanter and Royalist', ed. J. A. Fairley, *Trans. Buchan Field Club*, viii (1904-5), 156-8; Terry, *Leslie*, 108.
19. NLS, Wodrow Analecta Folio 31, 27, 34v.
20. Ibid., 33; PRO, SP. 16/464/59II, 134; SRO, GD. 25. Sec. 9, Box 2; P. W. Lilley, 'Rev. John Livingston, covenanter and scholar, minister of Ancrum, 1648-62', *Hawick Arch. Soc.*, lxvi (1934), 50; Terry, *Leslie*, 108.
21. Stevenson, *Covenanters*, 66, 206.
22. PRO, SP 28/120, 814v.
23. *Minute Book kept by the War Committee of the Covenanters in the Stewartry of Kirkcudbright in the Years 1640 and 1641*, ed. J. Nicholson (Kirkcudbright, 1840), 71; *Aberdeen Letters*, ii. 186.
24. SRO, B. 30, 21, 74; GD. 10. 749; *Baillie*, i. 260; *The Book of Caerlaverock; memoirs of the Maxwells, earls of Nithsdale, lords Maxwell & Herries*, 2 vols., ed. W. Fraser (Edinburgh, 1873), i. 363-4; Spalding, *Memorialls*, ii. 61, 65; *Stewartry of Kirkcudbright*, 71, 73; Cowan, *Montrose*, 105.
25. SRO, PA. 7.21, 74; *Baillie*, ii. 9; Cowan, *Montrose*, 125-6.
26. SRO, PA. 16.3.2, 2; *Register of the Privy Council of Scotland, 1635-43*, ed. P. H. Brown (Edinburgh, 1906), 2nd Ser. vii. 200-1, 353; Turner, *Memoirs*, 18-19; Stevenson, *Covenanters*, 67-70.
27. PRO, SP 28/120, 814v; 'Papers of Lord Sinclair', 179-82; *A True and Exact Relation of divers principall actions of a late Expedition in the north of Ireland, by the English and Scottish Forces* (London, 1642), 3; *A True Relation of the Proceedings of the Scottish Armie now in Ireland by Three Letters* (London, 1642), 4; Stevenson, *Covenanters*, 336.
28. Bod. Lib., Carte MS. 5, 195; *The Melvilles of Melville and the Leslies Earls of Leven*, 3 vols., ed. W. Fraser (Edinburgh, 1890), ii. 94; Stevenson, *Covenanters*, 131-2.

29. SRO, PA. 7.23/2.26; Stevenson, *Covenanters*, 203.

30. NLS, Adv. MS. 33.4.8, 96; *APS*, VI, i. 435; Stevenson, *Covenanters*, 206, 209.

31. *History of the War in Ireland from 1641 to 1653 by a British Officer of the Regiment of Sir John Clotworthy*, ed. E. Hogan (Dublin, 1873), 50; Stevenson, *Covenanters*, 231, 267.

32. *Ibid.*, 313.

33. Gordon, *History*, iii. 202; Spalding, *Memorialls*, i. 267; Foster, *Members*, 140.

34. *CSPD, 1640*, 480; J. W. Kennedy, 'The Teviotdale Regiment', *Hawick Arch. Soc.*, xxxv (1903), 57-8.

35. NLS, Wodrow Analecta Folio 31, 27, 30, 34v.

36. Ibid., 30, 33; PRO, SP 16/464/59II, 134; Hewison, *Covenanters*, i. 348; *Scots Peerage*, iii. 100; Terry, *Leslie*, 106, 108.

37. NLS, Wodrow Analecta Folio 31, 27v-8, 34v.

38. Ibid., 33; PRO, SP 16/464/59II, 134; *Baillie*, i. 247, 262; *Memoirs of Guthry*, 70; Cowan, *Montrose*, 98; *Scots Peerage*, vii. 51; Terry, *Leslie*, 107.

39. NLS, Wodrow Analecta Folio 31, 27-8, 29; SRO, KSR Bathgate, i. 15v, 16v; PR Linlithgow, 19 August, 2 September, 4 November 1640.

40. NLS, Wodrow Analecta Folio 31, 33; PRO, SP 16/464/59II, 134; Foster, *Members*, 110; Terry, *Leslie*, 108.

41. NLS, Wodrow Analecta Folio 31, 30.

42. SRO, KSR Tyninghame, i. 119; *APS*, VI, i. 86; Balfour, *Works*, ii. 407; *Baillie*, i. 259; Terry, *Leslie*, 108.

43. NLS, Wodrow Analecta Folio 31, 27, 30; SRO, PA. 7.21, 74; PA. 16.2 (Account of Lord Register's regiment of Edinburgh); *Kirkcaldie*, 182, 189, 193-4, 202-3; see also above Leslie's Life Guard of Foot.

44. NLS, Wodrow Analecta Folio 31, 33, 34; *Kirkcaldie*, 188, 206.

45. PRO, SP 16/464/59II, 134; *Memorials of the Family of Wemyss of Wemyss*, 3 vols. ed. W. Fraser (Edinburgh, 1888), i. 242.

46. NLS, Wodrow Analecta Folio 31, 30.

47. PRO, SP 16/461/57II, 121; SP 16/464/59II, 134; *Memoirs of Guthry*, 70; Cowan, *Montrose*, 98; Terry, *Leslie*, 108.

48. NLS, Wodrow Analecta Folio 31, 27; SRO, PR Lanark, 25 June, 30 July, 22 October 1640, 25 March, 6, 18 May, 17 June, 1 July 1641.

49. NLS, Wodrow Analecta Folio 31, 33; PRO, SP 16/464/59I, 134; SRO, PR Lanark, 25 June 1640; *Baillie*, i. 262; Terry, *Leslie*, 108.

50. SRO, RH. 13.18; *Aberdeen Letters*, ii. 223, 241-3, 245; Gordon, *History*, ii. 255; Spalding, *Memorialls*, i. 267, 308-9, 315-8, 331, 337-9, 350; *Ibid.*, ii. 3.

51. Gordon, *History*, ii. 196-7.

52. Spalding, *Memorialls*, i. 267.

53. SRO, GD. 112/39, 798-9, 806, 808, 812, 820-1, 823, 830.

54. Wilson, *History*, 22; W. Gordon, *The History of the . . . Family of Gordon*, 2 vols. (Edinburgh, 1727), ii. 349; *Scots Peerage*, iv. 315.

55. NLS, Wodrow Analecta Folio 31, 28, 29, 30.

56. PRO, SP 16/464/59II, 134; *Baillie*, i. 260; Cowan, *Montrose*, 98.

57. Balfour, *Works*, iii. 38.

58. PRO, SP 16/464/59II, 134; *CSPD 1640*, 480; Cowan, *Montrose*, 98; Terry, *Leslie*, 108.

59. NLS, Wodrow Analecta Folio 31, 28, 30.

60. PRO, SP 16/464/57II, 120v; SRO, KSR Tyninghame, i. 119; *CSPD 1640*, 534; *Ibid.*, *1640-1*, 136; Cowan, *Montrose*, 122-3; Terry, *Leslie*, 108.

61. NLS, Wodrow Analecta Folio 31, 30.

62. Ibid.; Balfour, *Works*, ii. 383; Cowan, *Montrose*, 98.

63. NLS, Wodrow Analecta Folio 31, 28, 30; *Stewartry of Kirkcudbright*, 9.

64. NLS, Wodrow Analecta Folio 31, 28, 30; SRO, PA. 7.2.71, 153, 210, 268; *Stewartry of Kirkcudbright*, 1-2, 5-6, 31, 127-9, 138-9; Turner, *Memoirs*, 16; Cowan, *Montrose*, 98.

65. NLS, Wodrow Analecta Folio 31, 28; NRH OPR Balmerino, 7 March, 9 June 1641; *Kirkcaldie*, 190, 194, 196, 203.

66. *Baillie*, i. 262; Gordon, *History*, iii. 159.

67. NLS, Wodrow Analecta Folio 31, 27-v, 33v; SRO, PA. 16.2 (Durie's company of Life Guards, 15 July 1640-25 August 1641).

68. NLS, Wodrow Analecta Folio 31, 30, 32, 33v; SRO, E 100/1/1.

69. PRO, SP 16/464/59II, SRO, E 100/1/12; PA. 16.2 (Life Guards of Horse, 12 August 1640-17 September 1641).

70. NLS, Wodrow Analecta Folio 31, 33v; Balfour, *Works*, ii. 386; Gordon, *History of Gordon*, ii. 343, 346.

71. S.A.U.L., Hay of Leyes Receipt 139; Balfour, *Works*, ii. 373; Somerville, *Memorie*, ii. 223, 225-6, 229, 247, 256.

72. NLS, Wodrow Analecta Folio 31, 30; Wodrow Letters Quarto 19, no. 68.

73. NLS, Wodrow Analecta Folio 31, 33; PRO, SP 16/464/59II, 134; *Baillie*, i. 256, 260; Gordon, *History of Gordon*, ii. 346.

74. *Selections from the Registers of the Presbytery of Lanark 1623-1709*, ed. J. Robertson (Abbotsford Club xvi, 1839), 22.

75. NLS, Wodrow Analecta Folio 31, 27.

76. Ibid.; SRO, KSR Livingston, 10 January 1641.

77. NLS, Wodrow Analecta Folio 31, 28-9, 30, 32, 33v; SRO, PR Jedburgh, 15 July 1640, 3 February 1641.

78. NLS, Wodrow Analecta Folio 31, 33; PRO, SP 16/464/59II, 134; SRO, GD. 237.17, no. 2; *Baillie*, i. 257; *Correspondence of Lothian*, i. 108; *CSPD 1640*, 480; Kennedy, 'Teviotdale', 57.

79. NLS, Wodrow Analecta Folio 31, 27, 30, 33v.

80. Ibid., 33; PRO, SP 16/464/59II, 134; Balfour, *Works*, ii. 407; *Baillie*, i. 256; Gordon, *History of Gordon*, ii. 346.

81. NLS, Wodrow Analecta Folio 31, 28, 29, 30, 32v, 34; SRO, KSR Pencaitland, i. 14-15v.

82. NLS, Wodrow Analecta Folio 31, 33; SRO, KSR Pencaitland, i. 15; Terry, *Leslie*, 106, 108.

83. *Aberdeen Letters*, ii. 211-12, 249-50; *Council of Aberdeen*, i. 222-5; Gordon, *History*, iii. 160; Spalding, *Memorialls*, i. 267, 282-3, 287-8.

84. NLS, Acc. 6026, 3/10, 31v; *Aberdeen Letters*, ii. 188, 216, 218, 220-1; Gordon, *History*, iii. 225; Spalding, *Memorialls*, i. 295-6, 315-6.

85. *Baillie*, ii. 470; *Council of Aberdeen*, i. 241; Spalding, *Memorialls*, i. 315-6, 357; *Ibid.*, ii. 6; Cowan, *Montrose*, 98.

86. NLS, Wodrow Analecta Folio 31, 28, 29, 30, 33-4v.

87. PRO, SP 16/464/59II, 134; *Baillie*, i. 256; W. M. Metcalfe, *A History of Paisley 600-1908* (Paisley, 1909), 258; W. M. Metcalfe, *A History of the county of Renfrew from the earliest times* (New Club, 13, 1905), 258; Terry, *Leslie*, 108.

88. NLS, Wodrow Analecta Folio 31, 28, 30, 34v; SRO, PR Perth, ii. 646, 648, 653, 656-7, 669-60, 662-3, 665, 667-8, 671, 674, 677, 681, 683, 685, 690, 699.

89. NLS, Wodrow Analecta Folio 31, 27-v, 33; PRO, SP 16/464/59II, 134; Balfour, *Works*, ii. 384; *Baillie*, i. 247; Gordon, *History*, iii, 257; Terry, *Leslie*, 108; G. Wishart, *The Memoirs of James, Marquis of Montrose, 1639-1650*, eds. A. D. Murdoch and H. F. M. Simpson (London, 1893), 19-21.

90. *Baillie*, i. 262; Cowan, *Montrose*, 108, 112-15, 128.

91. Spalding, *Memorialls*, i. 267.

92. PRO, SP 28/120, 82v, 896v; SRO, PR Stranraer, i. 17, 26, 44; J. Livingston, *A Brief Historical Relation of the Life of Mr. John Livingston*, ed. T. Houston (Edinburgh, 1848), 11; Stevenson, *Covenanters*, 160, 330.

93. NLS, Adv. MS. 29.2.9, 131; SRO, PA. 16.1 (Account of Munro's); *Aberdeen Letters*, ii. 186, 211; Gordon, *History*, iii. 167, 169, 196-7, 200-3; Spalding, *Memorialls*,

i. 273-85, 289-90.

94. SRO, PA. 16.1, 36; Balfour, *Works*, ii. 281-2; Gordon, *History*, ii. 210-3, 251-4; Spalding, *Memorialls*, i. 297-9, 305-6, 314-15, 320, 332-3.

95. *Aberdeen Letters*, ii. 223, 249; *Council of Aberdeen*, i. 226; Gordon, *History*, ii. 255; Spalding, *Memorialls*, i. 338-9.

96. SRO, GD. 188.19/1.2; PA. 7.2.66, 146; *CSPD 1640-1641*, 242; Spalding, *Memorialls*, i. 350.

97. SRO, PA. 16.3.12, 1; PA. 7.2.74, 157; *APS*, VI, i. 673; *Privy Council*, 2nd Ser. vii. 200-1; Spalding, *Memorialls*, i. 350; Turner, *Memoirs*, 17; Stevenson, *Covenanters*, 66, 69-70, 72.

98. Stevenson, *Covenanters*, 74-5, 80; see above.

99. Bod. Lib., Carte MS. 3, 239v; 'Papers of Lord Sinclair', 179-82; *True Relation of principall actions of Scottish Forces*, 3-4; Stevenson, *Covenanters*, 330-1.

100. Bodl. Lib., Carte MS. 6, 277; Carte MS. 10, 153v; Stevenson, *Covenanters*, 138, 157.

101. SRO, PA. 7. 23/2.26, 1; *A full relation of the late expedition of the Right Honourable the lord Monroe, Major-General of all Protestant Forces in the Province of Ulster* (London, 1642), 2; Stevenson, *Covenanters*, 231, 249.

102. Adair, *Narrative*, 150-1; R. Clark, *A Letter concerning General Monk's surprising the Town and Castle of Carrickfergus and Belfast, in Ireland, and his Taking General Major Monro prisoner* (London, 1648), s.s.; Stevenson, *Covenanters*, 266, 269-70, 273.

103. Spalding, *Memorialls*, i. 267; Foster, *Members*, 144.

104. NLS, Acc. 6026, 13, 1/524; *Baillie*, i. 256.

105. NLS, Wodrow Analecta Folio 31, 28, 30, 31, 32-33v; SRO, KSR Monimail, i. 11; *Kirkcaldie*, 189; see Elcho's foot for other ministers.

106. NLS, Wodrow Analecta Folio 31, 30, 33; PRO, SP 16/464/59II, 134; *Kirkcaldie*, 188; Terry, *Leslie*, 108.

107. NLS, Dep. 175, Box 87.1; PRO, SP 28/120, 305v, 1157v. Henry and David Sinclair served concurrently 1640-1, then Henry alone from 1642. SRO, PR Dalkeith, 6 June, 6 July 1642; Stevenson, *Covenanters*, 337.

108. NLS, Dep. 175, Box 87.1; SRO, PA 16.3.12, 3; *Aberdeen Letters*, i. 245, 294; *Council of Aberdeen*, i. 243-4, 265-7; *CSPD 1640-1641*, 102; 'Papers of Lord Sinclair', 170-1; Spalding, *Memorialls*, i. 351-2; *Ibid.*, ii. 6-7, 55.

109. *Ibid.*, ii. 101-2; Turner, *Memoirs*, 17-18; Stevenson, *Covenanters*, 70, 78.

110. SRO, PR Dalkeith, 6 July 1642; 'Papers of Lord Sinclair', 181-2; R. Pike, *A True Relation of the proceedings of the Scots and English forces in the North of Ireland* (London, 1642), 5; *True Relation by Three Letters*, 6; Turner, *Memoirs*, 19, 21-5.

111. Bod. Lib., Carte MS. 6, 277; *Melville and Leven*, ii. 93-4; Turner, *Memoirs*, 25-8; Stevenson, *Covenanters*, 140.

112. Bod. Lib., Carte MS. 8, 59, 61; Carte MS. 9, 199v, 213; Turner, *Memoirs*, 33; Stevenson, *Covenanters*, 153-6.

113. *Glasgow*, ii. 69; Metcalfe, *Paisley*, 260; Metcalfe, *Renfrew*, 262.

114. SRO, B.66.25.367; *Army of the Covenant*, ii. 305; *Memoirs of Guthry*, 154; Turner, *Memoirs*, 35-6; Wilson, *History*, 37; J. Barber, 'The Capture of the Covenanting Town of Dumfries by Montrose', *Dumfries and Galloway Natural History and Antiquarian Society*, xxi (1908-9), 32.

115. NLS, Wodrow Analecta Folio 27, 78; SRO, KSR Dron, 6 December 1646; *L. J.*, vii. 707; Turner, *Memoirs*, 39, 41-3; J. N. Buchanan, 'Charles I and the Scots, 1637-49' (Toronto Univ., PH.D. thesis 1965), 530, 583.

116. NLS, Adv. MS. 33.4.8, 141; SRO, GD. 2.53; *APS*, VI, i. 693, 723; *Correspondence of Lothian*, i. 204; Turner, *Memoirs*, 44.

117. *CSPD 1640*, 480; Kennedy, 'Teviotdale', 57-8.

118. NLS, Wodrow Analecta Folio 31, 28, 29, 30, 33v; SRO, KSR Tyninghame, i. 113, 118v-9.

119. PRO, SP 16/464/59II, 134; SRO, KSR Tyninghame, i. 113, 118v-9; Balfour, *Works*, ii. 407; Foster, *Members*, 178; Terry, *Leslie*, 108.

120. *List of Regiments*; Foster, *Members*, 181; Terry, *Leslie*, 108.

121. *CSPD 1640-1641*, 23; R. A. Hay, *Geneaologie of the Hayes of Tweeddale* (Edinburgh, 1835), 27.

4

Ulster Army

Marquis of Argyll's Foot

Colonel: Archibald, 1st marquis of Argyll

Lieutenant Colonels: Sir Duncan Campbell of Auchinbreck (1642-5), Sir Dugald Campbell of Auchinbreck (1645-8), Duncan Campbell of Inverliver (1648)

Majors: William Campbell (1642-8), Alexander MacAulay (1648)

Ministers: Dougal/Dugald Campbell, Archibald MacCallum[1]

The marquis of Argyll was the only colonel of a regiment bound for Ulster who received a royal commission. The king presented it on 18 March 1642, nearly five months after the outbreak of the Irish rebellion. Three days later Argyll appointed his lieutenant colonel, to whom he granted the authority to act as colonel in his absence. Between March and May the marquis recruited his men from Argyll and the surrounding islands, principally from his clansmen and allies. By some time in May the regiment was ready to embark upon its first campaign.[2]

The objective chosen by Argyll was the island of Rathlin. The king's commission had granted the island as a base for the regiment and had specifically stated that all rebels in occupation of the island were to be expelled or killed. Auchinbreck chose the latter course. At Port-na-Cailliagh his men threw or pushed the local women off the cliffs. There is a story that one soldier cared for a woman who had survived the fall, later marrying her. The regiment numbered 1,099 men and officers at this time. Although the regiment was part of the Ulster Army and as such was subject to orders from Leven or Munro, Auchinbreck adopted an independent stance when his men landed in north Antrim. The reason for this was that the regiment's first loyalty was to clan Campbell, which meant in practical terms opposing the Clan Ian Mor and its allies (in Ulster the MacDonnells under the earl of Antrim), and extending the territory of the Campbells. When two companies reached Ballycastle from Rathlin in late May they demanded to be garrisoned in Dunluce Castle. However, Munro stationed them in Donswerie. As more of the regiment arrived they were quartered in Portnaw, Cross, and Cominge Ferry. Despite Munro's orders to the contrary the regiment quartered on the earl of Antrim's lands and scoured the Glens of Antrim in search of MacDonnell cattle. Munro deemed the regiment so insubordinate that he wrote Argyll asking him to tell it to follow his commands.[3]

Almost from the start the regiment earned a reputation for rapaciousness. In early July George Campbell, Tutor of Calder, wrote his brother Colin of Ardersier that the officers in the army

> 'say that there is noe wrong done in Ireland bot onlie that quhilk is done be these men that comes out of Illa . . .'

These were volunteers who freely travelled between Argyll and Ulster. The Tutor instructed his brother to inform the Islaymen that if they came without passes signed by Ardersier they would be detained. Among the local inhabitants the regiment as a whole soon gained a reputation for oppression. In Antrim Auchinbreck was cessing oats, barley and cattle by 1643. In the same period the regiment assumed control of half of Coleraine's unplanted liberties.[4] Further evidence does not exist to indicate the extent of the regiment's oppressiveness, however the poor state of the army's supply system would have forced the regiment to maintain itself off the people until 1648.

Although Munro had attempted to prevent Argyll's regiment from quartering in the lands of its enemies at first, he eventually relented. By mid November 1642 the regiment was quartered as follows: Dunluce Castle (the regimental headquarters) 473 men and officers in four companies; Ballycastle 228 men and officers in two companies; Ballymoney 220 men and officers in two companies; Ballanatree 121 men and officers (the major's company); and Ballintoy 115 men and officers (the colonel's company). The strength of the regiment then stood at 1,172 men and officers.[5] It would retain control of the area delineated until disbanded in 1648.

There is little information about the regiment until 1644. In 1643 Argyll provided £12,000 as part of the loan to succour the Ulster Army. By 1644 it was rumoured that Auchinbreck was recruiting Scots and Irish men into the regiment 'without examing of what Cuntry or Nation or Religion they are, soo as they take the Covenant'. If that was the case it suggests that the regiment required fresh recruits. By mid May 1644 Alastair MacDonald had captured Rathlin Island from its Campbell garrison. This was the start of the regiment's involvement in warfare against Alastair, which nearly caused its ruin. However, in 1644 Ulster remained the centre of the regiment's activities. On 1 July part of the regiment joined Munro at Armagh to take part in his Leinster campaign. Again on 29 July most of the regiment rendezvoused with Munro in the Kilwarlin Woods for over two months of campaigning against Castlehaven's Irish army.[6]

The invasion of Argyll by Montrose and Alastair forced Argyll to recall his regiment to Scotland between late 1644 and early 1645. Most of the regiment reached Scotland and Auchinbreck received the command of Argyll's forces due to the marquis' physical disability. One of the captains, Ewan MacLean of

Treshnish, deserted to Montrose's army upon his arrival in Scotland. On 2 February 1645 at the battle of Inverlochy Auchinbreck placed his regiment in the centre. However, the addition of these regulars was insufficient to stem the advance of the royalist army and many of the regiment must have fallen fighting and fleeing. Auchinbreck was captured and confronted by Alastair with two means of execution, to which the Lieutenant Colonel responded, 'dà dhiù gun aon roghainn', or two evils and no choice. Alastair personally executed him. Treshnish saved the life of Campbell of Skipness after the battle by interposing himself between Skipness and his assailant, thereby incurring a wound. The remnants of the regiment limped back to Ulster. There are no estimates on the losses of the Argyll's regiment in this battle, however his army lost half of its combatants. Thus one may exterpolate that if 900 men crossed to Scotland about 450 of them returned. In 1645 each regiment of the Ulster Army provided 200 men to fight Montrose, which would have disastrously weakened this regiment unless it was levying new recruits. On 2 April 1646 Argyll arrived in Ulster for his only visit with the army. He hoped to persuade Munro to release a substantial force to help reconquer the parts of Argyll held by the MacDonalds. In the event he only received permission to use his own regiment. Sometime in April or May Skipness led the regiment on an invasion of Islay. Men of the Clanranald repulsed them, forcing the regiment to return to Ulster which they reached on 31 May. Fortunately for the regiment the abortive invasion of Islay prevented it from partaking in the debacle of Benburb.[7]

Until the acceptance of the Engagement by the Ulster Army there is no mention of Argyll's regiment. The Lieutenant Colonel Sir Dugald Campbell of Auchinbreck and Major William Campbell opposed the Engagement, but the men and the officers supported it. However, Auchinbreck's control of the regiment was so rigid that as late as mid June it was refusing to provide men for the Engager contingent of the Ulster Army. Nevertheless, Colonel George Munro (leader of that force) circumvented Auchinbreck's opposition by cashiering him and the major. In their places Captains Duncan Campbell of Inverliver and Alexander MacAulay received their respective ranks. The regiment then supplied Munro with about 200 men, who disbanded after the Treaty of Stirling in late September 1648. The remnant in Ulster disbanded following Monck's capture of Carrickfergus. However, seventeen of the regiment's kirk party officers remained in Ulster. In December they signed a petition stating their opposition to the Engagement and their desire for arrears. By early October 1649 Auchinbreck, the cashiered major, and twelve other officers were in Scotland receiving pay as reformadoes from the kirk party regime.[8]

The history of Argyll's regiment in the Ulster Army was not a glorious one. Gaining a reputation for oppression in the area where they quartered, the men did not compensate for that by feats of arms. The regiment served chiefly to extend Campbell power and as a reservoir of manpower for Argyll's campaigns against his enemies. In the end loyalty to the Covenants was espoused by only a minority within the regiment.

Train of Artillery

Commander: General Sir Alexander Hamilton

This arm was of little usefulness to the Ulster Army due to the terrain of the province and the nature of war in it. The former prevented the easy transport of artillery; the latter was such that there were few battles or sieges. On the Bann campaign (24 May - 6 June 1642) Munro had five guns. After 3 August ninety-six officers and artillerists arrived in Carrickfergus. In December 1643, due to the uselessness of artillery, Hamilton ordered six heavy cannon and other guns withdrawn to Scotland probably for the use of the Army of the Solemn League and Covenant. Munro used artillery in his Leinster campaign (27 June - 15 July 1644) and again in the campaign aginst Castlehaven (25 July - 7 October 1644). There is no further mention of the use of artillery in Ulster. It may have been taken on the Benburb campaign, but it is doubtful that the guns could have kept up with the speed of the advance on 5 June 1646. If they had, O'Neill would have seized them. Any remaining artillery would have been lost either by George Munro in his campaign in Enlgand and Scotland or by its capture by Monck in September 1648. In July 1649 the rights of the Scottish government to some artillery in Carrickfergus was recognised by the royalists in Ulster, who controlled the town. Sir Robert Adair of Kinhilt and another Scot arrived there on the orders of the Estates to reclaim the guns. However, their mission failed, leaving the cannon in Ulster to be captured by the Parliamentarians in December 1649.[9]

Auchinbreck's Horse Troop

Routmaster: Lieutenant Colonel Sir Duncan Campbell of Auchinbreck

This unit was raised to form part of a force of Ulster Army cavalry to replace that which had accepted the Cassation of 15 September 1643. The origin of its horsemen is unknown, however it is doubtful that they came from Argyll. Instead it may be assumed that they were raised either from the Scottish lowlands or from protestant settlers in Ulster. It numbered about 62 men and officers. The unit's only known military activity was service on the Leinster campaign. The troop quartered on all of the earl of Antrim's lands, the liberties of Coleraine and in several places in county Londonderry. It has been suggested that it disbanded after Auchinbreck's death. But the command may have devolved upon his son. On 17 January 1646 the English parliamentary committee for Irish affairs in Westminster claimed that it had been illegally raised, constituted a burden on Ulster and should be disbanded.[10] As there is no further mention of the unit it may be assumed that it ceased to exist sometime in 1645 or 1646.

Balfour's Horse Troop

Routmaster: Colonel Sir William Balfour

Balfour began his military career in the Dutch army. From 1630 to 1641 he was Governor of the Tower of London. In 1640 he became a naturalised Englishman. The English parliament chose him as colonel of the regiment of horse which it was to provide to support the Ulster Army. In late 1642 Balfour became lieutenant general of horse in the parliamentarian army, to which most of his regiment belonged. But Balfour never took up his charge in Ulster. Only sixty-nine men and officers, which formed his own troop, ever reached Ulster.[11] There is no mention of them after early 1643. They may have disbanded or joined other cavalry forces in Ulster.

Campbell's Horse Troop

Routmaster: Captain John Campbell

This unit may have formed part of the parliamentarian forces in Ulster. However, there was a Captain John Campbell in Argyll's Foot. In 1646 the commander of the troop went to England and raised his men. The troop was in Ulster by 26 January 1647. Unlike the Scottish troops of horse raised in 1643, Campbell's possessed full approval of the English parliament.[12] If this troop was part of Monck's forces, this easily explains why it is not mentioned in Scottish sources.

Cunningham's Horse Troop

Routmaster: Lieutenant Colonel William Cunningham

Cunningham was the lieutenant colonel of the earl of Glencairn's Foot. This unit was raised after the Cessation in 1643 to replace those cavalry units which accepted the truce. There were approximately sixty-two men and officers in the unit. The troop served on the Leinster campaign in 1644. In 1645 it was quartered near and in Belfast, indeed probably remained in that vicinity after Munro's seizure of Belfast in May 1644. There is no mention of the unit's origin. In January 1646 it was condemned with the other four troops of the Ulster Army by an English parliamentary committee as being illegal and a pro-digious burden to the province. The English desired its disbanding.[13] However, the troop did serve on the Benburb campaign. In 1648 Cunningham was a warm adherent of the Engagement, but it is unknown whether he persuaded his horsemen to join George Munro's force.

Earl of Eglinton's Foot

Colonels: Alexander, 6th Earl of Eglinton (1642-3), James Montgomery (1644-8)

Lieutenant Colonels: Colin Pitscottie (1642-3), James Montgomery (1643-4)

Major: Andrew Bell

Minister: Thomas Peebles[14]

Eglinton received his commission to raise a regiment from the Privy Council on 11 March 1643. The men probably came from the southwest lowlands. The regiment had reached Ulster by May. The musters between May and June put its strength at 1,006 men and 110 officers in ten companies. The chaplain took part in the first presbytery meeting in Ulster on 10 June. Eglinton was with his men only from 4 August to November. During that time the regiment may have taken part in Leven's two expeditions. In September the regiment was based at Bangor, and had a strength of 1,062 men and officers (including sixty-two sick).[15]

Unlike other regiments in the army, Eglinton's has a shadowy history. In early 1643 the colonel provided £6,000 as a voluntary loan for the army. On 4 April at 11 a.m. or noon the regiment furnished men for a rendezvous in Clandeboy's Woods, bordering MacCartan's lands. This enterprise remained in the woods for two days, burning them in order to prevent the Irish from using them as a refuge. The regiment is next mentioned in March 1644 when Munro ordered Eglinton to make James Montgomery the colonel. (Pitscottie had left the regiment to become lieutenant colonel of the Midlothian Foot, and Eglinton was the colonel of a horse regiment in the Army of the Solemn League and Covenant at this time.) On 27 June the regiment joined Munro's forces at Lisnegarvy at the start of the Leinster campaign. It appears that the men did not take part in the campaign against Castlehaven's army. In 1645 200 men of the unit went to Scotland as part of Home's new regiment; they never returned to Ulster. The regiment contributed 500-560 men to the Benburb campaign; only 200-300 of these men survived the battle. The strength of the regiment now stood at 500-600 men (excluding losses due to disease and starvation). In 1648 Eglinton opposed the Engagement, but his replacement and the men of the regiment favoured it. They contributed about 200 men to Munro's expeditionary force; none of them returned to the regiment after the defeat of the Engagers. When Monck abolished the Ulster Army in September 1648, Montgomery's regiment was no stronger than 400 foot soldiers.[16]

Earl of Glencairn's Foot

Colonel: William, 8th Earl of Glencairn

Lieutenant Colonel: William Cunningham

Majors: Alexander Barclay, William Knox

Ministers: Hugh Cunningham, Gabriel Maxwell[17]

On 11 March Glencairn received his commission from the Privy Council to raise a regiment of foot for the Ulster Army. The men probably came from south-western Scotland. The regiment reached Ulster sometime in May. In the musters of May/June 1642 it was revealed that there were 1,018 men and officers in the regiment. In late May two companies of the regiment took part in the Bann campaign. In June the regimental chaplain was present at the first Ulster presbytery meeting in Carrickfergus. It may have taken part in the other campaigns in 1642 as it formed part of the Carrickfergus garrison. In September the regiment's strength stood at 988 men and officers with seventy-five sick.[18]

The following years present a full history of the unit. In early 1643 the colonel loaned £6,000 for paying the Ulster Army. While it is uncertain what campaigns the regiment served on in the first half of 1643, it is known that it was part of Munro's force based at Armagh in August-September for the siege of Charlemont. Then the lieutenant colonel signed a letter to the Committee of Estates requesting supplies and advice about the Cessation. After 15 September the siege broke up and the regiment returned to Carrickfergus. In 1644 the unit took the Solemn League and Covenant. It took the field in late June and marched to Armagh, where it joined Munro on 1 July for his campaign into Leinster. After staying on at Carrickfergus for less than two weeks Glencairn's men marched out on 25 July as part of Munro's original force for the campaign against Castlehaven's army. Glencairn's regiment remained in the field for this campaign until early October. In early 1645 200 men of the regiment went over to Scotland as part of Home's regiment. Like the other men that formed that unit, they never returned to the Ulster Army. In August Glencairn made his only appearance in Ulster following the defeat at Kilsyth, when he sought refuge from Montrose. The following year his regiment contributed about 500-560 men to the Benburb campaign. They suffered between 250 and 360 casualties in the battle. The active history of the regiment ends in June 1646 and the unit disappears from the records until 1648.[19]

The Engagement and its aftermath caused more difficulties to this regiment than to most of the others. Both Glencairn and Lieutenant Colonel Cunningham were strong advocates of the Engagement. However, the men of the regiment, led by Major Knox and Captain Brice Cochrane, refused to obey the orders of George Munro and the army's Engager Council of War. Consequently, they did not contribute any men to the Engager force sent to England. Instead the Council of War declared the regiment an enemy to the cause and refused it quarters and provisions. In August, when Monck decided to act against Robert Munro and the remaining forces of the Ulster Army, Knox and Cochrane joined him. They sought to revenge their ostracisation by the Council of War and also hoped to deprive George Munro (should he return) of the means to do further harm to the regiment. On 13 September knowing that the Major General kept Carrickfergus easily guarded, these officers organised an ambush of the north gate guard. When Monck appeared with his forces they let him in. Munro was taken in bed and sent to the Tower. The power of the Ulster Army lay broken due to the efforts of the kirk party adherents in Glencairn's regiment. In June

1649 Cochrane was a captain in Carrickfergus Castle for the parliamentarians. Probably some of Glencairn's men were serving under him. Cochrane later became the captain of the castle. Following a siege he surrendered it to the royalists on 4 July. Cochrane reached Scotland quickly after the surrender, where on 10 August he was appointed the major of the Irish Foot (also known as His Majesty's Life Guard of Foot).[20] Knox and Cochrane may have been aided in their support of the kirk party by the loyalty of the southwestern Scots (who probably made up the regiment) to the Covenants. From the royalist perspective this was one of the most disloyal regiments of the period; from the viewpoint of the kirk party Glencairn's was one which recognised the value of the godly cause.

Hamilton's Horse Troop

Routmaster: Lieutenant Colonel John Hamilton

Hamilton, the lieutenant colonel of Lindsay's Foot, raised his troops as part of the Scottish horse which replaced the pro-Cessation British cavalry after September 1643. The troop contained approximately sixty-two men. The unit served on the Castlehaven campaign in 1644. In 1645 the troop quartered in the Lecale, county Down. On 17 January 1646 the English parliamentary committee of Irish Affairs demanded that it be disbanded, because it had been illegally raised and constituted a burden on Ulster. Hamilton refused to accede to the demand. The troop's last known service with the Ulster Army was on the Benburb campaign. However, the fifty cavalrymen who fought under Hamilton at the battle of Lisburn on 26 November 1649 may have been men of this unit. Hamilton fell prisoner to the parliamentarian forces and his men suffered heavy casualties.[21]

Home's Foot

See above, Cochrane's Foot, 45-7.

Kinhilt's Horse Troop

Routmaster: Sir Robert Adair of Kinhilt

Kinhilt was a Scottish laird from Wigtonshire who had emigrated to Ulster. He held an estate in Ballymena and was an Ulster J.P. In 1638 he fled to Scotland to avoid swearing the Black Oath. Due to his activities in Scotland the king had him declared a traitor and forfeited his Ballymena estate. In 1642 he was commissioned a captain in Balfour's horse regiment and raised his troop from

Ulster. By 19 July the troop consisted of seventy-one men and officers, who were to provide cavalry support for the Ulster Army. In 1643 Kinhilt was one of the two Ulster petitioners sent to the General Assembly of the Church of Scotland to request a supply of permanent ministers for the province's parishes. That December Leven received permission to withdraw Kinhilt's troop. However, the earl does not seem to have ordered it to Scotland at that time. On 25 July 1644 Kinhilt's men provided part of Munro's original force which marched to Lisnegarvy at the start of the campaign against Castlehaven. On 12 August the unit may have taken part in a cavalry skirmish, which the Scots won. On 19 September Kinhilt's troop formed part of a force of horse which rode into Cavan and burned 3,000 barrels of corn. The next day the unit moved into Leinster to gather intelligence about the Irish forces. Shortly afterwards Kinhilt's troop retired to its quarters. The unit is not mentioned as forming part of the Scottish forces in Ulster in 1645 and so may have been in England by then. On 13 August 1646 the English parliamentary committee on Irish Affairs ordered Lieutenant James Lindsey to be cashiered from the troop in Ulster for crimes unspecified. The troop was part of Leven's horse regiment at the time of its disbanding in February 1647. It may be assumed that the troop ceased to exist at that time. By September 1648 Kinhilt was back in Ulster, where he joined the officers of Glencairn's regiment in their plot with Monck to render Carrickfergus to the parliamentary forces. Kinhilt returned to Scotland after the fall of that place and was accepted by the kirk party regime.[22] Subsequently he rose to command a cavalry regiment in the Army of the Covenants and the Western Association Army.

Lawers' Foot

Colonels: Sir Mungo Campbell of Lawers (1642-5), (Sir) James Campbell of Lawers (1645-51)

Lieutenant Colonels: Andrew Milne (1642-4), John Moncrieff (1644-?), (? Menzies 1649), Colin Campbell (?1650-?)

Majors: Colin Campbell (1642-4), (?) Moncrieff (1644-?), Duncan Menzies (?-1651)

Ministers: John Baird, William Kinninmonth, George Ogilvie, Andrew Donaldson, George Murray, John Durie, Alexander Spittal/Spittell.[23]

Lawers' Foot was the last of the Ulster Army regiments to disband. The laird of Lawers received a commission from the Privy Council on 3 February 1642 to levy 500 men for a regiment. Five days later Lawers was ordered by the Privy Council to have the men ready at Dumbarton on Thursday 3 March. To encourage enlistments veteran Covenanter recruits would receive their arrears upon joining; new soldiers would receive £5 6s. 8d. as levy money. The Privy Council presented Lawers with £4,000 to meet these financial requirements. On 11 March Lawers received a commission making him a colonel. On 23 March the regiment (most of whose men came from Strathtay) was ready to embark for Ireland. Lawers request for money to pay the men met with refusal from the Privy Council. Finally the regiment reached Ulster by 10 April. Between the 10th and 18th the army muster master enumerated the regiment. It stood at 932 foot soldiers. In late May five of the regiment's ten companies joined Munro for the Bann campaign. By September its headquarters were at Templepatrick. Another muster of the regiment in that month revealed a strength of 1,132 men and officers with seventy-eight sick. Besides the Bann campaign the military activities of Lawers' Foot in 1642 is unknown, though they may have taken part in most of that year's expeditions.[24]

For the remainder of the time the regiment was in Ulster its activities went unnoticed. In June 1643 Captain John Moncrieff was sent with two other officers of the Ulster Army to represent its needs to the Convention of Estates in Edinburgh. The extent of the regiment's military actions in that year is unknown, however the figures given for its strength in 1644 would suggest that two seasons of campaigning in Ulster took a massive toll. In February 1644 Lawers' men embarked for Scotland, which they reached in early March. The 300 survivors of the Ulster campaigns quartered first in Greenock, then moved on through Paisley to the earl of Carnwath's estates in Clydesdale. By 15 April Lawers' men were at Perth from where they were ordered to Dumfries via Carnwath with forty baggage horses and three field guns to oppose Montrose's first incursion into Scotland. This was just the beginning of several years of hard service against Montrose and his forces.[25]

The regiment returned from the Borders in time to join Argyll in his campaign against the marquis of Huntly. On 26 April Lawers' and Lothian's regiments at Dunottar Castle numbered 800 men. These two regiments with the Mearns Foot and some horse plus a group of women camp followers were quartered at Drum on 2 May. Argyll granted the two former Ulster Army regiments permission to pillage Gordon of Drum's house. Two days later these regiments marched to Inverurie. Before returning to Drum in early June the two 'Irish' regiments marched to Turriff, Banff and Auchindoun. Due to the arrears owed them both for their service in Ulster and Scotland the two regiments resolved to march on Aberdeen and pillage it, although it contained a Covenanter garrison. The burgesses learned of the plan and quickly amassed £20,000 which they sent to Drum. On 3 June the regiments were paid and the wives of some of Lawers' men previously quartered in Old Aberdeen joined the regiment. The paired regiments marched off to Fettercairn and out of the northeast for the moment.[26]

Lawers' men proceeded south to the border, where they joined the earl of Callendar's army for what proved to be a brief period of service in England. The regiment crossed the border in June and served at the siege of Newcastle. During the siege a deserter from the regiment was discovered to have joined and deserted another regiment for which he was tried and hung in Edinburgh. The successes of Montrose in Scotland led the Committee of Estates to request troops from Leven. On 2 September Lawers' men were on their way north to oppose Montrose.[27]

The regiment would initially see little active service. Lawers' reached Aberdeen on 19 September, staying there on free quarter until the 23rd. From there it was ordered with Buchanan's Foot to form the garrison in Inverness. Lawers' regiment remained there until early 1647. The two regiments used local labour to fortify the burgh. An earth wall was constructed, which was surrounded by a deep ditch and surmounted with ramparts and pallisades. The labourers also fortified the East port, the South port in Castle Street, the Bridge port, and the Church port. In January-February 1645 Lawers' men formed part of the earl of Seaforth's army, which disintegrated after hearing of Montrose's victory at Inverlochy. On 4 February the men received their first pay in months. Three weeks later the Estates appointed Lawers and his lieutenant colonel and major to the Commission for the Northern Shires. Two days after that the regiment received authorisation from the Estates to levy the eighth man in conjunction with Lothian's Foot from Aberdeenshire, Banffshire and Moray. Meanwhile Lawers' and Buchanan's regiments had sent out parties of commanded men from Inverness to the east. They pillaged Elchess, where the laird of Grant was staying, and the lands of Cokston. The soldiers then entered Elgin, capturing Mackenzie of Pluscardine and his brother, whom they sent back to Inverness.[28]

The strange coursings of Montrose and his opponent Major General John Urry set the stage for the virtual destruction of Lawers' regiment. After marching to Aberdeen Urry retreated from Montrose to Inverness, where he gathered an army of men from the Moray plain and the north, including Lawers'. Knowing that he possessed a superior force, Urry marched against Montrose, who was encamped at Auldearn. Lawers' men were in the centre of the front line. Due to Lawers' service in Ulster and the regiment's Campbell connections the Irish and Highlanders singled it out for harsh treatment. At the end of the battle Lawers lay dead, as did four of his captains, five lieutenants and 200 infantrymen. Their graves may still be seen in Cawdor kirkyard. Captain Archibald Campbell, a brother of the first lieutenant colonel, was a prisoner of war. The regiment had been practically wiped out.[29]

The process of rebuilding occupies the next few years of the unit's history and it is problematical whether it ever regained the strength it had in September 1642. On 10 July the Estates answered a petition to the survivors of the regiment. The Estates agreed that the regiment's losses should be made up, because they had ordered it to be diverted from Ireland. The new recruits would come from Perthsire; they were to rendezvous in Perth burgh and Dundee. The Estates promised to supply money for the levy and provisions for the Inverness garrison. On 1 August the Estates decided that Perthshire would supply 1,200 recruits for Lawers' regiment. Four days later the officers petitioned the Estates about the levy. The Perthshire Committee of War had been approached about supplying men and had refused to do so on the grounds that its levy quota was already filled. The officers wished the Estates to take action; their response is unknown. Several weeks later one of the surviving soldiers was cited for fornication with a Janet MacDougal of Petty, Inverness-shire. Silence then enshrouds the regiment for several months. On 5 January 1646 Sir James Campbell of Lawers petitioned the Estates that his father's infantry regiment and horse troop should receive their back pay and that he be allowed to succeed his father as colonel and routmaster. The Estates decided to discover a way to satisfy the needs of the soldiers, and it asked Leven and Lothian to appoint Lawers to his father's rank. The matter of arrears was not satisfied for on 29 January Lawers, now colonel, and his officers petitioned the Estates for the production of the account book and payment of some arrears. The Estates agreed to the first request (the book has not survived), and ordered the payment of a quarter of the arrears. Pay still continued to be an issue, however. On 4 February the officers requested two months' pay, 400 suits of clothing and 400 pairs of shoes for the soldiers. The Estates ordered the Committee of Money to supply these requirements. Apparently the Committee managed to produce something, because the petitions stopped. By late October Quartermaster Robert Andrews had raised one hundred men, whom he led into Aberdeen on the 31st. The quartering charges from then until 20 February 1647 cost Aberdeen £3,024. On 4 January Quartermaster Andrews arrived with fifty-six recruits, who remained until 16 February. Their quartering charges amounted to £51 5s. 4d.; the burgh also loaned £73 6s. 8d. to the recruits. On 11 February the Estates ordered the regiment to Ireland. By the 20th Lawers' men with Major Moncrieffe as their leader were in Aberdeen with Argyll's and the Clydesdale Foot under the command of Lieutenant Colonel William Hunter. They remained in Aberdeen for seven days and exacted a loan worth three days' quartering allowance from their hosts upon their departure.[30]

Following a petition from Lawers, the Estates reiterated their order to send the regiment back to Ulster. Lawers had requested that the regiment should receive its arrears, be sent to Ireland and be brought up to strength. The Estates ignored the desire for more troops, but made arrangements for satisfying the other points. On 1 April Lawers' Foot was back in Aberdeen, from which the Estates ordered Leslie to remove it for shipment to Ulster if it was not needed to make up the army to 6,000 infantrymen. The regiment returned to Ulster, but the length of its stay there is unknown. By March 1648 it was back in Scotland, presumably because of the difficulties in finding good quarters in the restricted area held by the Scottish army. Sometime after its return to Scotland, Lawers' Foot marched back to Inverness to form part of the garrison, which was ordered to be reduced to 150 foot in February 1648. On 8 June 1648 the Engager parliament order the regiment to Edinburgh. Although the regiment obeyed the order and proceeded from there into England and back to Lothian, Lawers and his men opposed the Engagement. In February 1649 the colonel told the Estates that his regiment was in danger of attack by the Engagers during the march from England to Lothian due to its support of the kirk party.

The regiment became part of the kirk party Army following the Whiggamore Raid. On the 28th February 1649 Lawers was commissioned colonel of the Linlithgowshire Foot; possibly he used his old regiment as the basis of the new.[31]

On 28 February 1649 Lawers received a commission as colonel of 250 foot to be raised from Linlithgowshire. However, the old remnants of the regiment were already in the field. On 1 March 173 men, presumably all or part of the original 'Irish' foot were quartering in the northeast. Following the pacification of the northern royalists the Estates, on 1 June, assigned the regiment quarters in St. Andrews, Crail, Silverdykes, the Anstruthers, Pittenweem and Leven. On the 21st the burgh and university of St. Andrews complained to the Estates that the 230 soldiers of Lawers' there would create a dearth and scarcity of food and indiscipline in the university. The Estates assisted the hard pressed authorities by ordering the surplus of St. Andrews' proportion of men removed. The next day a petition reached the Estates from Anstruther Easter and Pittenweem claiming that eighty-four men in the former and eighty foot in the latter were impoverishing the burghs. The Estates ordered the Fife committee of war to reduce the numbers to the correct quotas which were twenty and thirteen men respectively. Thus by late June there were at least 394 soldiers in the regiment. That the number was greater is suggested by the muster figure for 31 July of 644 foot. On 3 August the number of officers was reduced to six captains and six lieutenants, because Lawers' consisted of only six companies (averaging 107 men each). Three days later the Estates authorised the levying of 187 men for Lawers' from Linlithgowshire. The regiment retained its quarters in east Fife for several months as can be seen by cases of soldiers before local church courts. A Captain Menzies commanded the company quartering in Scoonie which contained a drunkard and two fornicators who appeared before the kirk session between 27 November 1649 and 10 February 1650. At St. Andrews a married soldier committed adultery in late autumn 1649. While in Kilconquhar a soldier committed fornication in spring 1650. On 19 March 1650 a private appeared before St. Monans session requesting permission to marry a local woman. He produced a testimonial from his ensign and a testimonial of eight years' good behaviour while with the regiment. The session acquiesced to his request. Sometime in early 1650 a commanded party of thirty-six musketeers under a Quartermaster Shaw went north to join Strachan's force at Tain. Consequently, it was the only regular infantry unit engaged at Carbisdale on 27 April. The entire regiment may have marched north under Leslie as part of the operation against Montrose, because on 19 June it was ordered back to Fife. The regiment was heavily engaged in successful skirmishing against Cromwell's troops in late July in Holyrood Park, Edinburgh. At Dunbar Lawers served as a brigade commander and his men were posted on the right flank. The regiment resisted to its utmost as the following English report indicates. (This may have arisen from the musketeers being armed with flintlocks which meant that they were always ready for action.)

onely Lawers his Regiment of *High-Landers* made a good defence, and the chief officer, a Lieutenant Colonel being slain by one of the Generals Sergeants, the Colonel was absent of the name of the *Campbells*, they stood to the push of the pike, and were all cut in pieces those were all the Foot that ingaged.

Lawers' men only fled the field when a horse troop joined the English musketeers and pikemen who had first attacked them. Lawers' seems to have retreated into the presbytery of Hamilton after the battle, because two parishes there aided stricken soldiers of the regiment. In any case Lawers' received order on 30 November to march to Stirling and exactly a month later its soldiers still quartering in St. Andrews were ordered to rejoin the others in Stirling. On 24 December the Estates allowed Lawers to recruit more men. Nothing further is heard of the regiment until 24 April 1651 when Lawers' with two other regiments of foot was assigned duty of guarding the Head of the Forth and the nearby passes. It is unknown how long the regiment remained there. By 10 June it was in the Stirling camp where it mustered 413 men, suggesting that Lawers' lost over 200 men or more than one-third of its strength at Dunbar. The regiment fell in size to 391 soldiers on 11 July, but recovered to 400 men on 18 July. Unfortunately, there is no indication as to where Lawers' served in the 1651 campaign. Thus, it is impossible to state which action caused the final destruction of this resilient, loyal and courageous regiment, which was the longest serving of any Covenanter unit.[32] Throughout its history Lawers' regiment had provided the Covenanters with valuable service. In return the men had suffered from heavy casualties and lack of pay.

Earl of Leven's Foot

Colonels: Alexander, 1st earl of Leven (1642-4); George Munro (1644-8)

Lieutenant Colonel: George Munro (1642-4)

Majors: John Home (1642-5), George Gordon (1645-8)

Minister: Andrew Fairfoul (1642)[33]

This regiment was initially the General of the Ulster Army's own regiment, but due to his presence in England as commander-in-chief of the Army of the Solemn League and Covenant the lieutenant colonel (nephew and son-in-law of the major general) became its colonel. Although Leven was only commissioned colonel of the regiment on 11 March 1642, he had been apparently recruiting men before then. On 31 January an inhabitant of Edinburgh was convicted of aiding a deserter from one of Leven's companies. The majority of the regiment appears to have been raised from eastern Scotland south of the Tay. However, Captain George Gordon raised his men from Sutherland. The regiment reached Carrickfergus sometime in May, which it retained as a base until October. The

first muster of the regiment in May-June 1642 revealed a strength of 995 men
and officers. Although desertion was now more difficult due to the water
barrier, six men secured a rowboat (which none could handle) and tried to reach
Scotland. However, they were captured and several of the deserters were
executed as an example to others. On its first campaign Lieutenant Colonel
Munro led two companies. On 26-28 May Munro led a force including men
from Leven's Foot, Upton's Horse (40 horse) and Sir John Clotworthy's Foot
(500 men) on a search and destroy mission from Lough Beg through the woods
and bogs of the Apperly Hills. Following Major General Munro's seizure of
Dunluce Castle on 29 May, George Munro was installed as captain of the castle
with a garrison of men from the regiment. Munro's force remained there until
sometime in the autumn when Argyll's Foot occupied the castle. On 4 August
Leven arrived in Ulster. He led one campaign into county Tyrone and another
through county Down before departing in November. The regiment, which
numbered 982 men and officers with forty-eight sick, probably took part in both
expeditions. On 23 October the regiment entered Coleraine, where it remained
until September 1648 during which time the town 'deeply suffered'.[34]

Unlike other regiments Leven's foot does not disappear from the records at
any point after 1642. In February 1643 the regiment mustered 1,012 men and
officers. That spring Leven loaned £6,000 for the use of the Ulster Army.
However, the Scottish efforts to aid the army did little to provide Leven's men
with regular supplies. Consequently they were forced to apply to Coleraine,
which had suffered from the Rising, for money and supplies. Within a few
months the publicans and artisans within the town had spent £1,500st. on the
officers alone. The enlisted men had ransacked houses for food. The captains
had cessed each acre of land cultivated by townsmen at 6s. (per month!). In
June Captain George Gordon went to the Convention of Estates with two other
officers as representatives of the Ulster Army. The main purpose of such
missions was to persuade the Scottish and English parliaments to provide money
and supplies to the army. That they were generally without result can be seen
from the complaints about Coleraine. On 7 February 1644 an Ormondist officer
wrote that

> 'The town of Colerane by the Scotts Garrison [was] opprest without pitty & even
> utterly ruinated'.

The mayor and aldermen petitioned Ormond for the removal of the regiment on
6 March. They claimed that its demand for supplies had forced many inhabitants to live off charity, as they had given their money and food to the garrison.
The petitioners stated they preferred not to have a garrison, because the town
had become greatly impoverished. However, if one was deemed necessary the
magistrates requested a force of English settlers (two-three companies of
Colonel Audley Mervin's Foot), which would be of the same nation as the
inhabitants. In the view of the magistrates the ten companies of Leven's Foot
was a burden much larger than could be reasonably borne. The relations
between Ormond and Munro were tense at this time due to the rumours that the

Solemn League and Covenant was to be sworn in Ulster, thus the marquis probably never issued the requested order.

In April 1644 Lieutenant Colonel Munro and two other field officers travelled to the Scottish parliament to present the army's grievances. They returned by 4 May. One result of the mission was that the lieutenant colonel received the commission of a colonel for both Balfour's Horse and Leven's Foot. During the lieutenant colonel's absence, one of his officers provided an escort for two of the ministers, administering the oath of the Solemn League and Covenant in Ulster, from Ballymena to Coleraine. The regiment swore the Covenant; probably its example coerced the inhabitants to accept the Covenant too. Due to the difficulties which arose in Ulster over the Solemn League and Covenant, the campaign season began late in 1644. On 1 July part of the regiment joined Munro's force at Armagh for his march into Leinster, which lasted until mid July. On 29 July the regiment rendezvoused with Munro's army at Kilwarlin Wood for his campaign against Castlehaven's Irish army, which lasted until early October.[35] With the return of Leven's men to their quarters in Coleraine, the campaign season ended.

While the regiment remained inactive for the next few months, its new colonel was very active in a diplomatic role. In December 1644 George Munro served as the Ulster Army representative to Edinburgh. He returned to Ulster either in late December or early January 1645. That month he was again selected as the army's representative to Edinburgh. Munro also travelled on to London, where he lobbied fruitlessly, and returned to Ulster by 21 March. The regiment remained in Coleraine throughout 1645, save for 200 men who went to Scotland under Colonel Home, never to return to Ulster. The next mention of the regiment occurred in 1646. In June 500-560 men of the regiment marched under Major General Munro on the disastrous Benburb campaign. Only one third to one half of these men returned from the battle. Simultaneously George Munro had advanced on the west side of Lough Neagh with a small force of horse and foot. On 5 June several miles to the west of Benburb O'Neill's cavalry halted Munro's advance and prevented him from reinforcing his uncle's exhausted men at Benburb. By mid-June the regiment probably had no more than 560 men. In February 1647 Colonel Munro set off again as a representative of the army to the Scottish and English parliaments, returning sometime after April.[36] Throughout 1647 the regiment kept to its quarters except for minor engagements against the Irish.

As with many other regiments in the Ulster Army the events of 1648 would cause Munro's Foot to disintegrate. In the spring George Munro became commander-in-chief of the Ulster Army's Engager expeditionary force, for which he received the rank of major general. The regiment provided about 200 men for his force. Following Cromwell's victory in the Preston campaign and the Whiggamore rising, Munro found himself at Stirling with the other Engager forces in September. On the 20th the Commission of the General Assembly told Munro to disband his forces or face excommunication. Several days later the Engager forces disbanded following a treaty with the kirk party army. Munro and his men were to return to Ulster. However, attacks on them by civilians and a lack of supplies led the force to break up before it even embarked. In December 1648 the king recommended Munro to Ormond, who gave him a command in Ulster, which he held until 1650. Munro's royalist activities made him one of the few former Covenanter officers who was not employed either in 1650 or in 1651.

The fate of the regiment in Coleraine was not as straightforward. After 16 September 1648 Monck captured the town. Most of the regiment agreed to serve in his army under Colonel Edward Conway, viscount Kilwatagh, the heir of Lord Conway. The soldiers, still forming the Coleraine garrison, mutinied against their new colonel, who fled. Instead the men chose the presbyterian Lord Montgomery of Ards. Monck, anxious not to antagonise the presbyterians, accepted this. In May 1649 George Munro captured Coleraine from his former regiment. Ards now openly declared his allegiance to the royalists cause and joined Munro. Indeed, Ards may have aided Munro in taking Coleraine. They joined forces for the siege of Londonderry, which the presbytery of Carrickfergus deplored as an activity undertaken by malignants and which Owen Roe O'Neill relieved on 7 August. It is possible that some of the men of Leven's-Munro's-Conway's-Ards' regiment may have deserted after hearing of the presbytery's condemnation of the siege. The remaining men of the regiment probably fell back to Coleraine. They held out there until March 1650 when parliamentary forces under General Venables captured the town. The tenacity with which the regiment retained its cohesion in Ulster suggests either that it had become a purely mercenary unit (the mutiny over Conway's appointment points against this), or that the men had decided to settle in Ulster. Major George Gordon, for one, remained in Ulster after marrying the earl of Antrim's sister.[37] The history of this regiment is similar to that of the other regiments until after the Engagement period. It is the only Covenanting regiment to have served four masters — the Covenanters, the Engagers, the English parliamentarians, and the Ulster royalists.

Earl of Leven's Life Guard of Foot

Commander: Colonel Robert Home

This is one of the more obscure units in the Ulster Army. It was on foot in Ulster by 21 June 1642, when it numbered 117 men and officers. It may be assumed that this unit took part in Leven's two September 1642 campaigns, if not others. On 14 September the Life Guards were quartered at Donahadee, county Down. There were then 133 men and officers in the unit with eight sick.[38] There are no further references to this unit. It is probable that it remained in Ulster until disbanding in 1648.

Earl of Leven's Life Guard of Horse

Commander: Major James Bannatyne

Bannatyne was the second younger brother of the laird of Corehouse. In 1640, when he was a captain, he had led a crucial cavalry charge at the battle of Newburn. The origin of his men for the Life Guard is unknown. To contemporaries 'he was the swords of the Scots cavillrie' in Ireland. The Life Guards reached Ulster by 1 July 1642, when they were first mustered. Ballantyne then commanded 93 men and officers. The Life Guards took part in the Charlemont campaign and Leven's two offensives in 1642. In mid May 1643 the Life Guards served on another campaign against Charlemont. During it the Irish believed they killed Bannatyne at Anaghfaury. However, the report was nothing more than a piece of propaganda. The Life Guards also took part in Munro's other expeditions against Dungannon and Charlemont. In mid September the unit stood at 113 men and officers with eleven sick. In December the Scottish Estates granted Leven permission to withdraw his Life Guards to form the basis for a regiment of horse in the Army of the Solemn League and Covenant. The general consequently brought his Life Guard over to Scotland. Ballantyne became the lieutenant colonel of Leven's Horse.[39]

Earl of Lindsay's Foot

Colonels: John, 1st Earl of Lindsay (1642-4), John Hamilton (1644-8)

Lieutenant Colonels: John Hamilton (1642-4), William Borthwick (1644-8)

Major: William Borthwick (1642-4)

Ministers: John Aird (?), George Hamilton[40]

The earl of Lindsay received his commission as colonel of foot in the Ulster Army on 11 March 1643. He was one of the noble commanders never to take up his command personally. It may be assumed that most of the men in the regiment came from Fife and other parts of the Lowlands. In May 1642 Major Borthwick was recruiting men in Aberdeen for the regiment. By the end of June there were 1,014 men and officers in ten companies in Lindsay's Foot. On 13 May elements of the regiment were quartered at Broadisland and Islandmagee, where they suffered from a lack of food. In the autumn a muster of the regiment at Bangor revealed a force of 1,030 men and officers with 102 sick. There are no details of the regiment's activities in 1642. A similar blank exists for 1643. Early in that year the colonel loaned £6,000 for the use of the army. In April the regiment provided men for a search and destroy mission in Clandeboy's Wood for two days. The regiment may have taken part in the other expeditions which Munro led in 1643.[41]

The information on the regiment is more extensive in the following year. On 14 March 1644 Munro and the Council of War at Carrickfergus selected Major Borthwick to represent the army to the Committee of Estates. He was to demand supplies, money, and clothing in order to keep the army from evacuating Ulster. However, by that time the Estates had determined to keep the army in Ireland even if it meant additional burdens on Scotland. In April Lieutenant Colonel Hamilton went over to Scotland with two other officers to act as representatives of the Ulster Army. Their mission ended by 4 May. One of the results was the promotion of Hamilton and Borthwick to the ranks of colonel and lieutenant colonel respectively. In May soldiers of the regiment in alliance with some of Colonel Sir James Montgomery's men stole the goods of an inhabitant of Ballyhoman, which forced him to flee to Dublin. On 27 June six companies of the regiment formed part of Munro's original force for his campaign into Leinster. A month later the regiment joined Munro's army at Kilwarlin Wood for service in the campaign against Castlehaven's Irish army. With the return of the regiment to its quarters in early October, an eventful year ended.[42]

Evidence for the history of Hamilton's Foot after 1645 is sketchy. In spring 1645 the regiment provided 200 men for Home's regiment; they never returned from Scotland. At Benburb regiment contributed 500-560 men to Munro's army; between 250 and 360 of them fell in the battle and rout. In August 1647 Lieutenant Colonel Borthwick served on two committees established by the Council of War. One was to make up articles of war for the Ulster Army; unfortunately their report does not survive. The other was to work out a union with the British protestant forces, but that failed entirely. Sometime in early 1648 Borthwick travelled to Scotland, where he received a commission from the earl of Lanark to submit the Engagement to the Council of War for its acceptance. Borthwick's arguments were effective and the Council declared for the Engagement on 4 April. The regiment provided over 200 men for Munro's Engager expeditionary force.[43] After late spring 1648 the regiment disappears from view for ever. It is unknown whether Monck had to disarm the approximately 300 men left in arms in September or if they merely blended into the general Scottish settler population as immigrants.

Earl of Lothian's Foot

Colonel: William, 3rd earl of Lothian

Lieutenant Colonel: Walter Scott

Major: James Riddell

Minister: John Scott[44]

This regiment was one of three sent to Ulster in 1642 and evacuated from there in 1644 for service in Scotland. On 28 March 1642 the earl of Lothian, already the lieutenant general of the Ulster Army, received a colonelcy from the Privy Council. Like other noble commanders, Lothian never personally commanded his men in Ulster. By the end of August 1642 Lothian and his captains had recruited nine companies of 897 men and officers from southern Scotland. The regiment was at Carrickfergus in time to serve on Leven's two September expeditions. Meanwhile in the presbytery of Jedburgh the officers of the regiment above the rank of lieutenant (represented by Lieutenant Colonel Scott and Major Riddell) requested the ordination of John Scott as their chaplain. The presbytery agreed and on 15 July Scott was ordained in the presence of the regiment at Jedburgh. By the end of November Lothian's Foot had increased in size to 902 men and officers with thirty-four sick. The military experiences of the regiment in Ulster remains a blank, although it probably took part in Munro's campaigns in 1643. Early in 1643 the colonel provided £6,000 as part of the loan for the Ulster Army. In June the lieutenant colonel with two other officers of the army attended the Convention of Estates to represent the needs of the army. He returned to Ulster by 18 September. In mid-November Captain Gideon Murray went on a similar mission to the Committee of Estates. By the end of 1643 the Estates had determined to withdraw the Ulster Army. In the event Lothian's Foot was one of the three regiments evacuated. His men reached Scotland in February 1644 after an undistinguished tour of duty in Ulster.[45]

The initial reception of the regiment boded poorly for the future. After landing at Greenock Lothian's Foot marched in company with Sinclair's towards Paisley. Their reception was hostile, but after negotiations Lothian's regiment received permission to quarter as follows: three companies in Renfrew, Govan and Pollock and two companies in Paisley. This diminution in strength strongly suggests that the regiment had suffered heavily from disease, poor supplies and desertion in Ulster. Lothian's men proceeded to Glasgow, after which they went on to Heiton, arriving on 10 February, and eventually reached Selkirk later in the month. During the early spring some of the captains plotted with Turner to place the regiment under Montrose. However, the marquis' failure to advance north of Dumfries led the scheme to collapse. With the marquis of Huntly's rising in Aberdeenshire Lothian's Foot received orders to rendezvous with Argyll in the Mearns. On the march the regiment sacked Kincardine Castle in Strathearn. Lothian's men (about 500 strong) joined Lawers' Foot (300 men) on 17 April. Nine days later the two regiments joined Argyll's army at Dunottar Castle. From there they proceeded to Aberdeen, where the army quartered before marching against the royalist estates. On 2 May Lothian's and Lawers' men were quartered at Drum with some cavalry and the Mearns Foot, as well as their female camp-followers. That day Argyll granted the two 'Irish' regiments permission to sack Gordon of Drum's house, which they did. On 4 May the force proceeded to Inverurie. The exact details of their movements now become inaccessible. However, a general picture can be reconstructed. The regiment quartered in Turriff, where it took food from the earl of Erroll and Stewart of Ardoch and their tenants. It may have been then that Argyll detached a company of Lothian's Foot to capture a Roman Catholic woman and destroy her home and furnishings. The company obeyed its orders and sent the woman under guard to Banff (from whence Argyll removed her to the care of the parish minister of Turriff). However, the dignity with which the woman carried herself changed the regiment's opinion of catholics and made the company's captain ashamed of his behaviour. The regiment also quartered itself in Banff and Auchindoun before returning to Drum at the end of May. Due to their arrears in pay Lawers' and Lothian's men determined to pillage Aberdeen (although it contained a Covenanter garrison). The burgesses upon hearing rumours of the intended depredations raised £20,000 which they sent to Drum as a bribe. On 3 June the infantry received their pay from this money. Their wives in Old Aberdeen left and joined the regiments, which marched to Fettercairn.[46] The regiment's first incursion into the northeast had ended on an inauspicious note.

The Covenanter government now allowed the regiment to rest and recruit. By 18 July the regiment was quartered throughout Roxburghshire. On that day the Estates granted the officers permission to bring in deserters. In August the regiment marched north to Linlithgow burgh, where it quartered for one day. The efforts of the officers in levying men and capturing deserters had been successful, for the regiment now stood at 700 men and officers. On 28 August the Committee of Estates ordered the regiment to Perth. Lothian was to go there himself and assume command of the Covenanter army being assembled against Montrose until Argyll arrived to take command. However, the earl remained with the Committee in Edinburgh. The regiment moved slowly to obey the order, consequently missing the debacle of Tippermuir. It is possible the men were in Glasgow, which spent £3,600 on the regiment before the end of September. Lothian's Foot only reached Perth on 10 September, remaining until the morning of the 13th when it marched to Stirling. On the 12th the Committee issued new orders to the effect that the regiment should support Argyll in suppressing the rebels and Irish under Montrose. Lothian himself joined the regiment for this expedition. The stage was set for the unit's longest stay in the northeast.[47]

There are few details of the regiment's activities during Argyll's autumn campaign against Montrose. From 19 to 23 September Lothian's Foot (still 700 strong) with Lawers' Foot and Hackett's Horse quartered in Aberdeen. On the last day the regiment apparently ran out of money and cost the inhabitants of the Cruikit and Green quarters of Aberdeen £210. On 27 October Lothian's Foot quartered at Kintore and Inverurie. After over a month of marching and plundering and burning, Argyll caught Montrose on 28 October at Fyvie Castle. The two armies skirmished until the morning of the 30th when Argyll withdrew. Previous to that action, on 26 October, two companies of Lothian's Foot numbering 180 men and officers had quartered in Aberdeen at the cost of £36. Throughout October men of Lothian's maintained a night watch in the burgh. By late November Argyll decided to end his campaign and he and Lothian proceeded to Edinburgh where they resigned their commissions. Then Lothian's Foot went into winter quarters.[48]

There is some controversy as to where the regiment spent the winter. One historian and a chronicler claim that Argyll placed Lothian's regiment in Inverness with Lawers' men to serve as the garrison. However, this cannot be substantiated. The Aberdeen chronicler, Spalding, states that 500 men of the regiment entered the burgh on 19 November; the local records support him. It seems that Spalding's estimate of the regiment's size is an under-statement. In 1647 the burgh of Aberdeen submitted a claim of money owed to it by the Estates for military expenses. The burgh magistrates estimated that Lothian's Foot, said to be 900 strong, had cost £47,242 10s. in charges from November 1644 to April 1645. A closer examination of other Aberdonian material reveals this estimate to have been an exaggeration probably contrived to gain tax relief for the burgh. It appears that the regiment consisted of only 776 men and officers, who quartered in the burgh continuously from 11 November 1644 to 7 March 1645 and for several days in April. During that time the burgh provided £118 13s. 4d. in money for fire and candles for the night watch, £3,629 9s. 4d. in forced loans, and an estimated £10,708 9s. (based on the assessment mentioned in the burgh petitions, 12s. x 776 men x 17 weeks), or a total of £14,456 11s. 8d. There would of course have been additional expenses arising from pillaging or destructive acts of the soldiers. Even that reduced amount presented a burden on Aberdeen as can be seen from petitions to the Estates. On 9 January 1645 the magistrates complained that the burgh was becoming impoverished because the shire was not contributing its promised money. In order to escape free quartering the inhabitants had to agree to pay each man 12s. per week. However, the regiment wished to recruit more men and needed more quarters for them, which would have caused suffering within the burgh. On 4 February Major Riddell, by threatening free quarter, coerced the townspeople to continue providing for the regiment at the same rate. On 27 February the Estates authorised Lawers' and Lothian's regiments to raise the eighth man from Aberdeenshire, Banffshire and the shire of Moray. Lothian's officers, however, only had a few days to take advantage of the act, if they had learned of it. In late February Lothian's Foot and the cavalry quartering in Aberdeen extorted £2,000 from the burgesses. Then hearing of rumours of Montrose's advance from Inverness-shire the officers of Lothian's Foot sent two cannon, some ammunition and the regimental baggage south by sea. On 7 March, fearing Montrose's army, the Covenanter garrison fled, followed by the town's ministers (Andrew Cant, John Row and William Robertson). Two days later the royalists entered and captured a Lieutenant Scott of Lothian's Foot, who had inexplicably remained behind.[49] Aberdeen certainly had cause to complain about Lothian's men, who had taken their quarters without providing protection to the burgh from the Irish (who although royalist were noted as bloody plunderers).

The next months were spent in preparation for the Auldearn campaign, where Lothian's Foot nearly met its demise. The whereabouts of the regiment during the middle of March is unknown. Later in the month Lothian's Foot was near Brechin under Lieutenant General William Baillie. After Montrose's capture and retreat from Dundee this unit, Loudoun's Foot and Hackett's Horse were placed under the command of Major General John Urry and ordered to Aberdeen. This force entered the burgh on 11 April. Lothian's Foot now numbered 750 infantry. On 15 April the men of the regiment mutinied upon marching out of Aberdeen, preventing their officers and Loudoun's men from leaving. The mutiniers demanded pay and clothing, which other regiments had received. Fortunately for Urry, a supply ship arrived two days later, and the men received their arrears and new uniforms. On 19 April Urry's army marched out towards Inverness, which they reached on 7 May. On the night of 8-9 May Urry led his army from Inverness to Auldearn, where he surprised Montrose. Lothian's and Loudoun's Foot formed the right flank of the first line of infantry. Initially all went well but royalist resistance stiffened and the commander of Urry's right wing cavalry treacherously entangled his men with the neighbouring infantry. The result was a great defeat. Lothian's men stood their ground against the Irish and Highlanders who had singled out this unit and Lawers' for especially bad treatment due to their service in Ulster. The losses in the army amounted to 50% of those present, so one may assume that this regiment lost at least 375 men. However, its casualties were probably higher due to its position and the hostility of the enemy. Two captains, Sir John and Sir Gideon Murray, fell in the fighting. The remnants of the regiment fled back to Inverness.[50]

Shattered, the regiment still maintained some cohesion. On 4 June it was back in Aberdeen. Several days later it entered Dundee. On 16 June the burgh council requested the earl of Crawford-Lindsay to replace Lothian's men with Lyell's regiment by the 30th. After this the quarters of the regiment are unidentifiable. On 7 August the officers petitioned the Estates that the regiment be given the same treatment as other broken units. Their chief desires were the right to recruit men and some arrangement for their quarters. There is no mention of the regiment for four months. On 18 December the Estates agreed to supply money so that it could be recruited up to strength. At that time a portion of the regiment garrisoned Home Castle in Berwickshire. On 3 January 1646 the Estates ordered the company in the castle south to strengthen the Berwick garrison. The Estates again determined to bring the regiment up to strength on 4 February, when it agreed to supply either money or men depending on which it thought most expedient. In early 1647 Lothian's men were at Peebles with Sinclair's Foot (a force of 500 men). The Estates ordered the two regiments to march to Portpatrick within ten days under Lord Sinclair's command. On 23 February Lothian's Foot received orders to leave their quarters and march directly to Lord Sinclair's regiment (which suggests that they had not united before 11 February) along the following route: Peebles-Moffat-Dumfries-Carlingwark-Ferry of Cree-Monigaff-Glenluce-Portpatrick. The troops were told to be orderly on their march and to obey Lord Sinclair. On 6 March the Estates ordered the two regiments from Wigtonshire to Ulster as soon as the weather allowed. This was not to be. On 26 March the Council of War of the Ulster Army wrote the Committee of Estates rejecting the return of any of the three evacuated regiments. The officers claimed that the army's quartering areas was insufficient to maintain this new burden. Consequently, the Estates disbanded Lothian's and Sinclair's regiments.[51] Although commanded by a dedicated Covenanter, this regiment was fatally flawed. The desertion of Aberdeen and the subsequent mutiny there prove this. Nearly wiped out in its only major battle, Lothian's regiment contributed little to the Covenanting military effort after 9 May 1645.

Munro's Foot

See above, Munro's Foot, 63-7.

George Munro's Horse Troop

Routmaster: Lieutenant Colonel George Munro

This was one of the troops raised after the Cessation to provide the Covenanters with a cavalry arm. The source of its recruits is unknown; but there were about sixty-two men in the unit. In 1644 Munro received the colonelcy of Balfour's Horse, which probably consisted at that time of Kinhilt's troop and the five troops commanded by Ulster Army officers. The troop served on the Leinster and Castlehaven campaigns in 1644. In 1645 this troop was quartered in Carrickfergus. The English parliamentary Committee on Irish Affairs declared this troop to have been illegally raised at a meeting on 17 January 1646. It was ordered to be disbanded. However, Munro ignored the directive. In June 1646 Munro advanced from Coleraine with several troops of horse and some infantry along the west bank of Lough Neagh. To prevent him from uniting with Major General Munro's army, Owen Roe O'Neill sent out a force of Irish infantry and cavalry on 5 June. The Irish successfully drove off Munro's force near Dungannon. The troop is not mentioned again, but it may have gone over to England as part of the Engager force led by its commander.[52] In any case it ceased to exist by the end of September 1648.

Sir Robert Munro's Horse Troop

Routmaster: Major General Sir Robert Munro

This unit was another of those raised after the Cessation to replace the cavalry which had accepted the truce. On 25 July 1644 it formed part of Munro's original force which marched from Carrickfergus to Lisnegarvy. On August 12 it was probably engaged at the cavalry skirmish in Dromore won by the Scots. On 19 September it proceeded into Cavan with other horse troops. The cavalry men burned 3,000 barrels of grain. Those weak or sick returned to quarters in Armagh that day. On the 20th the cavalry penetrated Leinster seeking information on the enemy. Although the infantry kept the field until early October, the cavalry retired to their quarters in late September. In 1645 this unit was quartered on Islandmagee, north of Carrickfergus. On 17 January 1646 the English parliamentary Committee on Irish Affairs ordered this troop disbanded as an illegally raised and burdensome unit. The major general ignored this order, as did his subordinates. On 2 June this troop under the effective command of Lieutenant Daniel Munro rode from its quarters to form part of Munro's army on the Benburb campaign. Two days later the troop served as the forward reconaissance unit of the army. On that day the lieutenant had orders to ride forward and make contact with George Munro, who was in eastern county Tyrone. Daniel Munro was to arrange a rendezvous for the next day at Glaslough. However, the presence of O'Neill's army prevented the meeting. That evening the lieutenant arrived at the major general's camp at Hamilton Bawn with the first news of the Irish approach.[53] Here evidence about the troop ends. It may be assumed that it was engaged at Benburb, from which most of the cavalry escaped with light losses. In 1648 it may have served under George Munro in which case it would have disbanded in Scotland, or it may have been disarmed by Monck when he took Carrickfergus.

Lord Sinclair's Foot

See above, Lord Sinclair's Foot, 68-73.

Wemyss' Horse Troop

Routmaster: Sir Patrick Wemyss

This unit may have properly belonged to the English parliamentary forces in Ulster. It was noted as having been raised in 1646 in Scotland under the auspices of the English parliament.[54] Its fate and combat record are equally unknown.

NOTES

1. PRO, SP 16/492/58, 144; SP 28/120, 169v; *Argyll*, i. 36, 43, 66, 91; *RCGA*, i. 203.
2. Stevenson, *Covenanters*, 62.
3. Bod. Lib., Carte MS. 3, 239v; *A True and Exact Relation of divers principall actions of a late Expedition in the North of Ireland, by the English and Scottish Forces* (London, 1642), 3, 5; 'Unpublished papers of John, seventh Lord Sinclair, Covenanter and Royalist', ed. J. A. Fairley, *Trans. Buchan Field Club*, viii (1904-5), 179-82; G. Hill, *An Historical Account of the MacDonnells of Antrim* (Belfast, 1873), 73.
4. Bod. Lib., Carte MS. 8, 215; Carte MS. 9, 301-v; *The Book of the Thanes of Cawdor 1236-1742*, ed. C. Innes (Spalding Club, xxix, 1859), 286.

5. PRO, SP 16/492/58, 146v, 149, 152, 155, 158v, 163, 167, 171v, 175, 179, 182v.

6. Bod. Lib., Carte MS. 11, 101; SRO, PA. 7.23/2, 26v; *A full relation of the late expedition of the Right Honourable the lord Monroe, Major-General of all Protestant Forces in the Province of Ulster* (London, 1644), 2; Stevenson, *Alasdair*, 101; Stevenson, *Covenanters*, 1.

7. Stevenson, *Alasdair*, 154-5, 159, 161, 221; Stevenson, *Covenanters*, 212, 231.

8. NLS, Adv. MS. 33.4.8, 165; *The Diplomatic Correspondence of Jean de Montereul and the Brothers de Bellievre, French Ambassadors in England and Scotland 1645-48*, 2 vols., ed. J. G. Fotheringham (Scot. Hist. Soc., 1st Ser., xxix-xxx, 1898), ii. 519; Stevenson, *Covenanters*, 258-9, 266, 281.

9. Bod. Lib., Carte MS. 11, 440-v, 625; *True Relation of principall actions of Scottish Forces*, 1; Stevenson, *Covenanters*, 72-3, 109, 124, 260.

10. *CSPI 1633-1647*, 428; *Letters and Papers Relating to the Irish Rebellion Between 1642-46*, ed. J. Hogan (Dublin, 1936), 186; Stevenson, *Covenanters*, 210.

11. Cambridge University Library, MS. Ee. 111.39(D); Stevenson, *Covenanters*, 70, 74, 159.

12. Bod. Lib., Rawlinson MS. A/258, 53; Stevenson, *Covenanters*, 338.

13. *CSPI 1633-1647*, 428; *Letters and Papers Relating to the Irish Rebellion*, 186.

14. PRO, SP 28/120, 277v, 855v.

15. Stevenson, *Covenanters*, 70, 74, 333.

16. Bod. Lib., Carte MS. 5, 195-6; *Late expedition of lord Monroe*, 2; Stevenson, *Covenanters*, 141, 157, 231, 259.

17. PRO, SP 28/120, 224V, 774; SRO, PR Ayr, 29 November, 20 December 1643; 17 January-31 July 1644.

18. 'Papers of Lord Sinclair', 179-82; Stevenson, *Covenanters*, 332.

19. *Late expedition of lord Monroe*, 3; Bod. Lib., Carte MS. 6, 277; SRO, PA. 7.23.2.26, 1; Stevenson, *Covenanters*, 75, 141, 231.

20. NLS, Adv. MS. 33.4.8, 165; Adair, *Narrative*, 150-1; *Diplomatic Correspondence*, ii. 519; Stevenson, *Covenanters*, 259, 263, 267, 273, 280.

21. *CSPI 1633-1647*, 428; *Letter and Papers Relating to the Irish Rebellion*, 186; Stevenson, *Covenanters*, 210, 277.

22. Bod. Lib., Rawlinson MS. A/258, 17-18; PRO, SP 16/539/217, 216; SRO, PA. 7.23.2.26, 5; *Acts of the General Assembly*, 74; Stevenson, *Covenanters*, 21, 74, 151, 256, 263.

23. NRH, OPR Dalgety, 7 July-11 August 1650; PRO, SP 28/120, 214v, 1026v; *Kirkcaldie*, 346-7; *RCGA*, ii. 180, 424; *Ibid.*, iii. 8, 25, 273.

24. 'Papers of Lord Sinclair', 179-82; *Privy Council*, 2nd Ser., vii. 192, 197, 221, 230; J. K. Hewison, *The Covenanters*, 2 vols. (Glasgow, 1913), i. 418; Stevenson, *Covenanters*, 72, 335.

25. Bod. Lib., Carte MS. 9, 560; *APS*, VI, i. 87; *Extract of Letters Dated at Edenburgh (sic), the 14, 16 and 17. of April. 1644* (London, 1644), 2; Turner, *Memoirs*, 33; J. Barber, 'The Capture of the Covenanting Town of Dumfries by Montrose', *Dumfries and Galloway Nat. Hist. Antiq. Soc.*, xxi (1908-9), 32; W. M. Metcalfe, *A History of Paisley 600-1908* (Paisley, 1909), 261; W. M. Metcalfe, *A History of the county of Renfrew from the earliest times* (New Club, xiii, 1905), 262; Stevenson, *Covenanters*, 143, 179.

26. Spalding, *Memorialls*, ii. 346, 349, 353, 355, 373, 375-6.

27. SRO, PA 11.2, 81; *Army of the Covenant*, i. ix; *Baillie*, ii. 226; *Selected Justiciary Cases, 1624-50*, 3 vols., ed. S. A. Gillon (Stair Soc., 28, 1974), iii. 623-5.

28. NLS, Adv. MS. 29.2.9, 160; *APS*, VI, i. 344, 356; J. Fraser, *Chronicles of the Frasers, 916-1674*, ed. W. Mackay (Scot. His. Soc., 1st Ser. xlvii, 1905), 287; Spalding, *Memorialls*, ii. 414, 416, 432, 446; Cowan, *Montrose*, 181.

29. *Memoirs of Guthry*, 184, 187; R. Monteth, *The history of the Troubles of Great Britain . . . 1633-56*, trans. J. Ogilvie (2nd edn., London, 1738), 207; Spalding, *Memorialls*, ii. 473-4; Stevenson, *Alasdair*, 184, 188; Stevenson, *Covenanters*, 179.

30. SRO, KSR Petty, 24 August 1645; *Aberdeen Letters*, ii. 65, 82, 84, 89-80; *APS*, VI, i. 436, 446, 501, 544, 586, 693.

31. SRO, PA. 15.10, 4; *Aberdeen Letters*, ii. 96; *APS*, VI, i. 717; *Ibid.*, VI, ii. 98, 219, 698.

32. NLS, Dep. 175, Box 87.1; PRO, SP 28/120, 373v, 990v; SRO, KSR Cambusnethan, i. 69v; KRS Hamilton, i. 40; KSR Kinconquhar, i. 106v-7; KRS North Leith, 26 July, 18 September 1642; KSR Scoonie, i. 181-2; KSR St. Monance, 19 March 1650; PA. 7.24, 111-v; PA. 11.11, 32v; PA. 16.5, 33; S.A.U.L., PR. St. Andrews, i. 203, 231; *APS*, VI, ii. 217, 219 (Colin but obviously a mistake for James), 389, 426, 431, 490, 521, 527, 582, 613, 627, 630; Wishart, *Montrose*, 304; J. Buchan, *Oliver Cromwell* (London, 1934), 378; W. S. Douglas, *Cromwell's Scotch Campaigns: 1650-51* (London, 1898), 44-6, 80, 111; C. H. Firth, 'The Battle of Dunbar', *Trans. Roy. Hist. Soc.*, 2nd Ser. xiv (1900), 45; T. Gumble, *The Life of General Monck* (London, 1671), 38; D. Mackinnon, *Origin and Services of the Coldstream Guards*, 2 vols. (London, 1833), i. 23; W. L. Mathieson, *Politics and Religion*, 2 vols. (Glasgow, 1902), ii. 14.

33. SRO, KSR North Leith, 18 September, 10 October 1642.

34. Bod. Lib., Carte MS. 9, 283; 'Papers of Lord Sinclair', 179-82; *The Records of Elgin*, eds. W. Cramond and S. Ree (New Spalding Club, xxvii/xxxv, 1903/1908), i. 272; *True Relation of principall action of Scottish Forces*, 1; H. Boyd, 'The History of Coleraine from the Londoner's Plantation to the Restoration' (Queen's Univ., Belfast M.A. thesis 1932), 119; Stevenson, *Covenanters*, 74-5, 78, 125, 328.

35. Bod. Lib., Carte MS. 8, 215; Carte MS. 9, 283, 436; Cambridge University Library, MS. Ee. 111.39(D); SRO, PA. 7.23/2.26, 1; Adair, *Narrative*, 105; *Extract of Letters Dated at Edenburgh*, 2; *Late expedition of lord Monroe*, 3; Stevenson, *Covenanters*, 141, 143, 159.

36. *Ibid.*, 201, 204, 225, 231, 248, 258, 269.

37. *RCGA*, ii. 66; Boyd, 'Coleraine', 125-30; Stevenson, *Covenanters*, 258, 269, 305.

38. PRO, SP 16/539/105, 230-lv; SP 28-120, 436.

39. *Ibid.*, 33, 1068; H. M. O'Neill, ' Journal of the Most Memorable Transactions of General Owen O'Neill and his party, from the year 1641 to the Year 1650', *Desiderata Curiosa Hibernica: Or A Select Collection of State Papers* (Dublin, 1772), ii. 490; Somerville, *Memorie*, 202-4, 210, 279; Stevenson, *Covenanters*, 151.

40. PRO, SP 28/120, 341v, 1112v; J. McConnell and S. McConnell, *Fasti of the Irish Presbyterian Church 1613-1840*, ed. F. J. Paul (Belfast, 1951), 5.

41. Bod. Lib., Carte MS. 5, 195-6; *A True Relation of the Proceedings of the Scottish Armie now in Ireland by Three Letters* (London, 1642), 6; Stevenson, *Covenanters*, 75, 141, 336.

42. Bod. Lib., Carte MS. 9, 560; SRO, PA. 7.23/2.18; PA. 7.23/2.26, 1; TCLD, MS. 837 (Depositions after the Rising, County Down), 35b; *Extract of Letters Dated at Edenburgh*, 2; *Late expedition of lord Monroe*, 2; Stevenson, *Covenanters*, 157.

43. NLS, Adv. MS. 33.4.8, 142-3; Stevenson, *Covenanters*, 231, 256.

44. PRO, SP 28/120, 597v, 953v; SRO, PR Jedburgh, 13, 15 July 1642.

45. Ibid.; *Army of the Covenants*, i. 38; Turner, *Memoirs*, 33; Stevenson, *Covenanters*, 70, 75, 141, 143, 147, 178, 329.

46. SRO, PA. 16.4.7, 28; *Aberdeen Letters*, iii. 85; J. Burns, *Memoirs of the Civil War, and During the Usurpation*, ed. J. Maidment (Edinburgh, 1832), 6; *Memoirs of the Scottish Catholics During the 17th and 18th centuries*, ed. W. Forbes-Leith, 2 vols. (London, 1909), i. 272-3; Spalding, *Memorialls*, ii. 346, 349, 353, 355, 366, 375-6; Turner, *Memoirs*, 35; J. W. Kennedy, 'The Teviotdale Regiment', *Hawick Arch. Soc.*, xxxv (1903), 58; Metcalfe, *Paisley*, 260.

47. *APS*, VI, i. 169; *Baillie*, ii. 226; *The Chronicle of Perth*, ed. J. Maidment (Maitland Club, xxii, 1831), 40; *Glasgow*, ii. 508; *Memoirs of Guthry*, 167; Stevenson, *Alasdair*, 125-6; C. S. Terry, 'Free Quarters in Linlithgow, 1642-47', *SHR*, xiv (1916), 77.

48. *Aberdeen Letters*, ii. 381, 386; *Ibid.*, iii. 86; Spalding, *Memorialls*, ii. 414, 424; Kennedy, 'Teviotdale', 58.

49. *Aberdeen Letters*, ii. 57; *Ibid.*, iii. 45, 87, 118; *APS*, VI, i. 356; *Council of Aberdeen*, ii. 37, 41-2; Fraser, *Chronicles*, 87; Spalding, *Memorialls*, ii. 431, 451, 453; Cowan, *Montrose*, 181.

50. *Aberdeen Letters*, ii. 83; *Ibid.*, iii. 87; *Memoirs of Guthry*, 187; Monteth, *History*, 207; Spalding, *Memorialls*, ii. 461, 463-7, 473; Stevenson, *Alasdair*, 184.

51. NLS, Adv. MS. 33.4.8, 141; *APS*, VI, i. 471, 491, 500, 590, 693, 704-5, 723-4; Spalding, *Memorialls*, ii. 479; A. Maxwell, *History of Old Dundee* (Edinburgh, 1884), 501.

52. *CSPI 1633-1647*, 428; *Letter and Papers Relating to the Irish Rebellion*, 186; Stevenson, *Covenanters*, 210, 231-2.

53. SRO, PA. 7.23/2.26, 132, 135; *CSPI 1633-1647*, 428; *Letter and Papers Relating to the Irish Rebellion*, 186; Stevenson, *Covenanters*, 210, 227.

54. Bod. Lib., Rawlinson MS. A258, 20-v.

5

Army of the Solemn League and Covenant

Aldie's Horse

Colonel: Sir James Mercer of Aldie

Aldie served as the lieutenant colonel of Lord Kirkcudbright's Horse from 1644-6. He represented the lairds of Perthshire in the Estates 1645-7. At the battle of Kilsyth Aldie fell prisoner to the royalists. Later he either escaped or was exchanged. On 6 June 1646 the army accounts mention him as colonel of four Perthshire troops, which initially belonged to Kirkcudbright's Horse. The combat record of the regiment is unknown. The men were stationed in Scotland over the winter of 1646-7. On 5 February 1647 the Estates commissioned Aldie a colonel in the New Model Army. They ordered him to disband all save forty troopers of his regiment. These men in addition to other troopers would form Aldie's new command. The remainder of the regiment disbanded in mid February.[1]

Angus Foot

Colonels: Sir James, 2nd Viscount Dudhope (1644), Lieutenant General Sir William Baillie (1644-47)

Lieutenant Colonel: (?) Bonar

Majors: William Scrimgeour, Thomas Moffat

Ministers: James Gardiner, David Campbell, Arthur Granger, John Robertson, Alexander Kinninmonth[2]

Dudhope received his commission from the Convention of Estates to command the Angus infantry regiment on 26 August 1643. Although the viscount was at heart a royalist, he became a colonel in the army to escape persecution by the Covenanters. In October the Angus Committee of War required Dundee to provide 205 men and officers for the regiment. The magistrates hoped that volunteers would appear from the inhabitants. However, by 11 December the burgh had assembled only 150 recruits. The magistrates approached both

Dudhope and the Committee of War with hope of reducing the number required. They were met with refusals, and on 26 December the burgh council decided to select the deficients by combing the lists of guild members, craftsmen and other occupations. The regiment entered England on 19 January 1644 with Leven's army and remained with the main body, serving at the siege of York.[3]

The battle of Marston Moor played an important role in the regiment's history. The Angus Foot was paired with the Ministers' Foot as part of the reserve line of Fairfax's infantry. The two regiments advanced against the second line of the royalist foot, but retreated upon making contact. It may be assumed that the regiment was one of those which fled the field, although it appears that the men were engaged, because Dudhope was mortally wounded. He died on 23 July. Also on the day of the battle the colonel-to-be acquitted himself well. Baillie, as lieutenant general of foot, commanded the Scottish infantry opposite the royalist centre. Throughout the battle he aided the front line by rallying broken troops and sending them forward to succour their comrades.[4]

Following Baillie's good acquittal at Marston Moor the lieutenant general sought command of a regiment. On 27 July the Estates noted that Baillie was still owed £2,828 15s. 4d. from the last war and that he deserved a colonelcy. On 29 July the Committee of Estates' Committee with the Army solved the second problem by giving Baillie the Angus Foot, which he commanded until it disbanded.[5] After the fall of York the army remained in the shire until early August when it returned north.

The Angus Foot took part in the siege of Newcastle, which opened about 16 August. The regiment had a battery in the line of circumvallation on the north side of the town. It seems, however, that the regiment withdrew to Scotland for several weeks. For on 7 September the the Estates ordered it to return to England. On 19 October the regiment (ten companies strong) took part in the assault. There is a disagreement concerning the target of the regiment's attack. An officer in Sinclair's Foot stated that the Angus and Stirlingshire Foot acted in concert and entered Newcastle after Sinclair's men had cleared the wall. Another contemporary account says that the Angus, Strathearn, Fife, East Lothian regiments and another regiment of infantry formed the first brigade which attacked the Newgate. Both Baillie and Lieutenant Colonel Bonar are noted as having fought bravely in the storming of the city.[6] With the fall of Newcastle detailed information of the military activities of the regiment ends.

From 1645 to the regiment's disbanding only glimpses of its story come to light. In 1645 Baillie returned to Scotland, where he commanded the Covenanter forces at Dundee, Alford, and Kilsyth. However, the regiment remained in England for that year. In the summer it donated £178 2s. 6d. to the Kelso charity fund to help rebuild the burgh which had been destroyed by fire. Sometime in late 1645 or early 1646 the Angus Foot returned to Scotland. On 24 March 1646 Glasgow advanced £6,000 to the officers of the unit. In the first part of April the earl of Cassillis ordered the provost and bailies to provide thirty baggage horses for the regiment. From this one can deduce that the Angus Foot probably served on an expedition against the northeastern royalists, who were in arms that year. On 25 April Glasgow spent £30 4d. when the regimental officers were made burgesses. By mid December the regiment had returned to Glasgow, where it quartered with the Kyle and Carrick Foot. The Estates issued an order on 12 January 1647 regarding the Angus Foot's quartering arrangements. Due to the presence of the plague on the burgh, the burgesses were instructed to find barns and other outbuildings to house the regiment. The regiment received orders to hold a muster every ten days and forego the uplifting of cess as it was receiving pay. On 5 February the officers were ordered to disband all except one company of the regiment, which was reserved for the General of Artillery's Foot in the New Model Army. By the 12th the Angus Foot had disbanded and the Estates ordered the remaining company to march to Dundee, where it would rendezvous with the other parts of the General of Artillery's regiment.[7]

Argyll's Regiment

Colonel: Archibald, 1st marquis of Argyll

Major: Hugh Crawford

Ministers: Dugald Darroch, Archibald MacCallum, Neil MacCallum, Murdoch McCurrie[8]

This is a most mysterious unit. As early as October 1643 the synod of Argyll appointed a chaplain to it. However, there is no information on its levying. In January 1644 Lieutenant Walter Denniston of the regiment quartered in Linlithgow, costing the burgh £12 13s. 4d. A modern historian claims it was a cavalry regiment and it took part in the battle of Marston Moor. A mention of the regiment on 1 August 1645 supports the view that this unit was an infantry unit, because Dunbartonshire was to levy 200 infantrymen for it. On 7 June it was quartering in Menteith. The regiment remained on foot in 1645 and 1646, the synod and Commission of the General Assembly appointing chaplains in those years.[9] This unit may be confused with other regiments commanded by Argyll, however fresh evidence is necessary to determine its exact status.

Marquis of Argyll's Life Guard of Horse

Routmaster: Archibald Campbell

Although existing for the entire career of the Army of the Solemn League and Covenant, this troop spent little time in England. On 6 January 1644 the

Estates, having selected Argyll as president of the Committee with the Army, decided that he should have a cavalry bodyguard. Gentlemen or others who provided themselves with a horse and arms were to receive pay equal to that of other cavalrymen. The Campbell gentry provided some of the men for the troop. Sir Robert Campbell of Glenorchy gave Patrick Campbell of Inneryeldies a horse, arms, clothing and money worth £666 13s. 4d. He also provided four other gentlemen going to the troop with £333 6s. 8d. The Life Guards accompanied the army until Argyll returned to Scotland to deal with Montrose's raid on Dumfries and Huntly's rising. On 10 April the Estates ordered the troop to quarter on the deficients in Perthshire. Sixteen days later the troop numbered thirty-two men at Dunottar Castle, from whence Argyll commenced his campaign. On 31 May the Life Guards, now sixty troopers strong, were in Aberdeen. With the Fife Foot they pressed heavily upon the burgh's resources. Spalding, the Aberdeen historian, claims the troop remained in the burgh after 1 June when the army departed. However, it was in Linlithgow for one night during that month, when its quartering charges amounted to £40 11s. 4d. (which suggests a strength of forty-five men). In July the troop was back in Aberdeen, the Estates issuing an order on the 20th for the troop to proceed to Elgin and return from there with the young laird of Drum and other prisoners of war. The Life Guards accompanied Argyll on his autumn campaign against Montrose. During that expedition the troopers stole £3 and grain worth £16 from Walter Hay, and a plaid worth £1 10s. from Robert Urquhart, both tenants in Turriff.[10]

The Life Guards disappear for several months, so it is uncertain whether they were at the battle of Inverlochy. The unit was in the lowlands by 19 February 1645 when the Estates ordered a corporal of the troop and fifteen men to transport Coll Ciotach MacDonald, two of his sons, and Stewart of Ascog from Dumbarton Castle to Edinburgh. The troopers were to receive 18s. per day for themselves and their horses on free quarters. This convoy proceeded from the castle to Glasgow and from there to Linlithgow, where it arrived on 20 March. The troopers left with their prisoners on the 27th, probably reaching Edinburgh Castle that night. The stay in Linlithgow cost the burgh £126. Mention of the Life Guards abruptly ceases. However, in June Argyll received permission to levy horsemen for his troop from Stirlingshire. A local royalist, Sir George Stirling of Keir, was forced to provide two mounted cavalrymen at this time. Unfortunately, there are no further records of troopers levied then. The Life Guards probably escorted Argyll to the battle of Kilsyth from which he fled in haste. On 7 November the Committee of Estates authorised the marquis to raise forty troopers from Teviotdale. Again the Life Guards disappear from the records only resurfacing on 5 February 1647. Then the Estates authorised the laird of Ludquharn to raise part of a New Model Army troop of horse from the Life Guards, who were quartered in northeast Scotland.[11] The troopers not selected by Ludquharn disbanded later in the month.[12]

Marquis of Argyll's Life Guard of Foot

Commanders: Provost of Kilmund and Archibald Campbell of Lerags

On 6 January 1644 the Committee of Estates decided that Argyll as president of the Committee with the Army should possess a Life Guard of Foot. The men who joined it were to be armed with firelocks and swords; they were guaranteed the same pay as other infantrymen. Argyll's kinsmen and allies in Argyll decided to raise a force of sixty men. They would be clothed in Highland dress and armed with swords, targes and muskets. George Campbell, Tutor of Calder, was assessed two healthy and armed men who were to join the others at Inveraray.[13] It is likely that he and other Campbell gentry responded positively, because Argyll was respected by his kin. However, we possess no further mention of the unit. It probably served with the marquis during his time in England (January-April 1644), on the two northeastern campaigns of 1644, and at the battle of Inverlochy. Any survivors of that great defeat would have been with him at Montrose's last victory at Kilsyth. If any of the Life Guards escaped the battle they might have formed part of Argyll's Highland Foot raised in the winter of 1645-6, or they could have continued to act as a bodyguard. In either case they would have been engaged in the campaign to clear Argyll of the MacDonald in 1646-47.

Train of Artillery

General of Artillery: Sir Alexander Hamilton

Lieutant Colonel: Thomas Hamilton

Sir Alexander Hamilton provided Leven with a powerful artillery arm for the Army of the Solemn League and Covenant. By the end of February 1644 Leven possessed eight brass 24 lbrs., one brass 18 lbr., three brass 12 lbrs., six iron 9 lbrs., forty-two iron 3 lbrs., eighty-eight case of frames (which fired several musket balls at once), and six petards. The first use of any of these cannons appears to have been on 7 March — the first day of the Battle of Boldon Hill. Then the earl of Newcastle's army surprised the Scots, who lacked artillery. However, the Sunderland seamen conveyed one large gun (probably a 24 lbr.) and some 3 lbrs. from the town, which served as the army's artillery park. At 5 p.m. both armies commenced a long and largely ineffective cannonade. During the siege of York Leven established a battery 160 yards from Skelders Gate. The guns placed there were 18 and 12 lbrs., which suggests that the English had given the Covenanters some artillery. At the battle of Marston Moor Leven placed his field pieces (3 lbrs.) in front of the centre. During the course of the fight one was lost. Later in July the earl of Callendar established five batteries south of Newcastle. These batteries probably contained the 24 lbrs. left in

Sunderland. After Leven's arrival in mid-August six batteries named after various officers were set up. The most powerful one was the General of Artillery's, which contained only 24 and 18 lbrs. Cassillis', Gask's, and Sinclair's had 24, 12 and 3 lbrs. Lieutenant General Baillie had 24 and 3 lbrs. in his battery, while Loudoun only had 18 lbrs. It was during this siege that the Covenanter artillery rendered its best performance.[14]

In 1645 the train of artillery received additional reinforcements. In January the train gained six brass 3 lbrs., and three iron ones, as well as two petards. However, in addition to the field piece lost at Marston Moor two more had broken during 1644. At the siege of Carlisle the Covenanters used three guns (possibly 3 lbrs. as transport of heavier guns across the Pennines would have been difficult). Unfortunately the town garrison captured two of them. In June or July the artillerymen contributed £239 2s. 2½d. to the Kelso rebuilding fund. In the summer campaign the train advanced to the siege of Hereford via Gloucester. Leven established five batteries for this siege. The General of Artillery's, Sinclair's and Livingston's contained 18, 12 and 9 lbrs.; Colonel William Stewart's had 18 and 12 lbrs., while Buccleuch's merely had 3 lbrs. The siege broke up before the artillery had achieved much. The siege of Newark saw the last use of this arm. By 28 November a battery of 3 lbrs. had been constructed. There is no sign of any heavier guns being used. On 17 January 1646 the muster at Muskham revealed that Lieutenant Colonel Hamilton commanded fifty-three men of the Train of Artillery and Wagons. That is the only estimate we have of the unit's strength. The last mentions of the train occurred on 3 August when the treasurer distributed £100 st. and £66 13s. 4d. st. to the widows of the captain of the cannon and of a cannonier. The train probably disbanded in February 1647 and the guns (now reduced to eight 24 lbrs., one 18 lbr., three 12 lbrs., six 9 lbrs., two 6 lbrs., and forty-two 3 lbrs.) would have been lodged in Edinburgh Castle.[15]

Aytoun's Foot

Colonels: Sir John Home of Aytoun (1644-45), Quartermaster General Ludovick Leslie (1645-47)

Lieutenant Colonels: James Dixon (1644-45), Robert Hamilton (1645-47)

Major: (?) Pringle

Ministers: Robert Melville, James Home, Robert Home, George Home[16]

Aytoun received his commission to raise this regiment in April 1644. The men were levied in Berwickshire, the shire which Aytoun represented in the Estates. On 14 June the Estates sent him to Fife for a four day mission to speed the levying of troops there, which suggests that his own regiment was already on foot. On the 25th the regiment entered England as part of Callendar's army. The siege of Newcastle is the only campaign in which the regiment is known to have taken part. On 19 October Aytoun led his men as part of the Fourth Brigade in the storming of the city. By 1 March 1645 Quartermaster General Leslie had assumed command of the regiment. He had served as the first Scots governor of Sunderland, and was appointed to the governorship of Tynemouth Castle on 23 November 1644 by the Committee with the Army. At that time the Committee ordered Aytoun's Foot to be reduced to a company to act as the garrison. That the regiment was so weak was due to the presence of the plague and other diseases in the castle, which had reduced its strength.

The first sign of an accurate measure of the unit's strength is an army account entry of 13 May 1645, which places the regiment at 425 men. Its strength continued to increase throughout the year, reaching a high of 632 men on 20 December. In June or July the colonel contributed £48 to the Kelso charity, while his men gave £216. On 7 November it was allowed 200 recruits from Berwickshire, but it is unknown whether any of them ever joined the regiment. The regiment reached a maximum size of 714 men in June 1646 and retained it until disbanding in February 1647. On 5 January 1647 in answer to a petition by Leslie the Estates ordered the Committee at Newcastle to repay him £1,400 6s. 10d. which he had spent on refortifying the castle. The regiment evacuated its fortress on 30 January 1647, and disbanded in the next month.[17]

Earl of Balcarres Horse

Colonel: Alexander, 1st earl of Balcarres

Lieutenant Colonel: Alexander Strachan of Thornton (1644)

Majors: Alexander Home, Patrick Scougall, Patrick Blair (1646-47)

Ministers: Walter Greig, David Forret, Patrick Skougall, Alexander Moncrieffe, William Oliphant, George Hamilton, William Livingston[18]

This regiment of horse was actively engaged in both England and Scotland between 1644 and 1647. In autumn 1643 the Convention of Estates authorised Balcarres to raise four troops from Fife, four troops from the Mearns and Marischal's portion of Aberdeenshire, and twenty cavalrymen from Angus. The earl was to raise two more troops from an unspecified location. By February 1644 he had only raised six troops, which formed part of Leven's army. The regiment's first major was a Scot with experience in the Continental wars. Balcarres' men served at the siege of York and the battle of Marston Moor (on the left wing under Leslie) as well as the siege of Newcastle. On 24 August the Committee with the Army noted that the regiment still lacked one troop from Mearns and two from Fife. These deficiencies were eventually made up. There is some difficulty in determining when the regiment departed from England for service against Montrose. The burgh of Linlithgow quartering accounts show that £368 6s. 2d. was spent on Balcarres' Horse in October. However, the Committee with the Army did not order the regiment north until 16 November, when it authorised the treasurer to supply clothing and a month's pay. The next mention of the regiment does little to resolve this controversy, for it is merely an order by the Estates that the regiment should receive £4,800 to repair its arms and other accoutrements due to hard service.[19]

While the regiment had been active in 1644, its pace of activity was absolutely frantic in 1645. On 4 February the regiment received some of its pay; however it is unknown how far in arrears the soldiers' wages were then. Later in the month the regiment was ordered to unite with Hackett's Horse (then quartered in Old Aberdeen) in New Aberdeen. Balcarres' men reached the burgh on 26 February, but only remained for a few days. With Lothian's 'Irish' Foot and Hackett's Horse this unit extorted £2,000 from Aberdeen, then abandoned it on 7 March at rumours of the royalists' approach. Balcarres' troopers appear to have been in poor shape then. On 2 March for instance the kirk session of Balmerino, presbytery of Cupar, presented £16 to three clothesless troopers. By mid March the regiment had recovered enough confidence to serve in the field. Although it had been placed under Major General John Urry's command in late February, the regiment did not serve under him until after the flight from Aberdeen. Urry concentrated his regiments at North Water Brig to the south of Aberdeen. He quickly learned of the lax security measures of the royalists occupying the burgh. On Friday 15 March he selected 160 troopers and some infantry from Balcarres' Horse and other regiments with which he proceeded to Aberdeen. Upon its arrival at 8 p.m. the force detached parties to watch the gates while the main body entered the burgh. Donald Farquharson, a leading royalist, and several others were slain. Urry's force managed to capture other royalists; in addition he seized all of their horses (which included Huntly's best mount). After this successful action Balcarres' and Hackett's Horse under Urry's command joined Baillie's army near Brechin in late March. This army proceeded southwards to the west of Dundee, where on 5 April Baillie learned that Montrose had captured that burgh. Hoping to catch Montrose's men in the midst of sacking their rich prize the lieutenant general dispatched Urry with Balcarres' and Hackett's Horse then followed with the infantry. The two cavalry regiments closed on Montrose's rearguard infantry and skirmished with them. However, in Baillie's view, Urry had been laggard in the pursuit, a charge which later became public. On the second day of the pursuit Urry's force acquitted themselves well. After resting their horses the troopers of Balcarres' and Hackett's regiments caught the royalist force at Careston Ford on the South Esk river. From there the cavalrymen pursued them up Glen Esk, which delivered the country from a rapacious army and more importantly inflicted casualties on Montrose's men. This was the marquis' first reverse and foreshadowed the Covenanter victory at Philiphaugh, where Montrose's lack of knowledge of his opponents and Leslie's use of cavalry destroyed his army. In April Balcarres'

Horse joined Baillie's army at Cromar. By mid May Balcarres himself, leading two regiments of redcoated infantry, rendezvoused with Baillie's army in the same village. Several months later, in July, Baillie encountered Montrose at Alford. Balcarres' men were the key to Baillie's plan for the battle. The regiment was split into three squadrons and placed on the left flank. Two of them were to expose themselves to draw out Lord Gordon's Horse. Then the third squadron with the support of Baillie's infantry would charge and drive off the royalist troopers. Unfortunately for Baillie the battle did not go as planned. Lord Gordon with one hundred of his mounted kinsmen charged Balcarres' two squadrons. However, despite its orders, the third squadron refused to advance. Balcarres refused to fall back and Gordon's troopers managed to cut a path through the Covenanters. This success in turn allowed the royalist foot under Nathaniel Gordon and Colonel Thomas O'Lachlan to come to the support of their cavalry. The Irish infantry attacked the horses of the regiment with their knives, causing further disorganisation. Montrose, sensing another victory, ordered a general advance and the Covenanter forces collapsed. The regiment, although heavily battered, maintained enough cohesion to form a part of the Covenanter army used at Kilsyth. Baillie placed the regiment on the extreme right of the first line adjacent to the Midlothian Foot. These two regiments, joined by the earl of Crawford-Lindsay's Fife Foot, made the infamous flank march. Nathaniel Gordon's royalist infantry put up the initial resistance to this Covenanter force until he was reinforced by viscount Aboyne, halting the Covenanters. Then the situation began to deteriorate in the centre and within a short time the entire Covenanter army was in flight. That any of Balcarres' men survived is due solely to the speed with which their horses allowed them to flee. From the church records we learn that the regiment passed into the presbytery of Haddington, where one of the troopers committed fornication in late August. By mid September (after Philiphaugh), Balcarres' Horse was quartering in the presbytery of Kirkcaldy. In November the regiment, now recruited close to full strength, was on its way back to England. It spent one night in Linlithgow, costing the burgh £368 6s. 2d. A year of nearly continual military activity ended with the regiment's arrival at the siege of Newark on 17 January 1646 after a month's stay in Yorkshire.[20]

In comparison with the previous two years of the unit's existence 1646 was one of rest. From 17 January to 5 March Balcarres' Horse was engaged in the siege of Newark. A muster of the regiment in mid January revealed a strength of 488 officers and men in nine troops. Although relatively strong in numbers everything was not as it should have been. On 4 February the earl petitioned the Scottish Estates for three yards of cloth for each man, the troopers' monthly pay, an additional 135 troopers or £2,000 in levying money, two hundred pairs of pistols and eighty horses for unmounted troopers, before going into action again. The Estates remitted the petition to the Committee of Estates. Several days later the lieutenant colonel and one of the routmasters were referred to the Committee of Estates for redress of their past sufferings. Meanwhile the regiment was earning a bad reputation for itself in Derbyshire due to the inadequate provision for supplies by the English. From Stavely the men took £270 14s. st. in quartering; from Matlock a Lieutenant Nicholson and forty-four troopers exacted free quartering and £9 17s. 5d. st. by threatening the use of force. Simultaneously in Garfield a Corporal Hunter was responsible for burning buildings, horse theft, and oppressive quartering practices. On 6 March the regiment was back in Yorkshire, where it remained, at least until 1 May if not until the evacuation, on free quarters. On 31 December the Scottish Estates noted that Balcarres had spent £6,000 of his own money on the regiment due to its desperate condition. The Estates ordered his repayment. On 6 March 1647, with the regiment now disbanded, the Estates declared that the officers' arrears would come out of the monthly maintenance. At least four men of the regiment were cited to church courts. Each appeared for a different cause: drunkenness, fornication, fathering a bastard, and adultery. In the last instance the trooper repented within the regiment, not the parish where the offence was committed.[21] This was a unique regiment in that it demonstrated a tremendous ability to survive despite numerous reversals.

Barclay's Horse

Colonel: Harry Barclay

Lieutenant Colonel: Sir Mungo Murray

Major: John Tours, Futhie (1646)

It is difficult to write a precise history of this unit due to the gaps in evidence. The first mention of it occurs on 13 February 1644 when the Committee of Estates authorised Barclay to raise one hundred troopers from Marischal's section of Aberdeenshire for his regiment. Silence abouts its whereabouts and activities lifts on 12 May 1645, when Sir Mungo Murray's troop is mentioned as quartering in Dundee. It was engaged at Philiphaugh. On 7 November it was ordered from Glasgow to form part of the Dundee garrison. On the next day it was allocated two troops from Ayrshire and Renfrewshire, while the regiment was sent to Kinross-shire. On 16 December the Estates ordered it to Aberdeenshire with two companies of dragoons accompanied by Eglinton's and Montgomery's cavalry regiments. The colonel does not seem to have moved with alacrity, because on the 27th he was ordered north again. The three cavalry regiments, totalling 1,200 horsemen and dragoons, reached Aberdeen at 2 p.m. on 2 January 1646. The regiments quartered on the burgh lands and within it for only twenty-four hours, which cost the burgh £1,300. On 14 May the colonel with his men and a regiment of foot stoutly but unsuccessfully defended Aberdeen against the marquis of Huntly. During Middleton's campaign the regiment quartered on the lands of the earl of Erroll, Lord Coupar and James Baird of Auchmedden and their tenants. In this campaign Middleton planned to quarter Barclay's sick and his mounted men in Aberdeen, a course from which the burgh magistrates tried to dissuade him. By early August Selkirk was petitioning for the re.noval of four troops of the regiment, otherwise the burgh would be 'uttlerlie undone'. Again the regiment disappeared, this time for five months, when it reappeared quartering in Linlithgow in January 1647. On 5 February the Estates ordered Barclay to disband all but forty troopers on the 9th. These men would form part of Barclay's troop in the New Model Army. The lieutenant colonel was also to have a troop in that force, but his men were to be found from amongst the cavalry regiments quartered in England. The last mention of this regiment occurs on 6 February when the Estates set the payment of arrears for the remaining troopers. On the 9th it passed out of the Army of the Solemn League and Covenant.[22]

Brown's Horse

Colonel: Sir John Brown (of Fordel)

Lieutenant Colonel: Robert Douglas

Major: Archibald Strachan

Minister: Thomas Johnston[23]

On 22 August 1643 Sir John Brown, a veteran of the continental wars and Fife laird, was commissioned as one of the first three cavalry troop commanders of the Army of the Solemn League and Covenant. Sometime in the autumn he received a commission to serve as the lieutenant colonel of Major General David Leslie's Horse. On 19 May 1645 Brown received a commission for his own regiment, which initially consisted of four troops. However, the Committee with the Army stated that Brown's Horse should be made up to eight troops. On 10 July he received fifty-five recruits as part of the process of upgrading his regiment. The regiment quartered in Cumbernauld after its founding. In the autumn of 1645 Brown's Horse took part in its only major action. On 14 October Charles I had dispatched George Lord Digby, and Sir Marmaduke Langdale with the Northern Horse from Welbeck Abbey to join Montrose. Having been defeated at the battle of Sherburn by the parliamentarian forces and picking up reinforcements from Skipton Castle, the royalists (about 500 or 600 strong) by-passed Carlisle on their way north. On 20 or 21 October Brown (with his regiment now numbering eight troops), stumbled upon Lord Digby's force on Annan Moor. Langdale commanded the royalist front line, while Digby commanded the reserve. Brown's horse routed Langdale's men, and Digby fled. The royalists lost 60 officers and 100 men killed, and 200 were taken prisoner. The Scots also took the royalist colours. While fleeing to Dumfries 100 more royalists fell into Scots' hands. Meanwhile Cumbrian levies were being raised;

more importantly, the morale of the Northern Horse had been shattered. Consequently, Digby retreated into Cumberland, seeking refuge in the Lake District fells. On the 24th Digby and his officers sailed from Ravenglass to Man, ending the one serious attempt to provide Montrose with English reinforcements. On the 30th the Committee of Estates allowed Brown's regiment 100 breast, back and head pieces, and 100 pairs of pistols, possibly to replace losses in the battle. Sometime later the Scottish Estates voted Sir John Brown a gold chain worth £1,333 6s. 8d. for his good services while the officer who brought news of the victory received £1,200. By the end of 1645 the regiment had moved south to support the siege of Newark. A muster on 17 January 1646 revealed that the eight troops contained 539 men and officers. After the withdrawal of the army on 7 May Brown's Horse returned to Cumberland. On 25 June Major Strachan addressed the Yorkshire County Committee requesting quarters in that county. However, the Committee refused to accept his request which would have increased the burdens on Clevelandshire, an area already under Scottish occupation. In February 1647, probably after the 11th, the regiment disbanded, although Brown continued in the service of the Estates, receiving command of a horse troop in the New Model Army. However, the accounts of the regiment were not closed, because on 6 March the colonel and some officers petitioned the Estates for a month's pay, that and the colonel's gold chain were granted. Brown's gold chain was mentioned again by the Estates on 24 March, when they authorised it to be paid for from the first surplus of the monthly maintenance. It is unlikely that Brown ever received the chain due to the financial embarrassment of the regime; however it suggests the degree of gratitude felt for the colonel's victory at Annan Moor.[24]

Earl of Callender's Foot

Colonel: James, 1st earl of Callendar

Lieutenant Colonel: William Livingston of Westquarter

Majors: Richard Douglas (1644-45), (?) Somerville (1646), (?) Hamilton of Parklee (1646-47)

Ministers: Thomas Thomson, James Livingston[25]

The earl of Callender began life as a younger son of the 1st earl of Linlithgow. He served as an officer with the Dutch army, where he became obsessed with Dutch methods and discipline. His service as a professional soldier made him egotistical about his own tactical knowledge. In 1633 he returned to Scotland; he was made a Gentleman of the King's Bedchamber and was created Lord Almond (during the royal visit). In 1634 he purchased the barony of Callendar. Three years later he bought that of Falkirk and afterwards other lands in

Stirlingshire. Lord Almond served as General Leslie's lieutenant general in the Second Bishops' War, but he also signed the Cumbernauld Bond (an early indication of where his true loyalties lay). In 1641 the king created him the 1st earl of Callendar during his second visit to Scotland. Callendar declined any charge in Leven's army in 1643. However, on 16 April 1644 the Estates commissioned him commander of all forces which would oppose foreign and internal enemies (reserving Leven's rights as commander of the Army of the Solemn League and Covenant). He was also named lieutenant general of Horse and Foot on both land and sea. These commissions in reality restricted his scope of command to Scotland alone.[26]

Callendar's Foot were raised sometime in early 1644 from Stirlingshire and the presbytery of Linlithgow. By late April it was garrisoning Stirling. English reports in May placed it in the southwest Borders as part of a force meant to seize Cumbria. On 5 June the Estates appointed a committee to organise the levying of an army for Callendar. Six days later the earl received a commission as lieutenant general of Horse and Foot in Scotland and England, which he accepted with the proviso that he would serve directly only under Leven's orders. About the same time the regimental major, a son of the sheriff of Teviotdale, received the appointment as Adjutant General of Callendar's army. Simultaneously Callendar arranged for the ordination of Mr. Thomas Thomson as the regimental chaplain. Also in June the regiment (700 men strong) quartered in Linlithgow at the cost of £167 14s. 8d.[27]

Callendar's army entered England on 25 June, marching initially to Lumley Castle. From there it proceeded to Hartlepool, which was garrisoned by 300 men under Sir Edmund Carew. It surrendered on 24 July and Stockton-on-Tees fell shortly afterwards. Callendar's force, minus six companies of his own regiment under Major Douglas which garrisoned Hartlepool, returned to Lumley Castle. From there the earl marched to Osworth. Callendar commenced operations against the Newcastle garrison with the capture of Gateshead on 28 July. He retained full command of the besieging forces until Leven's arrival at Elswick on 15 August. The Committee with the Army ordered Callendar's Foot to return to Scotland on 4 September. Subsequently, the Committee of Estates ordered it south on the 7th with the Midlothian Foot. However, the Estates altered their decision, authorising part of the regiment to garrison Stirling. On the 25th 500 men of the regiment entered Linlithgow from England. Their quartering charges amounted to £351 16s. 10d. From the 25th to the 2nd of October Captains Hamilton and Whitehead's companies remained in the burgh at a cost of £238 13s. 9d. to the inhabitants. It may be that some of the men remained behind in England to garrison Hartlepool and Stockton.[28]

The regiment's tour of duty in Scotland was fraught with difficulties and dangers. On 18 September the Committee of Estates ordered Lieutenant Colonel Livingston to muster his company and that of the earl of Moray, which were serving as the Stirling garrison. In early December the Committee of Estates wrote to the presbyteries of Linlithgow, Stirling, Dumbarton and Glasgow requesting that the parishes within Linlithgow presbytery and

Stirlingshire make voluntary contributions of money which would pay for 600 suits of clothing, and 600 pairs of shoes and socks. (This strongly suggests that only 600 men of the regiment had returned to Scotland in September.) Almost all of the parishes responded favourably. Linlithgow presbytery raised £762 14s. 8d., for instance. However, Fintry parish in the presbytery of Dumbarton refused to provide money, because the elders claimed the additional responsibility would impoverish the parish. The regiment remained in Stirling burgh and castle after the battle of Inverlochy, when Colonel John Cockburn became governor. On 24 March Captain William Livingston, captain lieutenant of Callendar's own company, petitioned the Estates for the establishment of a magazine of food and drink in the castle, as well as a supply of clothing (the collections having been insufficient), a quartering allowance for the officers and the provision of cannoniers to man the guns. The Estates agreed to establish a magazine and to tell the Committee of Money to pay for the necessary clothing. Meanwhile, in early May, there is definite evidence supporting the view that part of the regiment remained in Hartlepool. At the end of the month the Hartlepool garrison consisted of 332 men and officers of Callendar's Foot. Their numbers were initially larger, but disease and plague had reduced the size of the garrison. Sometime in the spring the Scottish portion of the regiment joined Lieutenant General Baillie's army. It was badly mauled at the battle of Alford on 2 July. As a result the Estates ordered Linlithgowshire to provide 250 infantrymen for the regiment on 1 August. Six days later the officers petitioned the Estates to be put on the same footing as other officers, as they had lost their baggage, clothing and other necessities at Alford. They were referred to the Committee of Money.[29]

Throughout this time Callendar remained in England, where he replaced Baillie as lieutenant general of the Army of the Solemn League and Covenant. In June or July he contributed £96 to the Kelso charity. However, he was not in fact a benign Covenanter, but was in reality holding secret negotiations with the royalists. On 5 August he met with Sir William Fleming, his nephew, and others to contrive a plot to aid Charles I. He did so in direct contravention of Leven's position. However, like many plots of the period it came to nothing. Nevertheless, Callendar remained ready to show his true colours and after Kilsyth he accepted a protection from Montrose, which suggests that he returned to Scotland, possibly to aid the marquis.[30]

Little is known of the regiment after Alford. On 28 October the Committee of Estates authorised Callendar to gather in all the deserters then in West Lothian and Stirlingshire. On 6-7 November he also received permission to levy 100 men each from West Lothian, Peeblesshire and Berwickshire. The Hartlepool garrison increased in strength from 336 men and officers in summer 1645 to 501 infantrymen in late June 1646, falling to 383 men on 3 July. An anti-Scottish pamphleteer claimed that 500 new troops joined the garrison on 1 July. Yet there is no evidence for this in the army account books. The regiment also had between 40 and 158 soldiers in Stockton, which it garrisoned from 4 June 1646 to 25 January 1647. The garrison also departed from Hartlepool on the 25th and both disbanded on 11 February. The remnants of the regiment in Scotland disappear from sight between August 1645 and February 1647. On 5 February the Estates ordered Lieutenant Colonel Livingston and Major Hamilton, whose two companies were quartered in Clackmannshire, to disband their men on Tuesday the 9th.[31] Callendar's regiment was quite peculiar in that large parts of the unit served simultaneously in England and Scotland.

Earl of Callendar's Life Guard of Horse

Routmaster: (?) Rollock

This troop of horse was undoubtedly raised in the spring of 1644, probably from Stirlingshire. There is no mention of its strength. In June or July 1645 the troopers provided £60 for the Kelso charity. On 28 October the troop was assigned quarters in Stirlingshire and allowed to raise fifteen men. From 15 June until 15/21 July 1646 the Life Guard was quartered in county Durham. After then it moved to Northumberland, where it presumably remained until the Scots evacuated England in January 1647. The troop probably disbanded on 11 February with the other cavalry untis. It may be assumed to have accompanied Callendar whenever he was actively campaigning.[32]

Clydesdale Foot

Colonel: General of Artillery Sir Alexander Hamilton

Lieutenant Colonels: William Carmichael, William Lindsay, Andrew Leslie

Majors: Walter Lindsay, Sir James Maxwell

Ministers: Alexander Forrester, Francis Aird, Alexander Livingston[33]

This regiment was commissioned to be raised on 26 August 1643 from Clydesdale (Lanarkshire). All of the field officers had experience in the continental wars. By February 1644 the presbyteries of Lanark, Hamilton, and Glasgow had recruited ten companies, which served in Leven's invasion force. Not all of the men readily accepted service in the unit. On 10 July the Peebles magistrates gave Sergeant John Grainger the choice of rejoining regiment within fourteen days or facing execution. The supply difficulties of the army once it entered England can be seen by looking at a complaint against the Clydesdale Foot. In February the regiment took eighty-four bolls of rye (value unknown) and other grain worth £29 4s. st. from Henry Hinde of The Stelling, Bywell Peter, Northumberland. The regiment also quartered on his estates at Newton Hall for five days and six nights. It may have been engaged at the Hilton skirmishes on 24-25 March. At Marston Moor the Clydesdale Foot was brigaded with the Edinburgh Foot in the front line. When they advanced to support the first line of parliamentarian infantry a charge by the left wing royalist horse broke and routed them. At the siege of Newcastle the General of Artillery possessed a battery which he commanded directly; the regiment was also involved in the siege. On the day of the successful assault Sir Alexander Hamilton led about five of his companies and the Edinburgh Foot against the breach in the White Friar section of the wall. It is uncertain whether the losses at Marston Moor had so reduced the regiment that it was only the equivalent of five companies, or whether the other companies had already retired to winter quarters.[34]

After the fall of Newcastle the regiment quartered in county Durham for the winter. In early December Sir George Vane wrote Sir Henry Vane about the oppressiveness of the Scots quartering on his lands. Sir George had already complained to Sir Alexander Hamilton, who had sympathised and ordered the soldiers removed. However, the officers were reluctant to carry out the orders and the men were disobedient. On 11 January 1645 a muster of the regiment revealed that the campaigns of the previous year had severely weakened it, for there were only 444 men and officers remaining. In June or July the colonel and the rest of the regiment contributed £84 and £300 8s. respectively to the Kelso charity. The regiment was engaged at the siege of Hereford, where its colonel again had command of a battery. By December the Clydesdale Foot was in Scotland, which suggests that it marched north with or shortly after David Leslie. On 15 December the Estates ordered the regiment to march to Falkland, where it was to collect its deserters and remain until further orders.[35]

The Clydesdale Foot had left the English theatre of war. On 2 April 1646 it arrived in Aberdeen, remaining until the 26th. There were then 400 men in ten companies plus officers. The regiment presumably served on the campaigns against the royalist forces in the northeast. On 26-27 August the regiment (still only 400 privates), quartered in Linlithgow. It returned to Aberdeen on 12 September where it remained until 20 February 1647. Lieutenant Colonel Leslie commanded 500 men in ten companies plus officers. They remained on free quarter and also made some exactions upon the burgh. For instance, they received a forced loan worth four days' maintenance. In December the provost and bailies complained to the Committee of Estates about an exaction of £3 4s. per day by the governor from John Strachan for Major Maxwell. The total cost of the regiment's occupation of Aberdeen over the winter was £25,750. On 5 February the Estates ordered that the regiment should disband on the 9th save for one company, which would form part of the General of Artillery's Foot in the New Model Army. On the 12th the regiment was ordered to northern Scotland, a strange order for it was already there. On the 19th the Estates ordered the company which had formed part of the Berwick garrison to be disbanded and its arms to be returned to the shires which had supplied them. The regiment continued to reside on free quarter in Aberdeen with Argyll's and part of Lawers' Foot from the 20th to the 27th. Upon their departure they exacted three days' money of maintenance from those who quartered them. On the evening of the 27th (between 5 and 6 p.m.) the Clydesdale and Argyll's Foot under Middleton's orders reoccupied the town to protect it from royalists. Within a short time the veterans of the Army of the Solemn League and Covenant would leave the regiment save for the one company previously mentioned. Two soldiers of the regiment were cited for sexual sins — one case of fornication (which was settled by the regimental kirk session), and one of fathering a bastard.[36] This regiment possessed an active albeit undistinguished service record.

Collairney's Horse Troop

Routmaster: Sir David Barclay of Collairney

Collairney was the hereditary bailie of the regality of Lindores in Fife. He had raised his troop as a part of Callendar's army by early July. In the first half of that month forty-six troopers and three officers passed through Haddington on their way to England. They received an allowance there of 4s. per man per day plus maintenance for their horses. The only known military activity of this troop was service on the Philiphaugh campaign. It was back in England by June 1646, when it mustered forty-one troopers and three officers. The troop disbanded on 11 February 1647.[37]

College of Justice Foot

Colonel: John, 9th Lord Sinclair

Lieutentant Colonels: James Somerville (1643-44), (?) Sinclair (1644-47)

Major: James Turner (1644-47)

Ministers: James Simpson, Francis Cockburn[38]

A good deal of mystery surrounds this regiment. It was known by a variety of names in addition to that given above — Sir Alexander Gibson of Durie's Foot, the Levied Regiment, or Lord Sinclair's Foot. Because Lord Sinclair was in command of another regiment (the one originally raised in 1640) which served in England from June 1644 there is some confusion as to which regiment is meant when the documents mention 'Sinclair's Foot'. Finally there seems to have been uncertainty in the mind of the son of the first lieutenant colonel, who wrote of the early stages of the regiment's history.

The *Memorie of the Somervilles* casts doubt upon the Commission which

Sinclair received on 25 August 1643 as the basis of the regiment. This family history claims that the College of Justice told parliament that it would raise an infantry regiment after early February 1644. Durie, who had commanded College of Justice Forces in earlier wars, was made colonel. Somerville, who received the rank of lieutenant colonel, had served as the major of Lindsay's Foot in the Second Bishops' War. It was the former captains of Lindsay's, attracted by Somerville, who filled that rank in this regiment. According to Somerville the Edinburgh clergy persuaded 1,200 writer-apprentices, servants and trades-youths to join for the protection of protestantism, their lives, and Scotland's freedom. The regiment reportedly marched south in February via Berwick. At that time Durie became the Commissary General and Lord Sinclair received his commission. Lieutenant Colonel Somerville supposedly served as governor of Berwick from February to March. Leven later placed Somerville in command of Morpeth Castle in order to protect his supply line. Somerville complained bitterly about his appointment, because the place was in ruins.[39]

There is much that is demonstrably incorrect in the preceding paragraph. There is no evidence outside of the Somerville account that Durie received command of a regiment in the Army of the Solemn League and Covenant, nor did he serve as its commissary general (Humbie held that position). Also it would have been impossible for the College of Justice to offer to raise this regiment as late as February 1644, for on 1 February Leven placed Somerville in command of Morpeth Castle. Nor could Somerville have served as governor of Berwick in February-March 1644, because on 1 February Colonel Lindsay of Bellstanes became the governor. The writer of the Somerville history has confused his dates but not his facts. Sinclair received command of the 'Levied Regiment' on 25 August 1643, a month after the unit was commissioned to be raised. The regiment mustered on the Links of Leith on 16 September. Subsequently, it garrisoned Berwick where Somerville was presumably governor.[40]

After Somerville was deposited in Morpeth Castle by an apparently jealous Leven, the other five companies of the regiment continued south to the Newcastle area. (Here again there is some difficulty with the Somerville account, which mentions a total of twelve companies, however reliable evidence suggests that the regiment contained only ten companies.) After 22 February Leven left these five companies with Lumden as part of his force to screen Newcastle.[41]

Returning to the Somerville history, one finds the fullest if not the most prejudiced account of the siege of Morpeth Castle. Lieutenant Colonel Somerville was dubious about his ability to hold the castle from the start. He believed that Leven had given him such a hazardous command because the Lord General held a grudge against him and looked forward to his humiliation if his post fell. In further support of this suspicion Somerville stated that Leven had provided an insufficient supply of ammunition. To support the garrison of 500 men Leven left Weldon's Horse and some dragoons in nearby villages; otherwise the place was isolated. For three months Somerville held his post without seeing any forces. Then in mid April that bugbear of Covenanter commanders — Montrose — received a field command. The marquis first failed in an attempt to invade Scotland via Dumfries, then he turned southwards in hopes of aiding the hard-pressed royalist garrison of York. Montrose had 2,000 English infantry, 500 English cavalry, and 200 mounted Scots nobles and gentry under his command. On 10 May he opened the siege of Morpeth Castle. The next day Montrose launched an assault, which was repelled with the loss of eight of the defenders. The siege continued until the morning of 29 May. During it the garrison inflicted significant casualties on the royalists; Weldon unsuccessfully tried to relieve his comrades. Somerville, out of supplies of food and ammunition, and with his fortress crumbling about him, surrendered on the 29th. The troops under his command promised never to serve against Charles I in the future. After a loss of one ensign, two drummers and twenty privates, the garrison marched out at 10 a.m. That evening Montrose dined Somerville and his four captains. The next day the garrison began its march north to Edinburgh. In late June Somerville rejoined Leven's army outside of York. The Council of War then examined his conduct during the siege and acquitted him of any charge.[42]

Somerville noted a marked change in the strength of the regiment before Marston Moor. He believed that the regiment had shrunk due to neglect of Sinclair and his captains. On 2 July the five remaining companies of the regiment formerly left with Lumsden fought at Marston Moor. They probably served as part of the reserve of Fairfax's infantry, which was routed by the royalists. The College of Justice Foot was probably a mere shadow of its former self when Somerville laid down his commission on the next day. The regiment proceeded north to the siege of Newcastle in August. Sinclair commanded his own battery during the siege. The College of Justice Foot formed part of the 4th Brigade under Callendar's command at the storming of Newcastle. On 10 July 1645 the regiment provided £480 for the Kelso charity. It was probably engaged in the siege of Hereford, where Sinclair also had a battery. After the siege Lord Sinclair was charged in the Scottish Estates with fraternising with the enemy. However, on 22 January 1646 he was cleared. After August 1645 the regiment quartered in Yorkshire. Then it moved south to participate in the siege of Newark with other regiments of the army. On 6 December 1645 the regiment contained 491 officers and men. Six weeks later there were only 436 of all ranks (thirty-three of them being ill). In late April a muster revealed 453 men and officers in the regiment. From July the regiment quartered in Northumberland until it departed from England in February 1647. Prior to that (but after May 1646), the regiment quartered in county Durham, where it was considered oppressive. Captain Patrick Hardie demanded and received £3 per day for fifteen privates and £2 4s. per day for his officers. Lindley Wren in Branchester, after being sequestered, had fifty men and officers quartered on him. The parliamentary commissioners (in answer to his petition) ordered the soldiers' maintenance from his sequestered goods. Yet the soldiers disposed of the goods as they wished. However, when the county committee came to take the remaining ones, the major threatened them with quartering if the goods were touched. There are few other details concerning the regiment. Sinclair was barred from the king's presence in December 1646 by Leven for his royalist leanings. There is only one case of kirk discipline involving a soldier of the regiment, who fathered a bastard.[43] Unlike many of the regiments in the army the College of Justice Foot served only in England, where it participated in most of the army's campaigns.

College of Justice Horse Troop

Routmaster: John Cockburn

This troop was also called after its commander. It was probably raised by the College of Justice from amongst its younger and more active members in spring 1644. The troop crossed the border as part of Callendar's army on 25 June. It probably served under the earl's command until 4 September when the Committee with the Army ordered it back to Scotland. There are no details about its service in Scotland nor is there any information on its military activities until January 1646. Then it was serving under Lieutenant General Leslie as part of the force besieging Newark. There were sixty-nine men and officers in the troop on 17 January. In June the troop consisted of five officers and sixty-two troopers. After returning to Scotland in February 1647 it disbanded completely on the 11th.[44]

Lord Coupar's Dragoons

Colonel: James, 1st Lord Coupar

It is not known when or from where this unit was raised. There are no details about its service in England. However, 'a party of dragoones under the Lord Cowpers comand' returned seventy broken muskets during their service in England. The dragoons presumably served at Philiphaugh as they are found in Aberdeen with Fraser's Dragoons in October 1645. The regiment then consisted of 480 dragoons and officers in seven companies. With Fraser's men they cost the burgh £3,345 for five days' quartering. From there Coupar's men accompanied Middleton's expedition to Banff. On 7 November they were ordered to quarter in Glasgow. They were in southern Scotland on 16 December when the Estates ordered the seven companies to be reduced to six. The larger companies were taken from Coupar's command (and the regiment was effectively disbanded), by giving two companies each to Barclay's, Eglinton's and Montgomery's Horse regiments.[45]

Master of Cranstoun's Foot

Colonel: William, master of Cranstoun

Lieutenant Colonel: Sir Walter Riddell

Major: (?) Middlemass

Ministers: John Halswell, Thomas Courtney, John Dees[46]

Both the colonel and lieutenant colonel commanded contingents in May 1644 against the Cumbrian royalists. The master of Cranstoun received a colonelcy in Callendar's army in spring 1644. That July the Estates appointed him a member of the committee of war for Midlothian. The regiment crossed the border on 25 June as part of Callendar's army. On 19 October it formed part of the 4th Brigade (under Callendar's command) at the storming of Newcastle. The master personally led his men against the Sandgate. In May 1645 the regiment contained 521 men and officers. Within ten days it had fifty-seven fewer men on the rolls. On 31 July there were 471 men and officers in Cranstoun's Foot. In June or July the regiment contributed £180 to the Kelso charity fund. From 27 July to 28 August a Captain Scott led a party of sixty commanded men under the command of Captain William Johnston (Yester's Foot). A more serious depletion of the regiment's manpower was the departure of 155 more commanded men to Scotland on 12 August, where they remained until 31 January 1646. The regiment reached its lowest recorded strength, 310 men and officers, on 21 August 1645. On 28 October the Committee of Estates assigned it 600 men from Teviotdale and Selkirkshire; few appear to have been raised. The numbers rose to 370 of all ranks on 10 December. With the return of the large commanded party or the arrival of new recruits in late January 1646 (presumably after service at Philiphaugh and against royalist forces in Scotland), the regiment stood at 485 men and officers. The numbers continued to climb, attaining the 500-plus mark on 4 March and exceeding 600 of all ranks on 12 June. On 15 July the regiment contained 626 men and officers, and it remained at that level at least until 29 November. In February 1647 the regiment was entirely disbanded.[47]

Crawford's Horse Troop

Routmaster: Major General Lawrence Crawford

Major General Crawford served as a high ranking officer in the English parliamentary armies until March 1645, when he and other Scottish officers departed followng the creation of the New Model Army. The first mention of his troop occurs in late July 1645, although it may have been in existence before then. It served at the siege of Hereford. There Major General Crawford was killed; he was buried at Gloucester on 5 September. Subsequently his troop was either disbanded or shared out to the cavalry regiments.[48]

Earl of Dalhousie's Horse

Colonel: William, 1st earl of Dalhousie

Lieutenant Colonel: John Innes

Majors: (?) Blair (1644-45), James Bickerton (1645-47)

Ministers: Robert Row, John Maghie/Makghie[49]

Berwickshire, Haddingtonshire and Edinburghshire were to provide the regiment with two troops each, and Linlithgowshire and Stirlingshire (under Sir William Bruce) were assessed one troop each on 23 November 1643 to form this regiment. Both Lieutenant Colonel Innes and Major Blair had served in European armies before joining the Covenanters. By early February 1644 the regiment consisted of only six troops. On the 16th the Committee with the Army informed the Committee of Estates that Dalhousie still lacked one of his Berwickshire troops. The regiment served at the siege of York, where on 30 May members of the garrison attacked its quarters. At Marston Moor Dalhousie's Horse and two other Scots cavalry regiments supported Fairfax's Horse on the right flank. During the battle the royalist cavalry routed this regiment. After the return of the army to Newcastle in mid August Dalhousie's received orders to move north into Scotland on 2 September. On the 19th three troops of this regiment (about 160 men and officers), three troops of Hamilton's Horse and their women camp followers entered Aberdeen as part of Argyll's army. The horsemen received 18s. per man per day. The total charge after three days' stay was £864. Lieutenant Colonel Innes was in effective command of the regiment during this campaign. On 19 November this regiment with Hackett's and Hamilton's Horse were quartered throughout Aberdeenshire. Dalhousie's men received some of their pay on 4 February 1645, this may have occurred just before their return to England.[50]

The regiment reached England by early March 1645 and then may have served at the siege of Carlisle. A muster of the regiment on 10 March revealed that it contained only 321 troopers. On 11 June it engaged a party of Carlisle foragers, who beat Dalhousie's men. After the fall of Carlisle the regiment apparently joined Leven's field army and served at the siege of Hereford. On 4 August Routmaster Sir William Bruce arrived from Scotland in northern England with 36 troopers he was leading to Hereford. However, the regiment did not stay with Leven until the siege ended. Instead, it returned to Scotland under Lieutenant General Leslie and fought at Philiphaugh. On 7 November the regiment was ordered to quarter in Stirlingshire. On 16 December a muster of Dalhousie's Horse on the Links of Leith revealed a strength of 324 troopers, who possessed only eighty-four horses fit for duty and sixty-nine pairs of pistols. However, there were more men in the regiment than the muster indicated. From October Routmaster Thomas Hamilton was in charge of thirty-nine commanded horsemen in Northamptonshire; also from 11 November Routmaster

George Hepburn led a commanded party of ten troopers at the siege of Newark. Therefore, in December 1645, the seven troops of the regiment contained 373 troopers.[51]

By mid January 1646 the entire regiment was back in England. The majority of Dalhousie's men quartered in Yorkshire. A commanded party of twenty-seven officers and men was serving at the siege of Newark. In August, if not earlier, the regiment returned to Scotland. From 29 August to 29 September Routmaster Thomas Hamilton commanded 125 troopers plus officers who quartered in East Lothian, where they received a quartering allowance of 14s. per day. Between 21 October and 26 November 125 troopers, excluding officers, stayed in the same shire on identical rates. From 16 December to 9 February 1647 200 troopers (or half the regiment) remained in East Lothian at 12s. per man per day. In January 1647 the Commission of the General Assembly issued a directive on the receiving of repentant soldiers from the regiment quartering around Tranent. Adulterers in the regiment were to attend the presbytery where the offence had occurred, fornicators were to appear at the kirk session of the parish where they had sinned. On 5 February the Estates ordered the officers to disband the regiment on the 9th save for one troop of eighty men, who would serve under Lieutenant Colonel Mungo Murray in the New Model Army. On the next day the Estates ordered the shires of East Lothian and Edinburgh to pay the regiment's arrears, which amounted to £6,901 13s. 4d.[52]

There are four cases of sexual sins committed by troopers of the regiment. In three cases the crime was fornication; in each instance the trooper escaped public penance, but his partner did not. The remaining case was one of fathering a bastard. The mother claimed that the father, a trooper, had bound her to a stake and forced her to commit fornication. However, after investigation by two of the regiment's chaplains the trooper willingly confessed and the woman withdrew her charge that she was forced against her will. The woman did public penance first, but the trooper was also received from 'the publict place testifying his repentance for his fornicating wt Margtt Elder'.[53]

Disney's Horse Troop

Routmaster: (?) Disney

This was one of the troops which formerly belonged to Colonel Devereux's regiment of parliamentarian cavalry. It is unknown when it joined the Scottish army. The troop consisted of four officers and forty-one troopers during the siege of Newark. From January to 6 March 1646, at least, Nottinghamshire paid free quarters for this troop. Simultaneously it was busy uplifting cess and quarter in Derbyshire. The exactions from that county were as follows: £78 9s 7d. st. from Wentbridge with two other troops, £89 18s. st. from Sherland and Higham with three other troops, £17 st. from Westhallum with one other troop, £37 7s. 8d. st. and free quarters from Denby with one other troop, £15 st. from Horselywood House with one other troop, £19 1s. st. and free quartering from Kilburne with two other troops, £10 st. from Sandiaire and £3 st. from Risley. The troop remained on foot until 31 July, but its subsequent quartering grounds are not known. It is uncertain whether this unit disbanded in Scotland.[54]

Drummond's Horse Troop

Routmaster: Henry Drummond

Routmaster Drummond had raised his troop by April 1644. On the 15th the Estates ordered the troop to accompany Lawers' Foot from Perthshire to Dumfries to oppose Montrose. In June the troop entered England as part of Callendar's army. It presumably served with the army throughout the campaign in the northeast. On 24 August Drummond was promoted to major of Sir Frederick Hamilton's Horse and his troop was added to that regiment which ended its independent existence.[55]

Dundas' Horse Troop

Routmaster: (? Robert) Dundas

This troop was raised in the spring of 1644 and formed part of Callendar's army. The last mention of the troop occurs in July. After that it may have been placed under Major General Sir James Ramsay's command to allow him to create his own regiment of cavalry.[56]

East Lothian Foot

Colonels: Sir Patrick Hepburn of Waughton (1643-45), Sir Adam Hepburn of Humbie (1645-47)

Lieutenant Colonels: William Home (1643-44), Claud Hamilton (1644-47), Alexander Glass (1647)

Majors: Robert Hepburn (1643-44), Patrick Hepburn (1644-45), George Wauchope (1645-47)

Ministers: John Hamilton, David Robertson, John Robertson, John Courtney, Thomas Hepburn, John Lauder, Andrew Ballantyne/Bannatyne, Archibald Douglas, Alexander Davidson, Andrew Wood, Andrew Makghie/Maghie[57]

The majority of the information on this regiment concerns its raising and first year of existence. Both Lieutenant Colonel Home and Major Hepburn were veterans of the European wars. Nevertheless, their ability at recruiting men was not one of their strengths. The parish of Tyninghame held its first meeting for choosing the fourth man on 4 November 1643. But it broke up in failure as the townspeople 'could not pirfuytlie agree'. Two meetings later on 21 December the parish finally managed to select its twenty-five recruits demanded by the committee of war. However, the levying of the regiment elsewhere in East Lothian (particularly in the presbyteries of Dunbar and Haddington) must have been going badly, because on 9 January 1644 Waughton petitioned the Estates. He claimed that his regiment lacked so many men that he would join the army as a private person. The Estates responded by ordering Leven to find a way to complete the regiment. The Lord General succeeded for in February Waughton's Foot contained the required ten companies.[58]

For much of the year the regiment served actively. During the siege of York Waughton held a portion of the siege line. On 1 June the garrison attacked Waughton's. The regiment served at Marston Moor, probably as part of the reserve for Fairfax's Foot. In the event the royalists drove it from the field. Waughton's Foot formed part of the 2nd Brigade at the storming of Newcastle on 19 October. Both Waughton and his lieutenant colonel behaved with conspicuous bravery at the attack on Newgate. However, Lieutenant Colonel Home, Major Hepburn and Captain John Home died in the assault. The Committee with the Army granted Captain Home's sister £108 as an act of charity.[59] Following the capture of Newcastle the regiment went into winter quarters in northeast England.

The subsequent history of the regiment is shadowy. In June or July 1645 the soldiers and officers contributed £258 12s. to the Kelso charity fund. The East Lothian foot did not take part in the Hereford siege or any actions in Scotland, thus it may be assumed that it did garrison duty in the northeast between March and August 1645. Its absence from the siege of Newark provides further evidence that this regiment was on garrison duty, probably in Newcastle. On 7 November the Committee of Estates allowed the regiment to recruit 400 men from East Lothian. The first muster of the regiment on 10 November revealed a strength of 631 officers and men. By the end of that year it had increased to 644 of all ranks. Sometime in 1645 Sir Adam Hepburn of Humbie replaced Waughton as colonel of the regiment. Humbie was also the treasurer of the Army of the Solemn League and Covenant and its commissary general. Throughout 1646 the regiment increased steadily in strength. On 23 February it stood at 651 men and officers; two months later there were 893 soldiers in the regiment. On 16 May the regiment stood at 954 men strong and passed the thousand mark on the 26th. From then until 15 September the regiment gradually increased in size to 1,030 men and officers, which it maintained until late November at least. After the regiment evacuated England in February 1647 it disbanded entirely. The only recorded case of a soldier being cited for church discipline involved Captain George Pringle, who was guilty of fornication with Agnes Hamilton in Haddington.[60]

Edinburgh Foot

Colonel: James Rae

Lieutenant Colonel: Andrew Milne

Majors: Thomas Logan (1643-45), Robert Logan (1645-47)

Ministers: George Leslie, Thomas Garvin, John Oswald, Andrew Fairfoul, Archibald Newtoun[61]

This was the only regiment in the Covenanter armies raised by the efforts of a single burgh. On 28 September 1643 the Edinburgh Council elected James Rae and Andrew Milne colonel and lieutenant colonel respectively of its regiment for the Army of the Solemn League and Covenant. The council determined that the regiment would have 1,200 men and officers, but it is unknown whether its ten companies contained that many men. An examination of the parishes served by the regiment's chaplains suggests that not all of the men came from the town of Edinburgh, but that they were also recruited throughout the presbytery of Edinburgh. Nevertheless the ability of one town to successfully levy a regiment on its own was a considerable achievement. The regiment formed part of Leven's army in January 1644. In January or February Captain Alexander Stirling of the regiment stole £18 12s. from Henry Hinde of The Stelling, Bywell Peter, Northumberland. The Edinburgh Foot formed part of Leven's besieging force at York. During the battle of Marston Moor it was coupled with the Clydesdale Foot on the right flank of the front line infantry upon advancing. They were swept off the field by a royalist cavalry charge. Again at the storming of Newcastle the two regiments were brigaded together to assault the mined White Friar Tower. The colonel, lieutenant colonel and major personally led about five companies of the regiment under the overall command of the General of Artillery. On 23 October the Committee with the Army appointed Colonels Rae and Home of Wedderburn to meet together with all the substantial Nova-castrian merchants to see what had been taken from them, by whom, whether they compounded for it, and the sums compounded. The two colonels had a clerk appointed to help them in gathering written declarations. They were also instructed to preserve ships, keels, and other goods. Throughout the winter of 1644-45 the Edinburgh Foot quartered in Northumberland.[62]

As with other regiments the amount of material covering the years 1645-47 is sparse. On 31 March 1645 a regimental muster indicated there were 482 men of all ranks in it. The regiment fluctuated in strength throughout the rest of the year. It reached a low point of 313 men and officers on 20 September after having been 506 men strong on 11 August. The last muster of the year on 20 December revealed a strength of 340 officers and men. In June or July the men and officers contributed £240 to the Kelso charity fund. On 4 August Captain George Melville led fifty-seven commanded men 'out of Carlile'. This regiment seems to have remained on garrison duty in northeast England from spring 1645 until leaving the country. The regiment experienced gradual increases in strength throughout much of 1646. On 31 January there were 433 men and officers in the unit, four months later it had risen to 516 men strong. The regiment reached a high of 550 of all ranks on 11 August, but by 2 September there were ten fewer in the regiment and the number stabilised at that point. After evacuating England the regiment disbanded entirely in February 1647.[63]

Earl of Eglinton's Horse

Colonels: Alexander, 6th earl of Eglinton (1643-45), Robert Montgomery (1645-47)

Lieutenant Colonel: Robert Montgomery (1643-45)

Major: John Montgomery

Ministers: Robert Urrie/Urry, Robert Wise, Andrew Dunlop, Hew Archibald[64]

When Eglinton was commissioned to raise this regiment of cavalry in autumn 1643 he was assigned recruits out of three counties. Ayrshire and Renfrewshire were to provide four troops (240 troopers and officers), Lanarkshire was to levy three-and-a-third troops (200 troopers and officers), and the Estates were to find forty troopers from other counties. Eglinton chose professional soldiers to serve as his lieutenant colonel and major (the former post went to his younger son Robert). The regiment crossed the border into England on 19 January 1644 with the rest of Leven's army. By some time in February all the troops had been successfully levied. The regiment served with Leven during the siege of York, and was engaged at Marston Moor. Eglinton's Horse formed part of the Scottish reserve of three cavalry regiments for Fairfax's cavalry on the right flank. Following the destruction of Fairfax's force by the royalist cavalry, Eglinton's Horse stood their ground as the enemy horsemen pursued the broken English forces. The regiment was heavily engaged. The lieutenant colonel and major were wounded and four lieutenants died due to the battle. After Marston Moor the regiment dropped from sight for fourteen months.[65]

Eglinton's Horse probably served on the Hereford campaign before returning to Scotland with Lieutenant General Leslie. The regiment fought at Philiphaugh on 13 September 1645. On 7 November Eglinton's new colonel Robert Montgomery was ordered to quarter in Ayrshire and Renfrewshire within eight or ten miles of Glasgow. By 11 December a commanded party of the regiment was serving at the siege of Newark under Cornet Calhoun of Dalhousie's Horse. The rest of the regiment was then scattered throughout lowland Scotland. For instance, Cornet Harry Montgomery quartered with twenty troopers in Linlithgow on 16 December. On the same day the Estates ordered the regiment to Angus, where it would pick up two companies of dragoons formerly of Lord Coupar's regiment. From there Montgomery's Horse was to ride north into Aberdeenshire in company with Barclay's and viscount Montgomery's Horse. this body of horsemen reached Aberdeen on 2 January 1646 at 2 p.m. They remained only one day, but returned on the 23rd. Then the colonel brought in six troops of horse and one company of dragoons into Aberdeen. His regiment of 580 cavalrymen quartered in the burgh until 15/16 April, costing the townspeople £53,120. By late March part of the regiment had left the burgh and quartered on Lord Lovat's lands. In April the entire regiment took to the field under Major General Middleton. During this campaign the regiment destroyed grain belonging to the earl of Erroll, Lord Coupar and their tenants. Major Montgomery's troop plundered grain and clothing from a tenant in Turriff. Lord Coupar and his tenants endured quartering by part of the regiment. After the completion of this campaign it is uncertain where the regiment quartered in Scotland until 5 February 1647. That day the Estates ordered Colonel Montgomery to disband his men on the 9th, save for 100 troopers. Eighty of these men were to form his troop in the New Model Army, the remainder were assigned to Aldie's troop. Thus from 9 February 1647 one of the staunchest regiments of the Army ceased to exist. Although it had served in Scotland for a year and a half not a single one of its men were cited for kirk discipline.[66]

Fife (Crawford-Lindsay's) Foot

Colonel: John, earl of Crawford-Lindsay

Lieutenant Colonels: Thomas Moffat (1643-44), John Hamilton (1644-47)

Major: Mungo Murray

Ministers: Robert Blair, James Bruce, William Row[67]

This was one of the few regiments in the army which failed to survive until February 1647. In the autumn of 1643 the Fife presbyteries of Cupar and St. Andrews raised ten companies of men for the earl of Crawford-Lindsay. Both his lieutenant colonel and major were veterans of the European wars. The regiment entered England in January 1644 as part of Leven's army. On 5 March the Committee with the Army ordered that Lieutenant Colonel Hamilton was to have a troop of which he would be routmaster. The regiment served at the siege of York as well as in the campaign in Northumberland and Durham. At Marston Moor this was one of only three front-line Covenanter regiments which held. It was brigaded with the Midlothian Foot, to the left of Fairfax's cavalry. The Scottish infantry of the first line cleared a ditch defended by musketeers in front of the royalist line. The Fife and Midlothian Foot were reckoned to have endured the worst of the battle. The brigade endured three royalist cavalry charges yet lost only three killed. The earl behaved bravely, and was instrumental in forcing the royalist horse to retreat. The brigade also managed to capture Sir Charles Lucas, lieutenant general of Newcastle's Horse. During the siege of Newcastle the two regiments were brigaded together in defending a stretch of the line of circumvallation. On 20 August the garrison made a successful sortie against this section. Two weeks later the regiment returned to Scotland upon the orders of the Committee with the Army.[68]

With the return of the regiment to Scotland it was solely concerned with campaigns against Montrose and his allies. On 7 September the Committee of Estates ordered the regiment to remain in Scotland and to advance with a troop of horse. The regiment formed part of Baillie's army in late autumn. For some reason the Fife Foot took some time to find proper winter quarters. From 28 September until mid November the regiment used Perth as its base. However, after 19 November, in accordance with orders of the Committee of Estates issued in either October or November, the regiment arrived in Dundee under its lieutenant colonel. The regiment withdrew from there to Perth by 10 December. From the 16th to the 23rd the Fife Foot (now 800 strong) quartered in Perth with the Midlothian Foot. They withdrew on the 23rd leaving a garrison of 200 men (a hundred from each regiment), only to return on 9 January 1645. Then the soldiers began an exaction of two pecks of milk per man per week. On 27 February the Estates authorised the Fife Foot to split the eighth man from Angus with the Midlothian foot. This new levy was to be ready by 8 March, however there is no evidence concerning its implementation. Desertion was a problem within the regiment. On 13 March the kirk session of Kilconquhar, presbytery of St. Andrews, ordered some soldiers to return to the colours. On 22 March the Fife and Midlothian Foot quit their winter quarters at Perth to join Baillie on his march near Brechin. Crawford-Lindsay was then present with his regiment. The two units were involved in the relief of Dundee on 5 April. In May the regiment was quartered in Newtyle. There in early June the earl arrived with 500 recruits (possibly of the Angus levy) and an order from the Committee of Estates. This order allowed Crawford-Lindsay to establish an independent command and forced Baillie to provide him with 1,000 veterans in exchange for the recruits. It is possible that his regiment formed part of the force which he led in a destruction of Atholl. On 16 June the earl requested that Lothian's Foot leave Dundee, so that his regiment could enter. This was done by 30 June.[69]

On 27 July Robert Blair, a former chaplain of the regiment delivered a sermon at Torgonderony to the Fife and Midlothian Foot. He said that he heard that the regiments had fallen into sinfulness since Marston Moor, when God had protected them. He prophesised that a lesser foe would beat them unless they repented. Five days later the Estates assigned the regiment 600 recruits out of a new Fife levy to bring it up to strength. On 5 August the Estates appointed Major Murray lieutenant colonel of Balcarres' new regiment of horse. The stage was set for the fulfillment of Blair's prophesy. On the morning of 15 August 1645 few could have guessed that the Fife Foot would cease to exist by the evening. The regiment must have received some recruits, because it was the only regiment in the second line. The Fife Foot covered the gap between Home's regiment of commanded men and the Midlothian Foot at Kilsyth. They and the Midlothian Foot were to support Balcarres' Horse on the flank attack. The brigade was attacked first by Nathaniel Gordon, then by viscount Aboyne and finally by the earl of Airlie leading the Ogilvies. This royalist onslaught broke the brigade which fled suffering heavy casualties. The battle was a disaster for the regiment. All of the officers, excepting the colonel and Major Murray, and most of the men died. Within two days of the battle, the kirk session of Ceres, presbytery of Cupar, recorded that the regiment had ceased to exist.[70] The earl of Crawford-Lindsay's regiment of Fife Foot had seen much hard service in its twenty-odd months of existence, and it was one of the few regular units to be destroyed in battle.

Fife (Dunfermline's) Foot

Colonel: Charles, 2nd earl of Dunfermline

Lieutenant Colonel: Robert Halsalm/Halsell/Halson/Halswell

Major: David Finnie/Phine

Ministers: Walter Bruce, Joshua Meldrum, Henry Wilkie, Andrew Donaldson, James Wilson, William Oliphant[71]

Dunfermline received his commission from the Estates on 26 August 1643. This regiment was raised from the presbyteries of Kirkcaldy and Dunfermline. Recruiting continued as late as 24 December 1643. The twenty-seven parishes involved raised ten companies, or a full regimental complement. Both the lieutenant colonel and major were veterans of continental wars. The regiment served with Leven in Northumberland, Durham and during the siege of York. At Marston Moor the Fife Foot was brigaded with the Strathearn Foot as part of the Scottish infantry reserve. Royalist cavalry broke and routed this brigade. The regiment recovered to serve at the siege of Newcastle. On 19 October the Fife Foot was in the 2nd Brigade under the command of its colonel and Lumsden. The regiment took part in the attack on the Newgate. Four days later the lieutenant colonel was one of three men appointed to receive oaths from the royalist common soldiers that they would never serve against parliament and then release them. A month later, the widow of Captain William Cockburn (who was killed in the storm of Newcastle) received a grant of £81 from the Committee with the Army. On 28 December the regiment was 862 men strong. It retained this strength until 31 March 1645 when it declined to 673 men and officers; the decline continued until 11 June when the the regiment mustered 632 men and officers. Between the 23rd of June and 31st July the numbers increased slowly from 685 men and officers to 730 of all ranks. During these two months the regiment raised £241 4s. for the Kelso charity. On 2 August a force of fifty-seven commanded men were sent to Carlisle, suggesting that the regiment was doing garrison duty in northeastern England. Ten days later Major Finnie led another commanded party of 228 men to Scotland. Thus, on 30 August there were only 550 men and officers in the main body of the regiment. The size of the regiment continued to decline until 10 November when it numbered 500 men and officers. Again the regiment recovered its strength, managing to muster 656 men and officers on 31 January 1646. By 20 February there were 719 of all ranks on the rolls, implying that Major Finnie had now returned with all of the surviving commanded men. In March when the regiment joined Lieutenant General Leslie at the siege of Newark the number of men and officers had fallen to 548, where it remained for the remainder of its service. By 15 May the regiment had reached county Durham after leaving the siege and quartered there until it departed from England. In January 1647 Dunfermline was one of the two colonels explicitly forbidden access to Charles I by Leven. The following month the regiment returned to Scotland, where it was entirely disbanded.[72]

Fraser's Dragoons

Colonel: Hugh Fraser (of Kynneries)

Lieutenant Colonels: Hugh Crawford (1644-45), Andrew Munro (1645-46), John Munro (1646-47)

Major: John Munro (1644-46)

Minister: Alexander Fergus[73]

This regiment originally consisted of dragoons but by 1646 it had become a horse regiment. The recruiting area of the unit is unknown. All the field officers were veterans of European armies. By May there were four companies in the regiment. When the number increased to seven during the siege of York the regiment was reckoned the 'stoutest' in the army. The regiment served with Leven's army in Northumberland and Durham. At the battle of Corbridge Fraser's Dragoons contributed three companies to the Scottish cavalry force. During the siege of Morpeth Castle Fraser's unit aided Weldon's Horse in confronting Montrose's army. After its fall the regiment proceeded to the Scottish camp outside York. The regiment's successes at Marston Moor provided it with an impressive reputation. The dragoons deployed to the left of the allied line (in a position perpendicular to the line), within the Sike Beck (a cross ditch near Tockwith). While the armies were still marshalling their forces some of Rupert's cavalry advanced and tried to gain the ground southeast of Tockwith. The dragoons drove them back towards York, securing the site for the allies' left wing body of horse. As the battle commenced the dragoons cleared the ditch in front of Cromwell's horse (which permitted them to charge the royalist horse) and routed their opponents. Fraser's was then able to rest before it fought one last engagement. After the royalist horse had fled, the Whitecoats of Newcastle's army had positioned themselves in White Sike Close in order to fight to the last man. Cromwell's and Leslie's horse were unable to break through their hedge of pikes. Fraser's Dragoons were called upon, they forced a gap in the royalist line by their musket fire. The allied cavalry charged home and the battle ended with the slaughter of the Whitecoats. Fraser's men played an instrumental part in the great allied victory at Marston Moor.[74]

After the fall of York the regiment was involved in only one major operation. On 1 August 1644 Lieutenant General Leslie led it and three regiments of horse from Doncaster to Callendar's siegeworks around Newcastle. From 1 September to 7 October Fraser's Dragoons accompanied Leslie with seven regiments of horse on an exploratory campaign in Cumbria. The regiment then returned to Northumberland, where it remained until sometime in December. Fraser's crossed the Pennines for a third time and became part of the Scottish force which besieged Carlisle. The regiment served until the town fell on 28 June 1645. It is improbable that it proceeded south to Hereford afterwards, but it is certain that Fraser's men crossed the mountains again. In late August or early September they joined Leslie as he rode into Scotland with a large force of cavalry to confront Montrose. Accordingly the regiment was engaged at Philip-haugh on 13 September. Afterwards it proceeded northwards to Aberdeen in company with Middleton's force of cavalry. On arriving in the burgh the regiment was reckoned to contain 450 officers and troopers. It remained there four days before moving on to Banff with the rest of the force. Supply problems vexed the regiment. The earl of Erroll and others in Turriff complained of general plundering by the regiment in a report made eighteen months later. Captain David Kennedy's troop was accused of stealing grain. On the way south men of the regiment seized £3 from a tenant of Erroll. The dragoons remained in Aberdeen for twenty-four hours before continuing southwards. Their exaction on the burgh and that of Coupar's Dragoons totalled £3,345. With the end of the campaign Fraser's men were scattered into garrisons in the Mearns, Angus and Perthshire, and later moved to west Fife, Clackmannanshire and Perthshire. On 31 October Fraser received permission to transform the regiment into one of horse on its return to England. In early December thirty-two troopers and six officers were selected to serve as part of a commanded party of cavalry under Cornet Calhoun of Dalhousie's Horse at the siege of Newark. They reached the besiegers' camp on 11 December and remained there until the town fell in May 1646. On 16 December the Estates ordered the Strathearn Foot to replace the regiment in the garrisons it controlled. Fraser's men received orders to return to England. By January 1646 the regiment had reached York-shire, where it settled into quarters. Until now the regiment had covered itself in glory; that changed during this occupation of England.[75]

Between January and May 1646 the actions of Fraser's Horse did much to exacerbate Scottish-English relations. The regiment apparently left Scotland poorly provided with horses. For a week the troopers stole horses in the Northumberland parishes of Chillingham and Newton, attacking any owner who tried to recover his beast. From there the regiment proceeded into the West Riding of Yorkshire, seizing money in Ripley. By 30 January it had reached Tickhill at the southern tip of the Riding. On that day Lieutenant Colonel Munro addressed letters to the constables of Sheffield, Rotherham, and Darnall demanding a total of £1,507 12s. per week for the maintenance of the regimental staff and three companies. If the inhabitants did not pay, they would be quartered upon. Information on these payments is hard to find, but it is known that on 9 February Rotherham provided the £485 6s. it was assessed for the support of Captain Muir's company. Rotherham also had to quarter the entire regiment of 400 men and horses on the 23rd. Meanwhile the officers had established two zones between Rotherham and Doncaster to provide for the regiment's weekly maintenance. To the south of the River Don the officers cessed a group of twenty-five parishes centred around Maltby (including the headquarters at Tickhill). There figures exist for two weeks of the cess. In the first week the parishes provided £4,545 9s., and in the second they gave £3,653 3s. The group of thirty parishes north of the river stretched from Wentworth to Bentley, and were assessed £3,798 9s. per week. Unfortunately, there is no information about the promptness of payment nor about the subsequent increase or decrease of demands by the officers. The regiment remained quartered in this area until early May when it retired further north after the fall of Newark.[76]

Besides monetary exactions, indiscipline was another grievance the English had against the regiment. The first material on the regiment's crimes concerns the trial of the reformado officers at Thirsk. Lieutenant Colonel Munro was in command of a special regimental guard of these men. In April Lieutenant General Leslie convened a court-martial at Tickhill to try the prisoners. Colonel Fraser served on the panel of judges. Munro, however, was unable to produce several of the prisoners. In a fit of anger Leslie had him arrested. On 21 April Fraser held his own court-martial with officers of the regiment at Laughton En Le Morthen to try eight offenders. The court acquitted three men of rape and two of assault. One trooper was sentenced to death for assault and robbery. Another accused of assault had his case delayed. The eighth man, a corporal stood charged of bigamy, but failed to appear. Two weeks later the English Commissioners at Balderton, Nottinghamshire, condemned Fraser's council of war as a mockery of justice. They claimed that no witnesses had been called, although they had appeared and waited at other times for appointed courts which did not sit. The Commissioners insisted upon another trial of the offenders, because justice was not done. It is unlikely that such a trial took place. For one thing the regimental officers had already shown little respect for English wishes by illegally cessing parishes for their support. Furthermore, the regiment departed the area for the North Riding or the northeastern counties after 7 May.[77]

The regiment remained quartered in England until February 1647 when it returned to Scotland. It disbanded entirely at Kelso on the 11th. Colonel Fraser received command of a troop of horse in the New Model Army. This regiment possessed an excellent service record, however its relations with English civilians failed to gain it the reputation of being 'godly'.

Galloway Foot

Colonel: William Stewart

Lieutenant Colonel: John Gordon

Majors: Alexander Agnew (1643-44), John Gordon (1644-47)

Ministers: William Hume, Thomas Wylie, Hugh Henderson, John Macmillan[78]

The ten companies or 1,200 men and officers of this regiment were raised from the Stewartry of Kirkcudbright and Wigtownshire at the end of 1643. Both the colonel and major had experience in the continental wars. The regiment formed part of Leven's army in January 1644. In February it guarded the building of bridge across the Tyne near Newcastle. On 20 March the colonel led a party from the regiment in the storming of the South Shields Fort. It may have fought in the Hilton skirmishes on 24-25 March. The Galloway Foot remained in the northeast as part of Lumsden's force after Leven pushed on to York with the bulk of the army. It initially garrisoned Durham, but on 5 May the Committee with the Army ordered the regiment to proceed to the south side of Newcastle. On the same day the Committee made Colonel Stewart governor of Sunderland, a post which he held until 23 November. The Committee also authorised Stewart to uplift a troop of horse, of which he would be routmaster. The troop would be part of the Scots army and subject to the *Articles and Ordinances of War*. By late June the regiment had joined Leven's army at the siege of York. During the battle of Marston Moor the Galloway Foot served as part of Fairfax's infantry reserve. The regiment returned to the environs of Newcastle with the rest of the army in mid August. The men took part in the siege of Newcastle, when they had the misfortune to be the only regiment of the army to lose a chaplain to enemy action in the course of the war. The Rev. William Hume was killed by a royalist cannonball before the assault occurred. The Scottish parliament granted his widow and orphan £1,333 6s. 8d. on the recommendation of the General Assembly. At the storming of Newcastle the Galloway Foot were brigaded with the Perthshire (Gask's) Foot to take the Westgate. The colonel, lieutenant colonel and major led the ten companies of the regiment in the attack, which caused heavy losses amongst the men. Four days later Colonel Stewart was one of a panel of three to accept the paroles of the royalist common soldiers and to release them. In November the regiment quartered in county

Durham, however it left for Scotland late in the month. From 28 November to 9 December the 569 men and 100 horses of the Galloway foot quartered in Linlithgow. It is not known whether the regiment took part in any campaigns during this stay in Scotland or for how long it remained there.[79]

Sometime in the spring of 1645 the soldiers returned to England, where they stayed only briefly. On 26 June they contributed £210 to the Kelso charity. In July and August the Galloway Foot served with Leven's field army, taking part in the siege of Hereford. It is uncertain whether the regiment returned to Scotland in time for Philiphaugh, but that is doubtful. On 7 November Stewart received permission to levy 300 from Dumfriesshire, but it is uncertain if any were ever raised. It was in Scotland by mid December. On 13 December the Estates ordered the regiment to Arbroath. Three days later it was instructed to proceed to Aberdeenshire in company with viscount Kenmure's Foot. The brigade reached Aberdeen on 3 January 1646. The two regiments numbered 800 soldiers altogether. The brigade quartered entirely in the burgh until 14 or 16 April. Then it despatched 150 commanded infantry to garrison Fyvie Castle. The remaining 650 soldiers quartered in Aberdeen until 14 or 18 May, costing £7,200. It is probable that the brigade took part in Middleton's campaigns after it left Aberdeen. The whereabouts of the Galloway Foot is unknown until 9 September, when it began to quarter in East Lothian. There were then 450 soldiers in the regiment. They received an allowance from the inhabitants of 4s. per man per day until 26 November, when the charges were absorbed by the parliament. The Galloway Foot remained in the shire until 9 February 1647. The colonel received a total allowance of £624 17s. in eighty-nine days. The lieutenant colonel and major were paid £748 19s. 10d. for their maintenance during the same period. The other officers of the regiment split £35 10s. 5d. each day for their quartering allowance. On 22 January 1647 the regiment mustered only 330 common soldiers. The Estates, on 5 February, ordered Stewart to disband the regiment on the 9th. Eighty men were to be retained to form a company for the General of Artillery's Foot in the New Model Army. Stewart was also assigned a regiment in that army to be formed out of men coming out of England. One of his captains (Alexander Agnew) was to be the major of Stewart's Foot. This regiment could hardly be said to be a crack regiment of the Army of the Solemn League and Covenant, yet its behaviour both on and off the field was not notorious.[80]

Gask's Horse Troop

Routmaster: (?) Oliphant of Gask

Almost nothing is known about this unit. It was in existence by June 1646, when it numbered thirty-nine troopers. The troop undoubtedly disbanded in February 1647.[81]

Earl of Glencairn's Foot

Colonel: William, 8th earl of Glencairn

Lieutenant Colonel: James Cunningham

Major: Hugh Wallace

Ministers: Alexander Blair, William Smith, James Taylor[82]

The Committee of Estates appointed Glencairn colonel of foot for the Ayrshire and Renfrewshire levies on 16 April 1644. The regiment of three to six companies was raised from the presbyteries of Ayr and Paisley. Glencairn's Foot stayed in Scotland, spending some of the time in Kelso, until it entered England as part of Callendar's army on 25 June. Glencairn's Foot served at the siege of Newcastle, but it does not appear to have taken part in the assault. It is unknown where it quartered in the winter of 1644-45. On 1 January 1645 the regiment was back in Scotland, where it remained for the rest of its existence. On 27 February the Estates granted Glencairn the power to convene the Ayrshire and Renfrewshire Committee of War to aid him in securing deserters and filling up the deficiencies in his regiment. The Estates ordered the committee of war to levy 200 armed infantry to replace the cavalry not called out for the spring 1644 levy and to give them to Glencairn's Foot. In mid June 1645 Captain Patrick Cunningham's company of sixty men quartered in Aberdeen for four days, costing the burgh £148. On 2 July the regiment was badly mauled at Alford. A month later the officers of this and three other infantry regiments petitioned the Estates that they be placed on equal footing with other officers. The basis for their petition was the loss of all their baggage, clothing and necessities at Alford. The Estates referred to request to the Committee of Money. The remnants of the regiment were engaged at Kilsyth. On 24 January 1646 the Estates considered that the unit had ceased to exist on 15 August 1645 (the day of Kilsyth). In February 1645 Lieutenant Colonel Cunningham had paid a fine of £26 10s. for fornication in the Canongate, Edinburgh. He was the only officer of such a high rank to be arraigned for a sexual offence in Scotland during the mid 1640s. This, with the Fife (Crawford-Lindsay's) Foot, was one of the few regular regiments destroyed by Montrose.[83]

Lord Gordon's Foot

Colonels: George, Lord Gordon (1643-44), Major General Sir James Lumsden (of Innergelly) (1644-47)

Lieutenant Colonel: Sir James Lumsden (of Innergelly) (1643-44)

Majors: John Hay (1643-44), Arthur Forbes (1644-47)

Ministers: Hugh Mackail, Andrew Honeyman, William Row[84]

This regiment was more commonly known as Lumsden's Foot, because he received command of it sometime in 1644. Lumsden had served in the wars in Germany. He was made governor of Newcastle on 23 November 1644. Lord Gordon was persuaded by his uncle the marquis of Argyll to support the Covenanters in 1643. Consequently he was nominated to command a regiment of infantry from Aberdeenshire and Banffshire. Before the troubles of the late 1630s he had served in Alsace and Lorraine under Marshal de la Force. The Covenanters imprisoned him in 1639 for royalism. He was noted for being 'brave, chivalrous and popular'. Lord Gordon rejoined the royalists after Argyll's defeat at Inverlochy. However, he worked hard to recruit his regiment in the winter of 1643-44. As early as October 1643 the Aberdeenshire ministers began listing the fencible men of the shire, so that the fourth man might be levied. On 3 January 1644 Gordon called a meeting of the Aberdeenshire Committee of War to forward the recruiting of his forces. However, the earl Marischal remained absent for eight days in an effort to sabotage Gordon's endeavours. The presence of Marischal was essential for Gordon to offset the hostility of the Forbeses, Frasers and Crichtons who made up the committee. The ministers produced their lists at this meeting. On 1 February the Estates assigned Gordon 1,600 foot out of Aberdeenshire and Banffshire, which were to rendezvous at Berwick on 10 March. However, this was not the first authorisation for raising the men, for on the same day the Committee with the Army at Morpeth complained that none of the regiment was yet in England. Meanwhile in Aberdeenshire Captain William MacNab had raised sixty men for his company, including twelve from Old Aberdeen. Captains MacNab and John Forbes departed from Aberdeen on 23 February, each in command of sixty soldiers. On 4 March the committee of war held a meeting for calling out the eighth man, still the recruiting of the regiment lagged. Nevertheless Lumsden as lieutenant colonel had 302 soldiers under his command in March. They were probably divided between four companies. Until 3 April this portion of the regiment quartered in county Durham. This corresponds well with Lumsden's career as an officer in the army. On 21 February Leven had left him with six foot regiments outside Newcastle to watch the garrison. In April he left the northeast bringing ammunition to Leven's besieging army at York. Gordon's Foot accompanied him and served at Marston Moor, where it earned the reputation for being one of the three best infantry units in the army. During the battle Lumsden commanded the reserve line of the Scottish Foot. The royalists broke this line, nevertheless he and Baillie managed to form reserves out of fleeing men with which they succoured the Scots infantry's first line. This was the first and only action of the war in which this regiment is known to have fought.[85]

Meanwhile in Aberdeenshire and Banffshire the Committees of War had been doing their job. In June they brought the regiment up to strength. (This despite few recruits appearing at a muster on Aberdeen links on 4 June for the shires of Aberdeen, Banff and Moray.) The progress of these new levies to the army is easily observable. On 28 June Major Forbes with three companies was ordered to England via Haddington. His men were to receive a quartering allowance of 4s. per day. On three occasions in July Haddington quartered men of the regiment. Forbes' companies of 302 men stayed in the burgh from evening of the 4th to morning of the 5th. Captain George Innes' company of ninety-six men and officers was in the burgh from the 7th to the 8th. Finally Captain William Erskine's company of seventy-five men and officers quartered there from the 13th to the 15th. They cost the burgh £119 4s. 8d. In August Lumsden's company of sixty foot and Captain Alexander Gordon's company of 119 foot joined the regiment. Thus, by September the regiment had received further recruits of 784 men and officers and its total strength would have been between that and 1,086 of all ranks.[86]

Details of the subsequent activites of the regiment become intermittent after summer 1644. From November to December 1644, at least, the regiment quartered in county Durham. Thereafter it probably served as part of the Newcastle garrison (Lumsden having been made governor there on 23 November and being recognised by the Estates as such on 6 March 1645). Mysteriously by 31 March there were only 321 of all ranks in the regiment. This may have been due to the effects of diseases, particularly the plague, which had afflicted some of the regiments. By the end of May there were 448 officers and soldiers in the unit. The number increased to 546 foot on 30 June and reached a peak for the year on 11 August with 627 men and officers. In June or July the regiment contributed £244 18s. to the Kelso charity. In August Captain Forbes led a commanded force of fifty-eight men out of Carlisle. Despite fluctuations the regiment kept up its strength, mustering 588 men and officers on 10 December. Seven days later Lumsden wrote the Estates complaining of an increase of Independents in Newcastle amongst other things. There is no surviving response from the Estates signifying what his course of action should be against these enemies of the Covenanters. The regiment regained some of its strength in 1646. On 16 March there were 614 men and officers in it. On 22 May the number reached 647 of all ranks, where it remained for the rest of the year. In January 1647 Leven showed Lumsden a signal honour by allowing him only, of all the colonels or nobles with the army, access to the king. On the 30th between 2 p.m. and 3 p.m. Lumsden and his garrison quit Newcastle. The regiment entirely disbanded in February.[87]

Lord Gordon's Horse

Colonel: George, Lord Gordon

Major: Walter Ogilvy

On 26 November 1643 the Estates commissioned Lord Gordon the colonel of a horse regiment of eight troops. Aberdeenshire and Banffshire were to provide four troops between them; Elgin, Nairn and Inverness-shire east of the River Ness were assessed two troops altogether, and Angus was to recruit the same number. However, the act was little obeyed in the northeast due to the enmity Marischal felt for Gordon and the Committee of War's hostility to the Gordons in general. Marischal was particularly obstructive at a January 1644 meeting of the Aberdeen Committee. On 1 February the Estates changed the levying quotas. The requirement remained the same for Aberdeenshire and Banffshire (240 troopers) and Elgin *et alia* (120 troopers). However, Seaforth's portion of Inverness-shire was to provide two troops of sixty troopers each, as were Sutherland's portions of Inverness-shire and Caithness. This force of 600 horsemen was to rendezvous at Berwick on 10 March. The Committee with the Army noted on 5 March that only the Angus troops of horse had arrived in England. They wrote to the Estates ordering the rest of the regiment south and authorising an inquiry. It is uncertain what happened to the Angus horse, they were no longer part of Gordon's according to the levy requirements of 1 February. They may have been dispersed among other horse regiments or given to those officers authorised to raise troops of horse. Delays in raising the regiment persisted. Major Ogilvy's discharges for horses and men supplied by those assessed does not begin until June. By 6 July Routmaster Patrick Murray had sixty horse in his troop, which stayed the night at Haddington on the way to England. The quartering allowance for horse being 9s. per day, this visit cost the burgh £27. Major Ogilvy managed to raise only forty-eight horse for his troop by 20 August. It cost Duns £274 9s. on the 22nd and 23rd. In addition to these two troops only forty-two other troopers were raised from Aberdeenshire and Banffshire. The regiment's activities in England are unknown, presumably it served as part of the covering force at the siege of Newcastle. In the event the army had the use of the regiment only for a short time; on 20 September it was quartering in Linlithgow on the way north. The quartering charge there of £42 17s. 6d. suggests there were only about ninety troopers in the regiment. In October the regiment was under Major General Ramsay's command with Keith of Ludquharn's troop. Gordon's men were noted for spoiling the countryside. In November the regiment quartered in Banff and Moray. It may be assumed that the regiment took part in Argyll's autumn campaign, which Lord Gordon attended. In late November a woman who committed fornication with Major Ogilvy was cited to the Elgin kirk session, suggesting that part of the regiment quartered there. In February 1645 Lord Gordon defected to Montrose; the fate of his horse regiment is unknown. The Gordons and their allies among the unit probably followed him, serving at Auldearn and Alford against their former comrades. Those loyal to the Covenant were most likely disbanded or co-opted into other regiments. Lord Gordon died on the field of Alford on 2 July, a hero to the royalists and a traitor to the Covenanters.[88]

Hamilton's Horse

Colonel: Sir Frederick Hamilton

Lieutenant Colonel: Sir Patrick Mackie of Larg

Majors: Harry Drummond (1644-?), Robert Hamilton (164?-47)

Minister: James Houston[89]

Sir Frederick was an Ulster Scot with close Scottish connections. In 1643 he served as the representative of the Londonderry British to Scotland. In February 1644 he served as a Scottish commissioner to the Ulster Army with Lawers. The Committee of Estates, on 7 February, commissioned him colonel of a regiment of horse for the defence of Scotland against foreign and domestic plots. That April he commanded western Ulster British forces totalling 2,000 men. Sir Frederick was instrumental in getting the Solemn League and Covenant accepted in Londonderry town. By August Sir Frederick and his son had brought their troops of Ulster horse over to Great Britain to join the army. On 24 August the Committee with the Army authorised Sir Frederick to raise a regiment of 480 horse, consisting of his own, his son's, Larg's, Major Drummond's, Lawers', Hamilton of Preston's, Omachies', and Auchterlonie's troops. Drummond's, Lawers', and Preston's troops had been raised in spring 1644 and formed part of Callendar's army. From 4-6 August Larg's and Sir John Kilpatrick's troops numbering only forty men and officers quartered in Haddington at a cost of £106 14s. Clearly more troopers needed to be levied to bring the regiment up to strength. Unfortunately, there is no information about the unit's recruiting or its earliest activities.[90]

Although Hamilton's was part of the Army of the Solemn League and Covenant, it spent most of its service in Scotland. In September 1644 the regiment proceeded there from northeast England. Hamilton's formed part of Argyll's army in the autumn. Some of Larg's troopers stole a plaid worth £3 from a tenant in Fortrie. In September three troops (approximately 160 horsemen) quartered in Aberdeen with three troops of the earl of Dalhousie's and their women. The troopers remained three days and received an allowance for themselves and their horses of 18s. per day or £864 altogether. From 16 to 19 October the entire regiment quartered in the burgh and within the vicinity. They received 2,476 loaves of bread, seventy-five gallons of beer and ale, and eight pounds of candles from Aberdeen worth £179 13s. 4d. The lieutenant colonel's and major's troops numbering 100 horse stayed in the burgh on 3-4 November, at a cost of £90. On the 19th Larg's was in Aberdeen with Hackett's horse and Lieutenant Colonel Innes' troop. From November to March 1645 Sir Frederick's troop received £256 2s. 8d. in money, hay and oats for quartering from Coming and Newton. In November the regiment under Larg's command went into winter quarters in the presbyteries of Ellon, Deer, and Aberdeen, as part of Major General Ramsay's command of horse. Larg's men were badly supplied. The local population complained of their activities in the inquests of 1646-7. A tenant of Baird of Auchmedden had goods and clothing worth £16 6s. 8d. stolen by these troopers in December 1644. Other tenants had the troop quartered on them; one suffering theft of cloth, blankets and shirts worth £16 6s. and another had his crops destroyed in December. On 1 March 1645 the regiment mustered 294 troopers, fifty-four officers, and fifteen others in seven troops. By then Lawers' troop had left the regiment. On 10 July the Estates ordered that it be put on an equal footing with Hamilton's and Balcarres' Horse and paid as the latter, being on the same service. The Estates further authorised that Lawers' be recruited to full strength and rejoined Hamilton's. On 1 August the Estates ordered Peeblesshire to levy twenty horsement for this troop. The activities of the regiment throughout 1645 are a mystery.[91]

By the end of 1645 or at the beginning of January 1646 Hamilton's had joined the Scots army outside of Newark. On 17 January it mustered 316 horse in eight troops. Larg was absent on leave, and Sir Frederick was personally in command. Three days later the Scottish Commissioners in London wrote Lieutenant General Leslie that Retford, Nottinghamshire was two weeks behind in paying the regiment's cess. In early 1646 Sir James Campbell of Lawers was made routmaster of his late father's troop. As in 1645, the regiment's whereabouts in 1646 are unknown. The last mention of the regiment occurs on 17 February 1647 when the Estates thanked it for its good and loyal service and ordered it disbanded. The only notorious member of the regiment, Trooper William McRie, was beheaded on 5 March 1650 for a rape committed five years earlier.[92]

J. Hamilton's Horse Troop

Routmaster: Lieutenant Colonel John Hamilton

On 5 March 1644 the Committee with the Army declared that Lieutenant Colonel Hamilton of the Fife (Crawford-Lindsay's) Foot was to have a horse troop and to be made its routmaster. There is no material on the recruiting of the unit or the actions in which it took part. An account of 17 June 1645 states that Hamilton spent £7,700 on levying the regiment, which suggests it initially numbered sixty-four troopers. A muster roll of 1644x1645 states that the troop contained fifty-two troopers, four officers and four others. The only information about the troop is that it received a month and a half of pay, or £3,362 in 1645. It may be assumed that the troop disbanded in February 1647.[93]

The following information applies either to this entry or the subsequent one or partially to both. On 18 February 1646 Laurence Tyas of Derbyshire complained of quartering by a Lieutenant Colonel Hamilton's troop. He paid the lieutenant colonel £44 18s. st., then £9 st. for quartering sixty men and horses for two days, and finally a further £1 3s. 4d. st. for quartering. In the same period the town of Derby quartered sixty-seven men and eighty horses of the troop at free quarter for thirteen days. A Lieutenant Colonel Hamilton's troop was involved in a riot at Ashburne, Derbyshire. It also took part in the following exactions: £89 18s. st. from Sherland and Higham with three other troops, £54 8s. 6d. st. from Ilkeston with two other troops, £27 st. and free quarter from Holbruck with one other troop, £55 1s. 4d. st. from Crich, and £1 7s. st. from Westhallum with one other troop.[94]

W. Hamilton's Horse Troops

Routmaster: Lieutenant Colonel William Hamilton

Hamilton commanded two troops which had formerly belonged to Devereux's horse (an English regiment of which he was second in command). On 17 January 1646 the strongest troop mustered sixty troopers and four officers at Muskham, indicating that the unit was part of Leslie's besieging army at Newark. Four days later the two troops forming Hamilton's second command mustered 101 troopers. By mid August the unit had been reduced to one troop. It disbanded in or before February 1647.[95]

Innes' Horse Troop

Routmaster: Quartermaster General Robert Innes

Innes was the quartermaster general to Callendar's army. He raised his troop after the army entered England in June 1644. It is not known where the troopers were raised. There is no further mention of the troop until February 1646. On 18 February the town of Derby recorded that it had given the troop £24 17s. 8d. st. as part of four weeks' pay. The troop mustered eighty horse on the 24th. Innes' made the following exactions from Derbyshire towns: £78 9s. 7d. st. from Wentbridge with three other troops and £37 7s. 8d. st. and free quarters from Derby with one other troop. The only campaign which the troop is known to have served on was that against Newark. It disbanded entirely in February 1647.[96]

Viscount Kenmure's Foot

Colonel: Robert, 4th viscount Kenmure

Lieutenant Colonel: (?) Fraser

Major: Alexander Leslie

Ministers: John Dixon, James Ferguson[97]

On 15 April 1644 the Estates ordered the General of Artillery or his deputy to deliver 600 muskets and 300 pikes to viscount Kenmure for the use of the Stewarty of Kirkcudbright. The next day the Estates appointed Kenmure colonel of foot for the Stewarty and the non-Cassillis part of Wigtonshire. The regiment was raised from these two shires and one company was levied in Annandale. It entered England as part of Callendar's army. During the siege of

Newcastle the regiment guarded a bridge of boats, which ensured communication between the besieging forces. There is no information about the unit's winter quarters in 1644-45. The regiment quartered in Linlithgow from 29 May to 29 June 1645. During this time it contributed £260 to the Kelso charity. Kenmure's later returned to England for the summer campaign against Hereford. During that siege it was brigaded with the Galloway Foot. In the autumn Kenmure's again returned to Scotland and fought against Montrose. On 7 November it was allowed 200 recruits from Dumfriessshire, which may have never been raised. From 13-19 December the 400 men of the regiment quartered in the burgh of Perth. The Estates initially ordered the unit to Montrose for winter quarters on the 15th. However, on the next day it was ordered to march to Aberdeenshire with the Galloway Foot. The two regiments under the command of Lieutenant Colonel Fraser quartered in Aberdeen from 3 January to 16 April 1646. The 800 men of these regiments cost the burgh £28,500. From 14x16 April to 14 May 650 men of the two regiments stayed in Aberdeen at a charge of £7,200. The other 150 men served as the garrison of Fyvie Castle. Kenmure's probably remained in the northeast under Middleton's command until sometime in the summer. By 10 August half of the regiment was quartered in Selkirk with Barclay's Horse. Kenmure's remained in Scotland over the winter of 1646-47. On 5 February 1647 the Estates ordered all but fifty-three men of the regiment to disband on the 9th. The remnant were to form part of the General of Artillery's Foot in the New Model Army.[98]

Lord Kirkcudbright's Horse

Colonel: Thomas, 2nd Lord Kirkcudbright

Lieutenant Colonels: James Mercer of Aldie (1643-46), (?) Agnew (1646-47)

Majors: Alexander Crook (1643-44), (?) Agnew (1644), Andrew Gray (1644-47)

Ministers: John Govan, Andrew Kirk, Alexander Balnaves[99]

On 26 November 1643 The Convention of Estates commissioned Kirkcudbright to raise a regiment of horse. He was to have four troops from Perthshire, two from the Stewarty of Kirkcudbright and Wigtonshire, and two from Dumfriesshire. The regiment entered England in January 1644 as part of Leven's army. At the battle of Corbridge on 19 February the seven troops forming the regiment were under the overall command of Lieutenant Colonel Bannatyne of Leven's Horse. Bannatyne led the horse in two successful charges against Sir Marmaduke Langdale's twenty-five horse troops and 300-400 musketeers. A third charge was unsuccessful, but in their retreat the Covenanter horse defeated Colonel Robert Brandling's ten troops of horse, which had been sent to take them in the rear. Major Agnew of this regiment fell prisoner. On 7 May the Committee with the Army sent a letter to the Committee of Estates in favour of Kirkcudbright recruiting his regiment to full strength. The unit went with Leven to York and served on the left wing of the allied cavalry under Major General Leslie. During the siege of Newcastle the regiment advanced into Cumbria at least once. From November 1644 to July/August 1645 Kirkcudbright's Horse was in Cumbria. During the siege of Carlisle Kirkcudbright commanded the Stanwick siege work. On 16 May at 9 a.m. he advanced from Stanwick with 300 horse to attack musketeers of the garrison, who were protecting their cattle. The fire of the royalists forced them to retreat, then the royalist horse chased Kirkcudbright's men from the field. In late May/early June 1645 Kirkcudbright became the centre of a dispute which showed the fragile nature of the Covenanter-parliamentarian alliance. Kirkcudbright ordered Lieutenant Colonel Beecher, of Sir Wilfred Lawson's Foot, to remove his men from Botcherby Mount near Carlisle, where they had quartered all winter. When the English did not move, Kirkcudbright appeared with 300 commanded men out of Newcastle to take possession of Beecher's sconces. Then Beecher persuaded Kirkcudbright to wait until Lawson was notified. The colonel said Beecher should stay put. The next day, a Sunday, Kirkcudbright ordered Beecher out again, claiming he was commander-in-chief of the besieging forces. Beecher replied that Lawson commanded the English in Cumberland and demanded to see a commission. Kirkcudbright said Beecher was saucy and promised to capture the works. Beecher tried to dissuade him by saying that bloodshed might ensue, but Kirkcudbright said he would welcome that. An order then arrived from Lawson telling Beecher to stay. Kirkcudbright subsequently surrounded the works with 300 foot and three troops of horse. That continued until 9 a.m. Monday morning when Lawson appeared and Kirkcudbright withdrew. Lawson ordered Beecher to Appleby to meet Leven, who received him well. The Lord General promised he would act favourably. Colonel William Stewart (Galloway Foot) then entertained Beecher and told him that Leven was angry with Kirkcudbright. The next day Leven held a conference with Kirkcudbright, Lawson, Beecher, and Richard Barwis, a parliamentarian commissioner. Kirkcudbright now saw that things were running against him, so he charged Becher with being anti-Covenanter. However, the lieutenant colonel retorted by saying that he had taken the Covenant twice. In the end Kirkcudbright failed to gain control of the English positions. The location and activities of the regiment is unknown for several weeks after the fall of Carlisle on 28 June.[100]

The regiment continued to be actively engaged in both England and Scotland after the incident with Beecher. On 13 September 1645 Kirkcudbright's formed part of the victorious Covenanter army at Philiphaugh. In October eight troops of the regiment went to Aberdeen with Coupar's, Fraser's, and Montgomery's cavalry under Major General Middleton. The 350 troopers of Kirkcudbright's Horse remained in the burgh and shire for four days before heading further north to Banff. On the way south it remained in the burgh for twenty-four hours. On 7 November it was assigned quarters around the Bridge of Earn. Two weeks later it was ordered to cease quartering in Fife. By 16 December the regiment was back in Aberdeen, but the Estates ordered it to England via Mearns and Angus. A party of twenty-six commanded horse had reached the forces besieging Newark by 17 January 1646. The remainder of the regiment returned to Cumbria to find quarters. On 11 May Leven, writing from Boroughbridge, Yorkshire, told Kirkcudbright or Lieutenant Colonel Agnew to bring the horse in Cumberland to the army in northeast England immediately. They were to march peaceably, keeping good order, and to avoid causing grievances. Thus, there was to be no extortion of money, or plundering, nor were the men 'to do wrong whatsoever'. In May or June Lieutenant Colonel Mercer of Aldie received command as colonel of the four Perthshire troops, leaving Kirkcudbright with only four troops in his regiment. The regiment seems to have returned to Scotland sometime in late 1646. On 5 February 1647 the Estates ordered Kirkcudbright to disband all save twenty troopers for the New Model Army on the 10th. The next day the Estates set the payment of nearly £13,000 of arrears due the regiment. While the regiment undoubtedly disbanded at this time, a local history maintains that John, 3rd Lord Kirkcudbright took it to Ireland, where on 6 December 1649 parliamentarian forces attacked the regiment at Lisnegarvy and nearly destroyed it.[101]

Kyle and Carrick Foot

Colonel: John, 6th earl of Cassillis

Lieutenant Colonel: John Kennedy

Major: Archibald Houston (1643-46)

Ministers: Alexander Turnbull, Patrick Colville[102]

The earl of Cassillis was commissioned the colonel of the central and southern Ayrshire forces in August 1643. This area raised ten companies which were at Dalkeith on 14 January 1644. The Kyle and Carrick entered England as part of Leven's army five days later. In early 1644 it heavily burdened Henry Hinde of The Stelling, Bywell Peter, Northumberland. The regiment took thirty-one cattle worth £46 10s. st., sixty sheep worth £15 st., five swine costing £1 5s. st., forty foother of hay valued at £20 st., three horses at £6 st., a bible worth 13s. st. and other goods amounting in total to £215 5s. st. Major Houston received £3 8s. st. in cess and billeting. The Kyle and Carrick Foot served with Leven up to the siege of York and Marston Moor. At the latter it was one of the three second-line Scottish infantry regiments which held its ground. The regiment was brigaded with the Nithsdale Foot with which it cleared the royalist foot placed in a ditch in front of the allied line. After Marston Moor and the fall of York the Kyle and Carrick returned to the Newcastle vicinity to take part in the siege. On 24 August the garrison made a successful sortie against the portion of the siegeworks held by this unit and the Nithsdale Foot. The royalists forced the Scots to flee, because the Covenanting officers were absent. The regiment went to Scotland shortly thereafter to serve under Lieutenant General Baillie. It stayed in Aberdeen for ten days in September, when there were 700 men in the unit. On 19 October the Kyle and Carrick Foot formed part of the 3rd Brigade, whose target was the Pilgrim Street Gate-Cariol Tower area. Cassillis personally led about seven companies of the regiment in the storming operation. Although the Kyle and Carrick probably spent some of the winter of 1644-45 in England, it returned to Scotland before the spring arrived.[103]

From spring 1645 until it disbanded this regiment served as part of the home army. In late March Cassillis and his men were with Baillie near Brechin. On 2 and 3 April the 800 men of the regiment quartered in Perth. A party of 160 commanded men returned to the burgh on the 4th. They may have taken part in the pursuit of Montrose from Dundee on 5 April. From 14 June (Saturday) in the evening to the 18th at 2 p.m. Lieutenant Colonel Kennedy was in command of 700 men of the Kyle and Carrick in Aberdeen. They cost the burgh £560. Before then the regiment probably formed part of Baillie's army. The Kyle and Carrick was certainly with Baillie after the 18th, if it had not been beforehand. On 2 July the regiment was badly mauled at Alford. The officers later joined in a petition with those of other regiments for replacement of baggage, clothing and necessities lost at the battle. On 1 August the Estates decided to recruit the regiment back to full strength. Wigtonshire and the Stewarty of Kirkcudbright received orders to levy 600 foot; Ayrshire and Renfrewshire were assessed 200 foot. Due to Montrose's victory at Kilsyth two weeks later, it is doubtful that any of these reinforcements reached the regiment. The whereabouts of the regiment for six months is not known. However, in November 1645 it was assigned several hundred recruits from Galloway. In February 1646 it was serving under Middleton in the northeast. Some men took grain worth 23s. from a tenant in Turriff. It may be assumed that the Kyle and Carrick served under Middleton in his campaigns against Montrose. The regiment is found quartered in Glasgow on 18 December. Due to the plague, on 14 January 1647 the Estates ordered the regiment to be quartered in barns and outbuildings of Glasgow. It was to muster its men every ten days and not to lift cess or live on free quarter but on the money provided. On 4 February the unsatisfactory state of these arrangements comes to light through a petition of the regimental officers for £2,000 owed them by the burgh of Glasgow. (This was paid on 20 February.) On the 5th the Estates ordered the regiment to disband on 9 February. That day all, save fifty foot which were retained for the General of Artillery's Foot in the New Model Army, were disbanded.[104]

Earl of Lanark's Foot

Colonel: William, earl of Lanark

Lieutenant Colonels: (?) Cunningham (1644), William Scott (1645)

Majors: Thomas Weir (1644), James Somerville (1645)

Ministers: John Colin/Collins, Matthew McConle, James Home[105]

The Estates commissioned the earl of Lanark colonel of a Lanarkshire regiment of foot on 16 April 1644. Parliament supplied the men with 1,000 muskets, 500 pikes and 200 swords. The bulk of his men came from the presbyteries of Glagow and Paisley. The regiment entered England on 25 June as part of Callendar's army. In the summer of 1644 Lanark's garrisoned Hartlepool. However, part of the regiment joined the besiegers of Newcastle. On the afternoon of 20 August a Newcastle garrison sortie captured Major Weir. There is no sign that the regiment took part in the assault on Newcastle. On 23 October Leven ordered two companies to quarter for the winter in Hartlepool, Stockton and the nearest villages with the Stirlingshire Foot under the command of Lord Livingstone. The winter quarters of the remainder of the regiment are unknown. By February 1645 the entire regiment was in Scotland. On 27 February the Estates ordered 200 foot of the regiment to be made along with Orchardton's company into dragoons. Lanark's fought at Alford, where it was apparently destroyed. Although the officers joined in a petition on 7 August for the baggage, clothing and necessities lost at the battle, there is no mention of the regiment after that.[106]

Earl of Lanark's Horse

Colonel: William earl of Lanark

Lieutenant Colonel: William Lockhart

Major: Francis Forbes

Minister: Matthew McKail[107]

On 16 April 1644 the Estates appointed Lanark the colonel of the Lanarkshire horse. The regiment consisted of both horsemen and dragoons. By early May part if not all of the regiment, six troops of horse and two companies of dragoons, had been raised. From 10 to 30 May the troops of Routmasters Calhoun and Carmichael quartered in Dumfries. Calhoun's troop occupied Caerlaverock Castle from 14 August to 8 October. Meanwhile, the rest of the regiment had entered England as part of Callendar's army. Like many other units Lanark's virtually disappeared for months. It re-emerged from the fog of war in September 1645, when it served with Leslie at Philiphaugh. Lanark personally captured Sir Robert Spottiswood, son of a former archbishop of St. Andrews and a royalist. On 20 September the regiment arrived in Glasgow, which was cessed £73 14s. per day for the staff officers. In 1645 or 1646 Lanark's served on a campaign in the northeast. The tenants of the earl of

Erroll, Lord Coupar, Stewart of Ardoch, and Archibald Thompson suffered from plundering of food and money and from quartering. The regiment was promised 200 new dragoons from Clydesdale on 7 November. The same day it was given quarters within ten miles of Glasgow in Clydesdale and Lennox. Sometime in November/December Cornet Calhoun led a commanded party of twenty troopers to Newark, which he reached on 11 December. It is not known when, if ever, this party returned to the regiment quartered in Scotland. On 16 December the Estates issued orders regarding the quartering of the regiment. Two troops of horse and the two companies of dragoons were to stay in Ayrshire, two troops were to quarter in Renfrewshire, and two troops were to remain in Lanarkshire. The Committees of War would appoint the quartering grounds. On 17 April 1647 the Ayrshire heritors petitioned the Committee of Estates concerning the troops of horse quartered. They stated that the two troops had been there since December 1646 with Argyll's Foot. They requested that the horse be removed. As Lanark had no command in the New Model Army, this regiment must have been disbanded shortly after the petition reached Edinburgh.[108]

Lawers' Horse Troop

Routmasters: Colonel Sir Mungo Campbell of Lawers (1644-45), Colonel Sir James Campbell of Lawers (1646-47)

There is no surviving commission for this troop, however recruiting for it probably did not begin before Lawers returned to Scotland in February 1644. The source of the troopers is unascertainable, as is the length of time required to levy them. On 7 June the Estates ordered a Major Fraser to muster the troop on Bruntsfield Links, Edinburgh. William Thompson, a commissary of the Army, was then to provide the men with a month's pay. The troop entered England on 25 June as part of Callendar's army. On 24 August the Committee with the Army ordered the troop to be incorporated into Hamilton's Horse. However, the troop regained its independent existence sometime between August 1644 and July 1645. On 10 July the Estates ordered that the troop be put on equal footing with Hamilton's and Balcarres' Horse and it was to paid as the latter, having seen the same service. The unit was to be recruited to full strength and re-united with Hamilton's Horse. After 5 January 1646 Sir James Campbell replaced his late father as official commander of the troop. For the disbanding of this unit see Hamilton's Horse.[109]

Leslie's Horse

Colonel: Major General (later Lieutenant General) David Leslie

Lieutenant Colonels: Sir John Brown (of Fordel) (1643-45), Thomas Craig (of Riccarton) (1645-47)

Majors: Thomas Craig (of Riccarton), William Oliphant, Alexander Dickson, William Stewart (d. 1645)

Ministers: William Kinninmonth, Robert Bennet, Alexander Moncrieffe, William Turnbull, Robert Traill[110]

In the summer of 1643 Colonel David Leslie, a veteran of the Swedish army's campaigns in Germany, returned to his homeland. On 28 July the Convention of Estates decided he should remain in Scotland for the public service. The Estates arranged a retaining fee for Leslie of £6,000 per annum for three years. On 26 November Leslie was commissioned colonel of a horse regiment of eight troops. (By January 1644 the Estates would make him Major General of Horse for the army.) Three of his troops had been raised in the summer. On 22 August Sir John Brown, Thomas Craig of Riccarton, and William Stewart, Master of Ochiltree, received commissions to raise horse troops by 13 September. From 26 November these troops became part of Leslie's Horse. The laird of Polmais, Stirlingshire, was to raise another troop. The origins of the other four troops are undiscoverable. Besides the colonel, both Lieutenant Colonel Brown and Major Craig were veterans of the European wars. This was one of the few regiments in the army to have a chaplain ordained specifically for its use. On 11 January 1644 Leslie and Quartermaster General Ludovick Leslie approached the presbytery of Edinburgh asking that William Kinninmonth be granted permission to serve as chaplain. The presbytery agreed as he had already passed his trials before it and the presbytery of Cupar. On the 12th Kinninmonth was ordained following a sermon he delivered before the two Leslies, Leven, Major Craig and other regimental officers. The regiment was now ready to commence active service.[111]

Leslie's Horse had an active military career both in England and Scotland. The regiment entered England as part of Leven's army, serving at the York siege. At Marston Moor Leslie commanded the three regiments of Scots horse, including his own (about 800 troopers), which supported Cromwell's Ironsides on the extreme left of the allied line. Early in the action against Prince Rupert's horse Leslie commanded the entire wing of horse, because Cromwell had to retire to have a wound dressed. After their forces had shattered Rupert's men, Cromwell and Leslie led the left wing horse between Wilstrop Wood and the infantry action to challenge Lord Goring's (left wing) horse on the ground from which the royalists had initially charged. The allied horse again routed the royalists, leaving only Newcastle's Whitecoats in active opposition to the allied forces. These infantrymen ensconced themselves in White Sike Close. The first charges of Cromwell's and Leslie's troopers proved ineffective. However, Fraser's Dragoons punched a hole in the royalist pikemen, allowing the allied horse to break and slaughter the Whitecoats. (Only forty of these men surrendered unwounded.) After this battle and the fall of York the regiment moved to Doncaster with the rest of the army to recuperate. On 1 August Leslie led his own and two other regiments of horse, and one of dragoons north to aid Callendar in the siege of Newcastle. From 1 September to 7 October Leslie made his first incursion into Cumbria with seven cavalry regiments, probably including his own. After the 7th and until 9 November Leslie retained two regiments of horse in Cumbria. Following the reduction of forces in the area in October, Leslie with Richard Barwis, a parliamenterian burgess of Carlisle, led 800 horse against Carlisle. Leslie ordered Colonels Sir Wilfred Lawson and (?) Chomedley to raise Cumbria for the parliament. The major general then returned to Newcastle, where he remained for a month before returning with three regiments of horse (including his own), one of dragoons and one of foot. Then he commenced building siegeworks at Newtown to the west of Carlisle. He made his headquarters at Little Dalston, four miles southwest of the city. The siege continued throughout the winter of 1644-5. On 8 March 1645 the Estates promoted Leslie to the rank of lieutenant general of horse. In March Leslie received command of three horse regiments and 2,000 commanded foot with which he was to join Sir William Brereton in Cheshire. Brereton received his Scottish reinforcements only for a few weeks (1 March-1 April), but the Scots remained separate from the English forces. By early May Leslie was again with the forces besieging Carlisle. The garrison surrendered to him personally on 25 June; three days later the Scots entered. On 30 June Leslie contributed £12 to the Kelso charity; there is no record of a gift by his regiment. In July Leslie with his cavalry joined Leven's army on the march to Hereford. The lieutenant general remained only a short time at this siege. Due to rumours of the king bringing an army in relief of the city, Leslie led 4,500-5,000 cavalry eastwards to intercept him on 12 August. On the 14th this force was at Stourbridge, on the 15th it reached Uttoxeter, the next day it rendezvoused with 1,600 horse under Sir John Gell at Ollerton. Five days later Leslie was at Rotherham, and Poyntz with parliamentarian forces was on Doncaster Moor. Hearing of Montrose's tremendous victory at Kilsyth, Leslie left the English to screen Leven's army and advanced northwards. On the 29th he was at Northallerton, from there he went to Newcastle and Berwick before arriving on the field of Philiphaugh early in the morning of 13 September. The story of that battle has been told many times and need be reiterated here. Suffice to say that Leslie's superior knowledge of the enemy, tactical skills and vastly greater numbers gave him a victory which destroyed Montrose's army. Afterwards Leslie's Horse advanced towards St. Andrews, Glasgow, the Carse of Gowrie and Forfar, from where it reached Aberdeenshire in October. Major Stewart had a tenant's house timbers burnt in Turriff. Troopers stole food from Stewart of Ardoch and his tenants and also from tenants in Easter Seggiden. Forty-two men of the regiment quartered on Haldane of Gleneagles' estates, where they destroyed crops and stole a horse. On 30 October the Committee of Estates passed an act awarding Leslie with a gift of £6,666 13s. 4d. and the following day it commissioned the purchase of a jewel worth £7,200 for him. The regiment was ordered south the same day and it reached England by late November, where it served at the siege of Newark. After Leven returned to Scotland during the siege, Leslie became commander-in-chief of the Scottish forces there. Thus, the regiment saw its last active service during the siege.[112]

Compared with earlier years, there is little information on the regiment in 1646. On 19 January the regiment mustered 538 horse and seventy dragoons. That spring Charles I sent Leslie a letter asking him to receive the king in the Scottish army. However, Leslie refused to accept the letter, which impressed his fellow Covenanters. After Charles reached the Scottish army, lacking an understanding with either the earl of Lothian or Leslie, this regiment moved northwards into Durham or Northumberland, where it remained until late January 1647. In either late December 1646 or early January 1647 Bellièvre, the French ambassador with the Scottish army, tried to bribe Leslie into supporting the king. He offered Leslie a title (duke of Orkney), with an annual pension of £75,600, captaincy of the king of England's Guards, with another annual pension of £25,200, and the honour of being a knight of the Garter. Leslie refused these impressive gifts, saying agreement on religion (by which he meant establishment of presbyterianism in England) was essential before he would aid Charles I. Probably as a recognition of his loyalty the Estates made Leslie lieutenant general of the New Model Army. He was also appointed commander of a staff troop of horse in the army. On 25 February 1647 the Estates allowed Leslie to retain his dragoon company for the New Model and to recruit seventy men. Leslie and his regiment departed from England between 30 January and 11 February. On the 11th at Kelso he disbanded the army's cavalry units.[113] Leslie and Lieutenant Colonel Craig probably selected men from this regiment for their troops in the New Model.

Leslie's Horse Troop

Routmaster: Quartermaster General Ludovick Leslie

Ludovick Leslie was a Scottish mercenary who had served on the continent. In late 1643 the Covenanters made him quartermaster general of the army. He entered England with Leven in January 1644. By 1 March 1645 he was governor of Tynemouth Castle and colonel of Aytoun's Foot. There is no information regarding the raising of his troop. By late November 1645 it was part of the besieging army at Newark. On 17 January 1646 the troop mustered eighty troopers (six absent) and four officers. It cannot be ascertained where the troop quartered after the withdrawal from the vicinity of Newark in early May. By 1 July it was in Northumberland, where it remained until 15 August. From 19 August to 15 November, at least, it quartered in both Northumberland and Westmorland. Leslie withdrew from Tynemouth Castle on 30 January 1647. It may be assumed that his troop evacuated England shortly thereafter. The unit disbanded on 11 February with the rest of the Scottish cavalry not retained for the New Model Army.[114]

Earl of Leven's Horse

Colonels: Lord General Alexander, 1st earl of Leven (1643-45), Alexander Lord Balgonie (1645), Robert Stewart (1646-47)

Lieutenant Colonels: James Ballatyne/Bannatyne (of Corehouse) (1643-45), Sir Robert Adair of Kinhilt (1647-47)

Majors: Sir Robert Adair of Kinhilt (1643-45), (?) Crook (1646-47)

Ministers: William Jamieson, Archibald Porteous, Frederick Carmichael, John Moncrieffe, John Hogg, James Scott, James Simpson, David Forret, John Duncan[115]

Sometime between late August and 26 November 1643 the Convention of Estates authorised the raising of two troops of horse, which formed the foundation for this regiment. Leven was also commissioned the Lord General of the army during the same period. On 26 November Leven received permission to withdraw his Life Guard of Horse (under Bannatyne of Corehouse) and Kinhilt's troop from Ulster. The Life Guards certainly reached Scotland by January 1644. However, Kinhilt's troop may not have joined the regiment until 1646. The other four troops or 240 troopers were to be raised by Teviotdale, Selkirkshire, and Peeblesshire. The regiment consisted of seven troops when it entered England on 19 January 1644. It was first engaged at Corbridge on 19 February. Lieutenant Colonel Bannatyne commanded the fifteen Scottish horse troops which were involved in the skirmish. He led two successful charges against Sir Marmaduke Langdale's 300-400 musketeers and twenty-five troops of horse. The royalists repulsed the third charge, however the retreat of the Scots worked to their advantage. Bannatyne's force ran directly into ten troops of royalist horse under Colonel Robert Brandling, which had been sent to take the Scots in the rear. The Scottish charge swept Brandling's force from the field, saving themselves from disaster. The regiment subsequently moved south into Yorkshire with the bulk of the army, and was present at the siege of York. On 5 June Leven led the regiment against a fort near Skelders Gate in the evening. The troopers, presumably dismounted, took the fort, causing 120 royalist casualties. Leven marshalled the allied army at Marston Moor because of his experience in the continent. However, soon after the battle began he fled to Leeds, believing the initial allied setbacks presaged a total defeat. Inexplicably Lord Balgonie commanded the regiment during the battle. Leven's Horse began the battle as part of Fairfax's horse reserve, where it was deployed in two squadrons. Following the defeat of Fairfax's force by Lord Goring's horse, the regiment found itself separated by royalist forces. The advanced squadron of Leven's, which was armed with lances, charged a royalist foot regiment, routing it. Then it and the other squadron, using two different routes, rode to the left wing allied horse. They arrived in time to be involved in attacks on Goring's horse and Newcastle's Whitecoats. There is no mention of the regiment for nearly a year. In November Leven returned to Scotland for the winter, however he was back in England by March 1645.[116]

Although there is no information on the regiment for much of 1645, it can be reasonably assumed that Leven's accompanied the field army from March, when it was in Yorkshire. On 30 June Leven contributed £120 to the Kelso charity, but there was nothing given by the regiment. Leven was always a loyal Covenanter. An example of his allegiance was his refusal to join in the royalist plots of summer 1645, in which his lieutenant general, the earl of Callendar, was involved. The regiment was present at the siege of Hereford from 30 July to 12 August, when it began a month long advance to the field of Philiphaugh with Leslie's force of cavalry. Despite being ordered south on 31 October the regiment remained in Scotland until December 1645, when it returned to England and the field army outside of Newark. There is no evidence that this regiment was engaged in the northeast under Major General Middleton. The one surviving muster of this regiment on 17 January 1646 shows that the eight troops possessed 539 men and officers. Although the information is lacking, it is probable that the regiment quartered in the two northeastern counties from May 1646 to February 1647. It evacuated England then and largely disbanded on 11 February at Kelso. Leven was rewarded for his loyalty by being appointed Lord General of the New Model Army, although he never took the field again. He was provided with a staff troop of horse from men who may have belonged to his regiment.[117]

Earl of Leven's Life Guards of Horse

Routmaster: Lieutenant Colonel James Bannatyne (of Corehouse)

Although Leven possessed a Life Guard of Horse in the Ulster Army, which was brought over to Scotland, it was not used as his Life Guards in the Army of the Solemn League and Covenant. Instead a new troop was raised for the earl's protection. On 24 December 1643 Carnock in the presbytery of Dunfermline selected nine men for Leven's bodyguard. It is probable that other parishes in Fife recruited men for the troop. This unit entered England on 19 January 1644 and accompanied Leven on all the subsequent campaigns. It was part of Bannatyne's cavalry force at the skirmish of Corbridge. This unit may have fled with the earl at Marston Moor. It is uncertain whether it accompanied Leslie's force of cavalry back to Scotland in August 1645. The troop was definitely part of the besieging army at Newark, when it numbered 102 horsemen. On 3 February 1646 a commanded party of the troop convoyed money for the Scottish army from Nottingham to the headquarters at Southwell. On the 27th the English parliamentary commissioners with the army announced that the muster of 17 January had included ten men of the Derbyshire horse. However, there is no sign of the officers being disciplined for this infraction of the muster rules. After the withdrawal from the Newark area, the troop eventually quartered in Northumberland. The last definite mention of the troop occurred on 5 January 1647, when the widow of the routmaster petitioned the Estates for £4,800 in arrears. The troop left England in late January and disbanded at Kelso on 12 February.[118]

Linlithgow and Tweeddale Foot

Colonel: John, Master of Yester

Lieutenant Colonel: William Johnston

Majors: William Hamilton (1643-44), William Lisle/Lyell (1645), Alexander Dickson (1646-47)

Ministers: James Simson, Patrick Fleming, John Hay[119]

After receiving a commission in late August 1643, the Master of Yester raised the ten companies of his regiment from West Lothian (principally the presbytery of Linlithgow) and upper Tweeddale (particularly from Peebles presbytery). He selected a professional soldier for his lieutenant colonel. On 15 January 1644 the Linlithgowshire companies of the regiment were in Midlothian. Four days later the regiment entered England as part of Leven's army. Yester's was first engaged in combat on 20 March, when Lieutenant Colonel Johnston led a commanded party in the attack against the South Shields Fort. The regiment served at the siege of York and at the battle of Marston Moor, where it was brigaded with the Stirlingshire Foot in the Scottish infantry's second line. After Marston Moor the Linlithgow and Tweeddale accompanied the rest of the army to Leeds, where it remained until 7 August, reaching the outskirts of Newcastle on the 15th. The regiment formed part of the 3rd Brigade, whose target area was the wall between Pilgrim Street Gate and Carliol Tower, at the storming of Newcastle. It is not possible to determine where the regiment kept its winter quarters after the fall of the town. However, it remained in England on garrison duty during 1645. Twenty-four men of the regiment, for instance, guarded Warkworth Castle. From 27 July until 27 August Captain William Johnston, with Captain Scott of Cranstoun's, led a commanded party of about sixty foot to Carlisle. On 10 July the men of the unit contributed £197 8s. to the Kelso charity fund. On 12 August a commanded party of 180 men departed from England for service against Montrose. The Committee of Estates assigned the regiment 300 recruits from Midlothian on 7 November. The first indication of the size of the regiment does not occur until 10 November, when it contained 299 officers and men. It went to 367 of all ranks on the 19th, rising to 429 men and officers on 20 December. At the end of January 1646 the regiment had increased to 516 soldiers and officers (probably indicating the return of part of the commanded men), and its strength continued to grow. On 15 July the regiment contained 632 of all ranks and on 11 August it reached a high of 686 soldiers and officers, which it retained until the regiment evacuated England in late January 1647. From late 1644 Captain William Leslie commanded a garrison of 24-66 soldiers in Warkworth Castle. The regiment disbanded entirely sometime after 12 February.[120]

Lockhart's Horse Troop

Routmaster: Alan Lockhart

The first mention of Lockhart is a reference to his being a reformado from 28 April to 19 May 1645. On the 21st he received £108 to cover his expenses for riding from the Scots army at Ripon to Sir William Brereton in Cheshire. The troop was on foot by August, however the source of its recruits is not ascertainable. The troop served as part of the field army at Newark, receiving (or taking) its supplies from Derbyshire. The regiment made the following exactions in late 1645 and early 1646 from that shire: £45 7s. 6d. st. and free quarter with three other troops from Sutton and Duckmanton, £25 5s. st. and free quarter from Beighton with one other troop, and £104 18s. 3d. st. from Barlborough. On 30 January 1646 the troop consisted of thirty-six horsemen. Lockhart must have been a good horseman because the army sent him to London on public business in May. He received £276 for his expenses on that occasion. There is no further mention of the troop after August, nor is there any other reference to its quartering area. It must be assumed that the troop departed from England in late January 1647 and disbanded at Kelso on 11 February.[121]

Loudoun-Glasgow Foot

Colonel: John, 1st earl of Loudoun

Lieutenant Colonel: Robert Home

Majors: John Haldane (1643-44), Alexander Dickson (1645-47)

Minister: Ninian Campbell[122]

This unit was also known as the Chancellor's regiment, because Loudoun was Lord Chancellor of Scotland. He received his commission in late August 1643. Both the lieutenant colonel and major had served with European armies. The men were recruited primarily from the presbyteries of Glasgow and Paisley. The regiment contained the usual ten companies. On 15 January 1644 it was quartered at Selkirk, and entered England four days later. The regiment remained with Leven's main field army after 21 February, serving at Hilton and the siege of York. At Marston Moor Loudoun's Foot was brigaded with the Tweeddale Foot in the Scotish infantry reserve. It saw little action and was routed by the left wing royalist horse. On 10 July a bailie of Peebles apprehended a deserter from Captain Sinclair's company. He and other deserters were ordered back to York, if they refused they were to be executed. The regiment proceeded to Doncaster and Leeds with the army after the fall of York. It returned to the Newcastle area in mid August and took part in the siege.

Loudoun's possessed its own siege battery in the line of circumvallation. The Loudoun Foot was again coupled with the Tweeddale Foot as part of the 1st Brigade in the storming of Newcastle on 19 October. The lieutenant colonel and major led the regiment into the Closegate breach, where it suffered moderate casualties. As with many other regiments it is impossible to determine where it spent the winter of 1644-5. As of 31 January 1645 the regiment mustered 895 men and officers. By early March most of the unit had left for Scotland. From 30 April to 30 May there were 114 sick soldiers of the regiment in England. They apparently recovered and formed two companies which remained in England until the army evacuated the country in early 1647. The size of these companies fluctuated between 114 and 151 soldiers, finally settling at 134 men. Leaving the two companies in England, it is now possible to concentrate on the major part of the regiment.[123]

Eight companies of Loudoun's served in Scotland from 15 March 1645 to February 1647. In late March 1645 the regiment was under Lieutenant General Baillie near Brechin. On the 31st the 800 men and officers of the regiment entered Perth, remaining until 3 April. After the pursuit of Montrose following his capture of Dundee (5-6 April), in which this unit may have taken part, the regiment was ordered to serve under Major General Urry. A significant portion of the regiment was detached to garrison service. Urry proceeded to Aberdeen with his force, entering it on 11 April. This regiment quartered with Lothian's (Irish) Foot in New Aberdeen. The regiments received forty days' free quarter from the burgh, which represented the sum of £645 10s. for this regiment. The two regiments split a loan of six days' quartering allowance (6s. per man per day), totalling £2,880 (suggesting there were 1,544 recipients), which the burgh was forced to provide. On the 15th the Chancellor's and Hackett's Horse left Aberdeen, but Lothian's men mutinied, forcing the others to quarter in Old Aberdeen for three days. Urry's force finally departed from Aberdeen on 18 April. On 11 February 1647 Lieutenant Colonel Home acknowledged a quartering receipt for this period for 500 soldiers, although the burgh claimed there were 700 men. It seems more likely that the lower figure should be accepted as it is substantiated by another source and the burgh was trying to represent as bad a picture as possible of the exactions it suffered. Urry's force moved north to Inverness, where it gained a large reinforcement. On the evening of 8 May he marched out against Montrose's army encamped at Auldearn. This regiment was present at the battle on the 9th, from which it probably escaped with heavy losses. The regiment returned to the north central part of Scotland sometime in the ensuing weeks. On 1 August the Estates ordered that Midlothian and Peeblesshire provide 200 recruits each and that Ayrshire and Renfrewshire raise another 600 men to replace the regiment's losses. It is unknown whether any of these men reached the regiment by the 15th, the day of Kilsyth. At that battle the Loudoun-Glasgow held the left of the front line adjacent to Home's Foot. These two regiments were ordered to hold their ground; instead they advanced against the Macleans positioned opposite them in enclosures. The Covenanters wasted much shot, but eventually they came to grips with the royalists. Clanranald reinforced the Macleans, and both regiments charged the Covenanters. The fiercest fighting of the battle took place here before the two Covenanter regiments broke and fled. The losses suffered at Kilsyth effectively destroyed the regiment. Nothing was heard of it again until 31 January 1646 when the officers petitioned the Estates for five months' pay. The Estates ordered the payment of £5,459 2s. 8d. The regiment continued to exist in 1646, for Alexander Neilson, regimental quartermaster, became involved in a dispute over his levying of men in Ayrshire in December 1646. However, it cannot be determined how many recruits the regiment received at this time. On 4 February 1647 the Estates issued an order for all save one company (which was reserved for the General of Artillery's foot in the New Model Army) to disband on the 9th. On the 19th the Estates ordered the sixty men retained for the New Model to march from their quarters in Ayr and Irvine (which suggests that the regiment had stayed in Ayrshire) to Dundee. By then the two companies in England, who had served in a garrison, had returned to Scotland and disbanded.[124]

Ludquharn's Horse Troop

Routmaster: Alexander Keith of Ludquharn

Ludquharn command both a troop in the Army of the Solemn League and Covenant and home army. Nothing is known about the activities of this troop in England. In October 1644 it was under the command of Major General Ramsay, which suggests that it had left the Newcastle area in company with other units in September. While in the northeast Ludquharn's men spoiled the lands of royalists. There is no further mention of the troop until 28 July 1646 when it received £14,400 in pay. The troop probably disbanded in February 1647. Ludquharn went on to command a troop in the New Model Army.[125]

Macbride's Horse Troop

Routmaster: (?) Macbride

It cannot be ascertained when or from where this unit was raised. It was serving at the siege of Newark on 17 January 1646. In late 1645 and early 1646 the troop made the following exactions from Derbyshire: free quarter and £97 7s. 7d. st. with three other troops from Sutton and Duckmanton, £78 9s. 7d. st. with three other troops from Wentbridge and £89 18s. st. with three other troops from Sherland and Higham. In March the troop moved to Nottinghamshire to take up quarters. As with other of independent troops of horse Macbride's disappears from the picture following the withdrawal from the Newark area. It may be assumed that this unit disbanded at Kelso on 11 February 1647.[126]

Maule's Foot

Colonel: (? Harry) Maule

This is the most mysterious of the foot regiments. It cannot be determined from what area or when it was raised. By 20 January 1646 there was a Colonel Maule serving as governor of St. Andrews Castle. On 10 May Maule's Foot entered Northumberland. By the 20th, although the regiment had marched five-six miles a day it was only fourteen miles from the border. The activities of this unit almost immediately received the disapproval of the English. They rampaged and burned towns, collecting *brandenschatz* according to the size of the place. On leaving a town in which the regiment quartered it demanded the following amounts: £7 4s. for captains, £3 12s. for lieutenants, £2 8s. for ensigns and 2s. for each soldier. Following a complaint about these activities to a local prominent parliamentarian there is no further mention of the regiment for eight months. On 29 January 1647 the Estates decided that the regiment should contribute men to the New Model Army. However, it is unknown which regiment they joined following the evacuation and disbanding of most of the regiment in February 1647.[127]

Mearns and Aberdeen Foot

Colonel: William, 7th earl Marischal

Lieutenant Colonel: Sir James Wood

Majors: Andrew Leslie (1643-46), William Graham (1646-47)

Ministers: Robert Cheyne, George Sharp, Andrew Melville, David Strachan[128]

Marischal received his commission to raise a regiment of foot from Mearns and his area of Aberdeenshire on 26 August 1643. A large portion of the men came from the presbyteries of Kincardine O'Neil and Turriff. On 30 January 1644 the magistrates of Aberdeen 'pressit and violentlie took upone the nicht about 28' apprentices and servants to help make up the burgh's quota of 120 soldiers, ten officers and a captain. Also in late January a Lieutenant Colonel Strachan appeared before the Commissioners of the Committee appointed for valuations within Aberdeenshire and presented an act of the Convention of Estates. The act gave Strachan, Marischal and the laird of Morphie the power to raise the full quota of men required from Mearns and Marischal's part of Aberdeenshire. However, Marischal himself was hesitant about aiding the recruiting, because of the 'want of moneys expended in the public affairs besides the extraordinary losses suffered by reason of devotion to the cause'. Consequently the raising of this regiment was delayed. On 1 February 1644 the Committee with the Army complained that none of the men had reached the army. However, on 16 February the town of Aberdeen's contingent (which had cost £10,000 to levy) under Captain John Strachan marched south. Before then between the 3rd and 21st three companies had reached the army outside Newcastle. After the 21st this regiment was assigned to Lumsden's force, which watched Newcastle. Meanwhile back in Aberdeenshire the regiment suffered a setback. On 23 February Lieutenant James Forbes with forty musketeers marched out against the estates of the laird of Tibberties, Mr. William Seyton and the goodwife of Artrocher. The Committee of War had ordered him to plunder their lands, because the first two were royalists and the last a Roman Catholic. However, the lairds of Gight, Haddo, Schethin, Tibbertie and Ardlogie and Nathaniel Gordon with eighty horsemen met and disarmed Forbes' party. Recruiting of the regiment continued. On 22 May the magistrates of Aberdeen promised to send Captain Strachan more recruits and requested the names and addresses of deserters. The Covenanters ordered a muster on Aberdeen Links for Aberdeenshire, Banffshire and Moray on 4 June in order to fill up the regiments from these shires. Unfortunately few appeared at the muster. Nevertheless, the regiment neared full strength due to other recruiting efforts in June. By 1 September Captain Hew Fraser's company of sixty-four men and officers was ready to march towards England. The company stayed in Haddington on 15 and 16 September, costing the burgh £15 14s. 10d. By mid October at least seven, if not ten, companies had joined the regiment in England.[129]

The Mearns and Aberdeen Foot saw all of its active service in England. It served at the siege of Newcastle from late July to 19 October. The regiment formed part of the 3rd Brigade which assaulted the Pilgrim Street Gate-Carliol Tower area. Marischal with the other officers of the regiment led seven companies in the attack. Following the fall of Newcastle, the regiment moved to Morpeth for winter quarters. On 19 June 1645 the regiment contributed £67 14s. to the Kelso charity fund. By early June the unit had joined the field army and was marching towards Hereford. It took part in the siege, then returned to county Durham before serving at the siege of Newark. The first muster of the regiment on 6 December revealed a strength of 505 officers and men. A month and a half later there were 450 able bodied soldiers and officers and thirty-six sick. The regiment was under the effective command of Major Leslie at this time. After the fall of Newark the unit quartered in county Durham until it withdrew from England (between 25 and 30 January 1647) and disbanded in early February.[130]

Merse Foot

Colonel: Sir David Home of Wedderburn

Lieutenant Colonel: George Home

Majors: (?) Lumsdale (1643-44), Archibald Douglas, (?) Pringle, (?) Dalgetty (1646-47)

Ministers: John Home, Patrick Watt, Patrick Home, Samuel Douglas[131]

The Convention of Estates nominated Wedderburn a colonel for Berwickshire on 26 August 1643. He selected professional officers for his lieutenant colonel and major. The county raised the usual ten companies by January 1644. The Merse Foot entered England on 19 January as part of Leven's army. After 21 February the regiment was detached to serve in Lumsden's force, which guarded the supply lines of the army and watched the Newcastle garrison. On 26 March the Committee with the Army made Thomas Craw in Coupland a captain since he had raised fifty men. Enough recruits were to be joined to them make a company. The Merse was involved in the siege of Newcastle from late July. On 17 October Wedderburn was one of the commissioners for making a treaty with Newcastle. The negotiations, however, were a ruse on the part of the royalists to lengthen the siege. Thus, on 19 October the Merse Foot formed part of the 3rd Brigade which stormed the Pilgrim Street Gate-Carliol Tower area. Wedderburn personally led his ten companies in the attack. On 23 October the Committee with the Army appointed Wedderburn one of the two commissioners to meet with all the substantial merchants. They were to examine the merchants to discover what losses they had suffered from plundering and to get written declarations of the losses. The commissioners also received instructions to preserve ships, keels, and goods of the merchants. The winter quarters of this regiment are unknown. The next reference to the regiment is not until June or July 1645 when the men gave £24 to the Kelso charity fund. From early June the Merse Foot was part of Leven's field army. It served at the siege of Hereford. The regiment vanishes from sight again after the withdrawal from Hereford. On 7 November it was allowed to take 200 recruits from the Merse. The regiment quartered in Clevelandshire before marching towards Newark in November. From late November 1645 to early May 1646 it formed part of the army besieging Newark. On 17 January 1646 the Merse Foot contained 507 soldiers. In early April there were 596 men in the unit. Following the withdrawal of the army into northeast England in May, information on this regiment ends. It probably quartered in either Durham or Northumberland until departing from England in early 1647. It appears to have disbanded entirely on reaching Scotland.[132]

Middleton's Horse

Colonel: Major General John Middleton

Lieutenant Colonel: Gilbert Kerr

Majors: Lewis Kerr, James Innes

Ministers: Robert Brown, James Barclay, Andrew Affleck/Auchenleck[133]

Middleton was a colonel and lieutenant general in the parliamentary armies from 1642 to March 1645, when he resigned due to the creation of the New Model Army. He spent close to £12,000 on raising his regiment, which included some Englishmen. Middleton and his regiment accompanied Leslie's cavalry force to Scotland in August 1645. Middleton's served at Philiphaugh and his English troopers were widely praised for their role in the battle. Although Middleton remained in Scotland, the regiment was ordered south on 31 October. A week later it was promised a new troop from the shires of Stirling and Clackmannan. During its time in Scotland a troop of 43 horse quartered in Linlithgow for one day at the cost of £207 12s. The regiment quartered in northern Yorkshire before joining the siege of Newark on 11 November. Meanwhile in Scotland Middleton had received command of a cavalry force of at least two horse and two dragoon regiments (approximately 1,680 horsemen). This army quartered on Aberdeen for four days before proceeding to Banff in search of royalist forces. Middleton's men quartered on the lands of the earl of Erroll, Stewart of Ardoch, Burnet of Leys and Burnet of Craigmill, and in Turriff. Middleton was possibly accompanied by Captain Harry Bruce's troop of his regiment, seventy-one horse, because they did not leave Scotland until December. On 17 January 1646 the regiment mustered 348 troopers and officers in seven troops. Six troops of Middleton's received their weekly maintenance from Nottinghamshire, while Captain Bruce's troop was paid by Derbyshire. On 4 February 1646 the Estates commissioned Middleton to command horse and foot within Scotland, making him a major general of horse. From then on Middleton served against Montrose and Huntly. His regiment remained in England until it withdrew in early 1647 and disbanded at Kelso on 11 February. Throughout 1646 Middleton gave passes and remissions to repentant royalists. On 19 January 1647 the Estates claimed that they owed Middleton £45,786 for raising his regiment and for his pay. They hoped that he could be given the money quickly. On 24 March the Estates voted him a gift of gold chain worth £2,666 13s. 4d. for his services out of the first surplus. In further recognition of his services Middleton was made a major general in the New Model Army. He and Lieutenant Colonel Kerr received horse troops in the New Model, presumably drawn from troopers of his own regiment.[134]

Midlothian Foot

Colonel: John, viscount Maitland and 2nd earl of Lauderdale

Lieutenant Colonel: Colin Pitscottie

Majors: John Hay (1643-44), (?) Brown (1644), George Windram (1644-47)

Ministers: Robert Carson, William Calderwood[135]

Maitland received his commission for this regiment on 26 August 1643. However, the recruiting of the men from Midlothian (especially from the presbytery of Dalkeith) probably rested with the lieutenant colonel and major (both mercenaries), because Maitland was in London on diplomatic business for much of later 1643. The regiment consisted of the standard ten companies. On 20 January 1644 the Midlothian Foot entered England from Coldstream. The regiment joined Leven's army and served at the siege of York. Lieutenant Colonel Pitscottie was the commander of the regiment at Marston Moor and was cited for bravery for his actions during the battle. The Midlothian Foot was one of the three front line Scottish regiments, which were on the right-centre, to hold its cohesion in the battle. It was brigaded with the Fife (Crawford-Lindsay's) Foot. The two regiments, in company with others, cleared the royalist forlorn hope from a ditch fronting the royalist line. Then things began to go badly and the allied front-line on the right and right-centre began to unravel. The Midlothian-Fife brigade found itself facing royalist foot to the front and royalist horse on the right flank. The brigade had the worst of three cavalry charges delivered by Lord George Goring's horse. However, it continued to hold and proceeded to win signal honours by capturing Lieutenant General Sir Charles Lucas. Throughout the summer of 1644 the Midlothian Foot suffered from desertion. In July Leven sent Captain Alexander Inglis of Ingliston with a letter to the Estates. The letter asked for the sending out of deficients and the return of deserters to this and all other regiments due to their weakening in the preceding campaign. On 12 September the South Leith kirk session ordered deserters of the regiment back to England. Meanwhile in England the regiment had moved from Yorkshire to the Newcastle area. The Midlothian and Fife (Crawford-Lindsay's) Foot manned the same section of the line of cirumvallation. On 20 August at 3 p.m. the garrison made a sortie against their portion of the line and broke through. On 4 September the Committee with the Army ordered the Midlothian Foot back to Scotland, ending its service in England.[136]

The regiment reached Scotland on 15 September and remained there for the rest of its existence. The Midlothian Foot quartered in the burgh of Perth on the 28th, where it was later joined by Crawford-Lindsay's Fife Foot. The two regiments served in Baillie's army in late autumn. They returned to Perth on 16 December and remained until the 23rd, then each regiment left a hundred men to form the garrison. The Midlothian Foot returned on 8 January 1645. On 27 February the Estates ordered the two regiments to split a levy of the eighth man from Angus; the new recruits were to be ready by 8 March. On 22 March the two regiments departed from Perth and joined Baillie in his march to Dundee. For several months (March-July) there is no mention of the Midlothian Foot, however it may be reasonably assumed that it formed part of Crawford-Lindsay's force on his campaign into Atholl. On 26 and 27 July the army, including both the Midlothian and Fife foot which camped together, held fast days. On Sunday the 27th Robert Blair, minister of St. Andrews and former chaplain of the Fife Foot, preached to both regiments. He rebuked them for growing sinfulness and warned them of God's wrath unless they mended their ways. (There was some truth in this allegation of sinfulness, because in early 1645 two members of the Midlothian Foot appeared before the presbytery of Perth for fornication.) On 1 August the Estates decided that Haddingtonshire should provide 600 foot and Edinburghshire 200 foot for the Midlothian regiment. At Kilsyth, on 15 August, the Midlothian Foot held the right centre, with Balcarres' Horse on its right and Home's Foot to the left. The Midlothian Foot received orders to support Balcarres' on the flank march to the right. Nathaniel Gordon's and viscount Aboyne's men attacked and routed the Midlothian men. The regiment managed to rally after the battle, however it is unknown where this occurred. For eleven days in September the Midlothian Foot quartered in Linlithgow, costing the burgh £486 7s. From 2 October to 20 December the 400 men of the regiment quartered in Perth. Pitscottie was the effective colonel; it was noted then that his men disliked him. It cannot be determined where the regiment quartered after December 1645. On 24 January 1646 the Estates filed a report on the money due to the regiment. The major, seven captains, three lieutenants, three ensigns, three sergeants and regimental quartermaster had received only £2,592 12s. of the £13,929 13s. 4d. owed them. The Estates declared this amount to be part of the public debt. On 28 January 1647 the Estates appointed Pitscottie a colonel in the New Model Army. It is uncertain whether his new regiment included men of the Midlothian Foot. The Midlothian Foot disbanded by late February 1647 after several years of hard service.[137]

Minister's Foot

Colonel: Sir Arthur Erskine (of Scottscraig)

Lieutenant Colonels: James Bryson (1643-44), John Leslie (1644-45), James Lundie (1645-47)

Majors: John Leslie (1643-44), James Lundie (1644-45), Thomas MacDougall (1645-47)

Ministers: James Campbell, Robert Traill, Ephraim Melville, Andrew Duncanson, John Maxwell, William Maxwell[138]

The initial order authorising the raising of 'ane regiment for maintainece of religion' under Colonel Erskine of Scottscraig reached the presbyteries from the General Assembly in September 1643. Although the colonel was not a professional soldier, the other two field officers were. In December the Commission of the General Assembly sent the presbyteries a letter reminding them that each minister must send out a fully-armed soldier. Nevertheless, the ministers failed to perform their duty. By February 1644 Erskine had only three companies under his command, instead of the ten which usually constituted a foot regiment. On three occasions (two in summer 1644 and one in February 1645) the Commission demanded that the ministers send out a man a piece or pay £40 for the outfitting of one. These additional orders increased the size of the regiment to 464 men in December 1644. The ministers were continually hampered by theft of their recruits by lay recruiters, by laziness, desertion, poverty, and by the difficulty of sending out men from vacant parishes. Of more than sixty presbyteries only seventeen refer to the regiment in their records. Only the presbytery of Dumbarton managed to complete its levy. Despite all their efforts the ministers compared unfavourably with laymen as military recruiters.[139]

The regiment remained in England throughout the period of its existence. It formed part of Leven's army on 19 January 1644. During its service at the siege of York, the regiment consisted of five companies. At Marston Moor the Ministers' Foot may have formed part of Fairfax's infantry reserve. The regiment and its chaplain, Robert Traill, fled from the field. But Traill at least returned when he heard of the victory. He met with other ministers and searched for Leven, who had fled. Afterwards David Forret (Leven's Horse) and he examined the battlefield. Lieutenant Colonel Bryson fell in the battle, and the Kirk decided to hold a collection for his widow. Presbyteries in the Synods of Lothian and Tweeddale and Fife raised money for Janet Dunbar, Bryson's widow. After the fall of York the Ministers' Foot quartered in Yorkshire until 7 August when it marched northwards to the outskirts of Newcastle. The regiment served at the siege of that town, and also took part in the storming of Newcastle on 19 October. The royalists inflicted moderate casualties on the Ministers' Foot that day. After the fall of Newcastle the regiment disappears from the records for several months. Presumably, it served on garrison duty in northeast England. The muster of the regiment on 31 March 1645 revealed that its strength had fallen to 385 soldiers. In November the Ministers' Foot formed part of the army which besieged Newark. A muster of the unit on 17 January 1646 registered a further fall to 256 soldiers. On 24 April about two weeks before the siege ended the regiment contained only 243 soldiers. The remainder of its history must be speculative. It probably quartered in the two northeastern counties until early February 1647. Then the regiment withdrew from England and disbanded.[140]

Viscount Montgomery's Horse

Colonel: Hugh, viscount Montgomery

Lieutenant Colonel: John Home

Major: David Barclay

Ministers: William Naismith, James Naismith, Andrew Abercromby[141]

There are no details about the raising of this regiment or about the commissioning of its colonel. Apparently, a contingent of the regiment came from the presbytery of Ayr. By May 1644 Montgomery's Horse was quartering in Carnesellock. On 25 June the regiment crossed the English border as part of Callendar's army. Montgomery's first experienced military action in late July, when Major General Ramsay led it and 800 commanded foot in an unsuccessful attack against Gateshead. In September Montgomery's left the Newcastle area for Scotland, where most of the regiment remained until early 1647. The location of the regiment cannot be ascertained for a year (September 1644–September 1645), although between November 1644 and March 1645 it took £132 2s. worth of quarters from Coming and Newton. It formed part of Leslie's army at Philiphaugh. In October Montgomery's moved north with Middleton's cavalry army. It quartered in Aberdeen for four days before riding on to Banff. The regiment contained 600 troopers and officers during this campaign. During the stay in the northeast some men of the regiment were involved in crop destruction. The unit quartered in Aberdeen for twenty-four hours on the way south, where it took up quarters. On 7 November it was ordered to quarter in west Fife, Perthshire and Clackmannanshire with Fraser's. On 14 November the Scottish Commissioners to the English parliament informed the House of Lords that Montgomery had been summoned to appear for corresponding with royalists. The commissioners requested that any incriminating letters be sent to Scotland. However, the colonel seems to have been cleared. In early December a commanded party of thirty-seven troopers left Scotland for the siege of Newark under the command of Cornet Calhoun (Dalhousie's Horse). The party reached the siege camp on 12 December and remained in England until early May 1646, if not later. Meanwhile on 16 December 1645 the Estates ordered Montgomery's to Aberdeenshire in company with Eglinton's and Barclay's Horse. This regiment was to gain a reinforcement of two companies of dragoons. Montgomery's men may not have been well supplied or paid then. From the earl of Erroll's lands in Stannell troopers took more than £20 of goods in plunder. In February 1646 troopers took at least £89 in grain, and also stole clothing from Turriff. In late March the regiment took part in the relief of Inverness. April saw Montgomery's in Turriff and Aberdeenshire again. From 28 August to 20 December half of the regiment or 230 troopers, under Lieutenant Colonel Home, quartered on the freedom lands of Aberdeen. This visitation cost the burgh £21,735. On 29 January 1647 the Estates selected Major Barclay to be a troop commander in the New Model Army. A week later the Estates issued orders regarding the future of Montgomery's Horse. It was to disband on 10 February, except for eighty troopers for the major's troop and twenty others for Colonel Harry Barclay's troop. Thus, on the 10th, one of the most experienced regiments in Scotland ceased to exist.[142]

Naismith's Horse Troop

Routmaster: (?) Naismith

This troop was raised in the spring of 1644, although the source of recruits cannot be determined. It entered England on 25 June as part of Callendar's army. After receiving supplies later in the month the troop disappears from the records.[143]

Niddrie's Foot

Colonel: Sir John Wauchope of Niddrie

Lieutenant Colonel: Robert Hamilton

Major: Andrew Abernethy

Ministers: Patrick Sibbald, William Calderwood, Andrew Bannatyne[144]

Niddrie was a member of the Committee of War for East Lothian and Lauderdale. The Estates commissioned him a colonel of foot on 19 June 1644. However, he must have already been recruiting his regiment, for on 21 June it had quartered in Kelso for four days. The men came largely from eastern Midlothian and East Lothian, principally the presbyteries of Dalkeith and Haddington. On 25 June Niddrie's entered England as part of Callendar's army. Consequently it served in all the actions of that force and in the siege of Newcastle. On 19 October at the storming of that town Niddrie led his men as part of the 4th Brigade under the command of Callendar against the Sandgate. After this action there is no further mention of the regiment's military activities. Niddrie watched the battle of Inverlochy as a representative of the Committee of Estates from Argyll's galley. In spring 1645 he released a minister appointed chaplain of the unit by the Commission of the General Assembly. After that Niddrie's vanished entirely from sight.[145]

Nithsdale and Annandale Foot

Colonel: William Douglas of Kelhead

Lieutenant Colonel: John Hogg

Major: Thomas Macburnie

Ministers: Alexander MacGowan, Alexander Smith, James Maxwell[146]

The Convention of Estates nominated Kelhead, a brother of the earl of Queensberry, colonel of foot for Dumfriesshire and Annandale on 26 August 1643. Kelhead selected professional soldiers as his lieutenant colonel and major. By

January 1644 they had managed to raise ten companies from the western borders. The regiment entered England as part of Leven's army on 19 January. The Nithsdale and Annandale served with Leven's main field army until 21 February when it was detached to form part of Lumsden's command. In April Lumsden led a convoy of ammunition to the besiegers of York, which this regiment and the Strathearn Foot escorted. Kelhead's command then contained about 1,000 men. After reaching the main army the two regiments remained to take part in the siege of York. The Nithsdale Foot formed part of the second line of the right-centre at Marston Moor, where it brigaded with the Kyle and Carrick Foot. Kelhead's men successfully cleared the royalist infantry from a ditch in front of the main royalist line. However, they and the men of the Angus Foot fled upon coming into contact with the second line of royalist foot. After the fall of York the Nithsdale and Annandale Foot quartered in Yorkshire, first around Doncaster and later near Leeds. On 7 August this regiment marched back towards Newcastle with the rest of the field army, arriving in the area on the 15th. During the siege of Newcastle the Nithsdale and Annandale, and the Kyle and Carrick Foot held adjacent sections of the siegeworks. On 24 August the Newcastle garrison attacked their section of the line. Due to the absence of their officers the Scots fled, allowing the royalists to level their works. Almost two months later the Dumfriesshire men had their chance for revenge. On 19 October the Nithsdale Foot formed part of the 3rd Brigade which stormed the Pilgrim Street Gate-Carliol Tower area. Kelhead personally led about seven companies of his regiment in the attack. After the fall of Newcastle the location of the unit cannot be determined until sometime in December when it entered Cumbria to take part in the siege of Carlisle.[147]

From December 1645 to February 1647 the Nithsdale and Annandale Foot remained in Cumbria, initially on offensive operations but later as a garrison. On 12 May 1645 the regiment numbered 548 soldiers. On 28 June it entered Carlisle after besieging the city for six months. Leslie made Kelhead the governor of Carlisle, and his regiment formed the permanent garrison. Between July and December the unit increased in strength from 671 men to 777 soldiers. This may be explained by the Committee of Estates' authorisation of 7 November for raising 200 men from Dumfriesshire. On 2 February 1646 Kelhead petitioned the Estates that 100 horse might be added to the three troops of horse previously levied by him for serving at Carlisle and for repayment of the £6,000 in levy money spent by him for raising those troops. The Estates agreed to all of his requests. On 6 April the regiment reached a strength of 797 soldiers. In the following months its size fluctuated between 695 and 767 men, finally settling at 720 soldiers at the end of 1646. On 12 February 1647 Kelhead's men evacuated Carlisle and disbanded after reaching Scotland.[148]

Perthshire (Gask's/Tullibardine's) Foot

Colonel: James, Lord Murray of Gask, later 2nd earl of Tullibardine

Lieutenant Colonel: Lachlan Roffe/Rosse/Roughe

Majors: Duncan Campbell (1643-44), William Murray (1645-47)

Ministers: Archibald Reid, John Rattray, David Drummond, James Graham, Colin Campbell, Robert Campbell[149]

On 26 August 1643 Lord Gask was appointed a colonel of the Perthshire Foot by the Convention of Estates. Both his lieutenant colonel and major had served in the European wars. On 19 January 1644 the regiment, ten companies strong, entered England as part of Leven's army. From 21 February the Perthshire Foot served under Lumsden's command as part of his force watching the royalists in the northeast. While the regiment remained relatively static desertion became a problem. On 3 July Gask wrote the laird of Grandtully ordering him to arrest and send back deserters from the regiment sheltering on his lands. The colonel threatened to report Grandtully to the Committee of Estates if he failed to act. Within a few weeks the regiment had a more serious concern, namely the siege of Newcastle. Although possessing a siege battery in its portion of the line of circumvallation, the Perthshire Foot did not remain to see the outcome of the siege, because it was one of the first regiments sent back to Scotland to combat Montrose. On 2 September six companies (between 405 and 607 men) quartered in Linlithgow at a charge of £121 9s. 8d. Unfortunately, it is impossible to trace the activities of the regiment during its sojourn in Scotland. On 22 March 1645 250 Highland recruits for the regiment arrived in the burgh of Perth. Between 9 June and 16 July the Perthshire Foot was marching to join Leven's field army in the Midlands. The regiment gave £70 10s. to the Kelso charity fund then. The Perthshire Foot served at the siege of Hereford, and retreated with Leven to Clevelandshire. By early December the regiment was besieging Newark with other elements of the army. On 6 December it mustered 653 able soldiers and four to five sick. A little over a month later, on 17 January 1646, the nine companies of the Perthshire Foot numbered only 482 men. This dramatic loss of manpower may be explained by increased desertion during the absence of all three field officers. After the fall of Newark the regiment reached county Durham on 15 May where it remained until late January 1647. Then the Perthshire Foot marched north and departed from England. The regiment disbanded sometime in February.[150]

Perthshire (Freeland's) Foot

Colonel: Sir Thomas Ruthven of Freeland

Lieutenant Colonel: James Breamer/Breimar/Bremer/Brymmer

Majors: David Donaldson, (?) Hadden

Ministers: William Row, George Belfrage[151]

Freeland received his commission as a colonel of the Perthshire Foot on 26 August 1643 from the Convention of Estates. This regiment was also known as the Stirlingshire Foot, because it was partially raised from the presbyteries of Dumbarton and Stirling. Although the regiment was meant for Leven's army it first served in Scotland. Freeland raised his men in spring 1644 to campaign against the marquis of Huntly. On 14 April Argyll wrote his kinsman Sir Robert Campbell of Glenorchy asking him to let Freeland have his proportion that was first appointed and also to have men from the shire of Argyll. Glenorchy was to supply these men despite the exemptions he had received from levying men. By Argyll's and his own exertions Freeland managed to recruit his regiment and rendezvous with Argyll at Dunottar Castle on 26 April. The Perthshire Foot then served on Argyll's expedition in the northeast which ended in late May. On 6 June the Committee of Estates ordered the regiment to England. Each soldier was to receive 4s. maintenance each day, and the officers were to have their entertainment at no greater than the equivalent of a day's pay. On 27-28 June the regiment, numbering 256 soldiers, quartered in Haddington. Freeland's men eventually joined Callendar's army, which had entered England on the 25th. They took part in the siege of Newcastle until 2 September, at least, when the regiment was ordered back to Scotland by the Committee with the Army. If the Perthshire Foot reached Scotland, it does not seem to have experienced active service. In the event it was back in England by early June 1645, when the lieutenant colonel led a commanded party of eight foot companies to aid the besiegers of Carlisle. On 25 June the regiment donated £112 3s. to the Kelso charity fund. By then the Perthshire Foot had presumably rejoined Leven's field army, because it served at the siege of Hereford. Following the retreat from Hereford, the regiment quartered in northern Yorkshire. In December, if not earlier, Freeland's men were at the siege of Newark, where they remained until the town fell. A muster of the regiment on 6 December revealed that the six companies contained 387 soldiers. At the muster of the army on 17 January 1646 the Perthshire Foot contained 349 men, and Freeland was absent. The last figure for the size of the regiment is a muster of 24 April, when it numbered 345 men. While it cannot be determined where the regiment went immediately following the army's withdrawal from Nottinghamshire, on 1 September (at the latest) the Perthshire Foot quartered in Durhamshire. The regiment remained in that county until late January 1647 when it marched back to Scotland and disbanded.[152]

Preston's Horse Troop

Routmaster: Sir James Hamilton of Preston

This troop of sixty-five men was raised by 1 February 1644 in Lanarkshire and mustered at Glasgow. The troop entered England on 25 June as part of

Callendar's army, and served in the northeast. On 24 August the troop ceased to have an independent existence, because the Committee with the Army united it to Sir Frederick Hamilton's Horse.[153]

Quarrell's Horse Troop

Routmaster: Sir Robert Elphinstone of Quarrell

Quarrell raised his troop in spring 1644 and it accompanied Callendar's army into England on 25 June. The troop served in England until early 1647, apparently remaining continually in the northeast. On 2 February 1646 the Estates appointed Quarrell to the Stirlingshire Committee of War, thus it may be assumed that the troop was raised from that shire. The unit disbanded on 12 February 1647 at Kelso.[154]

Ramsay's Horse

Colonel: Major General Sir James Ramsay

Lieutenant Colonel: John Leslie

Major: Alexander Ramsay

Ministers: Thomas Elliot, William Cunningham, John Maghie/Makghie[155]

Although there is no evidence about the levying of this regiment, it was probably raised in spring 1644. On 21 June the Estates made Ramsay a Major General of Horse (he had formerly served as a major general for the Covenanters). Ramsay was ordered to repair to Callendar and obey his orders. Ramsay was also told that his commission did not prejudice David Leslie's. Ramsay's Horse entered England on 25 June as part of Callendar's army. On 28 July Ramsay led viscount Montgomery's Horse and 800 commanded foot in an attack against Gatehead, which failed to take the Novacastrian suburb. In September Ramsay's Horse returned to Scotland to help crush the royalists. On 12 September Major Ramsay with four troops (of the regiment's eight) was ordered to quarter in the Borders. In October Major General Ramsay arrived at Aberdeen, but it is not clear whether his regiment accompanied him. However, the major general did have Lord Gordon's three and Ludquharn's troops under his command. They ruined the countryside through quartering. In November Ramsay found himself in command of a substantial force of cavalry. In addition to the men he led in October, Dalhousie's, Hackett's, and Hamilton's Horse were now under his command. They settled into winter quarters in Aberdeen-shire, Banffshire, and Moray. After the end of the winter Ramsay's Horse presumably returned to England, because from spring 1645 he was the governor of Berwick. For most of the year there is no reference to either Ramsay or his regiment. However, on 13 December the Estates ordered the major general to send Angus MacDonald from Berwick to St. Andrews for his trial. Shortly before this the regiment had moved south to take part in the siege of Newark. On 17 January 1646 it mustered 417 troopers (with six ill) in eight troops. Meanwhile on 3 January a petition from Ramsay reached the Estates. He requested money for repairs of the walls of Berwick, for setting up a court de garde, and the pay of the cannonier, the magazine keeper, and the garrison. The petition was accepted in its entirety. After the fall of Newark, the regiment took up quarters in Clevelandshire. On 2 June an English colonel complained to the local M.P. of a heavy cess imposed upon Kirkby-under-brough, where the regiment quartered. The regiment seems to have returned to Scotland and quartered in East Lothian at the end of 1646 (but see above, Dalhousie's, p. 130). In the event it disbanded in February 1647, and none of its field officers received a troop in the New Model Army. However, on 26 March the Estates passed an act of approbation for Ramsay's services under Argyll, Callendar and as governor of Berwick.[156]

Lord Sinclair's Horse Troop

Routmaster: John, 9th Lord Sinclair

Lord Sinclair raised his troop in spring 1644 probably from Fife. It entered England on 25 June as part of Callendar's army. The troop received some pay on 23 November. After that there is no further mention of the troop. If it remained in existence until the end of the war, it would have disbanded in February 1647.[157]

Stewart's Horse Troop

Routmaster: Colonel William Stewart

On 5 May 1644 the Committee with the Army allowed Colonel Stewart, of the Galloway Foot, to uplift a horse troop of which he would be routmaster. The Committee stipulated that the troop would be under the *Articles of War* and would be a unit in the army. Although there is no information on the activities of this troop, it may be assumed that it accompanied the Galloway Foot. The troop was still on foot as of June 1645, when it received thirty-six lances. Stewart's foot disbanded in Scotland and the troop probably did so, too.[158]

Stirlingshire Foot

Colonel: George, Lord Livingston

Lieutenant Colonel: Andrew Bruce

Major: Andrew Livingston

Ministers: John Knox, John Craigenvelt, Alan Fergusson[159]

The Estate commissioned Lord Livingston colonel of the Stirlingshire Foot on 26 August 1643. On the same day his lieutenant colonel was appointed to the Clackmannanshire Committee of War. Both the lieutenant colonel and major had experience in the European wars. The regiment was principally raised from the presbyteries of Stirling and Dumbarton. In January 1644 the Stirlingshire Foot, numbering 1,000 men (in ten companies), quartered for one day in Linlithgow at the cost of £200. On 19 January the regiment entered England as part of Leven's army. On 20 March Lieutenant Colonel Bruce led a party of his men in the successful assault against the South Shields Fort. Four days later the regiment fought in the Hilton skirmishes. During the siege of York eight companies of the regiment served with Leven's army. It was engaged at Marston Moor, probably forming part of Fairfax's foot reserves. After the surrender of York the regiment quartered in southern Yorkshire until 7 August when it marched northwards to the vicinity of Newcastle with the rest of the army. The Stirlingshire Foot served as part of the besieging force around Newcastle. There is some confusion as to where and with which regiments this unit attacked Newcastle. An officer with Sinclair's Foot wrote in the 1660s that this regiment was paired with the Angus Foot and failed to enter Newcastle until Sinclair's men cleared the wall. A contemporary account states that the Stirlingshire Foot formed part of the 4th Brigade under the command of Callendar, and that Lord Livingston personally led his ten companies against the Sandgate. On 23 October Leven ordered Livingston into winter quarters with two companies of Lanark's Foot in Hartlepool, Stockton and the nearest villages. Leven warned Livingston not to extend his quarters without special orders and to keep good discipline within the area. Leven made Livingston answerable to the laird of Humbie and his deputies, who would issue orders on their maintenance. Livingston was also personally responsible for any disobedience among the soldiers. The regiment may have left its winter quarters in March 1645, but it certainly had done so by mid June.[160]

Unlike other regiments the Stirlingshire Foot remained in England throughout the period. In June or July 1645 the regiment contributed £307 4s. to the Kelso charity fund. During the summer of 1645 it belonged to Leven's field army, and consequently took part in the siege of Hereford. During the siege the regiment had a battery in its portion of the entrenchments. Following the withdrawal from Hereford the Stirlingshire Foot quartered in northern Yorkshire. On 14 November the Scottish Commissioners in London informed the House of Lords that the Estates had summoned Lord Livingston to appear for corresponding with royalists. The parliamentarians were requested to send any incriminating evidence to Scotland. Shortly afterwards the regiment moved south to join the siege of Newark. The muster of 17 January 1646 revealed that Livingston was on leave in Scotland and that there were 230 able soldiers and fourteen sick in the regiment. On 27 February the English parliamentary commissioners in the area announced that at least two Englishmen had been wrongly placed on the muster rolls. However, the strength of the regiment legitimately increased during the siege. On 17 March there were 370 soldiers present, little over a month later the number had grown to 468 men. After the surrender of Newark the Stirlingshire men retired to the northeast. From 15 June, at the latest, they quartered in Durhamshire. For part of the time the men quartered on Lindley Wren, a royalist in Borchester. Their occupation cost him £2,400, forcing him to borrow more than the worth of his goods. In late January 1647 the regiment withdrew from the county and England, disbanding in February. One soldier found his way to the church courts for fathering a bastard.[161]

Stockdale's Horse

Colonel: (?) Stockdale

This is the most shadowy of the units in this army. The only mention of it is a reference that Stockdale's Horse received pay on 29 August 1645.[162]

Strathearn Foot

Colonel: James, 1st Lord Coupar

Lieutenant Colonels: John Brown (1643-45), William Lumsden (1645-47)

Majors: George Brown (1643-45), (?) Elphinstone (1645-47)

Ministers: John Strachan, John Barclay, Robert Malcolm, James Campbell, Alexander Ireland[163]

Coupar received his commission for a colonelcy of Perthshire foot on 25 August 1643. It appears that the men were levied from southern Perthshire and from the presbytery of Dundee. On 15 January part of the ten companies were in Haddington and the others were on the way towards the border. The Strathearn Foot crossed into England as part of Leven's army on the 19th. After 21 February Leven detached the regiment to serve under Lumsden. In April

Lumsden used the Strathearn and Nithsdale and Annandale Foot to convoy a train of ammunition to Leven's army in Yorkshire. The Strathearn Foot had about 1,000 rank and file at the siege of York. At Marston Moor Leven brigaded this regiment with Dunfermline's Fife Foot in the reserve of the Scottish infantry. Lumsden managed to rally these two regiments after the royalist left wing horse broke and routed them. He then used them to succour the three front-line regiments which held. After the fall of York the Strathearn Foot quartered in Yorkshire, first in the Doncaster area and then near Leeds. On 7 August it marched north with the army to lay siege to Newcastle. At the storming of the town Coupar personally commanded his ten companies, which belonged to the 2nd Brigade and attacked the Newgate. Following the fall of Newcastle the Strathearn Foot vanishes from the records until June 1645. During those eight months it may be reasonably concluded that the regiment quartered in the northeast. On 12 June the men contributed £171 to the Kelso charity fund. That summer it served on the Hereford campaign and then marched off to Scotland to take part in the battle of Philiphaugh. For two months the whereabouts of the regiment is a mystery. On 13 and 15 December the Estates ordered the regiment to march to the burgh of Perth immediately upon receipt of the order and to remain there until further instructions arrived. These were sent out on the 16th when the regiment was ordered to Montrose, and to keep the garrisons formerly manned by Fraser's dragoons in Perthshire, Angus, and Mearns. On the 18th Lieutenant Colonel Lumsden led the regiment into Perth, where it remained until 10 March 1646. On that day it marched out against Kincardine Castle, which Middleton attacked. From the conjunction of Middleton and the Strathearn Foot in March, it can be assumed that the regiment served under his command for all of his campaigns in 1646. On February 1647 the Estates issued an order to the regiment to disband on the 9th, save for eighty-three men who were reserved for the General of Artillery's Foot in the New Model Army. The next day the Estates assessed the areas which were to pay over £4,000 of arrears due the regiment for its service in Scotland.[164]

Teviotdale Foot

Colonel: William, 3rd earl of Lothian

Lieutenant Colonels: Patrick Leslie (1643-44), Sir George Douglas (1645), Archibald Douglas (1646-47)

Majors: Sir George Douglas (1643-44), Archibald Douglas (1645), (?) Riddell (1646), (?) Abernethy (1646-47)

Ministers: William Wemyss, James Ker, Thomas Wilkie, Robert Knox, John Scott, Andrew Pringle, John Langland[165]

On 26 August 1643, while out of the country, Lothian was named a colonel of foot for Roxburghshire (Teviotdale) and Selkirkshire. Due to the absence of Lothian the task of recruiting fell on the lieutenant colonel and major, who were veterans of the European wars. These two officers raised ten companies, chiefly from the presbyteries of Jedburgh and Kelso. The regiment was at Ancrum on 19 January 1644, and entered England shortly afterwards as part of Leven's army. On 24 March the Teviotdale Foot was first engaged in combat at the Hilton skirmish. The regiment was present at the siege of York. On 5 May the Committee with the Army ordered the regiment to Sunderland with a horse troop. At Marston Moor it probably formed part of Fairfax's infantry reserves. After the end of the York campaign the Teviotdale Foot quartered in southern Yorkshire before returning to the Newcastle area to take part in the siege. After the town's fall the regiment quartered in Durhamshire until February 1645. It returned to the county in May, presumably after having been in Yorkshire as part of Leven's field army. In June or July the men and officers of the regiment contributed £168 to the Kelso charity fund. The Teviotdale Foot joined the field army in June and served in the siege of Hereford. After the withdrawal from the siege the regiment returned to quarters in Durhamshire. In mid November the unit mustered 600 men. These numbers fell to 532 soldiers in late March 1646, despite receiving permission to raise over 300 men from Teviotdale on 4 November 1645. Although the regiment was not at the siege of Newark its colonel was. When Charles I arrived at the army headquarters at Southwell on 6 May Lothian ordered him to demand the surrender of Newark, sign the Solemn League and Covenant, establish presbyterianism in England and Ireland, and order Montrose to surrender. Charles refused, saying that he had made Lothian an earl and Graham a marquis. Lothian then placed him under close guard. After the arrival of the king in Newcastle, the Teviotdale Foot began to increase in strength. On 2 June it contained 770 men, three months later there were 795 soldiers in the regiment. In late January 1647 the Teviotdale Foot evacuated England and disbanded in early February.[166]

Tweeddale Foot

Colonels: Francis, 2nd earl of Buccleuch (1643-44), Walter Scott (1645-47)

Lieutenant Colonels: Walter Scott (1643-44), (?) Kerr (1645-47)

Majors: Thomas Moffat (1643-44), John Burne (1644-47)

Ministers: William Wilkie, David Fletcher, John Knox, John Colt, Andrew Duncanson[167]

Buccleuch received his commissions as a colonel for the Teviotdale and Selkirk-shire, and Dumfriesshire and Annandale foot from the Convention of Estates on 26 August 1643. He chose two professional officers to be his immediate subordinates. They levied ten companies from the shires allotted to Buccleuch, but the main body came from the presbytery of Selkirk. The regiment, numbering 1,200 men, rendezvoused at Hawick on 18 January 1644. The Tweeddale Foot entered England as part of Leven's army on the 19th. It was present at Hilton and the siege of York. At Marston Moor the regiment was brigaded with the Loudoun-Glasgow Foot in the Scottish infantry reserve. Both fled from the field after being broken by the left wing royalist horse. The Tweeddale Foot quartered in southern Yorkshire before taking part in the siege of Newcastle. On 19 October it was again coupled with the Loudoun-Glasgow Foot, this time in the 1st Brigade, which stormed the Closegate. Major Moffat was killed in the assault. On 27 February 1645 his father, Lieutenant Colonel Thomas Moffat (of Crawford-Lindsay's Fife Foot) petitioned the Estates. He claimed that his wife 'upon the report of his [Major Moffat's] Death conceaved such heavie griefe and Melancholie that shortlie thereftir shoe departed this Life'. Moffat's brothers and sister, who had depended upon him for support, were accordingly allocated his arrears. Back in England the regiment donated £168 12s. to the Kelso charity fund on 12 June. About the same time it joined the field army and the Tweeddale Foot served at the siege of Hereford. In August and September a commanded party of sixty-three men under Ensign Robert Boston rejoined the regiment from Scotland. After the lifting of the Hereford siege the Tweeddale Foot quartered in northern Yorkshire. On 7 November the Committee of Estates permitted the regiment to raise over 300 foot from Teviotdale and Ettrick Forest. In late November it was present at the siege of Newark. A muster of the regiment on 6 December revealed a strength of 354 men. About six weeks later it had dropped to 301 soldiers. However, by late April the regiment had 358 men on the rolls. The quarters of the Tweeddale Foot immediately after the withdrawal to the northeast cannot be determined. However, from 1 September 1646, if not before, it was stationed in Northumberland. The regiment evacuated England in early February 1647. Most of the men disbanded, but some were probably selected for Colonel Scott's foot in the New Model Army.[168]

Van Druschke's Horse

Colonel: Jonas van Druschke

Lieutenant Colonel: William Hurry/Urry

Major: Hans George van Strobell

Minister: John Percy[169]

Van Druschke's Horse was one of the most oppressive and infamous regiments in the army. The colonel was Dutch and the major a German. It cannot be determined from where or when this unit was raised. However it was in existence by 11 December 1645. In January 1646 the seven troops of the regiment were in Yorkshire. It stayed in Austerfield from the 8th to 22nd under the command of (Major) Captain John Elwes. By its departure no fodder remained and the animals of the inhabitants were being sold. Simultaneously the parish of Bawtry paid £120 to the regiment. Van Druschke's Horse was at the Muskham muster on 17 January, when it numbered 324 troopers, six sick and thirteen absent without leave. About this time English royalists began to join the regiment. Andrew Elvit, the former major of Thornton's royalist horse, was Van Druschke's captain lieutenant. A Lieutenant Keir was also in the unit. Along with this problem the regiment was becoming notorious for imposition of cess. From Sutton and Duckmanton, Derbyshire, it exacted £1,168 11s. with three independent horse troops. John Man and Robert Borken, constables of Epworth and Axholm, Lincolnshire, produced a petition detailing the excesses of the regiment. Adam Ramsay and George Edmonston, quartermasters to Lieutenant Colonel Urry's and Routmaster Robert Taylor's troops respectively, had seized the constables and placed them in chains. They were kept imprisoned for thirteen days in Bawtry. To gain their freedom the constables had to provide £684 in food and money to the regiment. Lieutenant General Leslie had assessed the village of Wroofe £90 a day in food and money, Druschke's men collected it by driving away the cattle. In addition to that, Taylor's troop had taken ten loads of hay and twenty-eight quarters of oats from the hamlet. The constables wished the hamlet discharged from further exactions before it was impoverished. Meanwhile in Yorkshire between 2 March and 20 April Routmaster Samuel Potts' troop had coerced £334 4s. from Whitley. On 23 April several inhabitants of Rawcliff, Snaith and surrounding villages petitioned the committee of the West Riding on behalf of themselves and others. They said that ex-royalist officers and soldiers pretended to be under Van Druschke's command. These men had committed violent acts and raised high cesses, causing the people to flee. On 27 April the English Commissioners with the army presented the Scottish ones with a list of offenders from the regiment in the Osgodcross Wapentake. They included Elwes' servants, thirty-five troopers, Corporals Hall, Hansprice and Simpson, Quartermasters Hugh Kennedy, John Stables, Richard Owen, William Wilkinson and Robert Scott, Cornets Christian Shaw, and Haworth, Lieutenants Ralph/Robert Smith, Bainbridge, Perry and Shepherd, the Regimental Quartermaster John Cullen, and Routmasters Alexander, Wilson and Grimsditch. There are no details of the charges against these men, however some idea of their nature can be gained from later complaints against the regiment.[170]

In May and June Van Druschke's Horse became the centre of criticism. On 25 May Thomas Smallwood (in Scarborough) wrote a description of the regiment to Luke Robinson, M.P. for the North Riding. Smallwood claimed that the regiment consisted of Roman Catholics, Irish, Scots, Dutch, French and English, and that four parts of them were ex-royalist officers. They behaved rudely, riding about robbing both men and women. No one could safely reach a town, market or fair, nor were there any horses to carry anyone as the troopers had stolen them. They had apparently promised to steal all of the inhabitants' goods before they departed. Their style of quarterng was very oppressive. The country people were beaten without cause. The troopers ate only mutton, lamb and chicken, and drank ale. Although the horses fed off the grass, the regiment assessed the people a peck of oats each day per horse. Many had already fled to Whitby Strand, or the English army, or the East Riding. In towns not quartering the regiment, the Scots exacted £84-£240 per day. So far only one trooper had been executed and that was for murder of a landlord. Rather than remaining in the same villages, the regiment changed its quarters daily, because of this Smallwood predicted the Riding would be destroyed within twenty days. The religious practices of Van Druschke's men also received censure, for they only read Bibles with Common Prayers and Apocrapha. They considered the prayers of the 'godly' tantamount to treason. On 31 May the earl of Lothian noted that measures had been taken to reduce the regiment. The next day the Scots received complaints from Major General Sydenham Poyntz and the County Committee of Yorkshire about the oppressions of the regiment. On 2 June Colonel Robert Fowlis wrote the M.P. for Cleveland concerning Van Druschke's Horse. The regiment was then quartered in Guisborough, imposing a heavy cess. With Weldon's Horse it was noted to have horse thieves, murderers, robbers and many former royalists of Newark garrison in its ranks. The regiment delighted in abusing Parliament and swearing (the latter was the leitmotiv of the royalists). On the same day the Scottish Commissioners in London wrote the Committee with the Army about the reports reaching the parliament about the behaviour of the army in general and Van Druschke's Horse in particular. The regiment had gained national infamy for containing many former royalists and for its plundering activities. On the 9th the council of the army met and decided to disband the regiment. Six days later the Commons heard that Van Druschke's Horse was disbanded, that he would leave for the continent, and that none of his men had been accepted into the Scottish army. This report appears to have been premature. On the 26th the County Committee of Yorkshire wrote the committee of the Lords and Commons from York. The County Committee complained of heavy Scots exactions and the fear of popular rebellion against them. Van Druschke's Horse was specifically mentioned as being disorderly and containing many English royalists. The regiment had moved from Clevelandshire to Richmondshire. It is not until 27 December that one can be certain the regiment had disbanded. On that day the Lord Lyon King of Arms recorded

> 'that they [the Estates] wold . . . thinke upon some recompence to be given to Vandrusche, quho for his love to the kingdome of Scotland hes, one hes auen proper charge, levied a regiment of horsse, and was with them in service of the Scots armey'.

Despite this mark of consideration by the Estates neither Van Druschke nor any of his field officers received commands in the New Model Army. Considering the generally good behaviour of most units in this army the indiscipline of this regiment can be laid squarely on its heterogeneous nature and inclusion of questionable elements.[171]

Weldon's Horse

Colonel: Michael Weldon

Lieutenant Colonels: Alexander Home (1643-45), Stephen Home (1646-47)

Major: Alexander Home

Minister: William Home[172]

Weldon was one of the few foreign colonels in the army. In autumn 1643 the English parliament sent him to Scotland. There he decided to levy a horse regiment on his own charge. To aid him he selected a Scottish mercenary as his lieutenant colonel. There is no evidence as to the area where the seven troops of the regiment were levied. Weldon's Horse was completely recruited on 25 December 1643. (However, it was not until 15 December 1645 that the Committee of Estates, acting upon the advice of Leven, commissioned Weldon a colonel of horse.) The regiment was part of Leven's army and it served as an advance element. On 20 January 1644 Weldon's was at Wark, Northumberland. The regiment remained in the northeast to protect the Scots line of supply. On 19 April the Committee with the Army ordered it to Durham to oppose the royalists attempting to implement the Commission of Array. On 5 May the Committee issued orders for the regiment to enter Northumberland. There it was to take dragoons from Morpeth, slight Blythsnook and protect the county from the Newcastle garrison. The execution of these orders engaged the regiment in a great deal of activity, from which it suffered losses. Weldon with his regiment and dragoons tried, albeit unsuccessfully, to raise the siege of Morpeth Castle. In mid June Weldon's Horse was quartered in Durhamshire. There is no further mention of the regiment until October 1645. It seems unlikely that Weldon's Horse was present at either the siege of Hereford or the battle of Philiphaugh. Instead it probably remained quartered somewhere in northern England. In mid October the parishes of Haltwhistle, Knarsdale and Kirkhaugh sent identical petitions to the Committee of Both Houses and the deputies lieutenants of Northumberland. On 13 October two troops of Weldon's had come to collect cess, but the parish constables refused it as illegal. The next day three troops appeared. They murdered one man and wounded many others. The troopers plundered High Constable Blankensopp of Belliston's house of goods worth £1,168 10s. The Scots said they would keep the goods until he paid £60 for the parishes to Captain Burton, governor of Thirwall Castle. In addition to the High Constable's losses, the regiment had taken £2,782 5s. in goods, animals and free quarter. The inhabitants asked for justice, claiming they had always been loyal to parliament. It is not known whether the parishioners' grievances were successfully redressed. In October, if not before, two troops formed part of the Berwick garrison. In November Weldon's Horse rode to the Newark area, and participated in the siege. The muster of the seven troops on 17 January 1646 revealed that they contained 170 troopers, a very weak regiment indeed. After the surrender of Newark the regiment took up quarters in Stockley, Danby, Westerdale and the dales of Blackmoor. On 2 June Colonel Robert Fowlis wrote to the Cleveland M.P. about this and Van Druschke's Horse. He complained that these were the two worst regiments in that area. They contained horse thieves, murderers and robbers, as well as many former members of the Newark garrison. The troopers and officers were noted for delighting in swearing and abusing parliament. The last mention of the regiment in this period is the muster of 21 June, which showed Weldon's to have 182 troopers. The regiment departed from England in February 1647, disbanding on the 11th at Kelso. None of the field officers received commands in the New Model Army. The story of the regiment does not end here, however. On 16 March 1648 Weldon petitioned the Estates for £43,848. Humbie was ordered to audit his accounts, after that the Estates would render some aid towards the payment of Weldon's charge. After Humbie's account was received, the Estates referred the matter to the Committee of Estates. Considering the poor state of the regime's finances and the national economy at this time, it is doubtful whether Weldon ever received a substantial portion of his claims.[173]

NOTES

1. *APS*, VI, i. 685; *Army of the Covenant*, i. 144; *Ibid.*, ii. 367; *List of Regiments*; Foster, *Members*, 250.

2. SRO, KSR Menmuir, i. 37-v; *Army of the Covenant*, i. 172, 174; *Ibid.*, ii. 382, 471-2; *RCGA*, i. 36; *Records of the Kirk*, 341.

3. *Memoirs of Guthry*, 158; A. Maxwell, *The History of Old Dundee* (Edinburgh, 1884), 477-8.

4. *Memoirs of Guthry*, 158; M. Russell, *Life of Oliver Cromwell*, 2 vols. (Edinburgh, 1829), i. 146-7; Terry, *Leslie*, 236-7, 246; P. Young, *Marston Moor 1644. The Campaign and the Battle* (Kineton, 1970), map between 144-5.

5. SRO, PA 11.2, 70; *APS*, VI, i. 228.

6. SRO, PA. 7.3, 56; *Army of the Covenant*, i. 117-9; Turner, *Memoirs*, 39.

7. SRO, KSR Old Kelso, 23 November 1645; PA. 7.4, 145; *APS*, VI, i. 634, 655, 685-6, 696; *Glasgow*, 92-3.

8. *Argyll*, i. 81, 96; *RCGA*, i. 156.

9. SRO, GD 205.18.19; *APS*, VI, i.449; *Army of the Covenant*, i. lxvii; C. S. Terry, 'Free Quarters in Linlithgow, 1642-47', *SHR*, xiv (1916), 78.

10. *APS*, VI, i. 686; Stevenson, *Alasdair*, 101, 163; Terry, 'Free Quarters', 76-7.

11. SRO, PA. 7.4, 4; PA. 16.4.7; *APS*, VI, i. 65, 84, 179, 327; *The Black Book of Taymouth*, ed. C. Innes (Bannatyne Club, c. 1855), 100; Spalding, *Memorialls*, ii. 349, 372; Terry, 'Free Quarters', 76-7.

12. *APS*, VI, i.686.

13. *The Book of the Thanes of Cawdor, 1236-1742*, ed. C. Innes (Spalding Club, xxix, 1859), 291.

14. *Army of the Covenant*, i. xc-xci, 117-20.

15. PRO, SP 41/2, 243; SRO, KSR Old Kelso, 23 November 1645; *Army of the Covenant*, i. xcii, 121-2, 124; *Ibid.*, ii. 390; M. Deane, *A true relation of the proceedings, of the Scotch army since their advance from Nottingham* (London, 1645), 2.

16. *Army of the Covenant*, i. 221; *Ibid.*, ii. 456-7, 621; *Fasti*, ii. 62.

17. SRO, KSR Old Kelso, 23 November 1645; PA. 11.2, 114; *APS*, VI, i. 111-2, 651; *Army of the Covenant*, i. lxi, 221-3; *Ibid.*, ii. 455-7, 640; *Correspondence of Scots Commissioners in London, 1644-1646*, ed. W. W. Meikle (Roxburghe Club, clx, 1917), 71; Terry, *Leslie*, 325, note on 330.

18. SAUL, PR St. Andrews, i. 56; SRO, KSR Balmerino, 22 January 1644; KSR Dunfermline, i. 41; KSR Scoonie, i. 113; PA. 11.4, 161; SR Fife, 2 October 1644; *RCGA*, i. 35; *Army of the Covenant*, ii. 374, 534; *Kirkcaldie*, 281.

19. NLS, Adv. MS. 29.2.9, 159; SRO, PA. 11.2, 78v, 110-4; *Army of the Covenant*, i. xlvii-ix; *List of Regiments*; Spalding, *Memorialls*, ii. 303; Terry, 'Free Quarters', 77; Terry, *Leslie*, 235.

20. NLS. Adv. MS. 29.2.9, 160, 173; SRO, KSR Balmerino, 2 March 1645; KSR Haddington, i. 78; *APS*, VI, i. 356; *Army of the Covenant*, ii. 533; *Kirkcaldie*, 289; Spalding, *Memorialls*, ii. 449, 451, 455, 461-3, 475; Cowan, *Montrose*, 195, 197-8, 206, 210-1, 218, 220, 233; Terry, 'Free Quarters', 78.

21. PRO, SP 16/513/52, 148; SP 16/513/53, 157; SRO, KSR Dunfermline, i. 41, 48; KSR Haddington, 15 February, 1 March 1645; KSR Kilconquhar, i. 74v-5v, 77v; *APS*, VI, i. 595-6; *Army of the Covenant*, ii. 533-4.

22. NLS, Acc. 6026, 515; SRO, GD 157.2642; PA. 11.4, 145, 158v, 161v-2; PA. 16.4.4, 7, 29; *Aberdeen Letters*, iii. 36-7, 46, 88; *APS*, VI, i.487, 684, 687; Balfour, *Works*, iii. 344; *Council of Aberdeen*, ii. 60; Maxwell, *Dundee*, 498; S. Reid, 'Aberdeen, 14th May 1646', *English Civil War Notes and Queries*, viii. 2-4; Terry 'Free Quarters', 80.

23. PRO, SP 41/2, 82; *Army of the Covenant*, ii. 485.

24. Bod. Lib., MS. Tanner 59/1, 366v; PRO, SP 41/2, 81-2; *APS*, VI, i. 45, 723, 779; *Army of the Covenant*, i. lxiii, cv, 134, 165; *Ibid.*, ii. 485; *List of Regiments*; *Truths Discovery of A black Cloud in the North: Shewing Some Antiparliamentary, inhumane, cruell, and base proceedings of the Scotch Army* (n.p., 1646), 6; S. R. Gardiner, *History of the Great Civil War, 1642-1649*, 4 vols. (new edn., London, 1894), ii. 369-71.

25. SRA, PR Glasgow, i. 333-4; SRO, PA. 11.4, 149, 165; PR Linlithgow, 2 April, 21 May 1645; *Fasti*, i. 228; *Records of the Kirk*, 433.

26. *APS*, VI, i. 859; *Scots Peerage*, iii. 360-1; A. Woolrych, *Battles of the English Civil War* (paperback edn., London, 1966), 160.

27. SRO, PA. 7.3, 89, 92; PA. 11.2, 82v; *Army of the Covenant*, i. 38, 234-5; *Baillie*, ii. 226; *Extract of Letters Dated at Edenburgh, the 14, 16 and 17. of April, 1644* (London, 1644), 2; Terry 'Free Quarters', 76-7.

28. SRA, PR Glasgow, i. 333; *APS*, VI, i. 98, 100-1; Turner, *Memoirs*, 37; Wilson, *History*, 37; Terry, 'Free Quarters', 76-7.

29. SRA, PR Glasgow, i. 320; SRO, B.66.25.368; KSR Fintry, 22 December 1644; PA. 7.3, 114; PR Dumbarton, 14 January 1644; PR Linlithgow, 4 December 1644, 12 March 1645; *APS*, VI, i. 449, 469; *Army of the Covenant*, i. 235; *Correspondence of Scots*, 71; Wilson, *History*, 43.

30. SRO, KSR Old Kelso, 23 November 1645; J. N. Buchanan, 'Charles I and the Scots, 1637-49' (Toronto Univ. Ph.D. thesis 1965), 528; Cowan, *Montrose*, 224.

31. *APS*, VI, i. 685; *Army of the Covenant*, i. 235-7; *Ibid.*, ii. 463-5, 652; *L.J.*, viii. 700; *Truths Discovery of a black Cloud*, 9.

32. SRO, KSR Old Kelso, 23 November 1645; PA. 11.4, 145, 159, 161v; *Army of the Covenant*, i. lxvii, 138; *Ibid.*, ii. 575, 647.

33. SRA, PR Glasgow, i. 352; SRO, PA. 11.4, 161v-2; PR Hamilton, 25 August 1646;

PR Linlithgow, 4 January 1644; *Army of the Covenant*, i. 187; *Ibid.*, ii. 473; *RCGA*, i. 45; *Records of the Kirk*, 454. It has been suggested that James Lindsay of Bellstanes, Governor of Berwick from 1 February till his death in March 1645, was a colonel of this regiment. However, the documents only state that Bellstanes commanded a company: SRO, PA. 11.2, 16; *APS*, VI, i. 69, 658, 700; *Army of the Covenant*, i. xxvii.

34. SRA, PR Glasgow, i. 354; *Charters and Extracts from the Burth Records of Peebles*, ed. W. Chambers (Scot. Burgh Rec. Soc., x, 1872), 378; 'The Hinde Papers', ed. W. H. D. Longstaffe, *Arch. Aeliana*, New Ser., ii. (1858), 132-3; W. Lithgow, *A True Experimentall and Exact Relation upon that Famous and Renowned Siege of Newcastle* (Edinburgh, 1645), 19; Russell, *Cromwell*, i. 147; Terry, *Leslie*, 246, 325.

35. *APS*, VI, i. 487; *Army of the Covenant*, i. 121-2, 186, 189; *Ibid.*, i. 429; *CSPD 1645*, 174; Young, *Marston Moor*, map between 144-5.

36. SRO, KSR Dunfermline, i. 51v-2; *Aberdeen Letters*, iii. 65, 69, 75, 84, 89; *APS*, VI, i. 685-6, 698, 700; *Council of Aberdeen*, ii. 68; Terry, 'Free Quarters', 80.

37. SRO, PA. 7.3, 29-30, 57-8; *APS*, VI, i. 662; *Army of the Covenant*, i. lxxvi; *Ibid.*, ii. 378.

38. SRO, KSR Old Kelso, 23 November 1645; *Army of the Covenant*, i. 216-7; *Ibid.*, ii. 476-7, 483, 555.

39. *APS*, VI, i. 47; *Army of the Covenant*, i. xxxv; Somerville, *Memorie*, ii. 275-9, 281-3.

40. *APS*, VI, i. 69, 658; *Army of the Covenant*, i. v; Terry, *Leslie*, 184.

41. *APS*, VI, i. 47; *List of Regiments*; Somerville, *Memorie*, ii. 285; Terry, *Leslie*, 196.

42. Somerville, *Memorie*, ii. 287, 289, 297, 308, 330, 332, 335, 339, 341.

43. SRO, KSR Old Kelso, 23 November 1645; *Army of the Covenant*, i. 117-9, 121-2; *Ibid.*, ii. 582, 652; Balfour, *Works*, iii. 365; Lithgow, *Newcastle*, 10; Somerville, *Memorie*, ii. 343-4; Terry, *Leslie*, 236, 326.

44. SRO, PA. 11.2, 82v; *Army of the Covenant*, i. lxxvi and note 3; *Ibid.*, ii. 376, 528.

45. *Aberdeen Letters*, iii.. 78, 88; *APS*, VI, i. 488; *Army of the Covenant*, i. 22.

46. SRO, KSR Old Kelso, 23 November 1645; PA. 11.4, 161v; *Army of the Covenant*, i. lx, 181-2; *Ibid.*, ii. 618; *Records of the Kirk*, 407.

47. SRO, KSR Old Kelso, 23 November 1645; *Army of the Covenant*, i. lx, 190-2, 243; *Ibid.*, ii. 435-6, 438, 552, 634-5; *Intelligence from the south borders of Scotland, Written from Edenburgh, April 24, 1644* (London, 1644), 4; Terry, *Leslie*, 326, 330.

48. SRO, PA. 11.4, 161; *Army of the Covenant*, i. 170, 245; *The Dictionary of National Biography*, eds. L. Stephen and S. Lee (reprint edn., Oxford, 1950), xiii. 52.

49. SRO, KSR Dunfermline, i. 47v, 51v; PR Linlithgow, 22 April, 20 May-16 June, 17 June, 1 July, 15 July, 2 September-14 October, 28 October 1646.

50. NLS, Adv. MS. 29.2.9, 160; SRO, PA. 11.2, 23, 81; *Aberdeen Letters*, iii. 86; *Army of the Covenant*, i. xlix-l; *Baillie*, ii. 226; *List of Regiments*; Spalding, *Memorialls*, ii. 294, 414, 432; Stewart, *A Full Relation of the late Victory obtained (through God's Providence)* (London, 1644), 4; Terry, *Leslie*, 217.

51. *APS*, VI, i. 487; *Army of the Covenant*, i. 167; *Ibid.*, ii. 487; I. Tullie, *A Narrative of the Siege of Carlisle in 1644 and 1645* (Carlisle, 1839), 45-6.

52. SRO, PA. 11.4, 161v-2; PA. 16.1 (Quartering Charges in East Lothian, c. 1646); *APS*, VI, i. 684-7; *RCGA*, i. 177.

53. SRO, KSR Dunfermline, i. 47v, 51v-2, 53; KSR Langside, i. 70v-1, 73v-4v.

54. PRO, SP 16/513/53, 158, 159, 160; *Army of the Covenant*, i. lxxii; *Ibid.*, ii. 533, 579.

55. SRO, PA. 11.2, 78; *APS*, VI, i. 67; *Army of the Covenant*, i. lviii.

56. *Army of the Covenant*, i. lvii, lxx; *Ibid.*, ii. 337; see above Ramsay's Horse, 177-8.

57. SRO, KSR Tyninghame, i. 145v, 148, 151v, 158, 159v, 162v; PR Haddington, 25 June, 13 November 1645; 2 April 1646; *Army of the Covenant*, i. xxviii, 212-4; *Ibid.*, ii. 442, 444, 552, 620, 637.

58. SRO, KSR Tyninghame, i. 139v-40; PR Haddington, 24 January 1644; *APS*, VI, i. 71; *List of Regiments*.

59. SRO, PA. 11.2, 104v; Terry, *Leslie*, 217, 236, 325, note on 330.

60. SRO, KSR Haddington, i. 100; KSR Old Kelso, 23 November 1645; *Army of the Covenant*, i. xxviii; *Ibid.*, ii. 442-5, 553, 574, 637.

61. SRO, KSR Canongate, 29 July-5 September, 10 October 1645; KSR Old Kelso, 23 November 1645; PA. 11.4, 161; WRH, CS 181/6/2; *Army of the Covenant*, i. 206; *Ibid.*, ii. 448, 451, 573, 635; *Fasti*, i. 70, 171, 389; *Ibid.*, vii. 321.

62. SRO, PA. 11.2, 96; *Army of the Covenant*, i. 208; *Edinburgh*, 34-5; 'Hinde Papers', 133; Stewart, *Full Relation*, 5; Russell, *Cromwell*, i. 147; Terry, *Leslie*, 246, 325.

63. SRO, KSR Old Kelso, 23 November 1645; *Army of the Covenant*, i. 204-8; *Ibid.*, ii. 449-52, 550, 572, 636; Young, *Marston Moor*, map between 144-5.

64. SRO, PR Paisley, 13 June 1644, 15 May 1645; *Army of the Covenant*, i. 163; *Ibid.*, ii. 534; *RCGA*, i. 7; Metcalfe, *A History of the county of Renfrew from the earliest times* (New Club, xiii, 1905), 263.

65. *List of Regiments*; Spalding, *Memorialls*, ii. 294; Stewart, *Full Relation*, 4, 7; Russell, *Cromwell*, i. 147-8.

66. SRO, GD. 1.38.26.6; PA. 16.4, 7, 9, 29; *Aberdeen Letters*, iii. 37, 88; *APS*, VI, i. 487, 684-6; *Army of the Covenant*, ii. 534; *Council of Aberdeen*, ii. 60; Terry 'Free Quarters', 80.

67. SAUL, PR St. Andrews, i. 47, 49, 56, 60, 62; SRO, KSR Ceres, i. 6v, 12-v; PA. 11.4, 161v; *Army of the Covenant*, i. 178; *Ibid.*, ii. 601.

68. SRO, PA. 11.2, 17, 82v; SR Fife, i. 65v; *Army of the Covenant*, ii. 377; *Baillie*, ii. 226; *List of Regiments*; Stewart, *Full Relation*, 5, 8.

69. This regiment may have been at the Hilton skirmish. SRO, KSR Kilconquhar, i. 62; PA. 7.3, 89; *APS*, VI, i. 356; *The Chronicle of Perth*, ed. J. Maidment (Maitland Club, xii, 1831), 40-1; *Memoirs of Guthry*, 173; Cowan, *Montrose*, 195, 207; Maxwell, *Dundee*, 489-90, 500-1.

70. SRO, KSR Ceres, i. 7; *APS*, VI, i. 449, 585; Cowan, *Montrose*, 218, 220; J. Howie, *Biographia Scoticana*, ed. W. MacGavin (reprint edn., Glasgow, 1828), 304; *The Life of Mr. Robert Blair, Minister at St. Andrews*, ed. T. McCrie (Wodrow Soc., xiii. 1848), 175.

71. NRH, OPR Dalgety, 3 August 1645-April 1646; SRO, SR Fife, 2 April 1644; KSR Old Kelso, 23 November 1645; *Army of the Covenant*, i. 197, 200-1; *Ibid.*, ii. 432, 434, 577-8; *Kirkcaldie*, 270-1, 283, 291; *RCGA*, i. 21.

72. SRO, B.9.12.8, 8v; KSR Old Kelso, 23 November 1645; PA. 11.2, 95, 115v; *Army of the Covenant*, i. 195-8, 209; *Ibid.*, ii. 431-4, 579, 652; *List of Regiments*; Stewart, *Full Relation*, 5; Buchanan, 'Charles I', 583; Russell, *Cromwell*, i. 147; Terry, *Leslie*, 247, 325, 393.

73. *Army of the Covenant*, ii. 536.

74. *Ibid.*, i. liii; *List of Regiments*; Somerville, *Memorie*, ii. 315; Stewart, *Full Relation*, 9; Terry, *Leslie*, 194 note 1; Woolrych, *Battles*, 69-71.

75. SRO, PA. 16.4, 7, 9; *Aberdeen Letters*, iii. 78, 81, 88; *APS*, VI, i. 487; *Army of the Covenant*, ii. 536, 645; E. Bowles, *Manifest Truths or an Inversion of Truths Manifest* (London, 1646), 55.

76. Bod. Lib., Tanner MS. 60/1, 416, 417, 418; PRO, SP 16/513/54, 5, 162; SRO, PA. 11.4, 149v, 162.

77. Bod. Lib., Carte MS. 80, 415v-7, 423-v; PRO, SP 16/514/4, 7.

78. SRO, PA. 11.2, 48, 95; *Army of the Covenant*, i. xxxii; *Ibid.*, ii. 472; *List of Regiments*; Turner, *Memoirs*, 31; *Fasti*, ii. 364; Terry, 'Free Quarters', 79; Terry, *Leslie*, 205, 236, 325.

79. SRO, GD. 6.1076.4; PA. 16.1 (Quartering Charges in East Lothian, c. 1646); *Aberdeen Letters*, iii. 37, 51, 89; *Council of Aberdeen*, ix. 60.

80. SRO, KSR Old Kelso, 23 November 1645; *APS*, VI, i. 487, 684-6; *Army of the Covenant*, i. 229.

81. SRO, PA. 11.4, 161; *Army of the Covenant*, i. lxxii; *Ibid.*, ii. 377.

82. SRO, KSR Canongate, iii. 268v-9, 270; PR Ayr, 17 April 1644; PR Paisley, 27 June 1645, 2 February 1646.

83. SRO, PA. 11.4, 163v; *Aberdeen Letters*, iii. 3, 60, 87; *APS*, VI, i. 192, 355, 469, 537; *Army of the Covenant*, i. lx; *Ibid.*, ii. 306.

84. *Army of the Covenant*, i. lxvii; *Ibid.*, ii. 621; *RCGA*, i. 36; *Fasti*, i. 126; *Ibid.*, v. 200.

85. SRO, PA. 11.2, 15v; *APS*, VI, i. 79; *Army of the Covenant*, i. lxvii, 78; *Ibid.*, ii. 638; Spalding, *Memorialls*, ii. 280, 320-2, 329, 383; Russell, *Cromwell*, i. 46, 48; *Scots Peerage*, iv. 546-7; Terry, *Leslie*, 237.

86. SRO, PA. 7.3, 32, 39-40, 47; PA. 16.3.8, 6, 11.

87. SRO, Old Kelso, 23 November 1645; *APS*, VI, i. 37, 810; *Army of the Covenant*, i. 192-4; *Ibid.*, ii. 438-41, 551; Balfour, *Works*, ii. 338; Buchanan, 'Charles I', 583.

88. NLS, Dep. 175, Box 87/2; SRO, KSR Elgin, vi. 101v; PA. 7.3.48, 28-v; PA. 7.3.56, 74; *APS*, VI, i. 79; Spalding, *Memorialls*, ii. 280-1, 294, 303, 421-2, 431-2; Terry 'Free Quarters', 76.

89. SRO, PR Paisley, 26 March, 22 April, 21 May-1 October 1646; *Army of the Covenant*, ii. 520.

90. SRO, PA. 11.2, 78; *APS*, VI, i. 698; Stevenson, *Covenanters*, 151, 155, 193, 207.

91. SRO, GD. 30.2055.91; PA. 16.2; PA. 16.3.8, 12; PA. 16.4, 4, 5; *Aberdeen Letters*, ii. 86, 384-5; *APS*, VI, i. 436, 449; *Memoirs of Guthry*, 167; Spalding, *Memorialls*, ii. 431-2.

92. PRO, SP 41/2, 108; *APS*, VI, i. 501, 698; *Army of the Covenant*, i. lxv; *Correspondence*, 154; *Selected Justiciary Cases, 1624-50*, ed. S. A. Gillon (Stair Soc., xxviii, 1974), iii. 843-4, 837.

93. SRO, GD. 30.2056.5; PA. 11.2, 17; *Army of the Covenant*, ii. 377.

94. PRO, SP 16/513/53, 155, 158, 159; *CSD 1645*, 310.

95. *Army of the Covenant*, i. lxxii; *Ibid.*, ii. 532, 578.

96. PRO, SP 16/513/53, 158, 159; *CSPD 1645*, 310; *Army of the Covenant*, ii. 538.

97. *Ibid.*, i. 181.

98. SRO, GD. 157.2642; KSR Old Kelso, 23 November 1645; PA. 11.4, 161; *Aberdeen Letters*, iii. 37, 51, 88-9; *APS*, VI, i. 88, 92, 486-7, 685-6; *Army of the Covenant*, i. lxi, 229; *Ibid.*, ii. 330; *Chronicle of Perth*, 42; *Council of Aberdeen*, ii. 60; Lithgow, *Newcastle*, 11; Terry, 'Free Quarters', 79.

99. *Army of the Covenant*, i. 164; *Records of the Kirk*, 432; *Fasti*, v. 68.

100. SRO, PA. 11.2, 51v; *Aberdeen Letters*, iii. 78, 88; *Army of the Covenant*, i. liii, 130-1; *Ibid.*, ii. 367, 484, 646; *CSPD 1645*, 552, 558-9; *List of Regiments*; Spalding, *Memorialls*, ii. 294; Tullie, *Carlisle*, 10-11.

101. Bod. Lib., Tanner MS. 59/1, 164; SRO, PA. 11.4, 162, 174; *APS*, VI, i. 487, 684-7; W. Mackenzie, *History of Galloway* (Kirkcudbright, 1841), 86.

102. *Army of the Covenant*, i. 179; *Fasti*, ii. 340.

103. This regiment may have fought at Hilton. SRO, PA. 11.2, 9v; *Army of the Covenant*, i. xxxiii; *Ibid.*, ii. 595; 'Hinde Papers', 132-3; *List of Regiments*; Stewart, *Full Relation*, 5; Terry, *Leslie*, 246, 299, 326; Young, *Marston Moor*, map between 144-5.

104. SRO, PA. 11.4, 158, 161v; PA. 16.4, 7; *Aberdeen Letters*, iii. 2-3, 45, 87; *APS*, VI, i. 449, 469, 634, 655, 681, 686; *Chronicle of Perth*, 41-2; *Glagow*, 113, 512; Cowan, *Montrose*, 195.

105. SRA, PR Glasgow, 16 July 1645; SRO PR Paisley, 15 May 1645; *Records of the Kirk*, 433; *Fasti*, iii. 314.

106. *APS*, VI, i. 86, 192, 449, 469; *HMC Report* lxxii, 216; Terry, *Leslie*, 299.

107. SRA, PR Glasgow ii. 332, 337, 340.

108. SRO, PA. 7.4, 21, 173; PA. 11.4, 161v-2; PA. 16.4, 7, 27-29; *APS*, VI, i. 92, 487; *Army of the Covenant*, i. lxv; *Ibid.*, ii. 535; *Glasgow*, 79, 511; Cowan, *Montrose*, 247.

109. SRO, PA. 11.2, 78; *APS*, VI, i. 436, 501.

110. NLS, Wodrow Letters Quarto 19, 68; PRO, SP 28/120, 164; SRO, KSR Scoonie, i. 141, 146; *Army of the Covenant*, ii. 525, 587; *Extracts from the Presbytery Book of Strathbogie, 1631-54*, ed. J. Stuart (Spalding Club, vii, 1843), 111; *Kirkcaldie*, 302; *RCGA*, i. 21, 36, 100; *Fasti*, v. 319.

111. William Kinninmonth was with the regiment until 17 January 1646 at least; PRO, SP 28/120, 164; *APS*, VI, i. 19,45; *Army of the Covenant*, i. liv-v; *List of Regiments*; Spalding, *Memorialls*, ii. 294; *Strathbogie*, 111.
112. Bod. Lib., Tanner MS. 60/1, 38; SRO, KSR Old Kelso, 23 November 1645; PA. 11.4, 150, 151; PA. 16.4, 7, 28, 46; RH. 15.64/10; *APS*, VI, i. 394; *The Letter Books of Sir William Brereton, 31 January-29 May 1645*, ed. R. N. Dore, (Rec. Soc. Lancs and Cheshire, cxxiii, 1984), 57-69, 91-106, 113-9, 141-2, 156-7, 391, 581, 605; Stewart, *Full Relation*, 5, 9; Tullie, *Carlisle*, 3, 10-11; Russell, *Cromwell*, i. 149; Terry, *Leslie*, 235, 241, 295; Woolrych, *Battles*, 70-1, 76-7.
113. NLS Wodrow Analecta Folio 27, 78; PRO, SP 41/2, 164; *APS*, VI, i. 709; *Army of the Covenant*, ii. 524; *The Diplomatic Correspondence of Jean de Montereul and the Brothers de Bellievre, French Ambassadors in England and Scotland 1645-48*, ed. J. G. Fotheringham (Scot. Hist. Soc., 1st Ser., xxix, 1898), i. 393.
114. *Army of the Covenant*, i. lxxii; *Ibid.*, ii. 580, 646; *List of Regiments*.
115. SRO, KSR Culross, 3 November 1646-24 March 1647; KSR Kinghorn, 10 April, 15 June, 29 September, 4 October 1645; PR Jedburgh, 2, 7 February, 1 May, 17 July, 18 September 1644; *Army of the Covenant*, i. 160, 249; *Ibid.*, ii. 483; *Kirkcaldie*, 279, 283, 285; *RCGA*, i. 57, 73.
116. *Army of the Covenant*, i. lv; *List of Regiments*; Spalding, *Memorialls*, ii. 294; Stewart, *Full Relation*, 7; Russell, *Cromwell*, i. 145, 147; Terry, *Leslie*, 192-3, 221, 339.
117. PRO, SP 41/2, 200; SRO, KSR Old Kelso, 23 November 1645; PA. 11.4, 150; *Army of the Covenant*, ii. 492; Buchanan, 'Charles I', 528.
118. PRO, SP 16/513/52, 152; *APS*, VI, i. 649; *Army of the Covenant*, ii. 488, 648; Somerville, *Memorie*, ii. 279; R. A. Bensen, 'South-West Fife and the Scottish Revolution: the presbytery of Dunfermline, 1633-52' (Edinburgh Univ., M.Litt. thesis 1978), 142; Terry, *Leslie*, 194 note 1.
119. SRO, KSR Bathgate, i. 34v-6; PR Linlithgow, 2, 16 April-10 October 1645; *Army of the Covenant*, i. 201; *Ibid.*, ii. 446, 591, 619; *Records of the Kirk*, 453; *The Records of the Synod of Lothian and Tweeddale, 1589-1649*, ed. J. Kirk (Stair Soc., xxxi, 1977), 189; *Fasti*, i. 286.
120. SRO, KSR Old Kelso, 23 November 1645; PA. 11.2, 9v; PA. 11.4, 161v; *Army of the Covenant*, i. xxxv, 202, 242; *Ibid.*, ii. 445-8, 460, 551; Bowles, *Manifest Truths*, 3; Terry, *Leslie*, 205, 236, 325; Young, *Marston Moor*, map between 144-5.
121. PRO, SP 16/513/53, 157-8; *Army of the Covenant*, i. 254, 281; *Ibid.*, ii. 507, 538, 579-80, 643.
122. SRO, Paisley, 13 June, 15 August-11 September, 12 December 1644, 2 January, 1, 2, 8 April 1645; Metcalfe, *Renfrew*, 262.
123. SRO, PA. 11.2, 9v; *Army of the Covenant*, i. xxxvi, 55-6, 117-9, 209-12; *Ibid.*, ii. 452-5, 553, 593-5, 619, 639; *List of Regiments*; Lithgow, *Newcastle*, 19; *Peebles*, i. 378; Stewart, *Full Relation*, 5; Russell, *Cromwell*, i. 147; Terry, *Leslie*, 247, 250.
124. SRO, PA. 7.5, 19; *Aberdeen Letters*, iii. 45, 78, 118-9; *APS*, VI, i. 449, 547, 681, 685-6, 700; *Chronicles of Perth*, 41; *Memoirs of Guthry*, 184, 187; Spalding, *Memorialls*, ii. 461-2, 463-7, 473; Cowan, *Montrose*, 281-21.
125. *Army of the Covenant*, i. lxxii, cv; *Ibid.*, ii. 379; Spalding, *Memorialls*, ii. 422-3.
126. PRO, SP 16/513/53, 157, 158; *Army of the Covenant*, ii. 539.
127. *APS*, VI, i. 672; Balfour, *Works*, iii. 364; *HMC Report* xxix. 363-4.
128. *Army of the Covenant*, i. 182-3; *RCGA*, i. 42.
129. NLS, Acc. 6026, 32; SRO, KSR Old Kelso, 23 November 1645; PA. 7.3, 51, 84; PA. 16.3.8, 19; *Aberdeen Letters*, ii. 266; *Army of the Covenant*, i. xxxvii; 'The Late Proceedings of the Scotish Army, certifying their passing over Tyne', *Reprints of Rare Tracts Chiefly Illustrative of the history of the Northern Counties*, ed. M. Richardson (Newcastle, 1846), ii. 9; *List of Regiments*; *The Miscellany of the Spalding Club*, iii. ed. J. Stuart (Spalding Club, xvi, 1846), 148-9; Spalding, *Memorialls*, ii. 309, 320-2, 379; Terry, *Leslie*, 325.

130. PRO, SP 41/2, 32, 39v; *Army of the Covenant*, i. xxxvii, 154; *Ibid.*, ii. 478-9, 650.
131. SRO, KSR Old Kelso, 23 November 1645; *Army of the Covenant*, i. 183-4; *Ibid.*, ii. 479-80, 624.
132. SRO, KSR Old Kelso, 23 November 1645; PA. 11.2, 36v, 96; PA. 11.4, 161v; *APS*, VI, i. 51; *Army of the Covenant*, i. xxxviii, 22; *Ibid.*, ii, 479-80; 'Late Proceedings of the Scotish Army in passing over Tyne', 9; *List of Regiments*; Terry, *Leslie*, 315, 326.
133. PRO, SP 41/2, 146; *Army of the Covenant*, i. 168; *RCGA*, i. 108; *Fasti*, ii. 277.
134. SRO, PA. 6.4, 5, 7, 9, 28, 68; *Aberdeen Letters*, iii. 46, 78; *APS*, VI, i. 581, 661, 669-71, 687, 779; *Army of the Covenant*, i. lxix, cv-vi; *Ibid.*, ii. 530, 625, 654; W. Thomson, *Montrose Totally Routed in Tividale in Scotland* (London, 1645), 6; M. Kishlansky, 'The Case of the Army Truly Stated: The Creation of the New Model Army', *Past and Present*, lxxxi (1978), 69; Terry, 'Free Quarters', 77, 79.
135. SRO, PR Dalkeith, 26 September 1644, 5, 12 June-13 November 1645.
136. SRO, PA. 7.3, 89; PA. 11.2, 82v; *APS*, VI, i. 861; *Army of the Covenant*, i. xxxix, 59-60, 172-3; *List of Regiments*; *South Leith Records*, ed. D. Robertson (Edinburgh, 1911), 51; Stewart, *Full Relation*, 8; Russell, *Cromwell*, i. 147-8; Terry, *Leslie*, 181, 246, 299.
137. SRO, PR Perth, i. 897, 912-3; RH. 16/64/10; *APS*, VI, i. 356, 449, 537, 673; *Chronicles of Perth*, 40-2; *Memoirs of Guthry*, 173; *Robert Blair*, 174-5; Cowan, *Montrose*, 218; Terry, 'Free Quarters', 77.
138. NLS, Wodrow Letters Quarto 19, 68; SRO PR Linlithgow, 24 April, 22 May 1644; PR Perth, i. 829, 844; *Army of the Covenant*, i. 219-20; *Ibid.*, ii. 381; R. H. R. Liddell, 'Saint Madoes and its clergymen: notes on a Perthshire parish, 1640-88', *SHR*, xxv (1928), 257.
139. *Army of the Covenant*, i. xl; *List of Regiments*; Furgol, 'Religious Aspects', 269.
140. NLS, Wodrow Letters Quarto 19, 68; PRO, SP 41/2, 3; SRO, PR Biggar, i. 20, 22; PR Haddington, 18 December 1644; PR Peebles, 19 June 1645; *Army of the Covenant*, i. 218; *Ibid.*, ii. 475; *Kirkcaldie*, 309; *Lothian and Tweeddale*, 166, 171; Terry, *Leslie*, 236; Young, *Marston Moor*, 20.
141. SRO, PR Ayr, 19 February, 5 June, 7 July, 1645; *Army of the Covenant*, i. 162; *Ibid.*, ii. 366; *RCGA*, i. 53; *Records of the Kirk*, 341.
142. SRO, GD. 1.38.26, 6; GD. 30.2055.9b; PA. 11.4, 162; PA. 16.4, 7, 8, 9, 29; RH. 15/64/10; *Aberdeen Letters*, iii. 71, 78, 81-2; *APS*, VI, i. 487, 673, 684-7; *Army of the Covenant*, i. lxvi; *Ibid.*, ii. 312, 535; *Baillie*, ii. 226; *L.J.*, vii. 707; Terry, *Leslie*, 291.
143. *Army of the Covenant*, i. lviii; *Ibid.*, ii. 313, 336-7.
144. SRO, PR Dalkeith, 6 June, 25 September 1644; *Lothian and Tweeddale*, 175.
145. *APS*, VI, i. 114; *Army of the Covenant*, i. lxiii-v; *Ibid.*, ii. 308; *Lothian and Tweeddale*, 175; Cowan, *Montrose*, 184; Terry, *Leslie*, 326.
146. *Army of the Covenant*, i. xli, 227; *Ibid.*, ii. 254.
147. *APS*, VI, i. 51; *Army of the Covenant*, i. xli; 'Late Proceedings of the Scotish Army in passing over Tyne', 8; *List of Regiments*; Lithgow, *Newcastle*, 12; Stewart, *Full Relation*, 5; Russell, *Cromwell*, i. 147; Terry, *Leslie*, 237 note 3, 246, 299, 325.
148. SRO, PA. 11.4, 161; *APS*, VI, i. 564; *Army of the Covenant*, i. 227-8; *Ibid.*, ii. 458-61, 594, 624, 656; *Covenanter Government*, 36.
149. NRH OPR Alyth, 21 July, 24 November 1644; PRO, SP 41/2, 21; SRO, KSR Old Kelso, 23 November 1645; *Army of the Covenant*, i. xlii, 175-7; *Ibid.*, ii. 470, 478, 575; *Fasti*, i. 218.
150. PRO, SP 41/2, 20; SRO, GD. 121, Box 104; KSR Holy Rude, Stirling, 9 June 1645; KSR Old Kelso, 23 November 1645; *APS*, VI, i. 51; *Army of the Covenant*, i. xliii, 76-7, 117-9; *Ibid.*, ii. 470, 574-5; *Chronicle of Perth*, 41; 'Late Proceedings of the Scotish Army in passing over Tyne', 9; *List of Regiments*; Terry, 'Free Quarters', 76.
151. PRO, SP 41/2, 228; SRO, KSR Culross, i. 231; SRO, PR Perth, i. 859, 880, 891-3, 906, 908, 911, 914, 916, 918, 929, 931; *Army of the Covenant*, i. 184-5.
152. PRO, SP 41/2, 221, 223; SRO, GD. 112.39, 847; KSR Old Kelso, 23 November

1645; PA. 7.3, 25, 53; PA. 11.2, 81; PA. 16.3.8; *Army of the Covenant*, i. lviii, lxiii, 185; *Ibid.*, ii. 523-4, 648; *Justiciary Cases*, iii. 623-5; *Memoirs of Guthry*, 151; Spalding, *Memorialls*, ii. 349-50, 352-3.

153. SRO, PA. 11.2, 78; *Army of the Covenant*, i. lviii; *Ibid.*, ii. 313.

154. *APS*, VI, i. 560; *Army of the Covenant*, i. lvii; *Ibid.*, ii. 343, 378.

155. *Ibid.*, i. lxx, 164; *RCGA*, i. 159-60.

156. SRO, PA. 7.3, 92; *APS*, VI, i. 115, 486, 500, 789-90; *Army of the Covenant*, i. lxx, 234; *Ibid.*, ii. 529, 547; *Memorials of the Great Civil War in England from 1646 to 1652*, 2 vols., ed. H. Cary (London, 1852), ii. 82; *RCGA*, i. 159-60; Spalding, *Memorialls*, ii. 422-3, 431-2; Terry, *Leslie*, 291.

157. *Army of the Covenant*, i. lvii, 169.

158. SRO, PA. 11.2, 48; *Army of the Covenant*, i. 65.

159. PRO, SP 41/2, 211; *Army of the Covenant*, ii. 522; *RCGA*, i. 114, 173.

160. *APS*, VI, i. 51, 54; *Army of the Covenant*, i. xliii; *HMC Report*, lxxii. 216; *List of Regiments*; Lithgow, *Newcastle*, 21; Turner, *Memoirs*, 39; Terry, 'Free Quarters', 75; Terry, *Leslie*, 205, 236, 326; Young, *Marston Moor*, 20.

161. PRO, SP 41/2, 211; SP 16/513/52, 153; SRA, PR Glasgow, ii. 319; SRO, KSR Old Kelso, 23 November 1645; *Army of the Covenant*, i. xliii, 121-2; *Ibid.*, ii. 522-3; 576, 655; *Calendar of the Proceedings of the Committee for Compounding*, 5 vols., ed. M. Green (London, 1888), ii. 924; *L.J.*, vii, 707.

162. *Army of the Covenant*, i. lxx, 168.

163. SRO, KSR Dron, 1 July, 8 July-9 November 1645; KSR Kinnard, i. 72-3; PR Perth, i. 833-4, 837, 839, 898, 908, 911, 914, 931, 944, 961, 968; *Army of the Covenant*, i. 180-1; *Ibid.*, ii. 382; *Fasti*, iv. 161.

164. SRO, KSR Old Kelso, 23 November 1645; PA. 11.2, 9v; *APS*, VI, i. 486-7, 686-7; *Army of the Covenant*, i. xliv, 181; *Chronicle of Perth*, 42; 'Late Proceedings of the Scotish Army in passing over Tyne', 9; *List of Regiments*; Stewart, *Full Relation*, 5; Russell, *Cromwell*, i. 147; Terry, *Leslie*, 237 note 3, 247, 325.

165. SRO, PR Jedburgh, 6, 20 November 1644-6 April, 29 October 1645; *Army of the Covenant*, i. 215; *Ibid.*, ii. 383, 467-8, 593; *RCGA*, i. 57, 144.

166. SRO, KSR Old Kelso, 23 November 1645; PA. 11.2, 48; PA. 11.4, 161; *APS*, VI, i. 51; *Army of the Covenant*, i. xlv, 121-2; *Ibid.*, ii. 466-9, 549, 592, 657; *List of Regiments*; Turner, *Memoirs*, 41; J. W. Kennedy, 'The Teviotdale Regiment', *Hawick Arch. Soc.*, xxxv (1903), 58; Terry, *Leslie*, 236.

167. *Army of the Covenant*, i. 255; *Ibid.*, ii. 481-2, 554; *Fasti*, ii. 188.

168. SRO, KSR Old Kelso, 23 November 1645; PA. 11.4, 161; *APS*, VI, i. 151, 351; *Army of the Covenant*, i. xlvi, 62, 226; *Ibid.*, ii. 481, 654; *List of Regiments*; Lithgow, *Newcastle*, 19; Stewart, *Full Relation*, 5; Kennedy, 'Teviotdale', 58-60; Russell, *Cromwell*, i. 147; Terry, *Leslie*, 247, 325.

169. PRO, SP 41/2, 70; *Army of the Covenant*, i. lxxi.

170. Bod. Lib., Carte MS. 80, 42v; PRO, SP 16/513/53, 157; SP 16/513/54, 160, 164-5; *Army of the Covenant*, i. lxxi; *Ibid.*, ii. 527; *HMC Report*, xxix, 354, 367-8; *L.J.*, viii. 349-50.

171. Quote from Balfour, *Works*, iii. 346; *C.J.*, iv. 577; *Correspondence of Lothian*, i. 184-5; *Correspondence of Scots Commissioners*, 189; *Memorials of the Great Civil War*, i. 66-8, 82; *Truths Discovery of A black Cloud*, 5-6.

172. *Army of the Covenant*, i. lvii.

173. Bod. Lib., Tanner MS. 60/1, 294; NLS, Wodrow Analecta Folio 67, 56; PRO, SP 41/2, 65; SRO, PA. 11.2, 28, 44; PA. 11.4, 148-v; *APS*, VI, ii. 342; *Army of the Covenant*, i. lvi-vii, 133; *Ibid.*, ii. 531; *List of Regiments*; *Memorials of the Great Civil War*, i. 82; C. H. Firth, 'The Battle of Marston Moor', *Trans. Roy. Hist. Soc.*, New Ser., xii (1898), 26; Terry, *Leslie*, 176-7 note 3, 181, 285.

6
Home Army

Aberdeen Burghs' Foot

Commander: Major Arthur Forbes

On Sunday 8 September 1644 the ministers of Old and New Aberdeen announced a levée en masse in the two burghs, which was to rendezvous on the links. The burghs contributed 500 foot in four companies on the 12th. At the battle of Aberdeen on the 13th the regiment formed part of the centre or left of the Covenanter line. After the Covenanter forces broke only this unit managed to retreat correctly. However, the cohesion and existence of the burgh's infantry ended when Alasdair MacDonald with 400 Irish infantry fell upon the townsmen. Few of the regiment escaped to return to their former occupations and peaceful daily life.[1]

Angus Foot

Joint colonels: John, 2nd earl of Kinghorn, and James, Lord Carnegie

Following Huntly's rising in March 1644 Angus raised a foot regiment for Argyll's expedition to crush the royalists. On 31 March Dundee had a company for the regiment on foot (with ten days' provisions and money for the soldiers), which was ordered to the Mearns immediately. On 2 May, after rendezvousing at Dunottar Castle on 17 April with other forces, the Angus Foot entered Aberdeen with the rest of Argyll's army. Two days later it marched out to take part in the campaign to put down the supporters of Huntly. On the 31st the army re-entered Aberdeen. The 600-800 soldiers of the regiment received a sum of £5,473 15s. from Aberdeen for the month's supplies. On the day of their return some soldiers killed an Aberdonian and injured another. The bailies imprisoned the men for their crimes. However, Kinghorn had them freed. On 1 June the regiment departed from Aberdeen and paid for its quarters. A few days later the Angus Foot disbanded permanently. However, Carnegie continued to act as the colonel of the shire until mid 1645 at least.[2]

Earl of Annandale's Regiment

Colonel: James, 2nd earl of Annandale

Lieutenant Colonel: James Scougall

On 7 August 1645 a petition reached the Estates from Lieutenant Colonels Scougall, Gibson, William Osburne and Blair asking for their pay. These four officers were all professional soldiers who had been sent to the four quarters of Dumfries. They were to organise forces for the crushing of any rebellions by royalists. In addition to Annandale, the earl of Queensberry, Lord Johnston and the laird of Lagg were colonels of these Dumfriesshire forces. There is no sign that any of these regiments were ever raised. For that reason they are only treated in this entry.[3]

Ardkinglas' Forces

Commander: James Campbell of Ardkinglas

Ardkinglas commanded Campbells on several occasions, but generally under the auspices of his chief Argyll. Following the descent of an Irish raiding party into the western Isles in late 1643 Argyll commissioned Ardkinglas his deputy lieutenant on 6 December. Ardkinglas levied 600 men, but does not seem to have proceeded against the rebels until either the late winter or early spring of 1644. Ardkinglas drove the Irish back to Ireland and then proceeded against their allies on Mull. Sometime after mid May Ardkinglas led his men against Alasdair MacDonald's garrison on Rathlin Island. Alasdair's men fled to Islay and Jura with the Campbells in pursuit. Ardkinglas proudly reported the results of his activities on the two islands.

> I took them [the Irish] and causit cut of[f] above ane hundredth and ffyifteine of them and took some prisoners.

During these operations against the anti-Campbell coalition, which lasted between two and a half and four months, Ardkinglas had had the aid of a frigate.[4]

Following the successful completion of this campaign Ardkinglas waited only a few months before receiving another commission. In early June 1644 Argyll had his commission as the king's lieutenant in the western Highlands and islands extended. Again Ardkinglas was deputed to raise 500 men from amongst the Campbells and their allies. It is likely that this regiment was part of the 2,600 men that Argyll led on a summer campaign against the royalist clans in Lochaber, Morvern, Ardnamurchan, and the isles. Sometime in September Ardkinglas joined Argyll's army at either Stirling or Perth for the marquis' second campaign in the northeast. Ardkinglas' regiment now numbered 800 foot. Their two-day stay in Aberdeen, 18-19 September, cost the burgh £320. The regiment formed part of Argyll's army for the entire campaign, which included a march to Inverness and from there back to Aberdeen via Badenoch and Atholl.[5] It is possible that Ardkinglas' men were part of the 1,000 Campbells who left for home from Huntly on 14 November. (This force plundered its way through Speyside, Badenoch and Lochaber.) While there is no mention of Ardkinglas leading men at Inverlochy in February 1645, it is extremely unlikely (given his service record) that he was not there.

Ardkinglas disappears from the scene for nearly a year after Inverlochy. In the winter of 1645-46 he gathered a force of Campbell refugees, possibly to form them into a new regiment. He led them south from Argyll to recapture the castle belonging to Campbell of Glenorchy in Loch Dochart, which the MacNabs had seized. Ardkinglas then besieged Edinample Castle in Loch Earn, which had a garrison of MacDonald allies. After the siege was lifted (or during it) men of Clan Menzies and some Stewarts of Balquhidder joined Ardkinglas. He reached Callander in February 1646 with about 1,200 men. However, Patrick Graham of Inchbrackie and John Drummond of Balloch raised a force of 700 royalist Atholl Highlanders. On 13 February the royalists suddenly struck, routing the Campbell force. Ardkinglas rallied part of his men and led them to Stirling. From there they went to Renfrewshire where the inhabitants disliked them. Ardkinglas' men were eventually assigned quarters in the Lennox. There he managed to impose some discipline and training on his men, transforming them from a group of homeless wanderers into a regiment. Ardkinglas' first use for his new regiment was to break the siege of Skipness Castle. While doing so his men killed Archibald MacDonald, a brother of Alasdair MacColla. The new unit then went to Ayrshire (probably Irvine) to prepare for the invasion of Cowal, homeland of the Lamonts. Until February 1645 the Lamonts had been Campbell allies, however, after Inverlochy they attached themselves to Alasdair MacDonald. In mid May 1646 a large force of Campbells (probably Ardkinglas' new regiment) landed in Cowal under Ardkinglas. The Lamonts fled into Toward and Ascog castles. The Campbells began to besiege them, but they initially lacked artillery. However, on 1 June the besiegers of Toward Castle received some guns and began to bombard it. Two days later Sir James Lamont, chief of the clan, surrendered the castle. The terms of the surrender allowed Sir James, the garrison and their families to repair to an area under Alasdair's control. Sir James then persuaded Ascog Castle to surrender. The Campbells plundered and burnt it before leading their prisoners to Dunoon. There in the kirkyard contrary to the terms of the two surrenders the men of Ardkinglas' command tried the Lamonts. The verdicts were known before the trials began. Ardkinglas' men butchered a hundred Lamonts and hanged thirty-six leaders. Sir James was spared. With that the bloody successes of Ardkinglas' force ended.[6]

Sometime in 1646 Ardkinglas' men were officially formed into a regiment of infantry which remained on foot until February/March 1647. On 14 January 1647 Ardkinglas led 1,500 men into the presbyteries of Dunblane and Auchterarder. He then imposed a tax of £2 13s. per plow and a firlot of meal for every twenty men for four days without the approval of the Committee of War. On 31 January the Estates ordered all of the regiment and officers to move to Stirlingshire and quarter there as the Committee of War would appoint. The regiment only marched south on 12 February. On the 26th the Estates set the payment of arrears owed the regiment. Although the men were owed £8,866 13s. 4d. for the period 1 February to 10 March, the cost of quarters in

Stirlingshire reduced the amount due in cash to £2,866 13s. 4d. On 28 February the earl of Tullibardine, the Lords Cardross and Drummond presented a petition to the Estates on behalf of the gentry of the Perthshire presbyteries which Ardkinglas had taxed in January. However, the Estates decided against the petitioners and the colonel went unpunished. Meanwhile on 29 January the Estates had commissioned Ardkinglas colonel of a regiment of Highland foot in the New Model Army. At least part of his regiment in the Home Army was retained for his new command. Ardkinglas' old regiment partially disbanded after 12 February.

Ardnamurchan's Force

Commander: Sir Donald Campbell of Ardnamurchan

The men in this unit initially belonged to the three regiments of Campbells and their allies which mustered at Dunstaffnage Castle on 22 July 1644. Sometime in August Argyll reached Ardnamurchan on his campaign against Alasdair and his allies. The marquis commenced the siege of Mingary Castle, which was garrisoned by soldiers of Alasdair's Irish infantry regiments. On the 20th Argyll left for Edinburgh, and placed Ardnamurchan in charge. The laird received no reinforcements, and probably, more importantly, lacked artillery. Thus, until early October Ardnamurchan concerned himself more with the prisoners held by the garrison than taking the castle. One of the major conflicts between the two forces was over who should provision the prisoners. Ardnamurchan finally accepted the responsibility when the garrison threatened to cease feeding them. On 20 September Ardnamurchan secured the release of three prisoners by promising to pay their ransom. Ten days later the two sides agreed to exchange three ministers for Coll MacDonald and two of his sons. Learning of Alasdair's approach, Ardnamurchan lifted the siege on the night of 5-6 October. It is likely that he held a detachment of Campbells at Inverlochy.[8]

Argyll's Regiments

Colonel: Archibald, 1st marquis of Argyll

Between April 1644 and February 1645 Argyll personally commanded four expeditions against royalist Scots and men of the MacDonald-Irish-Highland alliance. In some of these instances it cannot be definitely established that the marquis possessed his own regiment, however he was of such importance in all of them that it would be improper to exclude a discussion of the campaigns. Furthermore in certain instances Argyll is referred to in his broader context as a clan chief. Consequently, some of the military activities of Clan Campbell are discussed in this entry instead of being placed in a separate section. Argyll's first command in the Home Army came in late November 1643 when the Convention of Estates commissioned him the king's lieutenant in the western highlands and isles to crush Alasdair MacDonald, the MacDonalds and the Irish. The marquis could raise 600 men and appoint deputies to command them. (As stated above, he selected Ardkinglas for his deputy.) The marquis' first opportunity for a field command came in late March/early April 1644 when he received command of the expedition to crush Huntly's rising. By 17 April a regiment of 1,000 foot had been raised for the marquis from the Campbells and their allies in the shire of Argyll. On the 26th it was at the rendezvous of his army at Dunottar Castle. From there the regiment took part in the campaign which Argyll led to Aberdeen, Turriff, Cullen, Elgin and Strathbogie. During it the regiment stole and destroyed goods and grain. In late May Argyll's Foot, now only 800 men strong, quartered in Birse and Cromar. The regiment quartered in Aberdeen from 24-31 May. During the campaign Argyll's Foot received a quartering allowance of twenty-four bolls of meal, 120 wedders and £159 per day. On the 31st Argyll departed from Aberdeen for Edinburgh, but his men went into garrisons in Birse, Cromar, Glentanar, Glenmuick, Abergeldie, Aboyne and elsewhere. The soldiers plundered without discerning between royalist and Covenanter or Gordon and anti-Gordon. The Campbells constantly searched for plunder, even opening graves and dragging pools of water, if a hostile account can be believed. However, Argyll's Foot and subsequent Campbell formations seemed to have a predilection for stealing from Roman Catholics. During the regiment's stint on garrison duty it captured all the animals in the area and ransomed them back to their owners before departing. On 1 July all but one captain and eighty soldiers of Argyll's Foot marched out of their garrisons and headed for Dunstaffnage Castle. The remnant followed shortly thereafter, ending the first incursion of Argyll's men into the northeast in the mid 1640s.[9]

The reason for the regiment's removal from the garrisons in Deeside arose from developments on the west coast. On 16 June the Estates commissioned Argyll the king's lieutenant on land and sea against the Irish MacDonalds. Argyll could act on this commission until 1 November. The marquis soon found a use for his commission when Alasdair and three regiments of Irish foot landed in Ardnamurchan. Sometime in June Argyll sent out orders for a rendezvous at Dunstaffnage Castle of his clansmen and their allies. One of these must have gone to his regiment in the northeast. On 22 July it and 1,800 other men (in two regiments) were at Dunstaffnage. This force campaigned in the isles, Ardnamurchan, Morvern and Lochaber until 2 September doing little else but terrifying the inhabitants. On 3 August the preliminary action of the siege of Mingary Castle took place. Four days later Argyll with five ships and many boats arrived in the area. The next day the siege formally commenced. About the same time Argyll's men successfully attacked two ships belonging to the Irish. On the 20th Argyll left the area, placing Ardnamurchan in charge (see above, p. 198). He reached Stirling on 4 September and began to assemble an army, which included his regiment of foot, for his second campaign in the northeast.

From there Argyll proceeded to Perth and collected more men there. The march to Aberdeen started on the 14th; two days later Argyll met the leaders of the northeast Covenanters at Brechin. Due to their recent defeat by Montrose (on the 13th), he received little help from those who had joined him in the spring. The army took Aberdeen on the 18th without facing any opposition. From there Argyll led his army through Strathbogie, Strathisla, Boyne, Enzie and Auchindroun to Forres, then to Inverness. Throughout the march Argyll's men seized food, weapons and any other goods they could use. The soldiers destroyed the Gordons' grain and killed the sheep and cattle which they did not require, all in an effort to make the area unable to support royalist forces. From Inverness Argyll marched through Badenoch and Atholl, which he had his men burn. On 23 October the army was at Dunottar Castle preparing to move on to Aberdeen. It reached the burgh the next day and on the 25th it was at Inverurie. Learning that Montrose was at Fyvie Castle, Argyll for once moved quickly and surprised his opponent there on the 28th. Although Montrose was at Argyll's mercy if the latter made a sustained attack, only some skirmishing occurred. On the 30th Argyll withdrew having thrown away his best chance of defeating Montrose. Argyll's army was at Huntly on 6 November. Eight days later he disbanded his army there by sending 1,000 Campbells (possibly including his regiment) to plunder their way home through Strathaucin, Strathspey, Badenoch and Lochaber. Argyll ended the campaign by granting pardons to those royalists who were willing to leave Montrose's army. He then returned to Edinburgh, where he and his lieutenant the earl of Lothian handed in their commissions. Argyll's Foot marched back to its homeland at this time.[10]

While Argyll might think that he had severely reduced the ability of his enemies to carry on the war, they were already preparing for the invasion of the shire of Argyll which would devastate the power of the Campbells. Meanwhile in Edinburgh Argyll was involved in a dispute with Lieutenant General William Baillie over command of troops in his territory. In the end the Committee of Estates granted the marquis a commission to proceed against the Irish in the west of Scotland, making him independent of Baillie. By 13 December Argyll had left Edinburgh for Inveraray, but Montrose's army was on the fringes of Argyll's territory. Soon the royalists had penetrated deep into Campbell lands, burning, plundering and killing able-bodied men as they went. Following the burning of his capital, Argyll fled to Roseneath. There in early January 1645 he met Baillie, who had marched from Perth and Stirling with a force of regular infantry. Argyll refused to allow Baillie to lead his men into the marquis' bailiwick. Instead Baillie was forced to 'loan' Argyll 1,100 of his men. Returning to his lands the marquis began to muster his clan. By 22 January he was at Castle Stalker with a force of 1,900 highlanders and 1,100 lowland foot. The army marched to Inverlochy Castle via Lochaber, reaching the stronghold on the 31st. During the march Argyll suffered a riding accident which disabled him from personally commanding his army. He appointed Sir Duncan Campbell of Auchinbreck, the lieutenant colonel of his 'Irish' regiment, to lead the army, while he retired to his personal galley in Loch

Linnhe. Among the troops at Inverlochy were Argyll's Foot, which served in the centre during the battle. Montrose's and Alasdair's army attacked the marquis' army on the morning of 2 February and destroyed it. The Covenanter force lost 50% of its men or 1,500 killed, including fifteen Campbell barons. Twenty-two gentlemen of the clan fell prisoner and were held for ransom. Argyll's Foot ceased to exist after the battle. If the casualty figures for the army are extended to the regiment, then only 400 men survived the battle. Argyll served as an advisor at Kilsyth, albeit an inept one. The last mention of the regiment is on 5 November, when it was sent to Dundee to form part of the garrison.[11]

Argyll's Highland Foot

Colonel: Archibald, 1st marquis of Argyll

Lieutenant Colonel: James Menzies

Major: James Stewart

On 27 November 1645 the Estates commissioned Argyll colonel of a special regiment. Its purpose was to pursue and slay any rebels (Irishmen or highland royalists) and their allies. The regiment could convoke courts martial to try any rebel prisoners. The regiment was to consist of 932 men. They were to be levied as follows: 300 men from the shire of Argyll, 200 from the laird of Glenorchy's lands, 100 from the laird of Weem's lands of Fortingall, Bolfrachs, Kilhaffie and Balnabaird, 100 from the lands of the lairds of Lawers, Aberurchill, Cultiwragan and Clahaig, 60 from the earl of Perth's lands in Comrie and Callander, 60 from the earl of Tullibardine's lands in Bucharty, Auchtertyre and Struan, 40 from the laird of Buchanan's lands in Drymen and Strathyre with Leny and Ardinpryor, 30 from the laird of Macfarlan's lands, 20 from James Stewart of Ardvorlich and the earl of Airth in the parishes of Drymenport and Aberfoyle, 12 from Colin Campbell of Bochastell, and 10 from the laird of Luss' lands in Row. On 3 January 1646 the Estates delegated the following places to serve as possible garrison houses for the regiment: Castle Menzies, Garth Castle, Finlarig Castle, the castle on the Isle of Lochtay, Fordew, Aberurchill, Moynes, Trochrig [Trochry?], Dewchrie, Cambismoir, and Cragivarnie castles. From this arrangement and the powers given the regiment it may be assumed that Argyll's Highland Foot was to conduct operations which would liberate the parts of the Campbell empire lost to Alasdair and his allies. Unfortunately, this can only be an assumption because the regiment disappears from the record until November. In March Lieutenant Colonel Menzies caused Lord Cardross £2,164 4s. 10d. in losses by stealing food and fodder. On 23 November 600 soldiers, excluding officers, under Lieutenant Colonel Menzies marched into Aberdeen. In December Major Stewart and some of the soldiers extorted over £53 from George Farquhar, a burgess of Aberdeen. Farquhar should have quartered a captain of the regiment for twenty days, however the officer was absent due to illness. On 11 December the provost and bailie commissioned the Committee of Estates on Farquhar's behalf, but there is no sign that it redressed the complaint. On 26 January 1647 Major Stewart entered the town with twenty-three recruits, as did Captain John Campbell who brought in eighty newly levied men and their officers. The charge of the regiment, its women, boys, babies and horses to Aberdeen until 9 February was £15,200. The regiment remained on free quarters during its occupation of the burgh. Argyll's Highland Foot departed from Aberdeen on 20 February, with each officer and man receiving three days of maintenance allowance in cash from their hosts.[12]

Meanwhile in Edinburgh events were occurring which affected the regiment. On 29 January the Estates passed an act establishing the New Model Army, which made provision for changing the regiment. On 22 February the Estates received a petition from the officers. They requested their arrears in pay and better quarters, as well as clothing and shoes for the soldiers. The Estates agreed to provide the items and some of the pay. The next day the Estates ordered Lieutenant John Denniston of the regiment transported to the Edinburgh tolbooth from Leith. Denniston had just been apprehended redhanded after killing one of his men on the shore at Leith. On the 25th the Estates ordered that Denniston be delivered to Leven, so that the lieutenant could be tried by a council of war. Although there is no further evidence on the matter it can be safely assumed that Denniston was executed according to the *Articles and Ordinances of War*. Back in the northeast the regiment re-entered Aberdeen on the 27th between 5 and 6 p.m. with the Clydesdale Foot. Within weeks after that Argyll's Highland Foot would be reconstituted as a regiment in the New Model Army.[13]

Auchinbreck's Foot

Colonel: Sir Duncan Campbell of Auchinbreck

Auchinbreck was the lieutenant colonel of Argyll's 'Irish' foot. In September 1644 he was in command of a regiment of Campbells. It is likely, though unprovable, that Auchinbreck was colonel of one of the three Campbell regiments which rendezvoused at Dunstaffnage Castle on 22 July for a campaign against royalist and Irish sympathisers. On 18 September Auchinbreck's was one of Argyll's five infantry regiments which occupied Aberdeen for two days. The regiment took part in Argyll's marches through northeast and central Scotland. On 27 October the marquis imprisoned a group of stragglers, including one Donald MacNab of this regiment. Auchinbreck's men may have been part of the Campbell force of 1,000 men which plundered its way back to Argyll. At Inverlochy Auchinbreck was in command of the 'Irish' foot as well as the Covenanter army. It cannot be ascertained whether he commanded any other regiment at the battle which caused his death.[14]

Auchmedden's Retinue

Commander: James Baird of Auchmedden

On 24 July 1644 the Estates appointed Auchmedden a member of the Banffshire committee of war. On 12 September, in answer to a call of the 6th for all Covenanters in the northeast to rendezvous at Aberdeen, Auchmedden brought out his kinsmen, friends, servants and tenants. This retinue served at the battle of Aberdeen on the 13th, but its location cannot be discerned. Auchmedden never again stirred for the Covenanters.[15]

Lord Balcarres' Horse

Colonel: Alexander, 2nd Lord Balcarres

Lieutenant Colonel: Mungo Murray

Lord Balcarres was already a colonel of a regiment of horse when the Estates commissioned him to the rank on 1 August 1645. Balcarres was to raise 980 troopers according to the following quotas: 60 horse each from Haddingtonshire, Midlothian, Berwickshire, Linlithgowshire, Nithsdale, Stirlingshire and Galloway, 100 troopers each from Roxburghshire and Lanarkshire, and 120 each from Fife, Ayrshire and Renfrewshire. There was no standardisation in the size of the troops. A Routmaster McCulloch was to have the sixty horsemen from Galloway in one troop; Harry Bruce younger of Clackmannan was to have the same number from Stirlingshire. Balcarres' troop was to consist of the 120 horsemen from Fife. Lieutenant Colonel Murray (who was the major of Crawford-Lindsay's Fife Foot) was assigned a troop of 160 men from West Lothian and Lanarkshire. Hackett's Horse was to be broken up and made into three troops for this regiment. Due to the activities of Montrose only Murray seems to have had any time to raise even a part of his troop. Up to Kilsyth, which occurred on 15 August, Murray spent £1,200 on outrigging the regiment. At £120 per horseman that sum meant at least ten men were raised for the regiment. They were at Kilsyth, probably on the left flank of the first line. During the battle Murray lost ten of his own horses. On 4 February he petitioned the Estates for his recruiting money and for reimbursement for his horses. This matter was referred to the Committee of Money. A year later the arrears due the troop remained unpaid, but the Estates made provision for their payment. There is no indication of the regiment's activities after Kilsyth and with the arrival of cavalry regiments from England in September it was no longer needed.[16]

Balhalgardy's Retinue

Commander: Thomas Erskine of Balhalgardy

On 4 June 1644 the Estates made Balhalgardy a commissioner for Aberdeenshire. On 3 July he served as the cautioner for Thomas Seaton, who was imprisoned in the

Edinburgh tolbooth. On 12 September Balhalgardy appeared in Aberdeen with his retinue of kinsmen, friends, tenants and servants in answer to the call of the 6th for a rendezvous of the northeastern Covenanters. The retinue served at the battle of Aberdeen, although its activities in the battle cannot be determined. Balhalgardy brought out his retinue only on this occasion.[17]

Stewarts of Balquhidder

In the winter of 1645-46 some members of this clan, whose homeland was along the upper reaches of the Forth, joined Ardkinglas on his march into the central lowlands. Ardkinglas' force was subsequently routed on 13 February 1646 at the battle of Callander. For the subsequent history of that force, please see the Ardkinglas entry (see above, 196-8).[18]

Lord Banff's Retinue

Commander: George, 1st Lord Banff

Banff was a royalist and episcopalian, and the provost of Banff. In the Bishops' Wars he had suffered from the Covenanters. He probably joined Argyll with a group of his followers on 15 May 1644 at Turriff out of fear of further persecution by the Covenanters. This was his only time in the field for them. The £2,400 he paid the Army of the Solemn League and Covenant was probably the result of a fine or an extorted loan, and not given out of goodwill.[19]

Birkenbogs' Retinue

Commanders: Sir Alexander Abercromby of Birkenbog elder, and Alexander Abercromby of Birkenbog younger

On 26 August 1643 the Convention of Estates appointed Birkenbog elder to the Aberdeenshire committee of war. In 1644 the Estates placed both father and son on the committee. It is uncertain whether one or both led the retinue from their estates to Urry's army in spring 1645. The Birkenbog Retinue was engaged at Auldearn on 9 May, and its commander escaped. After Alford (2 July) the younger Birkenbog garrisoned Kemnay, which Craigievar had abandoned as a result of the defeat. In 1646 the Estates retained father and son on the Aberdeenshire committee. On 26 March 1647 Birkenbog petitioned the Estates that he had lost animals to plundering royalists. He was allowed, no doubt because of his faithful service, to reclaim any animals captured by Lieutenant General Leslie during his operations in the northeast.[20]

Blair's Dragoons

Commander: Lieutenant Colonel James Blair

There is no evidence regarding the commissioning or raising of this unit. It was also known as the Major General's Dragoons, after Major General Middleton. On 16 December 1645 the Estates ordered it to Dumbarton. On 13 January 1646 it entered Aberdeen, 200 men strong. The regiment left the burgh on 9 February to a destination unknown. However, it probably served under Middleton in his campaigns of 1646. Between 13 June and 15 September 198-256 dragoons were back in Aberdeen. They cost the burgh a total of £16,200. The fate of the regiment is unknown, however it probably disbanded in early February 1647.[21]

Boyndlie's Retinue

Commander: John Forbes of Boyndlie

Boyndlie was one of the many northeastern Covenanters who reacted to the call for a levée en masse issued at Aberdeen on 6 September 1644. The retinue served at the battle of Aberdeen on the 13th. Boyndlie fell prisoner to Montrose's army in the flight, and never led his men out for the Covenanters again in this period.[22]

Boyne's Retinue

Commander: Sir Walter Ogilvy of Boyne

On 26 August 1643 the Convention of Estates appointed Boyne, the commissioner for Banff, to that shire's committee of war. He responded to the call of Lord Burleigh to bring men to Aberdeen in early September 1644. They served at the battle on the 13th. In late April 1645 Boyne again brought his retinue into the field with the Crichtons and joined Major General John Urry at Enzie. Boyne and his men went with Urry's army to Inverness, which they reached on 8 May. The next day Boyne's men were engaged at Auldearn from which they seem to have escaped without serious losses. This was the last time during the mid-1640s that Boyne led a force for the Covenanters.[23]

Buchanan's Foot

Colonel: Sir George Buchanan of Buchanan

On 26 August 1643 Buchanan received a commission as a colonel of foot from the Convention of Estates. However, he did not levy any men for a regiment in the Army of the Solemn League and Covenant. Buchanan led his first force under a different commission. On 18 April 1644 the Estates gave Buchanan a commission to take his friends and followers to Mugdock Castle, where they were to remove the weapons, powder, iron windows and gates. The laird departed from Edinburgh on the 19th and mustered a company under Patrick Buchanan of Auchmaur. Buchanan led these men to Mugdock, which they reached on the night of the 20th. The next day being a Sunday the force did nothing. However on the 22nd Buchanan and his men entered the castle. They found a few pikes and muskets. The gates and windows were removed to the House of Duntreath. On 22 July Buchanan petitioned the Estates for the expenses he incurred due to the operation. It was not until August that Buchanan raised his regiment from western Stirlingshire. It accompanied Argyll on his second campaign in the northeast in the autumn of 1644. On 18 September the 500 foot and some cannon belonging to the regiment marched into Aberdeen. They stayed two days and returned on the 23rd, leaving the next day. In Turriff, if not elsewhere, the soldiers took grain and money, and destroyed crops. After marching around central and eastern Scotland under Argyll, Buchanan's Foot was ordered into winter quarters at Inverness.[24]

The regiment seems to have spent the rest of its time in that burgh. Buchanan's Foot shared the garrison duties with Lawers' Regiment. They used local labour to fortify the burgh with an earth wall, a deep trench, ramparts and pallisades. The east, south, Castle Street, Bridge and kirk gates were also strengthened. In February 1645 the two regiments sent out parties to the east. They pillaged Elchess, where the laird of Grant was residing, and the lands of Cokston. The soldiers also entered Elgin; there they captured the laird of Pluscardine and his brother, who they brought back to Inverness. On 27 February the Estates ordered the Stirlingshire committee of war to apprehend any deserters from Buchanan's Foot and to send them to Inverness. To encourage the local committee the Estates promised that it would view this work as Stirlingshire's third levy, which would be taken into account when the next levy was apportioned. To aid the process the Estates ordered Buchanan to return home from Edinburgh. In May Urry arrived in Inverness. He definitely used Lawers' Foot at the Battle of Auldearn, but it is possible that Buchanan's Foot may have remained in Inverness to protect it. There is no mention of the regiment until 10 July when Captain Harry Bruce the younger of Clackmannan petitioned the Estates. He requested satisfaction for his service in Buchanan's Foot and in the Inverness garrison. The final mention of the unit occurs in a petition from the colonel on 4 February 1646. Buchanan sought the arrears both for his garrison in Buchanan House and for his regiment. Meanwhile back in Inverness Montrose had laid siege to the burgh. However, Major General Middleton relieved the garrison in May. As there is no reference to Buchanan's Foot in early 1647 when the Estates were determining the fate of regiments still in existence in Scotland, it may be assumed that this unit disbanded prior to that period.[25]

Clan Campbell

Some of the material for this entry is treated elsewhere (see pp. 196-203, pp. 219-220), however this reference includes information that would be difficult to list under only one commander. The first instance of the clan mobilising under the authority of its barons or gentry occurred in August 1644. Then Alasdair's Irish regiments were in Badenoch uncertain as to where to head. To ensure that they did not enter Argyll by the eastern passes the clan gathered together those forces not engaged on the campaign led by its chief. In the event the Irish did not enter the Campbell territory until December when the clan was unprepared. As a result, in addition to the great loss of buildings, animals and grain, the Campbells lost 900 fighting men to Montrose's and Alasdair's army. However, Argyll rapidly organised a composite army of lowland foot, his 'Irish' regiment, Campbells and their allies. Unfortunately for the clan this army was destroyed at Inverlochy, the Campbells losing something under 1,500 men. In addition to that fifteen barons of the clan were killed. They included Auchinbreck, Glenfeochan, Glencarradale, the provost of Kilmun, Lochnell, the heirs of Inverawe, Lochnell and Barbreck, and the brothers of Lochnell and Ardchattan. Furthermore the royalists captured twenty-two members of the gentry. This group contained, among others, Barbreck, Pennymore, Inverliver, and the Captain of Skipness Castle, the heir of Glencarradale, and a son of Dunstaffnage. As can be imagined these losses severely disrupted the ability of the clan to carry out successful military activity.[26]

Initially that disadvantage was endurable because the royalists and Irish departed from the area (save for their garrisons) after February 1645. However, in September Alasdair and his army returned with the support of many who had been former Campbell allies. This forced the clan to adopt a defensive strategy. This meant flight into its castles and tower houses in hopes that the Covenanting regime would send a relief force. The Campbells had a long wait, for it was not until May 1647 that David Leslie led a portion of the New Model Army into Argyll to reconquer it from Alasdair and his allies. Meanwhile the Campbells had seen a great deal of military activity, as well as passively watching the destruction of their land by their enemies. The first to feel the blows of the new situation was Archibald Campbell, provost of Kilmun. In autumn 1645 Sir James Lamont led his clan against the tower house of Kilmun in Cowal. The provost surrendered on quarter, nevertheless the Lamonts killed some of his relations and followers. Throughout the winter the Lamonts, native MacDonalds, Irish and former allies of the Campbells ravaged Argyll; Kintyre, Mull, Islay, Jura and many minor isles became part of a new MacDonald empire.[27]

In 1646 the situation worsened. Alasdair besieged Kilberry Castle, Knapdale, for two weeks. But he lifted the siege after receiving a barrel of ale from the garrison, accepting that it was well-supplied. Alasdair also besieged Craignish Castle. The garrison was commanded by Archibald Campbell, Tutor of Craignish or Barrichbeyan, who had 250 men in the castle and surrounding area. While Alasdair had 1,500 men he lacked heavy artillery necessary to reduce the walls. A feature of the siege was the Tutor's continual challenges to Alasdair to single combat. Duntroon Castle may have been attacked, albeit unsuccessfully, in early 1646 as well. The only battle in this period took place at Lagganmore, Glen Euchar. There Donald Campbell the blue-eyed of Lochnell, and John Campbell of Bragleen (also known as 'Little John of the Glen' and as Ian Beg MacIan) gathered a force of Campbells. Alasdair marched against them with his Irish regiments, the MacDougalls, and the MacAulays of Ardincaple. Lochnell escaped following the defeat sustained by the Campbells. Bragleen was captured but gained his freedom after a series of adventures. Many of the prisoners, and some Campbell women and children, were killed by being burned to death in a barn at Lagganmore. Such grim incidents fuelled the Campbell desire for revenge over their enemies. The only other significant action before Leslie's invasion was the siege of Skipness Castle, Kintyre. Malcolm MacNaughton of Dundarave commanded a garrison of Campbells against the forces of the Irish and MacDonalds. The siege was certainly well under way by May 1646, when a relief column brought in supplies and killed the commander of the MacDonalds — Archibald MacColla MacDonald. Alasdair eventually lifted the siege sometime before August. However, it had been such a close run thing that Dundarave died afterwards due to the hardships he had endured. As a result of the losses sustained by the Campbells between 1644 and 1647 it would not be until well into the Restoration period that they regained their former power and prominence in Argyll and the western isles.[28]

Clachreach's Retinue

Commander: John Keith of Clachreach

The Estates appointed Clachreach to the Aberdeenshire committee of war in both 1643 and 1644. He apparently led a retinue out only once for the Covenanters. In early September 1644 Lord Burleigh, commander of the Aberdeen garrison, issued a proclamation calling for a levée en masse of all Covenanters in Mearns, Aberdeenshire, Banffshire and Moray. In response Clachreach led out the men from the earl Marischal's Buchan estates to Aberdeen. They arrived on the 12th and saw action at the disastrous battle fought on the next day.[29]

Cockburn's Foot

Commander: Lieutenant Colonel John Cockburn

It cannot be determined of what regiment Cockburn was lieutenant colonel. Thus, it is impossible to discover when and from where his men were levied. In late December 1644 Cockburn's Foot, approximately 550 men strong, set out from either Perth or Stirling under the command of Baillie. They marched to Roseneath via Dumbarton, where they were transferred to Argyll's command. At the battle of Inverlochy Auchinbreck positioned Cockburn's Foot on one of the flanks. They must have been rather green for the men fled at the first impact with the royalist army. Cockburn made his way to Inverlochy Castle and surrendered there to Montrose's men. He gave his parole that he would never serve against the marquis' forces. Consequently when he returned to the lowlands the Estates gave him command of Stirling Castle, a place not likely to be a target of Montrose. There is no further mention of the regiment.[30]

Corsindae's Retinue

Commander: William Forbes the younger of Corsindae

In 1644 the Estates appointed Corsindae to the Aberdeenshire committee of war. Like many of his clan he responded to the call of 6 September 1644 to bring his men to Aberdeen to oppose Montrose. Corsindae's Retinue took part in the battle, although its location is not known. There is no specific mention to Corsindae leading men out for the Covenanters after this, however, they may have come out under the command of Lord Forbes or the master of Forbes.[31]

Craigievar's Forces

Commander: Sir William Forbes of Craigievar

Craigievar was one of the principal Covenanters of Aberdeenshire. In summer 1643 he served as a commissioner for the shire to the Convention of Estates. On 26 August he was appointed to the Aberdeenshire committee of war. In early April 1644, out of fear of plundering by the Gordons, he fled into Craigievar Castle, where he also brought in the victuals of Fintray House. He was first in the field for the Covenanters on 26 April, when he led a retinue to join Argyll's army at Dunottar Castle. Craigievar's men subsequently took part in the march to Elgin via Aberdeen and Turriff, and the return to Aberdeen through Strathbogie. In July he raised a troop of horse for the Committee for the North (a regional committee of war). On 15 August at the command of the Committee he captured Harthill House. He then threw out the laird's wife, children and servants, earning himself a bad reputation among the royalists. On 17 August at 11 p.m. William Forbes, a trooper and a bastard son of John Forbes of Leslie, slew Alexander Irvine of Kincausie in Aberdeen. This action was highly significant, for the Estates had placed a reward of £3,333 6s. 8d. for the death of Kincausie. Trooper Forbes received £1,333 6s. 8d. and his commander gained

£2,000 from the estate of Kincausie. This further enhanced Craigievar's reputation among the Covenanters and darkened it even more with the royalists.[32]

In September 1644 Craigievar answered Burleigh's call for a general rendezvous. He brought in his troop of about 100 men to Aberdeen on the 12th. The next day his unit was placed in the centre of the Covenanter line. Remembering the new style of cavalry charge developed in France and Sweden, Craigievar abandoned the carracole. Instead his troop charged the Irish foot opposite. However, no other Covenanter cavalry commander supported him, either out of stupidity or from a belief that such an attack was rash. Thus, the Irish infantry safely broke ranks and allowed the troop to charge through. The Irish then closed in and destroyed the troop, allowing few to survive. Craigievar fell prisoner to Montrose. He continued with the royalist army until 15 October, when Montrose released him on a conditional parole. In early November Craigievar returned to Montrose as he was unable to secure the release of the prisoners Montrose desired. However, he did not stay long and escaped, breaking his parole, to Argyll's army. Craigievar fades from the scene for several months, re-emerging in late February 1645. On Sunday the 23rd the lairds of Gight, Harthill and others surprised ten of Craigievar's troops in bed in Inverurie. The royalists kept their equipment, but released the men. In March or April Craigievar took advantage of Montrose's absence in Angus and took the field again with his retinue. He plundered and burned Lethenty House, from which he also ejected the wife of the laird. He also sent the grain there to his house of Fintray. On 25 April Craigievar seized Kemnay House from the laird's widow. He garrisoned it and Pitcaple House at this time. Furthermore he plundered the laird of Kincraigie's lands and those of Newton and Harth House. Among his plunder were 160 oxen, which Craigievar sent to Fife for sale there. Finally during this period the laird captured George Gordon of Rhynie, a royalist. After the battle of Alford (2 July) Craigievar pulled his garrison out of Kemnay House. At this point the material on the laird dries up, but it would not be too presumptuous to think that he continued to harry the royalists of the northeast until early 1647.[33]

Master of Cranston's Retinue

Commander: William, master of Cranston

In April 1644 the master of Cranston mustered a force from the Borders for use against Montrose and the Cumbrian royalists. It rendezvoused at Douglas with other Covenanter retinues in May. From Douglas this combined force proceeded to raid Cumberland. It disbanded shortly afterwards. The master of Cranston went on to raise a regiment which entered England in late June as part of the earl of Callander's army (see p. 120).[34]

Earl of Crawford-Lindsay's Horse Troop

Routmaster: John, 17th earl of Crawford and 1st earl of Lindsay

There is no mention of this troop prior to 1645. However, the earl may have been allowed to raise a troop either for his campaign in Atholl in spring 1645 or as president of the Estates in the same year. On 7 November it was assigned twenty horsemen from Teviotdale and Ettrick Forest. The troop was quartering in Scotland on 5 February 1647. Then the Estates authorised the earl to retain some troopers for Ludquharn's horse troop in the New Model Army, when it disbanded on the 9th.[35]

Cummings

The Cummings were a kin group from inland Moray, who twice appeared in the field for the Covenanters. In January-February 1645 they formed part of the army at Inverness, which had the earl of Seaforth as its titular commander. In early May they joined Major General Urry either at Elgin or Forres, when he made his march to Inverness. The Cummings fought at Auldearn on the 9th, probably in the second line. They appear to have retired from active service for the Covenanters after this action.[36]

Douglas' Retinue

Commander: Sir William Douglas of Cavers, sheriff of Teviotdale

In 1644 the Estates appointed Douglas to the committees of war of Roxburgh-shire and Selkirkshire. In April he was one of the Covenanters who led a force of Borderers, in this case from Teviotdale, to a rendezvous at Douglas. In May they raided into Cumberland. Shortly afterwards this force of 'border raiders' disbanded. Douglas went on to serve as the M.P. for Roxburghshire/Teviotdale in 1644-46.[37]

Drum's Retinue

Commander: Sir Alexander Irvine of Drum

In the Bishops' Wars Drum had been a royalist. However, he seems to have undergone a change of heart. In August 1643 the Convention of Estates appointed Drum or Philorth the convener of the Aberdeenshire committee of war. On 17 January 1644 Drum, with Provost Alexander Jaffray of Aberdeen, and his sons led eighty-four horsemen to the laird of Haddo's son's house, which belonged to Haddo. They searched the house for weapons and departed from it. Jaffray paid for the meat and drink of the expedition. After this Drum mysteriously disappears from the picture. The Covenanters garrisoned his house in summer and autumn 1644, but the laird is not mentioned again until 1646. That February twelve soldiers with ammunition and thirty prisoners of war from the laird quartered in Aberdeen. Given his previous loyalties it is not surprising that Drum was not more active for the Covenanters.[38]

Dunbars

This family controlled the part of Moray south and west of Elgin. In January-February 1645 it contributed men to the Covenanter army under the supposed command of Seaforth at Inverness. In early May Dunbars again joined a Covenanter army, this time under Major General Urry. On the 9th they were engaged at Auldearn. This was the last time that the Dunbars raised men for the Covenanters.[39]

Echt's Retinue

Commander: Robert Forbes of Echt

On 26 August 1643 the Convention of Estates appointed Echt a member of the Aberdeenshire committee of war. In early April 1644 he fled with the laird of Skene into Skene House to escape plundering by the Gordons and their allies. On the 26th Echt led his retinue to the rendezvous with Argyll's forces at Dunottar Castle. The retinue consequently served on Argyll's first northeastern campaign. On 12 September Echt responded to the call to arms issued by Lord Burleigh on the 6th, by bringing his retinue into Aberdeen. It was engaged on the next day in the battle of Aberdeen. In October Montrose burned Echt's lands for his support of the Covenanting regime. While Echt is not known to have led troops personally in a Covenanting force again, he may have done so under the Lord or master of Forbes.[40]

Fife Foot

Joint Colonels: Robert, 2nd Lord Burleigh and David, Lord Elcho

Lieutenant Colonel: (?) Arnott

Minister: John Chalmers[41]

On 12 April 1644 the Estates commissioned Lord Elcho commander of foot on Argyll's expedition against Huntly. Elcho worked in conjunction with Burleigh to raise an infantry regiment from Fife for the campaign. On 6 April the burgh of Burntisland provided eighteen men for the unit. On the 17th the colonels had 800 foot at Dundee; nine days later the regiment was at the muster at Dunottar Castle. On 2 May the Fife Foot was on Aberdeen links with the rest of the army. Two days later Burleigh led out a force, including his own regiment, to Udny. On the 6th this force marched on to Kellie, which it left by the 13th when both Burleigh's and Argyll's forces returned to Aberdeen. From there on the 14th Argyll with the Fife Foot and other regiments set off for Elgin, returning to Aberdeen via Huntly on the 31st. The Fife Foot, now numbering 700 men, did extensive damage while quartering in Aberdeen with the sixty troopers of Argyll's Life Guard of horse. In June Elcho sent out a force of sixty troopers and sixty musketeers to garrison Kellie Castle and the Bog of Gight. The Fife Foot also sent out a body of men to replace the two 'Irish' infantry regiments which had garrisoned Drum Castle. Part of the regiment was also placed in Auchindoun Castle. The remainder of the regiment served as the Aberdeen garrison. During the occupation the burgh paid Burleigh and Commissary General John Denholm £18,666 13s. 4d. The quartering charges of the regiment to 13 September were £19,050. The burgh claimed that the regiment applied for quarters for 1,000 men, but the burgh officials 'comptit' only 500 foot. Meanwhile on 17 August Elcho and Lieutenant Colonel Arnott left the regiment and Burleigh headed south. Elcho was responsible for raising some of the Fife levies which served at Tippermuir. He commanded the army there and personally led his levies on the right wing at that battle with Arnott's help. During this period Burleigh had left Aberdeen as well. On 25 August the Estates ordered him to Perth from Fife. After Tippermuir Burleigh, Arnott and some Fifemen made their way to Aberdeen. The easy time the garrison had had through most of the summer was about to end.[42]

Burleigh was the commander-in-chief in Aberdeen and it was his decision that cancelled any chance of successful resistance against Montrose. On 26 August Burleigh addressed the Aberdonians at Greyfriar's kirk. He called upon the men to defend the Covenant, reformation, their lives, and their women, children and goods against the Irish and vagabonds who had come to destroy the country. Some citizens were bitter about the garrison's and regime's exactions and refused to respond to the appeal. However, 500 men did come forth to serve in the regiment of Old and New Aberdeen. Burleigh also recalled the garrisons of Auchindoun, Gight, Kellie and Drum Castles, bringing his regiment up to 500 men from 400. The Fife Foot had suffered from desertion throughout its occupation of Aberdeen, but particularly after Elcho went south. Burleigh as president of the Committee for the North was the commander-in-chief of the forces ordered to assemble at Aberdeen on 12 September. That day he made a fatal error by moving his men outside of a fortified town to face veteran troops. On the 13th Burleigh failed entirely to exercise command control and his subordinates acted without co-ordination in making their attacks. The result was a debacle; 800 of the 2,500 men in Burleigh's command were killed. Burleigh and Arnott fled north towards the Don, and then south. The regiment was shattered.[43]

Shattered but not destroyed, for the Fife Foot continued to limp on until 1646. The Fife Foot may have served on Argyll's second northeastern campaign. However, there is no record of the regiment quartering in Aberdeen between 14 September and 14 November, which suggests that if it did enter the burgh it was too insignificant for the magistrates to list. There is, however, an ordinance of the Burntisland burgh council of 20 September which orders all gentlemen and men in the burgh who served with Elcho to join the present expedition to the north. The captain of this contingent was Sir James Melville. In late autumn the Fife Foot was quartered in Aberdeen, and formed part of Baillie's army. On 23 December the Burntisland council ordered a search made for deserters from the regiment. Any found were to be returned to the unit. Two months later the Estates issued an order to the Fife committee of war concerning the regiment. The committee was to put out all deficients and to gather up deserters so that the Fife Foot could be brought up to a strength of 500 men. On 9 March four deserters from Scoonie appeared before the kirk session. They were ordered to return to the regiment or face kirk censure. The men promised to return. Two weeks later the supply minister in Scoonie issued the same warning to deserters from the regiment in the parish. They also promised to rejoin the unit. The same procedures had occurred in Kilconquhar. During the late spring and early summer of 1645 the Fife Foot formed part of Baillie's army. It was engaged at Alford, where the officers lost all of their belongings in the flight. There were probably heavy casualties among the soldiers, at least the Estates thought so. On 1 August 1645 the Estates assessed Fife 600 infantry for this regiment, which was now under Arnott's command. The new levy was a failure as it was called during the events leading up to the disaster at Kilsyth. After Philiphaugh the Estates had no need to recruit fresh men into their forces; it possessed an excellent body of veterans in the cavalry regiments brought north from England. On 30 January 1646 the officers of the Fife Foot petitioned the Estates for a clearing of the accounts. The government agreed; with that the regiment disappears from history.[44]

Fife (Cambo's) Foot

Colonel: Sir Thomas Myretoun/Myrton of Cambo

Minister: James Bruce[45]

Cambo was an east Fife laird who received appointments to the shire's committee of war in 1643 and 1644. In late July 1645 Cambo gathered an assortment of about 1,000 men, most possessing little military experience, for his regiment from east Fife. The St. Andrews contingent marched out before the parish minister, Robert Blair, had a chance to bless them. He took this as a bad omen. All of the Fife levies in the Kilsyth campaign became filled with fear as they marched westwards. They mutinied twice, on the second occasion at the Stirling crossing of the Forth. Their commanders ordered the chaplains to go to their parishioners hoping that they could force the levies by prayer, preaching and persuasion 'to go out to the help of the Lord against the mighty'. Using an appeal to religion, as well as a promise that the western levies under the earls of Eglinton, Glencairn and Lanark would relieve the Fifemen, the ministers persuaded the levies to march. At Kilsyth Baillie placed Cambo's men in the third line or reserve of his army with the other Fife levies due to their in-experience. As Home's and the Loudoun-Glasgow Foot fought for control of the centre, the Fife levies panicked. By the time Baillie reached their position, from which he hoped to deploy them in the battle, they had fled. Their losses, which included Cambo, occurred during their flight away from Kilsyth. The rural parish of Ceres, presbytery of Cupar, lost twenty-two men from this regiment during the rout. The regiment ceased to exist on 15 August 1645.[46]

Fife (Ferny's) Foot

Colonel: James Arnott of Ferny

Ferny was a central Fife laird and a Covenanter since the early period of the troubles. In late July 1645 he raised a regiment of men largely unaccustomed to military activity from the area around his estate. This force numbered about 1,000 men. It, with the other two Fife regiments, suffered from mutinies on the march to Kilsyth (see above, pp. 214-215). Baillie stationed Ferny's men with the other Fife troops in the reserve or third line before the battle. Like the other men from their shire Ferny's fled before becoming engaged in the battle. Ferny, himself, fell prisoner to the royalists. His unit suffered heavy casualties in the rout. The regiment was never reconstituted.[47]

Fife (Fordell's) Foot

Colonel: John Henderson of Fordell

On 26 August 1643 the Convention of Estates nominated Fordell to the Fife committee of war; an appointment which was reaffirmed by the Estates in 1644. In late July 1645 Fordell levied a force of about 1,000 men from western Fife who were more noted for their abilities in the economic than martial sphere. This regiment suffered from mutinies on the march to Kilsyth exactly as did the other Fife units. Like them it was also placed in the reserve line of the Covenanter army and fled before fighting at Kilsyth. The colonel escaped from the field, but losses amongst his men were presumably high although they had the shortest distance to run of any of the three Fife regiments.[48]

Earl of Findlater's Retinue

Commander: James, 1st earl of Findlater

In August 1643 the Convention of Estates appointed Findlater a member of the committee of war for Banffshire. On 15 May 1644 he joined Argyll with his retinue at Turriff. From there Findlater's force of kinsmen, friends, tenants and servants went on to serve in Argyll's first northeastern campaign. In February 1645 the Farquharsons burned his Cullen estates. The earl's wife saved their home by paying Montrose a ransom of £13,332 13s. 4d. In late April Findlater, probably hoping to avenge himself on the royalists, raised his retinue. He joined Urry in Enzie with Lord Crichton, the laird of Boyne, and others. Findlater remained with Urry's army and his men served at Auldearn. The earl escaped after the battle and does not seem to have taken the field again.[49]

Lord Forbes' Retinue

Commander: Alexander, 11th Lord Forbes

Lord Forbes was the chief of his name and a committed Covenanter. One contemporary noted that all the Forbeses 'were furious in the cause'. Lord Forbes had served in the Swedish army under Gustavus Adolphus. After 1632 he became a lieutenant general in that country's service. In 1643 he commanded an expedition under the auspices of the English parliament against Galway. In 1644 the Estates appointed him to the Aberdeenshire committee of war and the Committee for the North. In early April 1644, out of fear of plundering by the Gordons, he and the laird of Glenkindie secured themselves in Kildrummy Castle on the upper Don. Later in the month Lord Forbes assembled his retinue and brought it to the rendezvous with Argyll at Dunottar Castle on the 26th. After entering Aberdeen on 2 May Lord Forbes accompanied the expedition which took Kellie on the 8th. Marischal and Argyll led this march, which included the forces of Lords Forbes, Fraser and Gordon. On 15 May Lord Forbes brought a force of his clan to the rendezvous at Turriff. Afterwards they presumably served with Argyll on his march to and from Elgin. In the summer Lord Forbes received a reward of £2,000 for capturing the royalist Irvine of Lenturk. In the late summer Forbes was among those who refused to accept the Estates' commissioning of Lord Gordon as the lieutenant general of the northeast. This resulted in a serious diminution of the Covenanters' force in September, because Gordon disbanded most of his men. A Forbes was appointed a colonel to appease the longer-standing Covenanters in the northeast. Given the traditional rivalry between the Forbeses and the Gordons neither decision is surprising. With Gordon out of the picture Lord Forbes responded to Burleigh's call for a levée en masse of the northeastern Covenanters. On 12 September his men entered Aberdeen and fought in the battle on the 13th.

The losses among Lord Forbes' men must have been severe. Forbes met with Argyll on the 16th at Brechin, but he gave the marquis little support in his campaign against Montrose. Nevertheless the estates of the Forbeses did not escape from the plundering and burning carried out by Montrose's army. In March 1645, while Montrose was in Angus, the Forbeses, Frasers and Crichtons took the field against the local royalists. However, on 23 May a force of Highlanders routed a combined army of Forbeses and Frasers at the head of Strathdon. There is no sign that Lord Forbes raised his men again to serve in opposition to the local royalists after this event.[50]

Master of Forbes' Retinue

Commander: William, master of Forbes

Like his father, the master of Forbes was a landowner in Aberdeenshire. In April 1644 he raised a group of his kinsmen and tenants with which he joined Argyll at Dunottar Castle on the 26th. From that it may be assumed that the master's retinue accompanied Argyll on his first northeastern campaign. In September the master again raised a body of men, which he led at the battle of Aberdeen. In March 1645 the master joined with the viscount Frendraught, Lord Fraser (both strong Covenanters) and brought out a force of his friends and followers. The combined force of Crichtons, Forbeses and Frasers captured Hew, son of George Gordon of Cocklarachie, Hector Abercromby of Fettercairn, and William Fraser of Craigton, but later released them. The Covenanters then tried to take the earl of Airlie at Lethenty, but he was in Huntly Castle. (For other possible activities of the master, please see the entry on Lord Forbes.) In 1646 the Estates appointed the master to the Aberdeenshire committee of war. He does not seem to have taken the field again in this period.[51]

Lord Fraser's Retinue

Commander: Andrew, 2nd Lord Fraser

Lord Fraser was another Aberdeenshire Covenanter who was also a hereditary enemy of the Gordons. His kinsmen 'were furious in the cause', and had been so since 1639. On 12 April 1644 the Estates appointed Lord Fraser to the Committee for the North. In early April Fraser had fled into Cairnbulg House out of fear of being plundered by the marquis of Huntly and his army. Later in the month he raised a group of his friends and followers, which he brought to the Dunottar Castle rendezvous on the 26th. After entering Aberdeen on 2 May, Fraser led his men on Argyll's march against Kellie and Gight. The force was back in Aberdeen on the 13th, two days later Fraser was one of the northeastern Covenanters who brought a contingent of men to the Turriff rendezvous. It was probably then that his kinsmen stole a sum of money from a tenant in Turriff. Fraser was one of the northeastern Covenanters who opposed the appointment of Lord Gordon as lieutenant general for the north in September. He raised a large body of men in response to Burleigh's summons for a Covenanter rendez-vous in Aberdeen. At the battle of Aberdeen on 13 September Fraser shared command of the left flank with Lord Crichton. The troops opposing them were Highlanders under the command of the earl of Airlie and Sir James Rollo of Duncrub. Twice Fraser and Crichton led their foot against the royalists (their horsemen failed to support these attacks) and twice they were driven back. Eventually the two nobles fled from the field with their men. On 16 September Fraser was present at Brechin with other northeastern Covenanters in order to meet with Argyll. However, Fraser gave the marquis little aid during his campaign against Montrose. On 6 March 1645 the Estates commissioned Fraser colonel of the forces of Aberdeenshire if viscount Frendraught, or the lord or master of Forbes refused it. Throughout the winter of 1644-45 Fraser had kept to his fortified houses and castles. However, in March when Montrose left the area Fraser brought his friends and followers into the field and joined with the other 'gryte Covenanters' — the master of Forbes and viscount Frendraught. They seized, but later freed, the heir of George Gordon of Cocklarachie, Hector Abercromby of Fettercairn and William Fraser of Craigton. This force of Covenanters also made an attempt to capture the earl of Airlie at Lethenty House, but he was absent. On 23 May a combined force of Frasers and Forbeses was routed by a group of Highlanders at the head of Strathdon. Lord Fraser does not appear to have brought out a retinue again.[52]

Viscount Frendraught's Retinue

Commander: James, 1st viscount Frendraught and Lord Crichton

Viscount Frendraught was the effective head of the Crichtons in the northeast. He was connected by marriage to the earl of Leven and to Irvine of Drum. In 1644 the Estates appointed him to the Committee for the North and Aberdeen-shire committee of war. His career as a northeastern Covenanter paralleled that of his associates, the master of Forbes and Lord Fraser. He joined Argyll's army with a group of kinsmen and friends at Turriff on 15 May 1644. From there the viscount went on to serve with Argyll's army as it marched to Elgin and then back through Strathbogie. He, too, opposed Lord Gordon's commission as lieutenant general, and refused to join him. Frendraught, however, acted in accordance with Burleigh's appeal for a rendezvous at Aberdeen. He shared command of the Covenanters' left wing with Lord Fraser. The two nobles attacked the royalists under the command of the earl of Airlie and Sir James Rollo of Duncrub twice with their infantry. Whether out of stupidity or caution the Covenanter horsemen failed to support these efforts, which were repulsed. Frendraught fled from the field and reached Brechin on 16 September. He met

Argyll there, but provided him with scant aid for his campaign. In October Montrose had Frendraught's lands burned. During the winter the Crichtons kept to their homes, but in March 1645 Frendraught raised his friends and followers in conjunction with Lord Fraser and the master of Forbes. This force captured two royalist lairds and the heir of a third. The Covenanters also tried to seize the earl of Airlie, but failed. They subsequently released their prisoners. In late April Frendraught, with the earl of Findlater, the laird of Boyne and others joined their forces to Urry's army in Enzie. Frendraught was at Auldearn with his men, but he escaped. In late May he was in the field again, this time burning the raws of Strathbogie and Tullish. Unlike other northeastern Covenanters Frendraught's military activities continued after Auldearn and Strathdon.[53]

Viscount Frendraught's Horse

Colonel: James, 1st viscount Frendraught and Lord Crichton

Sometime after May 1645 Frendraught raised a force of horsemen, which were under the pay of the Estates. The source of the recruits was presumably Aberdeenshire and Banffshire. On 5 February 1647 the Estates ordered the viscount to retain some of his men for Ludquharn's horse troop in the New Model Army. Frendraught's Horse disbanded after the 9th. There is no mention of their military activities, although they probably served under Middleton during his northeastern campaigns.[54]

Glenkindie's Retinue

Commander: Alexander Strachan of Glenkindie

Glenkindie was another member of the Aberdeenshire committee of war who raised a force for the the Covenanters in 1644. In early April he and Lord Forbes stayed in Kildrummy Castle to escape from the marquis of Huntly's army. On the 26th Glenkindie joined Argyll's army at Dunottar Castle with a group of his friends, relatives, tenants and servants. This retinue served on Argyll's first northeastern campaign which ended on 31 May. In September Glenkindie brought out his retinue in answer to Burleigh's call for a muster at Aberdeen. This force was engaged at Aberdeen. Afterwards Glenkindie does not appear to have joined in any more military endeavours for the Covenanters.[55]

Glenorchy's Foot

Colonel: John Campbell the younger or fiar of Glenorchy

Minister: Archibald MacCalman[56]

Glenorchy was a member of the Perthshire committee of war and an associate of Argyll's. By 17 April 1644 Glenorchy had a regiment of 800 infantry under his command, which had been recruited in Perthshire. This unit probably served on Argyll's summer campaign against the Irish and their allies. On 5 September Argyll wrote Glenorchy from Stirling concerning military discipline. He ordered Glenorchy to convene courts-martial, which would consist of fifteen captains, lieutenants, sergeants and corporals, to try offenders. Plunderers, robbers and creators of disorder were to be put to death in accordance with military law. If several soldiers were found guilty of the same crime, they were to draw lots to see who would live. On the 6th and 7th Argyll addressed two letters to Glenorchy concerning the material care of his soldiers. Glenorchy was upset that his men had not received their pay and Argyll promised him money as soon as there was some. The marquis also told Glenorchy to raise his supplies from known enemies, but to issue them with tickets of receipt. Later in the month Glenorchy's Foot joined Argyll's army for the autumn campaign against Montrose. The regiment was on foot until at least 14 November. It may have served at Inverlochy. More probably it was used by Sir Robert Campbell, laird of Glenorchy, to maintain his garrisons. From November 1644 to January 1646 (and probably to a later date) the laird kept forty men each in the castles of the Isle of Lochtay and Finlarig. He also garrisoned Achallader, Barcaldine and Kilchurn Castles. Glenorchy had another garrison in the castles of the Isle of Lochdochart, but it surrendered to the MacNabs and was not recaptured until early 1646. Throughout the course of the depredations by the Irish and royalists under Alasdair and Montrose the laird and his tenants suffered £800,000 in losses. Following Inverlochy few Campbell forces kept to the field, most fled into stone and lime strongholds, where there was some safety from the Irish and their allies. Glenorchy's Foot was no exception to this rule.[57]

Gordons

In general the Gordons were a devotedly royalist clan; however there were two important exceptions — George, Lord Gordon, and his brother Lewis. Lord Gordon received commissions from the Estates as a colonel for both a foot and horse regiment, which served in the Army of the Solemn League and Covenant. In May 1644 Lord Gordon joined his uncle, Argyll, for the campaign aimed against his father, the marquis of Huntly, and other royalists. In the summer the Estates commissioned Lord Gordon lieutenant general of the North. He mustered 3,000 foot and horse at Kildrummy Castle to oppose Montrose. However, his force suffered from external hostility and internal instability. The Covenanters of the northeast, led by the Lords Forbes, Fraser, Frendraught and the master of Forbes, opposed the appointment of a man who was a Gordon (and as such a hereditary enemy) and was well-connected with the royalists. Meanwhile in his own camp 2,600 men deserted Gordon, because of their royalist sympathies. To pacify the northeastern Covenanters the Estates annulled Gordon's commission and appointed a Forbes to the rank of colonel. This naturally angered Lord Gordon and be began to work less for the Covenanters. In particular he did not respond to Burleigh's opinion to bring men to the Aberdeen rendezvous. The controversy over his commission was also thought to have more long-term effects, that is Gordon began to become disenchanted with the Covenanter regime. Lewis or Ludovick did not share his brother's anger. He was probably more attracted to the possibilities for adventure, being only eighteen in 1644. In September Lewis led a troop of a mere eighteen horsemen to Burleigh's army. He was stationed on the right flank with other cavalry units. During the battle he led his little band in a carracole down the slope against the royalists opposite. After the battle Lewis and Lord Gordon rode to join their uncle at Brechin. From there they accompanied Argyll on his campaign of depredation and plunder through their father's estates. Argyll explained that such measures were necessary to deprive the royalists of sustenance; the Gordon brothers saw it as the destruction of their heritage. After Inverlochy, where both the Campbells and Argyll had suffered a great loss of prestige and power, the Gordons switched sides again and rejoined the royalists. In mid February 1645 the two brothers rode into Elgin to meet Montrose with a force of 200 horse. Lord Gordon went on to become a valuable officer in Montrose's army, but he was killed leading a cavalry charge at Alford. Lewis continued leading the Gordon contingent until after Kilsyth, when his father called him home. It is hard to say whether the activities of Huntly's two sons as Covenanters was contrived by the marquis, or if it occurred because of Argyll's persuasive powers. In the event the Gordons were so disliked and distrusted by the main adherents of the Covenants in the northeast that they could contribute little. Furthermore their kinsmen refused to back them in their pro-Covenanting enterprises. Yet by serving with Argyll they deprived the royalists of the necessary leadership during a critical period.[58]

Grant's Retinue

Commander: James Grant of Freuchie, chief of the Grants

In 1643 the Convention of Estates appointed Grant to the committee of war for Elginshire, Nairnshire, Strathspey, Inverness-shire east of the Ness and the burgh of Inverness. In March 1644 the earl of Moray, Grant's brother-in-law, told him to raise all the men under his division. Grant brought 1,000 foot and horse to a rendezvous at Elgin, because Elgin and the surrounding area feared Huntly's rising. On 9 April Grant led an expedition of his clansmen and one company of lowland foot. They plundered Sir Thomas Cromby's house, broke its yetts and doors, stole £4,000, and took grain and other goods from the grounds. They also plundered the laird of Pittordrie's house, the laird of Bannochy's sheep and grounds, and the lands of Mr. Robert Farquhar. A contemporary said of the expedition 'that [it] began this plundering in Scotland'.

Grant later led his men to join Argyll at the Turriff rendezvous in May. Grant probably stayed with Argyll until he reached Elgin, if not for more of the campaign. In August the Grants joined the Lovat Frasers, Rosses and Munros against Alasdair's Irish regiments when they were in Badenoch. The earls of Seaforth and Sutherland supported this gathering of Covenanter clans. In September Seaforth posted Grant in Strathspey to protect the river crossings. Montrose met Grant in the Abernethy Woods after the battle of Aberdeen and sought safe passage over the river. But Grant denied it, citing Seaforth's orders. However, Grant's service with the Covenanters was limited. In January-February 1645 he may have led his men out to serve in Seaforth's army stationed at Inverness. However, after Inverlochy Angus MacQueen of Corrybough visited Grant and persuaded him to sign the Kilcumin Bond, which Montrose had drawn up. Grant then joined Montrose with a force of 300 men and entered Elgin. Although the burgh paid Montrose £1,300 in ransom, Grant plundered it upon the royalists' evacuation. Grant was now firmly in the royalist camp.[59]

Hackett's Horse

Colonel: Sir James Hackett/Halkett/Halkhead (fiar of Pitfirrane)

Major: John Lyall

Sir James Hackett was a leading Fife Covenanter and an elder of Dunfermline Parish Church. He was appointed to the Fife committee of war in 1643 by the Convention of Estates, a nomination which was reaffirmed throughout the period. By November 1644 he had raised a regiment of horse, probably from Fife. In November Hackett served under Major General Ramsay. The regiment quartered in the presbyteries of Aberdeen, Deer and Ellon with Dalhousie's and Hamilton's Horse. Sometime in the winter of 1644-45 Hackett's Horse moved its quarters to Old Aberdeen. On 26 February 1645 the regiment received orders to move into New Aberdeen when Balcarres' Horse arrived. For a short time the two horse regiments shared the occupation of Aberdeen with Lothian's 'Irish' Foot. In early March these three units extorted £2,000 from the citizens of Aberdeen, then fled the burgh on 7 March upon hearing rumours of a royalist approach. The two horse regiments remained together; in late March they were near Brechin under Baillie. Although they received orders to proceed to Aberdeen under Major General Urry, Balcarres' and Hackett's Horse failed to move there immediately. On 5 April Baillie dispatched Urry with the two regiments from near Perth to catch Montrose in Dundee. The Covenanters skirmished with the royalist rearguard that day as they pursued them northeastwards. However, Baillie charged Urry with failure to press the pursuit. On the second day of the pursuit, following a rest, Balcarres' and Hackett's men (still under Urry's command) caught the royalists at the Careston ford of the South Esk. They continued to pursue them up Glen Esk, thus inflicting casualties on Montrose's men and preserving the countryside from plundering. On 11 April Hackett's Horse with Lothian's and the Loudoun-Glasgow Foot reached Aberdeen. The horse quartered across the Dee about Torry. Some entered the burgh where they purchased food, while others plundered the countryside for eight miles around New Aberdeen. On the morning of the 12th the horse regiment took up quarters in Old Aberdeen. Three days later Urry led his force out of Aberdeen, but Lothian's men mutinied for pay and the other two regiments returned to Old Aberdeen. On the 19th the regiments departed from the burgh for Moray and from there to Inverness. On 9 May at Auldearn Hackett's Horse served with other cavalry units on the left wing of Urry's army. The regiment escaped from the slaughter, but it was not in the best condition. On 10 July the Estates ordered the regiment to be broken up and added as recruits to Balcarres' 'new' horse. Hackett's Horse then consisted of three full troops. Major Lyall and a Captain Lindsay were to have two of them in the new regiment, the other officers were to receive satisfaction for their services. Balcarres' new regiment does not seem to have been fully raised and was soon devastated at Kilsyth. There Hackett led an independent troop of horse, the last time he served in the field during the mid 1640s.[60]

Home's Foot

Colonel: Robert Home of Heugh

Lieutenant Colonel: (?) Dick

There is a good deal of disagreement about the size of this force which consisted of commanded men drawn from the Ulster Army's seven remaining foot regiments in 1645. Through February and March 1645 the Covenanting regime negotiated with the council of war of the Ulster Army about withdrawing a large body of men to oppose Montrose and Alasdair. On 4 April this force landed in Scotland under the command of Home, who was made colonel of what was treated as a new regiment. One royalist contemporary stated that the rumoured number of 1,500 redcoats was a gross exaggeration and that only 600 men crossed over to Scotland. Another royalist believed that only 1,000 foot entered the country under Home. In fact 1,400 men (200 commanded men from each of the seven regiments) formed the new unit. There is no mention of the regiment during its first three months in Scotland. The silence is broken on 10 July by a petition from the lieutenant colonel and other officers. They desired that the conditions made by Sir William Cochrane and the laird of Garthland for bringing the men over be kept. They included the payment of £6 per month to the soldiers. The officers received permission on this occasion to seek out deserters from the Ulster Army. The Estates also ordered the payment of June's and July's monthly maintenance to the Home's Foot. Desertion must have been a severe problem, because on 1 August the Estates ordered Dumfriesshire to provide 600 recruits for the regiment. While in Scotland Home's Foot fought in only one action — Kilsyth. The regiment held the centre of the first line between the Midlothian Foot to the right, and the Loudoun-Glasgow Foot to the left. Baillie ordered Home's and the Loudoun-Glasgow Foot to hold their ground opposite the royalist Macleans, who held some enclosures. However, both regiments ignored their orders and advanced. They became entangled in the fiercest fighting of the day before the Macleans and Clanranald broke them. The casualties suffered by Home's men were so high that the regiment was never mentioned again in the state papers. By 24 December Home was back in Belfast with his old regiment. On 2 February 1646 the Estates made him governor of Inverness in absentia. On 27 March 1647 he petitioned the Estates that he remain as governor of that burgh until his arrears were paid. The government agreed to this. This appointment may have arisen as a way of compensating Home for the loss of his new regiment, or as a means to ensure his loyalty to the Covenanting regime.[61]

Innes' Retinue

Commander: Sir Robert Innes of Innes

Sir Robert was the chief of his name and an Elginshire Covenanter. In 1643 the Convention of Estates appointed him to the committee of war of Elginshire, Nairnshire, Strathspey, Inverness-shire east of the River Ness, and Inverness burgh. On 16 May 1644 Innes led a retinue of horse and foot into Argyll's camp at Turriff. While there his men stole clothing worth £5 6s. 8d. from one tenant, a sum of money from another, and destroyed £6 6s. 8d. worth of corn belonging to a third. Innes and his men accompanied Argyll to Elgin, and they may have taken part in the marquis' incursion into Strathbogie. In January and February 1645 Innes led his men in Seaforth's army, which was based at Inverness. Later in February Innes attended a meeting in Elgin with other northern Covenanters. Upon hearing of Montrose's approach they fled to safety in Spynie Castle (which Innes owned). In May Innes took the field for the last time in the mid-1640s and brought out a retinue to Urry's army. Innes led his men at Auldearn, from which he managed to escape.[62]

Keith's Horse Troop

Routmaster: Alexander Keith

Keith was a brother of the earl Marischal. In July 1644 he raised a troop of horse to attend the Committee for the North. During that month the troop quartered in Old Aberdeen for two days and cut unripe berries for its horses. In September Keith brought his troop to Aberdeen to join Burleigh's army. It fought at the battle of Aberdeen on the 13th, where it may have been one of the units which could not comprehend how to deliver a cavalry charge. In the autumn Keith's troop served under Argyll on his marches against Montrose. Unfortunately, Routmaster Keith was one of the few casualties of the Covenanter army during the skirmishes at Fyvie Castle on 28-29 October. Later in the autumn the troop served under Ramsay, and it ruined the countryside. The troop went into winter quarters near Aberdeen. On Sunday 9 March 1645 the troop was stationed at Torry to protect some armaments owned by the Covenanters. However, a force of royalists seized the weapons and then routed the troop at a skirmish at Brig of Dee.[63]

Kinmuck's Retinue

Commander: John Kennedy of Kinmuck

Kinmuck was an Aberdeenshire Covenanter and a member of the shire's committee of war. In early April 1644 he fled into Kinmuck House to avoid plundering by the royalists. On the 26th he joined Argyll at Dunottar Castle with a retinue in order to gain revenge against Irvine of Drum's son, who had ravaged his lands. After serving on Argyll's first expedition Kinmuck disbanded his retinue until September. Then in answer to Burleigh's call for a general mobilisation of northeastern Covenanters Kinmuck raised a force of kinsmen, tenants and servants, and entered Aberdeen on the 12th. This retinue fought at the battle of Aberdeen, but never took the field again. [64]

Kerr's Retinue

Commander: Thomas Kerr (of Cavers)

Thomas Kerr was a Roxburghshire Covenanter with strong credentials. In 1638 he married a sister of Sir James Hackett (see above, pp. 222-223). He was a commissioner for the shire at the Covention of Estates, which appointed him to the Teviotdale committee of war in August 1643. In spring 1644 he raised a body of men and led them to the rendezvous at Douglas. From there this unit with others attacked the Cumberland royalists in May. It disbanded after only a few weeks' existence.[65]

Lord Kinpont's Retinue

Commander: John, Lord Kinpont

Lord Kinpont was the heir of the earl of Airth and Menteith. He was a member of the Perthshire committee of war, and was thus, at least, a nominal

Covenanter. In late August 1644 he raised 500 Highlanders with the aid of Sir John Drummond, a son of the earl of Perth, and the master of Maderty, heir of Lord Maderty, from Monteith and western Perthshire. This force was stationed at the Hill of Buchanty to intercept Montrose as he descended the Sma' Glen. Instead Montrose caught them unprepared and they joined his army. This may have been a plot by all parties involved, because the loyalty of Kinpont and friends was suspect. Kinpont's Highlanders fought at Tippermuir. Shortly afterwards James Stewart of Ardvorlich murdered Kinpont for reasons still unknown. Kinpont's men then left the royalist army to bury their commander, which weakened Montrose's army.[66]

Kinnadie's Retinue

Commander: Patrick Strachan of Kinnadie

Kinnadie was an Aberdeenshire Covenanter who brought his retinue into Aberdeen in response to the general levy of September 1644. Kinnadie led his men at the battle of Aberdeen, and does not appear to have taken the field again.[67]

Clan Lamont

Chief: Sir James Lamont

This clan was traditionally allied to the Campbells, and had its centre of power on the Cowal peninsula. In January 1645 Sir James Lamont raised men of his clan to serve in Argyll's army. The Lamonts fought in the centre of the battle line at Inverlochy. Sir James and Robert Lamont of Silvercraigs fell prisoner to the royalists after the battle. They later joined the royalists and were particularly active in the second invasion of Argyll in late summer 1645. The Campbells exacted their revenge against this clan at Dunoon in spring 1646, when they killed thirty-three leaders and over a hundred others.[68]

Largie's Retinue

Commander: (?) Forbes of Largie

Largie raised a retinue in response to Burleigh's call to arms in early September 1644. The unit fought at the battle of Aberdeen on the 13th. Largie fell prisoner to Montrose, who released him on parole on 15 October. In early November Largie returned to the royalist army as he was unable to secure the release of the prisoners desired by Montrose. After Craigievar's escape from the royalist camp

Montrose released Largie. (For other possible appearances in the field by Largie, please see the entry on Lord Forbes.)[69]

Leslie's Retinue

Commander: John Forbes of Leslie

Leslie was an Aberdeenshire Covenanter who led a retinue to Argyll's army at Dunottar Castle on 26 April 1644. It may be assumed that he served with Argyll for the whole of that campaign. In September Leslie again took to the field following Burleigh's proclamation of a general rendezvous at Aberdeen. Leslie led his men in the battle on the 13th. Although there is no future mention of Leslie's Retinue, he may have been in the field under Lord Forbes.[70]

Lockhart's Horse

Colonel: William Lockhart (of Lee the younger)

Major: Andrew Munro

There is very little information on this regiment of horse. It was in existence by late January 1647, but there is no information on the levying of the troopers or about the actions in which they served. On 29 January 1647 the Estates appointed Colonel Lockhart the commander of an independent troop of horse in the New Model Army. On 5 February the Estates ordered Lockhart to disband the regiment on the 10th. However, he was to retain the best one hundred men. Eighty were assigned to his own troop; the other twenty were reserved for Barclay's troop.[71]

Lovat Frasers

Colonel: Hugh, 7th Lord Lovat, Chief of Lovat Frasers

Lieutenant Colonel: Sir James Fraser of Brea, Tutor of Lovat

Brea was a staunch Covenanter who managed to persuade the entire clan to support his party. In 1644 the clan busied itself fortifying its lands in Inverness-shire. William Fraser of Culbokie, with the aid of his brother, Major Hugh Fraser (a veteran of the Swedish army), built a sconce on the Carse of Kingillie. Lovat Castle was surrounded with a deep ditch and rampart. Alexander Fraser of Phioneas garrisoned the castle with a company of men. John Fraser of Clunavacky fortified Beauly Castle with a sconce. In August the Lovat Frasers joined the other northern Covenanting clans to oppose Alasdair's army. On 19 August the burgh of Inverness sent out eighty musketeers to join Lord Lovat's men in Stratharrick. In late September Brea with the earl of Sutherland and the sheriff of Moray joined Argyll with 1,000 men at Forres. It is uncertain whether or not the northern Covenanters continued with Argyll after he departed from Inverness. In January-February 1645 the Lovat Frasers were again in the field, this time as part of Seaforth's army. In May the Lovat Frasers under Brea and Struy joined Urry's army at Inverness. The Frasers fought at Auldearn, losing eighty-seven husbands whose wives required Lord Lovat's aid to maintain themselves. The losses among the unmarried men engaged in the battle are not known. Following the battle Alasdair's foot occupied Beauly, the Macleods quartered in Kilernan, Kilmoor Wester and Siddey, and Seaforth's men stayed in Urray, Contin, Dingwall and Fotterty. The Lovat Frasers had several months to recuperate before Montrose returned in early 1646. He laid siege to Inverness and his men plundered the surrounding area. However, the Frasers' forts provided safety for many. Besides Beauly, the Frasers controlled Wardlaw Sconce, Culbokie's sconce, the Isle of Aigas and Little Struy. After Middleton lifted the siege in May, Brea entertained him and his officers at Lovat Castle. During this campaign Middleton delivered Chanonry Castle, whose Mackenzie garrison surrendered, to Brea. (Brea garrisoned the castle with Frasers in spring 1647.) Sometime afterwards Brea went south and Seaforth took the opportunity to press his Remonstrance on the Frasers by sending Roderick Mackenzie of Davochmaluag to meet with their leaders. The lairds of Struy, Culbokie, Belladrum, Clunavacky, Foyers, Farraline, Reelich and Phoineas received Davochmaluag at Lovat Castle. After hearing his proposal for an alliance, Struy and Phoineas (the latter was governor of all the Fraser forts, captain of the Lovat garrison, mustermaster of the clan, and captain of its watch) spoke against it. Their opposition kept the Frasers in the Covenanter camp. Throughout 1646 and 1647 the Frasers maintained their garrisons. However, they suffered a reverse in 1647 when the Mackenzies recaptured Chanonry Castle from Lieutenant Hugh Fraser, its commander. During the mid-1640s the allegiance of the Frasers to the Covenants played an important rôle in ensuring the safety of Inverness, which was an important garrison.[72]

Lyall's/Lyell's/Lyes' Foot

Colonel: Arthur Lyall/Lyell/Lyes

Another mysterious regiment whose origin and sphere of action is not known. In early November 1644 fifteen men of the regiment stayed in the Aberdeen tolbooth for thirteen days at a cost of £28. In mid-June 1645 the earl of Crawford-Lindsay replaced Lothian's Foot in Dundee with this regiment. However, the soldiers and burgesses rioted on the 30th. The regiment was ordered from the burgh and the Edinburgh Foot replaced it. On 5 November

Lyell was ordered to bring his regiment from Dundee to Glasgow. The last reference to the regiment is to the 300 foot in it quartering in Perth between 10 and 19 March 1646.[73]

Clan MacDougall

The MacDougalls were the only clan other than the Lamonts to join the Campbells at Inverlochy. They, too, were traditional allies of Argyll's kinsmen. Their centre of power was northern Lorne. At Inverlochy the MacDougall's served in the centre. The clan suffered heavy casualties, which included the heir of MacDougall of Reray. In autumn 1645 they joined Sir James Lamont and Alasdair in the second invasion of Argyll. For that campaign the MacDougalls managed to field 500 men. The Campbells exacted their revenge on the MacDougalls at Dunaverty Castle in May 1647, when nearly fifty were massacred.[74]

Clan MacGregor

Commander: Patrick Roy MacGregor of that Ilk

The laird of MacGregor led his clansmen out for the Covenanters in September 1644. From 11 to 19 September they quartered in Perth. However, the clan joined Montrose's invasion of Argyll in December 1644. In early 1645 the laird signed the Kilcumin Bond. The early co-operation with the Covenanters may have been a ruse or motivated by fear, for the clan was steadfastly royalist.[75]

Mackintoshes

Some members of this clan (which belonged to the great alliance of Clan Chattan) from eastern Inverness-shire joined Urry at Inverness in early May 1645. They fought as part of the Covenanting army at Auldearn on the 9th. There was no further military activity by the clan until 1651.[76]

Mearns Foot

Joint Colonels: William, 7th earl Marischal, and Robert, 1st viscount Arbuthnott

Marischal and Arbuthnott were the leading Covenanter peers from the shire of Mearns. On 16 April 1644 the Estates commissioned Marischal the commander of horse on Argyll's expedition against Huntly. However, the two noblemen had already been at work raising foot soldiers, for by the 17th they could muster 500 men. The regiment joined Argyll at Dunottar Castle on 26 April. Six days later it entered Aberdeen, from where it departed on the same day to Drum. The expedition proceeded from there to Inverurie and Kellie. On the 8th Kellie surrendered to Marischal's summons on the Estates' quarters. It appears that Gight Castle fell on the same day. On the 13th Marischal and Arbuthnott were back in Aberdeen with their regiment. The two nobles accompanied Argyll with their regiment for the remainder of his campaign in the northeast. The regiment returned to Aberdeen on the 29th and disbanded between then and the 31st. Neither noble gave such active support again to the Covenanting regime in the mid-1640s. Marischal did meet with Argyll on 16 September at Brechin, but he rendered little military support. This did not exempt the earl's estates from being ravaged by Montrose's army. However, he was growing discontented with the Covenanting movement and he ceased to actively aid its military endeavours.[77]

Milne's Dragoons

Colonel: George Milne

There is no evidence concerning the levying of this regiment which was on foot by August 1645. It probably served at Philiphaugh. On 6 November it was ordered to Dundee and Milne received the governorship of that burgh. The regiment is last mentioned on the 17th when the Estates ordered 100 men from Dundee to St. Andrews as a guard for parliament.[78]

Clan Menzies

The Menzies were a pro-Covenanting clan located in central Perthshire astride the upper Tay. In the winter of 1645-46 some members of the clan joined Ardkinglas on his march to the lowlands. They were present at the battle of Callander on 13 February 1646, where a force of Atholl Highlanders routed Ardkinglas' force. The survivors continued with Ardkinglas and may have formed a contingent in his regiment of foot.[79]

Montgomery's Horse

Commander: Lieutenant Colonel Hugh Montgomery

There is no information on the commissioning or raising of this regiment. It was on foot by April 1646. From 27 April to 15 May 200 troopers in four troops quartered in Aberdeen. The regiment probably served on Middleton's campaigns in 1646. On 29 January 1647 the Estates appointed Montgomery the

Adjutant General of the New Model Army. However, on 15 March he declined the position, ending all references either to this unit or its commander.[80]

Monymusk's Retinue

Commander: Sir William Forbes of Monymusk

Monymusk was an Aberdeenshire Covenanter who possessed a tower house on the middle reaches of the Don. In early April 1644 he fled into Monymusk House to avoid plundering by the royalists. On 26 April Monymusk joined Argyll at Dunottar Castle with a body of men raised from his estates. After serving on Argyll's first northeastern campaign, Monymusk disbanded his men. However, in September he raised them again and took part in the battle of Aberdeen. In October Monymusk's wife dined Montrose, which saved her husband's lands from pillaging. Although there is no other explicit reference to Monymusk raising men for the Covenanters again, he may have served with Lord Forbes or the master of Forbes on their expeditions.[81]

Earl of Moray's Foot

Colonel: James, 4th earl of Moray

Lieutenant Colonel: James Grant of Freuchie

Major: James Grant

Again this is a regiment about which little is known. The first mention of the regiment occurs on 1 February 1644 when the Estates assigned Moray 1,500 foot out of Elginshire, Nairnshire and southern Inverness-shire. They were to rendezvous at Berwick on 10 March. However, there is no evidence that any of Moray's men ever joined the Army of the Solemn League and Covenant. Instead they always seem to have served in the Home Army. In mid-September 1644 a company or several companies formed part of the Stirling garrison. On 27 February 1645 the Estates ordered all deficients and runaways to attend the regiment. Moray's Foot formed part of Baillie's army from May to July. It fought at the battle of Alford, where the royalists inflicted heavy casualties. On 5 August the officers of the regiment petitioned the Estates. They claimed that they had previously submitted petitions, but that the Estates had ignored them. The officers stated that the regiment was broken and that they could no longer serve. They desired that Moray's Foot be dismissed from service and that the officers receive their arrears. The matter was referred to the Committee of Estates, which decided to maintain the regiment on the establishment. Indeed sometime between August 1645 and February 1647 Moray's Foot received new recruits. In autumn 1645 the officers of Moray's, while garrisoning Perth, seized 164 bolls and 1 firlot of meal from a Perth burgess. On 5 February 1647 the Estates ordered the regiment to disband on the 9th save for one company which would be retained for a regiment in the New Model Army. On the 12th the Estates issued further orders to the officers of the company still on foot. It was to march to Dundee, paying for its quarters on the way, and to join the General of Artillery's Foot there.[82]

Clan Munro

Commander: ? Sir Robert Munro of Obsdale, Master and Tutor of Foulis, or Colonel John Munro of Lemlair

Clan Munro controlled two stretches of territory north of Inverness. One was astride Strathoykell, and the other was a stretch of land between Strath Rannoch and Cromarty Firth. In August 1644 the Munros joined other Covenanter clans (the Grants, Rosses and Lovat Frasers) and the earls of Seaforth and Sutherland to oppose Alasdair MacDonald and his army. In January-February 1645 the Munros formed part of the earl of Seaforth's army at Inverness. In May they mobilised for the final time and joined Urry at Inverness. They fought at Auldearn on 9 May, after which they retired from active participation in the wars.[83]

Muiryfold's Retinue

Commander: James Hay of Muiryfold

Muiryfold held the barony of Delgaty in Aberdeenshire. In September 1644 he responded to Burleigh's request for a general rendezvous by raising the earl of Erroll's Buchan men and brought them to Aberdeen. They served at the battle on the 13th. Afterwards Muiryfold refrained from military activity.[84]

Orchardton's Company of Foot

Captain: Robert Maxwell of Orchardton

Orchardton was a professional soldier from Galloway. He served in both the Covenanter and English parliamentary armies in the mid-1640s. Sometime before February 1645 he raised a company of foot for the Covenanters. On the 27th the Estates ordered that his company be converted into one of dragoons. After this it disappears from the records. In early March Orchardton petitioned the Estates for relief. He had served as a colonel of horse under the earl of Warwick and had suffered property losses in Ireland. The Estates wrote the English parliament on his behalf.[85]

Perthshire Foot

Colonel: James, 2nd earl of Tullibardine

On 25 August 1644 the Committee of Estates ordered the levying of all fencible men of Perthshire. Tullibardine received the commission as colonel. He concentrated his forces at Perth. On 1 September they marched from the burgh to Tippermuir, where they formed the centre of Elcho's army. After initially resisting the Irish regiments the Perthshire men fled the field, and suffered heavy casualties.[86]

Phantiland's Retinue

Commander: Duncan MacCorquodale of Phantilands, chief of the MacCorquodales

Until 1646 the MacCorquodales had remained neutral and both sides had spared their lands. However, sometime in 1646 Alasdair and his army were marching through the clan lands in Lorn when the chief and some of his men opened fire from a fortified house on an island in Loch Tromleg. Alasdair responded in the manner typical of his age. He burnt the clan's houses, captured the island and had the chief shot.[87]

Philorth's Retinue

Commander: Alexander Fraser of Philorth

Philorth was an Aberdeenshire Covenanter who had an estate in Buchan. In 1643 he served as a commissioner for Aberdeenshire at the Convention of Estates. On 26 August the Convention appointed him a member of the Aberdeenshire committee of war. In early April he fled into Philorth House to escape plundering by Huntly's men. Subsequently he re-emerged and raised a force of men which he led to Dunottar Castle. Philorth served on Argyll's first northeastern campaign before disbanding his men. In September he brought out his retinue again and fought at the battle of Aberdeen. While there is no further mention of Philorth leading an independent force he may have served in Lord Fraser's retinue.[88]

Tutor of Pitsligo's Retinue

Commander: Alexander Forbes, Tutor of Pitsligo

In 1643 the Convention of Estates appointed the Tutor of Pitsligo to the Aberdeenshire committee of war. In early April 1644 the Tutor fled into Pitsligo

Castle to escape the plundering of Huntly's army. Later in the month he raised Lord Pitsligo's men from Buchan and marched south to Dunottar Castle. There he joined Argyll's army on the 26th and served with him until the end of May. In September the Tutor again levied Pitsligo's men, and went with them to Aberdeen. They served at the battle on the 13th, but never took the field again as a separate unit. However, the Tutor and his men may have served in the future with the Lord or master of Forbes.[89]

Poltalloch's Retinue

Commander: Zachary MacCallum of Poltalloch

Poltalloch was the last Campbell ally to remain loyal to Argyll. Following the expulsion of the Irish a proverb developed — 'None remained loyal to Argyll but stone and lime and Malcolm' (an alternative spelling of Poltalloch's surname). There are two stories which relate the death of Poltalloch. Both are placed sometime in 1646. In one version he led his clansmen to join the Campbells at Lagganmore. He fought Alasdair there and broke his sword. However, Poltalloch was eventually surrounded by his foes and died fighting. The other account takes place in Glen Euchar. There Poltalloch led an attack to recover some stolen cattle, but he fell in the fighting. With Poltalloch's death the Campbells became truly isolated in Argyll.[90]

Riddell's Retinue

Commander: Sir Walter Riddell of Riddell

In 1643 Riddell attended the Convention of Estates as a commissioner for Roxburghshire. On 26 August the Convention named him to the shire's com- mittee of war. In April 1644 he raised a body of kinsmen and tenants from the shire and marched to the rendezvous at Douglas. He participated in the raids against the Cumberland royalists. Afterwards Riddell received the commission as lieutenant colonel of the master of Cranston's Foot in the Army of the Solemn League and Covenant.[91]

Roses

Commander: Hugh Rose of Kilravock, chief of the name of Rose

The Roses were a Nairnshire family whose holdings were concentrated along the western bank of the lower Nairn. In January-February 1645 they came out and joined Seaforth's army at Inverness. In May they served in Urry's army at Auldearn. There is no subsequent reference to any military activity by the family in the mid-1640s.[92]

Clan Ross

Commander: David Ross of Balnagowan, chief of Clan Ross

Clan Ross possessed extensive holdings between the Moray Firth and Ben More Assynt in eastern Inverness-shire and the shire of Ross. In January-February 1645 the Rosses took the field against Montrose and formed part of Seaforth's army. In May they joined Urry's army and fought at Auldearn. This was their last service for the Covenanters until Carbisdale in 1650.[93]

Rosyth's Foot

Colonel: Sir James Scott of Rosyth

Rosyth served as the commissioner for Clackmannanshire at the Convention of Estates. He was also a member of the shire's committee of war, and of the Committee for the North. Before the 1640s Rosyth was a mercenary in the European wars. In August 1644 he received a commission to command some of the levies to be used against Montrose. They probably came from Clackmannanshire and western Fife. At the battle of Tippermuir he commanded the left wing, which held the longest before breaking.[94]

Roughe's/Rosse's/Roche's Foot

Commander: Lieutenant Colonel John Roughe/Rosse/Roche

Major: Patrick Grant

In December 1644 Roughe led a force of about 550 foot in Baillie's army during the march to Roseneath. There Baillie loaned Roughe and his men to Argyll. The regiment served on one of the flanks at Inverlochy and were shattered by the Irish. Roughe fled into Inverlochy Castle where he was captured. Montrose released him on parole; upon returning to the lowlands the Committee of Estates appointed him to the governorship of Perth so that he would not have to take the field against the marquis. On 7 August 1645 Major Grant petitioned the Estates that the regiment be recruited to strength for the defence of Stirling or that the men be paid off due to the regiment's low strength. In November Roughe was governor of Perth when part of the garrison, presumably his regiment, stole 126 bolls and two firlots of meal from William Blair of Williamstein. Following that incident the regiment vanished until November 1646; in the meantime it was probably recruited to a greater strength. On 6 November the people of Culross and Tulliallan, and Edward Bruce of Carnock asked the Estates to remove the regiment. The government concurred and ordered Roughe to march to the Carse of Gowrie without extorting any money before his departure. The Perthshire committee of war was to assign quarters to the regiment throughout the shire. On 28 January 1647 Roughe received an appointment as the lieutenant colonel of Pitscottie's Foot in the New Model Army. On 5 February the Estates issued an order for Roughe's Foot to disband entirely on the 9th.[95]

Sanda's Retinue

Commander: Archibald Mor MacDonald of Sanda

Sanda was the only MacDonald to bring a force to Argyll's army at Inverlochy. His men were posted in the centre of the army's line. After the battle Sanda fell prisoner to the royalists. After securing his release Sanda joined Alasdair and rose to the rank of governor of Dunaverty Castle.[96]

Scott's Retinue

Commander: Sir William Scott

There were at least three Sir William Scotts in 1644. One was the laird of Clerkington in the Borders. The other two were father and son. It is more likely that it was one of them that brought out a retinue in April 1644. Sir William the younger of Harden was the sheriff of Selkirkshire, thus he was able to levy men to oppose the invaders. Sir William the elder of Harden had served as a commissioner for Selkirkshire at the Convention of Estates. He possessed a commission (dated 26 August 1643) to be the colonel of the Selkirkshire Horse. In the event one of these men responded to Montrose's incursion into Scotland by leading a retinue to Douglas. From there he raided Cumberland with other Covenanters, and then disbanded his force.[97]

Scottscraig's Horse Troop

Routmaster: Colonel Sir Arthur Erskine of Scottscraig

Scottscraig was the colonel of the Ministers' Foot in the Army of the Solemn League and Covenant. He apparently received a commission to levy a troop of horse sometime in 1644. On 7 August the heritors of nine parishes of eastern Stirlingshire petitioned the Committee of Estates regarding the troop. They claimed that the troop had been present in their area since it had been levied and that it had received orders to remain there indefinitely. The heritors claimed that better parishes for grazing existed in the shire than theirs. They wished the

Committee to order the colonel and the committee of war to order the troopers away 'that we be not blallie overburdent . . .' There is no other reference to this unit which suggests that it was broken at Tippermuir.[98]

Earl of Seaforth's Foot

Colonel: George, 2nd earl of Seaforth, and chief of the Mackenzies

Seaforth was the leader of one of the largest northern clans. His power extended from Moray Firth in the east to the Isle of Lewis in the west and covered large sections of Inverness-shire and of the shire of Ross. Both the Covenanters and Montrose were to find in Seaforth one of the most self-serving and duplicious men of the age. In August 1644 he joined the earl of Sutherland and the northern Covenanter clans to oppose Alasdair and his men. He was probably motivated by fear of persecution by the Covenanters who were uncertain about his loyalties. The earl's apprehension as well as pressure from his allies led him to bring out his men again in January and to accept the post of commander-in-chief of the Covenanters at Inverness. He was probably in touch with Montrose at this time in order to protect himself against royalist successes. After learning of the royalist victory at Inverlochy the army broke up. In mid-February the northern Covenanters convened a meeting at Elgin, which Seaforth and his brother Thomas Mackenzie of Pluscarden attended. Hearing of Montrose's approach the Covenanters fled, and Seaforth reached his home north of Inverness. However, the earl returned to Elgin where Montrose seized him. Seaforth gained his liberty by signing the Kilcumin Bond, and by promising to raise the Mackenzies for Montrose and to hold Inverness for the king. But Seaforth betrayed Montrose and did not fulfil one of his promises. On 27 February, in the midst of the earl's flirtations with the royalists, the Covenanters authorised him to raise the eighth man from his district to strengthen his regiment. In early May Seaforth took the field again for the Covenanters. He raised a force of Mackenzies, MacLennans and Macaulays of Lewis to join Urry. While Seaforth escaped after the battle his men suffered heavily. Captain Bernard Mackenzie and his company from the Chanonry of Ross died fighting. Seaforth's chamberlain in Lewis and John Mackenzie of Kernsary also died in the battle. The Lochbroom and Lewis men suffered heavy casualties, because they fought to the death. The MacLennans were also badly hit. Roderick MacLennan, chief of the clan and bannerman of Kintail, was killed after refusing quarter. His brothers Donald and Malcolm, eighteen MacLennans of rank, and Duncan MacIan Og Macrae died with him defending the standard. While some might have been angered by such high losses among their kinsmen and followers Seaforth rushed to achieve an accommodation with Montrose. He joined Alasdair's regiments and the Macleods in quartering on the lands of the Lovat Frasers. Seaforth's men were assigned the parishes of Urray, Contin, Dingwall and Fotterty. However, Seaforth did not lead his men south to aid Montrose in conquering the lowlands. After May 1645 it was anyone's guess as to who Seaforth really favoured. During the siege of Inverness in spring 1646 Seaforth does not seem to have aided Montrose. But strangely when the siege ended he renewed the Kilcumin Bond with the marquis. He was subsequently excommunicated for this action. Of a greater threat to Seaforth's power was the arrival in the north of Middleton with a strong force. Lady Seaforth surrendered Fortrose/Chanonry Castle to Middleton during this campaign. The earl later gave himself up to the major general. Later in that year Seaforth journeyed to Edinburgh where he underwent repentance for his offences in St. Giles. By the end of 1646 Seaforth and all the Mackenzie lairds who had joined Montrose received pardons.[99]

Skellater's Retinue

Commander: William Forbes of Skellater

In March 1645 Skellater raised a force of 200 men to plunder the lands of royalists in the northeast. However, to escape the revenge of the Gordons Skellater joined them. Lord Gordon ordered him to aid Alasdair during his plundering and recruiting. Consequently Skellater marched to Coupar Angus with Alasdair. There he devastated Lord Coupar's estates, beat up a troop of horse and killed Robert Lindsay, a minister. Skellater then disbanded having gained the distinction of being the only Forbes to actively aid the royalist war effort.[100]

Skene's Retinue

Commander: James Skene of Skene

Skene served as a commissioner for Aberdeenshire at the Convention of Estates in 1643. Subsequently he was appointed to the Aberdeenshire committee of war. In early April 1644 he fled into Skene House with Forbes of Echt to escape plundering by Huntly. Shortly afterwards he raised a body of men from his estates and rendezvoused with Argyll at Dunottar Castle on 26 April. Skene disbanded this force after accompanying the marquis on his first northeastern campaign. In September Skene brought out his retinue for the last time in response to Burleigh's proclamation of a general muster of northeastern Covenanters at Aberdeen. Skene and his men fought against Montrose's army on the 13th, before fleeing back to their homes.[101]

Earl of Sutherland's Foot

Colonel: John, 13th earl of Sutherland, chief of Clan Sutherland

The earl of Sutherland was a Covenanter of long standing and the most loyal northern peer to that party. During 1642 the earl maintained a regiment in readiness due to his suspicions of the earl of Seaforth. On 1 February 1644 the Committee of Estates assigned Sutherland a force of 1,600 foot to be levied from his section of Inverness-shire and from Caithness to form an infantry regiment (which was to be at Berwick on 10 March). This regiment saw its first service in August when Sutherland joined the northern Covenanter clans and Seaforth to oppose Alasdair's Irishmen. Sutherland's Foot remained in the field until October when it went into winter quarters (probably on the clan lands). In January-February 1645 Sutherland and his foot soldiers were at Inverness as part of Seaforth's army. It returned to its quartering grounds after learning of Inverlochy. On 27 February the Estates authorised Sutherland to raise the eighth man from his district. The committee of war received instructions to assist the earl by putting into effect all acts on the eighth man, deficients and deserters. In early May the regiment was stationed at Inverness, which allowed it to join Urry's army. Both the earl and his men served at the battle of Inverness, from which they appear to have escaped with minor losses. The regiment vanishes from sight until December, then on the 18th the Estates issued several directives concerning Sutherland's men. The regiment was to march to Inverness and embark on the coal and meal ships there. The Estates left the choice of destination up to itself or the general officers of the army. The regiment was to receive arms and clothing on the public charge. There is no evidence suggesting that the earl's men ever departed from the north. Instead on 4 February 1646 Sutherland petitioned the Estates for money, clothing and shoes for his 800 foot. The Estates agreed to supply £4,240, 800 pairs of shoes, and a like number of suits of clothing. Robert Gray of Ballon received instructions from the government to muster the regiment. Sometime in the summer Sutherland disbanded his regiment at Invershin, ending its two years of service.[102]

Tolquhon's Retinue

Commander: Walter Forbes of Tolquhon

Tolquhon was another member of the great Covenanting family of Forbes. He served on the Aberdeenshire committee of war from August 1643. In early April 1644 Tolquhon secured himself in Tolquhon House to escape Huntly's army. Later in the month he raised a force of men which joined Argyll at Dunottar Castle and served on the first Covenanter campaign in the northeast. In September Tolquhon and his men took the field again, fighting at the battle of Aberdeen. Although Tolquhon does not appear to have raised an independent body of men again, he may have served either with Lord or the master of Forbes.[103]

Udny's Retinue

Commander: John Udny

In response to Burleigh's call to arms of early September 1644 Udny raised the men from the earl of Kinghorn's Belhelvie estate (Aberdeenshire). They served at the battle of Aberdeen on the 13th and then dispersed.[104]

Udny of Udny's Retinue

Commander: John Udny of Udny

Udny was a reluctant Covenanter. He served in the royal army in England between 1642 and 1644. Upon his return to Scotland he was forced to take the Solemn League and Covenant. In September 1644 Udny raised a body of kinsmen, tenants and friends to oppose Montrose. Udny and his force served at the battle of Aberdeen on the 13th, and never took the field again. In 1645 Udny served as an M.P. for Aberdeenshire.[105]

Urry's Dragoons

Colonel: Major General Sir John Urry

Urry had a very chequered career as both a royalist and Covenanter officer. In 1642 he served in the English parliamentary forces, then deserted to Prince Rupert. Charles I knighted him for providing information on the parliamentarian armies' manoeuvres. At Marston Moor Urry held a command with Rupert's army. Following the defeat he switched sides, but not before the Estates had forfeited his possessions. On 27 February 1645 the Estates made a volte face and commissioned Urry a major general of horse and foot, and colonel of the Aberdeenshire and Banffshire dragoons. Urry received instructions to go to Aberdeen with letters from Baillie (who hated him) and to commence raising his regiment of 240 men. During March Urry made a surprise attack on the royalists in Aberdeen. In early April he led the Covenanter horse in the pursuit of Montrose from Dundee. Baillie charged him with being overtly cautious on the first day of the pursuit. On 20 April the minister of Old Aberdeen read an order for the levy of 600 dragoons from Aberdeenshire. But none appeared for the levy. However, Urry managed to raise 400 dragoons by using local horses, which suggests that he merely mounted infantrymen instead of levying new recruits. Urry's Dragoons served with his army on the march to Inverness and then at Auldearn. They may have served on the left wing with Hackett's Horse, but as dragoons were incapable of charging they could have remained in the reserve with Urry. Following Urry's escape from Auldearn and his resignation from the Covenanter army, the Estates passed an act of approbation on his behaviour as an officer on 11 July 1645. On 7 August the Estates granted his petition asking for £6,000 for killing Donald Farquharson during the attack on Aberdeen. Urry joined Montrose in 1646. He was one of the few men excluded from the pardon extended to royalists and subsequently went into exile with the marquis. Urry returned to Scotland in 1650 to serve in Montrose's expedition. He was captured at Carbisdale and later executed in Edinburgh.[106]

Waterton's Retinue

Commander: Thomas Forbes of Waterton

Waterton belonged to the Forbes network of Covenanters and served on the Aberdeenshire committee of war. In early April 1644 he fled into Waterton House to escape plundering by the royalists. On 26 April Waterton led a force of his kinsmen and retainers into the Covenanter camp outside Dunottar Castle. He served with Argyll on the latter's first northeastern campaign, and disbanded his force in late May. In September Waterton raised his men again and served with Burleigh's army at Aberdeen. He did not take the field independently again, but may have served with either Lord or the master of Forbes.[107]

NOTES

1. Spalding, *Memorialls*, ii. 405-7; Stevenson, *Alasdair*, 184.

2. SRO, GD. 137, 2130-1; *Aberdeen Letters*, iii. 85, 118; *Memoirs of Guthry*, 151; Spalding, *Memorialls*, ii. 346, 353-4, 356, 365, 371-2; A. Maxwell, *The History of Old Dundee* (Edinburgh, 1884), 483.

3. *APS*, VI, i. 468-9.

4. Balfour, *Works*, iii. 198-9; *Muniments of the Royal Burgh of Irvine* (Ayrshire and Galloway Arch. Assoc., 1890-1), i. 10; Furgol, 'Religious Aspects', 152; Stevenson, *Alasdair*, 100-1.

5. *Aberdeen Letters*, iii. 85.

6. Stevenson, *Alasdair*, 216, 222, 226.

7. SRO, B.66.25, 370; *APS*, VI, i. 672, 705, 711.

8. Stevenson, *Alasdair*, 125, 138-9.

9. SRO, PA. 16.4, 7, 27; *APS*, VI, i. 61; *Memoirs of Scottish Catholics During the 17th and 18th centuries*, ed. W. Forbes-Leith (London, 1909), i. 274; Spalding, *Memorialls*, ii. 346, 360, 368-70, 381.

10. SRO, PA. 7.3, 92; PA. 16.4, 7, 9, 27, 46; *APS*, VI, i. 159; P. Gordon, *A Short Abridgement of Britaine's Distemper from 1639-49*, ed. J. Dunn (Spalding Club, x, 1844), 86, 89; *Irvine*, i. 102-3; Spalding, *Memorialls*, ii. 417-28; Wilson, *History*, 40; Stevenson, *Alasdair*, 124-5, 138, 142.

11. For details of losses at Inverlochy among the Campbells, see above, 207. Gordon, *Britaine's Distemper*, 102; Stevenson, *Alasdair*, 153-4, 157, 160. While Guthry suggested that there were men of Argyll's regiment at Kilsyth, the best modern authority disagrees, Cowan, *Montrose*, 218-21.

12. SRO, PA. 16.4, 28; *Aberdeen Letters*, iii. 39, 69, 72, 78, 83-4, 89-90; *APS*, VI, i. 494-5, 600.
13. *APS*, VI, i. 663, 672-3, 704, 707; *Council of Aberdeen*, ii. 75.
14. NLS. Dep. 175, Box 87.2; *Aberdeen Letters*, iii. 85; *APS*, VI, i. 361.
15. *APS*, VI, i. 203; Spalding, *Memorialls*, ii. 402.
16. *APS*, VI, i. 449, 585, 783; see above, 135, 137.
17. *APS*, VI, i. 137, 195; Spalding, *Memorialls*, ii. 402.
18. Stevenson, *Alasdair*, 216.
19. *Army of the Covenant*, ii. 370; Spalding, *Memorialls*, ii. 365.
20. *APS*, VI, i. 155, 293, 561, 811; Spalding, *Memorialls*, ii. 471, 473-5.
21. *Aberdeen Letters*, iii. 57-8, 89; *APS*, VI, i. 488; *Council of Aberdeen*, ii. 60, 63.
22. W. Gordon, *The History of the . . . Family of Gordon* (Edinburgh, 1727), ii. 440.
23. *APS*, VI, i. 55; Spalding, *Memorialls*, ii. 402, 470, 473-5.
24. SRO, PA. 16.4, 7, 9; *Aberdeen Letters*, iii. 85-6; *APS*, VI, i. 51, 184; *Memoirs of Guthry*, 167; Spalding, *Memorialls*, ii. 416, 432; J. K. Hewison, *The Covenanters*, 2 vols. (Glasgow, 1913), i. 418.
25. *APS*, VI, i. 354-5, 437, 590; J. Fraser, *Chronicles of the Frasers, 916-1674*, ed. W. Mackay (Scot. His. Soc., 1st Ser., xlvii, 1905), 287; Spalding, *Memorialls*, ii. 450, 473.
26. Stevenson, *Alasdair*, 117, 160.
27. *Ibid.*, 214-7.
28. *Ibid.*, 217-9, 221-2.
29. *APS*, VI, i. 55, 203; Spalding, *Memorialls*, ii. 401-2.
30. Stevenson, *Alasdair*, 153-4, 156, 158, 161.
31. *APS*, VI, i. 203; Spalding, *Memorialls*, ii. 402; see above, 216-7.
32. *APS*, VI, i. 55; Spalding, *Memorialls*, ii. 306, 338, 349, 372, 392; see above, 216-7.
33. SRO, PA. 16.4, 68; *Army of the Covenant*, i. lxxii; *Ibid.*, ii. 378; Spalding, *Memorialls*, ii. 402, 405, 410, 421, 427, 449, 467-8, 471; Cowan, *Montrose*, 165; Stevenson, *Alasdair*, 133.
34. *Intelligence from the south borders of Scotland. Written from Edenburgh, April 24, 1644* (London, 1644), 2.
35. SRO, PA. 11.4, 161v; *APS*, VI, i. 686; Cowan, *Montrose*, 205-6.
36. *Ibid.*, 181; Stevenson, *Alasdair*, 177.
37. *APS*, VI, i. 201-2; *Intelligence from the south borders of Scotland*, 2; Foster, *Members*, 67.
38. *APS*, VI, i. 55; *Council of Aberdeen*, ix. 60; Spalding, *Memorialls*, ii. 304-5; Cowan, *Montrose*, 163, 169.
39. *Ibid.*, 181; Stevenson, *Alasdair*, 177.
40. *APS*, VI, i. 55; Spalding, *Memorialls*, ii. 338, 349, 402; Cowan, *Montrose*, 170; see above, 216-7.
41. *Kirkcaldie*, 283.
42. SRO, B.9.12.8, 17; *Aberdeen Letters*, ii. 390-1; *Ibid.*, iii. 45, 85, 118; *APS*, VI, i. 90; *The Chronicle of Perth*, ed. J. Maidment (Maitland Club, xii, 1831), 39-40; *Memoirs of Guthry*, 151, 163; *Memorials of the Family of Wemyss of Wemyss*, 3 vols., ed. W. Fraser (Edinburgh, 1888), i. 248-9; R. Monteth, *The history of the Troubles of Great Britain . . . 1633-50*, trans. J. Ogilvie (2nd trans. edn., London, 1738), 172-3; Spalding, *Memorialls*, ii. 346, 353-5, 357, 363, 371-3, 378, 397; Stevenson, *Alasdair*, 125-6.
43. *Memoirs of Guthry*, 167; Spalding, *Memorialls*, ii. 397-9, 402, 404; Cowan, *Montrose*, 167; Stevenson, *Alasdair*, 131-2.
44. SRO, B.9.12.8, 31, 39; KSR Kilconquhar, i. 62; KSR Scoonie, i. 112, 113; *APS*, VI, i. 356, 449, 469, 547; *Memoirs of Guthry*, 167, 173.
45. SAUL, PR St. Andrews, i. 85.
46. SRO, KSR Ceres, i. 7; *APS*, VI, i. 54, 202; *The Life of Mr. Robert Blair, Minister of St. Andrews*, ed. T. McCrie (Wodrow Soc., xiii, 1848), 45; *Memoirs of Guthry*, 192-4;

Memorials of Montrose and his Times, ed. M. Napier (Maitland Club, lxvi, part i, 1848), i. 229; R. Chambers, *History of the rebellions in Scotland, from 1638 till 1660*, 2 vols. (Edinburgh, 1828), ii. 89; Cowan, *Montrose*, 218, 221.

47. *Memoirs of Guthry*, 192; *Memorials of Montrose*, i. 229; Cowan, *Montrose*, 218, 221.

48. *APS*, VI, i. 154, 202; *Memoirs of Guthry*, 192; Cowan, *Montrose*, 218, 221; see above, 214-5.

49. *APS*, VI, i. 52; Spalding, *Memorialls*, ii. 365, 469, 475; Cowan, *Montrose*, 189.

50. *APS*, VI, i. 190, 203, 242; *Memoirs of Guthry*, 167; Spalding, *Memorialls*, ii. 338, 349, 357-8, 365, 399-401, 469, 477-8; Cowan, *Montrose*, 168; *Scots Peerage*, iv. 62.

51. *APS*, VI, i. 562; Spalding, *Memorialls*, ii. 349, 402, 469.

52. SRO, PA. 16.4, 7; *APS*, VI, i. 190, 371; Spalding, *Memorialls*, ii. 338, 349, 357-9, 363, 365, 399, 402, 469, 477-8; Cowan, *Montrose*, 165-6; Stevenson, *Alasdair*, 133.

53. SRO, PA. 16.4, 7; *APS*, VI, i. 90, 203; Spalding, *Memorialls*, ii. 365, 399, 402, 462, 469, 475; Cowan, *Montrose*, 165-6; *Scots Peerage*, iv. 130; Stevenson, *Alasdair*, 133; see above, 217-8.

54. *APS*, VI, i. 686.

55. *Ibid.*, VI, i. 55, 203; Spalding, *Memorialls*, ii. 338, 349, 402.

56. SRO, GD. 112.39, 857.

57. *Ibid.*, 855, 857, 859; *Aberdeen Letters*, iii. 85; *APS*, VI, i. 202, 500; *The Black Book of Taymouth*, ed. C. Innes (Bannatyne Club, c. 1855), 101, 103.

58. *Memoirs of Guthry*, 167; Spalding, *Memorialls*, ii. 357, 363, 365, 399-402; Cowan, *Montrose*, 165, 168, 188; Stevenson, *Alasdair*, 166.

59. *APS*, VI, i. 55, 203; Spalding, *Memorialls*, ii. 341, 365; Cowan, *Montrose*, 169, 189; Stevenson, *Alasdair*, 117, 166.

60. *APS*, VI, i. 54, 202, 433, 562; *Army of the Covenant*, ii. 375; Balfour, *Works*, iii. 295; Spalding, *Memorialls*, ii. 432, 449, 451, 462; Cowan, *Montrose*, 197-8, 203.

61. *APS*, VI, i. 439, 449, 627, 823; *Memoirs of Guthry*, 183-4; Spalding, *Memorialls*, ii, 401; Cowan, *Montrose*, 218-21; Stevenson, *Covenanters*, 205-6, 209.

62. SRO, PA. 6.4, 7; *APS*, VI, i. 55, 203; Spalding, *Memorialls*, ii, 365, 473-5; Cowan, *Montrose*, 181, 188; Stevenson, *Alasdair*, 177.

63. Spalding, *Memorialls*, ii. 392, 402, 405, 421, 427, 453.

64. *APS*, VI, i. 203; Spalding, *Memorialls*, ii. 338, 349, 402.

65. *APS*, VI, i.154, 201; *Intelligence from the south borders of Scotland*, 2; Foster, *Members*, 203.

66. *APS*, VI, i. 202; *Memoirs of Guthry*, 163; Stevenson, *Alasdair*, 126, 130-1.

67. Spalding, *Memorialls*, ii. 402.

68. Stevenson, *Alasdair*, 156, 161; see above, 197-8.

69. Spalding, *Memorialls*, ii. 402, 410, 421, 427; see above, 216-7.

70. Spalding, *Memorialls*, ii. 349, 402; see above, 216-7.

71. *APS*, VI, i. 673, 684-5.

72. Fraser, *Chronicle*, 288-9, 294, 296, 316, 325-8, 332, 339; *Records of Inverness*, eds. W. Mackay and G. S. Laing (New Spalding Club, xliii, 1924), ii. 184; Spalding, *Memorialls*, ii. 473-4; Cowan, *Montrose*, 181; A. Mackenzie, *History of the Frasers of Lovat* (Inverness, 1896), 169-72, 174, 180, 183-5; Stevenson, *Alasdair*, 117, 177.

73. SRO, PA. 11.4, 158v; *Aberdeen Letters*, ii. 387; *Chronicle of Perth*, 42; Maxwell, *Dundee*, 501.

74. Stevenson, *Alasdair*, 156, 162, 214, 218, 228, 230, 235, 237.

75. *Chronicle of Perth*, 40; Stevenson, *Alasdair*, 150.

76. *Ibid.*, 116, 177, 271.

77. *APS*, VI, i. 190; Spalding, *Memorialls*, ii. 346, 353-9, 363, 371; Cowan, *Montrose*, 168.

78. SRO, PA. 11.4, 158v, 171v.

79. Stevenson, *Alasdair*, 216; see above, 197-8.

80. *Aberdeen Letters*, iii. 88; *APS*, VI, i. 673, 745; *Council of Aberdeen*, ii. 63.

81. Spalding, *Memorialls*, ii. 338, 349, 402; Cowan, *Montrose*, 170, see above, 216-7.

82. SRO, B.66.25, 368; PA. 11.4, 175; *APS*, VI, i. 79, 356, 450, 685-6, 696.

83. Spalding, *Memorialls*, ii. 475; Cowan, *Montrose*, 181; Stevenson, *Alasdair*, 117, 177.

84. *APS*, VI, i. 341; Spalding, *Memorialls*, ii. 401.

85. *APS*, VI, i. 356, 395-6.

86. *Memoirs of Guthry*, 163; Monteth, *Troubles*, 172; Stevenson, *Alasdair*, 125.

87. *Ibid.*, 218.

88. *APS*, VI, i. 55, 203; Spalding, *Memorialls*, ii. 338, 349, 402; Foster, *Members*, 144; see above, 217-8.

89. *APS*, VI, i. 55, 203; Spalding, *Memorialls*, ii. 338, 349, 402; see above, 216-7.

90. Stevenson, *Alasdair*, 218-9.

91. *APS*, VI, i. 55, 202; *Army of the Covenant*, i. lxi; *Intelligence from the south borders of Scotland*, 2.

92. Cowan, *Montrose*, 181; Stevenson, *Alasdair*, 177.

93. Spalding, *Memorialls*, ii. 473; Cowan, *Montrose*, 181; Stevenson, *Alasdair*, 177.

94. *APS*, VI, i. 90, 202; Monteth, *Troubles*, 172-3; Cowan, *Montrose*, 160.

95. SRO, PA. 11.4, 174v-5; *APS*, VI, i. 461, 614, 673, 685; Stevenson, *Alasdair*, 153, 157, 161.

96. *Ibid.*, 156, 161, 236.

97. *APS*, VI, i. 51; *Intelligence from the south borders of Scotland*, 2.

98. PRO, SP 46/129, 181; see above, 170-1.

99. *APS*, VI, i. 357; Spalding, *Memorialls*, ii. 473-4; Cowan, *Montrose*, 181, 188-9, 245; A. Mackenzie, *History of Clan Mackenzie* (Inverness, 1879), 186, 192; Stevenson, *Alasdair*, 117, 166, 178, 188-9, 196, 228.

100. *Ibid.*, 171.

101. *APS*, VI, i. 55, 203, 562; Spalding, *Memorialls*, ii. 338, 349, 402.

102. *APS*, VI, i. 79, 355, 491, 597; *Memoirs of Guthry*, 184, 187; Spalding, *Memorialls*, ii. 473-4; *The Sutherland Book*, 3 vols., ed. W. Fraser (Edinburgh, 1894), i. 239, 241-4; Cowan, *Montrose*, 181; *Scots Peerage*, viii. 349; Stevenson, *Alasdair*, 117, 178.

103. *APS*, VI, i. 55, 203; Spalding, *Memorialls*, ii. 338, 349, 402; see above, 216-7.

104. Spalding, *Memorialls*, ii. 402.

105. *Ibid.*, ii. 402; Foster, *Members*, 345.

106. *APS*, VI, i. 215, 356, 439, 470, 717; Spalding, *Memorialls*, ii. 466, 490; Cowan, *Montrose*, 190, 197-8.

107. *APS*, VI, i. 203; Spalding, *Memorialls*, ii. 338, 349, 402; see above, 216-7.

7
New Model Army

Aldie's Horse Troop

Colonel: James Mercer of Aldie

On 29 January 1647 the Scottish parliament appointed Aldie (who was a colonel in the Army of the Solemn League and Covenant) commander of a troop of eighty horse to be drawn from units in Scotland. A week later the Estates specified that the troop was to consist of twenty horse from Eglington's, the same number from Kirkcudbright's and forty troopers from Aldie's own regiment. On 5 March all troops of the New Model were ordered to be reduced to seventy-five men. This allowed the commissary general to recruit a troop. There is no information on the military activities of this unit in 1647. On 4 May 1648 the Engager parliament appointed Aldie to be colonel of a Perthshire troop of eighty horse in addition to this command. Aldie made his headquarters at Dunkeld for recruiting the new troop. The success of the levy is not discernable. Aldie's troops remained in Scotland during the summer. They probably served under Lanark at Stirling, after which they disappear.[1]

Ardkinglas' Highland Foot

Colonel: James Campbell of Ardkinglas

Ministers: Neill Cameron, Dugald Darroch[2]

On 29 January 1647 the Estates named Ardkinglas the colonel of a regiment of Highland infantry. He received the right to nominate his officers and levy 1,000 men in eight companies. Besides drawing men from his own regiment in the home army, Ardkinglas was to raise recruits from the Highlanders of the Perthshire (Tullibardine's) Foot, and from the lands of the lairds of Glenorchy and Weem. In May Ardkinglas' Foot marched into Argyll under David Leslie and participated in the campaign against Alastair MacColla and his allies. The regiment may have been heavily undermanned at this time. On 5 April 1648 the Engager parliament ordered that this regiment and Argyll's Foot provide a force of 600 commanded men to proceed by water against the Irish, Clanranald and their allies in the western Highlands and islands. There are no details concerning the campaign. By 3 June Ardkinglas and his regiment had declared for the kirk party. They refused to obey the Engagers' orders and remained in their quarters, which may have been in Perthshire, and Argyll, or at Selkirk. The possibility that it was at the latter is suggested by an order from the Estates to the garrisons of Inverawe and Inverlochy to proceed to their regiment in Selkirk. Ardkinglas' men remained in Scotland until September. The regiment seems to have become part of the Army of the Covenants for in February 1649 the presbytery of Dunblane sent a minister to the army to apprehend a private who was charged with fornication and fathering a bastard. The unit then vanishes from sight.[3]

Argyll's Highland Foot

Colonel: Archibald, 1st marquis of Argyll

Lieutenant Colonel: James Menzies

Major: Matthew Campbell, Captain of Skipness

Ministers: Archibald McClean, Donald McAllam/Macallum, (?) MacCalman[4]

Argyll received his commission to raise a regiment of Highland infantry with the ability to commission its officers on 29 January 1647. The regiment was to have eight companies of 133 men each. In addition to using his own regiment in the home army as a source of recruits, the marquis was also to take men from the Perthshire (Tullibardine's) Foot, and from the lairds of Glenorchy's and Weem's lands. In mid-April the regiment is reported to have started quartering in Ayrshire. Argyll and his regiment, which may have been below strength, accompanied David Leslie on his campaign into the western Highlands and Isles against Alastair MacColla and his allies. During the siege of Dunaverty Major Campbell was killed. Argyll is no longer credited with being a chief agent in inciting the massacre of Dunaverty. On 4 July he signed the surrender treaty of Dunyveg Castle, Mull as an officer on the expedition. In late September or early October, Argyll had Coll McDonald sent to Argyll from Edinburgh. There he was executed under the jurisdiction of the Campbell controlled shire court. On 9 November the regiment was quartering in the barony of Burrowfield and Alloway. This area was evidently used for its winter quarters in 1647-48, because on 2 March 1648 the presbytery of Ayr wrote Argyll informing him of the 'insolencie' of his regiment. However, the regiment also seems to have kept garrisons at Comrie, Finlarick Ballock, the Isle of Lochtay, Ruthven in Badenoch, and Weem until September 1648. On 5 April Argyll's and Ardkinglas' Foot received orders to draw out 600 men for an expedition by water against the Irish, Clanranald and their allies in the western Highlands. Sometime in April, Argyll and his political allies drafted the Tailors' Hall,

Edinburgh, petition of the officers in support of the Kirk and in opposition to the Engager party. Their endeavours failed to attract the mass support necessary. However, the regiment refused to follow orders of the Engager government and remained in its quarters. Some members of the unit did join Hamilton's march into England. Fifteen officers and men fell prisoner to the parliamentarians at Warrington Bridge. The House of Commons noted that their presence was contrary to the colonel's wishes, and that 'all the rest of his Three Regiments [were] oppossing it [the Engagement] to their greatest Hazard . . .'. The regiment may have served as part of Argyll's Whiggamore Raid force which was dispersed at Stirling.[5]

Argyll's Highland Foot appears to have survived the Whiggamore Raid. The marquis received no new commission to raise troops in 1649, but he had command of a regiment in the spring. On 29 January Lieutenant Colonel Menzies was noted to have left provisions at Garth. On 27 February two companies of Argyll's received orders to march north with part of Holburn's to suppress Pluscarden's rising. On 1 June 1649 its quarters are detailed as follows: garrisons in the north, but the main body in the town and presbytery of Glasgow, excepting Cathcart, Renfrewshire. Six days later we learn that Lieutenant Colonel Menzies was in command of the garrisons in Blair Atholl, Ruthven in Badenoch, and Garth. On 6 July the men at Glasgow were ordered to Tarbert. The levy of the regiment at the end of July mentions that part of it was on garrison duty at Ruthven. Garth was subsequently abandoned as a garrison, and Blair Atholl was turned over to Innes' Foot. The whereabouts of the main body of 600 foot is not given. Argyll's Foot disappears from the records for nearly a year, re-emerging on 19 June 1650. Then the Estates ordered it to Edinburgh, save for thirty men in the Ruthven garrison, twenty men at Inverlochy Castle, and twenty men at Duart Castle, Mull. On 3 July Argyll received a commission for himself or for a nominee of his choice to be colonel of foot regiment of 800 men raised from his section of Inverness-shire. During the summer campaign the activities of Argyll's regiment is not recorded. However, the marquis did support David Leslie in opposing further purging of the army. On 7 December the Committee of Military Affairs ordered the recruits of the regiment to go to Inverness and wait there for orders. Again there is no reference to Argyll's Foot for several months. During the winter Lieutenant Colonel Menzies took one hundred recruits into Seaforth's lands and plundered them. This caused most of Kintail's Foot to return to their homes to protect their families and goods. The Committee of Estates ordered an inquiry into the matter. On 29 April 1651 the Committee of Estates wrote a letter of complaint to Argyll concerning Lochaber men who had not come out in the levy. According to the laird of Grant this frightened the marquis' neighbours. Argyll was further upbraided for not sending in the accounts of the levy for the shire of Argyll, which was one of his duties as sheriff. The marquis was also admonished to send out his proportion of men from Argyll and Lochaber. By 20 June Argyll's Foot was described as a company of sixty-eight men in the army accounts. On 26 June the regiment consisted of two companies under the direct command of Lieutenant Colonel Menzies. As of 18 July the regiment contained 284 common soldiers.[6] This is the last mention of Argyll's Foot in the regular army.

There is no reference to Argyll's serving on the Worcester campaign, thus it may be supposed that the troops under the marquis' command in late 1651 and in 1652 belonged to his regiment. On 15 October 1651 Argyll made his first overtures to the English. On 9 November he sent the earls of Wemyss and Linlithgow to Monck as emissaries. They claimed that Argyll had made no new levies. However, as he still had men on foot the survival of this regiment is suggested. As of Christmas 1651 Argyll had 300 foot, a number close to that of the 18 July muster, in a garrison at Lochcarron. Argyll's regiment and his clansmen were not active, but they did present the English with an obstacle in subduing the western Highlands. However, Argyll made his first settlement with the English in August 1652, which was made permanent in October. With that the regiment would have been disbanded after five years under the colours.[7]

Train of Artillery

Commander: Lieutenant Colonel Thomas Hamilton

On 25 February 1647 the Estates authorised the raising of 120 horses and sixty horse-handlers for the purpose of carrying ammunition and drawing the artillery. In addition to the guns in Edinburgh Castle (which contained the castle's own pieces and those of the Army of the Solemn League and Covenant), there were five pieces at Fyvie Castle. The unit was to consist of seven officers, twelve artillery men, eleven artisans and five others. Hamilton received orders to convey six field pieces from Edinburgh to the Montrose rendezvous for the use of the forces assembling to crush the northeastern royalists. David Leslie did not possess a train of cannon for his campaign into Argyll. This was due both to the difficult nature of the terrain for transporting guns, and to his desire to flee the plague which was raging in central and southern Scotland. There is no further mention of the artillery in this army.[8]

D. Barclay's Horse Troop

Commander: Major (later Colonel) David Barclay

In late January 1647 the Estates appointed David Barclay the commander of a troop of eighty horse then present in Scotland. Shortly thereafter he was assigned that number of men from viscount Montgomery's Horse, of which he may have been the major. On 5 March the parliament had the troop reduced by five men to provide an additional unit for the army. The whereabouts and activities of the troop in 1647 are not specified. However, the wedding of Major Barclay on 26 January 1648 in Duffus, Moray, suggests that the unit may have served in Middleton's northeastern campaigns. From March 1648, if not before, parts of the troop were quartered in the garrisons of Bog of Gight, Strathbogie, and Lochkendar. On 4 May the Estates made Barclay a colonel of horse in Moray and Inverness-shire, authorising him to raise an additional eighty horsemen. A few days later his commission was altered. Barclay was now to levy fifteen troopers from Easter Ross, twenty men from Sutherland and forty-five more from Caithness. A week later Barclay received command of Sharp's Dragoons, which were added to his horse regiment. On 8 June the Estates appointed Barclay the governor of Strathbogie; he also received the responsibilities for the command of Gight and Lochkendar garrisons. However, the government diminished the importance of this promotion by reducing Strathbogie to fifty men and a captain, similarly weakening Gight to thirty men and a lieutenant, and by ordering the abandonment of Lochkendar. All the superfluous men were ordered to their regiments. There was some delay with regards to the last place, because it was included with the other two in the colonel's request for their pay in mid-August. Barclay's men remained in arms until the end of September and may have served under Lanark. Barclay later underwent repentance as an Engager colonel.[9]

H. Barclay's Horse Troop

Commander: Colonel Harry Barclay

Colonel Barclay received his commission as a troop commander in the New Model Army on 29 January 1647. A week later he was allotted men from the following units in Scotland: twenty troopers from Lockhart's Horse, the same number from viscount Montgomery's Horse, and twice that number from his own regiment. A month later the troop was reduced by five men. In October forty troopers and thirty-nine horses quartered for six days in Coull, Lochmens, and Stonyford in Cromar. The troop served under Major General Middleton in the autumn during his campaign against the marquis of Huntly and his clan. The service of Barclay's troop then suggests that it may have been in the campaigns against the northeastern royalists which commenced soon after it was raised. On 4 May 1648 Barclay received a colonelcy of the Aberdeenshire and Banffshire Horse from the Engager parliament with permission to levy eighty troopers from the two shires. Unfortunately, there is no information on the levying of this reinforcement to his command nor about the troop's activities in 1648. Barclay's command remained on the rolls until the end of September; a possibility exists that it was part of the Engager army at Stirling. The colonel later did public penance for supporting the Engager regime.[10]

Blair's Dragoon Company

Commander: Lieutenant Colonel Patrick Blair

In late January 1647 Blair was the lieutenant colonel of Balcarres' Horse. The Estates appointed him the overall commander of the dragoons in the New Model, and placed a company of 100 dragoons (which was to be made up from units in Scotland), under his command. On 25 February his company was reduced to seventy men so that David Leslie could retain his dragoons in the new army. Nothing is known of Blair's company nor of its commander for most of 1647. However, late in the year the Dundee burgh council complained that the quartering charges for its seventy-two dragoons amounted to £2,200. Blair's company served as part of the Engager army in Scotland until the end of September 1648. However, on 27 May the Committee of Estates gave eighteen troopers each to Lord Livingstone and Sir Robert Bruce of Clackmannan. During that month it was probably at Stirling with the bulk of the remaining Engager forces. It subsequently disbanded after the Treaty of Stirling.[11]

Bogie's Horse Troop

Commander: Commissary General Sir James Wemyss of Bogie

Bogie was a Fife laird with a conflicting background. Charles I had personally knighted him. However, Bogie married the daughters of two Covenanters — the lairds of Aytoun and Warriston. He served as a commissioner for Fife at the convention of 1643, and was an M.P. for the barons of the shire in 1645-47. In early 1647 the Estates appointed him commissary general of the New Model. On 5 March he was allowed to uplift a troop of seventy-five men by taking five men from each of the fifteen existing troops. This troop was to aid Bogie in collecting the maintenance (a sign of the warweariness and impoverishment of the country), by quartering on deficients in shires and burghs. On 5 May 1648 the Engagers reappointed Bogie to the position of commissary general, a sign of his loyalty to the new order if not of professional competence. Bogie's troop remained in Scotland during the summer, disbanding after the surrender of the Engagers in late September.[12]

Brown's Horse Troop

Commanders: Colonel Sir John Brown (of Fordell), (1647-48), Lieutenant General James, earl of Callander (1648).

On 29 January 1647 the Estates placed Colonel Brown in command of a troop in the New Model which was to consist of eighty men selected from his regiment in

England. The troop was on foot in mid-February, however, it was reduced to seventy-five men in March to provide recruits for the commissary general's troop. Unfortunately there is no information on the military activities or the quartering of this unit in either 1647 or in 1648. Sir John Brown was one of the signers of the original Tailors' Hall petition which supported the claims of the Commission of the General Assembly against the Engagers. As a result the Engager parliament assigned the troop to the earl of Callander on 11 May. Brown's troop remained in Scotland during 1648; it vanished from the records after late September.[13]

Fraser's Horse Troop

Commander: Colonel Hugh Fraser (of Kynnerie)

Lieutenant Colonel: Robert Gray of Balalon

Colonel Fraser received permission to retain a troop of eighty men (subsequently reduced to seventy-five on 5 March 1647), from his regiment in England on 29 January 1647. The activities of the troop in 1647 are a mystery. However, in 1648 Fraser supported the Engager party. As a reward the Engager dominated Estates appointed him a colonel of a troop of eighty Inverness-shire horse on 4 May. There is no evidence on the raising of the troop, although it does seem to have been levied. Fraser and his men may have remained in Scotland during Hamilton's campaign. They were probably with Lanark at Stirling, disbanding after the treaty between the Engagers and Whiggamore Raiders.[14]

Hackett's Horse Troop

Commander: Lieutenant Colonel Sir James Hackett

The only reference to this troop is a minute in the presbytery of Elgin records. On 5 February 1648 the presbytery undertook an investigation into the behaviour of the unit. The ministers issued bad reports only against the Regimental Quartermaster, James Wayne, for drinking, cursing and swearing. Another trooper had royalist tendencies. Possibly Hackett was the subordinate officer for one of the troops formed in 1647.[15]

Hamilton's Foot

Colonel: Sir Alexander Hamilton

Lieutenant Colonel: John Home

Major: James Innes

Ministers: Hugh Kennedy, William Rait, George Pittilloch[16]

This regiment was also known as the General of Artillery's Foot. On 29 January 1647 the Estates named the officers of the six companies of 133 men. The new unit was to receive recruits from the following regiments: fifty men from the Kyle and Carrick Foot, fifty-three from viscount Kenmure's, eighty from the Galloway Foot, eighty-three from the Strathearn Foot, and one company each from Moray's and the regiment in Dundee, the Angus Foot, the Clydesdale Foot, and the Loudoun-Glasgow Foot. Any deficients were to be made up from the Clydesdale Foot, which was Hamilton's regiment in the Army of the Solemn League and Covenant. On 12 February the Estates issued orders to these contingents to converge on Dundee, paying for their quarters on the march (save for the men from the Clydesdale Foot). The regiment was then to proceed north to campaign against the royalists in arms there. A week later the Loudoun-Glasgow Foot, quartered in Ayr and Irvine, received additional orders to march to Dundee. Part of the regiment reached Aberdeen on 10 March. On 1 April it was noted that the regiment was still under strength and recruiting men in the south. The Estates demanded that it be brought up to 800 men, or its pay would be withheld. There were 288 men present during the first thirty days of its occupation of Aberdeen. On 5 April Hamilton's received a recruit of thirty men, these with the original contingent were given twenty-one days' pay on 26 April. The military actions of the regiment are not recorded, but it would be safe to assign them to Middleton's forces in the northeast during the spring and summer. In July Hamilton's joined Leslie's force in the Western Isles as part of Middleton's reinforcement. On 7 September the unit was quartering in Douglasdale. Just over two months later the Glasgow burgh council appointed George Porterfield, the ex-provost, to seek out a means of repaying those in Lanarkshire who had quartered Major Innes' company. The council noted that Innes' men had injured Glasgow and its magistrates. In March and April 1648 Linlithgow spent £100 on quartering the regiment. A report of 3 April showed that Hamilton's own company contained only sixty men. If that figure held for the other companies then Hamilton's Foot contained only 480 men, which complements Major Turner's remark (of May or June) that it was a weak unit. In late March Hamilton joined Middleton in rejecting the Tailors' Hall petition in its original sense. He later supported Middleton's redrafting of the document. During the spring the regiment quartered in Glasgow until Holburn's Foot arrived. After that regiment's departure Hamilton's men once again formed the Glasgow garrison. Meanwhile on 11 May the Engagers commissioned Hamilton the General of Artillery. However, Hamilton had reached his dotage and made no provision for artillery to accompany the army when it entered England on 8 July. This was one cause for the delay in the army marching south and for its division into different commands. The regiment appears to have entered England with the bulk of the duke of Hamilton's army. There are no details concerning its activities until the surrender of the foot at Warrington Bridge by Lieutenant General Baillie on 19 August. The campaign had reduced Hamilton's Foot to three officers and fifty-one men. Hamilton, himself, suffered for his opposition to the kirk party. On 9 July 1649 the kirk party parliament purged him from the army and stripped him of his rank for voting and sitting in the Engager parliament and for supplying their army with artillery. For these reasons Hamilton was deprived of his offices under the second article of the Act of Classes. This also prohibited him from receiving a place of public office for ten years. However, as Hamilton died on 26 November 1649, he was not affected by the reversal of affairs after Dunbar.[17]

Holburn's Foot

Colonels: Major General James Holburn (1647-48), James Turner (1648)

Lieutenant Colonels: John Innes (1647-48), George Meldrum (1648)

Major: George Meldrum (1647-48)

Ministers: Henry Rymer, John Nevay, James Nasmith[18]

On 29 January 1647 the Estates appointed Major General Holburn colonel of a regiment of 800 foot consisting of six companies. This unit was also known as the Lowland Regiment, and its recruits were selected from regiments in Scotland on the 29th. Holburn's Foot accompanied David Leslie on his expedition against Alastair MacColla and his allies in May-August 1647. In late March 1648 Holburn and Lieutenant Colonel Innes signed the original version of the Tailors' Hall petition. Following the Engager coup d'état both men and the regiment's captains deserted. On 11 May the Engager parliament replaced Holburn with Major Turner. These developments caused the regiment to mutiny on the Links of Leith, however, the new colonel quelled the mutiny. Afterwards Turner led the regiment with eleven troops of horse to Renfrewshire. There it quartered in the anti-Engager town of Paisley, which submitted to escape further burdens from the forces under Turner. The regiment with three horse troops under Turner proceeded to the equally anti-Engager burgh of Glasgow. Turner again succeeded in converting a burgh to the Engager party by quartering two-three troopers and six musketeers for two-three nights in the homes of principal Covenanters. Turner also persuaded the Rev. Dick not to preach against the Engagement. However, Dick in a sermon, which Turner and his men attended, assailed the king and parliament. When Turner decided to leave with his men, Dick seems to have hesitated, but continued after the soldiers departed from the church. Dick complained to Hamilton; the Commission of the General Assembly took action against Turner. On 1 June it cited him for withdrawing his men from a kirk during the sermon. The

Commission also charged him with publically and verbally assaulting some ministers. This dispute started the bad feelings between the presbyterian ministers and Turner.[19]

After 12 June, the regiment and Turner marched with some other foot regiments to Dumfries in order to secure Carlisle against the parliamentarians. Before 8 July Turner and his men rendezvoused with Hamilton and the rest of the army at Annan. During the subsequent campaign Turner served as the effective Major General of Foot. Following the entry into England Turner with his regiment and another quartered at a village one-half mile from Appleby Castle, so that Sir Marmaduke Langdale could pursue the siege of the castle unhindered. Before the army commenced its fateful campaign into Lancashire Turner argued for a march through Yorkshire, which was better country for the Engager horse. He was overruled; and the next mention of Turner occurs on 17 August during the battle of Preston. As Langdale was battling Cromwell on Preston Moor, the duke of Hamilton ordered Turner to send him a reinforcement of several hundred men with gunpowder. This small reinforcement probably included men of Turner's own regiment. Later in the day Turner himself crossed over to Preston to join Hamilton and Langdale. As they sought to recross the river and join Baillie who had command of the bulk of the Scottish infantry, Turner attempted to rally some musketeers to oppose the English horse. But there was no fight in the broken men, and the officers had to cross using other resources. Later in the evening Turner argued with Baillie that the foot should not march from their prepared positions due to the dangers of a night march and the men's fatigue. The next day at Wigan Turner's men became so demented with fear that they formed up against a regiment of Scottish horse, supposing them to be Cromwell's men. Turner had the cavalry charge his pike men, so they could escape. The infantry broke in panic dropping their arms but Turner was wounded. On the 19th Lieutenant Colonel Meldrum, and 131 officers and men of the regiment fell prisoner to Cromwell at Warrington Bridge. Turner escaped with Hamilton, which was fortunate for the duke. For when the Scottish troopers mutinied and imprisoned the duke, Turner persuaded them to release him on the grounds of their own safety, the dishonour the seizure did to the duke, and the ignominy of the action. Later Turner was one of the three commissioners who arranged Hamilton's surrender. He blamed Hamilton for the disastrous campaign, particularly citing his leniency on the march and his disregard of discipline. Following his capture Turner was taken to Hull, where he ransomed himself for £540 in November 1649. He gained the right to hold a charge in the Army of the Kingdom by undergoing a false repentance for supporting the Engagement.[20]

Inverawe's Force

Commander: Lieutenant Colonel Dougal Campbell of Inverawe

On 25 May 1647 David Leslie ordered Inverawe to lead 300 men from Kintyre to Islay to pursue Alastair MacColla. However, a shortage of boats on Kintyre prevented Inverawe from acting immediately. He probably led the spearhead of Leslie's army (220 foot and 80 horse), in the campaign onto the Isles from Kintyre. On 19 June this force crossed from Kintyre to Gigha; four days later Leslie appeared with the main body of the army. From there the army moved to Islay via Jura, landing on the 24th.[21]

Kerr's Horse Troop

Commanders: Lieutenant Colonel Gilbert Kerr (1647-48), Major Alexander Ramsay (1648)

Major: George Simpson (1648)

On 29 January 1647 the Estates appointed Lieutenant Colonel Kerr the commander of a horse troop in the New Model. The troop of eighty horse (subsequently reduced to seventy-five men) was to be drawn from drafts not in Scotland. This strongly suggests that Kerr was allowed to recruit the men from Middleton's Horse, of which he was lieutenant colonel. There is no mention of the troop in action in either 1647 or 1648. Kerr supported the kirk party in 1648, and refused to serve in the Engager Army. On 11 May parliament appointed Major Alexander Ramsay commander of the troop, which he was to increase into a regiment of 180 horse. His troop remained on the army payroll until the end of September, and it probably served at Stirling.[22]

Leslie's Dragoon Company

Commanders: Lieutenant General David Leslie (1647-48), Captain John Ferguson (1648)

On 25 February 1647 the Estates granted Leslie permission to retain his company of dragoons from the Army of the Solemn League and Covenant. The company was to be made up to seventy men. In order to maintain the same numbers of dragoons on the establishment Blair's and Sharp's companies were reduced to the same number. Although there is no evidence concerning the company's history, it probably accompanied Leslie on his campaigns. Captain Ferguson took over command of the company following Leslie's resignation of his commission in spring 1648. On 9 May Jedburgh presbytery opened the case of a Trooper Gibson concerning a 'gross abuss comitted by him at Castleton Kirk'. One minister was to contact Ferguson; the minister of Langside was to try Gibson, who was residing in the parish. The company remained in the army until September, but the theatre of operations it served in is unknown.[23]

Leslie's Horse Troop

Commanders: Lieutenant General David Leslie (1647-48), General James, 1st duke of Hamilton (1648)

Ministers: Mungo Law, William Cockburn, Gabriel Maxwell[24]

Leslie received permission from parliament on 29 January 1647 to raise a troop of horse from his regiment in the Army of the Solemn League and Covenant. He was also appointed Lieutenant General of the New Model and due to Leven's ill-health he became the effective field commander. On 5 March the Estates ordered Leslie to select five men from his troop of eighty to help provide a troop for the commissary general. Five days later he departed from Montrose with a force to aid Middleton in suppressing the northeastern royalists. Wardhouse and Lesmoir Castles fell to Leslie by the 27th. He ordered and had executed forty-two members of the garrisons. On the 27th Leslie wrote the Committee of Estates from Lesmoir explaining that he planned to march again on the 29th, 'the morrow being the Lord's day . . .'. By the 31st the majority of royalist strongholds had fallen to Leslie and Middleton. Then Leslie departed from the northeast and headed to Dunblane, stopping first at Ruthven in Badenoch to establish a garrison. During the campaign Leslie's men had captured Father Andrew Leslie, S.J. When the priest was brought before the lieutenant general, he was forced to listen to an abusive discourse on Roman Catholicism. On 17 May Leslie set off to Argyll from Dunblane with a small army. The presence of the plague in southern Perthshire prevented him from amassing a larger force. Thus with a few thousand men Leslie began the task of subduing the Irish, the MacDonalds, and their allies. Sometime in August Leslie returned to Stirling having successfully reduced all of the enemy strongholds from Kintyre to Moidart. In the course of the campaign Leslie besmirched his reputation by following the urgings of his secretary, and Holburn's regimental chaplain (John Nevay), and ordered the execution of several hundred men from the Dunaverty Castle garrison. Leslie's troop served under him in the above-mentioned campaigns, but there are no direct references to its rôle in them.[25]

The troop and Leslie both disappeared from the records for several months before re-emerging in December 1647. In early December Trooper Robert Stewart killed William Tait, a servant of the laird of Harthill, in Jedburgh. The burgh magistrates imprisoned him in the tolbooth. But his comrades were not content to permit this to remain the case. On the night of 4 December sixty armed troopers of Leslie's troop) entered the burgh and wounded three men of the watch. Then they broke Stewart free and departed from the burgh. The next day the magistrates wrote the earl of Lothian requesting that he bring the case before Leslie and the Privy Council, so that they might take action. There is no sign of any steps being taken by the military or civil authorities. However, on 15 December the presbytery of Jedburgh ordered the matter reported to the Commission of the General Assembly. Months passed and nothing more occurred until 9 May 1648. Then the presbytery decided to commence excommunication proceedings against Stewart, and another trooper — George Cook — for murder. The presbytery tabled the matter on the 17th, but on 26 July, 9 and 23 August it ordered the ministers to read the first, second and third prayers of excommunication. These men probably never returned from their service in the Engager Army, for there is no further mention of them in the presbytery records. Meanwhile Leslie himself had strongly opposed the Engagement. In late March he signed the original Tailors' Hall petition in favour of the kirk party. The Engagers offered him the rank of General of the Engager Army, but the kirk party ministers persuaded him to refuse. On 11 May parliament assigned the troop to the duke of Hamilton's Life Guard. The remainder of the unit's history will be found under that account.[26]

Leven's Horse Troop

Commanders: General Alexander, 1st earl of Leven (1647-48), General James, 1st duke of Hamilton (1648)

On 29 January 1647 Leven became Lord General of the New Model Army due to a parliamentary appointment. The Estates also allowed him to raise a staff troop of horse from his own regiment in the Army of the Solemn League and Covenant. The troop originally consisted of eighty men, but it was reduced to seventy-five after 5 March. In 1647 Leven was a supporter of Argyll's party. The General does not appear to have taken part in any campaigns, and there is no information on his troop doing so either. In late March 1648 Leven signed the original draft of the Tailors' Hall petition. After the Engager coup d'etat he laid down his commission, but his troop continued in arms under the Engagers. On 11 May the Estates assigned the troop to the duke of Hamilton's Horse Guard, and its further history is under that entry. In September Leven became the official commander-in-chief of the Whiggamore Raiders. However, he does not seem to have done much more than lent his prestige to their cause. Afterwards the kirk party appointed him commander of the army of the Covenants, but he never actively led in the field again.[27]

Lockhart's Horse Troop

Commander: Colonel William Lockhart (of Lee the Younger)

Lockhart received a commission to retain eighty men from his regiment in the home army to form a troop in the New Model on 29 January 1647. The history of the unit in 1647 is obscure. The Engagers appointed Lockhart a member of the Lanarkshire Committee of War on 18 April 1648. On 4 May he received an appointment as colonel of horse for the same shire. Lockhart was permitted to raise eighty horse for his regiment from that shire. Three weeks later the Committee of Estates authorised Lockhart to levy thirty men from Roxburghshire previously assigned to Sir John Brown. After 12 June Hamilton sent Colonel Lockhart with some regiments of horse to Annan in order to protect Carlisle against Lambert's forces. His men crossed the border on 8 July as part of Hamilton's main army. Lockhart himself accompanied the duke throughout the Preston campaign. At Uttoxeter he served as one of the three commissioners for arranging Hamilton's surrender to the English. Lockhart was subsequently imprisoned in Hull. His troopers either fled north or fell prisoner to the parliamentarians by the end of August. In 1650, Lockhart secured his freedom from prison and underwent repentance for supporting the Engagement. Following a quarrel with Argyll he left the Army of the Covenants. During the summer of 1651 he attempted to join the Army of the Kingdom as a volunteer, but Charles II rejected his services. Thus in 1652 he turned his face against the king and joined the English. Between 1652 and 1657 Lockhart amassed offices for himself and his brothers under the Commonwealth and Protectorate.[28]

Ludquharn's Horse Troop

Commander: Colonel Sir William Keith of Ludquharn

The Estates appointed Ludquharn the commander of a troop in the New Model to be raised from men in Scotland on 29 January 1647. The troop originally was to number eighty men, but it was reduced on 5 March by five troopers. The Estates specified on 5 February that Ludquharn was to gather his men from a commanded party in the north, Argyll's and Crawford's horse troops, and Frendraught's regiment of horse. It is likely that this unit served in the northeast during 1647. Ludquharn supported the Engagers and was rewarded by them on 4 May 1648. He was appointed a colonel for the Stirlingshire, Clackmannanshire, and Lanarkshire Horse. The levy quota for Ludquharn's new troop was as follows: forty men from Stirlingshire and Clackmannanshire, twenty more from Lanarkshire, and an additional twenty from Dunbartonshire. Ludquharn's remained on the army rolls until the end of September, probably serving in Scotland, particularly at Stirling.[29]

Middleton's Horse Troop

Commander: Major General John Middleton

Ministers: Andrew Cant, Alexander Dunlop, John Robertson, John Nevay, Patrick Gillespie[30]

On 29 January 1647 the Estates granted Middleton permission to levy a staff troop from his regiment in England. The same day Middleton was appointed Major General of the New Model. On 5 March the Estates ordered the troop reduced by five men to seventy-five horse. Meanwhile, on the 2nd he had commenced the siege of Kincardine Castle (It is likely that his troop accompanied him in this and other campaigns in 1647). The castle fell on the 16th and Middleton had it levelled. Several days later he joined forces with Leslie to commence a campaign against the northeastern royalists. In April Leslie departed from the region, and Middleton was left in command. He continued in the field against the royalists until mid-May, when his men settled into quarters. Sometime in June Middleton led a reinforcement of two infantry regiments and some horse troops to Leslie in the west. He arrived in July, just as Leslie was crossing over to Mull. In August Middleton was back in the Lowlands with his men, who then dispersed into quarters. Although they did not partake in any more military operations that year, Middleton was active as an agent of the duke of Hamilton in the army, where many officers respected him.[31]

The next year looked to begin as one of success for Middleton. In late March 1648 he refused to sign the original draft of the Tailors' Hall petition. In speaking against it he complained that the petition seemed to be a mutiny like that done by Fairfax's men in 1647. Middleton altered the document to read in favour of obeying the parliament and supporting the Engagement. His version gained the signatures of many officers who had refused the earlier draft. Thus Middleton was responsible for bringing the officer corps and with it the army over to the Engagement. The Engager regime began to reward Middleton for his signal service in May. On the 4th he was given the colonelcy of horse for Selkirkshire and Teviotdale, as such he was permitted to levy eighty men from the shires. Five days later the Estates noted that an act of 1647 granted Middleton £45,000 in arrears but that they had remained unpaid. Consequently, Commissary General Sir James Wemyss of Bogie received orders to pay Middleton. On the 11th the Estates appointed Middleton Major General of Horse in the Engager Army, and on 10 June Lieutenant General. On the morning of 12 June Middleton took the field for the first time for the Engagers. On the 10th a body of 2,000 Lanarkshire and Ayrshire peasants (many of them mounted), and deserters from the army had congregated at Mauchline kirk, Ayrshire for communion and to discuss the possibilities of an anti-Engager rising. Two days later Middleton appeared on the scene with a few troops of horse (including his own), intending to disperse the 'rebels'. However, after negotiations with the ministers who acted as their spokesmen, Middleton allowed them (in a written document) to return to their homes unmolested. Suddenly as the negotiations were being concluded fighting erupted; the Engager cavalry charged. Some of the rebels fought, but most fled homewards. Middleton was wounded, and casualties on both sides were light. The ministers and officers who led the risers fell prisoner to Middleton, but they were later released. This exercise in crowd control did much to elevate Middleton in Engager circles, but it made him an object of hatred in the kirk party.[32]

With the battle of Mauchline Moor the struggle for control of Scotland ended in favour of the Engagers. On 8 July 1648 Middleton led the main body of seven regiments of 1,000 men each across the border into Cumberland. Before the army departed from northwestern England Middleton argued with Turner for a march through Yorkshire, claiming it was better country for the Scottish horse in which to operate. Although his council was sound on that occasion, on a subsequent one it led to disaster. As the Engagers moved southwards Callander and Middleton argued that the cavalry should be separated from the main body of the army due to its heavy quartering requirements. As a result on 17 August, the day of the battle of Preston, the Scottish horse were sixteen miles south of the foot on the Preston-Wigan road. Thus, Hamilton was unable to provide Langdale with sorely needed cavalry reinforcements. The lack of horse also allowed Callander to persuade Hamilton not to commit sizeable reserves of Scottish infantry to aid their English allies. On the night of 17-18 August as Hamilton and his infantry marched south to Wigan, Middleton returned northwards via the wrong road (the Chorley route). This led Middleton not to the infantry, which would have allowed the Scots to form a proper rearguard, but into the English. Middleton again headed south, this time in the path of the Scottish foot which must have made for rough going on the muddy roads for his cavalry. Two to three English parliamentarian regiments pursued the Scots, and there was skirmishing along the march. However, Middleton's men managed to kill Colonel Thornhaugh, one of the English leaders. On the 18th Middleton's horse joined the Scots foot at Standish. Together now they continued the flight from Cromwell's men. Middleton commanded the rearguard on the retreat. In the evening some English horse attacked the rearguard near Wigan. One of the Scottish cavalry regiments broke and fled towards the main body. But Middleton managed to control the rest of his men and held the English back. The rearguard then safely reached Wigan. Again on the 19th Middleton commanded the rearguard. In the evening he and Callander having brought Baillie and the infantry across Warrington Bridge told him to surrender the foot. The two generals then fled with the Scottish horse. Again Middleton led the rearguard of Hamilton's flight. However, near Stone after a fall from his horse Middleton fell prisoner to the English. His men may have kept together a bit longer but by the 25th Middleton's command had ceased to exist. Middleton was first imprisoned in Hull, and was later taken to Newcastle from which he escaped by spring 1649. Twice in 1650 he was active in leading royalist risings against the kirk party regime. After October 1650 he did public penance for his service against the kirk party and in the Engagement. In the Worcester campaign he was one of the staff officers.[33]

Montgomery's Horse Troop

Commander: Colonel Robert Montgomery (1647-48), Hugh, viscount Montgomery (1648)

Lieutenant Colonel: Hew Montgomery

Colonel Montgomery received a commission to raise a troop of eighty horse from his regiment (Eglington's) in the Army of the Solemn League and Covenant on 29 January 1647. On 5 March the troop was reduced by five men at the Estates' order. Montgomery and his troop served on both of Leslie's campaigns in 1647. In Argyll he successfully besieged MacKaill's House in Lorne. Montgomery opposed the Engagement and resigned his commission following the failure of the original Tailors' Hall petition to receive majority approval by the officers corps. On 11 May 1648 parliament assigned the troop to the colonel's eldest brother, Hugh, viscount Montgomery. The viscount added the troop to the regiment of horse he had been commissioned to raise from Renfrewshire and Ayrshire. Nothing further is known concerning it before its disappearance from the records in late summer.[34]

Murray's Horse Troop

Commander: Colonel Sir Mungo Murray

The Estates selected Murray to command a troop in the New Model on 29 January 1647. A week later he was ordered to select eighty men for the troop from Dalhousie's Horse (then in Scotland), of which he was lieutenant colonel. In early March the troop was reduced to seventy-five men at the order of the Estates. There is no further mention of the troop in 1647. The following year Murray supported the Engagement. On 4 May 1648 parliament appointed him a colonel of the Dumfriesshire Horse with a right to levy eighty troopers. The troops served under Murray at Stirling in September, disbanding after the treaty. In December 1650 Murray completed his public penance for serving in the Engagement.[35]

Pitscottie's Foot

Colonels: Colin Pitscottie (1647-48), John Toures (1648)

Lieutenant Colonel: John Roch/Rough

Major: John Toures (1647-48)

Ministers: Gabriel Maxwell, James Gardiner, Robert Cowden[36]

The Estates appointed Pitscottie (the lieutenant colonel of the Midlothian Foot), on 29 January 1647. On 5 February Pitscottie received orders to select a force of 800 foot in six companies from regiments not in Scotland. The unit largely disappears from the records until 1648. From August 1647 to 10 November 1648 Major Toures acted as governor of Bog of Gight; presumably men of the regiment provided the garrison. On 2 May at the synod of Lothian and Tweeddale, the Rev. James Granger, a member of the Commission of the General Assembly, reported that one private had lived with a woman using a false testimonial of marriage in Bervie parish. Granger asked the presbytery to search for the couple and told the regimental officers of the case. However, nothing else is known of the incident. Pitscottie opposed the Engagement, later receiving a regiment in the Army of the Covenants. His major, John Toures, replaced him as colonel on 11 May 1648. The regiment served under the Engagers until sometime in September, but it is not known where. Toures himself later did repentance for supporting the Engagement.[37]

Riccarton's Horse Troop

Commander: Lieutenant Colonel Thomas Craig of Riccarton

On 29 January 1647 parliament appointed Riccarton, who was the lieutenant colonel of David Leslie's Horse, commander of a troop in the New Model. The troop of eighty men was selected from Leslie's regiment. It was later reduced by five men. There is no further evidence concerning the unit. However, in 1648 Riccarton supported the kirk party for which he was rewarded in 1649 by a colonelcy.[38]

Scott's Foot

Colonels: Walter Scott (1647-48), Lieutenant General Sir William Baillie (of Lamington) (1648)

Lieutenant Colonels: John Hadden/Haldane/Haldean (1647-48), (?) Wood (1648)

Majors: (?) Blair (1647-48), (?) Livingston (1648)

Ministers: Patrick Fleming, James Simson, Andrew Pringle, John Forbes[39]

Colonel Scott, commander of the Tweeddale Foot, received his commission as an infantry colonel in the New Model on 29 January 1647. The new regiment was to consist of 800 men in six companies to be drawn from regiments in England (including the Tweeddale Foot). Scott's Foot may have served in the northeastern campaign of spring 1647. In late March 1648 Scott was one of the signers of the original Tailors' Hall petition. From 23-24 May the Committee of Estates had the colonel imprisoned in Edinburgh tolbooth as an enemy of the regime. In disgust with the Engager regime he requested and was granted a pass (written in Latin) to leave to the continent in order to seek employment there. The regiment continued in the service of the Engagers.[40]

On 11 May 1648 the Estates appointed Lieutenant General Baillie colonel of the regiment. Baillie was a veteran of the campaigns against Montrose. By 1648 he had not served as an officer for over two years. He served as an M.P. for Lanarkshire in 1645-47, and in 1648; in the latter instance he voted for the Engagement. Following the defection of certain high ranking officers in the spring the Estates commissioned Baillie as Lieutenant General of Foot on 10 June. Probably sometime in the late spring Lieutenant Colonel Wood and men of the regiment were involved in an incident in Kirkcudbright which came to light in a petition by the burgh council of 19 February 1649. Wood entered the burgh with 1,900 men during the Sunday sermon and quartered on all the inhabitants. His men behaved with hostility towards the townspeople; they plundered houses, even taking the household fixtures. Wood seized a Dutch ship in the harbour and had it plundered after threatening the crew with death. Losses in the burgh amounted to £800. In response Wood claimed that he acted under the orders of Hamilton and Callander, and that the Engager parliament had approved his actions and those of other officers. Wood also stated that he was a professional officer always ready to obey orders from his superiors. He also gave other reasons why he was not solely to blame for the behaviour of soldiers in Kirkcudbright.[41]

During Hamilton's campaign in England Baillie played an important rôle. In the council of war Baillie successfully argued for Lancashire. On the morning of 17 August Baillie led the Scots infantry, save for two brigades forming a rearguard, over Preston Bridge. During that afternoon he marshalled the foot in the enclosures of Walton Hall, one quarter mile south of Dawick. At the council of war that evening Baillie successfully overcame Turner's arguments against a night march to join Middleton's Horse. The regiment was engaged at the battle of Winwick on the 19th. That evening Baillie had the worst of many bad evenings of his life. Callander and Middleton instructed Baillie to surrender the surviving 2,600 infantry to Cromwell. They left the force to defend Warrington Bridge to cover their flight with the entire remaining cavalry and Hamilton. Baillie refused to surrender. First he tried to lead the infantry to the bridge in order to hold it, but only 250 men followed him. The rest downed their arms and ran to Warrington Moor. Their behaviour was not surprising; in the last six days there had been only two pounds of food for each man, and now there was no ammunition left. Eventually the infantry officers persuaded Baillie not to commit suicide and to surrender the remnant of the Engager Foot. Baillie and some of his officers then proceeded to parley with Cromwell, who offered them life and civil usage for the surrender of the men and their arms. Baillie was so disturbed over the surrender that he had a document signed by all the officers exonerating him of any fault in the action. At the capitulation his regiment contained only 128 officers and men. By 1651 he was back in Scotland where he satisfied the kirk for serving in the Engagement.[42]

Sharp's Dragoon Company

Commanders: Major William Sharp (1647-48), (Colonel) David Barclay (1648)

Major Sharp was appointed the commander of a dragoon company on 29 January 1647. The company was to contain 100 men, but when David Leslie received permission to retain and recruit his company of dragoons on 25 February Sharp's command was reduced to seventy men. There is no information on the unit's participation in military operations in either 1647 or 1648. Sharp supported the kirk party. However, the company formed part of the Engager Army. On 11 May 1648 parliament assigned the dragoons to Major Blair, who was a governor of three northeastern garrisons. The company was added to Barclay's horse regiment. It probably served at Stirling, disbanding after the treaty.[43]

Stewart's Foot

Colonels: William Stewart (1647), Ludovick Leslie (1647-48)

Lieutenant Colonel: David Weymss

Major: (?) Agnew

Ministers: George Thomson, Alexander Blair, Hugh Eccls, Robert Young[44]

On 29 January 1647 the Estates appointed Colonel Stewart, commander of the Galloway Foot, colonel of a regiment of 800 men in six companies. A week later he was given permission to retain one company from his old regiment. On 16 February Stewart demitted the new charge due to 'his infirmitie and weaknes of bodie . . . '. The Estates selected Colonel Ludovick Leslie, commander of an infantry regiment in the Army of the Solemn League and Covenant, in his place. The regiment may have served on the spring northeastern campaign. In 1648 Leslie supported the Engagers. On 8 June the Blair Atholl garrison was ordered to his regiment, but it does not seem to have departed from that place entirely because a garrison remained on the payroll until the end of September. The regiment was also to be augmented by 180 foot then quartering in the lands of the lairds of Glenorchy, Lawers, and Weem. This reinforcement probably reached the regiment before it marched into Berwick. Colonel Leslie was the Engager governor of that town until late in September when he withdrew. His regiment disbanded by the end of the month according to the provisions in the Treaty of Stirling.[45]

Strachan's Horse Troop

Commander: Lieutenant Colonel Alexander Strachan (of Thornton)

The Estates selected Strachan as a troop commander in the New Model on 29 January 1647. A week later he received orders to levy eighty horse. On 5 March the troop was ordered to be reduced by five men. There is no evidence concerning the troop's military activities in 1647-48. Strachan supported the Engagement; on 4 May 1648 the Estates appointed him a colonel of horse for Perthshire with the right to levy eighty men. As with so many other Engager units there is no information regarding the recruiting of these men. Strachan's troop remained in arms until sometime in September, when it disbanded probably having served at Stirling.[46]

Earl of Sutherland's Foot

Colonel: John, 13th earl of Sutherland

On 2 October 1647 Sutherland reported to Warriston from Dunrobin that the Estates had given the earl permission to levy and command 500 foot. This force was to oppose Lord Reay, a royalist and hereditary enemy of Sutherland. Later in the month the Inverness garrison sent a party into the Mackay's lands of Strathnaver. The earl's infantry probably assisted this operation which led to the submission of Lord Reay. It may be assumed that the regiment disbanded shortly afterwards. Sutherland supported the kirk party against the Engagers in parliament. However, the Estates named him as the colonel of 1,600 foot and 120 horse from Sutherland and Caithness. The earl refused the charge which Lieutenant Colonel John Munro of Lemlair took up. Sutherland then raised a force of his own clan and prevented the northern levies from reaching the Engager army. It is not known when he disbanded this kirk party force, but it was probably done by late October. Sutherland subsequently appeared at the kirk party parliaments of 1649 and 1650.[47]

NOTES

1. SRO, GD. 38.1, 193; PA. 15.10, 6; *APS*, VI, i. 673, 685, 719; *Ibid.*, VI, ii. 56; *Memoirs of Guthry*, 240.

2. *RCGA*, i. 205.

3. SRO, PA. 15.10, 1, 10; PR Dunblane, 21 February 1649; *APS*, VI, i. 672-4; *Ibid.*, VI, ii. 21-2, 92, 98; Stevenson, *Alasdair*, 232; see above, 196-8.

4. *RCGA*, i. 205; *Ibid.*, ii. 13.

5. SRO, B.6.18.2, 27v; PA. 7.4, 21; PA. 15.10, 3, 10; PR Ayr, 2 March 1648; *APS*, VI, i. 672-4; *Ibid.*, VI, ii. 21-2, 92; *C.J.*, vi. 685; *Three Letters Concerning the Surrender of many Scottish Lords to the High Sheriff of the County of Chester* (London, 1648), 4; Turner, *Memoirs*, 52; Stevenson, *Alasdair*, 231-40.

6. SRO, PA. 7.23, 12, 65; PA. 7.7, 163; PA. 11.8, 2v, 5; PA. 11.11, 25v; PA. 16.5; *APS*, VI, ii. 389, 506, 583, 599; Balfour, *Works*, iv. 295-6; J. Burns, *Memoirs of the Civil War, and During the Usurpation*, ed. J. Maidment (Edinburgh, 1832), 15.

7. F. Dow, *Cromwellian Scotland* (Edinburgh, 1979), 62-6.

8. *APS*, VI, ii. 710.

9. NLS, Dep. 175, Box 67, 647; SRO, KSR Duffus, i. 67; PA 15.10, 9; PR Elgin, i. 279; *APS*, VI, i. 623, 684, 719; *Ibid.*, VI, ii. 56, 62, 98, 122; see above, 241.

10. SRO, PA. 15.10, 5; *APS*, VI, i. 673, 684, 719; *Ibid.*, VI, ii. 56; *The Miscellany of the Spalding Club*, vol. 3, ed. J. Stuart (Spalding Club, xvi, 1846), 199-200; *RCGA*, iii. 170.

11. SRO, PA. 15.10, 9; *APS*, VI, i. 672-3, 709; A. Maxwell, *The History of Old Dundee* (Edinburgh, 1884), 527; see above, 114.

12. SRO, PA. 15.10, 11; *APS*, VI, i. 719; *Ibid.*, VI, ii. 74; Fosters, *Members*, 356.

13. SRO, PA. 15.10, 5; *APS*, VI, i. 673, 719; *Ibid.*, VI, ii. 122; Turner, *Memoirs*, 52.

14. SRO, PA. 15.10, 8; *APS*, VI, i. 673, 719; *Ibid.*, VI, ii. 56; R. Gordon and G. Gordon, *A Geneaological History of the Earldom of Sutherland* (Edinburgh, 1813), 542.

15. SRO, PR Elgin, i. 268.

16. SRO, PR Linlithgow, 10 March-2 June 1647; *RCGA*, i. 205, 272.

17. SRO, PA. 7.5, 27, 51; *Aberdeen Letters*, iii. 96, 98; *APS*, VI, i, 673, 685, 696, 698, 700; *Ibid.*, VI, ii. 73, 474; *The Diplomatic Correspondence of Jean de Montereul and the Brothers de Bellievre, French Ambassadors in England and Scotland, 1645-48*, ed. J. Fotheringham (Scot. His. Soc., 1st Ser., xxx, 1898), ii. 439; *Extracts from the Records of the Royal Burgh of Lanark with Charters and Documents Relating to the Burgh, AD. 1150-1722*, ed. R. Renwick (Glasgow, 1893), 137; *Glasgow*, 125; *Three Letters*, 4; Turner, *Memoirs*, 55; W. Wheatly, *A Declaration of the Scottish Armie concerning their immediate marching towards the Borders of England* (London, 1647), 5; *Scots Peerage*, iv, 309; see below, 285-6.

18. *RCGA*, i. 205, 272, 277-8.

19. SRO, PA. 15.10, 1; *APS*, VI, ii. 122; *Army of the Covenant*, i. civ; *RCGA*, i. 272, 277-8, 540; Turner, *Memoirs*, 52-5.

20. *Kirkcaldie*, 368; *Three Letters*, 4; Turner, *Memoirs*, 58-9, 61, 66-7, 70, 72-7; W. Gordon, *The History of the . . . Family of Gordon*, 2 vols. (Edinburgh, 1727), ii. 558; A. Woolrych, *Battles of the English Civil War* (paperback edn., London, 1966), 165, 172-4.

21. Stevenson, *Alasdair*, 236, 238.

22. SRO, PA. 15.10, 8; *APS*, VI, i. 673, *Ibid.*, VI, ii. 122; *Army of the Covenant*, i, cv; see above, 167.

23. SRO, PA. 15.10, 10; PR Jedburgh, 9 May 1648; *APS*, VI, i. 709; *Army of the Covenant*, i. 137; see above, 158.

24. SRO, KSR Tyninghame, i. 168v; PR Ayr, 14 July 1647; PR Dalkeith, 4 March 1647; *RCGA*, i. 204, 272; *Records of the Kirk*, 481.

25. SRO, KSR Tyninghame, i. 168v; *APS*, VI, i. 672-3, 719; *Memoirs of Guthry*, 240; *Memoirs of Scottish Catholics During the 17th and 18th centuries*, 2 vols., ed. W. Forbes-Leith (London, 1909), ii. 13; J. Thurloe, *A Collection of papers containing authentic memorials of English affairs, 1638-53* (London, 1742), i. 89; Stevenson, *Alasdair*, 229-40.

26. SRO, PA. 15.10, 4; PR Jedburgh, 15 December 1647, 17 May, 26 July, 4, 23 August 1648; *APS*, VI, ii. 122; *Correspondence of Lothian*, i. 222-3; G. Burnet, *The Memoirs of the Lives and actions of James and William dukes of Hamilton and Castle-Herald* (2nd edn., Oxford, 1852), 428; Turner, *Memoirs*, 49, 52; see below, 278-9.

27. NLS, Wodrow Analecta Folio 63, 74; SRO, PA. 15.10, 4; *APS*, VI, i. 674, 719; *Ibid.*, VI, ii. 122; *Memoirs of Guthry*, 240; Turner, *Memoirs*, 49, 52; see below, 278-9.

28. SRO, PA. 15.10, 7; *APS*, VI, i. 673, 684, 719; *Ibid.*, VI, ii. 56; *Memoirs of Guthry*, 240; Turner, *Memoirs*, 58, 74, 76; Dow, *Cromwellian Scotland*, 55, 59, 123, 148, 150-1, 165, 175, 177, 214.

29. SRO, PA. 15.10, 6; *APS*, VI, i. 673, 686, 719; *Ibid.*, VI, ii. 56; *Memoirs of Guthry*, 240.

30. SRO, PR Paisley, 18 February, 17 June, 15 July 1647; *RCGA*, i. 204-7, 272; for Nevay's service see above, 263.

31. NLS, Wodrow Analecta Folio 63, 74; *APS*, VI, i. 672-3, 719; *Memoirs of Guthry*, 240; Turner, *Memoirs*, 49; Stevenson, *Alasdair*, 231.

32. *APS*, VI, ii. 56, 65, 73, 120; *Diplomatic Correspondence*, ii. 439; *Memoirs of Guthry*, 269; Turner, *Memoirs*, 52; Woolrych, *Battles*, 160.

33. SRO, PA. 15.10, 5; 'A Declaration from Scotland Concerning the Advance of the Scots Army: Who are Come into England' (London, 1648), in *Reprints of Rare Tracts Chiefly Illustrative of the Northern counties*, 3 vols., ed., M. A. Richardson (Newcastle, 1845-9), ii. 10; *RCGA*, iii. 156; Turner, *Memoirs*, 76; *Scots Peerage*, vi. 184; Woolrych, *Battles*, 164, 167, 175-7, 179.

34. SRO, PA. 15.10, 5; *APS*, VI, i. 673, 685, 719; *Ibid.*, VI, ii. 56, 122; Turner, *Memoirs*, 47.

35. SRO, PA. 15.10, 8; PR Cupar, 23 December 1650; PR Stirling, 24 June 1650; *APS*, VI, i. 673, 686, 719; *Ibid.*, VI, ii. 56; *Memoirs of Guthry*, 240.

36. *RCGA*, i. 205, 226, 272; *Records of the Kirk*, 482.

37. SRO, KSR St. Cuthbert's, Edinburgh, v. 38, 42; PA. 15.10, 2; *APS*, VI, i. 673; *Ibid.*, VI, ii. 122; *Army of the Covenant*, i. civ; *Lothian and Tweeddale*, 237; *Memoirs of Guthry*, 240.

38. *APS*, VI, i. 673, 719; *Army of the Covenant*, i. liv, cv; *Memoirs of Guthry*, 240.

39. SRO, PR Peebles, 11, 25 March, 17 June 1647; *RCGA*, i. 205, 273; *Records of the Kirk*, 482.

40. *APS*, VI, i. 673; *Ibid.*, VI, ii. 105; *Army of the Covenant*, i. cv; *Memoirs of Guthry*, 240; Turner, *Memoirs*, 52; see above, 182.

41. SRO, PA. 7.6, 18; *APS*, VI, ii. 121-2.

42. SRO, PA. 15.10, 2; *Baillie*, iii. 457; *RCGA*, iii. 408; *Three Letters*, 3; Foster, *Members*, 20; Woolrych, *Battles*, 164, 172-4, 177-8.

43. SRO, PA. 15.10, 9; *APS*, VI, i. 673, 709; *Ibid.*, VI, ii. 122; *Army of the Covenant*, i. cvi.

44. SRO, PR Cupar, 4 March 1647; *RCGA*, i. 205, 273; *Records of the Kirk*, 480.

45. SRO, PA. 15.10, 2; PR Cupar, 4 March 1647; *APS*, VI, i. 673, 684, 698; *Ibid.*, VI, ii. 98; *Army of the Covenant*, i. cvi.

46. SRO, PA. 15.10, 8; *APS*, VI, i. 673, 719; *Ibid.*, VI, ii. 56; *Memoirs of Guthry*, 240.

47. *APS*, VI, ii. 55; *The Sutherland Book*, 3 vols. ed. W. Fraser, (Edinburgh, 1894), i. 249.

8
Engager Army, 1648

Earl of Atholl's Foot

Colonel: John, 2nd earl of Atholl

Lieutenant Colonel: William [Ogumye (sic)] Ogilvy

The Engager parliament appointed the seventeen-year-old earl of Atholl a colonel of the Perthshire Foot on 4 May 1648. The burghs of Perth and Culross and the wasted areas of the shire were exempted from providing any of the 800 men set out in the levy quota. Due to Atholl's youth the recruiting of the regiment probably fell upon his officers and the lairds of Atholl. Sometime between 8 and 31 July the regiment crossed the western border under its lieutenant colonel. Atholl's Foot served under Hamilton during the Preston campaign. It was certainly engaged at the battle of Winwick on 19 August, and may have fought at the skirmishes of Penrith, Appleby and Stainmore. On the evening of 19 August 168 officers and men, including Ogilvy, fell prisoner to the English at Warrington Bridge. With that the regiment ceased to exist. Atholl engaged in royalist plots and risings in 1649, and eventually received a colonelcy in the Army of the Kingdom.[1]

Lord Balcarres' Horse

Colonel: Alexander, 2nd Lord Balcarres

Lord Balcarres had been a firm Covenanter since inheriting the title in 1642. Before 1648 he had held a colonelcy of horse in the Army of the Solemn League and Covenant. From 1647-1648 he was the captain and keeper of Edinburgh Castle. Balcarres supported the Engagers in parliament. On 4 May he was appointed the colonel of a Fife horse regiment. Although the minimum number required for an Engager horse regiment was 180 troopers, Balcarres only received permission to levy 120 men. There is no information about the unit either concerning its recruiting or military activities. In the event it would have ceased to exist by the end of September. In 1649 Balcarres underwent repentance for supporting the Engagement. Subsequently he became a supporter of the kirk party.[2]

Lord Banff's Foot

Colonel: George, 1st Lord Banff

Sir George Ogilvy had begun his rise into the nobility in the reign of James VI. In 1624 he became the laird of Banff. Three years later he was made a baronet of Nova Scotia. From 1627 he was the provost of Banff. In 1639 Banff was a leading royalist in the northeast. The Covenanters destroyed his houses of Banff and Inchdrewer, but Forglen House escaped. The Engager parliament named him a member of the Banffshire committee of war on 18 April 1648. On 4 May he or his son was named the colonel of foot for Aberdeenshire and Banffshire outside of the earl Marischal's zone. The regiment was to contain 800 men. However, due to the plague, Aberdeen was exempted sixty men, Banff seven and Cullen six. The evidence that Banff raised his regiment was his repentance before the presbytery of Fourdoun on 19 June 1650.[3]

Lord Bargany's Foot

Colonel: John, 1st Lord Bargany

On 4 May 1648 the Estates appointed Bargany the colonel of the Linlithgow-shire and Peebleshire Foot. The shires were to provide 500 and 400 men respectively. Bargany's regiment entered northwest England in July. It may have fought at Penrith, Appleby and Stainmore, but certainly did so at Winwick. The campaign severely depleted the regiment's manpower (even assuming that only two-thirds of the quota was filled). On the evening of 19 August only ninety men and officers remained to surrender. Bargany, however, fled with Hamilton's portion of the army, falling prisoner at Uttoxeter. By December he had regained his freedom, for on the 12th of that month he underwent public repentance in Lanark presbytery.[4]

Earl of Buchan's Horse Troop

Colonel: James, earl of Buchan

Buchan received his commission as a colonel of a horse troop on 4 May 1648. Forfarshire was to provide him with seventy troopers, while Banffshire levied another ten. Again the only evidence concerning the levying of the troop was Buchan's public satisfaction of the Kirk.[5]

Earl of Callander's Foot

Colonel: Lieutenant General James, 1st earl of Callander

Lieutenant Colonel: Sir William Livingstone of Westquarter

Major: (?) James or William Livingston of Langston

Callander had previously served as the lieutenant general of the Second Bishops' War and Solemn League and Covenant armies. In 1648 he had drifted so far towards royalism that he was regarded warily by the Engagers. At the 1648 parliament he attempted to create a third party but was outmanoeuvred and forced to support the Engagers. The Estates appointed him colonel of the Stirlingshire and Clackmannanshire Foot on 4 May. The regiment was to consist of 1,000 men, and Stirling burgh was exempted from the levy due to the plague. A week later Callander was commissioned Lieutenant General of Horse and Foot. By mid-spring the regiment was quartering around Paisley. It was from there on 12 June that Callander lethargically set out to aid Middleton subdue the rebels on Mauchline Moor. His sloth ensured that his troops arrived too late. In early July the regiment and its colonel marched from Edinburgh to Annan with Hamilton. Callander was on very poor terms with Hamilton, and opposed him as a matter of policy. Hamilton, however, bowed to nearly all of Callander's arguments on the subsequent campaign. On 8 July when the bulk of the army crossed into Cumberland, Callander commanded the rearguard of 1,500 horse. Callander's Foot were saved the vicissitudes of the campaign, because they served as the Carlisle garrison. Callander was the governor of Carlisle town and castle, a task which he deputed to Westquarter, so that he could accompany the army.[6]

Callander's decision to remain with Hamilton was one of the chief causes of the disaster resulting in the surrenders at Warrington and Uttoxeter. First, Colonel George Munro refused to subordinate himself and his Ulster force to Callander. Therefore, Hamilton decided to allow Munro to remain in the northwest to guard the supply line and bring up the artillery. At the debate over the choice of a route through either Yorkshire and Lancashire Callander was undecided; it was the last occasion on the campaign when doubt entered his mind. He and Middleton argued for the separation of the horse from the foot on the line of march so that the quartering requirements of both arms could be met. This created a gap of sixteen miles between the infantry and cavalry on the morning of 17 August. On the previous evening Callander had discredited Sir Marmaduke Langdale's claim that Cromwell and his men were nearby. On the morning of the 17th Callander persuaded Hamilton to order the Scottish Foot south of Preston despite Langdale's pleas that it would leave his men on Preston Moor without hope of victory. Later in the day when Hamilton began to waver in this decision Callander again urged him to keep the Scottish forces south of the river. Indeed he insisted on a retreat south to join Middleton's cavalry, which had become separated from the infantry at *his* insistence. During the late afternoon Callander attempted to send 600 musketeers to reinforce the two Scottish infantry brigades at Ribble Bridge, but the English fire drove them back to Walton Hall. That evening at the council of war Callander's voice was decisive in persuading the officers to leave a prepared position to march wet, tired and hungry soldiers down an unknown road to join Middleton and the horse. On the evening of the 19th Middleton and Callander, now reunited, ordered Baillie to surrender the remains of the Scottish Foot. They fled south with Hamilton and the cavalry. Callander and some men escaped to London, from there he fled to the Netherlands. He remained in exile there until the Restoration. His regiment evacuated Carlisle in late September and disbanded thereafter.[7]

Lord Carnegie's Foot

Colonel: James, Lord Carnegie

Lieutenant Colonel: William Hamilton

Alone among the Engager regiments Carnegie's has information on its levying. On 4 May 1648 the Estates appointed Carnegie colonel of the Angus Foot. His regiment should have contained 1,500 men. The burgh of Brechin had thirty men exempted from the levy. On 16 May Carnegie rejected an appeal of Dundee burgh council to reduce its quota of 150 foot. The council had problems in levying the required number due to the success of cavalry colonels levying men from the burgh. Consequently, the magistrates prohibited any burgess from joining the cavalry until the town levy was complete. Lord Carnegie complained to the council on 5 June that it was moving too slowly. As a result the council drew up the following quotas: maltmen to provide thirty men; merchants and sailors, twenty-two; braboners, fifteen; cordiners, twelve; tailors and bonnet-makers, eight each; baxters and fleshers, six each; litsters and skinners, four each; and hammermen, three, for a total of 120 foot. Apparently, the council had managed to recruit only thirty men within three weeks. On the 19th the quota had still not been achieved and the council received a communication from the Committee of Estates ordering it to put out the deficient men. Then a total of ninety men had been levied. On 11 July the council ordered the company's captain, William Kyd, to the south. There is no sign that the burgh completed the levy, which in mid-June was sixty per cent filled. Carnegie's regiment may be assumed to have been understrength when it crossed the border into northwest England after 8 July. It is not known whether the regiment served in any of the skirmishes in the northwest. However, it was probably engaged at Winwick. At Warrington Bridge the only survivors of the campaign were Carnegie, the lieutenant colonel and 158 officers and men (just over ten per cent of the levy quota). All of them fell prisoner to Cromwell's army. Carnegie remained a prisoner in England until sometime in 1649, when he made his way to the Netherlands. The next year he was back in Scotland, where he repented for going out on the Engagement.[8]

Lord Cochrane's Foot

Colonel: William, 1st Lord Cochrane

Major: (?) Lammes

William Cochrane was forty-three years old in 1648. In 1632 he was appointed sheriff-depute of Renfrewshire. Charles I knighted him the year later. He sat as an M.P. for Ayrshire in the 1640s. In 1645 he acted as a messenger for the Estates in Ulster. On 26 December 1647 Charles I elevated him to the peerage as Lord Cochrane of Dundonald. In spring 1648 Cochrane acted as a commissioner to the Ulster Army for the Engagers. On 4 May 1648 he received a parliamentary commission as a colonel of the Ayrshire and Renfrewshire Foot. Initially his regiment was to contain about 666 men. However, on 12 May the Committee of Estates authorised Cochrane to raise 1,000 foot from the county. A local history claims that he received the full complement of men from Ayrshire, which is doubtful considering the hostility of the people in that county to the Engagement. The regiment was in Kirkcudbright sometime in the spring with Scott's (Baillie's) Foot. It may have been one of those destroyed on the evening of 17 August whilst guarding Preston Bridge. There is no mention of it among the regiments at Warrington. In December 1650 Cochrane underwent repentance for being an Engager colonel, recruiter and money collector. He attended parliament in 1651, and levied men from Ayrshire in that year.[9]

College of Justice's Horse

Colonel: Sir Alexander Gibson of Durie, Lord Register

Minister: John Brown[10]

On 17 June 1648 a delegation from the College of Justice appeared in parliament. The members of the judicatory offered to raise a regiment for the Engagers as it had done on other occasions for the Covenanters. This proved acceptable and the Estates promised to help. The choice of Durie as colonel was mentioned and accepted. There is nothing further about the regiment itself. However, its chaplain received £200 in pay from the Estates. On 26 September the Commission of the General Assembly noted that he was a chaplain to the Engagers, but they were unable to find him. This suggests that the regiment may have entered England or it could have still been at Stirling.[11]

Lord Cranston's Horse

Colonel: William, 3rd Lord Cranston

Cranston had served as a colonel in the Army of the Solemn League and Covenant. On 18 April 1648 he was nominated to the Edinburghshire committee of war. Just over two weeks later (4 May), the Estates appointed him a colonel of foot for that shire. His regiment was to contain 600 men. The only reference to the recruiting of these men concerns the levying of a former soldier in Dunbar presbytery who was under process for prenuptial fornication. However, on 12 May the Committee of Estates ordered Cranston to raise a regiment of 180 horse in three troops, of which eighty men would come from shire levies and 100 men from his own efforts. On the 19th he was assigned eighty horsemen from the shires of Roxburgh and Selkirk. Cranston accompanied Hamilton in his flight. He was captured at Uttoxeter, and from there went to prison in Hull. By November 1650 he was in Scotland, where he did penance for supporting the Engagement. In summer 1651 he accompanied Charles II to Worcester, where he again became an English prisoner. He was initially lodged in the Tower, but regained his freedom. In 1656 Cranston received a licence to raise 1,000 infantry for the king of Sweden. He apparently succeeded in this endeavour for Charles X Gustavus interceded with the Protectorate to allow Cranston to regain his lands which had been confiscated in 1654.[12]

Earl of Crawford-Lindsay's Horse

Colonel: John, 17th earl of Crawford and 10th earl of Lindsay

Although Crawford-Lindsay was a firm Covenanter from early 1647 he began to moderate his opinions. He then protested against surrendering the king to the English. In 1648 he was a strong supporter of the Engagers. On 26 May the Committee of Estates assigned the eight horse due to David Leslie from Perthshire to the earl. In September he was one of the leaders of the Engagers at Stirling. On the 20th the Commission of the General Assembly sent him a letter demanding that he disband the army or face excommunication. However, it was not this but the proximity of Cromwell's forces which persuaded him to submit. Crawford-Lindsay was stripped of his offices of state on 13 February 1649 and barred from public employment for life. However, he subsequently repented of his actions and regained military command in 1651.[13]

Earl of Dalhousie's Horse

Colonel: William, 1st earl of Dalhousie or George, Lord Ramsay

Minister: Simeon Knox[14]

On 4 May 1648 the Estates appointed Dalhousie or his son Ramsay as colonel of an Edinburghshire horse troop. The unit was to contain eighty men, but it would have been upgraded to a regiment of 180-240 troopers. Lord Ramsay accepted the commission, although the regiment was known under his father's name. It took part in the Preston campaign and would have been part of the cavalry force under Middleton's command. Lord Ramsay became a prisoner of the English at

Warrington Bridge. However, he was back in Scotland by early 1649, for on 8 February he petitioned the kirk. His father's repentance occurred after 1 June 1648. The unit ceased to exist sometime in August.[15]

Douglas' Foot

Colonel: Richard Douglas

Major: William Douglas

In some shires the Estates appointed several colonels of foot on 4 May 1648 out of fear that some nominees would refuse to accept the commission. Such was the case in Roxburghshire and Selkirkshire. There five men were listed in the leet; they included Sir William Douglas of Cavers and his son Richard. Cavers was himself an alternate, who refused the post, but Richard (who was the alternate for his father) accepted it. The levy quota from the two shires was 1,000 men. Douglas' Foot entered England sometime in July. The only action where it was definitely present was at the battle of Winwick, though it may have fought at skirmishes which took place in July. At Warrington Bridge there remained of the regiment only 142 officers and men. Major Douglas was one of the signators of Baillie's document expunging him of guilt for the surrender. On 14 December 1650 the Commission of the General Assembly recommended the services of Richard Douglas to the state.[16]

Viscount Dudhope's Horse

Colonel: John, 3rd viscount Dudhope

This is another Engager unit on which the information is sparse. Dudhope was commissioned as a colonel of a horse troop on 4 May 1648. It was to consist of seventy horsemen from Angus and ten from Banffshire. There is no further mention of the unit until Dudhope underwent repentance in 1650 for serving as a colonel. He was later employed in the Army of the Kingdom.[17]

Earl of Dumfries' Foot

Colonel: William, 2nd earl of Dumfries

Lieutenant Colonel: John Johnston

The Estates commissioned Dumfries as a colonel of Dumfriesshire Foot on 4 May 1648. The regiment was to contain 600 men. It served on the Preston campaign and was part of the force surrendered at Warrington Bridge. The only survivors of the campaign on 19 August were the lieutenant colonel, eight officers, four sergeants and forty-four men.[18]

Earl of Dunfermline's Horse

Colonel: Charles, 2nd earl of Dunfermline

Dunfermline was one of the colonels of horse commissioned by the Estates on 4 May 1648. He was to raise eighty horse from Fife. There is no further reference to the unit. Dunfermline, himself, went into exile with Charles II in the Netherlands from 1649-1650. He returned sometime in 1650 and repented for aiding the Engagement in late November.[19]

Earl of Erroll's Horse

Colonel: Gilbert, 11th earl of Erroll

Lieutenant Colonel: James Hay

Erroll, the seventeen-year-old hereditary High Constable of Scotland, received his commission as the colonel of an Aberdeenshire horse troop of eighty men on 4 May 1648.[20]

Forbes' Horse Troop

Colonel: Arthur Forbes

Yet another mysterious Engager unit. It is only mentioned as quartering twenty-four troopers in the barony of Lesmoir on 4 June 1648.[21]

Viscount Frendraught's Horse

Colonel: James, 1st viscount Frendraught

Frendraught had previously led the northeastern Crichtons against Montrose and had command of a horse regiment in the Home Army. On 4 May 1648 parliament appointed him the colonel of a horse troop. He was to levy eighty men from Aberdeenshire and Banffshire. As with many other units in this army there is no further reference to it until Frendraught satisfied the Kirk. In 1650 he allied himself to Montrose and was made prisoner after Carbisdale. After that he repented of his actions as an Engager and royalist.[22]

Fraser's Flintlocks

Colonel: Unknown

There is no information on this unit until the surrender at Warrington Bridge. The only Fraser nominated as colonel was a kirk party member, so there were no candidates for that post except Colonel Hugh Fraser, who was a cavalry officer. Units of men armed with flintlocks usually provided the baggage guard in the British wars of the mid-seventeenth century. At Warrington Bridge this consisted of 160 men and officers.[23]

Garthland's Horse

Colonel: Sir James MacDowall of Garthland

Major: John Macdougall

Garthland was an experienced Wigtownshire M.P., having sat for the shire at the convention of 1643, and the parliaments of 1645-47 and 1648. He had served as a routmaster in Kirkcudbright's Horse in the Army of the Solemn League and Covenant. Garthland had also acted as a commissioner to the Ulster Army from the Committee of Estates in 1646. On 4 May 1648 he received a commission as colonel of horse. Garthland was to recruit eighty troopers from Wigtownshire and Ayrshire for his unit. He may have received the full complement (forty men) from the latter county. However, Garthland's greatest service to the Engagement was acting as a commissioner to the Ulster Army with the earl of Glencairn and Alexander Crawford. They made the final arrangements for bringing over George Munro's contingent. Garthland satisfied the Kirk after the defeat of the Engagers. He then experienced a political conversion and became a supporter of the Protectorate. He served in the Westminster parliaments of 1654-55, 1656-58 and 1658-59 as a Wigtownshire M.P.[24]

Earl of Glencairn's Foot

Colonel: William, 8th earl of Glencairn

The earl of Glencairn had served as a colonel of foot in the Army of the Solemn League and Covenant. On 17 November 1646 he became Lord Justice-General. He was one of the leading Engagers. The Estates granted him a commission as a colonel of Ayrshire and Renfrewshire Foot on 4 May 1648. The regiment's strength was set initially at about 666 men. However, on 12 May Glencairn received orders from the Committee of Estates to levy 1,000 men. During May and June Glencairn served with Garthland and Alexander Crawford as a commissioner to the Ulster Army. This time in Ulster prevented him from taking much initiative in the recruiting of his men. It is reported that he levied a full complement from Ayrshire, but this is questionable due to the political proclivities of the inhabitants. Glencairn was one of the Engagers ordered to disband the army at Stirling on 20 September by the Commission of the General Assembly, or face excommunication. His regiment disbanded as a consequence of the Treaty of Stirling. He was stripped of his offices and title in 1649. By late 1650 he had satisfied the Kirk and was back in parliament. In 1651 Glencairn served on the Committee of Estates. In 1653 he instituted a rising for Charles II in the Highlands. The English exempted him from the Act of Grace and Pardon of 1654, although he subsequently surrendered. In 1659 Glencairn accompanied Monck to England. He favoured moderate episcopacy and opposed Archbishop Sharp. After the Restoration he was given important public offices.[25]

Grey's Foot

Colonel: Sir John Grey

Another obscure Engager regiment which is only mentioned once in the contemporary sources. At the surrender of the Scottish Foot at Warrington Bridge on 19 August 1648 this unit contained thirty-seven officers and men.[26]

Duke of Hamilton's Foot

Colonel: General James, 1st duke of Hamilton

Lieutenant Colonel: Claude Hamilton

Hamilton was one of the leaders of the royalist party in Scotland. Prior to his involvement in British politics he had raised troops for Sweden and served under Gustavus Adolphus (1631-32). He accompanied Charles I to Scotland for the coronation in 1633. In 1638 Hamilton acted as the royal commissioner to the Glasgow General Assembly. The following year he commanded a force of 5,000 men which attempted to land on the shores of the Firth of Forth. Two years later Hamilton was elevated from marquis to duke. From 1642-43 he attempted to moderate the Covenanters in favour of the king, but failed. Hamilton was always under suspicion of usurping the throne, because he possessed a claim to the Scottish crown as a descendant of James II. Due to his failure in altering the course of the Covenanters Charles imprisoned him from 1644-46. This action caused many nobles to change their allegiance to Covenanters. Hamilton's brother, Lanark, was one of the nobles who negotiated the Engagement, and Hamilton was the leader of the Engagers.[27]

Hamilton played important rôles in the military aspect of the Engagement as well as the political. On 4 May 1648 he was made colonel of the Lanarkshire Foot. The levy quota was set at 1,500 men. Following the refusal of Leven and

David Leslie to serve as General of the army, Hamilton received that post. In early July he went with his regiment and the other staff officers from Edinburgh to Annan for a rendezvous with Turner's force. On 8 July he led the vanguard of 2,000 cavalry in four regiments across the border into Cumberland. Throughout the campaign Hamilton was hampered by his willingness to bow to the arguments of Callander, who disliked him. As soon as his army entered England Hamilton was struck with mental paralysis. After remaining stationary for a week the army moved on again on the 14th, but with such sloth that its speed gave the Commonwealth army time to crush the other risings. Hamilton acquiesced to two fatal divisions in his forces: the first allowed Munro to keep the Ulster force in the north; the second created a gap between the infantry and cavalry of the main army. Hamilton also made the fatal decision to march through Lancashire, because he was fixated by the desire to capture the presbyterian town of Manchester and the hope of uniting his army with Lord Byron's forces from north Wales. During the day of the Preston battle Hamilton changed his mind continually. He initially ordered Baillie to keep the Scottish Foot north of the Ribble and commanded Middleton to bring the horse north from Wigan. However, Callander caught his ear and persuaded the duke against fighting north of the river. Instead, on the morning of 17th August the foot were sent south of the Ribble despite Langdale's pleas that this would mean the destruction of his own forces north of Preston (which did occur). As the day progressed Hamilton sent Turner with some infantry and powder to Langdale's assistance, but this aid was too little to stem the tide. Hamilton also ordered the rearguard horse north to Munro, which deprived Langdale of much needed cavalry. From this point on, although Hamilton displayed personal bravery, he abdicated the position of commander-in-chief. His infantry regiment which served at Penrith, Appleby, Stainmore and Winwick surrendered at Warrington Bridge. There were only 397 men and officers remaining in a unit which might have contained 1,500 infantry when it crossed the border. Hamilton's fate is covered in the subsequent entry.[28]

Duke of Hamilton's Horse Guard

Colonel: General James, 1st duke of Hamilton

On 11 May 1648 the Estates assigned Leslie's and Leven's horse troops to the duke. Consequently this unit had a nominal strength of 150 men. On 8 July when the army crossed the border this unit provided the protection for the train of wagons. On the morning of 17 August when Hamilton decided to fight north of the Ribble, the Guards were the only horse on that side of the river. In the afternoon Hamilton, Langdale, Turner and some gentlemen found themselves isolated north of the Ribble. They tried a ford west of Preston, but found it impassable due to the recent heavy rains. Then two troops of English horse attacked them. Hamilton led his Horse Guards three times against the pursuers.

Finally on the third attack they retreated, allowing the Engagers to escape and reach Baillie and the infantry at Walton Hall. After reaching Warrington on the 19th Hamilton with Callander and Middleton rode to Chester. They then turned south near Malpas, Salops, continuing the retreat through Market Drayton, Stone and finally to Uttoxeter. There Hamilton's men mutinied and held him prisoner until Turner persuaded them to release him. Hamilton was first captured by the Governor of Stafford and on the 25th handed over to Lambert. He was originally imprisoned at Windsor, where he had an interview with Charles I. Hamilton escaped from Windsor, but was recaptured. The Commonwealth government tried him and had him beheaded under his English title — the earl of Cambridge — on 9 March 1649.[29]

Earl of Home's Foot

Colonel: James, 3rd earl of Home

Lieutenant Colonel: Alexander Home

The earl of Home had been active for the Covenanters in the Bishops' Wars. His drift away from the mainstream began in 1640, however, when he signed the Cumbernauld Bond. In 1643 he became the Sheriff of Berwickshire. However, in 1645 he flirted with Montrose, which earned him a fine from the Estates. On 4 May 1648 the Engager parliament appointed him colonel of the Berwickshire Foot. The earl was to levy 1,200 men for his regiment. Sometime in July Home's Foot crossed the border under the earl's command. It may have served at the skirmishes of Penrith, Appleby and Stainmore, but it was engaged at Winwick. The earl escaped to Scotland following the surrender of infantry at Warrington Bridge. His lieutenant colonel and 276 officers and men, however, fell prisoner to the English. Lieutenant Colonel Home signed Baillie's apology for the surrender. In 1650 the earl of Home underwent repentance for serving on the Engagement. He later received a charge in the Army of the Kingdom.[30]

Home's Horse

Colonel: John Home

Home was appointed a colonel of Berwickshire horse on 4 May 1648. The troop was to contain eighty men. The next mention of the unit is Home's repentance for serving on the Engagement. Consequently, it cannot be determined how many men were in the unit or where it served.[31]

Innes' Horse

Colonel: Quartermaster General Robert Innes

Major: (?) Dunbar

Innes had served in the Army of the Solemn League and Covenant as a quarter-master general. He was commissioned to the same rank on 11 May 1648. Previously, on 4 May, the Estates had appointed Innes a colonel of horse for Elginshire, Nairnshire and Inverness-shire east of the Ness. The troop was to consist of eighty troopers. Five days later Innes was told to levy his horsemen from Elginshire alone. Later in the month Innes wrote Robert Gordon of Gordonston, a member of the Elginshire committee of war, informing him that his major was coming to Elgin to discuss the proportioning of the horse. (That Innes only had a major means that his regiment was to total only 180 troopers at full strength.) Innes also told Gordonston that he would be coming to attend the committee soon himself. Late in May Dunbar wrote Gordonston on the same matter, requesting a meeting place be set for the committee to discuss it. Innes' Horse probably served under Hamilton, surrendering at Uttoxeter. Innes later did public penance in the presbytery of Elgin for being an officer in the Engager Army.[32]

Keith's Foot

Colonel: George Keith (of Aden)

Keith was the brother and heir to the earl Marischal. Prior to 1648 he had served as a colonel in the French army. On 4 May 1648 parliament appointed him a colonel of foot for the Mearns and Marischal's area of Aberdeenshire. The regiment was to contain 600 men. While nothing is known of the levying of the regiment, it was at Preston. There Keith fell prisoner to the English. It may be presumed that the unit was one of those detailed to guard the Ribble bridge. By 1651 Keith was back in Scotland, where he received a colonelcy in the Army of the Kingdom.[33]

Kelhead's Foot

Colonel: William Douglas of Kelhead

Lieutenant Colonel: Laird of Applegirth

Kelhead was a Dumfriesshire laird who had commanded an infantry regiment in the Army of the Solemn League and Covenant. He received a commission as a colonel of Dumfriesshire Foot on 4 May 1648. The levy quota was to be 600 foot. Unfortunately, there is no further information about the regiment until Kelhead's repentance before the Dundonald kirk session.[34]

Earl of Kellie's Foot

Colonel: Alexander, 3rd earl of Kellie

Kellie had served as a colonel in the Home Army. In 1648, on 4 May, the Estates appointed him a colonel of foot for Fife and Kinross-shire. Kellie's regiment was to have 750 men. The regiment served on the Preston campaign and may have been involved in the skirmishes which occurred in July. It was certainly in a position to fight at Winwick. At Warrington Bridge 110 men and officers of the regiment belonged to the force which Baillie surrendered. Kellie satisfied the Kirk quickly after the Engagement. He was employed in 1649 as a parliamentary commissioner to Charles II. Kellie later commanded a regiment in the Army of the Kingdom.[35]

Viscount Kenmure's Horse

Colonel: Robert, 4th viscount Kenmure

Kenmure had been the colonel of an infantry regiment from the Stewarty of Kirkcudbright in the Army of the Solemn League and Covenant. On 4 May 1648 he received an appointment as colonel of a horse troop from Wigtonshire and the Stewartry. Kenmure's troop was to consist of eighty men. Once more there is no information as to its levying or subsequent military activities. However, Kenmure satisfied the Kirk in 1651 for his support of the Engagement. In December 1650 the English captured his seat — Kenmure Castle. The viscount was captured at Worcester, but later escaped, serving in Glencairn's Rising. Kenmure suffered during the Protectorate despite his marriage to the daughter of an English regicide. In 1661 he marshalled Montrose's funeral, a great royalist event.[36]

Earl of Lanark's Horse

Colonel: William, 1st earl of Lanark

In December 1647 Lanark was one of the three negotiators on the Isle of Wight who produced the Engagement. On 4 May 1648 he was appointed a colonel of horse for Lanarkshire with the right to levy eighty men. There were at least two troops in the regiment — Lanark's and John Murray of Polmaise's (from Stirlingshire). On 20 September the Commission of the General Assembly ordered Lanark to disband the army (including this regiment), or be excommunicated. However, Lanark, who was the chief of state and commander of the forces at Stirling, was more impressed by the approach of Cromwell than the Kirk's spiritual power. Lanark went into exile in the Netherlands where he remained until 1650. He was made a Knight of the Garter in 1650 (due to the execution of his brother he was already the duke of Hamilton). He returned from Scotland with Charles II in June, but he withdrew from the court until January 1651, when he repented for his previous actions. Before returning to the court Hamilton led raids against the English garrisons in Lanarkshire. He was then commissioned as a colonel in the Army of the Kingdom.[37]

Earl of Lauderdale's Horse

Colonel: John, 2nd earl of Lauderdale

Lauderdale was one of the framers of the Engagement. His skills were political and diplomatic rather than military. However, on 4 May 1648 the Estates appointed him colonel of eighty horse from Haddingtonshire. On the 26th the Committee of Estates authorised William Borthwick, routmaster, to raise twenty men from East Lothian and ten from Berwickshire due Sir John Brown, and thirty others for his troop. His regiment was partially recruited by early July when some troopers ended a disturbance created by soldiers of Yester's Foot in Oldhamstock kirk. However, nothing more is known of the regiment. Lauderdale was sent on two diplomatic missions in the summer of 1648, one to the Prince of Wales, and another to the governments of the Netherlands and France. Although he persuaded the prince to sail to Scotland, the defeats of the Preston campaign led them both to take refuge in the Netherlands. Lauderdale remained there with a short break until he returned to Scotland with Charles, who had been persuaded to sign the Covenants by the earl. In December 1650 Lauderdale publically satisfied the Kirk at Largo. He held a command during the Worcester campaign.[38]

Lemlair's Foot

Colonel: John Munro of Lemlair

Lieutenant Colonel: Alexander Munro

Lemlair had served as a lieutenant colonel on the continent, and as a second cousin of the young chief he was a leading member of the clan. On 4 May 1648 the Estates named him an alternate to the earl of Sutherland should the earl refuse the colonelcy of Sutherland and Caithness. As a member of the kirk party Sutherland would not accept a command in the Engagement, thus Lemlair took it up. The force from Seaforth's area of Inverness-shire, Sutherland and Caithness was to include 800 foot and 120 horse. However, Sutherland raised a force of his own clan and obstructed the levy, which prevented the sending of any men south. On 5 August the Committee of Estates ordered Lemlair to raise men from the Mackenzie lands and bring them to Perth. There is no evidence that Lemlair either raised these men or departed for the south. Sutherland had successfully obstructed the northern levies.[39]

Lord Livingstone's Horse

Colonel: George, Lord Livingstone

Minister: Andrew Keir[40]

Livingstone had been the colonel of the Stirlingshire Foot in the Army of the Solemn League and Covenant. He received a commission as a colonel of Edinburghshire and Linlithgowshire Horse on 4 May 1648. The shires were to provide twenty and sixty horse respectively. About three weeks later the Committee of Estates allowed the colonel eighteen men from Blair's dragoon company. On 28 June Livingstone issued a receipt for three troopers to the laird of Dundas. Two months later the regiment's routmaster, Sir Archibald Stirling of Carden, presented Dundas with a discharge for another trooper. It appears that this regiment served at Stirling in September and disbanded following the treaty. In October 1650 Livingstone, then the earl of Linlithgow, repented for his service on the Engagement. He subsequently commanded a regiment in the Army of the Kingdom.[41]

Machanie's Foot

Colonel: Sir James Drummond of Machanie

Machanie was a son of the 1st Lord Madderty. He received a commission from the Estates on 4 May 1648 as a colonel of Perthshire infantry. Machanie had permission to levy 800 men from the shire, but the burghs of Perth and Culross, and the wasted lands were exempted from providing troops. The regiment entered England sometime in July. Other than the battle of Winwick it is uncertain where this regiment fought. When Baillie surrendered at Warrington Bridge only 110 men and officers were present.[42]

Earl Marichal's Horse

Colonel: William, 7th earl Marischal

Marischal had been a leading supporter of the Covenants in the northeast. He had commanded men in the field in both Bishops' Wars and against Montrose. However, by 1648 he was disenchanted with the movement and willingly joined the Engagers. He received a commission as a colonel of horse for the Mearns and his portion of Aberdeenshire on 4 May 1648. The troop of eighty horsemen was raised at his expense and served on the Preston campaign. It probably disintegrated during Hamilton's flight. On 8 July 1650 Charles II visited Marischal at Dunottar Castle. Five months later the earl publicly satisfied the Kirk. He attended the king's coronation on 1 January 1651. During the English occupation Marischal was imprisoned. He was freed at the Restoration and resided in London until his death although he was a Scottish officer of state.[43]

Maule's Foot

Colonel: Henry Maule (of Balmakellie)

Colonel Maule was a son of the first earl of Panmure, an Angus landowner. The Estates commissioned him a colonel of foot for the Mearns and Marischal's portion of Aberdeenshire on 4 May 1648. Maule was to levy 600 men. He personally led his regiment on the Preston campaign, but it is uncertain whether it was engaged in any actions other than the battle of Winwick. Maule and 128 officers and men of his regiment fell prisoner to the English at Warrington Bridge. However, the colonel managed to escape to Scotland. He repented for supporting the Engagement and commanded a regiment in the Army of the Kingdom.[44]

Viscount Montgomery's Horse

Colonel: Hugh, viscount Montgomery

Viscount Montgomery had experience as a cavalry commander in the Army of the Solemn League and Covenant. He was also a man known for his royalist leanings, unlike his father Eglinton. Montgomery received a commission as colonel of horse for Ayrshire and Renfrewshire on 4 May 1648. The viscount was to raise forty horse from each shire. A week later he received command of his brother's, Colonel Robert Montgomery, horse troop. It has been claimed he succeeded in levying the full Ayrshire contingent (which is a doubtful assertion). Nothing further is known of the regiment. The viscount underwent repentance for serving as a colonel. In 1651 he accompanied the army on the Worcester campaign and was taken prisoner.[45]

Earl of Moray's Foot

Colonel: James, 4th earl of Moray

During Montrose's campaigns Moray had served as a colonel in the Home Army. He became sheriff principal of Inverness-shire in 1647. Moray was made a colonel of foot for Moray, Nairnshire and Inverness-shire on 4 May 1648. His regiment was to consist of 1,500 infantrymen. The Engagers also appointed him Governor of Inverness. By 8 May it had been determined that 200 of his soldiers should replace Lawers' Foot as the garrison of Inverness. On the 16th Grant of Freuchie's Banffshire lands were placed within its levying bounds. There is no further mention of Moray's regiment, but it may be assumed that it disbanded by mid-October.[46]

Munro's Ulster Force

Commander: Major General and Colonel George Munro

Following negotiations in the spring of 1648 with the Engager parliament, the Ulster Army's council of war decided to send a commanded force to Scotland. The officers hoped to send at least 3,000 men from the army and some newly recruited troops as well as any British forces which might support the Engagement. Colonel Munro was given command of the operation and gained the rank of major general. The English, who had command of the sea, were determined to stop as many men from landing in Great Britain as possible. English ships captured 300 soldiers of the force and returned them to Ulster. Argyll fitted out a frigate for the same purpose. Munro was forced to send his men across to Galloway in small boats at night. Upon the soldiers' arrival in Scotland they were assailed by the ministers, ignored by the gentry and refused quarters. Eventually about 1,500 foot (from six regiments) and 400 horse in twelve troops crossed to Scotland. Although small in number these were veterans, which would have been a welcome addition to the Engager Army. However, Munro rode south to Kendal ahead of his men. There he refused to serve under either Callander or Baillie. Hamilton then ordered him to convoy the expected artillery from Scotland to the army when it arrived.[47]

There were now nearly 2,000 men from Ulster in England, but they were on a useless errand. Hamilton further weakened his army by providing Munro with 1,500 English infantry under Musgrave and Sir Thomas Tyldesly. The Anglo-Scottish force first concentrated at Kirkby Lonsdale and then advanced with the cannons south of Appleby. However, on 14 August Munro learned that Cromwell was at Skipton. Munro and his force retreated north via Appleby, reaching Kirkby Lonsdale on the 16th. Two days later fugitives from Preston reached Munro as well as the 1,200 horse of the rearguard, which rode by on their flight north. According to his orders Munro prepared to march to Scotland via Berwick. Musgrave and Tyldesly pleaded with Munro to remain with them, but he remained true to his orders. As a result the two English regiments surrendered to Cromwell's army at Appleby Castle. Meanwhile Munro's force continued the plundering it had begun as it entered Cumberland on the way to Berwick.[48]

As Munro and his force headed north, Lanark and the Engager troops in Scotland came south to meet him. The two forces rendezvoused and then marched north to Stirling via Linlithgow. Munro was determined not to yield to the Whiggamore Raiders, but of his own officers only Major Thomas Dalyell supported him. The Ulster force during the negotiations for a treaty plundered and extorted money and goods worth over £1,000 from the lands of the laird of Kilsyth. On the conclusion of the Treaty of Stirling the Ulster contingent was to return to their regiments in Ireland. On 28-29 August for twenty-four hours 362 horse and 1,099 foot quartered on Kilsyth's lands of Campsie and Monyabroch (at a cost of £726 5s. 6d.), on their way from Stirling to Glasgow. Munro's men failed to reach Ulster, however. On their march the people of the southwest attacked and plundered them, breaking the cohesion of the unit. When Munro learned that Monck had seized Robert Munro and the Scottish garrisons he disbanded his force. General Munro fled to the Netherlands. There he gathered a group of officers (who were judged to be enemies to the ministry and the people of God). In 1649 they reached Ulster with a force of Irish catholics and allied with Lord Montgomery of Ards. Munro served in the campaigns against the English parliamentary troops but demitted his charge when a Roman Catholic bishop was appointed to command the army. From Ulster he travelled to Scotland where he repented of his service on the Engagement. But he was too notorious a man to receive a charge in the Army of the Kingdom.[49]

Philorth's Foot

Colonel: Sir Alexander Fraser of Philorth

Philorth had experience as a military commander for the Covenanters in the Bishops' Wars, and in campaigns against Montrose. He served as a commissioner for Aberdeenshire at the convention of 1643; five years later he was an M.P. for the same shire. On 23 May 1648 the Committee of Estates wrote Philorth naming him colonel of foot for Aberdeenshire and Banffshire. This nomination occurred because the Master of Forbes refused to accept the commission (he was a member of the kirk party). Philorth was to levy 800 foot from the two shires. Although there is no further mention of the regiment in 1648, Philorth later did penance in the presbytery of Deer for serving as a colonel.[50]

Lord Riche's Foot

Colonel: Lord Riche?

This is yet another regiment whose existence is only confirmed by the list of prisoners taken at Warrington Bridge. Nothing is known of a peer named Riche, which suggests a problem of orthography for the English reporter. There were 143 officers and men in the regiment on 19 August 1648 when they fell prisoner.[51]

Earl of Roxburgh's Foot

Colonel: Robert, 1st earl of Roxburgh

Lieutenant Colonel: Andrew Ker

In 1648 Roxburgh was seventy-eight years old, which signifies that it was reputation, rather than his potential for taking the field personally, which led to his nomination as a colonel by the Estates on 4 May. Roxburgh had a long career in Scottish politics dating back to 1599. Since 1637 he had been Lord Privy Seal. His commission authorised the earl to recruit 1,000 foot from Selkirkshire and Roxburghshire (shires in which he was personally prominent). The regiment entered England sometime in July. It may have served at the skirmishes in the early part of the Preston campaign, but Roxburgh's Foot probably fought at Winwick. Lieutenant Colonel Ker signed Baillie's apologia for the surrender at Warrington Bridge. Only two officers and thirty-four men survived the campaign to become prisoner on 19 August. The kirk party stripped Roxburgh of his offices for sending out a regiment and supporting the Engagers; however, he satisfied the Kirk before his death on 18 January 1650.[52]

Earl of Seaforth's Foot and Dragoons

Colonel: George, 2nd earl of Seaforth

Seaforth was the leader of one of the largest northern clans — the Mackenzies. His political allegiance changed frequently, which meant he had experience as a field commander for both the Covenanters and Montrose. On 5 August 1648 the Committee of Estates ordered Seaforth to levy men from his lands. Eight hundred of these recruits were to be infantry who should arrive in Perth between 1 and 10 September. Following them were to be 300 men who would be mounted by the Estates as dragoons. The clan history claims that Seaforth led 4,000 men from the Western Isles and Ross to Lanark, but then returned for the harvest. If this is not a fabrication, it is a very intriguing fact. Supposing that these men had reached the earl of Lanark, it is doubtful that he would have permitted them to return north in the face of opposition by the Whiggamores and Cromwell. Also there is no mention of the Mackenzie force other than in the family history. In 1649 Seaforth fled to the Netherlands. Charles II made him Secretary of State for Scotland, but Seaforth died in 1651 at Schiedam after Worcester.[53]

Lord Sinclair's Horse

Colonel: John, 9th Lord Sinclair

Lord Sinclair was an experienced colonel in the Covenanting armies, but he was also a man with royalist sympathies. The Estates appointed him a colonel of horse for Fife on 4 May 1648. Sinclair was given permission to raise eighty horse from the shire. His men were presumably part of the Engager army at Stirling, because on 20 September Sinclair was one of the nobles ordered by the Commission of the General Assembly to disband the army or face excommunication. After the Treaty of Stirling his troop would have disbanded. Sinclair later repented for supporting the Engagement and accompanied the Army of the Kingdom to Worcester. There he fell prisoner to the English and was imprisoned in Windsor Castle until the Restoration.[54]

Earl of Traquair's Horse

Colonel: John, 1st earl of Traquair

Traquair was Charles I's chief lay officer of state before the Covenanters took over the government. He was impeached by them in 1641. Before the battle of Philiphaugh his son, Lord Linton, joined Montrose, but then deserted. Traquair refused Montrose shelter at his home after the battle. On 4 May 1648 the Estates commissioned him a colonel of horse for Peeblesshire and Dumfriesshire. Each shire was to provide the earl with forty troopers. Traquair spent £60,000 in raising 600 horse for the expedition, which he and his son accompanied. They were with Middleton's force of cavalry on 17 August. After leaving Baillie at Warrington Traquair fled with his horse and Hamilton to Malpas, Salops. Then the earl and his son surrendered themselves to the English. Traquair was warded for four years in Warwick Castle before returning to Scotland. The regiment was dispersed and the men became prisoners of the English after their colonel's defection.[55]

Earl of Tullibardine's Foot

Colonel: James, 2nd earl of Tullibardine

Tullibardine was a colonel both in the Army of the Solemn League and Covenant and the Home Army. From 1646 the earl had been the sheriff of Perthshire. In 1647 he voted against the surrender of Charles I to the English. On 4 May 1648 he received a commission as colonel of a Perthshire infantry regiment from the parliament. He was to raise 800 men from the country excluding the burghs of Perth and Culross, and the wasted lands. Sometime in July his regiment entered England without the earl. It served at the battle of Winwick, if not at the other skirmishes which involved the Engager Army. On 19 August 131 officers and men became prisoners of the English at Warrington

Bridge. Tullibardine was barred from holding a place of public trust by the kirk party, but returned to the government before Worcester.[56]

Urry's Horse

Colonel: William Urry

Urry had served as the lieutenant colonel of Van Druschke's Horse, a regiment notorious for its behaviour, in the Army of the Solemn League and Covenant. On 4 May 1648 the Estates appointed Urry colonel of horse. He was to levy forty troopers from Renfrewshire and twenty more from Dunbartonshire. The Estates provided Urry with £2,333 6s. 8d. to raise twenty more horse. However, on 26 May the Committee of Estates withdrew the money, ordering Urry instead to levy ten horse from Berwickshire and ten from Roxburghshire previously assigned to Sir John Brown. His unit was in arms by early June. It fought under Middleton at Mauchline Moor, where Urry was wounded. The troop entered England on 8 July, and probably served in all actions of the campaign. On Middleton's night ride of 17-18 August from Wigan to the Preston area and south again Urry was severely wounded. The troop ceased to exist in the following week. Most of the men became prisoners of the English.[57]

Lord Yester's Foot

Colonel: John, Lord Yester

Lieutenant Colonel: Sir James Hay of Linplumt

Major: William Lyall of Bassendean

Yester had served as a Covenanter colonel in the First Bishops' War and in the Army of the Solemn League and Covenant. However, from 1642-43 he had accompanied the royal army in England. On 4 May 1648 the Estates appointed Yester and the laird of Waughton (or if the latter refused, Yester alone) colonels of Haddingtonshire. The regiment was to consist of 1,200 foot. Waughton, who was a member of the kirk party, failed to take up the commission, thus Yester became the sole colonel. Yester raised his men from Haddingtonshire and Tweeddale. On 2 July some soldiers of the regiment entered Oldhamstocks kirk and made a great noise before the minister entered. One of the men stood on the stool of repentance. The disturbance was ended by some men of Lauderdale's Horse. Later in July Yester's Foot entered England with the colonel. At the surrender at Warrington Bridge only eighty-one men and officers were present. Yester escaped to Scotland, where he later satisfied the Kirk. In 1651 he defended Neidpath Castle against the English.[58]

NOTES

1. *APS*, VI, ii. 54-5; *Three Letters Concerning the Surrender of Many Scottish Lords to the High Sheriff of the County of Chester* (London, 1648), 6; *Scots Peerage*, i. 473.
2. NLS, Adv. MS. 29.2.9, 190-lv; *APS*, VI, ii. 54, 56.
3. SRO, PR Fordoun, 19 June 1650; *APS*, VI, ii. 55; *Scots Peerage*, i. 15-18.
4. SRO, PR Lanark, 12 December 1648; *APS*, VI, ii. 55; *Three Letters*, 4.
5. *APS*, VI, ii. 56; *RCGA*, ii. 379.
6. SRO, KSR Falkirk, 3 April 1650; *APS*, VI, ii. 55, 115; 'A Declaration from Scotland concerning the Advance of the Scots Army: Who are come into England' (London, 1648), in *Reprints of Rare Tracts Chiefly Illustrative of the History of the Northern counties*, 3 vols., ed. M. A. Richardson (Newcastle, 1845-9), ii. 11; Turner, *Memoirs*, 55, 58; *Scots Peerage*, ii. 360-2; A. Woolrych, *Battles of the English Civil War* (paperback edn., London, 1966), 159.
7. *Scots Peerage*, ii. 362; Woolrych, *Battles*, 164-5, 167-9, 172-4, 177, 180-1.
8. *APS*, VI, ii. 55; *RCGA*, iii. 161; *Three Letters*, 1, 5; A. Maxwell, *The History of Old Dundee* (Edinburgh, 1884), 515-6; *Scots Peerage*, viii. 69.
9. SRO, PR Ayr, 27 December 1650; *APS*, VI, ii. 55; J. Paterson, *History of the county of Ayr*, 2 vols. (Edinburgh, 1847), i. 163; *Scots Peerage*, iii. 344-5.
10. SRO, PA. 15.10, 3; *RCGA*, ii. 74.
11. *APS*, VI, ii. 95; and note preceding.
12. SRO, KSR Oldhamstocks, 28 May, 2, 11 June 1648; PA. 11.6, 8v; *APS*, VI, ii. 55; *RCGA*, ii. 145; *Ibid.*, iii. 136; Turner, *Memoirs*, 76; *Scots Peerage*, ii. 595-6.
13. *RCGA*, ii. 66; R. Gordon and G. Gordon, *A Geneaological History of the Earldom of Sutherland* (Edinburgh, 1813), 42; *Scots Peerage*, iii. 35-6.
14. SRO, PA. 15.10, 3.
15. *APS*, VI, ii. 56; *RCGA*, ii. 199-200, 280, 367; *Three Letters*, 1.
16. *APS*, VI, ii. 54; *Baillie*, iii. 457; *RCGA*, iii. 161; *Three Letters*, 4.
17. *APS*, VI, ii. 56; *RCGA*, iii. 170.
18. *APS*, VI, ii. 55; *Three Letters*, 3.
19. *APS*, VI, ii. 56; *RCGA*, iii. 136.
20. *APS*, VI, ii. 56; *Scots Peerage*, iii. 578.
21. NLS, Dep. 175, Box 87/2.
22. *APS*, VI, ii. 56; *RCGA*, iii. 68; *Scots Peerage*, iv. 477.
23. *A Letter Concerning the Souldiers and their Orders about the Commissioners sent from Parliament, to treet with the Kings Majesty* (London, 1648), 2-6; *Three Letters*, 4; see above, 251.
24. SRO, PR Stranraer, i. 179v; *Army of the Covenant*, ii. 289, 401; Foster, *Members*, 225; Paterson, *Ayr*, i. 163; Stevenson, *Covenanters*, 257-8.
25. *APS*, VI, ii. 55; *RCGA*, ii. 66; *Ibid.*, iii. 272; Paterson, *Ayr*, i. 163; *Scots Peerage*, iv. 247-8; Stevenson, *Covenanters*, 258-60.
26. *Three Letters*, 4.
27. *Scots Peerage*, iv. 376-7.
28. *APS*, VI, ii. 55, 72; 'Declaration from Scotland', ii. 10; *Memoirs of Guthry*, 269; *Three Letters*, 3; Turner, *Memoirs*, 64; W. Gordon, *The History of the . . . Family of Gordon* (Edinburgh, 1727), 558-9; *Scots Peerage*, iv. 176-7; Woolrych, *Battles*, 163-5, 169, 172.
29. *APS*, VI, ii. 122; *Scots Peerage*, iv. 377-8; Woolrych, *Battles*, 160, 172-3, 179.
30. *APS*, VI, ii. 54; *Baillie*, iii. 457; *RCGA*, iii. 242; *Three Letters*, 5; *Scots Peerage*, 477-8.
31. *APS*, VI, ii. 56; *RCGA*, ii. 187, 195, 313.
32. NLS, Dep. 175, Box 67, 609, 633; SRO, PR Elgin, i. 252; *APS*, VI, ii. 56, 62, 736; *Army of the Covenant*, i. lviii.
33. *APS*, VI, ii. 55; Foster, *Members*, 200; *Scots Peerage*, vi. 60.

34. SRO, KSR Dundonald, i. 38v; *APS*, VI, ii. 55; *List of Regiments*.

35. SAUL, PR St. Andrews, i. 144; *APS*, VI, ii. 55; *Three Letters*, 5; *Scots Peerage*, v. 85, 87.

36. *APS*, VI, ii. 56; *Selections from the Minutes of the Presbyteries of St. Andrews and Cupar, 1641-48*, ed. G. R. Kinloch (Abbotsford Club, vii, 1837), 163; *Scots Peerage*, v. 120-2.

37. SRO, KSR Gargunnock, i. 45; *APS*, VI, ii. 56; *RCGA*, iii. 66; *St. Andrews and Cupar*, 61; *Scots Peerage*, iv. 379.

38. NRH, OPR Largo, 23 December 1650; SRO, KSR Oldhamstocks, 9 July 1648; *APS*, VI, ii. 56; *Scots Peerage*, v. 303.

39. SRO, PA. 7.23/2.57; *APS*, VI, ii. 55; *The Sutherland Book*, 3 vols., ed. W. Fraser (Edinburgh, 1894), i. 249.

40. SRO, PA. 15.10, 2; *Fasti*, i. 198.

41. SRO, GD. 75, 655, 657; PA. 15.10, 2; *APS*, VI, ii. 56; *Ibid.*, VII, 52; *List of Regiments*; *RCGA*, iii. 85.

42. *APS*, VI, ii. 55; *Three Letters*, 4; *Scots Peerage*, viii. 216.

43. *APS*, VI, ii. 55; *RCGA*, iii. 161; *Scots Peerage*, vi. 57-9.

44. *APS*, VI, ii. 55; *RCGA*, iii. 170; *Three Letters*, 5; *Scots Peerage*, vii. 20-1.

45. *APS*, VI, ii. 56, 122; *Army of the Covenant*, i. lviii; *RCGA*, iii. 179; Paterson, *Ayr*, i. 163; *Scots Peerage*, viii. 450-1.

46. NLS, MS. 2961, 131; SRO, PA. 11.6, 6; *APS*, VI, ii. 55; *Scots Peerage*, vi. 320.

47. G. Burnet, *The Memoirs of the Lives and actions of James and William, dukes of Hamilton and Castle-Herald* (2nd edn., Oxford, 1852), 453; 'Declaration from Scotland', ii. 11; Stevenson, *Covenanters*, 260-1; Woolrych, *Battles*, 161-2, 164-5.

48. 'Duke of Hamilton's Expedition to England 1648', ed. C. H. Firth, *Miscellany of the Scottish History Society*, ii. (Scot. His. Soc., 1st Ser., xliv, 1904), 310; Woolrych, *Battles*, 180-1.

49. SRO, PA. 7.6, 154, 295; PR Perth, iii. 180; Adair, *Narrative*, 149, 167; Stevenson, *Covenanters*, 262, 269-77.

50. SRO, PR Deer, ii. 9; *APS*, VI, ii. 55; Foster, *Members*, 144; A. Fraser, *The Frasers of Phillorth*, 3 vols. (Edinburgh, 1879), i. 176; *Scots Peerage*, vii. 441.

51. *Three Letters*, 5.

52. *APS*, VI, ii. 54; *Baillie*, iii. 457; *RCGA*, ii. 386; *Three Letters*, 5-6; *Scots Peerage*, vii. 341, 343-5.

53. SRO, PA. 7/23.2.7; A. Mackenzie, *History of Clan Mackenzie* (Inverness, 1879), 193-4; 204; *Scots Peerage*, vii. 508.

54. *APS*, VI, ii. 56; *Kirkcaldie*, 328; *RCGA*, ii. 66; 'Unpublished papers of John, Seventh Lord Sinclair, Covenanter and Royalist', ed. J. A. Fairley, *Trans. Buchan Field Club*, viii. (1904-5), 149, 151; *Scots Peerage*, vii. 576.

55. *APS*, VI, ii. 56; *Ibid.*, VII, 236-7; *Three Letters*, 1; Gordon, *Family of Gordon*, ii. 563; Woolrych, *Battles*, 179.

56. *APS*, VI, ii. 55; *Three Letters*, 4; *Scots Peerage*, iii. 414.

57. SRO, PA. 15.10, 7; *APS*, VI, ii. 56; *Army of the Covenant*, i. lxxi; *Ibid.*, ii. 527, 537; Turner, *Memoirs*, 57, 65.

58. SRO, KSR Oldhamstocks, 9 July, 1648; *APS*, VI, ii. 55; *RCGA*, ii. 339; *Three Letters*, 3; R. A. Hay, *Geneaologie of the Hayes of Tweeddale* (Edinburgh, 1835), 27, 29. One soldier satisfied the kirk on 7 January 1649 and paid £1 4s. to the poor box, SRO, KSR Oldhamstocks, 27 August, 31 December 1648, 7 January 1649.

9
Whiggamore Raid, 1648

Marquis of Argyll's Forces

Commander: Archibald, 1st marquis of Argyll

In spring 1648 Argyll had been one of the leading opponents of the Engagement. However, after a series of meetings with lairds and nobles from Fife and the southwest he decided against actively opposing the Engagement in the field. In late August as the news of Hamilton's defeat filtered north to the territory of Clan Campbell Argyll decided to join those already stirring in the southwest. On 8 September Argyll was at Dumbarton with a force of 300 Campbells, 300 foot from the Lennox and western Stirlingshire, and 100 horse. (This assembly may have contained men of Argyll's Highland Foot). Two days later the force stayed in Gargunnock. At 11 p.m. on the 10th Argyll entered Stirling, having possibly received 400 foot as reinforcements. He treated with the castle garrison, and set guards at the Bridge, the Burgh Mills, and gates. While Argyll was eating dinner with the earl of Mar word reached him of Lanark's and Munro's approach with 4,000 men. Argyll and his horse escaped south to the Whiggamore forces at Falkirk. His other men were not so fortunate. The foot soldiers fled north towards the bridge and escape. But the Engagers caught up with them and Munro's troops killed 100 foot. These included forty of the men raised by Glenorchy under the command of William Campbell of Glenfalloch. Others from Argyll's force fell prisoner to Lanark's, Glencairn's and Crawford-Lindsay's men. However, the rout at Stirling was to be the Engagers' last victory.[1]

Earl of Buccleuch's Retinue

Commander: Francis, 2nd earl of Buccleuch

Buccleuch had served as the colonel of the Tweeddale Foot in the Army of the Solemn League and Covenant. More importantly he was the head of the Scotts, and from 1647 the sheriff of Selkirkshire. In September he was one of the first raisers of Whiggamore forces when he brought out the Scotts. They reached the main body on 12 September at Falkirk. After the Treaty of Stirling Buccleuch's men returned home to bring in the harvest. Buccleuch himself was to be one of the kirk party nobles, attending the parliaments of 1649 and 1650. He also had a foot regiment in the Army of the Covenants.[2]

Earl of Cassillis' Horse

Commander: John, 6th earl of Cassillis

The earl of Cassillis was a Covenanter of long-standing. He had acted as a colonel in the Bishops' Wars and in the Army of the Solemn League and Covenant. Cassillis was one of the principal leaders of the Whiggamore Raid. In September he raised 600 horse (mounted bonnet lairds, tenants, and peasants), from Carrick and Galloway. His cavalry were posted to Linlithgow by the Whiggamores. During the Engagers march from Corstorphine to Stirling they surprised Cassillis and his force which fled east to Edinburgh. Later Cassillis and his troopers advanced with the main force to Falkirk. On 29 September they went home to harvest the crops. Cassillis became one of the prominent kirk party nobles in 1649.[3]

Earl of Eglinton's Force

Commander: Alexander, 6th earl of Eglinton

In 1648 Eglinton at sixty years old was one of the oldest leaders on either the Engager or Whiggamore side. He had commanded forces for the Covenanters since 1639. In 1648 one of his regiments (that in Ulster), disobeyed his orders and supported the Engagement. In late August his son, Colonel Robert Montgomery, on learning of Hamilton's defeat raised a force of Ayrshire men. With them he attacked a troop of Lanark's horse quartering in the county. This was the first incident in the Raid. Robert Montgomery became one of the major generals of the Whiggamore forces. During the course of the campaign his men destroyed £200 worth of corn outside of Lanark while pursuing one of the Barclays. Eglinton acted in conjunction with Loudoun in raising a force of 6,000 foot and horse from Kyle, Cunningham, Renfrewshire, Clydesdale, Avondale, and Lesmahagow. Eglinton marched on Edinburgh, taking the castle on 5 September. A week later Eglinton and the other Whiggamores advanced to Falkirk where they entered into negotiations with the Engagers. On 29 September Eglinton and his men returned to the southwest for the harvest, having successfully ended the rule of the Engagers with Cromwell's aid. Eglinton attended all of the kirk party parliaments, and received a prominent military command.[4]

Fife Forces

Of the Whiggamore forces these are the most mysterious. The earl of Leven, and Lords Balmerino, Burleigh, and Elcho probably led parts of this contingent. Nothing is known as to the size of the forces raised from Fife. On Sunday 10 September the ministers throughout Fife read an ordinance from the Lord Chancellor, the earl of Loudoun, that all men should join the well-affected in Edinburgh to oppose the Engagers. The minister of Ceres exhorted his parishioners to go out to the Whiggamores, and to encourage them he promised to leave with them on Monday. On 12 September the Fife contingent joined the Whiggamores at Falkirk. As there had been widespread opposition to the Engager levy in May, it would be reasonable to assume that men came from all over the county. On 29 September following the surrender of the Engagers, the Fifers returned home for the harvest.[5]

Lord Kirkcudbright's Forces

Commander: John, 3rd Lord Kirkcudbright

Lord Kirkcudbright raised reinforcements for the Whiggamores from Galloway in September. His force reached the main body at Falkirk sometime in mid-September, where they remained until the army disbanded on the 29th. In 1649 Kirkcudbright was one of the sixteen nobles to attend the January parliament.[6]

Earl of Loudoun's Forces

Commander: John, 1st earl of Loudoun

Minister: David Dickson[7]

Loudoun had been a prominent Covenanter from the beginning of the struggles. He had commanded regiments in the Bishops' Wars and in the Army of the Solemn League and Covenant. Since 1641 Loudoun had served as Lord Chancellor of Scotland. In 1647 he was one of the three nobles to negotiate the Engagement with Charles I on the Isle of Wight. In 1648 the earl was president of the Engager parliament. However, he was more committed to the Covenants and presbyterianism than Lauderdale. His principles led Loudoun to desert the Engagers in the summer. In late August and early September he was involved in raising men from Ayrshire, Renfrewshire, and Lanarkshire with the earl of Eglinton. This force eventually reached 6,000 men. The minister, David Dickson, aided Loudoun in bringing out the risers. Loudoun's and Eglinton's contingent, which formed the main body of the Raiders, disbanded on 29 September returning home for the harvest. Loudoun continued as Lord Chancellor for the kirk party regime and commanded forces in the Army of the Covenants.[8]

NOTES

1. *The Black Book of Taymouth*, ed. C. Innes (Bannatyne Club, c. 1855), 103; G. Burnet, *The Memoirs of the Lives and actions of James and William, dukes of Hamilton and Castle-Herald* (2nd edn., Oxford, 1852), 466, 471-2; *Memoirs of Guthry*, 288, 290-1; J. Lane, *The Reign of King Covenant* (London, 1956), 196.

2. *List of Regiments; The Scotts of Buccleuch*, ed. W. Fraser, 2 vols. (Edinburgh, 1878), ii. 235; *Memoirs of Guthry*, 292, 296; Wilson, *History*, 66; *Scots Peerage*, ii. 235.

3. Burnet, *Memoirs*, 466, 471; *List of Regiments; Memoirs of Guthry*, 296; Wilson, *History*, 66; W. Gordon, *The History of the . . . Family of Gordon*, 2 vols. (Edinburgh, 1727), ii. 565-6; *Scots Peerage*, ii. 478, 481.

4. *Army of the Covenant*, i. xiv; *List of Regiments*; Burnet, *Memoirs*, 465, 470; *Extracts from the Records of the Royal Burgh of Lanark with Charters and Documents Relating to the Burgh, AD. 1150-1722*, ed. R. Renwick (Glasgow, 1893), 465; *Memoirs of Guthry*, 285, 296; J. K. Hewison, *The Covenanters*, 2 vols. (Glasgow, 1913), i. 448; W. M. Metcalfe, *A History of the county of Renfrew from the earliest times* (New Club, xiii, 1905), 269; *Scots Peerage*, iii. 445-6.

5. NRH, OPR Anstruther Easter, 30 May 1648; SRO, KSR Ceres, i. 21; KSR Falkland, i. 74; KSR Kingsbarns, i. 18; KSR Newburn, 28 May 1648; PR Dunfermline, i. 40; *APS*, VI, ii. 124; *HMC Report* lxxii (Committee of War of Fife), 235, (Presbytery of Kirkcaldy), 236; *Memoirs of Guthry*, 292, 296; *Selections from the minutes of the Presbyteries of St. Andrews and Cupar, 1641-48*, ed. G. R. Kinloch (Abbotsford Club, vii, 1837), 41.

6. Burnet, *Memoirs*, 471; *Scots Peerage*, v. 268.

7. *Memoirs of Guthry*, 285.

8. *APS*, VI, ii. 124; *Memoirs of Guthry*, 285, 296; Metcalfe, *Renfrew*, 269; *Scots Peerage*, v. 506-7.

10
Army of the Covenants, 1648-1650

Viscount Arbuthnott's Foot

Colonel: Robert, 1st viscount Arbuthnott

Minister: William Cheyne[1]

Arbuthnott was a Mearns nobleman who in 1644 had shared the command of a foot regiment from the shire with the earl Marischal. On 28 February 1649 the Estates commissioned him colonel of foot for the Mearns and Marischal's portion of Aberdeenshire. The two shires were to provide 800 men for Arbuthnott. On 14 June Arbuthnott's Aberdeenshire Company of Foot was ordered to quarter in Old Aberdeen burgh and landward. On 6 July the regiment was ordered to Perth, where it was to receive further orders. A muster of 31 July revealed that only one company of eighty men had been raised in the preceding five months. Six days later the Estates gave Arbuthnott permission to raise a further 450 foot to bring the regiment up to a reasonable size. In the course of 1649 Aberdeen raised thirty men for the regiment, the outrigging of each man costing the burgh £33 6s. 8d. On 3 July 1650 Arbuthnott received permission to levy a further 900 men from the two shires. Aberdeen provided thirty men, but the burgh was still deficient by sixty men in early September. The last mention of the regiment was on 1 October, when a Major Straquhan refused a charge in the regiment as being unworthy of him. This suggests either that Arbuthnott's Foot was never properly raised or that it suffered heavy losses at Dunbar. The former hypothesis probably is correct.[2]

Arnot's Horse Troop

Routmaster: (?) Arnot of Arnot

A mysterious unit which was first mentioned on 31 July 1649 as consisting of sixty troopers quartered in Fife. On 20 May 1650 it received orders to go north to an unknown destination. On 19 June the troop is mentioned for the last time as being ordered to Fife.[3]

Arnott's Horse

Colonel: Charles Arnott

Major: William Johnston

On 1 June 1649 Lieutenant Colonel Arnott's horse troop is listed as an 'old troop'. Then a corporalship was ordered to quarter in Lanarkshire, Ayrshire, and Renfrewshire except for the burgh and presbytery of Glasgow. The troop was expanded into a regiment by September 1650 and fought at Dunbar. On 19 September Arnott's Horse and another cavalry regiment were ordered to Burntisland to protect the burgh from the English. The next day the Committee of Estates' minute refers to Arnott's Horse as one of five cavalry regiments ordered to Fife for the same purpose. It was still quartering in southern Fife on 12 November. On 31 March 1651 Major Johnston, who had served in garrisons in the north and in Edinburgh Castle, was cited for treason regarding the surrender of the latter. Five days later the Commission of the General Assembly noted that Johnston had gone over to the English, but nonetheless cited him to appear at Perth. On 7 May the regiment was assigned to the 3rd Cavalry Brigade with Balcarres' and Sir Walter Scott's Horse. This brigade was under the command of Sir John Brown. Its position in the line of battle was to be the third from the extreme left flank. The last reference to Arnott's Horse occurs on 17 June when it was ordered to Stirling, with the other horse regiments in Fife. Each trooper was to receive £3 on his departure from the landlords in Fife.[4] While the regiment is not mentioned again it ceased to exist sometime in September 1651.

Train of Artillery

General of Artillery: James Wemyss (of Caskieberran)

In February 1649 the Covenanters had eight cannon at Dumbarton Castle, while at Stirling there were five 18 lbrs., one 12 lbr., three 9 lbrs. and ten 3 lbrs. Wemyss like Sir Alexander Hamilton before him had gained his experience as an artillerist on the continent. In 1650 he became the General of Artillery for the Army of the Covenants. Besides the artillery planted in the Leith-Calton Hill line and that in Edinburgh Castle and within the walls of the burgh, the army had a train of field pieces. During the 1650 campaign they were used at the skirmish of Gorgie. At Dunbar the artillery accompanying Leslie's army was not put to use due to the surprise attack by the English. The number of guns captured has been given as follows: thirty guns, or thirty-two guns including small calibre, leather-bound, and great guns, or twenty-two field guns plus smaller calibre ones. (Field guns ranged in size from 3 lbrs. to 24 lbrs.) With the loss of the guns at Dunbar, Wemyss was forced to strip burghs and castles of artillery pieces to provide guns for the army.[5]

Balbegno's Foot

Colonel: James Wood of Balbegno

Minister: Thomas Lindsay[6]

Balbegno served as a Mearns M.P. in 1649. On 5 September 1650 the Committee of Estates nominated him colonel of foot for the Mearns and Marischal's portion of Aberdeenshire. In December Balbegno petitioned the Committee for Military Affairs that the regiment be allowed to quarter for eight to ten days in Montrose as he awaited for the last levies to come in, lest the others flee the colours. To supply the regiment the Committee ordered Aberdeen to provide one and a half pounds of meal per man per day. It also ordered that Balbegno's remain in Aberdeen until it was made up to strength. On 18 December the burgh of Aberdeen received a receipt for the last twenty of the sixty men required for the regiment. On 16 April 1651 the Committee of Estates received a petition from Baledgarno parish asking relief from quartering by the regiment, which was granted. On 7 May the regiment was in or near Stirling, and Balbegno received orders to muster it. On 24 May the Committee of Estates ordered the regiment to quarter at the Head of Forth and the nearby passes with Lawers' and Valleyfield's Foot. At the musters which took place between 10 June and 18 July the strength of the unit remained constant at 244 foot soldiers. There is no further reference to the regiment, but it would have ceased to exist sometime in September, either being destroyed in England or in Scotland.[7]

Balnagowan's Foot

Colonel: David Ross of Balnagowan

Ministers: Arthur Forbes, David Ross[8]

Balnagowan was chief of the Rosses. In April 1650 he raised a force of Rosses and joined Strachan's force. Balnagowan's men were few in number, as the total force of Rosses and Munros was only 400 men. They were unreliable allies, whose loyalty depended on the ability of Strachan's cavalry to gain victory. When the Covenanter horse scattered Montrose's army at Carbisdale on 26 April, the Rosses and Munros proceeded to slaughter the fleeing royalists. On 20 December 1650 parliament appointed Balnagowan colonel of foot for his family and for Ross and Inverness-shire. Balnagowan impoverished his estates by raising the regiment. Unusually, details survive of the soldiers' clothing; the men wore a uniform of red Ross tartan trews with blue French bonnets. Balnagowan's was near Stirling by 13 May 1651. Although the clan history claims that Balnagowan raised 800 men for the regiment, the muster rolls tell another story. By 11 June the regiment, consisting of 416 men, was in or near Stirling. On 5 July the regiment received sixty-six recruits. The last recorded muster gives the unit a strength of 476 common soldiers. Balnagowan's Foot served on the Worcester campaign, and the regiment was destroyed at the battle on 3 September. Balnagowan was taken prisoner and warded in Windsor Castle and the Tower. He was paroled but died soon afterwards, being buried on 29 December 1653 in Westminster Abbey.[9]

Lord Brechin's Horse

Colonel: George, Lord Brechin

Lieutenant Colonel: Sir Thomas Nairn

Ministers: James Stratoun, Robert Rule, Lawrence Skinner, Alexander Mill/ Mylne[10]

Lord Brechin was abroad for most of the struggles of the mid-seventeenth century. However, in 1649 on 28 February he received the commission as colonel of horse for Angus, the Mearns, and Marischal's portion of Aberdeenshire. Besides Brechin the Estates also named his lieutenant colonel and one routmaster. Angus was to provide 280 troopers for the regiment, while the Mearns and Aberdeenshire levied 200 more. On 31 July there were sixty troopers in the colonel's troop and fifty each in Lieutenant Colonel Nairn's and Routmaster Robert Arbuthnott's troops. On 6 August the Estates ordered the levying of more troopers. Mearns was to raise forty-four men, Angus would contribute 160 men. Aberdeenshire would levy 186 men which would be split with the master of Forbes. The next mention of the regiment occurs on 19 June 1650 when the Lieutenant Colonel's troop was ordered to Perthshire; Brechin's was sent to Linlithgowshire; and Arbuthnott's to Haddingtonshire. On 3 July Brechin was given permission to raise more troopers to bring the regiment up to the strength it should have achieved in summer 1649. Angus was to levy 160 troopers, but Dundee was exempted from contributing men. Mearns was to provide forty-four men, Aberdeenshire 186 men, again to be split with the master of Forbes. These would be made into six troops, as follows: 150 of the Angus men into two troops, the ten remaining Angus men and the Mearns recruits into one troop, and Aberdeenshire levy into three troops of 62 men each. It is impossible to determine the success of this levy. Brechin's Horse served as part of Leslie's army in summer 1650, and was at Dunbar. Lieutenant Colonel Nairn with officers of Montgomery's Horse discovered Charles II sheltering in a cottage on the land of Clova on 5 October, following the king's abandonment of The Start. On 15 October the regiment was ordered to serve under Leslie against the royalists in the northeast. On Monday 21 October, Brechin's was part of Sir John Brown's force which was out against Middleton. Following the battle of Newtyle, half of the regiment deserted to Middleton. It is not known whether they rejoined the loyal members of the regiment after the Treaty of Strathbogie. In April 1651 Brechin's Horse was noted as being one of the regiments which had been in and out of Angus since September. On 7 May Brechin's was assigned to the 1st Cavalry Brigade with Rothes' and Riccarton's Horse under Leslie on the extreme left wing of the battle line. The regiment was quartered in Fife, probably in the presbytery of Dunfermline, as the following incident suggests. On 4 June the presbytery learned that a woman had been 'abused' and raped on the way to Inverkeithing by a routmaster in the regiment. The presbytery instituted proceedings, but nothing more is heard of the case. On 17 June Brechin's with the other cavalry regiments in Fife was ordered to Stirling. The Fife landlords were to provide each trooper with £3 on the departure of the regiments. On 20 July the regiment was back in Fife, fighting at the battle of Inverkeithing. Brechin was wounded during the battle, but the regiment managed to escape. In August some troopers seized £25 from one Guy, an agent of Samuel Atkins in Leith. On 30 November Atkins requested the return of the money as he had heard Brechin was a 'gentleman of much honor'. The regiment remained on foot in the north until sometime in 1652 when Brechin surrendered to Monck.[11]

Brodie's Horse Troop

Routmaster: Brodie

Another little known unit, which is first mentioned as containing forty-six troopers on 31 July 1649. On 19 June 1650 it was ordered to Linlithgowshire, and is not referred to again.[12]

Brown's Horse

Colonels: Major General Sir John Brown (of Fordell), Sir Arthur Forbes

Lieutenant Colonel: William Bruce

Ministers: Samuel Row, Robert Young, George Murray, John Knox[13]

Major General Brown had served as a lieutenant colonel and colonel in the Army of the Solemn League and Covenant and as a troop commander in the New Model Army. He was an M.P. for Perthshire in 1649-50. On 28 February 1649 Brown received a commission as colonel of the Perthshire Horse. The shire was to levy 480 troopers. However, by 31 July the regiment consisted of only Brown's and Bruce's troops of seventy-five and fifty-eight troopers respectively. On 2 August the Estates ordered an investigation into the finances of Brown's troop to determine if it owed a refund to the monthly maintenance. Four days later Perthshire was ordered to put out 228 troopers for the regiment. On 16 January 1650 Captain Lieutenant John Oliphant, the effective commander of Brown's troop, asked the presbytery of Perth to provide a testimonial for his troop. The presbytery ordered the ministers to contact the heritors and elders of their parishes to learn of the troop's behaviour. It must be assumed that its conduct was satisfactory for no more is heard regarding the matter. In May 1650 a case of fornication regarding trooper David Lin of Bruce's troop reached the kirk session of Cumnock. Although the incident had occurred in summer 1649, it dragged on without resolution until early July 1650. With that, information on the peacetime activities of the regiment ends.[14]

In 1650-51 Brown's Horse was involved in a series of military activities. On 19 June 1650 Brown's troop was ordered to Perthshire. On 3 July Perthshire received instructions to levy 288 troopers to make up three troops of ninety-five men each. The burgh of Perth was exempted from the levy. As with other units in the Army of the Covenants Brown's Horse included former Engagers. In this unit one cornet, if not other men, had served on the Engagement. On 13 August Brown was one of those who presented the West Kirk Declaration to the Committee of Estates. However, the regiment was quartering north of the Tay. On 18 August a case of bastardy reached the Alyth kirk session in the presbytery of Meigle that one trooper had fathered a child. An elder was assigned to attend the officers of the regiment in Boat of Borders to try the matter. The trooper eventually confessed the crime, but no action was taken against him. On 2 September the regiment was with Leslie's army. On that night Brown supported Ker and Strachan in arguing with Leslie that he fight at Dunbar. The regiment was engaged the next day, but due to being mounted it escaped to Stirling. The English claimed that Brown was captured, although this was just magnifying their victory. Due to Middleton's rising Brown received orders to take his regiment and Castle Stuart's north from Stirling on 15 October. On Monday six days later Brown sent a trumpeter to Middleton, who was in command of 1,000 foot and horse, to lay down his arms or face attack. (Brown had now been reinforced by Brechin's Horse.) Instead of waiting to be set upon, Middleton with half of his force attacked Brown in Newtyle. The royalists killed one officer, fifteen troopers, and took 120 prisoners. Half of Brechin's men deserted as did other men in the area. Brown's defeat was seen to herald the restoration of Charles II to his regal authority. By 12 November Brown's Horse was quartering in southern Fife. Meanwhile in the presbytery of Dunblane a trooper had a fruitful liaison with an inhabitant of Port parish. However, when the case reached the presbytery in February 1651 it was learned that the trooper was beyond jurisdiction of the church courts, as the man had been killed or captured at Dunbar. Of more immediate interest in the church records was the announcement at Kinglassie, presbytery of Kirkcaldy, on 23 March that anyone having complaints against the soldiers should put them into Brown, who would redress them. The regiment was also partially quartered in Dunfermline presbytery. For on 30 April the Committee of Estates ordered the colonel to report on the regiment's receipts in the presbytery, which were badly overburdened. On 7 May Brown was made commander of the 3rd Cavalry Brigade, which consisted of three regiments. In mid-June Brown's Horse was ordered from Fife to Stirling with the other horse regiments in the shire. His troopers were to receive £3 per man on their departure. On 27 June the Committee of Estates dealt with a singular action regarding the murder of Lieutenant John McCracken, a recruiter for the regiment in Atholl. McCracken's widow requested that the Committee obtain a horse of her husband's, which had been taken by one of the murderers' accomplices. The Committee ordered the horse returned within forty-eight hours, threatening the new owner with legal proceedings if it was not. On 20 July Brown and his regiment were back in Fife. Brown was commander of the Scottish Horse at the battle of Inverkeithing. The overall commander, Holburn, was a friend of Brown's, but both men disliked the Macleans which were serving in their force. Holburn led 200 horse and two foot regiments against the English right flank. Although the right wing Scottish Horse charged well and regrouped afterwards, those on the left under Brown's personal command were too raw to regroup and most of them scattered after their initial success. Brown was wounded and fell prisoner to the English. He died in captivity in Leith on 1 September. A portion of the regiment regrouped and came under the command of Sir Arthur Forbes. Although these men were heading north from Angus at the end of August, they soon dispersed.[15] Inverkeithing was the last action of Brown's Horse.

Brymer's Foot

Colonel: (?) Brymer

Minister: John Hogg[16]

This unit was also known as the (Town of) Edinburgh Regiment. It was one of the few units in the Army of the Covenants on foot in 1648. On 21 September 1648 Leven ordered Brymer's men to quarter in the West Port area of Edinburgh. However, Brymer is listed as a reformado on 8 February 1649. But on 9 and 23 July 1650 the kirk session of the Canongate, Edinburgh, issued fourteen of his soldiers testimonials. On 26 July the Edinburgh council ordered Brymer to have his men cess and quarter on those in arrears for their taxes. The last reference to the regiment was the appointment of a chaplain on 5 August.[17] This suggests it was destroyed at Dunbar.

Buchanan's Foot

Colonel: George Buchanan of Buchanan

Lieutenant Colonel: Sir James Douglas

Ministers: Matthew Ramsay, Daniel Douglas, John Veitch, Alexander Livingston, Robert Carson[18]

Buchanan was a Covenanter of long-standing and had commanded regiments in the armies since 1639. On 3 July 1650 the Estates appointed him colonel of foot for Linlithgowshire, Clackmannanshire and Stirlingshire. Linlithgowshire was to levy 374 men. The other two shires were assigned a quota of 750 men, although Stirling burgh was exempted due to the plague. Nothing is known about the levying of the regiment, however, it served on the Dunbar campaign. There is no information about the losses it sustained at the battle, and no mention is made of the regiment or Buchanan until 20 December. Then the parliament appointed him colonel of foot for Clackmannanshire, Stirlingshire and Dunbartonshire. On 7 May 1651 the regiment was in or about Stirling burgh. Buchanan received orders to muster his men. The first muster roll is from 9 July and the last one is dated the 18th. In the course of that time the regiment maintained a constant strength of 896 common soldiers. On 20 July Buchanan's Foot was engaged in the battle of Inverkeithing. Buchanan's and Maclean's Foot were brigaded together on the right of the Scottish line. They suffered badly from the English artillery fire. With the flight of left wing horse and foot these two regiments were left alone to face the English. The Macleans with 700 Buchanans and others were encircled together. The Macleans were destroyed and Buchanan's Foot met with a similar fate. Buchanan was taken prisoner, dying at the end of the year.[19]

Lord Burleigh's Foot

Colonel: Robert, 2nd Lord Burleigh

Ministers: John Hogg, John Gray[20]

Burleigh was a Covenanter active in both the military and political spheres. In 1650 he acted as vice-president of parliament. On 28 June Burleigh was appointed to the Purging Committee. On 3 July he received a commission as colonel of foot for Roxburghshire, Selkirkshire and Peeblesshire. The first two shires were to provide 750 men, while the last was to raise 150 men. On 13 August Burleigh was one of the colonels who presented the West Kirk

Declaration to the Committee of Estates. There is no reference to his regiment during the summer campaign. However, on Christmas Eve he received orders to place twenty of his men into the House of Lochleven. From that date Burleigh's Foot disappears from the records.[21]

Campbell's Dragoons

Colonel: Colin Campbell

Colin Campbell was commissioned colonel of the Perthshire dragoons on 30 September 1650. On 17 December Campbell petitioned the Committee of Military Affairs concerning his regiment. Perthshire had been ordered to put out 200 horses for the regiment, but the committee of war had refused. Then Campbell decided to accept an offer of 100 horses with armed riders. However, the committee of war took no action on the matter. The Committee of Military Affairs attempted to resolve the impasse by ordering the Perthshire committee to raise 100 horses worth £50 each and a like number of armed riders. By February 1651 the regiment was partially raised. Between 22 February and 16/30 April the regiment received £960 13s. 4d. for maintenance from Dumbarton burgh. The Dumbarton area was the chief quartering ground for the regiment. On 18 April the Committee of Estates ordered it to aid Sir Charles Erskine, governor of Dumbarton Castle, in raising grain for his garrison from Eastwood, Mearns, Renfrew, Aschumnan, Kilbarchan and Glasgow. Ten days later the regiment received orders to send a detachment of eighty men to the island of Little Cumbrae. It was to remain there under the orders of viscount Montgomery, who owned the castle. The soldiers' horses were to be left on the mainland. The islands of Great Cumbrae and Bute were to provide the garrison's maintenance, which would be refunded them by the first maintenance from Ayrshire and Renfrewshire. In the course of the English conquest the castle of Little Cumbrae was taken and burned. Back on the mainland the regiment was extending its quarters. In May it received £54 13s. 4d. from Paisley. On 9 June the Committee of Estates mentioned that the regiment might be moved into Ayrshire and Renfrewshire depending upon the success of Major General Montgomery. Part of the regiment was then quartering in Clackmannanshire, where it was ordered not to uplift £180 in cess, as the amount had already been levied. The last mention of the dragoons is a note of the Committee of Estates on 24 June. An investigation was ordered to determine whether the regiment had taken quarters for more men than were present. If that fraud had occurred the regiment would have to repay the amount uplifted. It is conceivable that this regiment either accompanied the army on the Worcester campaign or remained in Scotland. In either case it ceased to exist after September.[22]

Earl of Cassillis' Foot

Colonel: John, 6th earl of Cassillis

Ministers: William Guthrie, Hugh Eccles[23]

In 1648 Cassillis had been one of the leaders of the Whiggamore Raid. During 1649 he became Lord Justice General of Scotland and acted as a commissioner for the Estates to Charles II in the Netherlands. On 28 June 1650 Cassillis was appointed to the Purging Committee. Five days later the earl received a commission as colonel of foot for Ayrshire, Renfrewshire and Dunbartonshire. The first two shires were to recruit 750 men, while the third levied 120 men for the regiment. Cassillis' Foot appears to have been destroyed at Dunbar, for it is not mentioned after the battle. Cassillis eventually became a supporter of the Protectorate, and remained loyal to his presbyterian ideals in the 1660s.[24]

Castle Stuart's Horse

Colonels: Quartermaster General William Stewart of Castle Stuart (1649-50), Robert, 4th viscount Kenmure (1651)

Lieutenant Colonels: John Bannatyne of Corehouse (1649/51), (?) Crawford, (1651)

Minister: Samuel Row[25]

Castle Stuart was a professional officer who had served as a colonel of foot in the Army of the Solemn League and Covenant, and New Model Army. He owned land in Galloway (Castle Stuart), and in Durham (Littleburn). In 1650 he acted as an M.P. for Wigtonshire. On 28 February 1649 the Estates appointed Castle Stuart colonel of horse for Wigtonshire and the Stewartry of Kirkcudbright. The shires were to levy 240 troopers for the regiment. Although there is no sign of any men being levied by August, the levy quota for 6 August was only 130 troopers, which suggests some men had already been raised. On 1 May 1650 the town of Edinburgh provided Castle Stuart, now Quartermaster General, with twelve men for his regiment. On 3 July the Estates ordered Galloway to levy 110 men for the regiment. Fifty-five men would be formed into one troop, while the others would be combined with Dunbartonshire levies to form a troop. Although nothing precise is known about the size of the regiment, fully recruited it would not have contained more than 260 troopers. Castle Stuart's served on the Dunbar campaign. At the battle on 3 September it was posted on the left flank, far from the point of the initial English attack. Castle Stuart barely escaped with his life. and never returned to command the regiment after the battle.[26]

For the next nine months the effective commander of the regiment was Lieutenant Colonel Bannatyne of Corehouse. After Dunbar Corehouse went to Stirling to rally the regiment, which had fled there. On 20 September Castle Stuart's and four other horse regiments were ordered to southern Fife to protect Burntisland. On 15 October Corehouse received orders to take the regiment north under Major General Brown in order to crush Middleton's rising. The regiment was engaged in the internecine battle of Newtyle. It probably served under Leslie in the campaign leading up to the Treaty of Strathbogie. Castle Stuart's horse went into winter quarters in Angus, and had its headquarters at the laird of Grange's house. The regiment departed from the shire at least once by late April 1651. In December 1650 it quartered with Kinhilt's horse troop in Kincarne and Dunblane on its way to join Major General Montgomery at Port and Kilmadock. On 20 May 1651 the Committee of Estates ordered Leslie to have the regiment restore money taken as a loan for ten days supply of corn and straw from Angus, as it had previously refused to do so. In early May Castle Stuart's Horse was assigned to the 5th Cavalry Brigade under Major General Massey with Erroll's and Drummond's Horse. Corehouse continued to act as commander of the regiment until late June.[27]

On 27 June the Committee of Estates dismissed Corehouse, making the viscount Kenmure colonel. Kenmure was an Engager, who had commanded a cavalry unit in 1648. The English had besieged and taken his seat, Kenmure Castle, in December 1650. On the day of his appointment he was given a new lieutenant colonel. The regiment received permission to recruit eighty troopers from Galloway. There is no information on this levy, but the English presence in the region suggests it was not undertaken. In July Kenmure led his regiment into England on the Worcester campaign. Kenmure's Horse formed part of the body of horse under Leslie's command at Worcester, which was stationed to the north of the city. It fled northwards after battle; the regiment disintegrated and its colonel fell prisoner. Kenmure himself later returned to Scotland and joined Glencairn's rising (1653-54). He married the daughter of an English regicide in 1655. However, in 1661 he marshalled the royalist event of the century in Scotland, Montrose's funeral in Edinburgh.[28]

Lord Coupar's Foot

Colonel: James, 1st Lord Coupar

Minister: John Cruikshank[29]

Lord Coupar received his first commission as a colonel of foot under the kirk party regime on 28 February 1649. He had previously commanded units in the armies of the First Bishops' War, and of the Solemn League and Covenant. His commission in 1649 made him colonel of the Angus Foot, which was to contain 750 men. However, he took no action to raise the regiment, concentrating his attention on the court of session to which he was newly appointed in 1649. On 3 July 1650 Coupar was appointed a colonel of Perthshire Foot. The shire was to raise 920 men, and Perth was exempted from contributing. There is no reference to the regiment's service in 1650. On 6 April 1651 a private in the regiment was cited for fathering a bastard in the parish of Culross. That is the last mention of the regiment, which presumably ceased to exist from September. Coupar was fined by both the Protectorate and Restoration regimes, in the first case for his royalism, in the second for his presbyterianism.[30]

Cragg's Horse

Colonel: Cragg

The most mysterious unit in the army, it is only mentioned in the English list of regiments engaged at Dunbar.[31]

Darroch's Foot

Colonel: Archibald Douglas of Darroch

Lieutenant Colonel: John Crichton of Crawfordton

Minister: James Brotherstaines[32]

The only mention of this regiment, other than the appointment of the chaplain, was the colonel's commission. Darroch was appointed colonel of foot for Dumfriesshire on 3 July 1650. He was to raise 900 men. The regiment was probably destroyed at Dunbar, as it disappears from the records in early August.[33]

Duffus' Foot

Colonel: Sir Alexander Sutherland of Duffus, later 1st Lord Duffus

Ministers: James Park, Alexander Symmer, William Fullerton[34]

In 1640 Duffus accompanied the earl of Sutherland to England. The next year Charles I knighted him during his Scottish visit. Duffus possessed estates in Moray; however, from 1646-47 he served as a Sutherland M.P. Between 1647 and 1650 he travelled on the continent. In 1650 Duffus returned to Scotland and then served as an M.P. for Elgin and Forresshire. On 3 July 1650 Duffus received a parliamentary commission as colonel of foot for Elginshire,

Nairnshire and part of Inverness-shire. He was to levy 750 men for the regiment. There is no information on the recruiting of men in summer 1650, or the regiment's military activities. In mid-September Duffus was on his way north presumably to levy more men for the unit. Two months later the regiment was part of the army at Stirling. On 8 December Charles II ennobled Duffus as Lord Duffus. Fifteen days later the new peer was appointed a colonel of the Moray Foot. He was to raise the last men of the previous levy from the shire. Sometime in the winter of 1650-51 the regiment was mustered. It then contained thirty non-commissioned officers, six scribes, a drum major, two pipers, five drummers, 318 privates, and fourteen sick men plus officers. On 7 May 1651 the regiment was in or near Stirling, and another muster was ordered. Between 10 June and 2 July the size of Duffus' Foot hovered around 470 men. It declined to 451 common soldiers on the 9th, but between the 11th and 18th eighty-four recruits arrived. After the army moved south Duffus and his regiment garrisoned Perth with seventy other men. Duffus was the governor of the burgh, and surrendered it to Monck after offering only light resistance on 2 August. Two companies made their way to Dundee and formed part of the ill-fated garrison. On 1 September the English stormed the burgh and the last survivors of Duffus' Foot were cut down at the great steeple of St. Mary's.[35]

Edzell's Foot

Colonel: John Lindsay of Edzell (and Canterland)

Ministers: David Campbell, Thomas Small, Thomas Pierson[36]

Edzell began his public service as an Angus J.P. in 1623. He acted as an M.P. for the shire in 1649. On 3 July 1650 the Estates commissioned him colonel of the Angus Foot. Dundee was exempted from providing men by the Estates, but this was not adhered to by Edzell. He was given permission to levy 1,214 foot from the shire. On 14 July the Dundee burgh council received orders to provide a company of men. Due to difficulties in finding men, only half of it was raised, that is ninety men. Edzell's Foot served on the summer campaign and was at Dunbar. On 3 October, or later, another company was to be raised from Dundee. The burgh council sought an exemption, but failed to receive one from the committee of war. Consequently, Dundee contributed another eighty men to the regiment. In winter 1650-51 the regiment was mustered, it was found to contain 334 privates and twenty-two sick soldiers. On double allowance were two captains, twelve sergeants, one scribe, a drum major, and a piper, on one and half allowance were the six drummers, and the nineteen corporals were on half allowance. Sometime in the first half of 1651 Edzell received the appointment as sheriff of Angus. His regiment was in or near Stirling on 7 May, when it was ordered to hold another muster. On 11 June there were 403 men in the regiment, and its strength increased to 438 soldiers by

18 July. There is no further mention of the regiment, suggesting that it served in Scotland during the summer. In the event it was disbanded or destroyed by mid-September.[37]

Lord Elcho's Horse

Colonel: David, Lord Elcho, later 2nd earl of Wemyss

Ministers: William Oliphant, Patrick Wemyss[38]

Lord Elcho was a firm Covenanter and had commanded forces in the mid-1640s. On 28 February 1649 he was appointed colonel of horse for Fife and Kinross-shire. Those two shires were to levy 440 troopers for the regiment, while Ayrshire and Renfrewshire recruited forty men for it. In April the regiment consisted of three troops: Elcho's, Routmaster Andrew Arnot of Capeldrae's and Routmaster Alexander Fraser's. The regiment then levied 100 troopers from Fife. On 31 July the regiment is listed as containing two troops, Elcho's with sixty-one men, and Capeldrae's with fifty-one men. On 6 August the Estates gave Elcho permission to levy 290 horsemen from Fife and Kinross-shire. It is doubtful that these men were raised, because on 3 July 1650 the same number (in four troops) were to be levied from both shires. Meanwhile on 19 June the Colonel's troop had been ordered to Fife. Between 15 and 22 July Fife raised 360 troopers, enough to meet its commitments to Wemyss' regiment, as well as to others. Thus by late July Wemyss had about 400 troopers under his command. While the regiment probably served on the summer campaign, there are no explicit references to it, nor are there any until mid-March 1651. From the following evidence it is certain that the regiment was quartering in Fife. On 16 March the earl of Wemyss reported to the Wemyss kirk session that his quartermaster, a Major Barclay, had perturbed worship and profaned the Sabbath by molesting God's people. The kirk session referred the matter to the presbytery so that it could be brought before the king and parliament. On 30 March Issobell Smart complained against a trooper that had wounded her in her house on a Sunday. The case was sent to the regimental officers, so that the trooper would be punished. There is no further mention of the regiment, but as Wemyss was with Argyll in the autumn it suggests that the earl's men disbanded or were taken prisoner before October.[39]

Master of Forbes' Foot

Colonel: William, master of Forbes

This regiment was probably commissioned to be raised from Aberdeenshire and Banffshire in late February 1649. On 1 June it was ordered to quarter in

Aberdeenshire, Banffshire, and the burgh of Banff; the burgh and Liberties of Aberdeen were exempted from supporting the regiment. An example of this is that nine soldiers quartered on Robert Gordon's lands in Botarns from 9 to 11 June. On 31 July the estates ordered Forbes' 200 men to be disbanded as unnecessary. However, it was still on foot on 3 February 1650 when the Aberdeen burgh council received a warrant ordering the collection of taxes and monthly maintenance for the regiment. The regiment was to receive free quarters in the burgh until the deficiency in taxes and maintenance were paid. After this date there is no further reference to the regiment.[40]

Master of Forbes' Horse

Colonel: William, master of Forbes

Lieutenant Colonel: Arthur Forbes of Echt

Ministers: Robert Davidson, Thomas Hepburn, Oliver Colt, Gabriel Maxwell, Robert Keith[41]

The master of Forbes was a loyal Covenanter and had commanded troops in various armies since 1639. His lieutenant colonel had also led retinues for the Covenanters. On 28 February 1649 the master received a commission to raise a horse regiment of 480 men from the area of Aberdeenshire outside of the earl Marischal's zone, and from Banffshire. On 6 July the regiment was ordered to Perth to receive further orders. At the end of the month it consisted of fifty-nine troopers under the master, and fifty-one men under Echt. On 6 August the master was given permission to raise fifty-six troopers from Banffshire. He was to split a recruit of 186 men from Aberdeenshire with Lord Brechin. The next references to the regiment concern soldier-sinners. On 11 November the fornication case of trooper James Cullen and Jeanne Movat reached the Echt kirk session, presbytery of Kincardine O'Neil. On 9 December the master sent Cullen back to the parish. There he paid £2 13s. 4d. to the kirk session as a fine and promised to do repentance at the pillar. The other case was not so usual. On 22 November the presbytery of Turriff requested that the master send trooper John Prerie to the presbytery for 'upbraiding' the Rev. Alexander Gordon. On 20 December the trooper appeared. Gordon had refused to baptise Prerie's child until the marriage certificate was produced. When it was the minister kept his promise. However, after a subsequent Wednesday meeting Prerie stood up and said he would make the minister sorry he had not baptised the child at once. If the child had died, Prerie continued, Gordon would never have preached again. Prerie confessed this to the minister. The presbytery ordered him to repent in sackcloth at Forgan parish church on Sunday morning, and the minister would receive him. Silence descends upon the regiment's activities until June 1650. However, it probably continued to quarter in Aberdeenshire and Banffshire. On

19 June 1650 the master's troop was ordered to Perthshire, while the lieutenant colonel's was sent to quarter in the three parishes of Angus adjacent to Perth. On 3 July the master received permission to levy more troopers. The quotas are such that it strongly suggests nothing had been done about levying men assigned in August 1649. Again the master was to levy fifty-six men from Banffshire. He was to split three troops of sixty-two troopers each from Aberdeenshire with Lord Brechin. The division probably allotted two troops to the master's regiment, as Brechin's was larger to begin with. The master's horse served on the summer campaign and at Dunbar. It is not mentioned after the battle, but it may have been transferred to Sir Alexander, Lord Forbes' command as part of the Army of the Kingdom.[42]

Freeland's Foot

Colonel: Thomas Ruthven of Freeland

Freeland had long supported the Covenants, and had also commanded military units in the armies. From 1649-51 he served as an M.P. for Perthshire. In 1649 Freeland was appointed a commissioner to the Exchequer. The only mention of his regiment is in the English list of Scots forces engaged at Dunbar. As there is no commission for Freeland, this suggests that the list is in error. Between 28 March 1651 and 1 January 1661 Freeland was elevated to the peerage as Lord Ruthven of Freeland.[43]

General of Artillery's Foot

Colonel: General of Artillery James Wemyss (of Caskieberran)

Minister: David Durie[44]

Wemyss had gained his professional training as an artillerist by serving under Gustavus Adolphus. In 1630 he settled in England. He was an inventor and innovator in artillery, small arms and mining. Wemyss was appointed Master Gunner of England in 1638. Although he apparently supported the Engagement, the kirk party regime employed him as General of Artillery and Master of Ordnance for Scotland from 1648/49. On 3 July 1650 the Estates appointed the lairds of Brodie and Cesnock, and Sir John Cheisley to consider a way to provide Wemyss with an infantry regiment. The committee must have taken positive action, because the General of Artillery's Foot fought at Dunbar. On 10 September the Committee of Estates gave Wemyss permission to levy 700 foot from Fife. By late October his regiment was quartering in southern Fife along the coast from Burntisland to Wemyss, in order to protect it from an English attack. On 28 January 1651 Ensign Andrew Hanna appeared before the kirk session of Burntisland and confessed he had tried to rape Christian Rind. On

4 February the session charged him with attempted rape and scandalous carriage, and ordered him to repent as for fornication. On the 23rd Hanna completed his repentance and was received. This is the only mention of poor behaviour by members of the regiment. On 7 May the regiment was in or about Stirling and the Committee of Estates ordered a muster. The first one occurred on 10 June and revealed a strength of 296 common soldiers; by 2 July the numbers had risen by only three men. On 7 July the Committee of Estates noted that the Fife burghs had not paid the regimental officers' entertainment money for April to June, and ordered they do so. The final muster of the regiment on 18 July placed its size at 391 men. Wemyss and his regiment took part on the Worcester campaign. The unit may have formed part of the garrison on 3 September; in any case it was destroyed at the battle. Wemyss himself was captured, but the Protectorate government appointed him Master Gunner of England. In 1660 Charles II made him General of Artillery for Scotland, but he resigned that and his other offices six years later due to the expenses involved.[45]

Gleneagles' Foot

Colonel: Sir John Haldane of Gleneagles

Lieutenant Colonel: Robert Melville

Major: John Cockburn

Ministers: Thomas Lundie, Robert Campbell, George Murray[46]

On 3 July 1650 the Estates appointed Gleneagles, a Perthshire laird, to be a colonel of the Perthshire Foot. Gleneagles was to raise 920 men from the shire, excepting Perth. The regiment served on the summer campaign and fought at Dunbar. It may have been the other regiment with Lawers' Foot, which fought until nearly all of its men were dead. Gleneagles, his lieutenant colonel, and major were all killed at the battle. The regiment is not mentioned after Dunbar, further reinforcing this idea.[47]

Greenhead's Foot

Colonels: Andrew Ker of Greenhead (1649-50), Richard Douglas (1650-1651)

Major: John Rutherford (1651)

Ministers: John Meyne, Robert Ker[48]

Greenhead had long been prominent in Covenanter affairs nationally and in

Teviotdale when he received his first commission in 1649. On 28 February the Estates appointed him colonel of foot for Teviotdale and Selkirkshire. The shires were to raise 800 men for the regiment. As of 24 May the regiment consisted of only two companies. On 1 June the unit received orders to quarter in Montrose. A muster of the regiment on 31 July placed its strength at 200 soldiers. The regiment served on the summer 1650 campaign and was engaged at Dunbar. The colonel was reported as killed, but on 5 September Ker of Greenhead was present at Stirling as colonel of Teviotdale and Selkirkshire Foot. However, Greenhead joined the Western Association Army, relinquishing his command. On 11 December the regiment was quartering in Dundee. The town council requested 200 bolls of meal from the Mearns committee of war which had previously been assigned to Greenhead's Foot. Before then the burgh had refused to quarter the regiment, which appears to have become its permanent garrison. By 3 January 1651 Richard Douglas, a son of the sheriff of Teviotdale and a former colonel in the Engager army, was in command of the regiment. There is no further mention of the regiment, suggesting that it remained in Dundee and was destroyed as a result of the successful English attack on 1 September.[49]

J. Hackett's Horse

Colonel: Sir James Hackett (fiar of Pitfarrane)

Lieutenant Colonel: Robert Hackett

Sir James Hackett had served as a colonel of horse in the home army. More importantly he was a brother-in-law to the marquis of Argyll. In 1649 Hackett served as an M.P. for Fife. Hackett received several commissions as a colonel on 28 February, but he only raised a single regiment. The shires of Nairn, Elgin, and southeastern Inverness were to levy a regiment of 240 horse. Seaforth's and Lovat's areas of Inverness-shire received orders to provide an infantry regiment of 500 men and a cavalry one of 240 men for Hackett. However, by late July Hackett had not received men for any of these regiments. Instead he received a full complement of sixty troopers from Fife, and part of the 120 troopers from Linlithgowshire, a portion of the eighty men from Peeblesshire, and some of the eighty men of Dunbartonshire. The Fife contingent was raised in April. However, by 16 February the lieutenant colonel and his troop were ordered from Moray to Ross to assist the Inverness garrison. Sometime in April-June forty-three troopers of the colonel's troop quartered twice on the lands of George Leith of Threefields in the northeast. On 9 May Lieutenant Colonel Hackett and his troop of about forty men took part in the battle of Balvenie. Robert Hackett was one of the officers who signed the letter written by the victors to the Commission of the General Assembly (see Ker's Horse). On 1 June Lieutenant Colonel Hackett received orders to quarter in Moray,

Nairnshire, and Inverness-shire between the Ness and Spey. On the 7th this troop was ordered instead to quarter in Fife, Angus, or Mearns for a month due to a request from the lieutenant colonel. The Estates ordered him to remain with his troop during that time. The troop was to rendezvous with Ker's and Strachan's troops on 6 July at Coupar Angus. The muster of the regiment on 31 July revealed that both the colonel and lieutenant colonel had sixty men in their troops. Routmaster Cranston of Glen had forty-four troopers, while Routmaster Cranston the younger had a troop of thirty-four men. On 6 August the Estates produced new levy quotas for Hackett's regiments. Linlithgowshire was assessed sixty-six men, Peeblesshire forty-nine men, and Dunbartonshire thirty troopers. Moray was to levy fifty-four troopers, and Nairnshire fourteen more. Seaforth's and Lovat's sections of Inverness-shire were ordered to levy 138 horse and 375 foot. There is no evidence that any of these new recruits were raised. On 21 October troopers of the lieutenant colonel's troop, who were not Engagers, renewed the Solemn League and Covenant after the service at Duffus, presbytery of Elgin, swearing it with uplifted hands. Then the men or the clerk signed the Covenant. A week later 'the most part' of the officers and troopers were admitted to Holy Communion in the congregation 'upon their pious and earnest desire', they being free of 'scandallous conversationn' according to the testimony of their officers. This troop appears to have gone into winter quarters in the Duffus area. Routmaster Cranstoun's troop had been in the presbytery of Forres, possibly quartering in Edinkillie parish, before early November. However, it had returned south to take up winter quarters somewhere there. The colonel's troop, and perhaps others of his regiment spent the winter in the presbytery of Dunfermline, some in the principal burgh. On 6 January 1650 Sir James appeared before the Dunfermline kirk session, asked it to bring in reports of his men to aid in purging the regiment. The elders were ordered to make their reports in eight days. On the 15th the elders reported

> . . . that they carried themselves honestlie christianlie frie of anie scandall to ye knowledge except against ane John Dalgleish who so soone as report was made of him for his drunknes & swearing was put out of service by the sd Sir James Halkett.

A day later the colonel appeared at a meeting of the Dunfermline presbytery requesting that the ministers tell him of scandalous and disorderly veterans in his regiment within their parishes. The ministers were to report to Hackett on this matter. There is nothing to suggest that their findings were worse than those of the Dunfermline kirk session. In early February Elgin presbytery investigated the conduct of Lieutenant Colonel Hackett's troop. The ministers only returned bad reports against Quartermaster James Wayne for drinking and swearing, and a trooper with royalist tendencies. With this the first phase of the regiment's history ends.[50]

Throughout 1650 Hackett's Horse was involved in military operations. In April Lieutenant Colonel Hackett's troop moved north to join Strachan's command in Inverness-shire. The troop took part in the battle of Carbisdale on

27 April. After the battle it returned to Moray, quartering in the presbytery of Elgin. On 29 May two troopers appeared before the presbytery requesting testimonials as they 'have beine religiouse and sober . . .'. The testimonials were granted. On 19 June the colonel's and lieutenant colonel's troops were ordered to Fife. The two other troops received orders to proceed to Peebles. On 3 July parliament issued further levy quotas for Hackett's regiments. Elginshire and Nairnshire were to provide one troop of sixty-eight men, fifty-four men coming from the former and the remainder from the latter. Inverness-shire was to recruit a troop of sixty-nine men. Galloway was to levy fifty-five men and combine them with thirty troopers from Dunbartonshire to form a troop of seventy-five men. The remaining ten plus two men from Selkirkshire and forty-nine troopers from Peeblesshire would make up another troop. Linlithgowshire was to levy a troop of sixty-six horse. Thus, Hackett's northern horse, which probably did not exist, were to receive 178 troopers; the southern horse which was on foot would gain a reinforcement of 200 men. Hackett's Horse served on the summer campaign, but sometime during it Lieutenant Colonel Hackett's troop with its commander were detached to form a separate regiment. The lieutenant colonel may have made use of some of the recruits for Sir James' regiment for his new one. Sir James led his men on the Musselburgh raid against the English quarters, 30-31 July, but retreated causing a potential success to fail. This was remembered by the army when Charles II visited it in August, as there were cries that the colonel be hung for his action. Hackett tried to purge his regiment further as new recruits arrived, but he seems to have been unsuccessful. Hackett's Horse was present at Dunbar, but at least part of it escaped. On 10 September the Committee of Estates authorised the colonel to levy about ninety-six troopers from Fife. The regiment was ordered from Stirling to Burntisland on 19 September. The order was repeated the next day to this and four cavalry regiments, who were to aid in the defence of that burgh. Meanwhile since July Sir James had been governor of Inchgarvie, an islet whose importance increased tremendously after Dunbar, and the retreat north of the Forth. In early January 1651 Sir James resigned his commissions due to the triumph of the royalist party. Part of the regiment was quartered in the presbytery of Kirkcaldy until sometime in June, but there is no further mention of it. It is probable that the regiment remained in Fife, as it is not listed among those cavalry regiments ordered to Stirling in mid-June. Wherever it ceased to exist it is fairly certain that the regiment was no longer under the colours by mid-September.[51]

R. Hackett's Horse

Colonel: Robert Hackett

Minister: Gilbert Hall[52]

This was one of the four regiments which transferred from the Army of the

Covenants to the Western Association Army. It was a change over that could be hardly described as accidental. Robert Hackett although commanding a troop in J. Hackett's Horse and acting as its lieutenant colonel seemingly had little to do with it. Robert Hackett was a committed radical, believing strongly in the Gideonite army defeating the hosts of the ungodly. This could have hardly been otherwise as he had personal experience of such victories at Balvenie and Carbisdale. By mid-July 1650 Lieutenant Colonel Hackett had a regiment of his own, which may have taken recruits assigned to Sir James' regiment (see above for the numbers and sources of the July 1650 levy). The new regiment was at Dunbar, but managed to escape with the majority of the cavalry units to Stirling. On 10 September the Committee of Estates assigned R. Hackett's Horse about ninety-six troopers from Fife. It is questionable whether these men ever joined the regiment, for five days earlier colonels Hackett, Ker and Strachan had been sent to the shires of the Western Association with their regiments to raise an army from among the radical bonnet lairds and peasants. At the Kilmarnock meeting of the Association Hackett was commissioned a colonel for any men he might levy in the southwest. His regiment, which included the survivors from Dunbar, was one of three horse regiments in the army. It was well-manned, consisting of about 400 troopers, and well-armed. The troopers wore buff-coloured coats, and no armour. All three regiments were noted for containing many Dutchmen and High Germans. Hackett supported the Western Remonstrance, and did not agree with Strachan's republican tendencies. At the battle of Hamilton on 1 December Hackett commanded the reserves. He and his regiment fled; the troopers dispersed or fell prisoner to the English. Hackett's career as a soldier ended with the failure of the radicals to recreate the victories of Balvenie and Carbisdale.[53]

Hartwoodburn's Horse

Colonels: Walter Scott of Hartwoodburn (1649-50), George, 3rd earl of Linlithgow (1651)

Lieutenant Colonels: William Ker of Newton (1649-50), Archibald Scott (of Syntoun) (1651)

Major: (Archibald?) Scott (of Syntoun?)

Minister: William Durrant[54]

Hartwoodburn was a Selkirkshire laird, who served as M.P. for the shire in 1646-47, and in 1648-49. Parliament commissioned him the colonel of horse for Teviotdale and Selkirkshire on 28 February 1649. The two shires were to recruit 400 troopers. On 1 June the Estates ordered Hartwoodburn to quarter his troop in Nithsdale. From 20 June to 1 August Lieutenant Colonel Ker was on a mission to Carlisle and Berwick to recover the arms and ammunition left there by the Engagers. The muster of the regiment for 31 July gave its strength as follows: sixty men in the colonel's troop, fifty-three in the lieutenant colonel's and fifty in Captain Archibald Scott of Syntoun's. On 6 August the Estates issued orders that Selkirkshire raise forty-seven troopers and Teviotdale levy 180 men for the regiment. There is no further mention of the regiment until 19 June 1650. Then the colonel's and lieutenant colonel's troops received orders to go to Selkirk, and Syntoun's was sent to Lauderdale. The 3 July levy quota assigned the regiment two troops of ninety men each out of Teviotdale and one troop of forty-five men from Selkirkshire. The regiment served on the summer campaign and was at Dunbar. Until 16 October it dropped from sight; on that day the lieutenant colonel received orders to bring the regiment to Stirling, if it had not joined the Western Association Army. In December the transition of this regiment from the control of Hartwoodburn and Newton to the earl of Linlithgow began. On 20 December Linlithgow was commissioned colonel of the Perthshire Horse. Two weeks later the earl received the colonelcy of this regiment, for the colonel had died. Linlithgow was to receive reinforcements for the regiment from Perthshire and from Colonel Kennedy of Kirkhill's Horse. Linlithgow had served as an infantry colonel in the Army of the Solemn League and Covenant. He supported the Engagement in 1648, but returned to parliament on 5 December 1650. His new regiment quartered in Angus sometime between September 1650 and April 1651, spending part of November in Alyth. On 7 May 1651 Linlithgow's Horse was assigned to the 2nd Cavalry Brigade which consisted of three regiments under Major General Montgomery. It was to serve on the left wing of the line of battle. Linlithgow and his regiment took part in the Worcester campaign. During the battle the regiment formed part of the cavalry stationed north of the city under Leslie. The earl's unit fell to pieces on the flight northwards. Linlithgow went on to have an impressive career in Protectorate and Restoration affairs, both political and military.[55]

His Majesty's Life Guard of Foot

Colonel: Archibald, Lord Lorne

Lieutenant Colonel: James Wallace of Achens (1649-50)

Major: Brice Cochrane (1649-50)

Ministers: Hugh Peebles, Francis Aird, Harie Forbes, John Veitch, James Nasmith, Thomas Charteris, John Hamilton[56]

This unit was originally constituted solely of soldiers of the Ulster Army, who had fought the royalist conquest of Ulster in March-July 1649. They then fled to Scotland, where the kirk party government recognised they would resist all royalists and were prize recruits for the Army of the Covenants. In June the Estates ordered that the 'well-affected officers and soldiers fled out of Ireland' were to be recruited into the army. On 6 August the Estates ordered that four companies of not more than 500 foot soldiers be recruited from the refugees. Their officers must have testimonials from Irish ministers or from well-affected officers who had served in Ireland. Argyll, Lothian and Kinhilt were to screen the officers. Maintenance for the new regiment was set for three months from 15 August. The committees of war were recommended to use those refugees not recruited to replace purged soldiers and officers. On 10 August the Estates created six companies of foot containing 396 men from the refugees. Lieutenant Colonel Wallace, who had served in Argyll's Foot and had been taken prisoner at Kilsyth was to command the regiment. Major Brice Cochrane, formerly of Glencairn's Foot and one of the conspirators who had aided Monck's capture of Carrickfergus, was appointed second-in-command. Most of the officers were veterans of the Ulster Army, but there were some settlers who had commissions in the regiment. Chief amongst these men was Colonel Sir Alexander Stewart, a landowner from the province. On the 14th the Estates made a grant to the officers of the regiment and forty-seven other officers from Ulster, including many settlers. In order to pay the new regiment the kirk party regime had to reduce the numbers in the older horse and foot regiments. By October there were ninety-seven officers from Ireland receiving pay to retain their services. These included the lieutenant colonel and major of Argyll's Foot and twelve other officers of the regiment. In November the former Surgeon General Andrew Brown was added to the list of officers. These officers and the nearly 400 foot soldiers continued to receive pay until June 1650.[57]

In mid-1650 the regiment entered a new phase of its existence when parliament elevated it to the Life Guard of Foot for Charles II. The kirk party believed that the regiment contained the perfect men to protect the king from his royalist friends. Outside of the officers already mentioned, this unit did not include any men from Argyll's Foot. Lord Lorne, the heir of Argyll, was, however, commissioned colonel of the Life Guards. In 1647-49 Lorne had travelled in Italy and France, and had missed the upheavals of those years. When he received his commission from the Estates, Lorne refused it, only taking command of the regiment when Charles II granted him a commission on 22 July. The regiment was then reconstituted to contain seven companies of about fifty-nine men each. Being a royal bodyguard, each company had different colours. Lorne's on one side were blue with the royal arms, which were not surplanted by a crown; the other side had the motto 'Covenant; for Religione, King and Kingdomes' in gold. All the other banners had the same motto on one side but they differed from Lorne's and each others. Achens' possessed a blue field with a silver unicorn, while Cochrane's had a blue field with a lion rampant. The first captain had three fleur de lys on the blue field; on the blue field of the second captain was a lion rampant guelles; the third had three lioncells gradien and gold; while the fourth sported a gold harp fringed with silver. The regiment served throughout the summer campaign. By

8 August Major Cochrane had fallen prisoner to the English. Because he signed the Engagement against the House of Stewart, the Commission of the General Assembly condemned him. At Dunbar the Life Guards suffered heavy losses. Colonel Stewart was killed, and Achens fell into the hands of the English. These losses were important as they weakened the radical character of the regiment. Any new recruits would be more royalist than the original members of the regiment. This situation quickly developed, for on 3 October Warriston and Brodie purged the Life Guards at Kinross. From 5 October to 5 December the Commissary General allotted quarters to the regiment in Perth and the adjacent parishes. On the 14th Lorne petitioned the Committee for Military Affairs, requesting a new allotment of quarters. The Committee responded by placing the Life Guards on an equal footing with the other regiments. On 25 March 1651 Lorne petitioned the king and parliament. On this occasion his demands were much greater; he required shoes, clothing, and recruits from other foot regiments to make up the Life Guards to 1,200 men. Lorne further specified that all their coats should be of one colour. The regiment never reached anything near the size of 1,200 men. From June the Life Guards were quartered near Stirling, and they contained only 283 men. The last muster on 18 July revealed that desertion had shrunk the Life Guards to 236 soldiers. The Life Guards served on the Worcester campaign, from which they did not return. Lorne led a chequered career throughout the Commonwealth, Protectorate, and Restoration periods, before he met his death as a Whig martyr in 1685.[58]

His Majesty's Life Guard of Horse

Colonels: Alexander, 6th earl of Eglinton (1650-51), Sir James, 1st viscount Newburgh (1651)

Lieutenant Colonel: Sir James, 1st viscount Newburgh (1650-51)

Major: (?) Gib

Minister: Andrew Fairfoul[59]

As with the Life Guard of Foot, this regiment was originally created from refugees from the Ulster Army who had opposed the royalists in 1649. On 10 August 1649 the Estates decided to retain one troop of forty men plus officers under a Captain Cullace. This new unit was known as the 'Irish troop'. In April 1650 it was quartering in the Inverness area, and it joined Strachan's force to oppose Montrose. The troop fought at Carbisdale. On 22 July the Estates commissioned Eglinton as colonel of the Life Guards. Eglinton had a sound military and political background for such an appointment. His lieutenant colonel, Newburgh, does not appear as a Covenanter prior to this time. On 28 June Eglinton had been appointed a member of the Purging Committee, a further illustration of his contemporaries' view that the earl was not tinged with royalism. Besides the 'Irish troop' Eglinton had permission to recruit more men into the regiment. Like the Life Guard of Foot the Horse Guards had more elaborate banners than those in the other cavalry regiments. Eglinton's troop had a blue field with a sword and sceptre in the saltire under an imperial crown in gold. That side of the banner was completed by the motto: 'Nobis haec in victa miserunt' in gold. The other side of the banner sported a saltire with the motto: 'Covenant; for Religione, King and Kingdomes', which was the same for all the other banners. The flag of the lieutenant colonel's troop had an imperial crown of Britain on a field of blue with the motto: 'Nemo me impune lacessit' in gold. The major's banner had a blue and gold saltire, and the motto 'Pro Religione, Rege et Patria' in gold. All the other troops' flags were the same on both sides: blue with the motto 'Covenant, Religion, King and Country'. Eglinton quickly brought his regiment up to strength, but the earl does not appear to have paid much attention to the quality of his recruits despite his allegiance to the kirk party.[60]

The Life Guard of Horse soon became notorious for its poor discipline and behaviour. On 22 August Major General Montgomery, a son of Eglinton, wrote the earl from the camp at Corstorphine. The Life Guards were not then with the field army, but had accompanied Charles II to Perthshire. The following excerpts from the Major General's letter reveal the behaviour of the regiment.

> I thought fitt to acquaint yor. Lo. that the shyre of perth cryes mightily out against yor. Lo. regt.

The county had promised the army 2,000 bolls of grain, if the Life Guards were removed. Montgomery continued in a similar vein.

> Ther is many lykwyse for the bringing them over to purge them. Wherfor yor. Lo. wold see that ye have none but such as ye can be ansrable for. Ther is some who spares not to vent publickly that ther is no need of a guard, and that his Majestie wold rather be content to quyt them, than to have the countrey oppressed.[61]

Two days later the Committee of Estates decided to discharge the regiment, except for the men reserved to Eglinton's troop by act of parliament, due to the abuses and insolencies it committed. The shires were exempted from providing further recruits for the regiment. However, on 13 September, probably owing to Dunbar, the Committee authorised the restoration of the regiment to full strength. This decision was not accompanied by an improvement in behaviour. By mid-September the regiment was quartering in the presbytery of St. Andrews. On 25 September a trooper of Routmaster Forsyth's troop swore oaths and beat up a tenant of David Beaton in Anstruther Easter. On the same day a trooper in Major Gib's became drunk in Anstruther Easter, and quartered in Andrew Strange's house. He forced his host with threats of having the house burned down to stay up giving him drink all night. The trooper also broke glasses and anything which came into his sight. At about the same time a

Captain Dunbar in the regiment brought further complaints from the parish. He was quartering in John Oliphant's house, and one night the captain demanded that Oliphant convey him to Balcastrie. Oliphant refused, and the captain threw Oliphant's wife down the stairs, trampled on her and broke her chamber's door. News of such disorders appears to have reached the Committee of Estates, because it appointed the earl of Sutherland, Lord Ross, and the lairds of Humbie, Brodie and Obsdale to purge the regiment on 30 September. On 11 October the Commission of the General Assembly appointed the ministers Samuel Rutherford, John Robertson, Walter Greig, and George Bennet, and the lairds of Creich and Lochtour to investigate and report on the misconduct of the regiment and of the excesses it committed in quartering. On the 16th the Committee appointed Argyll, Cassillis, Lothian, Humbie and Brodie to speak with Eglinton about the behaviour of the regiment. Despite all these efforts there does not seem to have been any improvement in the carriage of the regiment.[62]

The regiment quartered in southern Fife throughout the autumn of 1650, the winter of 1650-51, and the spring of 1651, but it did not experience a return to order or quiet during the period. After the battle of Newtyle Newburgh joined Middleton's rising, which suggests that the lieutenant colonel may have been supplying the regiment with Engagers and royalists, whose standards of behaviour were poor. In November Corporal James Nasmith, an ex-captain and a member of Routmaster Harrie Gibson's troop, drew his sword on the Anstruther Easter watch at 1 a.m. On 1 March 1651 Corporal Nasmith came to the town drunk and threatened to open the prison door, where there were two women imprisoned for theft. He promised to kill the bailies if they would not give him the keys. With his companions, he brandished his sword, received the keys, and released the women. The corporal then carried one of them out of town on his horse. The case was continued in the presbytery of St. Andrews on 23 April. Then the woman, Helen Clark, who had ridden off with Nasmith (now a quartermaster) confessed fornication with him. The case was referred back to the Anstruther Easter kirk session. The regiment as a whole drew the fire of the Committee of Estates upon it for its quartering practices in the presbytery of Dunfermline. On 30 April the Committee ordered the colonel to report on the maintenance received by the regiment in that presbytery. About this time Eglinton and his son James were captured in the burgh of Dumbarton while on a recruiting mission. They were taken first to Edinburgh Castle, then to Hull, and finally to Berwick where Eglinton remained until 1660.[63]

The regiment continued to quarter in Fife under the effective command of its lieutenant colonel. On 7 May the Life Guards were assigned to the 8th Cavalry Brigade; it was the only regiment in this brigade which was to be posted on the extreme right of the battle line. By early June Newburgh was officially commissioned as the colonel of the Life Guards. He had been a Gentleman of the Bedchamber for Charles I, and was ennobled by him on 13 September 1647. Newburgh went into exile in 1649, only returning to Scotland in June 1650 with Charles II. On 11 June 1651 the Estates assessed Dumfriesshire 120 troopers and Teviotdale seventy-three men as recruits for the regiment. Six days later the Life Guards were ordered to Stirling with the other horse regiments quartering in Fife. Each trooper was to receive £3 on his departure. On the 20th the levy quotas for Teviotdale and Dumfriesshire were increased to 133 troopers and 130 men respectively. It is uncertain and doubtful whether any of these new levies were uplifted. Newburgh and the Life Guards participated in the Worcester campaign. Newburgh escaped capture, but the regiment was destroyed. After the Restoration Newburgh served as the colonel of the Scottish Life Guards for ten years.[64]

Holburn's Foot

Colonel: Major General Sir James Holburn

Minister: (Michael?) Gilbert[65]

This regiment was on foot during the winter of 1648-49. On 1 January 1649 Sir James Livingston of Kilsyth submitted a petition for the recovery of quartering money spent on the regiment. Thirty foot, a sergeant and corporal had remained on his lands for ten days, incurring a cost of £101 3s. 4d. During that time Kilsyth had spent £8 on officers of the regiment. On 27 February three companies of Holburn's were ordered to join with part of Argyll's to march north to suppress Pluscarden's uprising. The next day the Estates commissioned Holburn colonel of foot for Stirlingshire and Clackmannanshire. The two shires were to levy 500 soldiers for the regiment. On 1 March Holburn arrived at Stirling Castle to find that the common soldiers had mutinied. He quelled the rising by paying them a month's means out of his pocket. To secure the castle he ordered out three foot companies, retaining his own as the garrison. Holburn requested the despatch of Strachan's troop to aid him in disciplining the mutineers; the Estates agreed to this measure. On 1 June Holburn's was ordered to quarter in Stirling and throughout Linlithgowshire. The strength of the regiment as of 31 July was 380 men. On 6 August the Estates assessed Stirling-shire and Clackmannanshire a further 375 men. Unusually Holburn was one of the three commissioners appointed to hear James Guthrie preach for the call of Holy Rude parish, Stirling on 7 October. On 5 November Holburn was nominated with another man to attend the Commission of the General Assembly on the 14th to agitate for Guthrie's translation to Stirling. Holburn's inter-cession was successful, and Guthrie went to Stirling, where he caused a great deal of trouble in late 1650 to mid-1651 preaching against the Public Resolutions and the acceptance of former Engagers and royalists in offices of state. This was just one of many causes for slander against Holburn, although the others existed more in men's imaginations than in reality. By the summer of 1650 the regiment was fully recruited, and it was not allotted any men from the levies at that time. In August Holburn was one of the colonels who presented the West Kirk

Declaration to the Committee of Estates, further emphasising his radical leanings. At Dunbar the Major General acted as a brigade commander, and was blamed by rumour for ordering all save a few men in each regiment to extinguish their matches, thus making them easy prey for an English attack. Holburn's own regiment escaped with losses of about 300 men. A regimental muster of winter 1650-51 revealed that it contained 400 able and twenty-four sick privates. There was also one captain, fourteen sergeants, three scribes, a drum major, twenty corporals, and six drummers for a total strength of 469 men and officers. On 7 May 1651 the regiment was quartering in or near Stirling, when another muster was ordered. By 10 June Holburn had recruited his regiment up to 667 men. On 18 July, two days before the battle of Inverkeithing the unit contained 646 soldiers plus officers. Shortly after that muster Holburn was appointed commander-in-chief of a force to oppose a landing at North Queensferry by Lambert. Holburn was a protegé of Argyll and David Leslie, thus despising those who had supported Montrose. Unfortunately included in his battle group was the regiment of Maclean Foot under the clan chief. Holburn's activities at Inverkeithing have led to charges of treachery towards this unit. However, as Buchanan's Foot (a pro-Argyll unit) shared the debâcle of the Macleans one must seriously consider the possibilities of a royalist campaign of slander against the major general. Holburn marshalled his regiment and other Lowland regiments on the left flank, which was based on the Hill of Salvage. This flank consisted of veteran soldiers with a large leavening of untried recruits. After an initially successful charge by the horse, things disintegrated. The cavalrymen were too raw to rally after the charge, and fled from the English Horse. This exposed the infantry to attack by the English Horse on the left flank and by infantry to their front. Not surprisingly Holburn and the Scots foot ran from the field, leaving the Macleans and Buchanan's Foot to suffer grievous losses. Holburn's regiment never recovered from the battle. Holburn himself was barred from holding further commands because he was distrusted by too many in the army.[66]

Innes' Foot

Colonels: John Innes (1648-51), James Innes (1651)

Lieutenant Colonel: (?) Jardine (1650-51)

Ministers: James Park, Robert Watson, Alexander Fraser, James Gordon, Robert Irvine, Robert Jamieson[67]

This regiment was originally recruited in August/September 1648 either from kirk party soldiers who had belonged to the New Model Army, or from men who joined the Whiggamore Raid, or both. On 21 September Leven ordered Innes to quarter his men in the Canongate, Edinburgh. From 10 November

Innes was governor of Bog of Gight; the regiment provided its garrison. On 5 January 1649 Innes' Foot arrived in Arbroath. However, the 400 soldiers of the regiment should have received quarters throughout Angus. The presence of the regiment in the burgh for five weeks caused the council to petition the Estates for its removal. The Committee of Estates obliged Arbroath by ordering Innes' men to Dundee, where they arrived on 13 February. On the 28th Innes was commissioned colonel of foot for Moray, Nairnshire, and Inverness-shire south and east of the Spey. This area was to recruit 500 men for the regiment. Meanwhile the regiment moved south of the Tay into Fife, where it took up quarters. On 1 March Innes learned that his regiment had fled and broken up except for one company. He arrived in Cupar and placed some deserters he apprehended there into the tolbooth. His officers, particularly the major, said the mutiny and dispersal had occurred because the men had heard they were to march to Inverness. Innes informed Major General Holburn of the situation, warning that other regiments might do likewise. He asked Holburn to check for deserters in Perth and Stirling, and capture and punish them. Innes requested Holburn tell parliament 'least in this intended expedition they trust in a brokin bow'. Innes explained he and his officers would hunt down the deserters. To him the cause of the problem was the Engagement. He ended his letter to Holburn with a pious declaration.

> The Lord turn all to his glorie and his kirks comfort, for humane helpe is now verie low.[68]

Eventually Innes regrouped the regiment, but it is not known how many men deserted. On 1 June 1649 Innes' Foot was ordered to quarter in the Highland garrisons established after the royalist risings. The regiment was again ordered to garrisons on 6 July. At the end of the month there were 100 men and officers under a Lieutenant Scott, the governor of Brahan Castle, quartering there and in Chanonry Castle. Four other companies of the regiment, containing 245 soldiers, were quartered in Moray and Banffshire. On 3 August Innes petitioned the Estates due to difficulties with the committees of war of those two shires. They had refused to provide money to the regiment since 1 July, because they claimed the monthly maintenance should be reduced if they were quartering soldiers. The Estates supported the colonel and ordered the committees to aid him in collecting the monthly maintenance. On the 6th Moray, Nairnshire and eastern Inverness-shire were ordered to put out 375 soldiers to the regiment. However, it is uncertain whether shires levied these men. On 30 January 1650 the first case of church discipline involving a soldier of the regiment reached the presbytery of Strathbogie. A private in the Strathbogie garrison confessed fornication, and then deserted to escape penance. A private from the Bog garrison was cited before the presbytery of Elgin on 13 March. The presbytery accused John Byres of being a royalist, an Engager, a profaner of the Sabbath, and of having deserted his wife. He appeared two weeks later; denying he was a royalist, Byres admitted to having served as a trooper on the Engagement. Byres further stated he had no part in an incident on the Sabbath, but was merely a witness. He ingeniously claimed that he had to desert his wife in Alves, because he had no money. However, he did send her what he had. A minister was appointed to question his wife, and Byres was ordered to return on 17 April. Then he continued to deny subscribing a band with Montrose or Huntly. The presbytery ordered him to behave as a 'christian husband' by providing for his wife during the famine. On 15 May Colonel Innes appeared before the presbytery concerning services at the Bog garrison. The presbytery had already refused to provide a preacher on Sundays, as they thought that prejudicial to their own parishes. Innes asked for a minister to come to preach on a weekday. In addition he desired a minister to tender the Solemn League and Covenant and to give communion to the garrison. The presbytery set aside Tuesdays as the day for sermons and appointed a minister for the first Tuesday. He was also instructed to see if there were any Engagers in the garrison and to see if they had repented. The presbytery decided to give further consideration to the question of communion. Due to the threat of an English invasion the days of the regiment solely doing garrison duty were about to end.[69]

Innes' Foot was established in several garrisons throughout northern and central Scotland. On 19 June the entire regiment was ordered to Edinburgh save for reduced garrisons. Fifty men would continue in Brahan, another fifty would continue at Blair Atholl; Strathbogie and Eilean Donan would have twenty men each as garrison; while thirty men would stay in Bog. The remainder of the regiment served on the summer campaign against Cromwell. Innes served as a brigade commander at Dunbar. The regiment lost its lieutenant colonel due to the battle, but there are no more details on casualties. During the autumn royalist rebellion Major General Middleton unsuccessfully attacked the garrisons in Bog of Gight and Strathbogie. On 11 November the Committee of Estates issued instructions to Banffshire and the near parts of Aberdeenshire to levy 500 men for the regiment. However, Inverness burgh still owed recruits to the regiment from the earlier levies. In December the burgh council petitioned the Committee of Military Affairs concerning Innes' demands. The colonel desired the burgh to put out the number of men proscribed by the 1643 levy quota; he had threatened the burgh with quartering if it did not comply. However, Inverness had recruited the levy quota as of 1648, and refused to levy more. The Committee agreed with the burgh and issued orders that Innes desist from his actions. This set-back to bringing the regiment up to strength was followed by another. On 30 January a report reached a sub-committee of the Committee of Estates from Lieutenant Colonel Jardine and five gentlemen in Aberdeen. The townspeople of Aberdeen had attacked the regiment earlier in the month. The council claimed that the assault was the fault of the soldiers. But that '. . . the Regiment is ruined by the sad tulmult and almost all disarmed . . .'. One soldier was killed, a lieutenant had been wounded, and two soldiers were at the point of death. The sub-committee ordered the incident to be more straitenly tried. The next day the Committee of Estates ordered a full investigation into the incident. The perpetrators were to be summoned before the Lord Justice General or the Committee and tried. Unfortunately nothing further is known about the 'tumult'. By June the regiment had a new colonel, James Innes. On the 24th the Committee of Estates instructed him to abandon the Bog and Strathbogie garrisons, bringing them to the rest of the regiment at Stirling. Innes' Foot had been in the Stirling area since 11 June, if not before. The regiment numbered 355 men on muster undertaken then. On 3 July there were 414 soldiers in the unit, but the numbers dropped by seven men on the 18th. There is no further mention of the regiment, but it may be assumed that it ceased to exist sometime in September. As an epilogue in 1652 Lieutenant Colonel Jardine received £9 16s. from two kirk sessions as aid to keep him in food and shelter.[70]

Ker's Horse

Colonel: Gilbert Ker

Lieutenant Colonel: Archibald Strachan

Ministers: Gilbert Hall, James Park[71]

Ker's Horse was one of the four regiments from the Army of the Covenants which formed the foundation of the Western Association Army. As the history of the regiment and Ker's life will show this was not unexpected. Ker had served as the lieutenant colonel of Middleton's Horse in the Army of the Solemn League and Covenant. He later held a command in the New Model. In 1648 Ker refused an Engager commission to raise a regiment and supported the kirk party, serving in the Whiggamore Rising. On 28 February 1649 parliament granted him a commission to raise a regiment of 240 horse from Dumfriesshire. On 1 March Major General Holburn requested Strachan's troop to aid him in disciplining the Stirling mutineers. It was dispatched by the Estates for that purpose on the 2nd. By April Ker's own troop (if not the lieutenant colonel's and routmaster's), was at least partially raised. On the 12th twenty-five troopers of Ker's quartered in the northeast. On Robert Gordon's lands in Botarns another twenty-three troopers and the colonel quartered. Presumably the regiment was on the way north to Ross from which it marched to Balvenie in the northeast. On the Balvenie campaign Ker commanded a force of three troops of 120 men and twelve musketeers. Although there were other foot soldiers they could not maintain the same rate of advance as the few musketeers. The three troops were Ker's, Strachan's and Lieutenant Colonel Hackett's.[72] After the battle, on 8 May, Ker wrote to the Commission of the General Assembly:

> We in oure weak maner beged the Lords direction, that Hiss blissing might wait His owne and our labours . . .[73]

Ker's small force surprised and defeated a royalist army of 1,060–1,180 men. The Covenanters killed sixty–eighty of their foes and captured 800 others. Upon learning of this victory the Commission declared 25 May as a day of thanksgiving. Balvenie laid the basis for the ideal of the small, godly, Gideonite army defeating large hosts of profane royalists, which strongly influenced both Ker and Strachan.[74]

After Balvenie the regiment settled into inaction for the remainder of 1649. On 1 June Ker's and Strachan's troops were ordered to quarter in Ross, Cromarty and Inverness-shire. On the 7th the two officers petitioned that their troops might quarter in the south due to the long march from their assigned area with Lieutenant Colonel Hackett's troop. All three troops were granted quarters in Fife, Angus and Mearns. However, they were ordered to rendezvous at Coupar Angus on 6 July for the march north. At the end of July Ker's Horse consisted of three troops. His own and Strachan's had sixty men each, while routmaster the laird of Craigdarroch's mustered fifty-four men. On 6 August the Estates instructed Dumfriesshire to raise another 146 troopers for the regiment. This is the last mention of the regiment in 1649. However, it is known to have remained in its northern quartering grounds until spring 1650 when the regiment gained further laurels.[75]

The Carbisdale campaign provided further ammunition for those who argued in favour of a small, godly army. The commander of the Covenanter forces on this campaign was the regiment's lieutenant colonel. Strachan was the son of a craftsman. Earlier in the 1640s he had been known for his profane behaviour, but had become convinced of the folly of such behaviour, converting to being a committed puritan. In 1648 Strachan acted as Argyll's liaison with Cromwell. In early 1650 Strachan wrote the radical minister of Stirling, James Guthrie, from Inverness. He complained of the financial demands on the lower classes, of royalism in army, and of his men's low pay and arrears. He confidently stated that God would give Montrose into his hands if he appeared nearby. When Montrose began his march south from Caithness Ker's and Strachan's troops were quartering in Brahan, Chanonry and Ross. After 16 April Strachan advanced to Ross, where he was joined by some musketeers of Lawers' Foot, and Lieutenant Colonel Hackett with his troop. Colonel John Munro of Lemlair and David Ross of Balnagowan, both formerly out in Pluscardine's Rising, joined Strachan with 400 foot from the two clans. Both of these local leaders came out because they had become clients of the earl of Sutherland. On the morning of 27 April the council of war of Strachan's force met at Tain. Several officers objected to marching that day for fear that they must fight on the next day — the Sabbath. However, news reached the council that Montrose was marching south towards them. The council determined to fight that day. Before setting out, the troops increased their fervour by singing psalms, reading scripture and being led in prayer by Gilbert Hall, the chaplain of Ker's Horse and Lawers' company of foot. The departure of the 230–280 horse (in five troops) and 436 foot was further delayed by Strachan delivering the only known exhortation by a Covenanting officer.[76]

> Gentlemen, yonder are your enemeis, and they are not only your enemies, they are the enemies of our Lord Jesus Christ; I have been dealing this last night with Almighty God, to know the event of this affair, and I have gotten it: as sure as God is in heaven, they are delivered into our hands and there shall not a man of us fall to the ground.[77]

Strachan was correct. Only one of his troopers drowned while pursuing the royalists across the Oykel. Montrose lost 400 men killed, 200 more drowned, and 450 fell prisoner. The survivors fled to Caithness and from there to Orkney and back to the continent.[78] This total victory provided confirmation of the idea born at Balvenie, and was not forgotten by Ker or Strachan.

While Ker's Horse was actively engaged against the English in the summer, the loyalty of its colonel and lieutenant colonel were in doubt. On 19 June Ker's and Strachan's troops were ordered to Lanark, and Craigdarroch's was sent to Stirlingshire. On 3 July Dumfriesshire was instructed to levy two troops of seventy-three men each for the regiment, which indicates that the levy of summer 1649 had not been fulfilled. About the same time Strachan departed from the regiment, receiving command of the Ministers' Horse. Throughout the summer Ker strongly supported the further purging of the army;[79] he was encouraged in his views by Samuel Rutherford, the leading radical theorist. On 10 August Rutherford wrote Ker from St. Andrews. The minister desired that God would give him a 'sword . . . and orders from heaven . . .'. He promised that Christ would overcome the English sectaries, and that God planned to make Britain his throne. Rutherford strongly stated that a pure army was desired

> that the shout of a King who hath many crowns may be among you; and that ye may fight in faith, and prevail with God first.

The letter ended with a piece of pastoral advice to Ker.

> Though He need not Gilbert Ker, nor his sword, yet this honour have ye with His redeemed soldiers, to call Christ High Lord-General, of whom ye hope for pay all arrears well told. Go-on, worthy Sir, in the courage of faith, following the Lamb . . . He will place salvation in Britain's Zion for Israel's glory.[80]

On 13 August, possibly inspired by this letter, Ker was a presenter of the West Kirk Declaration to the Committee of Estates. The colonel also carried out secret meetings with Cromwell and his officers during the campaign in an effort to let the godly of Scotland rid the country of malignants. These talks led to nothing but planted hopes of persuading Ker to change his allegiance in the minds of the English. Despite Ker's well-known radical sympathies or possibly due to them, he was appointed a groom of Charles II's bedchamber on 14 August by the Committee of Estates. On 2 September Ker and his colleague Strachan argued for fighting at Dunbar in the council of war. The regiment served at the battle, but managed to escape the disaster which overtook the army. The English initially reported that Ker was killed in the fighting, but unfortunately for both the moderate Covenanters and the invaders this was untrue.[81]

The final and most controversial chapter of the regiment's history covers the last months of 1650. On 5 September the Committee of Estates commissioned Ker to raise troops in the southwest for service there. On the same day Ker received another letter from Rutherford. The minister declared that both the royalists and sectaries were God's enemies, and that it was wrong to join either. Rutherford believed that God would grant victory to the Covenanters over the English. He stated that the army lost at Dunbar 'through the sinful miscarriage of men'. Victory, however, would only come when the sins of the English had incited God's wrath, and when the Scots had hauled themselves before Him. Ker became the commander-in-chief of the Western Association Army. His regiment was recruited to about 400 troopers, who dressed in buff coats. They contained many Dutchmen and High Germans in addition to the southwestern bonnet lairds, tenants, sub-tenants, and labourers who volunteered. The army contained at least 1,200 horse and 400 dragoons, but these men did little to relieve the pressure on Stirling. On 1 October the Committee of Estates ordered Ker to send 100 troopers raised from Dumfriesshire to Major General Montgomery; he refused to obey. On the 7th Ker's Horse quartered in Paisley, at the cost of £80. Ten days later the army issued the Western Remonstrance from Dumfries. The Remonstrance effectively declared the Western Association's independence of the English, and the Committee of Estates. Afterwards Paisley became the headquarters of the army, which was rent by arguments. Strachan and other officers, including Major Govan and Scoutmaster Dundas, entertained hopes of establishing a Scottish republic. Strachan entered into correspondence with Cromwell on this matter, and some of the officers were purged by the Association. However, Strachan remained to pull the loyalty of the army away from Ker's radical royalism. The army avoided any contact with the English during the autumn. On 23 November Rutherford wrote his last letter to Ker. He promised him victory or a martyr's death in attempting it, and pointed out that the people of three kingdoms prayed for Ker's success. Meanwhile the Committee of Estates had appointed Montgomery to go west with a force and take over the army. Ker weakened the ideological unity of his force by allowing Govan and Strachan to retain their commands. Upon hearing of Montgomery's advance to Campsie, Ker became determined to eliminate the English Horse in the region, then quartering at Hamilton, before turning on this former colleague. On 30 November the army was quartering at Carmunock. That night Ker told his officers that he would only serve with those who supported the Western Remonstrance and opposed the Committee of Estates. The army then prepared to attack what it thought was only 1,200 cavalry under Lambert in Hamilton. At 4 a.m. on Sunday 1 December the Scots attacked an enemy consisting of 3,000 cavalry, who had been horsed since 3.30 a.m. in preparation to march to Glasgow. Strachan's lieutenant colonel, however, managed to surprise the English and cleared the town. Ker then appeared with 200 reinforcements. Meanwhile the English formed up at the end of the town behind a ditch. Because of the cramped terrain Ker ordered a small withdrawal. However, the new recruits thought it was a flight, and 'yea, the whole rest fled apart; not one would stay'. Twenty troopers died and eighty fell prisoner. Ker was wounded and captured. Strachan took command of the survivors only to surrender them to the English before he joined Cromwell. Although the English attempted to use Ker after the conquest as a J.P. for Teviotdale, he flatly refused the post. In the end the failure of Ker was that of Montrose, inadequate intelligence of the enemy.[82]

Kinhilt's Horse Troop

Colonel: Sir Robert Adair of Kinhilt

Minister: John Meyne[83]

Kinhilt served as a troop commander in the Ulster Army, and as lieutenant colonel of Leven's Horse in the Army of the Solemn League and Covenant. He acted as an M.P. for Wigtownshire in 1649-50. On 31 July Kinhilt is mentioned in the army muster roll as commanding a troop of eighty horse. There is no surviving commission for this troop, which suggests that it may have been formed from Ulster refugees, as Kinhilt had strong connections in the province. On 19 June 1650 Kinhilt's troop received orders to move to Lanark. The troop served on the Dunbar campaign, but managed to escape destruction. On 20 September the troop was ordered to Fife with four other cavalry regiments to defend Burntisland. Kinhilt, however, had deserted his unit and was appointed a colonel in the Western Association Army. On 11 December the troop was noted as being at Kincarne and Dunblane with Castle Stuart's Horse, on the way to join Major General Montgomery at Port and Kilmadock. On 3 January 1651 the regiment was cast into Massey's Horse, after having quartered in Angus.[84]

Lord Kirkcudbright's Foot and Dragoons

Colonel: John, 3rd Lord Kirkcudbright

Kirkcudbright brought a cavalry regiment over to Ulster from Scotland in 1649, which was surprised and nearly destroyed at Lisnegarvy in December. On 28 February 1649 Kirkcudbright was appointed a colonel of foot for Galloway, Ayrshire and Renfrewshire. Galloway was to levy 600 foot for the regiment, and the other two shires would raise 200 men. There is only evidence that a lieutenant, ensign, two sergeants and fifty-four foot were levied from Galloway. On 6 August the Estates ordered Galloway to levy 450 men; these men were probably not levied. Again on 3 July 1650 parliament ordered Galloway to recruit 900 foot. This time the men were raised, serving on the Dunbar campaign. Those who survived Dunbar were sent west to the Western

Association Army, where they were mounted as dragoons. The regiment consisted of 400 buff-coated men, including many Dutchmen and High Germans. The lieutenant colonel and major commanded the regiment, although Kirkcudbright had his commission as colonel. The dragoons dispersed after the battle of Hamilton on 1 December, and the survivors were surrendered to the English by Colonel Strachan. Kirkcudbright carried the king's train at the coronation on 1 January 1651. He remained a staunch presbyterian until his death, opposing the admittance of episcopalian ministers in his region.[85]

Kirkhill's Horse

Colonel: (?) Kennedy of Kirkhill

This regiment is first mentioned on 14 December 1650 as having been granted a proportion of the Ayrshire and Renfewshire Horse levy of 500 men in Major General Montgomery's and Lord Mauchline's petition. As of then none of the horse had been received. On Christmas Day the remainder of the regiment (suggesting that it had received some recruits), was ordered to be cast into the Lord General's regiment. It would then be given to Major General Massey, to make up for the troop given to Lieutenant Colonel Hamilton. Part of this regiment was given to Hartwoodburn's (later the earl of Linlithgow's) Horse.[86]

Kirkness' Foot

Colonel: Sir William Douglas of Kirkness

On 3 July 1650 the Estates appointed Kirkness a colonel of foot for Fife and Kinross-shire. The two counties were to levy 700 men, having been excused ninety-six men for this regiment. Between 15 and 22 July Fife raised 2,700 foot, which suggests that this regiment received its full complement. It served on the Dunbar campaign and was present at the battle. There it certainly resisted the English, because Kirkness was taken prisoner. He later died of his wounds. The regiment ceased to exist after the battle.[87]

Leslie's Horse

Colonel: Lieutenant General David Leslie

Ministers: James Ferguson, George Bennet, Robert Young, John Smith, Robert Home, William Home[88]

Leslie was one of the finest generals to serve in the Covenanting armies. He led troops in the Army of the Solemn League and Covenant and the New Model Army, but he demitted his post during the time of the Engagement. In September 1648 Leslie acted as lieutenant general and active field commander of the Whiggamore forces. He was employed in the same capacity by the kirk party regime. On 28 February 1649 the Estates appointed him colonel of horse for Lanarkshire, Renfrewshire and Ayrshire. The latter two counties were to provide only twenty troopers, while Lanarkshire levied 360 more. Between 13 February and sometime in March three men and two horses of Leslie's troop quartered on George Leith of Threefield's lands. On 5 May part of the troop quartered on Robert Gordon's lands in Botarns. Meanwhile in late February Leslie had taken the field against Pluscardine and his allies. After subduing them by 21 March, he had to turn south to deal with the earl of Atholl's rising. On 31 March the Atholl gentry submitted to Leslie, however, Pluscardine had risen again. But it was to be Colonel Ker and not Leslie who crushed this rebellion on 9 May at Balvenie. Following that battle Leslie proceeded north to the Inverness area in order to establish garrisons on the earl of Seaforth's lands. Those campaigns appear to have ended by 1 June for Leslie's troop was then ordered to quarter in Banffshire and Aberdeenshire. At the end of July the regiment consisted of three troops of sixty men each: Leslie's, and Routmasters James Carmichael's and the laird of Allanton's. On 6 August parliament ordered Lanarkshire to recruit 117 troopers for the regiment in order to increase its strength. On 5 and 7 September Leslie's Life Guards took three bolls of meal and bere, and twenty-two fowls from the laird of Cubine's Balnaboth and Kinbath lands. After the 27th Leslie moved north with his regiment and other forces to oppose the royalists who had captured Orkney. However, due to a lack of transport he was unable to invade the islands, and in late November Leslie brought his force south into winter quarters. Following the news of Major General John Urry's landing in Caithness with royalist forces from Orkney in early April 1650, Leslie was ordered north on the 16th. He held a general rendezvous of his forces at Brechin on the 25th. But the army was needed only to pursue the royalists due to Lieutenant Colonel Strachan's victory at Carbisdale on the 27th. With that the primary concern of Leslie and his regiment ceased to be royalists, and became the English sectarian army.[89]

The second half of 1650 saw Leslie in nearly continual military activity. On 19 June the Estates ordered his troop to Fife, and Allanton's and Carmichael's to Lanark. At the end of the month a relic of the regiment's occupation of Inverness-shire appears in the Petty kirk session records where a woman confessed fornication with one of the troopers. On 3 July Lanarkshire received instructions to raise one troop of seventy-five men for the regiment. Unfortunately, there is no information about this levy or the preceding ones of 1649. From late July until 2 September Leslie was in the field guarding the Edinburgh Castle–Leith line against Cromwell. Indeed, Leslie bested Cromwell in the strategic manoeuvres of this campaign. Throughout the summer Leslie opposed those in the army and state who wished to further purge the army, but his wishes were disregarded. Nevertheless by the evening of 2 September total victory lay within Leslie's grasp as his men on Doon Hill overlooked Cromwell's poorly supplied and illness-racked army. That afternoon the Committee of Estates and the ministers with the army ordered Leslie down the hill. This he did without protest as he lacked the supplies and tents to occupy the hill in the worsening weather, while a prolonged stay on the summit would result in sickness and desertion. Leslie himself blamed the defeat on the failure of the soldiers to stand to arms all night (this order originated with Holburn), and the officers' desertion of their units to find shelter from the rain. Leslie's Horse fought at Dunbar, but escaped to Stirling with the rest of the cavalry. Following the battle of Newtyle on 21 October Leslie commanded an army of only 2,500 foot and horse. His problems were intensified by being pinned in Stirling by Cromwell. On the 22nd Leslie received orders from the Committee of Estates to proceed north to crush the malignants under Middleton with all possible speed. On the 24th he led 2,500-3,000 horse in thirty-two troops through Perth on the way northeastwards. The Committee of Estates began to moderate its policies towards the royalists on 26 October when it promised a general pardon to any who disbanded in the next fifteen-twenty days and subsequently behaved well. As Leslie advanced, Middleton retreated until he came to Huntly's seat of Strathbogie. There on 4 November Leslie and Middleton signed a treaty which permitted the royalists to disband under the general pardon previously offered. Shortly afterwards Leslie and his regiment returned south and settled into winter quarters.[90]

Due to Leslie's loyalty to the kirk party his power and prestige diminished as the royalists began to insinuate themselves into positions of authority. His regiment went into winter quarters in Fife during November 1650. Leslie, however, remained at Stirling with the army. Throughout the winter the Committee of Estates and the army staff became filled with Leslie's former foes and he became a staff officer of secondary importance. Meanwhile the regiment fell foul of the authorities on several occasions. On 26 April 1651 a trooper was accused of fornication with an indweller of Culross, presbytery of Dunfermline on 3 March. The session wrote to the regimental officers to have the offender punished in the army. On 29 April the Committee of Estates summoned another member of Leslie's to answer for insolencies. The next day the Committee ordered the regiment to refund money to Culross for taking excessive quarters. On 7 May Leslie received command of the 1st Cavalry Brigade of three regiments, which excluded his own. This brigade was to be posted on the extreme left wing of the line of battle. The Committee of Estates ordered Leslie's Horse to depart from Fife to Stirling on 17 June. Each trooper was to receive £3 upon his departure. Three days later new levy quotas were issued for the regiment. Teviotdale was to recruit ten troopers, and Midlothian and Berwickshire were to provide thirteen and 133 men respectively. On 31 July Leslie and his regiment moved south from Stirling on the march to Worcester. Throughout August Leslie, jealous of Middleton's rapport with the officers, quarrelled with his comrade in arms. Leslie repeatedly stated that the horse 'as well as they look they will not fight'. On 1 September Charles II attended an

Anglican service, and the Scottish chaplains were quick to attack this action. They claimed that no true Covenanter could support such a king. Thus, prior to Worcester Leslie was confused in his mind as to what to do. He may have been further plagued by the image of another disastrous defeat at the hands of Cromwell. Prior to the 3rd all of the horse were stationed at Pitchcroft, north of the city under Leslie's command. On the morning of 3 September he issued, revoked and contradicted his own orders. During the battle Leslie failed to send succour to either Middleton at Powick, or Hamilton in the centre. Instead he rode about as 'one amazed'; nothing would persuade him to commit the vast body of the cavalry to an attack. Finally, at the end of the day Leslie escaped northwards with 4,000 demoralised horsemen. On the 9th Colonel Birch reported from Manchester that he had captured Leslie and Middleton with 1,000-1,200 troopers at Blackstone Edge in the moors between Paysdale and Halifax. Leslie was initially imprisoned in Liverpool. Meanwhile back in Scotland Leslie's own troop had served as a guard for the Committee of Estates. On 28 August it was broken up at Alyth when an English cavalry detachment surprised the Committee. Leslie spent the years of the interregnum in the Tower. He was released in 1660; in the following year Charles II created him Lord Newark and provided him with a pension of £500 per annum.[91] Leslie contributed greatly to the Covenanter victories in the 1644-50 period. Yet his nervous breakdown at Worcester sealed the destruction of their last army.

Earl of Leven's Horse

Colonel: Lord General Alexander, 1st earl of Leven

Ministers: Norman Leslie, David Campbell, John Veitch, George Pittiloch, Andrew Makghie[92]

In 1649 Leven was one of the most experienced commanders in the kirk party, but he was too old to take a field command. Nevertheless, the Committee of Estates reappointed him as Lord General due to his officially leading the Whiggamore forces. On 28 February the Estates commissioned Leven colonel of horse for Berwickshire and Haddingtonshire. Both shires were to levy 200 troopers. On 1 June Leven's troop was ordered to quarter in Angus. The troop of Routmaster the laird of Ormiston was provided two-thirds of its quarters in Berwickshire, and the other third in Tweeddale. At the end of July Leven's and Ormiston's troops mustered sixty men each, and Routmaster Swinton the younger of that Ilk had sixty-two men in his troop. On 6 August the Estates ordered both shires to recruit 133 troopers for the regiment. However, there is no evidence that the shires levied these men. The regiment disappears from the records until spring 1650. On 9 April David Wilson, an indweller in Haddington, deponed that a trooper in Ormiston's troop (then quartered in the tolbooth), had abused his wife and household, and had blasphemed the name of

God. The kirk session appealed to the bailies to prevent the trooper's escape. Five days later the elders judged trooper Robert Tait guilty of the above mentioned crimes, which included calling Wilson's wife a 'lying devill'. He was remanded to the burgh magistrates until he became sensible of his guilt. On the 18th Tait appeared and confessed, then asked forgiveness on his knees. The presbytery of Peebles found a trooper in Leven's Life Guard guilty of supporting the Engagement and scandalous carriage. However, he seems to have escaped repentance due to the summer campaign.[93]

As the summer of 1650 neared, Leven's Horse only had a few more months to exist as a separate unit. On 19 June the Estates ordered Leven's troop to Midlothian, and the other two troops to East Lothian. On 3 July East Lothian and Berwickshire were ordered to produce two troops of sixty-seven men each. Five days later a committee of the Committee of Estates asked the presbytery of Haddington for aid in mustering forty horse from the presbytery's portion of East Lothian. Leven took little part in the summer campaign, but his horse served at Dunbar. After the battle Routmaster Swinton served in the Western Association Army, then joined the English. On 7 January 1651 the Commission of the General Assembly cited him to appear at St. Andrews on the 21st for these crimes. That body cited him again on 5 April to come to Perth on 14 May. On 31 March the Estates cited him for treason. Not surprisingly Swinton failed to answer any of these summonses. Ormiston, however, remained loyal to his country and became a member of the Committee of Estates. On Christmas 1650 the Committee of Estates gave Major General Massey permission to take over this regiment. This was to be done because Massey's troop was given to Lieutenant Colonel Hamilton. Furthermore, the remainder of Kirkhill's Horse would be cast into this regiment before it went to Massey. On 6 January 1651 the Committee issued orders regarding mutineers belonging to Leven's troop. These men had thrown away their standard and had fled. Lord Cranston received orders to apprehend them. The deserters were to be punished, discharged, and barred from joining other regiments. Their action may have arisen from the dislike of serving under an Englishman or of being under orders from a man more royalist than Leven. The men in Leven's Horse who remained with Massey participated on the Worcester campaign. Despite Leven's physical incapacity he remained with the Committee of Estates. The earl and routmaster Ormiston were captured on 28 August at Alyth. The English sent Leven to the Tower, but he gained his full liberty in 1654.[94]

Lemlair's Retinue

Colonel: John Munro of Lemlair

Lemlair had received his military experience on the continent, where he rose to the rank of colonel. In 1639 he led members of clan Munro in Seaforth's host which marched to Elgin. Ten years later he joined Pluscardine's Rising.

Sometime between May 1649 and April 1650 Lemlair became a client of the Covenanter nobleman, the earl of Sutherland. Consequently, in April 1650 when Strachan was mustering a force to oppose Montrose's army Lemlair took the field with his son, Andrew. (Probably due to Sutherland's influence Andrew had been appointed captain of the Ross militia.) Lemlair combined his men with those of Balnagowan. Thus on 27 April Strachan assigned this force of 400 foot to the fourth division of his tiny army. Lemlair's allegiance was suspect by both sides, and it has been said he would have sided with whoever was initially successful. Fortunately for the Covenanters Strachan quickly gained the upper hand. The slaughter of Montrose's men at Carbisdale is attributed to the decision of Balnagowan and Lemlair to throw in their forces. After Carbisdale Lemlair did not take the field again.[95]

Logan's Force

Commander: (?) Major Logan

On 5 September 1650 the Committee of Estates appointed Logan organiser for forming the Scots who fled from England into military units. There is no further information regarding this venture which was necessitated by the disaster at Dunbar. Logan may have been the major of the same surname who received that rank in the Master of Gray's Foot on 30 December 1650.[96]

Earl of Loudoun's Horse Troop

Commander: John, 1st earl of Loudoun

Although one of the original Engagers Loudoun defected to the kirk party and led men in the Whiggamore Rising. There is no commission for his troop, which was also known as the Lord Chancellor's troop due to Loudoun's office. It is first mentioned as an old troop on 1 June 1649, when the Estates ordered it to quarter in East Lothian. On 3 July a trooper appeared before the Haddington kirk session, where he confessed fornication with two women. He then craved forgiveness on his knees. The session set his penance at four Sundays on the pillar and a fine of £5 6s. 8d. He was also to produce a testimonial from his regiment saying he was single, and had not fallen into sin before. At the end of July Loudoun's troop consisted of 100 men and a trumpeter. It disappears from the records until 19 June 1650, when it was ordered back to East Lothian. The troop served on the summer campaign with Leslie's army. On 28 August Loudoun went through the camp saying that the cause of God could not be maintained by wicked men (that is royalists). An Englishman considered him either a mad man or a traitor for speaking on behalf of purging. The troop served at Dunbar and is not mentioned again. However, Loudoun remained in the government and it is possible that the remnants of his troop stayed with him. On 1 January 1651 he attended Charles II's coronation at Scone. In June the Commission of the General Assembly accused the earl of adultery with a Major Johnson's wife. This action had serious military consequences, because Johnson deserted to Cromwell and told him of a plan to attack the quarters of part of the English forces. Loudoun accompanied the army to Worcester, but he managed to escape to the Highlands. In 1653 Loudoun joined Glencairn's rising, after which his military career ends.[97]

Lovat's Foot

Colonels: Sir James Fraser of Brea, Tutor of Lovat (1650), Hugh, 8th Lord Lovat

Lieutenant Colonel: Alexander, Master and Tutor of Lovat

Major: Hugh Fraser of Struy

The Lovat Frasers were one of the northern clans loyal to the Covenants from 1639. On 22 February 1649 Mackenzie of Pluscardine attacked and took Inverness with the help of the magistrates. This was a blow to the prestige of the Lovat Frasers as Sir James of Brea was the burgh's governor. However, he was in the south at that time. Lieutenant Hugh Fraser held Lovat Castle against the royalists. Unhappily he could do little more because one hundred men of the 200 man garrison were in Strathspey. The clan passes out of the Covenanter military annals until July 1650. On the 3rd parliament commissioned Brea colonel of foot for Seaforth's and Lovat's areas of Inverness-shire. The regiment was to contain 750 men. It served on the Dunbar campaign and at the battle. Brea's death sometime in late 1650 may be ascribed to wounds inflicted at the battle. His regiment disappears from the records in September. On 20 December parliament appointed Alexander Fraser, Master and Tutor of Lovat, colonel of foot for Inverness-shire and Ross. However, the clan history suggests that the commission actually went to the seven-year-old Lord Lovat, and that his uncle the tutor acted as lieutenant colonel. Certainly there is some confusion about the name of the regiment. It is known as the Master of Lovat's, the Tutor of Lovat's, and Lord Fraser's Foot. The effective commander, Alexander Fraser, had been Master of Lovat from 1643, and in 1651 he became the Tutor. He had received a previous commission in the Covenanter forces due to the patronage of his uncle the earl of Wemyss. Thus when he received his commission the Tutor had both prestige in the recruiting area and some military experience.[98]

Although the Tutor probably received his commission in January 1651 at the latest, he waited for the winter to end before mustering his regiment. In April the Tutor held a rendezvous at Inverness of 800 men. He selected half of them, and placed them in six (or seven) companies under the command of (the major?), a captain lieutenant, and five captains. The regiment marched south through Badenoch, Appin, and then to Stirling, arriving on 6 May. The next day the Committee of Estates ordered a muster of the regiment. On 16 May the Committee informed the Tutor to have the regiment ready to march in a few days according Major General Middleton's orders. The men were to take the forty days' loan and pay for entertainment with them. However, the destination of the march is unknown. Sometime before the army marched south Struy acted as captain of the Life Guard of Foot for a day. He met Charles II after overhearing the Rev. Thomas Colville tell the king that of all the clans the Frasers had been the most loyal to the monarchy throughout its history. Struy then told Charles

> Do but command us in any service prestable, we shall compeat with any clan within your Majesties camp.

The surviving muster rolls of the regiment show that its strength remained stable. On 12 June it contained 528 men, and on 18 July there were 522 common soldiers in the regiment. The Tutor of Lovat's Foot served on the Worcester campaign, which led to its destruction. The Tutor was initially taken prisoner on 3 September, but managed to escape.[99]

Lumsden's Foot

Colonel: Lieutenant General Sir James Lumsden (of Innergelly)

Ministers: John Gray, Patrick Colville, George Ogilvy[100]

Lumsden was a professional soldier who had served on the continent and in the Covenanting armies before 1649. In 1649 he raised a regiment of foot from the presbytery of St. Andrews. Lumsden's Foot served on the summer 1650 campaign. At Dunbar Lumsden served as a brigade commander. The regiment was so placed that it was entirely destroyed and Lumsden fell prisoner to the English. On 10 June 1651 the Committee of Estates granted the lieutenant general £240 from voluntary contributions for prisoners of war to maintain himself.[101]

Lord Mauchline's Horse

Colonel: James, Lord Mauchline

Major: (?) Staiger

Ministers: Alexander Blair, Robert Campbell, Alexander Livingston

Although this regiment was meant to be one of infantry it was raised as cavalry. On 3 July 1650 the Estates commissioned Mauchline, or his father Loudoun, a colonel of foot for Lanarkshire. The shire was assessed 900 men. However, at Dunbar Mauchline commanded a regiment of horse. On 5 September the Committee of Estates allocated a portion of 500 cavalry to be raised from Ayrshire and Renfrewshire to him. On 15 October the Committee ordered Mauchline's men to Perthshire. They may have subsequently served under Brown and Leslie against Middleton's Rising. Mauchline's quartered in Fife from 22 November 1650 to 28 February 1651. On 14 December 1650 Mauchline and Major General Montgomery petitioned the Committee and king regarding the reinforcements for their regiments. Ayrshire and Renfrewshire had levied slightly more than a fifth of the quota assigned them in September, but none of these men had joined Mauchline's Horse. Instead the only recruits he had received were thirty-nine men from Fife originally assigned to Colonel Robert Hackett. Mauchline and Montgomery requested the right to take recruits from the broken and scattered elements of the Western Association Army in order to bring their regiments up to strength. The king and Committee granted this request, unfortunately it is uncertain how successful they were in gathering men from this dubious source. In late April Major Staiger, a High German, landed in Zealand with letters for Lady Morreton. Staiger then sailed for England. The royalists in the Netherlands suspected him of being a spy, as he had claimed he was returning to Scotland. On 7 May 1651 Mauchline's Horse was placed in the 6th Cavalry Brigade with Innes', Erskine's, and Forbes'. On 10 June the Kyle district of Ayrshire was ordered to levy eighty troopers for Mauchline. Sometime prior to spring 1651 the regiment had taken up quarters in Fife and on 17 June Mauchline's received orders to proceed to Stirling with the other cavalry regiments in the shire. Each trooper was to receive £3 on his departure. Unfortunately, there is no further mention of the regiment, so it is unknown where it met its destruction.[102]

Melville's Dragoons

Commanders: Lieutenant Colonel Melville (1650). Colonel James Braibner/ Brainner (1650-51)

This is another relatively obscure unit which was commissioned to be raised following the debâcle of Dunbar. On 14 October 1650 the Committee of Estates appointed a Lieutenant Colonel Melville to levy a force of dragoons from Inverness-shire, Ross, Cromarty, Sutherland and Caithness. By early December Melville had demitted this charge, being replaced by Colonel Braibner. (Melville may have been the man of the same name and rank who was the Captain of the Castle of North Leith. He was captured by the English at the storming of Dundee.) On 9 December Braibner petitioned the king and Committee of Estates regarding his regiment of 272 dragoons — the levy quota.

The colonel claimed that much had been accomplished towards levying a regiment, however, problems did exist. Braibner complained that the Captain of Clanranald, and Sir James MacDonald of Sleat had opposed his levying men from Lochaber. The colonel requested that letters be sent to these men ordering them to allow him to gather recruits there. Braibner also requested a proportion of the Orkney levy so that his regiment did not fall far behind Campbell's and Menzies' dragoons in strength. Braibner also asked for Captain Wardlaw's force of dragoons, which had been levied in Moray and Nairn. On Christmas Day the Committee for Military Affairs agreed to all of Braibner's requests, ordering the Orkney men to be given to the regiment. On 30 January 1651 the Committee of Estates authorised the Committee of Grievances to examine the behaviour of the regiment, which had created disturbances in Ross. There is no further reference to the regiment, but it may be assumed that it ceased to exist sometime in September.[103]

Menzies' Dragoons

Colonel: William Menzies

Menzies was a younger son of the Covenanter, Menzies of that Ilk. On 10 September 1650 the Committee of Estates issued instructions to Fife to raise 350 men for Menzies' dragoons. On 12 October Cupar burgh council received orders to levy six dragoons from the committee for the regiment. The Committee of Military Affairs mentioned Menzies' dragoons in their proceedings on 9 December, suggesting the regiment was partially raised. On 12 June 1651, the Committee of Estates ordered Menzies to quarter his men on Airth, Baldernock, Killearn, Inchcailloan and Balfron. The laird of Kilsyth was to be freed of further quartering by the regiment, when it moved to these quarters. Five days later Colonel Sir James Douglas of Mouswall appeared before the Estates with a grievance against Menzies. At the battle of Dunbar Mouswall had loaned Menzies his horse, with saddle, bridle, and pistol to escape. Nearly nine months later these items were still in Menzies' possession. The king and Committee ordered Menzies to return the horse, or pay Mouswall 'fifty pieces'. The dragoons served on the Worcester campaign. Colonel Menzies lost his life and his regiment ceased to exist as a result of the battle.[104]

Ministers' Horse

Colonel: Archibald Strachan

Lieutenant Colonel: William Ralston of Ralston

Major: (?) Govan

Minister: John Carstairs[105]

This regiment was under the command of the notorious republican radical — Archibald Strachan. From February 1649 until early summer 1650 he served as the lieutenant colonel of Ker's Horse. As early as May 1649 Leslie had wished to cashier him as a sectary, but the Rev. Mungo Law had dissuaded him from taking that sensible step. Strachan's feelings towards Leslie were as suspicious, thinking him too much of a royalist. On 3 July 1650 the presbytery of Edinburgh sent out a letter to all the presbyteries calling for the levying of a regiment of 550 horse

> to joyne in so necessarie a worke for the Incouragement of others, and the stopping of the mouths of the Malignants and profane who speak evill of the Ministers as though they did onlie keep themselves free of public burdens . . . and to give a public testimonie of their willingness to resist those sectaries . . .

The letter proceeded to set the contribution of each minister: those with stipends of £1,000 or over were to supply £133 6s. 8d., all other ministers were to give in £66 13s. 4d. The remaining presbytery records suggest that the ministers acted with alacrity, for several had made the assessment and delivered the money before Dunbar. There is some difficulty in determining the amounts collected and disbursed. Only the presbyteries of Brechin, Elgin, Perth, St. Andrews, Kirkcaldy and Stranraer mention the sums gathered in. These six presbyteries contributed £5,840 or less than ten per cent of the £66,666 13s. 8d. the Commission wished to raise. However, the presbyteries had less difficulty in arranging for the ministers to supply the money for the horse regiment than it did in having them send out infantrymen in 1643-45. A contemporary observer stated that the ministers raised their regiment of horse 'freelie and franklie'.[106]

Strachan played a prominent part in the Dunbar campaign for good or ill. On 31 July he and his regiment (or the portion that had been raised by then) formed part of Major General Montgomery's force which attacked the English in Musselburgh. Throughout the summer Strachan pushed for further purging of the army. He probably signed the West Kirk Declaration on 13 August. Certainly he and Ker held secret talks with Cromwell's officers. On the evening of 2 September Strachan and Ker agreed with those on the council of war who wished to fight. On the 3rd Strachan's Horse was posted on the Scottish right flank, the front rank of which were lancers. Initially these cavalry units repulsed Lambert, and to his credit Strachan fought desperately. The regimental chaplain was wounded, stripped, and left for dead by the English. However, Strachan and his regiment extricated themselves and retreated to Stirling. Their career with the Army of the Covenants had ended.[107]

Strachan had only a short wait before being relieved of further connections with Leslie. On 5 September the Committee of Estates commissioned Strachan and Ker to proceed with the remnants of their regiments to the Western Association where they were to raise a new army. Eventually Strachan's Horse consisted of about 400 troopers well mounted and armed, being dressed in buff.

There were as many Dutchmen and High Germans in this regiment as there were in the others of this army. Prior to the promulgation of the Western Remonstrance Strachan was in communication with Cromwell. His major was also writing to the English. On 17 October Strachan refused to sign the Western Remonstrance. Instead he wished Charles II to be made a prisoner or banished, which would cause Cromwell to leave. This extraordinary action caused consternation in the army and the Committee of the Western Association. The immediate response was to order him not to attend his regiment, but Strachan disobeyed. Some counselled his arrest so he would not join Cromwell. But the Committee decided to do nothing for fear of affronting Ker and other officers. However, the Committee cashiered Major Govan, and Scoutmaster Dundas, a friend and ally of Strachan. Although Strachan departed from his regiment he remained in the background to take action. At 4 a.m. on 1 December Lieutenant Colonel Ralston led 100 troopers of the regiment into Hamilton driving out the English cavalry. However, the regiment fled when Ker tried to regroup. The English pursued the army to Paisley and Kilmarnock. On the 2nd 200-300 men rallied at Kyle, but Strachan persuaded them to disband. He failed to convince them to join the English. The army was past saving in any case and most Scots were glad of it. Later that day Strachan and Routmaster Swinton led thirty men over to Lambert. Strachan's military contribution to the Covenanters had ended, but he was not forgotten by them.[108]

The Covenanters still had to deal with Strachan and part of his regiment after his defection. On 14 December the Commission of the General Assembly ordered him to appear before it in Perth for refusing to fight, corresponding and speaking with the English. On Christmas Day the Committee of Estates allocated the recruits due to Strachan's regiment from Clydesdale to Lieutenant Colonel Hamilton's Horse. On 3 January 1651 the Commission of the General Assembly meeting in Perth commenced proceedings of excommunication against Strachan for desertion of his charge (which was for the defence of God and the kingdom), and for fraternisation with the enemy. On the 12th the Commission formally excommunicated him. The Committee of Estates cited Strachan for treason on 31 March. He naturally failed to appear, however, he was probably sentenced in absentia.[109] Between 1648 and 1650 Strachan had been of great assistance to the kirk party and to the Remonstrants-Protesters. His actions after the battle of Hamilton earned him the hatred of all but the minute republican element in Scottish politics.

Montgomery's Horse Troop(s)

Commander(s): Routmaster (?) Montgomery, Captain George Montgomery

Two very obscure troops, or one mentioned only in June 1650. On the 7th the Estates ordered Routmaster Montgomery's troop to Moray from Fife. Twelve days later Captain George Montgomery's troop was ordered to Fife.[110]

Montgomery's Horse

Colonel: Major General Robert Montgomery

Lieutenant Colonel: James Chalmers of Gadgirth

Ministers: Thomas Ramsay, John Edmonston, David Brown[111]

By 1649 Major General Montgomery had gained considerable military experience in Scotland and had also demonstrated his loyalty to the kirk party by initiating the Whiggamore Raid. The kirk party dominating parliament commissioned him a major general of horse in the Army of the Covenants, as well as making him colonel of horse for Ayrshire and Renfrewshire. The two shires were to provide 400 troopers for Montgomery's regiment. On 1 March Montgomery with the advice of the parliamentary commissioners of Ayrshire nominated the laird of Gadgirth as his lieutenant colonel. Gadgirth was also to have a troop in the regiment. On the same day the commissioners of Renfrewshire nominated John Shaw the younger of Greenock to be lieutenant colonel 'to the Lord Cathcart when he shall be needed'. Greenock was assigned a troop as well. However, the situation never arose which made Cathcart's and Greenock's troops independent of Montgomery's Horse. Montgomery's Horse was in the northeast for part of spring 1649. Between April and 7 May troopers of the regiment took five kids, five lambs, ten pecks of bere, and three firlots of black oats from the laird of Cubine's lands. They also received £11 in quartering allowance from Culgishie. On 1 June the Estates ordered Montgomery's troop to quarter in Aberdeenshire and Banffshire. At the end of July the regiment consisted of four troops — Montgomery's, Gadgirth's, Cathcart's and Greenock's — of sixty men each. On 6 August parliament instructed Ayrshire to levy 173 horsemen and Renfrewshire to provide 58 troopers for Montgomery's Horse. As with many other regiments this one disappeared from the records for a number of months.[112]

For Montgomery's Horse 1650 was a year of intense activity, mainly of a military nature. On 16 January Lord Cathcart appeared before the presbytery of Ayr requesting an examination of the troopers under his command. The presbytery informed the ministers to report to it on the 30th. On that day the ministers received further instructions from the presbytery to render their reports on Cathcart's and Gadgirth's troops to the committee of the shire on 6 February. However, nothing is known about the substance of these reports. On 22 April a trooper of Gadgirth's was mentioned as the correspondent in a case of fornication in the parish of Ayr. Meanwhile Montgomery's troop had continued to quarter in the northeast and it was able to rendezvous with Strachan's force at Tain. This unit took part in the battle of Carbisdale on 27 April. The Estates issued orders to the regiment to change its quartering grounds on 19 June. Montgomery's troop was to proceed to East Lothian, while Gadgirth's went to Kyle, Cunningham, and the parts nearest Stirling, and

Greenock's was sent to Renfrew. On 3 July the Estates ordered Ayrshire and Renfrewshire to levy 173 and 58 troopers respectively to be made into three troops of 73 men for the regiment. Unfortunately, there is no evidence regarding the raising of these men. By late July Montgomery's Horse was with Leslie's army at Edinburgh. On the 31st Montgomery led a force of 2,000 horse (presumably including his own), and 500 foot against the English quartering in Musselburgh. The Scots withdrew after scoring an initial success. Montgomery's Horse was engaged at Dunbar, but the regiment escaped northwards. By 22 September it was quartering in the parish of Dron, Perth presbytery. On the 5th the Committee of Estates had instructed Ayrshire and Renfrewshire to levy 500 horse, some of whom were to reinforce Montgomery's Horse. On 4 October the Committee sent Montgomery with his regiment north to find the king, who had fled on The Start. On the 5th Lieutenant Colonel Nairn of Brechin's Horse and officers of this regiment found Charles II in a cottage belonging to the laird of Clova. In late November the Committee used Montgomery again to deal with opponents of the regime, this time on the left of the political spectrum. Montgomery was ordered into the Western Association with a force of cavalry under instructions to take over or disperse its army. Montgomery had only reached Campsie on 30 November, when on the next day he learned of the defeat of Ker's army at Hamilton and ended his operation. However, several days later Montgomery set out towards Glasgow, where the English were, but by 11 December they had retired to Hamilton. On this march Montgomery quartered first near Loch Lomond, but as the country was becoming impoverished he moved on to Port and Kilmadock. By the 11th Montgomery had garrisoned Craigbarnet House with a cornet and twenty troopers; the laird of Glover had already placed twenty foot in that place. On the 14th Montgomery and Lord Mauchline petitioned the Committee of Estates regarding the recruits due from the southwest. Although 500 troopers had been allotted to regiments near Stirling, the men had gone instead to the Western Association Army and were now broken and scattered. Montgomery had received 146 troopers raised by his father, the earl of Eglinton, from Ayrshire, but he hoped for more. Montgomery and Mauchline requested permission to recruit the former elements of the Association's army, which the Committee allowed. Nothing more is heard of these recruits and it is uncertain whether they were levied. Montgomery's Horse again disappeared from the records for several months.[113]

When the regiment is again mentioned, in February 1651, it had only a few more months remaining. On 2 February a trooper was mentioned in the Burntisland session meeting as being guilty of fornication which indicates at least part of the regiment spent the winter in Fife. On 22 April Montgomery's Horse was mentioned as one of the regiments which had quartered at some time in Angus between then and September. A week later a corporal was cited to appear before the Committee of Estates for insolencies he had committed. On 7 May Montgomery received command of the 3rd Cavalry Brigade of three regiments (excluding his own), which was to serve on the left flank of the battleline. Montgomery's is one of the few cavalry regiments for which a contemporary estimate of its strength survives. On 16 May the Committee recorded that there were 415 men and officers in the regiment. On 9 June Montgomery received orders to remove his or Colin Campbell's dragoons from Dunbartonshire to Ayrshire and Renfrewshire. It is uncertain whether either regiment moved south. On the next day the Committee of Estates instructed Galloway to raise forty troopers, Renfrewshire 114 men, and Cunningham near Renfrewshire six horsemen for Montgomery's. Again there is no evidence regarding this levy. Montgomery and his regiment served on the Worcester campaign. On the day of the battle Montgomery commanded the Scots forces holding Powick Bridge to the south of the city against Fleetwood and Ingoldsby. The major general only retreated his forces after they had run out of ammunition. Montgomery and his men were forced back into the city, because Pitscottie, who had been securing their left flank, had also fallen back. During the battle Montgomery was wounded, depriving his men of leadership; the English later took him prisoner. His regiment served with Leslie's body of cavalry which did nothing, and ceased to exist as a fighting force after the battle.[114] It was a sad end to Montgomery's career as a Covenanter officer, for he and his men had always distinguished themselves.

Mouswall's Foot and Dragoons

Colonel: Sir James Douglas of Mouswall

Minister: Alexander Smith[115]

Mouswall was a Covenanter from Dumfriesshire, who served as an M.P. for Dumfriesshire and the Stewartry of Annandale in 1644, 1649 and 1650-51. On 28 February 1649 parliament commissioned him the colonel of a regiment of Dumfriesshire foot. The shire was to levy 600 men for Mouswall's command. On 1 June the regiment was ordered to quarter in Dundee. Unfortunately, there is no muster of the regiment in 1649, however, on 6 August the Estates instructed Dumfriesshire to raise 450 men. This suggests that Mouswall's Foot consisted of 150 men in summer 1649. The regiment served on the summer campaign in 1650 and was at Dunbar. During the battle Mouswall loaned his horse with saddle, bridle, and pistols to William Menzies to allow him to escape. Mouswall also managed to avoid capture and reached the army at Stirling. The fate of his regiment is not known, but the survivors would have been co-opted into Mouswall's new regiment. Initially Nithsdale was ordered to provide Mouswall with 900 foot as reinforcements for his regiment. However, the committee of war instead offered a force of 500 dragoons. This was accepted by the Committee of Estates on 23 October. Subsequently Mouswall proceeded to Annandale and Dumfriesshire where he raised 400 dragoons. These recruits were sent north towards Stirling under the major. However, before they reached

Glasgow the major received an order from Colonel Ker, backed by the Committee of Estates, for the men to march back in order to assist the levying of deficients. Before Mouswall could petition the Committee to change the order the battle of Hamilton took place. Mouswall ordered his recruits disbanded as he thought it unlikely that they would successfully avoid Lambert's cavalry. From December to June 1651 there is no reference to Mouswall or his regiment. However, on 17 June the colonel petitioned the king and Committee that Menzies return his horse and gear. They responded favourably and ordered their return or the payment of 'fifty pieces' by Menzies. Nine days later Mouswall again approached the Committee, on this occasion bringing up the matter of his disbanded recruits. Mouswall suggested that he levy them again, which he thought an easy thing, because the English had departed from the region. However, he required a warrant to do so; this the Committee granted him. There is no information on whether Mouswall was correct in his supposition, and both he and his regiment disappeared from the records on 21 June.[116]

Murkill's Foot

Colonel: Sir James Sinclair of Murkill

Murkill served as an M.P. for Caithness in 1641, and 1646-47. There is no surviving commission for him, nor is there much material about the regiment. It is mentioned once in the muster roll of 31 July 1649, when it contained 160 foot.[117]

Pitscottie's Foot

Colonel: Major General Colin Pitscottie

Ministers: Robert Young, John Mak(c)gill, Hugh Kennedy, Gabriel Maxwell, Henry Rymer, Alexander Rollock, John Murray, Alexander Moncrieffe, Thomas Ramsay, William Jack, Alexander Dickson[118]

Pitscottie was both a veteran officer and one of the supporters of the kirk party against the Engagement in spring 1648. On 21 September 1648 Leven ordered Pitscottie to quarter the Whiggamores under his command in the Canongate and Pleasance sections of Edinburgh. This unit seems to have disbanded, and on 28 February 1649 the Estates commissioned him a colonel of Fife and Kinross-shire Foot. The two counties were to levy 400 men for the regiment. By early May Pitscottie's Foot formed the Perth garrison. On 2 May Captain Lieutenant Mark Home appeared before the presbytery for fathering a bastard. After questioning him, the presbytery ordered Home to do repentance so that his child could be baptised. In late May a private in the garrison (one of those who had fled Ulster after the royalist takeover), petitioned for the right to marry a local resident. On 1 June parliament ordered the regiment to remain in Perth. At the end of July the garrison totalled 400 men in four companies. Thus, Pitscottie's Foot was one of the only regiments to reach its prescribed size. One reason for Pitscottie's ability to raise a full regiment may be his recruitment of former Engagers. On 23 November the Commission of the General Assembly wrote the Committee of Estates and Lieutenant General Leslie requiring the purging of public offices and the army. The Commission paid particular attention to Perth, claiming its government and garrison were full of malignants. The chaplain appointed at that time, John Makgill, received orders to be strict in purging the regiment. On 5 December two privates from the garrison (one of whom was from Ireland), petitioned the presbytery for the right to marry. The matter, however, was delayed until they could produce full testimonials. Two weeks later those soldiers in the garrison who had not served on the Engagement requested to swear the Solemn League and Covenant. The presbytery appointed a minister for them, but ordered them repent of their sins before taking the Covenant. On 10 January 1650 the ministers appointed to speak with Leslie concerning purging the garrison reported back to the presbytery. Leslie had told them he would speak with the garrison's major granting him the power to implement the act of parliament against royalist soldiers. The matter dropped from sight for several months until Hugh Kennedy, the regiment's chaplain, reported that the Solemn League and Covenant had not been tendered to the garrison. The presbytery ordered him to administer the Covenant with the aid of three other garrison chaplains. On 5 June the case of adultery between Janet Akison and regimental quartermaster Robert Forbes reached the presbytery. However, before Forbes could be brought to do penance the case was delayed on 7 August until military operations ended. In early July a private of the regiment appeared before the Elgin kirk session where he confessed the sin of fornication. He petitioned to be received that day as it was his first offence, and the kirk session agreed. During the summer Pitscottie and his men served in Leslie's army. They were present at Dunbar, where Pitscottie served as a brigade commander. Extrapolating from the 1651 muster rolls, the regiment seems to have lost about 170 men in the battle. There is no mention of the regiment from then until 7 May 1651 when it was quartering in or near Stirling and received orders to hold a muster. There was little variation in the strength of Pitscottie's Foot. On 13 June it contained 230 men, over a month later it had increased by only one man. The regiment and Pitscottie served on the Worcester campaign. During the battle Pitscottie commanded the left flank of the Scots forces south of the city and west of the Severn. When his men retreated from their positions Major General Montgomery was forced to withdraw into the city, because Pitscottie's men uncovered his left flank. The regiment probably served under its colonel and suffered destruction through casualties and capture. Pitscottie himself fell prisoner to the English, which ended his nine years of service with the Covenanter armies.[119]

Riccarton's Horse

Colonel: Adjutant General Thomas Craig of Riccarton

Lieutenant Colonel: Alexander Inglis of Ingliston

Minister: David Liddell[120]

In 1649 Riccarton was one of the professional officers on whom the kirk party could rely. He had served as the major and lieutenant colonel of Leslie's Horse in the Army of the Solemn League and Covenant, and as a troop commander in the New Model. However, he had refused a charge in the Engager Army. On 28 February 1649 parliament commissioned him colonel of horse for Midlothian. The shire received instructions to levy 200 troopers. Both Riccarton and Ingliston were to have their own troops. However, the muster of 21 July reveals that only Ingliston had a troop, which contained fifty-seven men. On 6 August the Estates ordered Midlothian to levy a further 133 troopers. By mid-June 1650 Riccarton had a troop. It and Ingliston's were ordered to quarter in Midlothian. On 3 July parliament again instructed the shire to levy 133 horsemen. Edinburgh was exempted from providing men for the regiment. The troopers were to be divided into one troop of sixty-six men, and another of sixty-seven. Riccarton's Horse served under Leslie in the Dunbar campaign and were present at the battle. With the exception of the appoinment of a chaplain in mid-January 1651 the regiment disappeared from the records until the spring. On 16 April Riccarton's Horse was ordered to Angus to relieve the shire it was quartering in, unfortunately it is not known which one it was. On 7 May Riccarton's Horse was assigned to the 1st Cavalry Brigade under Leslie's command. It was to serve with Rothes' and Brechin's regiments on the extreme left of the battleline. On 20 June the Committee of Estates authorised Midlothian to provide 120 troopers for the regiment. This order was a piece of wishful thinking, and it is unlikely in the extreme that Riccarton received a single trooper due to the English occupation. It is not known where the regiment served in summer 1651, but it most certainly ceased to exist sometime in September.[121]

Scottscraig's Horse

Colonel: Sir Arthur Erskine of Scottscraig

Lieutenant Colonel: Sir Charles Erskine (of Alva)

This regiment is of particular interest because its lieutenant colonel was one of the last garrison commanders to surrender to the English. In the course of this entry attention will be paid first to the history of the regiment and then to

Sir Charles Erskine's defence of Dumbarton Castle. The regiment's colonel, Scottscraig, was both a professional soldier and a former colonel in the Covenanter army. In 1648-49 he sat as a Fife M.P., and opposed the Engagement. On 28 February 1649 he received a parliamentary commission as a colonel of foot for Fife and Kinross-shire. However, he failed to act on this commission. Instead he used his parliamentary commission as colonel of horse for Stirlingshire and Clackmannanshire. These two shires were to provide Scottscraig with 240 horse. By 1 June Routmaster Campbell of Lundie's troop was recruited, and received orders to quarter in the Mearns. At the end of July the regiment contained three troops — Scottscraig's, Erskine's and Lundie's — with sixty, fifty, and sixty men respectively. The Estates issued further instructions to Stirlingshire and Clackmannanshire to raise ninety and twenty-eight troopers on 6 August. The results of this levy are unknown, and the regiment drops from sight for nearly a year. On 19 June 1650 parliament ordered Scottscraig's troop to Stirlingshire, while Erskine's and Lundie's went to Dumbarton and Linlithgowshire. Parliament desired to raise three further troops for the regiment, issuing levy quotas on 3 July. Clackmannanshire was to levy twenty-eight men, who would be combined with forty-two men from Lanarkshire to form a troop. Stirlingshire, excluding Stirling, would recruit ninety and they would join with thirteen troopers from Bute to make up two troops. Again there is no information on the success of these levies; it may be assumed that some of the men were raised. Scottscraig's Horse served at Dunbar, but managed to escape to Stirling. The Committee of Estates ordered Fife to provide about ninety-six men for the regiment on 10 September. Ten days later Scottscraig's was ordered to Fife with four other cavalry regiments to protect Burntisland. The regiment was still quartered in southern Fife on 14 November, but it departed from the shire about March 1651. It may have taken up winter quarters in Angus, but that is merely supposition. On 4 December 1650 Routmaster Lundie was ordered to be tried by the presbytery of St. Andrews for aiding Charles II's escape in early October. No verdict was ever returned, which is not surprising considering the change of policy in the Kirk on 14 December when it decided to allow the use of royalists. On 7 May 1651 Scottscraig's Horse was assigned to the 4th Cavalry Brigade under Major General Middleton. The regiment served on the Worcester campaign and was engaged at the battle. Scottscraig was killed and Lundie taken prisoner. The regiment was destroyed, however, Sir Charles Erskine fought on in Scotland.[122]

In general the defence of fortresses is beyond the scope of this work, but in this case an exception is made as the commander can be identified with a regiment. Sir Charles Erskine served as the governor of Dumbarton Castle from 1649 to early 1652. In summer 1650 when he and his troop were ordered to the burgh, his command also included Dunglas Castle. The garrison of Dumbarton Castle consisted of fifty-four men under a lieutenant, sergeant and corporal. A gunner and drummer were also in the garrison. Dunglas contained thirty foot under an ensign and corporal. Neither garrison withstood a siege in 1650. On 11 November the Committee of Estates ordered Sir Charles to repair to

Dumbarton Castle to prepare its defence. In mid-April 1651 three ministers received a commission from Dumbarton presbytery to speak with Erskine about his men's behaviour. The presbytery charged them with Sabbath breaking, swearing, drunkenness, and oppressive quartering. The ministers were to have Erskine promise to restrain his men in the future. It is uncertain whether there was any improvement in their carriage. Also in April the Committee of Estates instructed Campbell's dragoons to aid Sir Charles in uplifting supplies of grain for his garrisons from Glasgow, Renfrew, Mearns, Kilbarchan and Eastwood. In July the provost of Dumbarton persuaded Erskine not to gather cess from the burgh. However, in mid-October Erskine decided the situation would have to change as his men had received no supplies for three months. In regards to the burgh, after 16 October all goods in it were liable to be seized by the garrison until the arrears in cess was collected. Throughout the month Erskine raided the countryside demanding food and money. Not only Dumbarton, but also Glasgow was forced to contribute or suffer loss of goods. General Monck persuaded the duke of Lennox and Richmond, the hereditary captain of the castle, to have Erskine surrender. But the governor refused to accept these orders. In December General Lambert sequestered Erskine's estates, then summoned him to surrender. Again the English were refused. However, on 29 December due to lack of supplies and the impossibility of relief Erskine signed articles of surrender with Lambert. The English marched in on 5 January 1652.[123] Erskine's defence after September 1651 was not altogether pointless, for the control of Dumbarton Castle prevented the English from free use of the Clyde and provided a debarkation point for any royalist forces brought over from Europe.

Earl of Sutherland's Foot

Colonel: John, 14th earl of Sutherland

Minister: Hero Gordon[124]

Sutherland was one of the few nobles who supported the kirk party. Prior to 1649 he had commanded a regiment of foot in the home army. On 28 February 1649 he received three parliamentary commissions to raise troops. The earl was to receive 500 foot and 240 horse out of Orkney which would form two regiments. Sutherland also shared the colonelcy of foot for the area of Inverness-shire outwith Seaforth's and Lovat's zones, Sutherland and Caithness with the laird of Dunbeath. Sutherland was to have a regiment of 400 infantry from these shires. Nothing more is heard of these regiments until 6 August when the Estates ordered out more levies for the earl. Inverness-shire, Sutherland, Ross and Cromarty were to provide 300 men for an infantry regiment. Orkney would raise another 375 foot soldiers for Sutherland's regiment from that area; while Orkney and Shetland would provide the earl with fifty-four horse. However, nothing was done towards levying these forces in 1649. Not until the landing of Urry in early April 1650 did Sutherland take action to raise any of the men assigned to him, but by then it was too late. The earl raised a force of infantry which he led north from his lands to Caithness. However, Sutherland's lack of cavalry forced him to retreat from Helmsdale to Dunrobin. From there he retired into Ross with 300 foot, having left garrisons in Dunrobin, Skibo, Skelbo and Dornoch. While Sutherland's protegés Lemlair and Balnagowan took part in the Carbisdale campaign there is no further reference to the earl's own men until mid-June. Then the Estates ordered his infantry regiment south to Edinburgh to oppose an English invasion, but they were not at Dunbar. On 3 July parliament authorised Sutherland to levy the cavalry forces assigned to him in the previous August from Orkney and Shetland. He also received a commission for himself or for a colonel of his choice to raise 1,200 infantry from Seaforth's and Lovat's sections of Inverness-shire, Ross and Cromarty. The earl spent June-August raising a regiment of 1,000 foot for the kirk party regime. Fortunately for them the earl brought them south only after Dunbar. Sutherland's Foot quartered in Stirling, where they formed the backbone of the Army of the Covenants' foot regiments as the others had been badly mauled at Dunbar. Sometime in the autumn Sutherland had a meeting with the king in Perth. On 20 December the earl received another commission, this time he was to raise a foot regiment from Sutherland. Throughout the winter he levied men for the new army and by sometime in March 1651 the earl was able to send a force of Sutherland and Strathnaver men south to Stirling. On 25 April the Committee of Estates ordered the regiment to quarter at Errol and Carrde. Five days later 250 men of Sutherland's Foot (probably the recently arrived recruits), were granted a ration of two pounds of meal per day. The first muster of the regiment took place on 10 June and reveals that desertion was a tremendous problem. Sutherland's Foot mustered a mere 449 common soldiers on that day. The last recorded muster of the regiment on 18 July indicates further desertions, because there were only 375 foot present. Sutherland's Foot served on the Worcester campaign without its colonel. The regiment ceased to exist as a result of the battle on 3 September. Sutherland never received another military command.[125]

Thornton's Horse

Colonel: Sir Alexander Strachan of Thornton

Minister: John Munro[126]

This is another obscure unit. It is first mentioned on 29 November 1650 when the Commission of the General Assembly appointed a chaplain to it for three months' service. On 20 December parliament reserved one troop from Mearns, Aberdeenshire, and Banffshire for Thornton. Three days later the Estates determined that Thornton's new troop should come from south of the Mearns. However, they contradicted this decision in the act of levy issued on the same day which again authorised Thornton to have a troop from those counties mentioned on the 20th. There is no further mention of the regiment. The last reference to Thornton (M.P. for Mearns) occurs on 28 March 1651 when he was appointed to the committee for managing of the affairs of the army. This regiment ceased to exist sometime in September.[127]

Valleyfield's Foot

Colonel: Sir George Preston of Valleyfield

Major: James Stewart

Ministers: Thomas Swinton, James Edmonston, John Edmonston[128]

Valleyfield had gained his military experience as a routmaster in the Army of the Solemn League and Covenant. On 28 February 1649 he received a parliamentary commission as colonel of 1,200 Perthshire Foot. He had not raised any of these men by 6 August when the levy quota was reduced to 900 foot. Valleyfield finally carried out his commission in summer 1650. His regiment served on the Dunbar campaign and escaped from the battle with heavy losses. On 16 April 1651 one company was quartered in Dumbarton burgh. Eight days later the Committee of Estates ordered Valleyfield's, Lawers' and Balbegno's Foot to quarter at the Head of the Forth and the nearby passes. The regiments were to receive their supplies from the Stirling magazine. On 7 May Valleyfield's Foot was in or near Stirling, and it was ordered to hold a muster. Later in the month it received orders to protect the burgh and shire of Renfrew. However, it appears to have rejoined the army at Stirling by 10 June. The regiment mustered only 234 men then, and the last muster of 18 July reveals the same strength. Nothing further is known about Valleyfield's Foot; it certainly ended its military career sometime in September.[129]

Wedderburn's Foot

Colonel: Sir David Home of Wedderburn

Lieutenant Colonel: George Home of Wedderburn the younger

Wedderburn the elder had commanded regiments in the Second Bishops' War and Solemn League and Covenant armies. He also sat as a Berwickshire M.P. for the lairds in 1639-41, 1645-46 and 1649-50. His son had served as his lieutenant colonel in the Second Bishops' War. Wedderburn the younger acted as M.P. for North Berwick in 1639-41, 1643-44 (at the convention), and 1644-45. On 28 February 1649 parliament commissioned Wedderburn the elder colonel of a foot regiment. Berwickshire was to levy 600 men, while Teviotdale and Selkirkshire levied 200 foot together. On 1 June the Estates ordered Wedderburn's Foot to quarter in Arbroath. At the end of June 100 men of the regiment quartered in Berwickshire were assigned their pay as well as the maintenance due them since 18 May. By 17 July Wedderburn's had arrived in Arbroath, which elicited a petition from the Arbroath commissioner to parliament. He complained that the burgh had been overburdened with quartering since 1648. The petitioner suggested that Greenhead's Foot be removed from the burgh to lighten its suffering. Furthermore, he asked that Wedderburn's Foot have its quarters extended to all the Angus burghs and Montrose, or to the presbytery of Arbroath and adjacent parishes. The Committee of Estates disagreed with these proposals, however, they gave the Quartermaster General charge of solving the problem. There the matter rested and no further mention is made of the regiment's quarters. On 31 July Wedderburn's Foot still mustered only 100 men. However, a week later the Estates authorised Berwickshire to levy merely 450 foot. This is the last act of levy for the regiment, and there is no evidence regarding its success. It is probable that Wedderburn took no further action towards raising his regiment until the threat of English invasion in summer 1650. Wedderburn's Foot formed part of Leslie's army during his campaign against Cromwell. The regiment was present at the battle of Dunbar where it was destroyed. Both the colonel and lieutenant colonel died in the fighting.[130]

Whitslaid's Horse

Colonel: Sir Walter Scott of Whitslaid

Lieutenant Colonel: Gilbert/William Elliot of Stobs the younger

Minister: John Shaw[131]

Whitslaid was a Selkirkshire M.P. (1645-46, 1650-51), without a record of military experience in the Covenanter armies when he received his commission. The Committee of Estates appointed Whitslaid colonel of horse for Teviotdale, Selkirkshire and Peeblesshire on 5 September 1650. Whitslaid and Stobs soon went south to these shires where they successfully raised a body of horse. On 16 October the Committee of Estates ordered the regiment to Stirling, if it had not already joined the Western Association Army. Within a week Whitslaid had united with Ker's force, and the Committee instructed him to remain with that army until it sent further orders. These must have arrived quickly, for by 14 November the regiment was quartering in southern Fife. On the 22nd Whitslaid's Horse received orders to move from Fife to the south of Stirling burgh to cover the town against an English advance. By 30 April 1651 Whitslaid's Horse was back in Fife, quartering in Dunfermline presbytery. Due to the sufferings of the parishes in that presbytery Whitslaid received orders to issue a report on the exactions of his men. Unfortunately, the report no longer survives, but from the absence of mentions of the regiment in the records of the church courts it may be assumed that this was not a notorious unit. On 7 May Whitslaid's Horse was assigned to the 3rd Cavalry Brigade with Balcarres' and Arnott's Horse under the command of Major General Sir John Brown. On 17 June the regiment was again ordered from Fife to Stirling. Each trooper received permission to be paid £3 on his departure. Whitslaid's Horse quartered in the Stirling area for about a month. On 19 July it was sent once again into Fife as part of Holburn's and Brown's force which was to oppose the English under Lambert on the Inverkeithing peninsula. On the 20th Whitslaid's Horse formed part of the left wing cavalry which supported the Lowland infantry at the battle of Inverkeithing. Initially the regiment charged well but its inexperience soon told. Whitslaid's men failed to regroup after their first success; instead they turned and fled from the field with the other horse on that flank. This exposed the Lowland infantry to a flank attack and it too retreated from the field. Whitslaid's Horse never recovered from the retreat and ceased to exist after the battle of Inverkeithing.[132]

NOTES

1. *RCGA*, iii. 52, 68.
2. SRO, PA. 7.24, 27; PA. 11.8, 94; *Aberdeen Letters*, iii. 167; *APS*, VI, ii. 218-9, 506, 527, 599.
3. *Ibid.*, VI, ii. 190, 507, 567, 582.
4. SRO, PA. 7.24, 20-1; *APS*, VI, ii. 389, 658; Balfour, *Works*, iv. 164, 300, 308; *RCGA*, iii. 328; D. Mackinnon, *Origins and Services of the Coldstream Guards*, 2 vols. (London, 1833), i. 123.
5. SRO, PA. 11.11, 96; *Mercurius Politicus*, 229; *A True Relation of the routing the Scottish army, near Dunbar, Sept. 3, instant* (London, 1650), 2; C. H. Firth, 'The Battle of Dunbar', *Trans. Roy. Hist. Soc.*, 2nd Ser. xiv (1900), 46 note 6.
6. *RCGA*, iii. 463; *Fasti*, iv. 343.
7. SRO, PA. 7.7, 183v-4; PA. 7.8, 40; PA. 7.24, 14v, 111-v; PA. 11.11, 32v; PA. 16.5, 57, 59; *Aberdeen Letters*, iii. 171-2; Foster, *Members*, 359.
8. *RCGA*, iii. 25, 463; *Fasti*, vi. 221.
9. SRO, PA. 11.11, 33v; PA. 16.5, 73, 79; *APS*, VI, ii. 623; Balfour, *Works*, iv. 211; G. Wishart, *The compleat history of the warrs in Scotland under the conduct of . . . Montrose* (London, 1720), 304-5; D. Mackinnon, *The Clan Ross* (Edinburgh, 1957), 20-1.
10. *RCGA*, iii. 10, 85, 134, 342; *Fasti*, i. 155.
11. NLS, Adv. MS. 23.7.12, 119v-20; SRO, GD. 16.50, 61; GD. 45/5.14, 116; PR Dunfermline, i. 162; *APS*, VI, ii. 218-9, 507-8, 527, 582-3; Balfour, *Works*, iv. 126, 299, 308; Mackinnon, *Guards*, i. 23; *Scots Peerage*, vii. 21.
12. *APS*, VI, ii. 507, 583.
13. SRO, PA. 16.2; *RCGA*, iii. 8, 86, 463; *Fasti*, i. 155; *Ibid.*, ii. 88.
14. SRO, KSR Cumnock, 12 May, 2 June, 7 July, 1650; PR Perth, iii. 95; *APS*, VI, ii. 219, 507, 518, 527, 582, 598-9; Foster, *Members*, 36.

15. Bod. Lib., Carte MS. 28, 314v; NLS, Adv. MS. 23.7.12, 119v-20; NRH, OPR Alyth, 18 August 1650; SRO, KSR Kinglassie, i. 33v; PA. 7.24, 116; PA. 11.11, 82; PR Dunblane, 28 February 1651; Balfour, *Works*, iv. 126, 164, 300, 308; *Scotland and the Commonwealth*, ed. C. H. Firth (Scot. His. Soc., 1st Ser., xviii, 1895), 23; *Selections from the minutes of the Presbyteries of St. Andrews and Cupar, 1641-48*, G. R. Kinloch (Abbotsford Club, viii, 1837). 152; *True Relation of Routing Scottish army*, 2; *Original Memoirs during the Civil War*, ed. W. Scott (Edinburgh, 1806), 278; R. A. Bensen, 'South-West Fife and the Scottish Revolution; the presbytery of Dunfermline, 1633-1652' (Edinburgh Univ. M.Litt. thesis 1978), 221, 223, 225; W. S. Douglas, *Cromwell's Scotch Campaigns, 1650-51* (London, 1898), 102-3; Foster, *Members*, 36; Mackinnon, *Guards*, i. 23; A. M. Sinclair, *The Clan Gillean* (Charlottetown, 1899), 194; [J. C. Sinclair], *An Historical and Geneaological Account of the Clan Maclean* (Edinburgh, 1838), 163.

16. *RCGA*, iii. 13.

17. SRO KSR Canongate, iv, 54, 55; *Edinburgh*, 168, 250; *RCGA*, iii. 13.

18. SRO, PR Dumbarton, 30 July 1650; *RCGA*, iii. 8-9, 24, 30-1.

19. SRO, PA. 11.11, 32v; PA. 16.5, 130; *APS*, VI, ii. 510-11, 599, 623; Bensen, 'South-West Fife', 223, 226; Mackinnon, *Guards*, i. 23; Sinclair, *Clan Gillean*, 194; [Sinclair], *Clan Maclean*, 162-3.

20. *RCGA*, iii. 110.

21. Bod. Lib., Carte MS. 28, 314v; *APS*, VI, ii. 594, 599, 626.

22. SRO, PA. 7.7, 187; PA. 7.24, 26; PA. 11.11, 16v, 52, 56, 74; *Dumbarton Burgh Records, 1627-1746*, ed. J. Young (Dumbarton, 1860), 63-4; W. M. Metcalfe, *A History of the county of Renfrew from the earliest times* (New Club, xiii, 1905), 276; J. Paterson, *History of the county of Ayr*, 2 vols. (Edinburgh, 1847), i. 128.

23. *RCGA*, iii. 13.

24. *APS*, VI, ii. 594, 599; Mackinnon, *Guards*, i. 23; *Scots Peerage*, ii. 478, 480-1.

25. *RCGA*, iii. 9.

26. SRO, B.51.15, 38; PA. 3.2, 3; *APS*, VI, ii. 218-9, 528, 598; *Calendar of the Proceedings of the Committee for Compounding, &c., 1643-1660*, 5 vols., ed. M. Green (London, 1890), iii. 2619-20; *List of Regiments*; Somerville, *Memorie*, ii. 421, 432; Firth, 'Dunbar', 39; Foster, *Members*, 334; Mackinnon, *Guards*, i. 23; *Scots Peerage*, iv. 162.

27. SRO, GD. 16.50, 61; PA. 7.7, 165; PA. 7.24, 21; Balfour, *Works*, iv. 126, 300; Somerville, *Memorie*, ii. 421, 432.

28. SRO, PA. 11.11, 82v; J. W. Willis-Bund, *The Civil War in Worcestershire, 1642-1646, and the Scotch Invasion of 1651* (Birmingham, 1905), 239-47; *Scots Peerage*, v. 120, 122-3.

29. *RCGA*, iii. 24.

30. SRO, KSR Culross, ii. 66v; *APS*, VI, ii. 218-9; *List of Regiments*; *Scots Peerage*, ii. 576.

31. Mackinnon, *Guards*, i. 23.

32. *RCGA*, iii. 13.

33. *APS*, VI, ii. 599; *RCGA*, iii. 13.

34. SRO, KSR Duffus, I/ii. 36, 38; PA. 16.2; PR Elgin, i. 301-3, 305, 308, 313; *RCGA*, iii. 31; *Fasti*, vi. 427.

35. SRO, KSR Duffus, I/ii, 36; PA. 11.11, 32v; PA. 16.3.1, 13; PA. 16.5, 21, 23; *APS*, VI, ii. 599, 623; Foster, *Members*, 338; *Scots Peerage*, iii. 207-8; R. Small, 'Town and Parish of Dundee', *The Statistical Account of Scotland*, ed. J. Sinclair, (New edn., Wakefield, 1976), xiii. 159-60.

36. SRO, PA. 16.2; PR Brechin, i. 56, 57-v; *RCGA*, iii. 111; *Fasti*, v. 285.

37. SRO, PA. 11.11, 32v; PA. 16.3.1, 11; PA. 16.5, 85, 87; *APS*, VI, ii. 599; Foster, *Members*, 214; Mackinnon, *Guards*, i. 23; A. Maxwell, *The History of Old Dundee* (Edinburgh, 1884), 533-4.

38. SRO, KSR Dunfermline, i. 113v-4, 115; *RCGA*, iii. 9, 25; *Fasti*, v. 99.

39. SRO, KSR Wemyss, 16, 30 March 1651; *APS*, VI, ii. 217, 219, 507, 527, 582, 598; Balfour, *Works*, iii. 398; *Ibid.*, iv. 81; *Memorials, of the Family of Wemyss of Wemyss*, 3 vols., ed. W. Fraser (Edinburgh, 1888), i. 254.

40. NLS, Dep. 175, Box 87/2; *APS*, VI, ii. 389; *Council of Aberdeen*, ii. 113.

41. SRO, PR Deer, ii. 44, 54; *RCGA*, iii. 25, 31.

42. NRH, OPR Echt, i. 14-v, 16-v; SRO, PA. 7.23/2.65; PR Turriff, 22 November, 20 December 1648; *APS*, VI, ii. 218-9, 507, 527, 582-3, 598; Mackinnon, *Guards*, i. 23.

43. Foster, *Members*, 302; Mackinnon, *Guards*, i. 23; *Scots Peerage*, vii. 386.

44. SRO, PA. 16.2; *RCGA*, iii. 46.

45. SRO, KSR Burntisland, v. 195v; KSR Wemyss, 26 October 1650; PA. 11.11, 32v, 96v; PA. 16.5, 41, 43; *APS*, VI, ii. 597; Balfour, *Works*, iv. 164, 338; Mackinnon, *Guards*, i. 23; *Scots Peerage*, ii. 282; Willis-Bund, *Worcestershire*, 239-47.

46. *RCGA*, iii. 9, 13, 31; *Fasti*, iv. 171.

47. *APS*, VI, ii. 599; Balfour, *Works*, iv. 98; Firth, 'Dunbar', 45 note 5; Mackinnon, *Guards*, i. 23.

48. *RCGA*, iii. 29.

49. SRO, PA. 7.7, 171; PA. 7.24, 14v, 65; *APS*, VI, ii. 219, 389, 507, 613; Balfour, *Works*, iv. 98, 278; Foster, *Members*, 202; Maxwell, *Dundee*, 528.

50. NLS, Dep. 175, Box 87/2; SRO, KSR Duffus, I/ii. 14v-5; KSR Dunfermline, i. 105-v; KSR Edinkillie, i. 19; PA. 11.8, 3v; PR Dunfermline, i. 109; PR Elgin, i. 268; *APS*, VI, ii. 217, 219, 397, 506-7, 527; Balfour, *Works*, iii. 398; *RCGA*, iii. 263; Bensen, 'South-West Fife', 211; Foster, *Members*, 167.

51. SRO, KSR Wemyss, 15, 29 June, 6 July, 26 October 1651; PA. 7.24, 20, 21; PR Elgin, i. 289; *APS*, VI, ii. 582-3, 598; Balfour, *Works*, iv. 338; *Mercurius Scoticus*, 10; Wishart, *Montrose*, 304; Bensen, 'South-West Fife', 196, 211; Mackinnon, *Guards*, i. 23.

52. *RCGA*, iii. 7.

53. Balfour, *Works*, iv. 338; *Baillie*, iii. 111; J. Nicoll, *A Diary of Public Transactions and other occurrences chiefly in Scotland from January 1650 to June 1667*, ed. D. Laing (Bannatyne Club, lii, 1836). 36; *RCGA*, iii. 7; Somerville, *Memorie*, ii. 441-2; Mackinnon, *Guards*, i. 23.

54. NRH, OPR Alyth, 9, 16 November 1650.

55. NRH, Ibid.; SRO, GD. 16.50, 61; PA. 7.24, 37, 65-V; PA. 11.8, 94-v, 97, 98; *APS*, VI, ii. 217, 219, 389, 507-8, 583, 589; Balfour, *Works*, iv. 210, 300; Foster, *Members*, 215, 307; Mackinnon, *Guards*, i. 23; *Scots Peerage*, v. 447-8.

56. SRO, PA. 16.2; *RCGA*, iii. 7-8, 13, 19, 74, 156.

57. *APS*, VI, ii. 535; J. Howie, *Biographia Scoticana*, ed. W. MacGavin (reprint edn., Glasgow, 1828), 422; Stevenson, *Covenanters*, 280-2.

58. SRO, PA. 7.7, 172; PA. 16.5, 25; Balfour, *Works*, iv, 85-6, 97, 272-3; *RCGA*, iii. 24; E. Walker, *Historical Collection of Several Important Transactions Relating to the Late Rebellion and Civil Wars of England* (London, 1707), 165, 196; Howie, *Biographia*, 423; Mackinnon, *Guards*, i. 23; *Scots Peerage*, i. 361-6; Stevenson, *Covenanters*, 281.

59. SRO, PA. 16.2; *RCGA*, iii. 282.

60. *APS*, VI, ii. 594; Balfour, *Works*, iv. 81, 85; Wishart, *Montrose*, 304; Stevenson, *Covenanters*, 280-1.

61. Paterson, *Ayr*, i.126.

62. NRH, OPR Anstruther Easter, 11 March 1651; SRO, PA. 7.24, 13, 16v, 26, 37; *RCGA*, iii. 75.

63. NLS, Adv. MS. 23.7.12, 120; NRH, OPR Anstruther Easter, 11 March 1651; SAUL, PR St. Andrews, i. 237; SRO, PA. 7.24, 116; Balfour, *Works*, iv. 164, 290, 298.

64. SRO, PA. 11.11, 57v, 66; Balfour, *Works*, iv. 301; *Scots Peerage*, vi. 452-3.

65. *RCGA*, iii. 463.

66. Bod. Lib., Carte MS. 28, 314v; SRO, KSR Holy Rude, Stirling, 7, 29 October, 15 November 1649; PA. 7.5, 46, 74; PA. 7.6, 154, 295; PA. 11.8, 5; PA. 11.11, 32v; PA. 16.3.1, 12; PA. 16.5, 29; *APS*, VI, ii. 218-9, 389, 507, 527; Bensen, 'South-West

Fife', 221, 223, 226; Douglas, *Cromwell's Campaigns*, 102; Mackinnon, *Guards*, i. 23.

67. SRO, PR Elgin, i. 286; *Extracts from the Presbytery Book of Strathbogie, 1631-54*, ed. J. Stuart (Spalding Club, vii, 1843), 135-6; *Fasti*, vi. 301, 303, 331-2.

68. SRO, PA. 7.6, 106, 218; *APS*, VI, ii. 170, 218-9; *Edinburgh*, 168; D. Forbes, *Ane Account of the Familie of Innes With An Appendix of Charters and Notes*, ed. C. Innes (Spalding Club, xxxiv, 1864), 240-1; Maxwell, *Dundee*, 527.

69. SRO, PR Elgin, i. 273, 276, 277, 281, 286; PR Strathbogie, ii. 227; *APS*, VI, ii. 507, 527, 532-3.

70. NRH, OPR Anstruther Easter, 11 May 1652; SRO, Kinglassie, 30 January 1652; PA. 7.7, 174; PA. 7.8, 61; PA. 7.24, 27, 85, 152; PA. 11.11, 72v; PA. 16.5, 89, 91; *APS*, VI, ii. 583, 705-6; Mackinnon, *Guards*, i. 23.

71. SRO, PR Linlithgow, 27 March-c. 5 June 1650; *RCGA*, ii. 308, 348 *A true relation of the happy victory obtained . . . upon April 27, 1650, against . . . James Grahame* (Edinburgh, 1650), 5.

72. NLS, Dep. 175, Box 87/2; *APS*, VI, ii. 219, 705-6; *Army of the Covenant*, i. lxix, cv; *RCGA*, ii. 263.

73. *RCGA*, ii. 263.

74. *Ibid.*

75. *APS*, VI, ii. 389, 397, 489, 508.

76. *True Relation Grahame*, 5; Wishart, *Montrose*, 304; Cowan, *Montrose*, 285-6; Furgol, 'Religious Aspects', 146.

77. Nicoll, *Diary*, 9; *True Relation Grahame*, 5; R. Chambers, *History of the rebellions in Scotland . . . from 1638 till 1660*, 2 vols. (Edinburgh, 1861), ii. 225.

78. Cowan, *Montrose*, 289.

79. *APS*, VI, ii. 582-3, 598; J. Burns, *Memoirs of the Civil War and During the Usurpation*, ed. J. Maidment (Edinburgh, 1832), 15; see above, 340-2.

80. *Letters of Samuel Rutherford*, ed. A. Bonar (Edinburgh, 1891), 649-51.

81. Bod. Lib., Carte MS. 28, 314; NLS, Adv. MS. 23.7.12, 106v; *Correspondence of Lothian*, ii. 283; Douglas, *Cromwell's Campaigns*, 103; Mackinnon, *Guards*, i. 23.

82. SRO, PA. 7.24, 14, 27; *Baillie*, iii. 124-5; *Letters of Rutherford*, 651-2, 654-5; Nicoll, *Diary*, 37; Somerville, *Memorie*, ii. 471-2; F. Dow, *Cromwellian Scotland* (Edinburgh, 1979), 181; W. L. Mathieson, *Politics and Religion*, 2 vols. (Glasgow, 1902), ii. 132; W. M. Metcalfe, *A History of Paisley 600-1908* (Paisley, 1909), 269-70.

83. *RCGA*, iii. 42.

84. SRO, PA. 7.7, 165; PA. 7.24, 21; *APS*, VI, ii. 507, 582; *Baillie*, iii. 111; Mackinnon, *Guards*, i. 23.

85. SRO, PA. 11.8, 93v-4; *APS*, VI, ii. 219, 527, 599; Somerville, *Memorie*, ii. 441-2; Douglas, *Cromwell's Campaigns*, 182; Mackinnon, *Guards*, i. 23; *Scots Peerage*, v. 268.

86. SRO, PA. 7.7, 211; *APS*, VI, ii. 620; see below, 390-1.

87. *APS*, VI, ii. 590, 599; Balfour, *Works*, iv. 81, 97; *True Relation of Routing Scottish army*, 2, 7-8.

88. SRO, PA. 16.2; *RCGA*, iii. 73, 86, 242, 446, 463; *Fasti*, ii. 18.

89. NLS, Dep. 175, Box 87/2; *APS*, VI, ii. 218-9, 389, 506-7, 527; *List of Regiments*; *Scots Peerage*, vi. 440-1.

90. NLS, Adv. MS. 23.7.12, 120; SRO, KSR Petty, 30 June, 21 July 1650; *APS*, VI, ii. 582, 598; *Baillie*, iii. 198; Burns, *Memoirs*, 15; *Correspondence of Lothian*, ii. 317-8; Douglas, *Cromwell's Campaigns*, 102, 161, 163; Mackinnon, *Guards*, i. 23; D. Stevenson, *Revolution and Counter-Revolution in Scotland, 1644-1651* (London, 1977), 178-9.

91. Bod. Lib., Tanner MS. 55, 56, 57; PRO, SP 18/16/40, 80, 81v; SRO, KSR Culross, i. 67v; PA. 7.24a, 112, 116; PA. 11.11, 66; PR Deer, ii. 80; Balfour, *Works*, iv. 299, 308; E. Hyde, *The History of the Rebellion and Civil Wars in England*, 6 vols., ed. W. D. Macray (Oxford, 1888), v. 189-90; Lane, *King Covenant*, 240; *Scots Peerage*, vi. 442; Willis-Bund, *Worcestershire*, 226, 239, 244, 247.

92. *RCGA*, iii. 8, 32, 52, 73.

93. SRO, KSR Haddington, i. 166, 167v, 169; PR Peebles, 18 April, 2 May, 4 July 1650; *APS*, VI, ii. 217, 219, 389, 507-8, 528.

94. SRO, PA. 7.7, 211; PA. 7.24, 73v; PA. 11.11, 40v; PR Haddington, vi. 124; *APS*, VI, ii. 583, 598, 658; *Baillie*, iii. 125; *The Diary of Mr. John Lamont of Newton, 1649-1671* (Maitland Club, xii, 1830), 34; *RCGA*, iii. 243; *Scotland and Commonwealth*, 9; Mackinnon, *Guards*, i. 23; *Scots Peerage*, v. 376, see below 368.

95. Wishart, *Montrose*, 304-5.

96. SRO, PA. 7.24, 15; *APS*, VI, ii. 640.

97. SRO, KSR Haddington, i. 144; *APS*, VI, ii. 389, 507, 583; *CSPD 1650*, 309; *Diary of Lamont*, 31; *Scots Peerage*, v. 507.

98. *APS*, VI, ii. 599; J. Fraser, *Chronicles of the Frasers, 916-1674*, ed. W. Mackay (Scot. His. Soc., 1st Ser., xlvii, 1905), 336-7; Mackinnon, *Guards*, i. 23; *Scots Peerage*, v. 533-4.

99. SRO, PA. 11.11, 32v, 39; PA. 16.5, 93, 95; Balfour, *Works*, iv. 211; Fraser, *Chronicles*, 378-81; A. Mackenzie, *History of the Frasers of Lovat* (Inverness, 1896), 187-8.

100. *RCGA*, iii. 8, 32.

101. NLS, Adv. MS. 23.7.12, 106v; SRO, PA. 11.11, 54; *Collection of Original Letters and Papers concerning the Affairs of England, 1641-51*, 2 vols., ed. T. Carte (London, 1739), i. 383; *True Relation Routing of Scottish Army*, 2, 7-8; Douglas, *Cromwell's Campaigns*, 102; Mackinnon, *Guards*, i. 23.

102. SRO, PA. 11.11, 54-v; *APS*, VI, ii. 599, 620-1; Balfour, *Works*, iv. 126, 300, 308; *Collection of Original Letters*, i. 454; Mackinnon, *Guards*, i. 23.

103. SRO, PA. 7.7, 209, 210; PA. 7.24, 35, 84; *Scotland and Commonwealth*, 13.

104. SAUL, Cupar Court and Council Records, 12 October 1650; SRO, PA. 7.3, 209; PA. 11.11, 58v, 67; Balfour, *Works*, iii. 338.

105. *RCGA*, iii. 7; *Fasti*, iii. 460.

106. Wishart, *Montrose*, 301; Furgol, 'Religious Aspects', 269-70.

107. Burns, *Memoirs*, 15; Douglas, *Cromwell's Campaigns*, 103; *Fasti*, iii. 460; Firth, 'Dunbar', 42-3; Mackinnon, *Guards*, i. 23; Metcalfe, *Paisley*, 267; Paterson, *Ayr*, i. 125.

108. SRO, PA. 7.24, 14; *Baillie*, iii. 113, 122, 124-5; Nicoll, *Diary*, 36-7; Somerville, *Memorie*, ii. 441-2; J. K. Hewison, *The Covenanters*, 2 vols. (Glasgow, 1913), ii. 22.

109. SRO, PA. 7.7, 211; *APS*, VI, ii. 658; *Diary of Lamont*, 27; *RCGA*, iii. 215.

110. *APS*, VI, ii. 574, 582.

111. *RCGA*, iii. 70, 86, 156; *Fasti*, ii. 157.

112. *APS*, VI, ii. 219, 389, 506-7, 702.

113. NLS, Dep. 175, Box 87/1; SRO, KSR Ayr, 22 April 1650; KSR Dron, 22 September 1650; PA. 7.7, 165; PR Ayr, 16, 30 January 1650; *APS*, VI, ii. 583, 598, 620-1; Wishart, *Montrose*, 304; Douglas, *Cromwell's Campaigns*, 102; Hewison, *Covenanters*, ii. 24; Mackinnon, *Guards*, i. 23; Mathieson, *Politics*, ii. 132; Paterson, *Ayr*, i. 125, 127.

114. SRO, GD. 16.50, 61; KSR Burntisland, v. 195v; PA. 7.24, 112; PA. 11.11, 39, 52, 54-v; Balfour, *Works*, iv. 300; *A List of the Prisoners of war who are officers in commission, in custody of the marshall-general* (London, 1651), 4; Paterson, *Ayr*, i. 128; Willis-Bund, *Worcestershire*, 239-47.

115. *RCGA*, iii. 10; *The Session Book of Dundonald, 1602-1711*, ed. H. Paton (Edinburgh, 1936), 45-7; *Fasti*, ii. 260-1.

116. SRO, PA. 7.24, 43; PA. 11.11, 67, 79-v; *APS*, VI, ii. 219, 389, 527; Foster, *Members*, 101.

117. *APS*, VI, ii. 508; Foster, *Members*, 314; *Scots Peerage*, iii. 341.

118. SRO, KSR Carluke, i.13; KSR Scoonie, i. 186, 187; PR Cupar, 6 December 1649, 22 January 1650; PR Linlithgow, 1 March 1650; PR Perth, iii. 75, 98, 108; *RCGA*, ii. 325, 327, 365; *Ibid.*, iii. 8, 462; *Kirkcaldie*, 361; *Fasti*, ii. 57.

119. SRO, KSR Elgin, vii. 64v; PA. 11.11, 32v; PA. 16.5, 113, 115; PR Perth, iii. 55-6, 64-5, 86, 89, 98, 108, 111, 115, 117-8, 120, 126; *APS*, VI, ii. 219, 389, 507; *Edinburgh*, 168; *List of Prisoners*, 2; *RCGA*, ii. 325-6; Mackinnon, *Guards*, i. 23.

120. *RCGA*, iii. 253.

121. SRO, PA. 7.8, 40; PA. 11.11, 66; APS, VI, ii. 217, 219, 507, 528, 583, 598-9; *Army of the Covenant*, i. liv, cv; Balfour, *Works*, iv. 229; *List of Regiments*; Mackinnon, *Guards*, i. 23.

122. SAUL, PR St. Andrews, i. 229; SRO, GD.16.50, 61; PA. 7.24, 21; *APS*, VI, ii. 218-9, 389, 507, 527, 583, 598-9; Balfour, *Works*, iv. 164, 300, 308; *Diary of Lamont*, 35; Foster, *Members*, 125; Mackinnon, *Guards*, i. 23; *Scots Peerage*, v. 621-2.

123. SRO, PA. 7.24, 52; PA. 11.11, 52, 73v; PR Dumbarton, 22 April 1651; *APS*, VI, ii. 507; *HMC Report*, lxxii. 270; Dow, *Cromwellian Scotland*, 16.

124. SRO, PA. 16.2.

125. SRO, PA. 11.11, 22, 26v; PA. 16.5, 17, 19; *APS*, VI, ii. 218-9, 527, 583, 599, 623; *The Sutherland Book*, 3 vols., ed. W. Fraser (Edinburgh, 1894), i. 254, 263, 265, 267; R. Gordon and G. Gordon, *A Geneaological History of the Earldom of Sutherland* (Edinburgh, 1813), 552, 558-9; *Scots Peerage*, viii. 349-50.

126. *RCGA*, iii. 156; *Fasti*, vii. 25.

127. *APS*, VI, ii. 632-3, 654; *RCGA*, iii. 156; Foster, *Members*, 338.

128. *RCGA*, iii. 8, 462; *Fasti*, iv. 347.

129. SAUL, Hay of Leyes Papers, 926; SRO, PA. 7.24, 111-v; PA. 11.11, 32v; PA. 16.5, 13; *APS*, VI, ii. 217, 219, 528, *Dumbarton Burgh*, 67; Mackinnon, *Guards*, i. 23; Metcalfe, *Renfrew*, 276.

130. SRO, PA. 7.6, 106, 218; *APS*, VI, ii. 217, 219, 389, 443, 508, 527; Balfour, *Works*, iv. 97; *List of Regiments*; Foster, *Members*, 181; Mackinnon, *Guards*, i. 23.

131. SRO, PA. 16.2; *RCGA*, iii. 463.

132. PA. 7.24, 14v, 37, 43, 116; Balfour, *Works*, iv. 164, 168, 300, 308; Bensen, 'South-West Fife', 225; Foster, *Members*, 307.

Army of the Kingdom, 1650-1651

Aldie's Horse

Colonel: Sir James Mercer of Aldie

Ministers: Robert Malcolm, Robert Mercer[1]

Aldie had served the Covenanters as a colonel of horse in the Army of the Solemn League and Covenant, the New Model Army and the Engager Army. His support of the Engagement led to his exclusion from serving in the army until after the Public Resolutions, 14 December 1650. On the 20th Aldie was commissioned colonel of horse for Perthshire. Nothing is known about the levying of the regiment which was in existence by 1 May. On that day twenty troopers arrived in Alyth. They had gone to that parish, because one of the recruits from it had deserted. The troopers threatened to quarter on one house from the 2nd, if the deserter did not reappear. Nothing further is known regarding this incident, but it does indicate the difficulties faced by this army in raising and keeping recruits. On 7 May Aldie's Horse was assigned to the 4th Cavalry Brigade under Major General Middleton with Marischal's, Ogilvy's and Scottscraig's Horse. Aldie's Horse served on the Worcester campaign, in which it was destroyed. Its chaplain, the Rev. Robert Mercer, fell prisoner to the English after the battle.[2]

Train of Artillery

General of Artillery: James Wemyss (of Caskieberran)

Lieutenant Colonel: (?) Lymburne

Following Dunbar the Army of the Covenants ceased to possess any field artillery. The loss of the cannon foundry at Potterrow, Edinburgh meant that Wemyss had to strip fortresses of guns as well as purchase them from overseas. Undoubtedly, the poor financial state of Scotland and the blockade by the English navy prevented full recourse to the second source. By February 1651 Wemyss had assembled only sixteen field pieces. Before 2 April James Menteith in Stirling had cast the brass cannon for the army. On the 5th four field pieces at Strathbogie were ordered south, and on the 24th the two guns at Bog of Gight were ordered to Stirling. On 12 June the train of artillery had extensive quarters assigned in the parishes of Airth, Larbert, Dunipace, Denny, Strathblane, Baldernock and Campsie. As of 4 July the establishment of the train contained 120 men and officers; this included seven gunners, twenty-five cannoniers and fifty mattrosses. The monthly pay of the artillery was set at £3,017 6s. 8d. The train of guns accompanied the army on the Worcester campaign and probably saw extensive action in the battle. For the artillery Worcester was a second Dunbar, but on this occasion there was to be no recovery.[3]

Earl of Atholl's Foot

Colonel: John, 2nd earl of Atholl

Lieutenant Colonel: (?) Murray of Polmais

Major: Adjutant (?) Murray

Minister: Robert Campbell[4]

In October 1650 Atholl joined Middleton's rising out of fear of discovery and punishment for his rôle in The Start. Due to the Public Resolutions the Estates could employ the earl, and on 20 December he received a commission as colonel of foot for Perthshire. Royalist rumours concerning the strength of this regiment, which was under the command of one of their number, are exaggerated. One guess placed the strength of Atholl's Foot at 1,000 men in early 1651. Another in a letter dated 5 February stated that the regiment contained 2,000 foot soldiers. While the reality of the situation appears to have been much different, it cannot be disputed that Atholl raised a large number of foot. Indeed, too great a number if one can judge by a letter of the Committee of Estates to Lord Drummond on 18 April. The Committee plainly stated that Atholl had raised a larger number of foot than demanded by the levy quota. However, no horse had been levied from his section of Perthshire. In fact the earl requested that it be excused levying any horse due to his feat in levying a large force of infantry. The king refused to honour this request. By 7 May Atholl's Foot had arrived in or near Stirling, and they received orders to hold a muster. The first muster of the regiment occurred on 11 June, revealing that Atholl's contained 856 men, well below earlier estimates. A week later the number had dropped to 715 foot. On the 20th two companies numbering 164 joined the regiment in the Stirling camp. By 2 July Atholl's Foot had lost eight men by desertion. Three days later the Committee of Estates granted Atholl command over 100 foot with their money and food to be raised from the presbytery of Dunkeld. The parishes which contributed to this new burden were to be free of all maintenance and public dues, certainly a generous incentive to speed the levy. However, from the muster rolls it appears that these men were not raised (at least by 18 July). The size of Atholl's Foot on the 18th was 859 men. Strangely, this powerful regiment did not accompany the army on the Worcester campaign. Instead it withdrew to the Atholl region of Perthshire where the earl was levying more men in late August. The regiment remained on foot until 2 September 1654 when Atholl defected from Glencairn's rising and surrendered to Monck.[5]

Lord Balcarres' Horse

Colonel: Alexander, 2nd Lord, later 1st earl of Balcarres

Minister: William Jamieson[6]

Balcarres had supported the Engagement and accepted a commission in its army; consequently he was barred from public employment until mid-December 1650. On the 20th parliament appointed him a colonel of horse for Fife. On 9 January 1651 (the same day he was elevated to an earldom) the Committee of Estates wrote him a letter encouraging him to raise his regiment and assigned him twenty-three horse from Fife. By 30 April the regiment had taken shape; indeed Balcarres was ordered to investigate the amount of maintenance it had received from the overburdened presbytery of Dunfermline, where it quartered. On 7 May Balcarres' was assigned to the 3rd Cavalry Brigade under the command of Major General Brown. Balcarres' Horse received orders to depart from Fife to Stirling on 17 June. Because the regiment was from the shire each trooper was to receive £15 and one boll, one firlot of oats on his departure. In mid-July a lieutenant in the regiment was cited for fornication, but due to the military activity of the unit he never appeared before the session. Balcarres' Horse formed part of the Scots force at the battle of Inverkeithing on 20 July. It was posted on the left flank, which covered the left flank of the Lowland infantry. The cavalry on this wing charged well, but the English Horse destroyed them as they failed to rally. However, Balcarres kept his regiment together following the battle. Unlike many members of the nobility the earl remained in Scotland during the summer, since he was the royal commissioner to the General Assembly at St. Andrews and Dundee. He opposed the Killin meeting of parliament on 10 September, because it had been called by Loudoun, a member of the kirk party. The meeting ordered Balcarres to be at Dumbarton on the 25th and in Dunkeld on the 29th. However, he refused to accept orders from the kirk party regardless of the necessity for co-operation between all Scots if they hoped to preserve their independence. In late September Balcarres had 250 horse under his command. On 31 August he had joined in alliance with the royalist marquis of Huntly. However, they did little more than make great demands on their countrymen while falling back before the English advance. On 17 November Balcarres held talks with the English.

Six days later he disbanded his regiment. On 3 December the earl formally surrendered to the English.[7]

Master of Banff's Foot

Colonel: George, Master of Banff

Minister: John Kinninmonth[8]

The Master of Banff was one of the many former Engagers who received a command in the Army of the Kingdom. On 20 December 1650 the Estates appointed him colonel of foot for Banffshire. In early January 1651 the Committee of Estates sent him a letter urging him to raise the regiment. Six days later the committee of war for the shire addressed a letter to the Committee of Estates regarding the colonel's behaviour. The master was charged with obstructing the levy, because he refused to act until he saw a copy of the act (which had not yet arrived). The shire committee requested a copy be sent to it in order to solve this difficulty. Apparently the master heard of the committee's missive, for on the 16th he sent his own to the Committee of Estates. In his letter the master reversed the rôles described in the Banffshire committee's. He claimed that it had baulked at levying any men until a copy of the act arrived, so he too requested that it be sent north. Such disagreements were not unusual in this year of national danger. In addition to the act, the master also desired the right to nominate his own men to the committee to increase its capability. It is doubtful that the Committee acquiesced to such a request; indeed it would have been an illegal act, as only parliament could appoint members of shire committees. On 20 May the Committee of Estates granted Lieutenant General Leslie authority to decide a case of wrong done by the regiment's major to Alexander Seaton of Thornton, Angus. Nothing is known concerning the details of this case. But it would not be assuming too much to consider that the action had something to do with illegal exactions undertaken by the major. By 18 June the Master of Banff's Foot was in or near Stirling. A muster on that day revealed that the regiment contained 526 common soldiers. Desertion reduced this number by eleven men as of 9 July. The regiment served under its colonel on the Worcester campaign. The master fell prisoner to the English, but unlike the majority of his men he escaped. As with other regiments engaged at Worcester this one ceased to exist as a result of the battle.[9]

Duke of Buckingham's Horse Troop

Colonel: George, 2nd duke of Buckingham

(?) Major: (?) Dochtie

The Duke of Buckingham was the only English peer to hold a command in the armies of the Covenanters. He arrived in Scotland from the Netherlands with Charles II in June 1650. However, due to his royalist attitude he was not given a military command until February 1651. On 11 February the Committee of Estates assigned a proportion of the Englishmen levied to the duke so he could have a troop. A week later the Quartermaster General and David Leslie were appointed to consider how best to raise Buckingham's troop. The next day the duke's proportion of the English recruits was set at a number not mentioned. On 19 April the Committee gave him command over English deserters without prejudice to Major General Edward Massey's recruiting. By 7 May the troop was in existence for it was then assigned to the 7th Cavalry Brigade with the Duke of Hamilton's and the Earl of Home's Horse. On 19 July the Committee of Estates decided that the troop should be increased in size. Buckingham was to have 100 horse from Perthshire and Stirlingshire with the deficients to be made up by adjacent counties. The heritors who appeared at the Stirling camp from those counties were to provide one horseman per £2,666 13s. 4d. of annual rent as of the 1649 valuation. The heritors who failed to turn up were assessed one horseman per £1,333 13s. 4d. of rent according to the same valuation. Each trooper was to have a sword, pistols, back and breast armour, a helmet, and a horse worth £266 13s. 4d. Buckingham was to send out his officers to raise the men from the heritors. Perthshire and Stirlingshire were to have their recruits ready on 30 July, while the other shires were to have their men out by 20 August. As the army left for England on 31 July the troop could have only received the recruits from the shires of Perth and Stirling. Buckingham and his troop served on the Worcester campaign and fought at the battle. He subsequently escaped to the Netherlands and returned to England in 1657. The duke played an important part in Restoration politics.[10]

Burntisland Defence Regiment

Colonel: Harry Barclay

Burntisland had been recognised as a key part of the Fife defence system when it was first fortified in 1639. In the summer of 1650 its fortifications were rebuilt by order of parliament. Throughout the autumn of 1650 and the winter-spring of 1650-51 the burgh had been garrisoned by various units. However, with the coming of summer and a more active campaigning season it was decided to withdraw the veteran troops to the field army and provide the burgh with a garrison of new recruits. Accordingly on 17 June the Estates ordered Perth and Dundee to send out and supply men for the garrison. On 7 July the Committee of Estates appointed Colonel Harry Barclay, a veteran of the Covenanter forces in 1644-48, commander of the garrison and governor of Burntisland. On the same day the Committee took action to raise a regiment for the defence of the burgh. By then Perthshire had levied 210 foot for the garrison; however, they had not occupied the burgh yet, which was then without regular troops. The Committee made the following assessments for the regiment: Peeblesshire — 40 men, Angus — 150 men, Dundee — 50 men, Mearns — 40 men, Aberdeenshire — 250 men, and Banffshire — 60 men. Three days later the heritors of the shires assessed to levy the regiment requested that they be excused due to the danger of English attacks on their coasts. The Committee denied the petition, claiming as the act of levy was done by parliament it lacked the authority to overturn it. However, the heritors were promised that men put out for this levy would be deducted from the next levy. On 19 July the burgh of Montrose petitioned for an exemption with success. The burgh council claimed that the place had suffered from plague and transient quartering, and was now under immediate threat of an English landing. The security of this burgh was probably the decisive factor in convincing the Committee to grant an exemption. The preparations for the defence of Burntisland proved to have been in vain. The burgh surrendered without a fight on 29 July. Little else could have been expected following the defeat of Inverkeithing which signalled the inability of the army to drive out a relatively small English force from Fife. If any men of the Defence Regiment were still in the burgh they either disbanded or went to the nearest Scottish garrison. In the case of Burntisland the planning by the Committee of Estates was too little, too late.[11]

Master of Caithness' Foot

Colonel: Francis (of Keiss and Northfield), Master of Caithness

Minister: Robert Brown[12]

The Master of Caithness (or Berriedale) was a son of the fifth earl. On 20 December parliament appointed him colonel of foot for Caithness. In spring 1651 the master led his regiment south through the lands of the Lovat Frasers. The regiment reached the Stirling camp around 23 April, when it received Forgandenny, Inchture and Rossvens for quarters. On 10 July it mustered 644 common soldiers, and on 18 July the regiment contained only seven fewer men. The Master's Foot served on the Worcester campaign, but it is not known where they fought on 3 September. The regimental chaplain and many men became English prisoners either on the 3rd or later as they attempted to reach Scotland.[13]

Lord Carnegie's Foot

Colonel: James, Lord Carnegie

Minister: David Auchterlonie[14]

Lord Carnegie had supported the Engagement and raised a regiment for the army in 1648. He fell prisoner to the English on the Preston campaign, but managed to escape to exile in the Netherlands in 1649. He returned to Scotland in 1650, but was denied public employment until after the Public Resolutions. Parliament appointed Carnegie a colonel of foot for Angus on 20 December. The Committee of Estates sent him a letter on 9 January 1651 requesting that he speed up his levy. The regiment seems to have been on foot by 20 February when Carnegie asked the presbytery of Brechin to provide a chaplain for it. On the same day the presbytery began the case of two troopers of Lord Ogilvy's Horse and a soldier of Carnegie's for raping Christian Folly, an unmarried woman living in Montrose. The soldiers had been apprehended and placed in Montrose gaol, where they awaited trial. As the months passed it became apparent to the presbytery that Folly was a whore. However, parliament was not as well informed as the local authorities, and on 3 June it ordered the general officers to do speedy justice on the soldiers. By then the men were probably back with their regiments for Folly had fled from prison herself between 1 and 22 May. On 3 April the Angus committee of war was ordered to levy the remaining quota of men. The regiment was either disbanded or destroyed by sometime in September. Certainly, Carnegie quickly changed his tack, because in 1652 he acted as a commissioner for the union with England. That suggests he withdrew from or played only a minor part in the military affairs of 1651.[15]

Lord Cranston's Horse

Colonel: William, 3rd Lord Cranston

Minister: Andrew Makghie/McKie[16]

Lord Cranston had served as a colonel of infantry regiments in the Army of the Solemn League and Covenant, and the Engager Army. In December 1650 he satisfied the Kirk for his accession to the Engagement, thus he was once again liable for public employment. There is no surviving commission for Cranston as a colonel of horse in this army. The first mention of his regiment occurs on 7 May 1651 when it was assigned to the 2nd Cavalry Brigade with two other horse regiments under Major General Montgomery. On 17 June the 240 troopers of Cranston's Horse were ordered to quarter in St. Ninian's and Kippen. Three days later the Committee of Estates ordered Haddingtonshire to levy 133 troopers for the regiment. It is extremely doubtful that Cranston received any men from this shire, because it lay under English occupation. Cranston and his regiment fought at the battle of Worcester. Both the colonel and chaplain became English prisoners; the regiment was destroyed. Cranston was removed to the Tower, but he was freed in 1656 when he received a licence to raise 1,000 foot for the king of Sweden. His friendship with the king led to successful pressure by Charles X Gustavus on Cromwell to return Cranston's forfeited estates.[17]

Earl of Crawford's Foot

Colonel: John, 17th earl of Crawford and 1st earl of Lindsay

Minister: David Rait[18]

Until the triumph of the kirk party the earl of Crawford-Lindsay had been one of the leading Covenanters, playing an important rôle in both political and military affairs. However, on 13 February 1649 he was stripped of his offices by the kirk party parliament and barred from holding a position in the public trust. Six days after the Commission of the General Assembly passed the Public Resolutions the earl returned to public life. On 20 December the Estates appointed him a colonel of foot for Fife. Just under three weeks later the Committee of Estates wrote him a letter urging him to take action regarding the recruiting of the regiment. On 22 January 1651 the burgh of Cupar enlisted its quota of twenty for Crawford's Foot and made them burgesses. By the end of January a royalist source estimated the strength of the two foot regiments from Fife — Crawford's and Kellie's — at 2,400 men. On 5 February another royalist stated that Crawford's alone consisted of 1,500 foot. As shall be seen from the summer muster rolls either these figures were exaggerated or the regiment had suffered heavily from desertion. Crawford's Foot appears to have quartered in central and eastern Fife after being raised. On 26 February a taverness appeared before Ceres kirk session, presbytery of Cupar, being charged with selling drink to a soldier during time of sermon. She denied the action, claiming she had only given some broth to one of Crawford's men beforehand. Anstruther Easter, presbytery of St. Andrews, had complaints against several men in the regiment. A lieutenant was guilty of playing, drinking and swearing with men of the regiment in the house where he was quartered until 1 a.m. A private brought a woman and child into the house where he was billeted and then forced the aged owners to stay up all night providing food and ale. Another private became drunk; afterwards he threatened and swore at a poor woman as well as cutting up her clothes. There is no evidence that either the regimental officers or the local sessions took action against these offenders. As of 28 April each company lacked two men. By 7 May Crawford's Foot had moved from Fife to in or near Stirling. On 20 May and again on 20 June the Committee of Estates appointed Crawford to its committee which was to meet with the Commission of the General Assembly over their differences. The first muster of the regiment occurred on 12 June and 1,011 men were present. The numbers in the unit rose to 1,123 foot on 2 July, but fell to 1,045 men on the 18th. After Charles II and the Committee of Estates departed from Stirling on 31 July bound for England, Crawford became the effective commander-in-chief of forces in Scotland. Nothing is known of the fate of his regiment other than it ceased to exist sometime in that summer. Crawford was taken prisoner by the English with other prominent Scots at Alyth on 28 August. He was sent to Windsor Castle, remaining there until 1654. Although he initially served the Restoration regime he soon resigned due to his presbyterian scruples.[19]

Dalyell's Foot

Colonel: Major General Thomas Dalyell (of the Binns)

Minister: Colin Campbell[20]

Dalyell was a hard-drinking soldier who had received his military training with the Ulster Army. In 1648 he served in that army's contingent which came to England under George Munro. Dalyell returned to Ireland after the dispersal of Munro's force in early autumn. The royalists in Ulster made him governor of Carrickfergus, which he defended against the Commonwealth troops. He surrendered to the English in December 1649, but did not return to Scotland until after August 1650. The kirk party regime initially ordered his exile, but Dalyell was permitted to remain. On 30 December he petitioned the king and Estates to serve the kingdom. At some date between then and 10 June 1651 Dalyell was either commissioned to raise a regiment or given command of one already on the establishment. Dalyell's Foot mustered 658 common soldiers on 10 June. The last muster of the regiment on 18 July placed its strength at 664 foot. Dalyell led his regiment south with the field army. At the battle of Worcester Dalyell became an English prisoner and his regiment ceased to exist. Although imprisoned by the English Dalyell escaped back to Scotland and served as a major general in Glencairn's rising in 1654. Afterwards he went to Russia where he served in the Tsar's army until Charles II recalled him in 1665. Upon his return to Scotland the king made him commander-in-chief of the Scottish army. Dalyell was victorious against the Pentland risers at Rullion Green in 1666. He continued as Lord General until his death in 1685.[21]

Douglas' Foot

Colonel: Robert Douglas

On 28 March 1651 the Committee of Estates appointed Robert Douglas colonel of foot for Teviotdale, Selkirkshire and the five parishes of Eskdale. Despite the English control of the Lowlands, Douglas was able to raise a small regiment. On 7 May it was quartering in or adjacent to Stirling. The musters for Douglas' Foot, which took place between 1 and 18 July, gave its strength as merely 181 common soldiers (or less than two companies). The fate of this regiment, other than it no longer existed after September, is not known.[22]

Lord Drummond's Horse

Colonel: James, Lord Drummond

Lieutenant Colonel: Gilbert Blair

Major: Harry Drummond of Pitcairne

Minister: William Clyde[23]

Lord Drummond had commanded infantry regiments in the Covenanting armies in the Bishops' Wars. He joined Montrose in 1645, but was taken prisoner at the battle of Philiphaugh. His strong royalist sympathies led to his being ignored for military commands until 20 December 1650, when the Estates nominated him colonel of the Perthshire Horse. Ten days later they appointed his chief field officers. However, nothing seems to have been done towards raising the regiment until the spring of 1651. On 18 April the Committee of Estates informed Drummond by letter that the earl of Atholl had raised so many infantrymen from Perthshire that he was requesting the shire be exempted from putting out any horse. However, the king rejected Atholl's request which opened the way for Drummond to raise his regiment. On 7 May Drummond's Horse was assigned to the 5th Cavalry Brigade with two other regiments under Major General Massey. On the 14th news of a crime committed by men of this regiment and Macleod's Foot reached the Committee of Estates. During a march between Stirling and St. Ninians soldiers of the regiments destroyed and plundered the house of a weaver. The artisan's losses amounted to £304 12s., but there is no evidence that he received any reparations. Also on the 14th the Committee ordered Drummond's to send out two parties of twenty troopers each under a corporal or quartermaster to quarter on those deficient on the forty and twenty days loan as well as the monthly maintenance in Perthshire. The commanded parties rejoined the regiment in time to serve on the Worcester campaign and at the battle. The regiment's minister was captured by the English after the battle; the regiment itself failed to survive the 3rd of September.[24]

Drummond's Foot

Colonel: William Drummond

Lieutenant Colonel: Thomas Marshall

Major: William Drummond of Corewauchter

Ministers: Robert Lawrie, James Row[25]

William Drummond was a younger son of Lord Madderty, who began a long military career after attending St. Andrews University. He served as a captain in Major General Munro's Foot from 1642 to 1648. During the Engagement Drummond was in George Munro's Ulster force. He witnessed Charles I's execution on 30 January 1649, going afterwards to join the Marquis of Ormond in Ireland. Drummond fought with the royalist forces in Ulster during 1649, before returning to Scotland in 1650. On 23 December parliament appointed him a colonel of foot for Perthshire. Drummond had his regiment partially raised by mid-February. It was quartering in or adjacent to Stirling on 7 May when the Committee of Estates ordered it to hold a muster. As of 18 June Drummond's Foot contained 1,005 men, but the regiment declined in size to 985 foot as of the last muster on 18 July. Drummond led his regiment into England as part of the field army. At the battle of Worcester the colonel became a prisoner of war and the regiment suffered destruction. By 1654 Drummond had escaped to Scotland where he served as a major general in Glencairn's rising. After its collapse he received permission to go to Russia and serve in the Tsar's army. There he rose in rank from a captain to lieutenant general until his recall by Charles II in 1665. However, he was later imprisoned for twelve months in Dumbarton Castle. Throughout the Restoration period Drummond acted as a Perthshire M.P. In 1684 Charles made him General of Ordnance for Scotland. On 6 September 1684, having already succeeded as 4th Lord Madderty, he was created Viscount Strathallan. The following year the king promoted Drummond to be Lord General of the Scots army and a lord of the treasury, posts which he held until his death in 1688. Drummond had a reputation as a harsh martinet, a characteristic he may have developed in Russia. In addition to his military and political achievements he wrote a history of the House of Drummond.[26]

Earl of Dunfermline's Horse

Colonel: Charles, 2nd earl of Dunfermline

Lieutenant Colonel: John Shaw of Greenock

Major: (?) Stewart

Minister: Robert Bruce[27]

Since 1639 the earl of Dunfermline had served as a colonel in the Covenanting armies. Due to his allegiance to the Engagement he was barred from holding any offices of state in January 1649. As a result he fled to exile in the Netherlands with Charles II, remaining there until the king's arrival in Scotland in June 1650. On 9 January 1651 the Committee of Estates wrote Dunfermline ordering him to raise a cavalry regiment from Fife. Dunfermline had raised at least part of his regiment from the presbytery of Dunfermline by late February. On 2 April Dunfermline's regiment was ordered to swap its inland quarterings with Massey's which was quartering on the south Fife coast. Meanwhile on 25 February the Dunfermline kirk session addressed a letter to the lieutenant colonel and major regarding a certain Katherine Bulbie who had had carnal relations with many soldiers from the area. This matter rested until 3 June when the session wrote Major Stewart and other officers in the regiment asking that a trooper be sent to Dunfermline and undergo repentance for fornication with Bulbie and Janet Campbell. A week later it sent more letters to the regimental officers requiring that troopers appear before the kirk session for their sins. On 24 June Trooper Jamieson appeared before the session for his dilapse into fornication. However, he claimed his duty with the regiment prevented him from satisfying the church in the parish where he committed his offence. This elicited another letter from the session, which went to the moderator of the presbytery of the army. The kirk session desired that Jamieson satisfy either in Dunfermline or the army. However, by 8 July it had received no answer to the letter of 24 June. Again the session wrote requesting information on the Jamieson case. Another letter on the same day demanded the appearance of Quartermaster Kingell for fornication. This was supported by a missive to the presbytery of the army asking it to take action against Kingell, if he could not come to Fife. Finally, the session wrote to Lieutenant Colonel Shaw and Major Stewart regarding 'a vile harlot', namely Katherine Bulbie. The session accused her of committing fornication with many soldiers, chiefly men of Dunfermline's and Massey's Horse. The officers were asked to search the army for Bulbie, as she had followed it from Dunfermline, and to send her back with a note of her infamies. Despite all these activities there is no evidence that any of the offenders ever satisfied the Kirk. The efforts of Dunfermline kirk session indicate that Dunfermline's men were raised within its bounds. On 7 May Dunfermline's Horse was placed in the 2nd Cavalry Brigade with two other regiments under Montgomery. This regiment served on the Worcester campaign and was engaged in the battle. Due to his valour and loyalty at Worcester Charles II knighted Lieutenant Colonel Shaw in the field. As with other regiments on this campaign Dunfermline's was destroyed on 3 September. The English captured a Major Stewart in Liverpool a few days after the battle. If he was the same man as Dunfermline's major it indicates that the regiment tried to flee back to Scotland after the debâcle.[28]

Earl of Erroll's Horse

Colonel: Gilbert, 11th earl of Erroll

Erroll had supported the Engagement in 1648 and Middleton's rising. As a result he was unable to receive any position in the public employ until mid-December 1650. On the 20th parliament appointed him a colonel of horse for Kincardineshire, Aberdeenshire and Banffshire. On 10 April the Committee of Estates ordered Erroll to quarter his men in the northeast in order to train them. On 7 May 1651 Erroll's Horse was put into the 5th Cavalry Brigade with two other regiments under Massey. A week later Erroll received permission to quarter on those who had failed to put out their quota in Aberdeenshire. The last reference to Erroll's Horse occurs in late August when the colonel was levying troops north of the Tay.[29] The regiment presumably ceased to exist shortly thereafter.

Lord Erskine's Horse

Colonel: John, Lord Erskine

Lord Erskine initially sided with the Covenanters; however, in 1644 he joined Montrose. This led to his exclusion from serving as an officer under both the Engager and kirk party regimes. On 20 December 1650, however, the Estates nominated him a colonel of horse for Dunbartonshire, Stirlingshire and Clackmannanshire. It was not until 29 January 1651 that the king and Committee of Estates granted Erskine a commission to raise the regiment. Two days later the Stirlingshire committee of war wrote the Committee of Estates claiming that it could not put out the proportion of men demanded by Erskine. On 3 March Erskine requested the Committee of Estates remove the exemption for Dunbartonshire, because without the men from that shire his regiment would never reach full strength. The Committee acquiesced to this petition. On 7 May Erskine's Horse was assigned to the 6th Cavalry Brigade under Major General Van Druschke. On 15 May the earl of Glencairn, Lord Cochrane, and the laird of Kilbirnie complained to the Committee of Estates that officers and men of Erskine's had illegally uplifted cess from Renfrewshire. The Committee plainly forbade officers of this and other regiments from doing so in the future. All money previously seized was to be returned. Future offenders were to appear before the Committee of the Army to face trial. The next day the earl of Abercorn and John Wallace of Ferguslie also complained that Erskine's officers had taken cess from their Renfrewshire lands. The Committee repeated its orders of the previous day and demanded that all offenders appear before the Committee of the Army to answer for their actions. On 22 May the Committee of Estates ordered Leslie to remove Erskine's Horse from Dunbartonshire, which had suffered due to the presence of three cavalry regiments. From this point Erskine's Horse vanishes from the records; as with other such regiments it was destroyed or disbanded by mid-September.[30]

Lord Forbes' Horse

Colonel: Alexander, 11th Lord Forbes

Minister: Robert Cheyne[31]

There is no surviving commission for this regiment, although Lord Forbes may have taken over command of his heir's cavalry regiment in the Army of the Covenants. On 16 April 1651 the Committee of Estates ordered Forbes' Horse to move to Angus. The regiment was assigned to the 6th Cavalry Brigade on 7 May; this brigade was under the command of Van Druschke. On 20 May the behaviour of the regiment became a matter for the Committee, because it had refused to restore the money taken for the ten days' supply of corn and straw from Angus despite Leslie's orders. The Committee informed Leslie that he must ensure that Forbes' Horse made good their exactions. In July the Slains kirk session, presbytery of Ellon, dealt with a woman of Cruden charged with scandalous conversation with some of Forbes' troopers. The regiment was present at Worcester where it was demolished. Forbes was taken prisoner by the English which put an end to his long military career.[32]

Earl of Galloway's Foot

Colonel: James, 2nd earl of Galloway

Lieutenant Colonel: (?) McDowell

Major: (?) Hamilton

The Committee of Estates appointed Galloway a colonel of foot for Wigtownshire and the Stewartry of Kirkcudbright on 26 June 1651. The levy quota was set at 600 men, 240 of whom would be musketeers while the remainder would be pikemen. The levies were to be put out with ten days' food as well as a baggage train. Within a short time the earl had raised at least part of his regiment. On 26 August he requested a chaplain from the presbytery of Stranraer, but it refused to provide one claiming that the presbytery of Wigtown owed the first chaplain. On the same day in a letter to Wigtown presbytery from that of Stranraer concerning the appointment of a minister, the latter presbytery mentioned the conduct of Galloway's men. Stranraer presbytery requested that Wigtown join them in censuring the 'enormities both of severall officers and souldiers within my Lord Galloway's regiment'. This is the last mention of the unit, but it remained in the area until the English conquered it in late August-early September.[33]

Earl of Glencairn's Horse

Colonel: William, 8th earl of Glencairn

Glencairn was one of the leading Engagers in 1648; because of this the kirk party stripped him of his offices and title in 1649. However, in 1651 the earl was back on the Committee of Estates. He was one of the members appointed on 20 May to meet with the Commission of the General Assembly over the differences between the two bodies. On 10 June Glencairn received a commission to raise a cavalry regiment from Renfrewshire and Ayrshire. The former shire was to levy forty troopers, while Cunningham, Carrick and the parts of Kyle not assigned to Viscount Montgomery and Lord Mauchline were to levy 160 troopers. There is no evidence regarding the raising of this regiment and it was not present at Worcester. In 1653 Glencairn started a royalist rebellion in the Highlands for Charles II; however, he deserted it in 1654. After the Restoration Glencairn held the Chancellorship until his death in 1664.[34]

Grant's Foot

Colonel: James Grant of Freuchie (and Grant)

Lieutenant Colonel: Patrick Grant of Cluniemore and Clunebeg

Grant was the chief of his name and an important laird in Strathspey. Until 1645 he had sided with the Covenanters, but after Inverlochy Grant had brought his clansmen out for Montrose. Consequently, his services were ignored by both the Engagers and kirk party. On 20 December 1650 parliament appointed him a colonel of foot for Nairn, Moray and his own lands. On 17 January 1651 the committee of war at Elgin requested that the laird of Grant have charge over the earl of Moray's men as well, because they were more willing to serve under him than under a Lowlander. On 24 April the Committee of Estates ordered the regiment south with all possible speed. It was to bring forty days' supply of meal and an additional twenty days' worth, if the smaller amount did not cause the regiment to delay its march. The regiment only arrived at the Stirling camp in late June. On the 27th it mustered 330 common soldiers, but by 9 July eight men had deserted. While the laird of Grant had raised the regiment he had not marched with it, instead his brother Grant of Cluniemore and Clunebeg acted as the effective commander. Grant's Foot was at Worcester, where few, besides the lieutenant colonel, escaped, the rest becoming prisoners.[35]

Master of Gray's Foot

Colonel: William, Master of Gray

Lieutenant Colonel: Thomas Lyell/Lyon

Major: (?) Logan

Ministers: John Ramsay, Robert Blaiklaw, Robert Barclay[36]

The master was the eldest son of Sir William Gray of Pittendrum, a rich Edinburgh merchant. The master initially received a commission to raise an infantry regiment from Perthshire on 20 December 1650. However, on 9 January 1651 the Committee of Estates instructed him by letter to raise a foot regiment from Angus instead of Perthshire. The master levied his men at his own expense, which amounted at least to £25,000. By 7 May the Master of Gray's Foot was quartered either in or about Stirling. On 12 June the regiment consisted of 607 men, a figure which rose to 636 foot on 2 July, but then declined to 610 men as of 18 July. On 28 June the petition of a Perthshire laird concerning oppressive behaviour of Captain Lieutenant Patrick Gray and Lieutenant William Stuart reached the Committee of Estates. The laird had already complained to the Perthshire committee of war, but without result. The two officers quartered some men on the laird's lands, because they claimed he had not paid money owed to the state. The laird showed his discharge to the lieutenant colonel, but the troops remained. Indeed the two officers kidnapped two of his husbandmen for the regiment. The committee ordered that the two men be returned to their homes, and summoned the offending officers. Unfortunately, no more is heard of the case. The Master of Gray's Foot may have fought on the left wing at Inverkeithing, as his brother Robert was killed in the battle. However, if the regiment was engaged it escaped only to meet its destruction at Worcester.[37]

Hamilton's Horse

Commander: Lieutenant Colonel (?) Hamilton

This is one of the more obscure units in the army. On Christmas Day 1650 the Committee of Estates organised a swapping of units. Lieutenant Colonel Hamilton was given Major General Massey's troop. In turn Massey received the remnants of Kinhilt's, Kirkhill's and Leven's Horse. In order to bring Hamilton's Horse up to strength he was assigned Strachan's Clydesdale recruits (originally meant for the Western Association Army), and any other men he could raise in Clydesdale. The only other reference to the unit occurs in the Dumbarton burgh records of 14 April 1651. On that day the council paid out £162 for fifteen days' maintenance for twelve troopers. Hamilton's Horse probably ended its existence sometime in September.[38]

Duke of Hamilton's Horse

Colonel: William, 2nd duke of Hamilton

As the earl of Lanark, Hamilton had played an important rôle in the events of 1648. After agreeing to the Treaty of Stirling with the Whiggamore Raiders, Lanark left for the Netherlands. In 1649 after his brother, the duke's, execution in London Lanark succeeded to the title. Charles II granted Hamilton a knighthood of the Garter in 1650 before he went to Scotland. That June Hamilton returned to Scotland with the king, but he withdrew from the court until January 1651. On 27 March Hamilton was appointed one of the colonels of the forces to be raised from Clydesdale. By 7 May the duke had levied a regiment of horse which was put in the 7th Cavalry Brigade with two other regiments. On 20 May and later on 20 June Hamilton was one of the members of the Committee of Estates selected to confer with the Commission of the General Assembly over their disagreements. On 18 June the Committee nominated him to be colonel of the Clydesdale Horse. The shire was to levy 180 troopers. Two days later the Committee re-issued its instructions to Clydesdale and also ordered West Lothian to provide Hamilton with sixty-six troopers. On the 24th Glasgow received an exemption from levying any men for the regiment. Meanwhile throughout the winter and spring Hamilton had used the regiment to harass the English garrisons in Clydesdale. The duke personally commanded his men on the Worcester campaign. On the eve of the battle he filled three sides of quarto paper meditating on death, and the soul's immortality. Among these writings Hamilton stated that to die 'poorly, basely & sinfully' makes a man miserable. During the battle he charged with his regiment against Cromwell's men to the east of Worcester. As a result of this brave action the duke was wounded and fell prisoner to the English. Hamilton died of his wounds on 12 September; the cause for which he died lay shattered along with his regiment.[39]

Hamilton's Foot

Colonel: Major General John Hamilton

Hamilton was yet another former Engager who received a command in this army. He satisfied the Kirk at the presbytery of Cupar's meeting on 16 January 1651. On 6 June the Estates appointed him a major general of foot. Following an offer by Clydesdale committee of war of 900 foot, the Committee of Estates appointed Hamilton a colonel on 18 June. Six days later the Committee relieved Glasgow of putting out men for the horse levy. However, the burgh was ordered to levy its proportion of foot as if the shire quota was 1,200 men. By the end of the month Glasgow had raised 200 foot for Hamilton. These men must have formed the bulk of the regiment. The only regimental muster, for 10 July, gives its strength at merely 160 foot. Nothing more is recorded regarding this unit, which must have disappeared in September.[40]

Hoffman's Horse

Commander: Captain Augustine Hoffman

Captain Hoffman had initially served the Covenanters as the quartermaster of Leslie's Horse in the Army of the Solemn League and Covenant. This was a reversal of the usual rôles for Hoffman had come from Germany to seek military employment in Britain. In the autumn of 1650 he raised a force of moss-troopers which operated in the Lothians. His most famous exploit of that time was the provision of reinforcements and supplies to the besieged Edinburgh Castle in early December. On 20 July 1651 Hoffman commanded 200 horse at the battle of Inverkeithing. Although his men charged well, their failure to regroup allowed the English to sweep them from the field. Afterwards Hoffman rallied his men and joined forces with a Captain Gordon. They commanded the moss-troopers between Aberdeen and Inverness. Although they harried the English, this force was more of a nuisance to the English advance than an actual threat. In recognition of the futility of further resistance Hoffman fled to Norway in January 1652. Thus, his men were some of the last to disband in this army.[41]

Earl of Home's Horse

Colonel: James, 3rd earl of Home

Home was another noble tainted by commanding forces in the Engager Army. He was not given a command until 28 March 1651 when the Estates made him colonel of Berwickshire. The earl appears to have raised a regiment of horse which was assigned to the 7th Cavalry Brigade on 7 May. There is no further information on this unit, nor on Home's activities in 1651. The regiment was undoubtedly a victim of the English successes of the summer.[42]

Home's Horse Troop

Commander: Colonel John Home

The little that is known concerning this unit reflects to its discredit. The troop was first mentioned in a letter of Archibald Johnston of Warriston to Guthrie of Guthrie on 30 January 1651. Warriston wrote asking for clemency for Trooper William Boyd, who had opposed 'that basse and Insolent action comitted by some of Coll. hoome's troup . . .' at Guthrie's house. On 23 April the Committee of Estates requested the king to find Home a regiment of horse, but nothing more is heard of this. The final reference to the troop occurred in the meeting of the Angus committee of war on 21 May. From this the exact nature of the 'barbarous and villanous action' becomes clear. The committee ordered Home to apprehend those troopers who had broken into Guthrie's house. There they had killed a mason, and wounded Francis Guthrie of Guthrie, his wife Bathia, and his servant, John Forrester. While no further information survives regarding the crime or the troop, it may be assumed that this unit ceased to exist in September.[43]

Marquis of Huntly's Forces

Colonel: Lewis, 3rd marquis of Huntly

Following his defection to Montrose in early 1645 Huntly (then merely Lord Lewis Gordon) was denied employment by the Covenanters. In 1650 the General Assembly sought to have him imprisoned. That October he joined Middleton's rising out of fear of punishment for being implicated in The Start. The marquis signed the royalist declaration issued during the rebellion. It was at Huntly's castle of Strathbogie on 4 November that Leslie and Middleton signed the treaty which led to the disbanding of the royalists. Huntly was restored to a place of honour in Scotland on 25 March 1651 by the king and Committee of Estates. His contemporaries thought him a 'brave, impetuous, but fickle and untrustworthy man'. As the events would show Huntly was not the best man to lead the Scottish resistance in the northeast. There is no surviving commission for Huntly to raise either an infantry or cavalry regiment. However, on 24 June the Committee of Estates made the marquis responsible for mustering the heritors of Aberdeenshire and Banffshire. The Committee demanded that he bring out all the heritors save those possessing a royal exemption. Huntly was also ordered in cases of overlapping feudal superiority to allow the heritors to serve under the man 'they lyik best'. On 5 July the Committee sent Huntly instructions to bring his men to the Stirling camp. He was specifically cautioned against quartering men on those deficient in providing men or money from Aberdeenshire or Banffshire. The necessity of such an order becomes apparent from a minute of the Committee on 8 July. Messengers of arms were sent north that day to summon Huntly to answer charges of levying cess from the Banffshire heritors. The Committee ordered that the goods and money taken be restored. It also warned the marquis, his officers and men not to uplift cess in the future. Despite the benefits the army would have received from Huntly's reinforcements, the marquis never brought them south. This may have been caused by the slow response of the localities in putting out men as is illustrated by Aberdeen. It was only on 21 August that the burgh provided any of the ninety men (sixty musketeers and thirty pikemen) which it had been assessed. Finally, on 6 September Aberdeen completed its part of the levy. By this time Huntly commanded a force of 600 horse and 1,000 foot. Meanwhile, on 31 August he had united with Balcarres' and his horse. Although the marquis lacked the numbers to oppose Monck's army in a pitched battle, he could have done more for the Scottish cause than raising cess in the northeast. In late September and again in mid-October Huntly quartered ineffectually in Rothiemay. The English had already captured Aberdeen on 7 September, but the marquis does not appear to have been interested in investing the burgh or preventing the English from advancing. In addition to the unwelcome imposition of cess, Huntly's men committed at least one murder. Such activities did a great deal towards convincing the inhabitants to accept the orderly rule of the English. On 6 November the Gordon lairds surrendered to the invaders.

Huntly began his negotiations with them three days later and spun out the talks for twelve days before surrendering and disbanding his forces. For the little that the marquis accomplished his men would have been better levied into the other northeastern regiments.[44]

Innes' Horse

Colonel: Robert Innes of Innes the younger

Minister: David Robert/Robeson/Robieson/Robison/Robson[45]

On 20 December 1650 the Estates appointed Innes the younger colonel of horse for Nairnshire, Moray and the laird of Grant's lands. On 17 January 1651 the Moray committee of war informed the Committee of Estates that Innes was absent, and in any case his regiment would be small. In April the Committee of Estates ordered Innes to bring his men and the mounted gentry of Ross south. This order was issued first on the 26th, then renewed on the 29th when Innes was told to hurry south and that the Committee would make up his regiment when he arrived. The next day the Committee reissued the orders, pronouncing its displeasure at Innes' disobedience. On 7 May Innes' Horse was one of the four regiments assigned to the 4th Cavalry Brigade under Major General Brown. Six days later the Committee informed the earl of Findlater and the commissioners in the north that Innes' men were at their disposal in order to force civilians to provide horses for the necessary transport of grain by land to Brechin. On the same day Innes was given orders to proceed north, where he was to quarter on delinquents and obey the orders of the northern commissioners. Furthermore, on the 22nd the Committee issued new orders regarding the levying of gentlemen and heritors from Moray, Nairnshire, Inverness-shire and Ross. Although these men had been told to come south before, none had arrived in Stirling. The Committee sent them and the nobles instructions to do so immediately. They were to bring forty days' supply of food with them. The Committee placed these reinforcements under Innes, who was then heading north. On 7 July the Committee issued further orders that the northern levies and heritors be sent south as the former were deficient and the latter delinquent. There is no further mention of Innes' Horse, but they may have kept in the field until November before disbanding.[46]

Lord Johnston's Foot

Colonel: James, Lord Johnston

Lieutenant Colonel: Andrew Drummond

The Committee of Estates appointed Lord Johnston (sheriff of Dumfriesshire) a colonel of foot for Dumfriesshire and Nithsdale on 26 June 1651. The regiment was to consist of 600 men. In late August Johnston had 100 men in arms in Dumfriesshire. An English attack broke and scattered the regiment when it was marching to a local rendezvous.[47]

Keith's Foot

Colonel: George Keith (of Aden)

Minister: David Leitch[48]

Colonel Keith was yet another Engager who received a commission in this army. On 20 December 1650 parliament nominated him a colonel of foot for Aberdeenshire and Banffshire. His regiment was on foot by 8 May, when its chaplain joined it. On the 21st the Committee of Estates ordered the Aberdeenshire committee of war to provide Keith's officers with food and part of the shire's forty days' loan. On 10 June the Committee demanded that Aberdeen put out its deficients. The burgh was cautioned that as many of its recruits were hired and not local, that it was liable to replace any deserters or bounty hunters from other regiments. By that day Keith's Foot had arrived at the Stirling camp. The regiment then numbered 758 men, but on 18 July desertions had reduced it to 731 common soldiers. Keith's Foot fought at the battle of Worcester where it was destroyed. Both the colonel and the chaplain fell prisoner to the English.[49]

Kelhead's Foot

Colonel: Sir William Douglas of Kelhead

Lieutenant Colonel: John Hamilton of Boreland

Major: William Maxwell of Borbhouse

Kelhead had commanded regiments from Nithsdale in the Solemn League and Covenant and Engager Armies. On 27 March 1651 he was appointed as an alternate to his brother the earl of Queensberry as a colonel of foot for Nithsdale. On 26 June the Committee of Estates gave the command of two infantry regiments to be raised from Dumfriesshire and Nithsdale to Kelhead and Lord Johnstone. Both units were to have 600 foot. In late August Kelhead had 300 men in Dumfriesshire, but they fled when an English force based at Drumlanrig approached them. Following a skirmish near Maxwellton only forty foot remained in the regiment. However, they would have dispersed shortly afterwards because the English captured Kelhead and Boreland at the skirmish.[50]

Earl of Kellie's Foot

Colonel: Alexander, 3rd earl of Kellie

Ministers: George Belfrage, Joshua Meldrum[51]

Although Kellie served as a colonel in the Engager Army, he quickly satisfied the Kirk after its disbanding. In 1649 he acted as a parliamentary commissioner to Charles II. In autumn 1650 he plotted to place the king under the care of the royalists. For his part in The Start St. Andrews presbytery planned to try him on 4 December. However, on the 20th the Estates appointed him a colonel of foot for Fife. The Committee of Estates sent him a letter on 9 January 1651 urging him to raise his men. By the end of January Crawford's and Kellie's Foot were estimated to have 2,400 men. However, another contemporary guess of 5 February stated the two regiments contained only 1,500 foot. Kellie's Foot was large enough on 12 March to receive a chaplain. As of 28 April the regiment lacked two men per company. It joined the Stirling camp between 7 May and 12 June. On the second date Kellie's Foot consisted of 898 soldiers. On the 21st the number rose to 985 men, but as of 18 July it contained only 961 foot. The earl commanded his regiment at the battle of Worcester where it was broken. Kellie fell prisoner to the English and was lodged in the Tower. However, he was later exiled to the Netherlands. In 1657 the earl was permitted back to Scotland for six months before returning to exile. He attended Charles II in London in 1660.[52]

Lord Kintail's Foot

Colonel: Kenneth, Lord Kintail

Lieutenant Colonel: Thomas Mackenzie of Pluscardine

Major: Simon Mackenzie of Lochslin

Minister: John McCrae[53]

In December 1650 Lord Kintail, the heir of the earl of Seaforth, was a fifteen-year-old bejant at King's College, Aberdeen. Kintail had spent the previous nine years of his life as a student of the Rev. Farquhar Macrae, chieftain of the Macraes, chamberlain of Kintail, and constable of Eilean Donan Castle. As Seaforth had remained in the Netherlands after Charles II's arrival in Scotland, the Estates were forced to appoint his son, and brother, Pluscardine, the colonel and lieutenant colonel of a regiment of foot to be raised from Seaforth's family and friends. The parliamentary commission was issued to Kintail on 20 December. It appears that Kintail raised his regiment with the help of his uncles — Pluscardine and Lochslin — as well as the Mackenzie lairds of Dochmalvag/Davochmalvag, Coul, Fairburn and Tarbat the younger. From the evidence of the muster rolls Kintail and his aides were remarkably successful. However, there were problems which vexed the Mackenzies and their allies. During the winter of 1650-51 Lieutenant Colonel Menzies of Argyll's Foot brought one hundred recruits into Seaforth's lands and plundered them. This wanton disregard for the public good caused most of Kintail's Foot to return to their homes to protect their families and goods. When Lord Kintail and his helpers tried to raise the men of Kintail they met with a flat refusal. The Kintail men claimed that his lordship was too young, and that if Charles II wanted them to come out he would send for the earl. This may explain Lochslin's strange reluctance to march from the west unless the Rev. Farquhar Macrae be evicted from Eilean Donan. Lochslin may have believed that Macrae supported the sentiments of the Kintail men, or that his loyalty to Seaforth's heir was insufficient. (Both suppositions are rather bizarre in relation to Macrae's offices, but there does not seem to be any other explanation for Lochslin's hostility.) In the end Lochslin won his point and Macrae was forced to move to Inchchurter. On 16 May 1651 the Committee of Estates noted that Kintail's Foot was to march on Monday next according to Middleton's orders. The regiment was to bring the forty days' loan south and to pay for its entertainment on the march. Kintail's Foot marched through the lands of the Lovat Frasers on the way south, and probably proceeded to Stirling via Badenoch. It crossed the Tay at Inchyra on or after 19 May. By 10 June the regiment, numbering 800 foot, had arrived at the Stirling camp. Between 27 June and 2 July 300 recruits joined Kintail's Foot. However, within a week one hundred men had deserted, and as of 18 July the regiment's strength had dropped to 982 foot. Kintail and his uncles led the regiment at the battle of Worcester. The regiment failed to survive the battle and Kintail became an English prisoner, only gaining his freedom in 1660.[54]

Lagg's Foot

Colonel: Sir John Greer of Lagg

Lieutenant Colonel: (?) Cockburn

Major: John Kilpatrick

This is yet another regiment which was commissioned to be raised from the southwest on 26 June 1651. Lagg was appointed a colonel of foot for Wigtownshire and the Stewartry of Kirkcudbright with the earl of Galloway. The region was to provide Lagg with 240 musketeers and 360 pikemen with ten days' food and a baggage train. Although there is no evidence that Lagg levied any of the regiment, it would not have been impossible, because Galloway successfully raised part of his.[55]

Lochiel's Foot

Colonel: Sir Ewan Cameron of Lochiel

This regiment was also known as Lochaber's, or Mackalduey's, or the Clan Cameron Foot. Parliament commissioned Lochiel colonel of an infantry regiment to be raised from his clansmen on 20 December 1650. Lochiel accordingly levied his regiment, but contrary to his image as the beau chevalier of the royalists used it for ends that were contrary to the national interest and solely benefited the Camerons. Rather than bringing his regiment south to the Stirling camp, Lochiel first marched against Clanranald in order to gain payment of his feu duty. Then this great clan chief turned on MacDonald of Keppoch, who owed Lochiel a mortgage payment. After harrying the lands of his fellow Scots Lochiel disbanded his regiment.[56]

Clan Macduggan

The Macduggans were a minor Highland clan which joined forces with the Macgregors, Mackinnons and MacFarlanes. In late December 1651 this coalition had 800 men in the field against the English. However, they restricted their activities to minor attacks on the invaders. The coalition appears to have broken up without offering sustained opposition to the conquest.[57]

Clan MacFarlane

Chief: Walter MacFarlane of MacFarlane

In the mid-1640s the MacFarlanes had been supporters of Montrose. The clan's lands were centred between Tarbet and Arrochar and around Loch Sloy. The MacFarlanes joined in alliance with the Macduggans, Macgregors and Mackinnons against the English in late 1651. Near the end of December these clans had 800 men in the field. They avoided large scale conflicts with the English, concentrating instead on small raids and ambushes. Twice during the 1650s the English attacked the MacFarlane's house of Inveruglas. After the second capture it was destroyed, and the chief moved his seat to Arrochar.[58]

Clan Macgregor

Commanders: Callum and Ewan Macgregor

The Macgregors were another clan which had served in Montrose's army during his year of victories. For that reason they were ignored as a source of recruits by the Engagers and kirk party. However, on 11 June 1651 the clan made a major step forward towards regaining the legitimacy it had lost during the reign of James VI. On the 11th the king and the Committee of Estates ordered Callum and Ewan Macgregor to bring their servants and followers to Stirling by Tuesday the 17th, or to be answerable for their failure to act. These two leaders of the clan complied with this request, probably with alacrity as it gave them a chance to redeem the tarnished image of the Macgregors. The clansmen fought at the battle of Worcester, from which few could have returned. However, in December the remaining Macgregors in Scotland allied with the Macduggans, Mackinnons and MacFarlanes against the English. These four clans had 800 men in the field near the end of 1651. However, they caused more worry than harm to the English before disbanding.[59]

Clan Mackay Foot

Colonel: William Mackay of Borley

The Mackays were a royalist clan which controlled the region of Strathnaver. They were the hereditary enemies of the earl of Sutherland, who had used his position as a leader of the Covenanters to pursue his claims against the Mackays. From the end of the 1640s until 1651 the Covenanters had maintained garrisons on their lands. However, the first and second Lords Reay were ardent royalists who had sacrificed much for the cause. On 20 December 1650 the Estates appointed either Hugh Mackay, brother to Lord Reay, or Hugh Mackay of Scourie to be colonel of a foot regiment raised from the clan. In the event the colonelcy was given to Captain William Mackay of Borley, Scourie's nephew, probably in a clan council. Borley raised his regiment and led it south through the Lovat Fraser lands on the way to Stirling. The regiment was destroyed at the battle of Worcester.[60]

Clan Mackinnon Foot

Colonel: Lachlan Mor Mackinnon of Mackinnon and Strathsuardal

In 1645 the Mackinnons, probably due to their hostility to the Campbells, had joined Montrose's army. The Mackinnons launched an unsuccessful raid against the Campbells in 1649. However, on 20 December 1650 parliament appointed the Mackinnon colonel of his family and friends. The chief raised his men from the clan lands on Skye, then led it south to Worcester. Charles II reportedly knighted Lachlan for saving his life. However, this battlefield promotion was not confirmed in 1660. In any case the chief was a casualty of the battle. It is doubtful whether many of his men returned home. However, in late December the Mackinnons entered into a coalition with the Macgregors, Macduggans and

MacFarlanes against the English. This alliance put 800 men into the field, but accomplished little before disbanding.[61]

Clan Mackintosh Foot

Colonels: Lachlane Mackintosh of Mackintosh, or Lachlane the younger, or Duncan Mackintosh

On 20 December 1650 parliament appointed Lachlane Mackintosh, chief of the clan, or his brother Duncan, colonel of foot for Badenoch. However, the news of the commission had not reached the chief by late January 1651. On the 25th the Inverness-shire committee of war wrote the Committee of Estates on the chief's behalf. The letter noted that commissions had gone out to clan chiefs in remote areas, but that the Mackintoshes had been left out. The committee requested that he or his son, Lachlane, be appointed to bring out Clan Chattan. There is no further information on this regiment, suggesting that it may not have been raised.[62]

Maclean's Foot

Colonel: Sir Euchunn (Hector) Ruadh Maclean (of Duart)

Lieutenant Colonel: Donald Maclean of Brolas

(? Major: Ewen Maclean of Treshnish)

Unlike many of the clan regiments a great deal of material exists regarding the Macleans, which is due to their tragic destruction at Inverkeithing. On 20 December 1650 parliament appointed the Maclean or the Tutor (his uncle) colonel of an infantry regiment to be raised from Argyll and Bute. Estimates of its size vary from 500-1,500 men, but the regiment appears to have consisted of 700 Macleans and 100 Macquarries and others in six-seven companies. Although it had reached the Stirling camp sometime in July, there is no surviving muster of Maclean's Foot which would dispel the problem of its size. Between 17 and 20 July Maclean's Foot was assigned to Holburn's and Brown's force which had the mission of driving Lambert's landing party of 4,000-5,000 men from Fife. The Scottish force suffered from a variety of problems including insufficient numbers and inexperience. In addition Holburn and Brown were proteges of the marquis of Argyll which made the relationship with Maclean one of hostility. Because of this Maclean had a 'virtually independent command' consisting of his and Buchanan's seasoned foot regiments. They were marshalled on the right wing on Casland Hill. To the right of this force was a body of cavalry, and on its left was Holburn's Lowland infantry regiments. The

Highlanders were anxiously awaiting this battle in which they may have hoped to recreate the victories of Montrose. However, unlike those battles the enemy's artillery caused a significant number of casualties, and the army lacked training and skill. The Scots cavalry was the first part of the advance to be broken; the horse on the left fleeing before those on the right were also driven off. The Lowland infantry, deprived of protection on its left flank and facing a combined attack by the English foot and horse, retreated from the field in some disorder. These withdrawals left Maclean's command isolated, despite its own successes. The English forces encircled and fought the Scots for four hours without offering quarter. At the end of the day the attempt to drive Lambert from Fife had failed, several regiments of the Scots had been destroyed or were past rallying and the Macleans had acquired a legend. In order to protect their chief from death the Macleans interposed themselves between him and the English. As one man fell another took his place, until Sir Hector, already wounded, died from an English musket shot. This gave birth to the Maclean battlecry — 'Fear eil airson Eachuinn!' or 'Another one for Hector!' Of the 800 men in Maclean's Foot only thirty-five lived to see their homes again. Major N. M. Bristol details the following casualties: Coll/Tiree company — a son of Maclean of Coll, two sons of Hynish, one of Muck and one of Borreray killed and two sons of Coll wounded; Ross of Mull company — Ardchraoishnish and his three brothers (officers) and 140 men killed; Ardgour company — two brothers of the fiar of Ardgour and a son of Inverscadell killed and the fiar (captain) probably wounded; Morvern company — John Maclean of Kinlochaline wounded; Kingerloch company — no known losses among officers; and northwest Mull company — a brother of Torloisk killed and its captain Ewen Maclean of Treshnish wounded. Brolas and Neil Maclean of Ardtanish also suffered wounds in the battle. For at least one family the story of the battle of Inverkeithing took a long time to forget.[63]

Clan Maclennan

The Maclennans were a subject clan of the Mackenzies with their chief residence in Kintail. In mid-November 1651 they allied with the neighbouring Macraes against the English. Their opposition did little to delay the English conquest.[64]

Tutor of Macleod's Foot

Colonel: Roderick Macleod of Talisker, Tutor of Macleod

Lieutenant Colonel: Norman Macleod of Bernera

Minister: Alexander Clark/Clerk[65]

On 20 December 1650 the Estates appointed the Tutor of Macleod (Talisker) colonel and his younger brother Bernera lieutenant colonel of a clan regiment of foot. Besides the Macleods of Harris and Skye, Macdonald of Sleat reportedly contributed men to the regiment. By 7 May the regiment had been partially raised and the first elements were in or near Stirling. On 14 May soldiers of this unit with troopers of Lord Drummond's Horse destroyed and plundered a weaver's house on their march from Stirling to St. Ninians. The damages amounted to £304 12s. The first muster of the regiment on 12 June reveals a strength of only 297 men; as of 18 July the Tutor's Foot had grown to 596 soldiers. These figures, although more accurate, disagree with the estimates of clan histories of 700-1,000 men. It may be that 700 men were raised, because when a report of this reached the Committee of Estates the Tutor was ordered to levy 300 more foot. At the battle of Worcester Major General Pitscottie placed this regiment at the junction of the Severn and the Temet. The English forces under Lambert and Fleetwood only carried the position after several attacks. The regiment was destroyed in the battle and ensuing pursuit. While the Tutor escaped, his second fell prisoner. Bernera was imprisoned until March 1653 when the English tried him for treason as a Welshman. This legal error saved his life and Bernera escaped later in the year. The Macleod's losses so severely reduced the clan's strength that the royalists did not ask for their assistance in Glencairn's rising. The financial demands on Talisker in purchasing the regiment's armaments were such that he was pursued by a creditor until a special act of parliament in 1661 freed him of the obligation. The losses and troubles associated with serving the royalist cause on this occasion combined with the lack of rewards following the Restoration made the Macleods one of the few Whig clans.[66]

Clan Macnab

Chief: Ian ('Smooth John') Macnab of Macnab

The Macnabs were another clan which had supported Montrose in the mid-1640s. Their lands extended from Killin through Glen Dochart towards Tyndrum, and along the south bank of Loch Tay. The chief's seat was Eilean Ran Castle in the River Lochay. In 1651 the chief (on his own or possibly as part of another regiment) led 300 of his clansmen to Worcester. The Macnabs as with others at that battle did not return to Scotland. The chief was rumoured to have been killed in action. However, in 1653 an English officer recorded his death in a battle against the English in Perthshire. As a result of 'Smooth John's' royalism his lands and castle were forfeited and given to the Campbells. However, in 1660 Charles II restored the lands, but not the castle.[67]

Macneil's Foot

Colonel: Neil Óg Macneil of Barra, chief of the Macneils

On 20 December 1650 the Estates appointed the protestant Barra colonel of his largely Roman Catholic clan. The chief successfully raised a regiment which fought at Worcester on the right flank of the Macleods, who were posted at the confluence of the Severn and Temet. Few of the Macneils returned to their homelands in the outer Hebrides. This regiment was unique in the annals of the Covenanter regiments, because it was the only predominantly catholic one.[68]

Clan Macrae

Chief: The Rev. Farquhar Macrae, Chamberlain of Kintail and Constable of Eilean Donan Castle

Like the Maclennans the Macraes were a subject clan of the Mackenzies which was concentrated in Kintail. A close connection existed between the chief and the second earl of Seaforth, who had made the former tutor of his son, Kintail, in 1641. However, in 1651 Simon Mackenzie of Lochslin, one of Kintail's uncles, had the chief evicted from Eilean Donan. The Macrae removed himself to Inchchurter. In mid-November his clan was out with Maclennans against the English. However, this alliance was too weak to accomplish much. In 1654 Monck arrived in the area and his men stole 360 of the chief's cattle with impunity.[69]

Earl Marischal's Horse

Colonel: William, 7th earl Marischal

Marischal was another former Engager who received a colonelcy in this army. In July 1650 he had entertained Charles II at Dunottar Castle, but remained out of public events until joining Middleton's rising in October. Parliament appointed him a colonel of horse for the Mearns, Aberdeenshire and Banffshire on 20 December. On 1 January 1651 the earl attended the king's coronation at Scone. In the first half of February the committees of war responsible for raising Marischal's regiment met and allocated the proportions to be recruited. Mearns was to raise 100 troopers, and Banffshire sixty more. Aberdeenshire was to levy eighty horse as follows: Strathbogie presbytery — ten, Deer — forty-four, Turriff — fourteen, Aberdeen — seven, and Kincardine — fifteen. The entire regiment appears to have been raised, although on 14 May Marischal received permission to quarter on those deficient in Kincardineshire. On 10 April orders were issued to have Marischal's quarter in the northeast for training. On 7 May it was assigned to the 4th Cavalry Brigade with three other regiments under Middleton. Marischal was one of the members of the subcommittee of the Committee of Estates appointed to meet with the Commission of the General Assembly on the 20th. Two days later the earl received orders to provide parties of horse to the laird of Ormiston and John Auchterlonie so that they could use the troopers to force out those who had refused to supply baggage horse for carrying the Mearns grain. Marischal fell prisoner to the English at Alyth on 28 August with other members of the Committee of Estates. It is not known whether his regiment was dispersed there or at Worcester. The earl spent the remainder of the interregnum in prison.[70]

Massey's Horse

Colonel: Major General Edward Massey

Minister: Harry Knox[71]

Major General Massey was an English presbyterian who had served as the parliamentarian governor of Gloucester in the first English civil war. Sometime in 1650 he made his way to Scotland, where he received command of a troop of horse. On Christmas Day the Committee of Estates decided to provide Massey with a regiment. He was to surrender his own troop to Lieutenant Colonel Hamilton. In return Massey would receive Leven's Horse with Kennedy of Kirkhill's Horse being added to it. On 3 January 1651 Massey was given command of Kinhilt's Horse and Lieutenant Andrew Ker's horse troop. He was also to receive all the Englishmen in the camp. (However, this reinforcement was partially taken away on 19 April when Buckingham received command of all the English deserters.) Between Christmas and 6 January some of Leven's men threw away their standard and deserted. This may have been in reaction to being placed under an Englishman. The Committee of Estates would not let the incident pass and appointed Lord Cranston to apprehend the deserters. The men were to be punished, then discharged and prohibited from rejoining the army. In February it was decided to bring Massey's Horse up to 800 troopers, who would be largely English and foreigners. On the 19th the Committee of Estates ordered that the regiment be provided with horses. The major general must have been allocated a portion of the Fife levies, because the Committee appointed Lord Burleigh, the laird of Bogie, and James Snord to join that committee of war to speed up the recruiting of this regiment. Throughout the winter Massey's guarded the south Fife coast, but on 2 April it received orders to take over Dunfermline's inland quarters. Their occupation was not without complaint, for on 30 April Massey received orders to report on the regimental receipts for the overburdened presbytery of Dunfermline. On 7 May Massey was given command of the 5th Cavalry Brigade consisting of Erroll's, Dunfermline's and Stewart's Horse. Twice on 3 and 10 June Dunfermline kirk session wrote Massey demanding the appearance of two troopers for fornication with two whores. However, on 17 June Massey's Horse was ordered from Fife. Each trooper was to receive £3 before leaving for Stirling. Meanwhile since the 10th thirteen English troopers of the regiment had been quartering in Stirling. The removal of the regiment from Fife did not lessen the determination of Dunfermline kirk session to bring the two troopers to justice. On 8 July the session wrote Massey a letter. He was requested to produce the troopers in Dunfermline or have them satisfy the Kirk before the presbytery of the army. The session also mentioned Katherine Bulbie, 'a vile harlot', who had committed fornication with his men as well as those of other regiments. Massey was asked to search the army for her and after capturing her to return her to Dunfermline with a note of infamy. However, the major general was too busy to bother about bringing sinners to repentance. Massey was sent into England ahead of the army (it is uncertain if his regiment accompanied him) to recruit forces from the English presbyterians. When the Resolutioner ministers learned of this they despatched letters to Massey which seriously affected his ability to recruit men. The Resolutioners reminded him of the king's and the army's zeal for the Solemn League and Covenant and their willingness to implement it. Furthermore, Massey was told to accept only those who upheld the Covenant. Believing that the king had authorised the ministers' action Massey proclaimed their views. However, when Charles II learned of Massey's activities he ordered him to ignore the ministers' injunctions. But it was too late; the English had taken Massey's statements to heart and refused to join him. Massey's Horse perished in the debâcle of Worcester. As in the early 1640s he had contributed to the royalist defeat, but this time unintentionally.[72]

Maule's Foot and Horse

Colonel: Harry Maule (of Balmakellie)

Lieutenant Colonel: John Towers

Major: John Durham

Minister: David Liddell[73]

Colonel Maule had commanded regiments in the Solemn League and Covenant and Engager Armies. Although taken prisoner on the Preston campaign he had escaped back to Scotland. On 20 December 1650 the Estates nominated him a colonel of foot for the Mearns. The Committee of Estates wrote Maule on 9 January 1651, confirming the appointment and ordering him to raise the regiment. The levying of Maule's Foot and their subsequent behaviour provides a certain amount of interest. To persuade the laird of Leyes to provide the men stented by the committee of war one Captain Inglis quartered his men on Leyes and his tenants. This certainly had the desired effect, Leyes making a bond with Maule to deliver the men. Following their agreement the king ordered Inglis to withdraw and no longer trouble Leyes or his tenants. The regiment appears to have been levied by early April, because on the 8th Leslie and Quartermaster

General Stewart advised the quartering of Maule's Foot on Dunfermline town and presbytery. Four days later the regiment was installed in southern Fife, and Dunfermline presbytery was ordered to provide for it. In addition to local supplies one hundred bolls of meal would be sent every ten days from Newburgh by packhorse. Some troops of the regiment were still in Kincardineshire. On 18 April the Committee of Estates wrote the committee of war to tell the officers and soldiers to be sparing in their demands and satisfied with little for entertainment, as 'the country is almost exhausted with burdens'. The Committee warned that officers demanding extortionate quarters would be punished. Ten days later the Committee had more concrete complaints against Maule, which had been provided by the local committee. Maule received orders no longer to trouble the shire over the forty days' loan. Nor was he to quarter on those whose recruits had deserted without first complaining to the committee of war. Maule was also reprimanded for levying fifty-four baggage horses to the regiment, which was greatly above the correct number. The Committee finally informed the colonel that the shire's loan of twenty days' meal would be given at Montrose. By 7 May the portion of the regiment south of the Tay had moved to or near Stirling, and it was told to hold a muster. On the 12th the Committee received a lengthy petition of complaint from the Mearns committee which dealt largely with Maule and his men. The local committee complained of being burdened by 40-120 of Maule's troopers and others, which it requested be removed from the shire. The shire committee wished its provision of the forty and twenty days' loans be used for the army not swallowed up by Maule's men. The petitioners also asked that Maule's demand for the forty days' loan be rescinded, as it had been paid at Stirling. The return of forty baggage horses obtained by questionable means was another demand. In general the petitioners were anxious to find a way round meeting all of Maule's demands, which he claimed were for the good of the public service. One method around this was to have Maule removed from having anything to do with shire business. The Committee of Estates was quite obliging to meet all of the grievances. Maule's Horse was ordered from the shire; the shire's bond for the forty days' loan was returned to it; having raised 540 men for the infantry regiment Mearns was discharged from levying more; finally Maule was to return thirty-four baggage horses. On 13 May Mearns requested the appointment of a member of the Committee of Estates to hear the list of its grievances against the heavy burdens it had carried in preceding months. Two days later the Committee had shifted to Maule's side. While all of his men and the colonel were ordered from the shire, permission was granted to leave thirty men and an officer to collect £976 owed the regiment by the shire. It was also discovered that the 540 men had not been fully recruited. Maule was ordered to provide a list of the deficients and the shire was given until the 22nd to recruit the men, or it would face quartering on delinquents. The first muster of Maule's Foot occurred on 10 June. The regiment then contained 575 common soldiers, but by 9 July eleven had deserted. Maule led his regiments at Worcester, where they were destroyed. The colonel, major and chaplain fell prisoner to the English.[74]

Middleton's Horse

Colonel: Lieutenant General John Middleton

Minister: Robert Knox[75]

Middleton was one of the most interesting officers of the period. Having become a major supporter and beneficiary of the Engagement, he was also one of the victims of the Preston campaign. However, having recovered from a wound received before his capture he escaped from Newcastle to Scotland. In 1649 he joined Ogilvy's and Huntly's rising, but acted as one of those appointed to reach a settlement with Leslie. In October 1650 Middleton raised the royalist standard of rebellion again and was joined by a large number of nobles. On 21 October he defeated Major General Brown at the battle of Newtyle. But just two weeks later he signed a treaty at Strathbogie with Leslie agreeing to disband the royalists. Meanwhile on 24 October the Commission of the General Assembly excommunicated Middleton for all his activities from March 1648. However, due to the change in the Commission's attitude, Middleton was allowed to satisfy the Kirk in Dundee at the end of January 1651. Middleton appears to have spent the first quarter of 1651 in the northeast, probably with his royalist friends. On 19 April the Committee of Estates ordered him to send his forces to Stirling. Five days later the Committee asked Charles II to find Middleton a regiment of horse. On 7 May Middleton was given command of the 4th Cavalry Brigade, which consisted of four regiments excluding his own. The Committee ordered him on 22 May to bring out the heritors, gentlemen and nobles of Aberdeenshire and Banffshire with the forty days' loan of food from the two shires. In order to provide Middleton with more recruits for his regiment the Committee hit upon various schemes. On 20 June it ordered Teviotdale to levy thirty-seven horse, while Selkirkshire and Peeblesshire would raise forty-seven and forty-nine troopers respectively. On 19 July the Committee devised a means whereby the heritors would provide Middleton with recruits. All heritors who had private or public business to attend to, or who did not appear in the camp, were to send Middleton a trooper armed with sword, pistols, back, breast and helmet on a horse worth £266 13s. 4d. For the shires north of the Forth each heritor or group of them who did not serve in the army worth £1,333 13s. 4d. annual rent as of 1649 was to supply a trooper. Heritors in Renfrewshire, Dunbartonshire and Bute were assessed one horseman per every £2,666 13s. 4d. annual rent. If the heritors of the last named shires did not have their men out by 1 August they were to pay £266 13s. 4d. per man. Middleton received orders to send his officers to the shires north of the Forth to recruit the troopers, save a hundred allocated to Buckingham from Perthshire and Stirlingshire. The new recruits were to join the army between 30 July and 10 August, depending on the distance of the shire from Stirling. Any heritor who failed in his duty would have the penalty of the act of levy used against him without mitigation. Unfortunately nothing is known concerning the success of this method of recruiting.

Furthermore, the army departed from Stirling on 31 July, giving only Perthshire and Stirlingshire time to send their men. Also on the 19th the Committee authorised Middleton to send one of his officers to Caithness and Orkney to recruit the deficient horse from those shires. It is unlikely that any of those men ever took the field against the English. On the Worcester campaign Middleton became very popular with the officer corps. This has been largely attributed to his ability to keep from his usual vice of drunkenness during the campaign. At Worcester Middleton was one of the chief officers who led the Scottish forces in action. As a result of this he was wounded. Following the battle he joined Leslie and his cavalry force in trying to return to Scotland. However, on 9 September Colonel Birch captured Leslie and Middleton at Blackstone Edge in the moors between Parsdale and Halifax. Middleton was initially imprisoned in Liverpool, but was then sent to the Tower. The fate of the regiment is uncertain in that it is not known whether it was destroyed at Worcester or on the retreat northwards. By the end of 1651 Middleton had escaped from the Tower, and in 1652 he joined the king in exile. However, Middleton returned to Scotland in 1653 to take part in Glencairn's rising. The following year he fled again to the continent and remained with Charles II until the restoration. In 1656 the king elevated him to the peerage as the earl of Middleton. From 1660-63 Middleton was the chief political and military agent of the crown in Scotland. During that time he served as governor of Edinburgh Castle. Following his political demise in 1663, Middleton went to England where he acted as governor of Rochester until 1667. In that year the king despatched him to Tangiers as governor, and the earl served there for two years. Middleton died four years after his return to Britain. He was remembered as a brave soldier and good officer, but also as a man addicted to the bottle and dissolution, a friend of the episcopalians and an implacable foe of the presbyterians.[76]

Viscount Montgomery's Horse

Colonel: Hugh, viscount Montgomery

Until 1648 Montgomery had been willing to support the more radical policies of his father; however, he broke with Eglinton in that year and joined the Engagers. He was excluded from military command until after the repeal of the act of classes on 4 June 1651. On the 10th the Committee of Estates appointed him a colonel of Ayrshire Horse. Kyle was to levy forty horse for the regiment, while Carrick and Cunningham recruited 160 troopers. Montgomery was to split the surplus of horse raised from Kyle with Glencairn, and they were also to share out the Carrick levy. While it is uncertain whether Montgomery received any recruits, the viscount did accompany the army on the Worcester campaign. He was taken prisoner after the battle, and if his regiment had existed it was destroyed at Worcester or shortly afterwards.[77]

Sheriff of Moray's Foot

Colonel: Thomas Dunbar of Westfield, sheriff of Moray

Minister: Alexander Spens[78]

On 20 December 1650 the Estates appointed the sheriff of Moray colonel of foot for Nairnshire, Moray and the laird of Grant's lands. The regiment was on foot by late March 1651, but it did not reach the Stirling camp until late June. Its first muster on 21 June gave a strength of 437 foot. As of 18 July the number in the sheriff's regiment had dropped to 421 men. Nothing more is known of the regiment, except that it no longer existed after early September.[79]

Lord Ogilvie's Horse

Colonel: James, Lord Ogilvie

Lieutenant Colonel: William Sinclair of Dun

Major: Walter Boswell

Lord Ogilvie, heir of the earl of Airlie, had been an ally of Montrose in the 1640s. The Covenanters captured him at Philiphaugh, then tried him for treason, but Ogilvie escaped. Parliament pardoned him in 1649, and he subsequently satisfied the Kirk. On 20 December 1650 the Estates nominated him colonel of the Angus Horse. Ogilvie was present at Charles II's coronation on 1 January 1651. Eight days later the Committee of Estates sent him a letter urging Ogilvie to raise his regiment. About the same time his lieutenant colonel began the procedure for satisfying the Kirk, which suggests he was an Engager. The regiment was partially levied by mid-February, with some troopers quartered in Montrose. On the 20th Brechin presbytery took up a case of rape involving two troopers and a soldier of Carnegie's Foot. The men had been imprisoned in Montrose tolbooth for allegedly raping Christian Folly. On 15 March the presbytery heard the testimony of the alleged victim and criminals, which was contradictory. However, further investigations determined that Folly was a whore and by 1 May was imprisoned in Montrose. Folly escaped by the 22nd clearly establishing that she had acted voluntarily as the soldiers had said. Yet parliament had not been informed of the change in events, because on 3 June it called for a speedy trial of the three men, who had presumably been released already. Meanwhile the regiment at large had not been idle. On 7 May Ogilvie's Horse was assigned to the 4th Cavalry Brigade under Middleton with three other regiments. A week later the Committee of Estates ordered Ogilvie to call out two parties of twenty horse and a corporal or quartermaster. Each of these commanded parties was to quarter on those deficient in the forty and twenty days' loans in Angus. On 22 May the Committee told Ogilvie to provide parties of horse to aid the laird of Ormiston and John Auchterlonie. Their mission was to coerce those who had failed to provide baggage horses to carry the grain from the Mearns to do so. By late May part of the regiment was quartering in Menmuir, presbytery of Perth. During June a Trooper Andrew Simpson appeared before the kirk session for threatening a married woman with violence. Although he denied it, the woman claimed he was drunk. There the case ended due to the absence of witnesses. Apparently, Ogilvie's Horse remained in Scotland during the summer, because the colonel was captured at Alyth on 28 August. His men would have then been taken prisoner or dispersed. Ogilvie was sent to the Tower where he remained until 1657. In 1660 the king appointed him a Privy Councillor, and commander of a horse troop; in addition he received a royal pension.[80]

Earl of Rothes' Horse

Colonel: John, 7th earl of Rothes

Ministers: John Oswald, John Makghie/Mckie[81]

On 20 December 1650 parliament appointed Rothes colonel of a Fife cavalry regiment. The earl attended the coronation at Scone on 1 January 1651. The Committee of Estates sent him a note on the 9th telling him to speedily raise his regiment and permitted him to levy twenty-nine men in Fife. By mid-March the regiment was under the colours. Rothes' Horse quartered in southern Fife, partially if not exclusively in Dunfermline presbytery. On 30 April the Committee of Estates, in response to the overburdened condition of the presbytery, instructed the earl to send in a report of his regiment's exactions. On 7 May the regiment was put in the 1st Cavalry Brigade with two other regiments under Leslie. The Committee of Estates ordered it from Fife to Stirling on 17 June. On the unit's departure each trooper was to receive £15 and one boll, one firlot of oats. Rothes led his regiment at Worcester, where he was captured and it was destroyed. Rothes spent four years imprisoned in the Tower and Newcastle. He was sequestered and imprisoned in Edinburgh Castle in 1658, gaining his liberty in 1659 having paid a £48,000 fine. Between 1660 and 1663 Rothes held a number of appointments in Middleton's government. The earl was made Lord General of the Scottish army for a short time in 1666. Although he held political appointments after that he no longer served as an officer. Rothes died in 1681, having been elevated to a dukedom in the previous year.

Rothiemay's Foot

Colonel: John Gordon of Rothiemay

Ministers: William Keith, James Merk/Mirk[83]

Parliament appointed Rothiemay a colonel of foot for Aberdeenshire on 20 December 1650. By 19 March the regiment had been levied and was ready to march south. However, the colonel was guilty of two accidental slaughters and the presbytery of Strathbogie would not permit him to march until he had repented. Consequently, he was ordered to Rothiemay parish church where he was to repent in sackcloth before the minister. The regiment eventually went from Aberdeenshire, but its immediate destination is unknown. On 21 May the Committee of Estates authorised Rothiemay to receive part of the forty days' loan and the food for officers raised by the Aberdeenshire committee of war. By 10 June Rothiemay's Foot was in the Stirling camp. As of 18 July the regiment numbered 423 men, having lost only six deserters. Rothiemay's Foot served at Worcester where it was destroyed. Its chaplain, James Merk, was one of the ministers captured by the English.[84]

Sinclair's Foot

Colonel: Henry Sinclair

Minister: James Lyon[85]

Henry Sinclair was the second son of the eighth Lord Sinclair. In 1644 he served as a captain in his brother Lord Sinclair's regiment of foot. Henry Sinclair accepted a high ranking commission (colonel or lieutenant colonel) in the Engager Army for which he repented in spring 1651. There is no surviving commission for him in this army; however, by 7 May Sinclair had raised an infantry regiment from Angus. On the 7th it was quartering in or adjacent to Stirling. The first muster of the regiment on 11 June revealed a strength of 654 men. On 7 July the Committee of Estates ordered that the 110 foot due from Dundee be split between this and Spynie's regiment. However, Sinclair's Foot received no more recruits, and as of 18 July it consisted of 635 common soldiers. Nothing further is known concerning the regiment. It may have served on the Worcester campaign for the colonel's brother, Lord Sinclair, was taken prisoner there. In the event the regiment ceased to exist sometime in September.[86]

Sleat's Foot

Colonel: Sir James MacDonald of Sleat, chief of the MacDonalds

This is a slightly mysterious regiment as there is a possibility that its recruits may have served in Macleod's Foot. On 20 December 1650 parliament appointed Sleat, as chief of his clan, colonel of a regiment of MacDonald Foot to be raised from Skye and the Uists. The regiment was reportedly on foot by the end of January 1651. It cannot be determined who commanded the unit once it left the isles, which provides further support for the theory that it was amalgamated into the Tutor of Macleod's Foot. In any case the men joined the royal army and fought at Worcester, from which few returned home.[87]

Lord Spynie's Foot

Colonel: George, 3rd Lord Spynie

Minister: Robert Reynolds

Lord Spynie was another former Engager employed in this army. Although parliament appointed him a colonel of foot for Angus on 20 December 1650, Spynie did not satisfy the Kirk for his political sins until 1651. He was also appointed a member to the Committee for Regulating the Army. On 9 January 1651 the Committee of Estates sent Spynie a letter telling him to raise his regiment. On the same day Dundee noted that it would have difficulty raising the two foot companies which were its quota. However, the Angus committee of war decided to levy 1,200 foot for the shire's infantry regiments, and it assigned Dundee the responsibility for raising only one strong company. The burgh council produced a muster roll with 300 names. It also decided to stent those who were not called out £13,332 13s. 4d. to outrig the company. As the company was to consist of 108 common soldiers, plus officers, drummer and messenger-at-arms, and the cost of outfitting one man was £66 13s. 4d. or £7,830 for the privates, the stented sum would probably be applied to other needs of the company such as food and baggage horses. The burgh council did in fact provide the company commander, a Captain Davidson, with seven and one-fifth baggage horses. On 3 April Angus committee of war was ordered to raise the deficients for the regiment. By 7 May Spynie's Foot was in the field and quartered in or about Stirling. As of 11 June the regiment consisted of 514 common soldiers, of whom four deserted by 2 July. On the 17th the Committee of Estates decided that 110 foot due from Dundee be split between this and Sinclair's Foot. Sinclair's regiment does not appear to have received any of them; however, Spynie's did gain fifty-nine recruits on the 9th. When the regiment set off for England it contained 567 soldiers. Spynie's Foot was destroyed at Worcester and the colonel fell prisoner.[89]

Tolquhon's Foot

Colonel: Walter Forbes of Tolquhon the younger

Minister: David Leitch[90]

On 20 December 1650 parliament appointed Tolquhon the younger colonel of an Aberdeenshire foot regiment. By 7 May the regiment was raised and in the

Stirling area. On 21 May the Committee of Estates gave Tolquhon permission to receive part of the forty days' loan and supply of food for officers raised by the Aberdeenshire committee of war. The first muster of the regiment on 10 June indicates it contained 651 men, on the 18th Tolquhon's Foot reached its greatest strength — 659 soldiers. The numbers dipped to 603 foot on 9 July, but rose to 608 men on the 18th. The regiment fought at Worcester, where it disintegrated. Its chaplain, which it shared with Keith's Foot, was taken prisoner.[91]

Urry's Horse

Colonel: William Urry

Urry began his career as a Covenanter officer as lieutenant colonel of Van Druschke's Horse in the Army of the Solemn League and Covenant. He commanded a troop in the New Model Army, and was made a colonel of horse in the Engager Army. In October 1650 he joined Middleton's rising, which provoked a threat of excommunication from the Commission of the General Assembly if he did not quit the rebellion. On 23 April 1651 the Committee of Estates requested that Charles II find Urry a cavalry regiment. On 6 May the quartermaster general received orders to find Urry a place where he could mount and outrig his regiment. There is no other mention of the regiment, but Urry does not disappear from sight. On 7 June the Committee of Estates sent the committees of war of Aberdeenshire and Banffshire a notice to pay Urry and Van Druschke three months' quartering amounting to £2,000 owed from 8 May. The committees were to pay up on sight of the letter, or face quartering on their members by soldiers in Aberdeenshire, Banffshire and the Mearns. Urry led his regiment on the campaign into England. At Worcester Urry was captured and his regiment ceased to exist.[92]

Van Druschke's Horse

Colonels: Major General Jonas Van Druschke (1651); (?) Cochrane (1651)

Van Druschke had begun his career as Covenanter officer as colonel of a regiment of horse in the Army of the Solemn League and Covenant which was known for its indiscipline and oppressive behaviour. In October 1650 he had joined Middleton's rising. The Commission of the General Assembly threatened him with excommunication if he did not desist in supporting Middleton. However, Van Druschke remained loyal to the royalist rebels. On 7 January 1651 the Committee of Estates gave him permission to draw together the officers and men without employ or regiment to be under his command. This group presumably included men from regiments broken at Dunbar, and veteran soldiers and officers who had drifted into the army camp in hope of employment. On 23

April the Committee asked Charles II to find Van Druschke a cavalry regiment. Just under two weeks later the quartermaster general was ordered to find Van Druschke a place where he could mount and outfit his regiment. On 7 May Van Druschke was placed in command of the 6th Cavalry Brigade, which consisted of four regiments. A month later the Committee of Estates took action on his and Urry's behalf to get the three months' quartering money owed them from Aberdeenshire and Banffshire. The two shires received orders to provide the £2,000 owed the officers immediately or to face quartering on the committee-men by the soldiers in the northeast. Upon the entry of the army into England Charles II appointed a certain Cochrane colonel of Van Druschke's Horse with the responsibility of levying men in the southwest. By 17 August the laird of Blantyre had raised a troop for Cochrane's. Disaster struck when Colonel Okey entered the area, and Cochrane with Blantyre and his troop fled to the Highlands. Van Druschke, meanwhile, had remained with the main army and fell prisoner to the English at Worcester.[93]

Train of Wagons

Strictly speaking, this unit was not a regiment. Its men were probably drawn from several regiments. As of 3 July 1651 seventy men had been assigned to guard the wagon train. The number rose to a high of 279 foot on the 9th, falling to 247 men on the 18th. This unit undoubtedly served on the Worcester campaign, and due to its duties it is unlikely that any of the men escaped capture, or death.[94]

NOTES

1. SRO, PA. 16.2; *A List of the Prisoners of war who are officers in commission, in custody of the marshall-general* (London, 1651), 8; *RCGA*, iii. 282, 463; *Fasti*, v. 91, 253.

2. SRO, GD. 16.50, 62; *APS*, VI, ii. 623, 685; *Army of the Covenant*, ii. 367; Balfour, *Works*, iv. 300; *List of Regiments*; *List of Prisoners*, 8.

3. SRO, PA. 11.11, 4, 7, 21, 59, 90v-1; *Collection of Original Letters and Papers Concerning the Affairs of England, 1641-51*, 2 vols., ed. T. Carte (London, 1739), i. 409.

4. *RCGA*, iii. 463.

5. Bod. Lib., Carte MS. 29, 199; NLS, Adv. MS. 23.7.12, 120v; SRO, PA. 11.11, 17v, 32v, 93; PA. 16.5, 77, 79; *APS*, VI, ii. 623, 640; *Baillie*, iii. 117; Balfour, *Works*, iv. 300; *Collection of Original Letters*, i. 408; *Scotland and the Commonwealth*, ed. C. H. Firth (Scot. His. Soc., 1st Ser., xviii, 1895), 6.

6. SRO, PA. 16.2; *RCGA*, iii. 439.

7. SRO, KSR Clackmannan 13 July 1651; PA. 7.24, 116; *APS*, VI, ii. 623; Balfour, *Works*, iv. 300, 308-9; *Correspondence of Lothian*, ii. 330; R. A. Bensen, 'South-West Fife and the Scottish Revolution: the presbytery of Dunfermline, 1633-52' (Edinburgh Univ., M.Litt. thesis 1978), 225; Dow, *Cromwellian Scotland* (Edinburgh, 1979), 14, 17-18.

8. *RCGA*, iii. 462.

9. SRO, PA. 11.11, 41; PA. 16.5, 1; Balfour, *Works*, iv. 211; *Correspondence of Lothian*, ii. 331; J. Thurloe, *A collection of papers, containing authentic memorials of English affairs, 1638-53* (London, 1742), i. 165; *Scots Peerage*, i. 18-19.
10. SRO, PA. 7.24, 92, 94, 95, 109v; PA. 11.11, 44, 101v-2; Balfour, *Works*, iv. 301.
11. SRO, PA. 11.11, 81v, 94, 99v, 103.
12. Bod. Lib., Tanner MS. 55, 58; SRO, PA. 16.2; *RCGA*, iii. 463.
13. Bod. Lib., Tanner MS. 55, 58; SRO, PA. 11.11, 20v; PA. 16.2; PA. 16.5, 45, 47; *APS*, VI, ii. 623; J. Fraser, *Chronicles of the Frasers, 916-1674*, ed. W. Mackay (Scot. His. Soc., 1st Ser., xlvii, 1905), 378.
14. SRO, BR Brechin, 20 February 1651.
15. SRO, PA. 11.11, 5; PR Brechin, 20 February, 15 March, 1, 22 May 1651; *APS*, VI, ii. 623; *Correspondence of Lothian*, ii. 331; *Scots Peerage*, viii. 69.
16. SRO, PA. 16.2; *List of Prisoners*, 8; *Fasti*, i. 351.
17. SRO, PA. 11.11, 61v, 66; Balfour, *Works*, iv. 300; *List of Prisoners*, 8; *Scots Peerage*, ii. 595-6.
18. SRO, PA. 16.2; *RCGA*, iii. 439; *Selections from the minutes of the Presbyteries of St. Andrews and Cupar, 1641-48*, ed. G. R. Kinloch (Abbotsford Club, vii. 1837), 164.
19. Bod. Lib., Carte MS. 29, 199; NRH, OPR Anstruther Easter, 1 March 1651; SAUL, Cupar Court and Council Records, 22 January 1651; SRO, KSR Ceres, i. 37v; PA. 11.11, 23v-4, 32v, 40v, 64v; PA. 16.5, 97, 99; *APS*, VI, ii. 623; Balfour, *Works*, iv. 309; *Correspondence of Lothian*, ii. 331; *The Diary of Mr. John Lamont of Newton, 1649-71* (Maitland Club, xii, 1830), 34; *Scots Peerage*, iii. 35-6.
20. *RCGA*, iii. 463; *Fasti*, iv. 144.
21. SRO, PA. 16.5, 5, 7; *APS*, VI, ii. 638; Turner, *Memoirs*, 95; Foster, *Members*, 94; Stevenson, *Covenanters*, 283, 311-2.
22. SRO, PA. 11.11, 32v; PA. 16.5, 126; *APS*, VI, ii. 655.
23. SRO, PA. 16.2; *List of Prisoners*, 8; *RCGA*, iii. 463.
24. SRO, PA. 7.8, 47, 48; PA. 11.11, 17v, 35v; *APS*, VI, ii. 623, 649; Balfour, *Works*, iv. 226, 300; *List of Prisoners*, 8.
25. SRO, PA. 16.2; *RCGA*, iii. 439, 485; *Fasti*, ii. 126.
26. SRO, PA. 11.11, 32v; PA. 16.2; PA. 16.5, 117, 119; *APS*, VI, ii. 625, 640; Balfour, *Works*, iv. 227; W. Drummond, *The Genealogy of the Most Noble and Ancient House of Drummond* (Edinburgh, 1831), 187, 296-8; Foster, *Members*, 105; *Scots Peerage*, viii. 219, 222; Stevenson, *Covenanters*, 311-3.
27. *RCGA*, iii. 462.
28. Bod. Lib., Tanner MS. 55. 57; SRO, KSR Dunfermline, i. 118, 120-1; PA. 11.11, 3v, 36; Balfour, *Works*, iv. 300; *Correspondence of Lothian*, ii. 330; *RCGA*, iii. 462; Foster, *Members*, 313; *Scots Peerage*, iii. 373-4.
29. NLS, Adv. MS. 23.7.12, 120; SRO, PA. 11.11, 10; *APS*, VI, ii. 623; Balfour, *Works*, iv. 300; *Scotland and the Commonwealth*, 6; *Scots Peerage*, iii. 578.
30. SRO. GD. 124.13, 4-6; PA. 11.11, 37v, 39v, 43v; *APS*, VI, ii. 623; Balfour, *Works*, iv. 300; *Scots Peerage*, v. 625-6.
31. *RCGA*, iii. 463; *Fasti*, vi. 130.
32. SRO, KSR Slains, i. 219-20; P. A. 7.8, 40; PA. 11.11, 41; Balfour, *Works*, iv. 300; *List of Prisoners*, 2; *Scots Peerage*, iv. 62.
33. SRO, PA. 11.11, 80; PR Stranraer, i. 239.
34. SRO, PA. 11.11, 40v, 54-v; *Scots Peerage*, iv. 247-8.
35. SRO, PA. 11.11, 21; PA. 16.5, 123; *APS*, VI, ii. 623; Thurloe, *Papers*, i. 170; W. Mackay, *Urquhart and Glenmoriston* (Inverness, 1893), 166-7; *Scots Peerage*, vii. 473-4.
36. SRO, PA. 16.2; *RCGA*, iii. 439, 463.
37. SAUL, Hay of Leyes Papers, 930; SRO, PA. 11.11, 32v, 85v; PA. 16.5, 101; *APS*, VI, ii. 623; *Correspondence of Lothian*, ii. 331; *Scots Peerage*, iv. 288, 290.
38. SRO, PA. 7.7, 211; *Dumbarton Burgh Records, 1627-1746*, ed. J. Young (Dumbarton, 1860), 64.

39. PRO, SP 18/16/40, 81v; SRO, GD. 45/5, 26, 126; PA. 11.11, 40v, 63v, 64v, 66, 72; Balfour, *Works*, iv. 278, 301; E. Hyde, *The History of the Rebellion and Civil Wars in England*, 6 vols., ed. W. D. Macray (Oxford, 1888), v. 190; *Scots Peerage*, iv. 378-80.

40. SRO, PA. 11.11, 63v, 72-v; PA. 16.5, 132; PR Cupar, 16 January 1651; *APS*, VI, ii. 685; W. S. Shepherd, 'The Politics and Society of Glasgow 1648-74' (Glasgow Univ. Ph.D. thesis 1978), 85.

41. *Army of the Covenant*, i. liv; Bensen, 'South-West Fife', 225; Dow, *Cromwellian Scotland*, 19.

42. *APS*, VI, ii. 655; Balfour, *Works*, iv. 278, 301; *Scots Peerage*, iv. 477-8.

43. SRO, GD. 188.2/5, 4, 25/6, 1; PA. 11.11, 20.

44. NLS, Adv. MS. 23.7.12, 120-v; NRH, OPR Rothiemay, i. 59-60; SRO, PA. 11.11, 73v, 92v, 97; PR Deer, ii. 81, 83, 87, 90; *Aberdeen Letters*, iii. 181-2, 185; *Baillie*, iii. 117; Dow, *Cromwellian Scotland*, 14, 17-18; *Scots Peerage*, iv. 548.

45. SRO, PA. 16.2; *RCGA*, iii. 463.

46. SRO, PA. 11.11, 24v, 26, 39, 43-v, 94; *APS*, VI, ii. 623; Balfour, *Works*, iv. 300; Thurloe, *Papers*, i. 170.

47. SRO, PA. 11.11, 80v; *Scotland and the Commonwealth*, 321-2; see above, 380.

48. SRO, PA. 16.2; PA. 16.3, 24; *List of Prisoners*, 8.

49. SRO, PA. 11.11, 41v, 54v-5; PA. 16.3, 24; PA. 16.5, 49, 51; *APS*, VI, ii. 623; Balfour, *Works*, iv. 211; *List of Prisoners*, 8; Foster, *Members*, 200; *Scots Peerage*, vi. 60.

50. SRO, PA. 11.11, 80v; *Army of the Covenant*, i. xli; Balfour, *Works*, iv. 278; *Scotland and the Commonwealth*, 321-2; see above, 379-80.

51. SRO, PA. 16.2; *RCGA*, iii. 261, 424.

52. Bod. Lib., Carte MS. 29, 199; SAUL, PR St. Andrews, i. 229; SRO, PA. 11.11, 23v-24; PA. 16.2; PA. 16.5, 109, 111; *APS*, VI, ii. 623; Balfour, *Works*, iv. 309, 339-40; *Correspondence of Lothian*, ii. 330; *List of Prisoners*, 8; *Scots Peerage*, v. 85, 87.

53. *RCGA*, iii. 474; *Fasti*, vii. 33; W. Makey, 'Ministers in Scottish Parishes, 1648', 99.

54. SRO, PA. 11.11, 39; PA. 16.5, 37, 39; *APS*, VI, ii. 623; Fraser, *Chronicles*, 378; A. Mackenzie, *History of Clan Mackenzie* (Inverness, 1879), 204, note on 204-5, 207; A. Macrae, *History of the Clan Macrae* (Dingwall, 1899), 62-3; Stevenson, *Alasdair*, 271; see above, 247.

55. SRO, PA. 11.11, 80; see above, 374.

56. *APS*, VI, ii. 623; Stevenson, *Alasdair*, 272.

57. Dow, *Cromwellian Scotland*, 19.

58. *Ibid.*; R. W. Munro, *Kinsmen and Clansmen* (Edinburgh, 1971), 99.

59. SRO, PA. 11.11, 56v; Dow, *Cromwellian Scotland*, 19; Stevenson, *Alasdair*, 271.

60. *APS*, VI, ii. 623; Fraser, *Chronicles*, 378; Stevenson, *Alasdair*, 271.

61. *APS*, VI, ii. 623; Dow, *Cromwellian Scotland*, 19; G. Eyre-Todd, *The Highland Clans of Scotland* (London, 1923), 331-2; Stevenson, *Alasdair*, 271.

62. *APS*, VI, ii. 623; Thurloe, *Papers*, i. 172.

63. *APS*, VI, ii. 623; Balfour, *Works*, iv. 211; J. Nicoll, *A Diary of Public Transactions and other occurrences chiefly in Scotland from January 1650 to June 1667*, ed. D. Laing (Bannatyne Club, lii, 1836), 53; Bensen, 'South-West Fife', 223, 225-7; A. M. Sinclair, *The Clan Gillean* (Charlottetown, 1899), 160, 162-3, 165-7; [J. C. Sinclair], *An Historical and Geneaological Account of the Clan Maclean* (Edinburgh, 1838), 194; letter of N. Maclean-Bristol to the author, 26 July 1985.

64. Dow, *Cromwellian Scotland*, 19.

65. *RCGA*, iii. 462; *Fasti*, vi. 149, 456; I. F. Grant, *The Macleods* (London, 1959), 293 note 2.

66. SRO, PA. 7.8, 47-8; PA. 11.11, 32v; PA. 16.5, 105, 107; *APS*, VI, ii. 623; Grant, *Macleods*, 292-3, 296-7; [Sinclair], *Clan Maclean*, 196; Stevenson, *Alasdair*, 271.

67. Munro, *Kinsmen*, 129; Stevenson, *Alasdair*, 271.

68. Balfour, *Works*, iv. 211; R. L. MacNeil, *The Clan MacNeil* (New York, 1923), 81, 149.

69. Dow, *Cromwellian Scotland*, 19; Macrae, *Clan Macrae*, 62-3.

70. NLS, Acc. 6026.14, 1/528-30; Adv. MS. 23.7.12, 120; SRO, PA. 11.11, 10, 36, 40v, 42v; *APS*, VI, ii. 623; Balfour, *Works*, iv. 300; *Diary of Lamont*, 34; *Scots Peerage*, vi. 58-9.

71. SRO, PA. 16.2.

72. SRO, KSR Dunfermline, i. 120-1; PA. 7.7, 211; PA. 7.24, 65, 95, 109v-10, 116; PA. 11.11, 3v, 55v; Balfour, *Works*, iv. 300, 308; *Collection of Original Letters*, i. 408-9; Hyde, *History*, v. 178; see above, 331, 334-5.

73. NRH, OPR Channelkirk, 29 November 1651; SRO, PA. 16.2; *List of Prisoners*, 8.

74. Bod. Lib., Tanner MS. 55, 57; SRO, PA. 7.8, 31/1, 72-3, 75; PA. 7.24, 105v; PA. 11.11, 13, 15, 24v, 32v, 33v-4; PA. 16.5, 9, 11; WRH, RH. 1.14, 25; *APS*, VI, ii. 623, 640; Balfour, *Works*, iv. 227; *Correspondence of Lothian*, ii. 331; *Scots Peerage*, vii. 20-1.

75. SRO, PA. 16.2; *RCGA*, iii. 463.

76. Bod. Lib., Tanner MS. 55, 56b-7; NLS, Adv. MS. 23.7.12, 119v-20; PRO, SP 18/16/40, 80v, 81v; SRO, PA. 7.24, 109; PA. 11.11, 20, 43v, 66, 101v-2v; *Baillie*, iii. 118; Balfour, *Works*, iv. 300; Hyde, *History*, v. 189-90; *RCGA*, iii. 90, 171-3; W. S. Douglas, *Cromwell's Scotch Campaigns: 1650-51* (London, 1898), 163; *Scots Peerage*, vi. 183-5.

77. SRO, PA. 11.11, 54-v; *Scots Peerage*, iii. 450-1.

78. SRO, PA. 16.2; PR Elgin, i. 314, 317, 324, 326, 328, 329.

79. SRO, PA. 16.2; PA. 16.5, 121-2; *APS*, VI, ii. 623.

80. SRO, KSR Menmuir, i. 61; PA. 11.11, 35v, 42v; PR Brechin, 20 February, 15 March, 1, 22 May 1651; *APS*, VI, ii. 640, 678; Balfour, *Works*, iv. 210, 227, 300; *Correspondence of Lothian*, ii. 331.

81. *RCGA*, iii. 335.

82. SRO, PA. 7.24, 116; *APS*, VI, ii. 326; Balfour, *Works*, iv. 299, 308-9; *Correspondence of Lothian*, ii. 330; *List of Prisoners*, 2; *RCGA*, iii. 335; *Scots Peerage*, vii. 299-301.

83. SRO, PA. 16.2; *List of Prisoners*, 8; *RCGA*, iii. 463.

84. SRO, PA. 11.11, 41v; PA. 16.5, 65, 67; *APS*, VI, ii. 623; *Extracts from the Presbytery Book of Strathbogie, 1631-54*, ed. J. Stuart (Spalding Club, vii, 1843), 178.

85. SRO, PA. 16.2; *RCGA*, iii. 463.

86. SRO, PA. 11.11, 32v, 96v; PA. 16.5, 81, 83; *Army of the Covenant*, i. xxxiv; *RCGA*, iii. 311; *Scots Peerage*, vii. 576.

87. *APS*, VI, ii. 623; A. MacDonald and A. MacDonald, *The Clan Donald* (Inverness, 1904), 62; see above, 386-7.

88. SRO, PA. 16.2; *RCGA*, iii. 462.

89. SRO, PA. 11.11, 5, 32v, 96v; PA. 16.5, 69, 71; *APS*, VI, ii. 623; *Correspondence of Lothian*, ii. 331; *List of Prisoners*, 2; A. Maxwell, *The History of Old Dundee* (Edinburgh, 1884), 534-5, 538, 542; *Scots Peerage*, viii. 105-7; see above, 396.

90. SRO, PA. 16.2; PA. 16.3; *List of Prisoners*, 8.

91. SRO, PA. 11.11, 32v, 41v; PA. 16.5, 61, 63; *APS*, VI, ii. 623; *List of Prisoners*, 8.

92. SRO, PA. 7.24, 118; PA. 11.11, 20, 51; *Army of the Covenant*, i. lxxi; *List of Prisoners*, 2; *RCGA*, iii. 93.

93. SRO, PA. 7.24, 80, 118; PA. 11.11, 20, 51; *Army of the Covenant*, ii. 527; Balfour, *Works*, iv. 300; *Diary of Lamont*, 35; *RCGA*, iii. 93; *Scotland and the Commonwealth*, 5.

94. SRO, PA. 16.5, 128.

Chronology of Events, 1639-1652

1639

February Lovat Frasers and Mackenzies seize Inverness for the Covenanters.

13 February Marquis of Huntly musters the northeastern royalists.

March Covenanters occupy Dunglas and Tantallon Castles.

21 March Edinburgh Castle falls to the Covenanters.

26 March Covenanters capture Dumbarton Castle.

Late March the earls of Home, Lothian and Dalhousie with Lords Balmerino and Cranston go to the eastern Borders with 3,000 horse accompanied by Major General Sir Robert Munro's 2,000 foot.

28 March 2,000 northeastern Covenanters rendezvous at Kintore. 29th the northeastern lairds join the earl of Montrose's army at Tullo Hill near Aberdeen. 30th 10 a.m. Montrose's army enters Aberdeen and is mustered on the Queens Links then proceeds to Kintore. 1 April Montrose's army (minus Kinghorn's) marches to near Inverurie and remains there. 4th Huntly signs a modified National Covenant and is seized. 6th Montrose departs for and arrives in Aberdeen. 11th Argyll's men enter Aberdeen. 12th Montrose's Foot under General Leslie departs from Aberdeen. 13th Montrose with Huntly as his prisoner and accompanied by his horse and Argyll's men leaves Aberdeen.

25th April earl Marischal occupies Aberdeen.

May Expedition of northern Covenanters reaches Elgin. Returns north and disbands following negotiations with northeastern royalists.

10 May siege of Towie-Barclay Castle, royalists repulsed and suffer first casualty of the wars.

14 May Trot of Turriff, a royalist victory. 15th royalists occupy Aberdeen.

20 May General Leslie concentrates his forces on the eastern border.

23 May Marischal reoccupies Aberdeen and is joined by Montrose. 30th Marischal and Montrose leave Aberdeen for Udny. 31st Covenanters march to Kellie House. 1 June Montrose's men march to Gight House and remain until the 3rd when they return to Aberdeen, which they leave on the 5th.

6 June royalists under viscount Aboyne occupy Aberdeen. 15th Marischal wins a skirmish against Aboyne's men at Megra Hill near Stonehaven.

18-19 June Battle of Brig of Dee and Montrose's army occupies Aberdeen on 19th. 21st Montrose's occupation ends and he disbands his army.

20 June Leslie's army disbands at Duns Law after the Treaty of Birks is signed.

25 June Ardnamurchan returns from his raid on Colonsay, during which he captured Coll MacGillesbuig MacDonald and goes to Islay.

1640

5-8 May Marischal's occupation of Aberdeen.

28 May Marischal reoccupies Aberdeen with Munro and they extort the Articles of Bon Accord from the burgh. 2 June they capture Drum House. 10th their troops pillage laird of Gight's house of Ardessie. 13 x 18th Marischal's men leave Aberdeen. 27th Munro's plunder Houses of Lethenty and Newtown of Culsalmond. 5 July Munro marches on Strathbogie. 10th the castle falls to him. 11th Covenanter victory at Auchindoun skirmish. Spynie Palace taken during the occupation of Strathbogie. 10 August Munro marches to Banff and laird of Banff's house is destroyed. 18th Munro's men vandalise Inchdrewer House. 4 September Munro marches to Aberdeen arriving by the 9th. 12th he marches to the borders.

Late May siege of Edinburgh Castle begins. July mine under the Spur exploded. 19 September Edinburgh Castle surrenders.

18 June earl of Argyll's forces rendezvous and commence campaign against Highland royalists. 6-13 July the expedition takes action against the earl of Airlie's lands and houses. 2 August Argyll's campaign ends.

July Leslie's army mustered at Links of Leith. 20 x 27th rendezvous Choicelee Wood. 17 August army at Coldstream. 18 x 20 it marches to Hirslaw. 20th army invades England. 21st reaches Milfield Moor area. 22nd marches to Middleton Haugh near Wooler. 23rd after hearing sermons the army marches to Newton Edyliefordmuir/Brandon Field near Bramford. 24th it marches to Newton of

Boglingham and New and Old Edlingham via Whittingham. 26th advance to Creich/Trelbirk. 27th advance to Thirkly/Newburn. 28th Battle of Newburn, Covenanters successfully force the Tyne. 30th army enters Newcastle.

27 August Argyll captures Dumbarton Castle after a siege.

September Caerlaverock and Threave Castlés surrender after sieges.

2 October Ripon negotiations begin. 16th and 26th Treaties of Ripon.

1641

June Treaty of London concluded.

20 August Durham evacuated. 21st Leslie's army leaves Newcastle. 25th army disbands at Hirslaw. 27th final disbanding of remaining regiments, save four (later reduced to three).

23 October Ulster Rising. 28th Scottish parliament offers an army of 10,000 men to put down the rising. 3 December to April 1642 negotiations over army.

1642

3 February Scottish Privy Council orders recruiting of new levies for the three standing regiments and for Lawers' new regiment. 11, 18 and 28 March commissions issued to the infantry colonels of the Ulster Army by Charles I and the Council.

3 April the three standing regiments under Major General Munro land at Carrickfergus.

27 April Munro leads 1,600 infantry from Carrickfergus to Malone. 28th 1,400 British foot, two companies dragoons and three troops horse join Munro and march to Drumbo. 29th 800 British foot and two troops horse join force, which marches to Lisnegarvy and fights in Kilwarlin Woods. 30th army advances to Loughbrickland via Dromore. 1 May cavalry move to Newry; the infantry capture an Irish garrison in a lough. 2nd Newry town falls to Munro. 3rd Newry Castle surrenders to Munro. 6th leaving Newry garrisoned, Munro marches to Armagh. Then he takes 800 foot through the Mountains of Mourne, rejoining the army at Dundrum. The army splits up at Drumbo. 11 x 12th Munro back in Carrickfergus.

May Argyll's Foot takes Rathlin Island, massacring the inhabitants.

24 x 25 May Munro leaves Carrickfergus with about three Scottish foot regiments. They march to the Bann and are joined by five companies British foot and four troops horse. 26th-28th main army marches down the Bann to Coleraine and Ballymoney, while part moves through the Apperly Hills. 29th Munro with 400 foot captures the earl of Antrim in Dunluce Castle. 30th the army marches to Ballycastle via the Glens of Antrim, joined by part Argyll's. 1 June march to Glenarm. 2nd-4th army rests. 5th x 6th army returns to Carrickfergus.

16 June Munro with 2,000 Scottish infantry leaves Carrickfergus on 17th, reaches Lisnegarvy and is joined by 1,600 British foot and nine troops horse. 18th Munro leads part of the army to Dromore via the plains; the other portion moves via Killultagh Wood to Knockbridge-on-Bann. Munro proceeds to Toolish Banside to Newry to the Mourne Mountains and Maccartan's Wood, eventually returning to Carrickfergus.

12 July Munro marches south with 3,600 infantry, three troops horse and some artillery to Charlemont. He then retreats to Newry and raids Irish cattle herds from there before retiring to Carrickfergus.

4 August earl of Leven, general-in-chief of Ulster Army, arrives at Carrickfergus.

September Leven leads a force from Carrickfergus across the Bann to county Londonderry to county Tyrone and takes Dungannon. He then retires to Carrickfergus.

25 September Leven leads a force from Carrickfergus, reaching Lisburn on the 26th where British forces join him. The army marches via Tanderagee, Newry, Mourne Mountains and Maccartan's Wood to Carrickfergus.

November Leven leaves Ulster.

1643

4 April three Scottish and three British infantry regiments rendezvous at Clandeboy's Woods and burn them for two days before retiring to their quarters.

12 May Munro leads 2,000 infantry and 300 cavalry from Carrickfergus to Drumbo. 13th main force marches to Sir Charles Poynt's house, skirmishing at Tanderagee; Home with 600 men marches to Newcastle. 14th Munro marches to Armagh and from there to Lochgall where 300 foot and one horse troop join him. A three and a half hour skirmish against the Irish follows. After the Irish flee all the houses between Armagh and Charlemont are burnt. 15th Munro

after nearing Charlemont falls back to Armagh. 16th skirmish in Glencane Woods. 18th Munro marches to Newcastle, which is under siege. It surrenders and the earl of Antrim is captured upon landing from a ship. Munro returns to Carrickfergus by the 23rd.

July Munro leads a force from Carrickfergus. British units join him. 7th Dungannon falls to him. Munro returns to Carrickfergus.

28 July Convention of Estates orders levying of five foot companies and three horse troops.

August Munro builds a fortified camp at Armagh with a Scottish-British army. The army besieges Charlemont, raiding Irish territory to the south. After 16 September (The Cessation) the siege breaks up and Munro raids Irish grain-producing regions before wintering in Carrickfergus.

18 August all fencible men in Scotland put on 48-hour stand-by.

22 August routmasters commissioned. 25th foot commanders commissioned. 26th first nomination of colonels; Leven made commander-in-chief.

16 September the foot companies and horse troops rendezvous on the Links of Leith. c.20th they occupy Berwick.

November Alasdair MacColla MacDonald raids the Western Isles and captures Colonsay.

24 November Argyll appointed king's lieutenant in west until 1 June 1644.

26 November colonels of horse named.

29 November military treaty with English parliament made.

Mid-December Scottish levies marching into southern Lowlands.

1644

1 January Army of the Solemn League and Covenant rendezvous at Harlaw.

18 January the army moves from Dunbar to Berwick. 19th Tweed crossed; army moves to Adderstone by 22nd. 23rd Lieutenant General William Baillie crosses Tweed at Kelso with six regiments of foot and one of horse. 24th artillery reaches Adderstone, march to Alnwick. 29th Morpeth town and castle garrisoned. 3 February army reaches suburbs of Newcastle. 19th Corbridge

cavalry skirmish. 21st Leven leaves Sir James Lumsden with six regiments and some horse to watch Newcastle. 22nd army at Heddon-on-the-Wall. 23rd army quartering in the Ovingham-Corbridge area. 28th 15 foot regiments and six horse cross Tyne at Ovingham, Bydwell and Altringham, then cross Derwentwater at Ebchester. 1 March army near Chester-le-Street. 2nd Wear crossed at Newbridge/Lumley Castle. 3rd army in Harrington area. 4th Sunderland occupied. 7th-8th Boldon Hills skirmish. 13th two regiments foot garrison Sunderland; army on line of Wear from South Shields to south of Newcastle. 15th operations against South Shields Fort begins; an unsuccessful attack takes place. 19th army fasts. 20th South Shields Fort stormed. 23rd army at Hilton near Sunderland. 24th-25th skirmish at Hilton. 26th-8 April Easington occupied. 8th army at Quarrington Hill near Durham. 13th army reaches Ferryhill. 14th army moves from Darlington to Wetherby, reaching it on 17th. 18th rest day. 20th rendezvous at Tadcaster with Fairfax's forces and march to York.

February-March three regiments foot evacuate Ulster and Newry given to the earl of Ormond's forces.

19 March Gordon of Haddo raids Aberdeen and seizes some of the leading Covenanters.

Late March Huntly rises against the Covenanters and produces a band. 1,200 men appear at the Aboyne rendezvous and march to Aberdeen. The royalists create havoc from Deeside to Banff. 21 April they capture Montrose, but disband on 1 May.

April-May Ardkinglas chases the Irish from the isles; he captures Mull. He recaptures Rathlin after Alasdair had seized it in early May. Then he pursues the Irish to Islay and Jura in June.

4 April-25 May Solemn League and Covenant sworn in Ulster.

15 April Aboyne and Montrose capture Dumfries. 17th a force of 180 Border Covenanters go to Selkirk. 18th they move to Fanasch. 19th Covenanters at Crasmoor and joined by ten companies foot and eight troops horse; the royalists abandon Dumfries. 20th Covenanters pursue them to border, then retire to Teviotdale.

16 April the earl of Callander made lieutenant general and commander-in-chief of the forces in Scotland and colonels appointed for a new levy.

17 April Argyll musters an army of 4,700 foot in central and eastern Scotland. 26th Argyll holds a rendezvous at Dunottar Castle of his army and the north-eastern Covenanters. 2 May Argyll's army reaches Aberdeen. Part of the army

remains as a garrison but 400 horse with Argyll, Marischal and Lords Gordon, Forbes and Fraser move on to Drum. 4th the cavalry rides to Inverurie, while Lord Burleigh with most of the infantry marches from Aberdeen to Udny. 6th Argyll's force goes to Kellie and Burleigh marches there too. 8th Kellie House and Gight Castle surrender to Marischal and are garrisoned. 13th Argyll with Burleigh returns to Aberdeen. 15th-16th Argyll's army at Turriff where he holds a rendezvous of the northeastern Covenanters. 18th Argyll marches to Cullen and from there to Elgin. 24th Argyll returns to Aberdeen, having marched via Strathbogie. Huntly flees to Strathnaver. 29th two regiments foot disband. 31st Argyll leaves for the south. 1 June one foot regiment disbands. 3rd two regiments foot go south and Argyll's Foot goes into garrisons on Deeside. It finally departs the area on 1 July save for a small party which leaves shortly afterwards.

22 April siege of York begins. 5 June unsuccessful attack on York. 2 July after lifting siege of York, the allied army wins the battle of Marston Moor. 16th York falls.

28 April Callander holds a rendezvous of 5,000 Covenanters at Douglas and marches from there to Dumfries. May his men raid Cumberland.

14 May Belfast seized by Munro from Ormondist officers. He marches to Lisburn hoping to capture it, but fails and retires to Belfast.

29 May Morpeth Castle falls to Montrose after a siege. May-June Montrose captures South Shields Fort, Stockton, Hartlepool and Lumley Castle.

30 May Argyll's commission in west extended to 1 July.

25 June Callander's army enters England and retakes Lumley Castle. 24 July Hartlepool Castle (300 foot under Sir Edmund Carew) surrenders to him. Stockton recaptured. Army returns to Lumley, then moves to Osworth. 28th July Gateshead taken and siege of Newcastle begins.

27 June Munro leads four Scottish infantry regiments and a horse troop with three British infantry regiments to a rendezvous at Lisnegarvy. 28th four British horse troops join army which moves to Dromore. 30th the army marches to Armagh via Loughbrickland and six British horse troops and at least one infantry regiment join it. 1 July three Scottish infantry regiments and three troops horse as well as three and a half regiments British foot with three troops horse join the army, giving it a strength of 12,000 foot and 1,000 horse. Munro marches to Granard via Monaghan and Cavan, stopping on Sunday the 7th. 8th the army marches through Longford, Fyna Bridge and Kells to Navan. 10th advance to Bedloe Castle via Ardye. 11th the army at Castlehaven. 12th Munro attempts to gain entrance to Newry and fails. 14th Munro reaches Lisnegarvy. 15th army disbands.

8 July Kinlochaline Castle surrenders to Alasdair. 14th Mingary Castle surrenders to him.

17 July Leven's army at Doncaster; he later moves to Leeds and establishes a camp there. 1 August Lieutenant General David Leslie leads four cavalry regiments north to aid in siege of Newcastle. 7th Leven leaves Leeds. 10th army at Bishop Auckland. 14th it crosses the Tyne at Newburn.

22 July Argyll with 2,600 men at Dunstaffnage Castle commences a campaign in the Isles, Ardnamurchan, Morvern, Lochaber and the adjacent regions which lasts to 2 September. 8 August siege of Mingary Castle commences. Kinlochaline Castle also besieged and two ships belonging to Alasdair captured.

25 July Munro with three regiments Scottish foot and two troops horse marches from Carrickfergus to Lisnegarvy, where two British infantry regiments and one troop horse join them. 26th three British infantry regiments and three troops horse join the army. 27th the army marches to Kilwarlin Wood. 28th one regiment Scottish foot and two British ones with a horse troop join the army. 29th two Scottish infantry regiments and three troops horse join the army. 11 August Western Ulster British forces arrive. 12th Dromore skirmish. By the 16th the army moves to Armagh and makes a camp there. 8 September Black-waterford skirmish. 10th cavalry skirmish. 15th Irish army under the earl of Castlehaven retreats to Cavan and Leinster. 19th Scots and British cavalry move into Cavan. 20th the cavalry moves into Leinster to Kinnard, then returns to quarters. 21st Munro moves infantry to Tynan, remaining there until the 28th. 7 October Munro disbands army and enters winter quarters.

August Campbells muster in Argyll against Alasdair; Seaforth, Sutherland, the Moray and northern Covenanters rendezvous at Inverness against Alasdair in Kingussie and march up the Spey. Covenanters abandon Blair Atholl.

15 August Leven establishes siege camp at Elswick. 20 and 24 August Newcastle royalist sorties against siegeworks. 19 October successful attack on Newcastle. 22nd governor surrenders castle.

29 August Montrose rendezvouses with Alasdair at Blair Atholl. 31st Lord Kilpont with 500 foot defects to Montrose at Hill of Buchanty. 1 September Battle of Tippermuir, Montrose defeats Lord Elcho's army of 7,000 men which loses 1,300 killed and 800 captured. 1 September Montrose captures Perth and leaves it on the 4th.

1 September-7 October Leslie enters Cumbria with seven cavalry regiments.

2 and 4 September and 16 November five regiments foot and two regiments and one troop of horse withdrawn from Leven's army to Scotland.

2 September Covenanters rendezvous at Stirling. 4th Argyll appointed commander-in-chief of forces congregating there.

6 September Burleigh sets rendezvous for Mearns, Aberdeenshire, Banffshire and Moray Covenanters at Aberdeen on 12-13 September. Garrisons withdrawn from Auchindoun, Gight, Kellie and Drum Castles. 13th Battle of Aberdeen, Montrose with 1,500 men defeats Burleigh's 2,700 who lose 800 killed. Montrose's army occupies and sacks Aberdeen. They leave the burgh on the 16th.

11-13 September Argyll musters his army at Perth. 14th it leaves for Aberdeen. 16th Argyll at Brechin, meeting with northeastern Covenanters. 18th at Aberdeen, joined there by a few local Covenanters. 23rd Argyll's army burns Strathbogie. 27th 4,000 Covenanters burning Bog of Gight and Strathbogie. Argyll marches to Forres where he meets with the northern Covenanters. Then he moves to Inverness and from there to Badenoch, reaching Ruthven on 5 October. The army burns Badenoch and then Atholl. 23rd Argyll at Dunottar Castle. 24th Aberdeen reoccupied. 25th march to Kintore and Inverurie, remaining at latter for two days. 28th-29th skirmishes at Fyvie Castle. 30th Argyll withdraws. 6 November Argyll in Strathbogie. 14th 1,000 Campbells leave and plunder their way to Argyll via Strathspey, Badenoch and Lochaber. Argyll returns to Aberdeen, then to Edinburgh where he lays down his commission.

6 October the sieges of Mingary and Kinlochaline Castles lifted. Alasdair later slights the latter.

7 October-9 November two horse regiments of Leven's army remain in Cumbria.

27 October North Shields and Tynemouth Castle surrender.

Late November Baillie appointed commander-in-chief in Scotland.

December Leslie brings one regiment foot, three of horse and one of dragoons to Cumbria and commences siege of Carlisle. It surrenders on 25 June 1645 and is garrisoned on the 28th.

Early December Montrose and Alasdair enter Glenorchy then press on to Argyll. They capture Inveraray on the 13th and spend several weeks burning and plundering. 900 Campbell fencible men die in the campaign.

Late December Baillie marches from Perth to Dumbarton via Stirling.

1645

Early January Baillie reaches Roseneath where he meets Argyll and 'loans' him 1,000 foot. 8 January Baillie returns to Perth.

January the northern Covenanters muster at Inverness under Seaforth to oppose Montrose's march up the Great Glen.

22 January Argyll musters his army of Highlanders and Lowland foot at Stalker Castle, then proceeds through Argyll, Badenoch, Appin and Lochaber, reaching Inverlochy on the 31st. 2 February battle of Inverlochy, 3,000 Covenanters under Lieutenant Colonel Sir Duncan Campbell of Auchinbreck defeated by 2,000 men under Montrose and Alasdair. The Covenanters lose 1,500 killed. Montrose marches towards Inverness and Seaforth disbands his army. Montrose proceeds to Aberdeen via Elgin, where Gordon and his brother Lewis defect from the Covenanters.

7 March the Covenanter garrison flees from Aberdeen. 9th Montrose's men occupy it.

9-10 March Leven's army at Tadcaster, Wetherby and Ferrybridge. Leslie with 2,000 commanded foot and three regiments horse marches to Cheshire to rendezvous with Sir William Brereton. 18th Leslie reaches Stretford. 20th moves to Knutsford. 21st Leslie to Sandbach. 26th reaches Whitchurch. 29th returns to Sandbach and on 1 April Knutsford, then retires to Leven's army.

15 March Urry's surprise attack on Aberdeen, which he captures but abandons early a.m. on the 16th. 18th Montrose evacuates Aberdeen.

Late March Baillie with his army near Brechin. After the 22nd Baillie confronts Montrose along the Isla, shadowing him between Alyth and Coupar Angus. He moves south, blocking Montrose from descending from Dunkeld. Baillie moves to Perth.

4 April 1,400 infantry reach Scotland from the Ulster Army under Colonel Robert Home.

4 April Montrose storms Dundee and his men pillage the burgh. Baillie sets out from Perth with his foot, sending Urry in advance with two cavalry regiments. Baillie enters Dundee at 6 p.m. as Montrose is pulling his men out. 5th Urry with his cavalry catches Montrose's men at Careston Ford on the South Esk and chases them to Edzell.

11 April Urry occupies Aberdeen and Torry with two infantry regiments and one of cavalry. 15th Lothian's Foot mutinies as the army heads north, which

causes the other regiments to return to Aberdeen. 19th Urry marches to Kintore and Inverurie. 20th-1 May Urry's army ravages Strathbogie and Enzie. 2nd the army at Buckie. 3rd Urry moves west across the Spey and to Elgin where he receives local reinforcements and continues on to Forres. 7th x 8th Urry reaches Inverness. 8th p.m. Urry's army moves east via Cawdor, reaching the outskirts of Auldearn on the morning of the 9th. Battle of Auldearn, 4,000 Covenanters against Montrose's army of 1,700 men. The Covenanters lose 2,000 killed; Urry flees to Inverness, then rides to Wood of Cocklarachy near Huntly via Tomnahurich and joins Baillie there.

Mid-April Baillie with an army in Cromar.

25 April Craigievar garrisons Kemnay and Pitcaple Houses; he also plunders the lands of Harth and Kincraigie.

May Leven takes the field with his army, marching from Newcastle to Ripon to Doncaster, where he remains three days, then moves north to Bramham Moor, remaining there from mid-May and leaves by the 31st for Ripon, Stainmore and Appleby. Then he heads south back to Ripon.

3 May Baillie's army burns Atholl. Then it marches to Kirriemuir and Fettercairn. 10th at Birse. 11th at Cromar. From there it proceeds to Wood of Cocklarachy (see Urry's campaign above). Urry demits his commission. 21st Covenanters in battle formation awaiting attack by Montrose. 22nd they leave Strathbogie for Mortlach and Balvenie Castle, then march up Glen Rinnes and Glen Livet to Ruthven of Badenoch. Army withdraws north to Inverness, then moves east crossing the Spey. 3 June Newton in Garioch. 4th marches to Aberdeen.

23 May Forbeses, Frasers and Crichtons defeated at the battle of the Head of Strathdon by a force of Highlanders.

June Baillie moves up Deeside and is joined by the earl of Crawford-Lindsay who has advanced from Newtyle. Baillie gives the earl veterans in exchange for recruits.

June Crawford-Lindsay marches from Deeside into Atholl, which he ravages.

June Baillie marches to the site of Keith and entrenches; his army skirmishes with Montrose's. Baillie marches south along the Suie Road by the Coreen Hills. 2 July Battle of Alford, 2,000 Covenanters against 1,500 men under Montrose. The Covenanters lose 700 killed.

7 June Leven's army at Wakefield, 18th at Mansfield. Then marches through Nottingham and south Derbyshire, reaching Staffordshire and Warwickshire on 2 July. 3rd main army at Birmingham with a screening party at Lichfield. 8th

army at Alcester. 11th at Bromsgrove. 17th at Droitwich where it divides with the artillery moving to Pershore then crossing the Severn at Upton before reaching Ledbury. The main army marches to Bewdley then reaches Tenbury on the 19th. 20th to Bishop's Frome. 22nd a detachment storms Canon Frome (garrisoned with 120 foot and 20 horse). 23rd army in Bromyard-Frome-hope area. 24th headquarters at Ledbury, foot rendezvous at Newent and wounded and sick in Gloucester.

11 June Munro with some troops at Dundrum.

Early July Munro at Dundrum again.

July Munro leads an expedition to Enniskillen and back to Carrickfergus via Clannaboy, Armagh, Sliabh naMaol and Clogher.

July-August Baillie with the survivors of Alford withdraws to Stirling, where he gains reinforcements. Then he moves north to Perth and Methven Woods, where the Covenanters massacre some royalist camp-followers. Baillie entrenches at Kilgraston near Bridge of Earn. Then he withdraws to Lindores but advances to Alloa and Stirling. Meanwhile the southwestern Covenanters are being levied. 14 August Fife levies join Baillie at Stirling. The army marches across Bridge of Denny and encamps at Hollandbush Farm. 15th Baillie advances. After a council of war he determines to fight at Kilsyth. Battle of Kilsyth. 7,000 Covenanters face 5,000 royalists under Montrose. The Covenanters lose 3,000 killed.

30 July siege of Hereford begins. 12 August Leslie leaves siege with the cavalry. 27th Leven lifts siege. 28th army crosses Severn at Gloucester and moves north via Cheltenham and Warwick.

Late August Munro leads a force from Carrickfergus to county Armagh. 24th the army reaches Blackwatertown. It then proceeds to Granard via Glaslough and Monaghan before returning to Carrickfergus.

17 August Montrose takes Glasgow, then encamps at Bothwell. Leith falls to the royalists and Montrose secures the release of prisoners in Edinburgh Castle. Alasdair scatters the Covenanter levies in the southwest lowlands. September Alasdair leaves the Bothwell camp, giving Montrose only 500 men. The Gordons withdraw to the northeast. Montrose advances to the borders and camps at Philiphaugh. Meanwhile on 12 August Leslie with 4,500-5,000 horse leaves the Hereford siege. 14th reaches Stourbridge. 15th Uttoxeter. 16th Ollerton rendezvous with Sir John Gell's 1,600 horse. 21st Doncaster Moor rendezvous with Poyntz's, Rossiter's and Thornhaugh's Horse. Leslie moves to Rotherham. 29th Northallerton. Reaches Berwick on 6 September via Newcastle. Advances to Dunbar then Home Castle, Haddington, down the Gala

Water to Sunderland, arriving at Selkirk on the 13th a.m. Battle of Philiphaugh, 5,000 Covenanters defeat 2,000 men under Montrose, who flees to the northeast.

September Leven's army quartered in North and West Ridings of Yorkshire.

September Leslie advances to St. Andrews. October he moves to Glasgow, then into the Carse of Gowrie and reaches Forfar before heading south.

October Major General John Middleton with a force of cavalry ravages the earl of Mar's estates at Alloa after being at St. Andrews. Then he advances to Banff via Aberdeen. On his approach the Gordons lift the siege of Spynie Palace. Middleton returns south via Aberdeen, leaving it an open city.

October Covenanters garrison Carrick Castle and House of Rothesay.

2 October Leven's army headquarters at Stokesley with foot and horse in Clevelandshire.

20 x 21 October Lord Digby and Sir Marmaduke Langdale with 1,500 men of the Northern Horse enter Scotland. Battle of Annan Moor, Brown defeats the royalists, who take Dumfries only to abandon it. 24th Digby sails to Man from Ravenglas.

November Covenanters garrison Rossdhu, Douglas, Drummond and Glasgow Castles.

November Leven's army at Northallerton.

November-December Montrose marches on Inverness via the glens. Gordons attack Covenanter castles in Banffshire and Moray.

15 November Leven at Bramham Moor then marches to Newark via Texford. Siege of Newark and Scots man north side of siege works. Headquarters and camp at Southwell. 29th Battle of Muskham Bridge outside Newark.

December most of the cavalry Leslie had brought to Scotland return to England.

1646

January-February Ardkinglas with 1,200 men raids Menteith. He captures Isle of Loch Dochart Castle but fails to take Edinample Castle. 13 February Battle of Callander; Ardkinglas's men routed by 700 Atholl Highlanders. The

Covenanters flee to Stirling. Are then sent to Renfrewshire before quartering in the Lennox.

3 January a force of Scottish cavalry reoccupies Aberdeen.

17 January Army of the Solemn League and Covenant (nine regiments of foot, ten of horse, two companies of dragoons and thirteen troops of horse) mustered on Muskham Moor near Newark. 5 May Charles I joins the army. 6th Newark surrenders to Scots and parliamentarians.

12 February Alasdair raids Bute.

Winter-April Montrose and Gordons besiege Inverness.

Mid-April Middleton advances from Aberdeen to Banff via Turriff. Late April he relieves Inverness and pursues Montrose to Caiplich then to Farley Forest. Several Mackenzie castles surrender to Middleton. Middleton returns to the northeast and captures Fyvie Castle on the 29th.

April-May Argyll's 'Irish' foot invade Islay under Skipness from Antrim, but the Captain of Clanranald repulses them.

7 May Leven's army moves four miles north of Newark. 15th Charles I reaches Newcastle. Leven's Foot quarter in Northumberland and Durham, while the horse reside in north Yorkshire.

14 May Huntly storms Aberdeen, but quickly evacuates it.

May Middleton's army reoccupies Aberdeen, then Middleton heads south.

Late May-June Ardkinglas invades Cowal from Ayrshire. He besieges Ascog and Toward Castles which surrender on 3 June. The Campbells destroy them and then massacre over 130 prisoners at Dunoon. Ardkinglas advances to the head of Loch Fyne and possibly relieves Skipness Castle, which Alasdair is besieging.

2 June Munro with 3,400 Scottish infantry in six regiments, 2,000 British infantry and eleven troops of Scots-British cavalry (700-800 horse) takes the field, and marches to Dromore. 4th advances to Hamilton's Bawn. 5 June 4 a.m. Munro's army reaches Armagh and marches to the pass of Kinnaird, south up the Blackwater to Caledon Ford, then north down the Blackwater, arriving at Benburb at 6 p.m. Early that day near Dungannon an Irish force defeats Colonel George Munro's force of 240 musketeers and three troops of horse. Battle of Benburb. 5,000 Irish foot and 500 horse against 5,400 Scottish-British foot

and 700-800 horse. Scottish survivors flee first to Caledon then Armagh, suffer the worst of the casualties, which are 2,000-3,000 killed. Irish advance to Tanderagee, but then withdraw to Westmeath and Longford for a march on Kilkenny.

3 June Huntly disbands.

June Middleton leaves Dundee for northeast with permission to pardon all royalists save Montrose, Alasdair, the earl of Crawford and Urry who go into exile.

Spring-summer Alasdair besieges Kilberry and Craignish Castles, but lifts both sieges. Battle of Lagganmore, Campbells defeated by Irish and Highlanders under Alasdair.

22 July Middleton and Montrose meet on Water of Isla to discuss cessation for two hours. 30th Montrose disbands at Rattray. 3 September Montrose sails to Norway.

By August Alasdair's siege of Skipness Castle lifted.

August Blair Atholl falls to Covenanters.

By September Inveraray area solidly under Covenanter control.

After 3 September Huntly raises a new army and Middleton in the field against the Gordons.

December Huntly occupies Banff and remains there during the winter.

1647

1 January Middleton in the field with three regiments opposing the Gordons.

25 January Scots horse leave Yorkshire; Stockton and Hartlepool abandoned. 30th 2-3 p.m. Leven's army receives £100,000 st. and leaves Newcastle, South and North Shields and Tynemouth Castle. Parliamentarians gain king. 3 February second £100,000 paid to the army. 11th Leven's army crosses Tweed at Kelso. Horse disbanded. 12 noon Berwick and Carlisle garrisons leave England.

5 February the Estates orders reduction of regiments in Scotland. 6th arrears for regiments in Scotland set. 9th regiments in Scotland disband.

2 March Middleton commences siege of Kincardine Castle held by fifty royalists. 16th castle razed.

5 March New Model Horse troops reduced from eighty to seventy-five men.

10 March Leslie moves north from Montrose with New Model Army regiments. He joins forces with Middleton. They besiege and capture Wardhouse Castle. 27th Lesmoir Castle falls to Leslie. Covenanters capture Strathbogie, Bog of Gight, Auchindoun and Lochkendar Castles. Leslie leaves for Dunblane. April he establishes a garrison in Ruthven of Badenoch.

Mid-April Leslie in Dunblane and Middleton in the northeast.

17 May Leslie leaves Dunblane for Argyll. 21st at Inveraray. 22nd army rests. 23rd Leslie begins march south to Kintyre. 24th skirmish of Rhunahaorine Point, Kintyre. Leslie's Horse versus 1,300 Irish foot. Covenanters lose nine wounded and kill sixty-eight Irish, capture three captains and clear the route to advance. 25th Campbell of Inverawe ordered to invade Gigha which he does on 19 June with 220 foot and 80 horse. 26 May Leslie marches to House of Lochkillkerran and takes the abandoned Lochhead Fort. 31st siege of Dunaverty Castle begins. Covenanters capture water supply. Castle surrenders and 300 defenders massacred. Leslie returns to Lochhead, then to Loch Tarbert. 23 June midday Leslie lands on Gigha. 24th lands on Islay four miles from Dunyveg Castle. Castle besieged. 1 July Coll MacDonald, governor of castle, seized during truce. 4th castle surrenders. 5th garrison departs. Simultaneously Loch Gorm Castle besieged and it falls after 7 September. Leslie moves to Jura and is joined by Middleton with two regiments of foot and some horse troops. Leslie lands on Mull, where Sir Lachlan Maclean of Duart submits. His force sails to Moidart and takes Captain of Clanranald's Castle Tirrim. August Leslie returns to Stirling with his army.

October Inverness garrison sends a force to Strathnaver and Lord Reay submits.

15 October decision made to keep army on foot until March 1648.

November Middleton captures Huntly.

26 December the Engagement signed on the Isle of Wight.

1648

2 March the Estates convene and subsequently accept Engagement.

April Tailor's Hall, Edinburgh petition by army officers.

4 April the Ulster Army Council of War accepts the Engagement. 7th Council of War writes the Estates in favour of the Engagement.

5 April expedition against Clanranald ordered involving Argyll's and Ardkinglas's Highland foot.

18 April Engager committees of war appointed.

28 April English royalists seize Berwick. 29th English royalists capture Carlisle.

4 May new levy ordered for Engager Army.

8 June Scottish garrisons ordered reduced or abandoned.

12 June Battle of Mauchline Moor.

27 June Glencairn's Foot ejected from the Ulster Army.

Early July the duke of Hamilton rendezvouses with Turner's infantry at Annan.

8 July Hamilton with 6,000 foot and 3,000 horse crosses into Cumberland. 8th-14th army quarters at Carlisle and Sir Marmaduke Langdale joins with 2,500 English foot and 1,500 English horse. 14th Penrith skirmish against Lambert. 17th Appleby skirmish against Lambert, while English royalists besiege Appleby Castle. 17th-31st army at Kirkby Thore and reinforced by 4,000 foot and 1,000 horse. (Late July Major General George Munro reaches Scotland with 1,900 foot and horse from Ulster.) 26th Stainmore skirmish against Lambert. 2-9 August army at Kendal. 9th-14th army at Hornby. 14th army marches to Preston. 17th Battle of Preston, English Engagers under Langdale versus English Parliamentarians under Cromwell. Scottish foot form up at Walton Hall south of the Ribble p.m. Council of War is followed by march of Scottish foot south via Standish. Meanwhile Middleton's Horse are advancing north from Wigan on the Chorley Road. Middleton's cavalry turn south in tracks of infantry upon encountering English and skirmishes as they move south. 18th morning, horse stand at Standish, joining the foot there. Retreat continues to Wigan. Evening, foot leave Wigan. Scots horse skirmish with Cromwell's cavalry. Scottish cavalry reach Wigan and continue south. 19th Scottish army forms up at Winwick and fights until in danger of being outflanked. Scottish foot routed after losing 1,000 killed and 2,000 captured. Survivors retreat to Warrington. Evening, Scottish foot hold Warrington Bridge, but Callander and Middleton lead the cavalry away. Baillie surrenders 2,600 foot to Cromwell. Hamilton flees with horse to Cheshire then to Malpas, Salops, where Traquair and others surrender to the English. Hamilton proceeds to Market Drayton and Stone, where Middleton is captured. Hamilton reaches Uttoxeter where the soldiers mutiny and temporarily hold him prisoner. The English

capture Hamilton, but Callander escapes. 25th Hamilton becomes Lambert's prisoner.

19 August Munro commences return to Scotland from Kendal. He marches with 3,000-4,000 men to Berwick.

Late August the Whiggamores take the field in the southwest lowlands.

Early September Munro rendezvouses with 2,000 men under the earl of Lanark at Haddington. They proceed to Corstorphine via Musselburgh and Colinton.

5 September the earl of Eglinton takes Edinburgh Castle for the Whiggamores.

11 September skirmish at Linlithgow between Engager and earl of Cassillis' Horse.

8 September Argyll with 700-1,000 men at Dumbarton. 11th at Gargunnock. 12th Argyll in Stirling, but Engagers surprise his forces and retake town.

12 September Whiggamores advance to Falkirk, where they receive reinforcements from Fife and earl of Buccleuch.

13 September negotiations arranged but Whiggamores fail to appear. 14th Whiggamores appear and negotiations commence. 19th first truce to end at 6 p.m. 20th second truce to end at noon on the 22nd if treaty unacceptable. 26th x 27th Treaty of Stirling and Edinburgh. Stirling forces and garrisons of Berwick and Carlisle to disband by 1 October and Engagers north of the Tay to disband by 10 October. Leven and Leslie to disband on the 1st save 1,000 foot and 500 horse, which will disband on the 10th. Munro's force allowed to return to Ulster, but disbands on march to embarkation points.

16 September surprising of Carrickfergus by Colonel George Monck with aid from officers of Glencairn's. Belfast and Coleraine also taken. Ulster Army ceases to exist.

14 October levy of 2,930 foot and horse ordered.

22 November Western Association established.

1649

January Second Act of Classes enacted.

February Charles II proclaimed king of Great Britain, France and Ireland.

February Lord Reay, a royalist, in arms against the Covenanting earl of Sutherland.

9 February act for placing the kingdom in a posture of defence.

22 February Pluscardine, Redcastle, Cromarty and Lemlair with 700 men take the Covenanter town of Inverness and retreat after slighting the works. 28th act of levy for 18,840 foot and horse. February-March Leslie moves north and garrisons Chanonry Castle; he pursues the royalists into Ross; negotiations follow in which all royalists, save Pluscardine, submit on 21 March. Meanwhile on 1 March the Stirling Castle garrison and Innes' Foot at Cupar mutiny. Leslie returns south. Pluscardine retakes Chanonry Castle. 31 March Atholl gentry who had previously risen for the king submit. Their leaders flee north to Pluscardine.

March fortification of Leith and Burntisland begins.

Mid-April-early May Pluscardine, Reay, Ogilvy and Middleton march to Badenoch where Huntly joins them. They take Ruthven then march north to Balvenie Castle. Leslie moves north from Atholl. Pluscardine and Middleton negotiate personally with Leslie. But on 9 May Ker with three troops horse and some musketeers reaches Balvenie from Ross. Battle of Balvenie. Royalist army destroyed and Huntly, Ogilvy, Pluscardine and Middleton submit. Pluscardine and Reay are sent to Edinburgh Castle.

Mid-May-June Ker moves north and takes Redcastle. Leslie garrisons Brahan Castle and captures Chanonry again. Parties are sent out to Cromarty and Eilean Donan Castle, the latter is garrisoned. Ker destroys Redcastle.

27 March-19 May negotiations in Netherlands with Charles II.

21 June purging act for army. 6 August levy act for 10,000 foot and horse.

5 September earl of Kinnoull with 180 men lands at Kirkwall; he shares command of the royalist army with the earl of Morton. After 27 September Leslie moves north but is unable to invade Orkney. November Kinnoull and Morton die. Late November Leslie disbands his army and leaves garrisons in the north.

1650

Mid-March marquis of Montrose reaches Orkney with 1,200 continental mercenaries. Lord Eythin joins him with more. 19 March-1 May negotiations with Charles II and Treaty of Breda. Early April Major General John Urry lands in Caithness from Orkney and is quickly joined by Montrose with more men. Montrose moves south to Carbisdale. 16 April Leslie ordered north with an army against Montrose. Strachan sent north to command troops already there. At Inverness he musters five horse troops and advances to Ross. 25th Leslie's army rendezvouses at Brechin. 27th Strachan holds council of war at Tain and decision to advance is made, resulting in the Battle of Carbisdale. Casualties: one Covenanter drowned, 400-500 royalists killed, 200 drowned and 450 captured. Late April on news of Carbisdale royalists in Caithness flee to Orkney and then to continent. Early May Neil Macleod of Assynt captures Montrose, who is sent to Edinburgh for trial and execution.

May Noltland Castle, Westray, last royalist stronghold, captured.

21 June purging committee for army established. 25th act of levy.

24 June Charles II lands at Garmouth.

Late July Leslie with about 15,000 foot and horse behind Leith-Edinburgh Castle line; Berwickshire and East Lothian stripped of food and fodder. 22 July Cromwell crosses Tweed at Berwick with 16,000 foot and horse. After the 22nd Warriston, Ker, Strachan and others hold secret talks with Cromwell. 29th Charles received in the army. 30th-31st skirmish of Musselburgh. 2-5 August 80 officers purged and more go by the 31st. 11th-27th Cromwell outside Edinburgh. 13th West Kirk Declaration of radical officers. 18th English capture Colinton House. 24th English capture Redhall. Skirmishing at Gogar. By 2 September Cromwell retreats to Dunbar. Leslie takes up positions at Doon Hill and Cockburnspath. 2nd Leslie descends Doon Hill. 3rd 4 a.m. English attack an unprepared Scottish army, Battle of Dunbar. Leslie loses 4,000 dead and 10,000 captured and only 4,000, mainly horse, escape to Edinburgh.

After 3 September Coldingham, Dunglass, Fast and Hailes Castles abandoned.

5 September new levies ordered; Ker, Strachan and R. Hackett sent to Western Association with four units to raise an army.

17 September Cromwell within a mile of Stirling, but falls back to Edinburgh.

4 October The Start. 5th Leslie's officers find Charles at Clova; earl of Atholl disbands.

Mid-October Cromwell temporarily occupies Glasgow.

October Sir John Brown sent to Angus. 21st Battle of Newtyle, Sir David Ogilvy's royalists attack Brown's force. Some Covenanters desert to the royalists. Leslie ordered north. 24th Leslie passes through Perth with 3,000 horse. Northern Band signed by Huntly, Atholl, Seaforth, Pluscardine, Middleton, George Munro and Van Druschke. 4 November Treaty of Strathbogie, royalists submit and disband.

17 October Western Remonstrance promulgated in Army of Western Association.

November guerrilla activity starts south of the Forth. 8th Dirleton Castle surrenders after a siege. 10th-15th Roslin Castle surrenders. 18th Borthwick Castle surrenders.

Late November Cromwell with Lambert and cavalry regiments move to the west. Major General Montgomery with a cavalry force proceeds to Campsie from Stirling. 1 December 4 a.m. Ker attacks Lambert, Battle of Hamilton, Western Association Army routed. Cromwell moves to Glasgow then back to Edinburgh, leaving Hamilton garrisoned. 2nd Strachan gathers up remnant of Western Army and tells men to disband or join English. He deserts to Cromwell with 30 men.

December English capture Kenmure Castle.

Early December Captain Hoffman reinforces Edinburgh Castle. 24th Dundas the younger surrenders Edinburgh Castle after a three-month siege.

14 December Commission of General Assembly passes Public Resolutions. 20th new list of colonels produced by Estates.

1651

Early in year Neidpath Castle falls to English.

1 January Charles II crowned at Scone.

January Monck tries landing at Burntisland, but fails.

February Scots abandon Callander House.

Early February Cromwell advances west to the upper Forth, but retires to Edinburgh. Late February-June Cromwell ill in Edinburgh.

2 February Home Castle surrenders. 21st Tantallon Castle surrenders. March Blackness Castle captured by English. English garrison Callander House.

14 April Scottish raid on English-held Linlithgow.

April Montgomery with a cavalry force moves into the southwest lowlands. English abandon Hamilton. English raid Dumbarton and capture earl of Eglinton.

May Middleton brings in forces of north and northeast to Stirling camp.

19 May Paisley Skirmish, Scots victory. Late May Scottish victories in skirmishes at Carnwath and Linlithgow.

June Scots reoccupy Callander House.

4 June Acts of Classes repealed.

22 June ten cavalry regiments depart from Fife to Stirling.

28 June Scots army at Torwood. Early July Cromwell moves towards Stirling; Scots withdraw from Falkirk.

Early July Cromwell advances to Glasgow; English horse probe fords of Forth. Cromwell retreats to Edinburgh.

15 July English capture Callander House.

17 July Lambert crosses Forth with 4,000-5,000 men and captures North Queensferry fortalice on the Inverkeithing peninsula. 20th Battle of Inverkeithing. Lambert's forces versus 4,000 Scots under Holburn, Brown and Maclean. Scots lose 2,000 killed.

21 July royal army marches from Torwood to Stirling into Fife. Cromwell moves from Edinburgh to Bannockburn; Scots retreat to Stirling.

Late July Cromwell in Fife with 14,000 men, only eight English regiments south of the Forth. 29th Burntisland surrenders. 1 August Cromwell outside Perth. 2nd Perth falls to the English.

31 July Charles with the Committee of Estates and a 13,000-man army leaves Stirling for Cumbernauld; earl of Crawford-Lindsay appointed commander-in-chief, Scotland. August army marches to Worcester via Cumbria, Lancaster, Warrington, Nantwich, Whitchurch, Newport, Wolverhampton and Kidderminster. 22nd Worcester reached.

6 August Stirling burgh surrenders. 14th-15th Stirling Castle garrison mutinies and surrenders. Monck, English commander-in-chief, Scotland, marches to Dundee. 26th Dundee summoned. 28th p.m. Alyth raid, 800 English horse capture Crawford-Lindsay, Leven, Marischal and Ogilvy and disperse their

forces. 30th St. Andrews surrenders. 1 September 11 a.m. English storm Dundee. They kill 800 Scots and pillage burgh.

Late August Dumfries garrisoned by English and southwest lowlands cleared of Scottish troops.

31 August Huntly and Balcarres join forces.

3 September Battle of Worcester, 31,000 English under Cromwell against 13,000 Scots under Charles. Scots lose 2,000 killed and 10,000 captured. Leslie leads cavalry north, but he and his force are captured outside Manchester.

By 6 September English capture Montrose.

7 September English occupy Aberdeen.

Mid-November-December Highland clans in field against English.

21 November Huntly surrenders. 3 December Balcarres surrenders. December Elgin then Inverness surrender and receive English garrisons. By 31 December English occupy Ross, Sutherland and Caithness.

29 December Dumbarton Castle surrenders following a siege.

1652

5 January English garrison Dumbarton Castle.

January moss-troopers Captains Gordon and Hoffman disband.

28 January English invade and occupy Orkneys.

April Bass Rock surrenders. 6th Brodick Castle surrenders. 24 May Dunottar Castle surrenders after a siege.

Late June Monck's Highland campaign begins. August-October Argyll submits to English.

Bibliography

Manuscript Sources

Bodleian Library, Oxford.
Carte MSS. 3, 5-17, 19-20, 28-9, 32, 77, 80.
Rawlinson MS. A/258, Irish letters, September 1645-September 1648.
Tanner MSS. 54-5, 58/1-59/2, 60/2, 61, 65.

British Library, London.
Harleian MSS. 1460, Fisher, F., 'A perfect Registry of all the Colours taken from the
    Scots at Preston . . . and Dunbar'.

Cambridge University Library.
MS. Ee.111.39 (D), Pay of the Scottish Army in Ireland, 1642.

National Library of Scotland, Edinburgh.
Acc. 6026.
Adv. MSS. 23.7.12, Walker, E., 'A Short Journall of Severall actions performed in the
    Kingdom of Scotland'.
Adv. MS. 29.2.9, 104-216, Balcarres Papers.
Adv. MS. 33.4.8, Transactions of the Scotts army in Ireland from 1643 to June 1648.
Dep. 175, Gordon-Cumming Papers.
MSS. 2961, Culloden Papers.
Wodrow Analecta Folio 27, Church and State Papers, 1639.
Wodrow Analecta Folio 31, Presbytery of the Army, 1640.
Wodrow Analecta Folio 63, Church and State Papers, 1638-9.
Wodrow Analecta Folio 67, Letters, many of them originals, 1641-53.
Wodrow Letters Quarto 10 no. 68, Extracts from Mr. Robert Traill's Diary.

New Register House, Edinburgh.
Old Parish Registers: Alyth, Anstruther Easter, Channelkirk, Dalgety, Echt,
    Rothiemay.

Public Record Office, London.
SP 16/461/57III.
SP 16/464/59II, List of regiments, officers and numbers 1640 army.
SP 16/492/58, 2nd muster roll Argyll's regiment in Ulster.
SP 16/513/52, Meeting to hear complaints against Scots by inhabitants of Tickhill,
    Yorkshire.
SP 16/513/4, Trials at Tickhill.
SP 16/539/105, Leven's Life Guard, Ulster.
SP 16/539/217, Adair's horse troop.
SP 17/H/7, Mr. Auditor Collin's book on Ulster.
SP 18/16/40, Relation of the Defeat of the King's army, 17 September 1651.

SP 28/120, Muster Rolls of the Scottish Army in Ireland by Hew Kennedy, April-November 1642 and by Thomas Clayton, September, November 1642.

SP 41/2, Muster Roll of the Scots Army in England, January 1646.

SP 46/106, Payment and supply of the Scots armies in England and Ireland.

Scottish Record Office, Edinburgh.

Synod Records: Fife.

Presbytery Records: Ayr, Biggar, Cupar, Dalkeith, Deer, Dumbarton, Dumfries, Dunblane, Dunfermline, Elgin, Fordoun, Haddington, Hamilton, Jedburgh, Lanark, Linlithgow, Paisley, Peebles, Perth, Stirling, Stranraer, Strathbogie, Turriff.

Kirk Session Records: Ayr, Bathgate, Burntisland, Cambusnethan, Canongate, Clackmannan, Culross, Cumnock, Dron, Duffus, Dundonald, Dunfermline, Edinkillie, Elgin, Falkirk, Falkland, Fintry, Gargunnock, Haddington, Hamilton, Kilconquhar, Kinghorn, Kinglassie, Kingsbarns, Kinnard, Livingston, Menmuir, Monimail, Newburn, North Leith, Oldhamstocks, Old Kelso, Pencaitland, Petty, St. Cuthbert's (Edinburgh), St. Monance, Scoonie, Slains, Holy Rude (Stirling), Tyninghame, Wemyss.

B.6.18.2, Ayr Council Minutes, 1647-59.

B.9.12.8, Burntisland Council Minutes, 1643-6.

B.30.21.74, Haddington Account for Quartering South Regiment/Colonel Cochrane's Foot, April-May 1640, 14 July 1642.

B.48.13.4, Linlithgow Treasurer's Accounts, 1638/9.

B.51.15, Montrose Miscellaneous Documents.

B.66.25, 367-70, 373, Stirling Miscellaneous Military Documents.

E.100/1/1, Muster Roll of Sir Thomas Hope's Troop, 1640-1.

E.100/1/2, Muster Roll of the General's Life Troop, 1640-1.

GD. 1/38, Lloyd's Bank Ltd. MSS.

GD. 2/53, Miscellaneous MSS.

GD. 6, Biel MSS.

GD. 10, Broughton and Cally MSS.

GD. 16, Airlie MSS.

GD. 25, Aisla MSS.

GD. 30, Shairp of Houston MSS.

GD. 38, Dalguise — Perthshire MSS.

GD. 45/5, Dalhousie MSS.

GD. 75, Dundas of Dundas MSS.

GD. 112/39, Breadalbane Letters.

GD. 124, Mar and Kellie MSS.

GD. 137, Scrymgeour, Wedderburn of Wedderburn MSS.

GD. 157, Hume of Marchmont, Scott of Harden MSS.

GD. 188, Guthrie of Guthrie MSS.

GD. 205, Ogilvy of Innerquharity MSS.

GD. 237, Messrs Tods, Murray and Jamieson MSS.

PA. 7.2, Supplementary Parliamentary Papers, 1609-42.

PA. 7.3, Supplementary Parliamentary Papers, 1643-5.

PA. 7.4, Supplementary Parliamentary Papers, 1646.

PA. 7.5, Supplementary Parliamentary Papers, 1647-8.

PA. 7.6, Supplementary Parliamentary Papers, 1649.

PA. 7.7, Supplementary Parliamentary Papers, 1650.

PA. 7.8, Supplementary Parliamentary Papers, 1651.

PA. 7.23/2, Supplementary Parliamentary Papers, 1643-9.

PA. 7.24, Minutes of the Committee of Estates, July 1650-May 1651 and Parliamentary Papers, 1641-51.

PA. 11.1/12, Register of the Committee of Estates with the Army, January-November 1644.

PA. 11.2, Committee with the Army, 1643-4.
PA. 11.4, Register and Minute Book of the Committee of Estates, 1645-6.
PA. 11.6, Committee of Estates Acts and Orders.
PA. 11.8, Register and Minute Book Committee of Estates, 1649.
PA. 11.11, Register of the Committee for Managing the Affairs of the Army, April-July 1651.
PA. 15.10, Weems account books, Treasurer of the army, 1648.
PA. 16.1, Hepburne of Keith-Marischal Papers.
PA. 16.2, Army Pay and Equipment Receipts, 1640-5.
PA. 16.3.1, Army Pay, 1640-c. 1651.
PA. 16.3.2, Army Accounts, 1642-50.
PA. 16.3.3, Army Miscellaneous, 1642-51.
PA. 16.3.8, Army Accounts for Quarterings, 1644.
PA. 16.3.12, Papers relating to the Army in Ireland.
PA. 16.4.1-69, Report on Losses, 1646-7.
PA. 16.5, Book of Receipts of Foot Regiments, 1651.
PA. 16.6.2-3, Receipts by ministers to regiments and Precepts and receipts Miscellaneous Military 1651.
RH. 13/18, Diary, April 1639-October 1640.
RH. 15/64/10, Losses of Easter Seggiden, 1644.

Trinity College Library, Dublin.
MS. 837, Depositions after the Rising, County Down.

University of St. Andrews Library.
Cupar Court and Council Records.
Hay of Leyes Papers.
Presbytery Record, St. Andrews.

West Register House, Edinburgh.
CS 181/6/2, Weapons receipts, 1644-6.
RH. 1.14, 18-21, 23-5, Maintenance, levies and relief from quartering, laird of Leyes, 1645-51.

Printed Primary Sources

Aberdeen Council Letters, vols. ii-iii, ed. Taylor, L. B., (London, 1950).
Acts of the General Assembly of the Church of Scotland, 1638-1842, ed. Pitcairn, T. (Edinburgh, 1843).
The Acts of the Parliament of Scotland, 12 vols., eds. Thomson, T. and Innes, C. (Edinburgh, 1814-75).
Adair, P., *A True Narrative of the Rise and Progress of the Presbyterian Church in Ireland*, ed. Killen, W. D. (Belfast, 1866).
All the Transactions between the Noblemen and gentlemen now in arms for the Covenant and the officers and soldiers now in arms by authority of the Parliament, of the Kingdom of Scotland (Edinburgh, 1648).
Analecta Scotica: Collections illustrative of the Civil, Ecclesiastical and Literary History of Scotland, 2 vols., ed. Maidment, J. (Edinburgh, 1834-8).
The Army of the Covenant, 2 vols., ed. Terry, C. S. (Scot. His. Soc., 2nd Ser., xvi-vii, 1917).
Ashe, S., *A Continuation of True Intelligence From the English and Scottish Forces in the North . . . from the 16th of June to . . . the 10th of July 1644* (London, 1644).

Ashe, S., *A Continuation of True Intelligence From the English and Scottish Forces in the North . . . 10 July to 27 July* (London, 1644).
Balfour, J., *Works*, 4 vols. (Edinburgh, 1823-5).
The Black Book of Taymouth, ed. Innes, C. (Bannatyne Club, c, 1855).
The Book of Caerlaverock: memoirs of the Maxwells, earls of Nithsdale, lords Maxwell & Herries, 2 vols., ed. Fraser, W. (Edinburgh, 1873).
The Book of the Thanes of Cawdor 1236-1742, ed. Innes, C. (Spalding Club, xxix, 1859).
Bowles, E., *Manifest Truths or An Inversion of Truths Manifest* (London, 1646).
Boyd, Z., *The Battle of Newburne* (Glasgow, 1643).
Burnet, G., *Memoirs of the Lives and Actions of James and William, dukes of Hamilton and Castle-Herald* (2nd edn., Oxford, 1852).
Burns, J., *Memoirs of the Civil War, and During the Usurpation*, ed. Maidment, J. (Edinburgh, 1832).
Calendar of the Proceedings of the Committee for Compunding & c. 1643-1660, 5 vols., ed. Green, M. (London, 1889-92).
Calendar of State Papers, Domestic, 1639-49, 8 vols., ed. Hamilton, W. D. (London, 1873-93).
Calendar of State Papers, Domestic, 1649-1651, 3 vols., ed. Green, M. (London, 1875-7).
Calendar of State Papers, Ireland, 1633-1647, ed. Mahaffy, R. P. (London, 1901).
Charters and Extracts from the Burgh Records of Peebles, i, ed. Chambers, W. (Scot. Burgh Rec. Soc., x, 1872).
The Chronicle of Perth, ed. Maidment, J. (Maitland Club, xii, 1831).
Chronicles of the Atholl and Tullibardine Families, 5 vols., ed. Murray, J. (Edinburgh, 1908).
Clark, R., *A Letter Concerning General Monks surprising the Town and Castle of Carrickfergus and Belfast, in Ireland, and his taking General Major Monro prisoner* (London, 1648), s.s.
Collection of Original Letters and Papers concerning the Affairs of England, 1641-51, ed. Carte, T. (London, 1739).
Committee of Parliament, *Act Anent the out comming of Horses* (Edinburgh, 1640), s.s.
A Continuation of Papers from the Scots Quarters (London, 1646).
A Continuation of the Proceedings of the Scots Army before Hereford, 11 August (London, 1645).
Correspondence of Scots Commissioners in London, 1644-1646, ed. Meikle, H. W. (Roxburghe Club, clx, 1917).
Correspondence of Sir Robert Kerr, First Earl of Ancram and his son William, Third Earl of Lothian, 2 vols., ed. Laing, D. (Bannatyne Club, xcvi, 1875).
Deane, M., *A true relation of the proceedings of the Scotch army since their advance from Nottingham* (London, 1645).
The Declaration and Propositions of his Excellency the Lord Generall Leven and divers other Commanders of the standing Army . . . in Scotland (London, 1648).
A Declaration concerning Sir Edward Deering; with a true relation of the Scots proceedings about the surrendering of Newcastle (London, 1644).
A Declaration of His Excellency the Earle of Leven: Concerning the rising of the Scotish Army from the Seige of the City of Hereford (London, 1645).
A Declaration of the Proceedings of the New Model'd Army in the Kingdome of Scotland, against the Irish Army (London, 1647).
The Demands and Behavior of the rebels of Scotland (London, 1640).
Despatch on Philiphaugh (London, 1645), s.s.
The Diary of Mr. John Lamont of Newton, 1649-1671 (Maitland Club, xii, 1830).
'The Diary of Mr. Robt. Douglas when with the Scottish army in England, 1644', in *Memoirs of James Burns*, ed. Maidment, J. (Edinburgh, 1832).
The Diplomatic Correspondence of Jean de Montereul and the Brothers de Bellièvre, French Ambassadors in England and Scotland 1645-48, 2 vols., ed. Fotheringham, J. G. (Scot. His. Soc., 1st Ser., xxix-xxx, 1898).

Drummond, W., *The Genealogy of the Most Noble and Ancient House of Drummond* (Edinburgh, 1831).

Dumbarton Burgh Records, 1627-1746, ed. Young, J. (Dumbarton, 1860).

Extract of Letter Dated at Edenburgh, the 14, 16 and 17. of April. 1644 (London, 1644).

Extracts from the Burgh Records of Dunfermline in the Sixteenth and Seventeenth Centuries, ed. Shearer, A. (Dunfermline, 1951).

Extracts from the Council Register of the Burgh of Aberdeen, 1625-1747, 2 vols., ed. Stuart, J. (Scot. Burgh Rec. Soc., viii-ix, 1881-2).

Extracts from the Presbytery Book of Strathbogie, 1631-54, ed. Stuart, J. (Spalding Club, vii, 1843).

Extracts from the Records of the Burgh of Edinburgh, 1642-55, ed. Wood, M. (Edinburgh, 1938).

Extracts from the Records of the Burgh of Glasgow, ii, 1630-1662, ed. Marwick, L. (Scot. Burgh Rec. Soc., xii, 1885).

Extracts from the Records of the Burgh of Stirling, i, 1519-1666, ed. Renwick, R. (Glasgow, 1887).

Extracts from the Records of the Royal Burgh of Lanark with Charters and Documents Relating to the Burgh, A.D. 1150-1722, ed. Renwick, R. (Glasgow, 1893).

Forbes, D., *Ane Account of the Familie of Innes With An Appendix of Charters and Notes*, ed. Innes, C. (Spalding Club, xxxiv, 1864).

Fraser, J., *Chronicles of the Frasers 916-1674*, ed. Mackay, W. (Scot. His. Soc., 1st Ser., xlvii, 1905).

A full relation of the late expedition of the Right Honourable the lord Monroe, Major-General of all the Protestant Forces in the Province of Ulster (London, 1644).

A Full Relation of the Scots March from Barwicke to Newcastle (London, 1644).

A fuller Relation of the taking of Bath . . . Also the proceedings of the Scottish Army and their march towards Monmouth after the King (London, 1645).

General Assembly Commission Records, 1646-1652, 3 vols., eds. Mitchell, A. F. and Christie, J. (Scot. His. Soc., 1st Ser., xi, xxv, lviii, 1892-1909).

The Glorious and Miraculous Battle at York (Edinburgh, 1644).

Gordon, J., *History of Scottish Affairs from 1637-1641*, 3 vols., eds. Robertson, R. and Grub, G. (Spalding Club, i, iii, v, 1841).

Gordon, P., *A Short Abridgement of Britaine's Distemper from 1639-1649*, ed. Dunn, J. (Spalding Club, x, 1844).

A great Fight in Scotland between the Lord Gen. Cromwel's forces and the Scots upon the advance of Lieutenant Gen. Lesley, and Col. Massie from Sterling towards Glasgow (London, 1651).

A Great Victory God hath vouchsafed by the Lord General Cromwels forces against the Scots (London, 1651).

Gumble, T., *The Life of General Monck* (London, 1671).

Hardy, J., *The Fatal Blow given to the Earle of Newcastle Armie by the Scots* (London, 1644).

'The Hinde Papers', ed. Longstaffe, W. H. D., *Arch. Aeliana*, New Ser., ii (1858), 127-35.

His Majesties Passing Through the Scots Armie (n.p., 1641).

Historical Fragments, relative to Scottish affairs from 1635 to 1664, Maidment, J. (Edinburgh, 1833).

Historical MSS. Commission Reports, xxix, lxxii.

Historical Notices of St. Anthony's Monastery, Leith and Rehersal of Events . . . in the North of Scotland from 1635 to 1645 in relation to the National Covenant, ed. Rodgers, C. (Grampian Club, xiv, 1877).

History of the War in Ireland from 1641 to 1653 by a British Officer of the Regiment of Sir John Clotworthy, ed. Hogan, E. (Dublin, 1873).

Hope, T., *A diary of the public correspondence . . . 1633-45* (Bannatyne Club, lxxx, 1843).

Hyde, E., *The History of the Rebellion and Civil Wars in England*, 6 vols., ed. Macray, W. D. (Oxford, 1888).

Intelligence from the Scottish Army. Being the Extract of Letters sent to Master Bowles, dated April 14, 1644 (London, 1644).

Intelligence from the south borders of Scotland. Written from Edenburgh, April 24. 1644 (London, 1644).

The intention of the army of the kingdome of Scotland, Declared to their Brethern of England (Edinburgh, 1640).

'The Journal of John Aston, 1639', *North Country Diaries*, i, ed. Hodgson, J. C. (Surtees Soc., cxviii, 1910), 1-34.

The Journal of Thomas Cunningham of Campvere, ed. Courthope, E. J. (Scot. His. Soc., 3rd Ser., xi, 1928).

Journals of the House of Commons.

Journals of the House of Lords.

Kirkcudbright Town Council Records, 1606-1658, ii, eds. Stewart, J. and Armet, C. M. (Edinburgh, 1958).

A Large Relation of the Fight at Leith, Neere Edenburgh (London, 1650).

The Late Proceedings of the Scottish Army as also the taking of Cannow Froome (London, 1645).

A Letter Concerning the Souldiers and their Orders about the commissioners sent from the Parliament, to treat with the Kings Majesty (London, 1648).

A Letter from Edinburgh Concerning the difference of the Proceedings of the Well-affected in Scotland From the Proceedings of The Army in England (London, 1648).

A Letter of Great Consequences; sent by the Honorable Robert Lord Monro, out of the Kingdom of Ireland (London, 1643).

The Letter Books of Sir William Brereton, 31 January-29 May 1645, ed. Dore, R. N. (Rec. Soc. Lancs. and Cheshire, cxxiii, 1984).

The Letters and Journals of Robert Baillie, Principal of the University of Glasgow, 1637-1662, 3 vols., ed. Laing, D. (Bannatyne Club, lxxii, parts i-ii, lxxvii, 1841-2).

Letters and Papers Relating to the Irish Rebellion Between 1642-46, ed. Hogan, J. (Dublin, 1936).

Letters from the Head-Quarters of Our Army in Scotland: An Account of Col. Kerr and Staughan's Overture to the Lord Generall Cromwell (London, 1650).

Letters of Samuel Rutherford, ed. Bonar, A. (Edinburgh, 1891).

The Life of Mr. Robert Blair, Minister of St. Andrews, ed. McCrie, T. (Wodrow Soc., xiii, 1848).

A List of the Prisoners of war who are officers in commission, in custody of the marshall-general (London, 1651).

A List of the Several Regiments and Chief Officers of the Scottish Army quartered near Newcastle (London, 1644), s.s.

Lithgow, W., *A True Experimentall and Exact Relation upon that Famous and Renowned Siege of Newcastle* (Edinburgh, 1645).

Livingstone, J., *A Brief Historical Relation of the Life of Mr. John Livingstone*, ed. Houston, T. (Edinburgh, 1848).

The Marches of the Scots, under the Command of Lieut. Gen. Lesley (London, 1645).

The Melvilles of Melville and the Leslies Earls of Leven, 3 vols., ed. Fraser, W. (Edinburgh, 1890).

Memorials of Montrose and his Times, 2 vols., ed. Napier, M. (Maitland Club, lxvi, parts i and ii, 1848-50).

Memorials of the Family of Wemyss of Wemyss, 3 vols., ed. Fraser, W. (Edinburgh, 1888).

Memorials of the Great Civil War in England from 1646 to 1652, 2 vols., ed. Cary, H. (London, 1842).

The Memoirs of Henry Guthry, late bishop of Dunkeld, ed. Crawfurd, G. (Glasgow, 1748).

Memoirs of Scottish Catholics During the 17th and 18th centuries, 2 vols., Forbes-Leith, W. (London, 1909).

Mercurius Politicus, 1650.

Mercurius Scoticus, 1650.

Minute Book kept by the War Committee of the Covenanters in the Stewartry of Kirkcudbright in the Years 1640 and 1641, ed. Nicholson, J. (Kirkcudbright, 1840).

Minutes of the Synod of Argyll, i, 1639-1651, ed. MacTavish, D. C. (Scot. His. Soc., 3rd Ser., xxxvii, 1943).

Miscellany of the Scottish History Society, ii (Scot. His. Soc., 1st Ser., xxvii, 1904).

The Miscellany of the Spalding Club, iii, ed. Stuart, J. (Spalding Club, xvi, 1846).

Monteth, R., *The history of the Troubles of Great Britain . . . 1633-50*, trans. Ogilvie, J. (2nd trans. edn., London, 1738).

A More Perfect and Particular Relation of the Late Great Victorie in Scotland obtained over Montrose and the Rebels there (London, 1645).

Muniments of the Royal Burgh of Irvine, 3 vols., (Ayrs. and Galloway Arch. Assoc., 1890-1).

A New Declaration Setforth by the Lord Gen. Hamilton Wherein is declared, The full Resolution of the Officers and Soldiers in the Scottish Army (reprint edn., London, 1648).

Nicoll, J., *A Diary of Public Transactions and other occurences chiefly in Scotland from January 1650 to June 1667*, ed. Laing, D. (Bannatyne Club, lii, 1836).

O'Neill, H. M., 'A Journal of the Most Memorable Transactions of General Owen O'Neill and his party, from the year 1641 to the year 1650', *Desiderata Curiosa Hibernica: Or A Select Collection of State Papers, ii* (Dublin, 1772), 481-528.

Original Memoirs during the Civil War, ed. Scott, W. (Edinburgh, 1806).

Pike, R., *A True Relation of the proceedings of the Scots and English forces in the North of Ireland* (London, 1642).

The Presbytery Book of Kirkcaldie, ed. Stevenson, W. (Kirkcaldy, 1900).

The Records of Elgin, 1230-1800, 2 vols., eds. Cramond, W. and Ree, S. (New Spalding Club, xxvii, xxxv, 1903-8).

Records of Inverness, ii, eds. Mackay, W. and Laing, G. S. (New Spalding Club, xliii, 1924).

Records of the Kirk of Scotland, containing the acts and proceedings of the General Assemblies, from the year 1638 downwards, ed. Peterkin, A. (Edinburgh, 1838).

The Records of the Synod of Lothian and Tweeddale, 1589-1596, 1640-1649, ed. Kirk, J. (Stair Soc., xxx, 1977).

Register of the Privy Council of Scotland, 1603-43, 16 vols., eds. Mason, D., et. al. (Edinburgh, 1885-1906).

A Relation From the Right Honourable the Lord Viscount Conway, of the Proceedings of the English Army in Ulster from the seventeenth day of June to this present. 1642 (London, 1642).

Reprints of Rare Tracts Chiefly Illustrative of the History of the Northern Counties, 3 vols., ed. Richardson, M. A. (Newcastle, 1845-9).

Row, J., *The History of the Kirk of Scotland from the year 1558 to August 1637 with a Continuation by his son John Row* (Wodrow Soc., xxii, 1842).

Scotland and the Commonwealth, ed. Firth, C. H. (Scot. His. Soc., 1st Ser., xviii, 1895).

The Scotts of Buccleuch, 2 vols., ed. Fraser, W. (Edinburgh, 1878).

Selected Justiciary Cases, 1624-1650, ii-iii, ed. Gillon, S. A. (Stair Soc., xxvii-viii, 1972-4).

Selections from the minutes of the Presbyteries of St. Andrews and Cupar, 1641-48, ed. Kinloch, G. R. (Abbotsford Club, vii, 1837).

Selections from the Minutes of the Synod of Fife, 1611-87, ed. Kinloch, G. R. (Abbotsford Club, viii, 1837).

Selections from the Registers of the Presbytery of Lanark, 1623-1709, ed. Robertson, J. (Abbotsford Club, xvi, 1839).

The Session Book of Dundonald, 1602-1711, ed. Paton, H. (Edinburgh, 1936).

Somerville, J., *Memorie of the Somervilles*, 2 vols. (Edinburgh, 1715).

South Leith Records, ed. Robertson, D. (Edinburgh, 1911).

Spalding, J., *Memorialls of the Trubles in Scotland and England, 1624-1645*, 2 vols., ed. Stuart, J. (Spalding Club, xxi-ii, 1850-1).

Stewart, *A Full Relation of the Late Victory obtained (Through God's Providence)* (London, 1644).

The Sutherland Book, 3 vols., ed. Fraser, W. (Edinburgh, 1894).

Thomson, W., *Montrose Totally Routed at Tividale in Scotland* (London, 1645).

Three Letters Concerning the Surrender of many Scottish Lords to the High Sheriff of the county of Chester (London, 1648).

Thurloe, J., *A collection of papers, containing authentic memorials of English affairs, i, 1638-53* (London, 1742).

Tracts relating to the military proceedings in Lancashire during the Great Civil War, ed. Ormerod, G. (Chetham Soc., ii, 1844).

A True and Exact Relation of divers principall actions of a late Expedition in the north of Ireland, by the English and Scottish Forces (London, 1642).

A true relation of a second victorie over the Scots at Hamilton (London, 1650).

A True Relation of the Fight between Major-Gen. Lambert and the Scots army neer Appleby (London, 1648).

A true relation of the happy victory obtainted . . . upon April 27, 1650, against . . . James Grahame (Edinburgh, 1650).

A true relation of the proceedings of the Scottish army, from the 12th of March to the 25th (London, 1644).

A True Relation of the Proceedings of the Scottish Armie now in Ireland by Three Letters (London, 1642).

A True Relation of the routing of the Scottish army, near Dunbar, Sept. 3, instant (London, 1650).

Truths Discovery of A black Cloud in the North: Shewing Some Antiparliamentary, inhumane, cruell, and base proceedings of the Scotch Army (n.p., 1646).

Tullie, I., *A Narrative of the Siege of Carlisle in 1644 and 1645* (Carlisle, 1839).

Turner. J., *Memoirs of His Own Life and Times, 1632-1670*, ed. Thomson, T. (Bannatyne Club, xxviii, 1829).

Two Letters from Lieutenant General David Leslie to the Right Honourable the Commissioners of Scotland residing at London (London, 1646).

'Unpublished papers of John, seventh Lord Sinclair, Covenanter and Royalist', ed. Fairley, J. A., *Trans. Buchan Field Club*, viii (1904-5), 129-84.

Walker, E., *Historical Collections of Several Important Transactions relating to the late rebellion and civil wars of England* (London, 1707).

Walton, J., *The bloody battel at Preston in Lancashire* (London, 1648).

Wheatly, W., *A Declaration of the Scottish Armie concerning their immediate marching towards the borders of England* (London, 1647).

Wilson, J., *The History of Scottish affairs, particularly during the reign of Charles I* (Trans. Literary Antiq. Soc. Perth, i, 1827).

Wishart, G., *The compleat history of the warrs in Scotland under the conduct of . . . Montrose* (London, 1720).

Wishart, G., *The Memoirs of James, Marquis of Montrose, 1639-1650*, eds. Murdoch, A. D. and Simpson, H. F. M. (London, 1893).

Published Secondary Sources

Aiton, J., *The Life and Times of Alexander Henderson* (Edinburgh, 1836).

Barber, J., 'The Capture of the Covenanting Town of Dumfries by Montrose', *Dumfries and Galloway Nat. His. Antiq. Soc.*, xxi (1908-9), 26-42.

Broxap, E., *The Great Civil War in Lancashire 1642-51* (Manchester, 1910).

Buchan, J., *Montrose* (London, 1928).

Buchan, J., *Oliver Cromwell* (London, 1934).

Burne, A. H. *Battlefields of England* (London, 1950).

Campbell, A. H., 'Cromwell's Edinburgh Campaign', *Scots Mag.*, xviii (1933), 456-63.

Chambers, R., *History of the rebellions in Scotland . . . from 1638 till 1660*, 2 vols. (Edinburgh, 1828).

Corsar, K. C., 'David Leslie's defence of Edinburgh, July-August 1650', *Journ. Soc. Army Hist. Research*, xxv (1947), 96-105.

Corsar, K. C., 'The surrender of Edinburgh Castle, December 1650', *Scot. Hist. Rev.*, xxviii (1949), 43-54.

Cowan, E. J. *Montrose: for Covenant and King* (London, 1977).

The Dictionary of National Biography, xvii, eds. Stephen, L. and Lee, S. (reprint edn., Oxford, 1950).

Douglas, W. S., *Cromwell's Scotch Campaigns: 1650-51* (London, 1898).

Dow, F., *Cromwellian Scotland* (Edinburgh, 1979).

Eyre-Todd, G., *The Highland Clans of Scotland* (London, 1923).

Fasti Ecclesiae Scoticanae: The Succession of ministers in the Church of Scotland from the Reformation, 8 vols., ed. Scott, H. (Edinburgh, 1915-50).

Firth, C. H., 'The Battle of Dunbar', *Trans. Roy. Hist. Soc.*, 2nd Ser., xiv (1900), 19-52.

Firth, C. H., 'The Battle of Marston Moor', *Trans. Roy. Hist. Soc.*, 2nd Ser., xii (1898), 17-19.

Firth, C. H., *Cromwell's Army* (London, 1962).

Foster, J., *Members of Parliament, Scotland 1357-1882* (2nd edn., London, 1882).

Fraser, A., *The Frasers of Phillorth*, 3 vols. (Edinburgh, 1879).

Gardiner, S. R., *History of the Commonwealth and Protectorate, 1649-1653*, i-ii (3rd edn., New York, 1965).

Gardiner, S. R., *History of the Great Civil War, 1642-1649*, 4 vols. (new edn., London, 1894).

Gordon, R. and Gordon, G., *A Geneaological History of the Earldom of Sutherland* (Edinburgh, 1813).

Gordon, W., *The History of the . . . Family of Gordon*, 2 vols. (Edinburgh, 1727).

Grant, I. F., *The Macleods* (London, 1959).

Hay, R. A., *Geneaologie of the Hayes of Tweeddale* (Edinburgh, 1835).

Hayes-McCoy, G. A., *Irish Battles: a military history of Ireland* (London, 1969).

Hazlett, H., 'The Recruitment and Organisation of the Scottish Army in Ulster, 1642-9', *Essays in British and Irish History in Honour of James Eadie Todd*, eds. Crome, H. A., Moody, T. W. and Quinn, D. B. (London, 1969).

Hewison, J. K., *The Covenanters*, 2 vols. (Glasgow, 1913).

Hill, G., *An historical account of the Macdonnells of Antrim* (Belfast, 1873).

Howie, J., *Biographia Scoticana*, ed. MacGavin, W. (reprint edn., Glasgow, 1828).

Jones, G. F. T., 'The Payment of Arrears to the Army of the Covenant', *Eng. Hist. Rev.*, lxxiii (1958), 459-65.

Kennedy, J. W., 'The Teviotdale Regiment', *Hawick Arch. Soc.*, xxxv (1903), 57-64.

Kishlansky, M., 'The Case of the Army Truly Stated: The Creation of the New Model Army', *Past and Present*, lxxi (1978), 51-74.

Lane, J., *The Reign of King Covenant* (London, 1956).

Lawson, C. C. P., *A history of the uniforms of the British army*, 2 vols. (London, 1940).

Liddell, R. H. R., 'Saint Madoes and its clergymen: notes on a Perthshire parish, 1640-88', *Scot. Hist. Rev.*, xxv (1928), 255-69.

Lilley, P. W., 'Rev. John Livingston, covenanter and scholar, minister of Ancrum, 1648-62', *Hawick Arch. Soc.*, lxvi (1934), 49-51.

McConnell, J. and McConnell, S., *Fasti of the Irish Presbyterian Church, 1613-1840*, ed. Paul, F. J. (Belfast, 1951).

MacDonald, A. and MacDonald, A., *The Clan Donald* (Inverness, 1904).

MacGregor, A. G. M., *History of the Clan MacGregor*, 2 vols. (Edinburgh, 1898).

Mackay, W., *Urquhart and Glenmoriston* (Inverness, 1893).

Mackenzie, A., *History of Clan Mackenzie* (Inverness, 1879).

Mackenzie, A., *History of the Frasers of Lovat* (Inverness, 1896).

Mackenzie, W., *History of Galloway* (Kircudbright, 1841).

Mackinnon, D., *The Clan Ross* (Edinburgh, 1957).

Mackinnon, D., *Origin and Services of the Coldstream Guards*, 2 vols. (London, 1833).

MacNeil, R. L., *The Clan MacNeil* (New York, 1923).

Macrae, A., *History of Clan Macrae* (Dingwall, 1899).

Makey, W., *The Church of the Covenant 1637-1651* (Edinburgh, 1979).

Mathieson, W. L., *Politics and Religion. A study in Scottish history from the Reformation to the Revolution*, 2 vols. (Glasgow, 1902).

Maxwell, A., *The history of old Dundee* (Edinburgh, 1884).

Metcalfe, W. M., *A History of the county of Renfrew from the earliest times* (New Club, xiii, 1905).

Metcalfe, W. M., *A History of Paisley, 600-1908* (Paisley, 1909).

Munro, R. W., *Kinsmen and Clansmen* (Edinburgh, 1971).

Newman, P. R., *Marston Moor, 2nd July, 1644* (York, 1978).

Ogilvie, J. D., 'Bishop's Wars', *Glasgow Bibliog. Soc. Rec.*, xii (1938), 21-40.

Ó Tuathaigh Ghilleenn, 'The Battle of Benburb', *Ulster Journ. Arch.*, xvi (1911), 78-89, 140-52.

Paterson, J., *History of the county of Ayr*, 2 vols. (Edinburgh, 1847).

Paul, J. E., *Scots Peerage*, 9 vols. (Edinburgh, 1909-14).

Perceval-Maxwell, M. 'The Adoption of the Solemn League and Covenant by the Scots in Ulster', *Scotia*, ii (1978), 3-18.

Reid, S., 'Aberdeen, 14th May 1646', *English Civil War Notes and Querries*, viii.

Reid, S., *Scots Armies of the Civil War 1639-1651* (Norwich, 1982).

Roberts, M., *Gustavus Adolphus. A History of Sweden 1611-1632*, 2 vols. (London, 1958).

Roberts, M., *The Military Revolution, 1560-1660* (Belfast, 1958).

Russell, *Life of Oliver Cromwell*, 2 vols. (Edinburgh, 1829).

Sherwood, R. E., *Civil Strife in the Midlands 1642-1651* (London, 1974).

Sinclair, A. M., *The Clan Gillean* (Charlottetown, 1899).

[Sinclair, J. C.], *An historical and genealogical account of the clan Maclean* (London, 1838).

Small, R., 'Town and Parish of Dundee', *The Statistical Account of Scotland*, ed. Sinclair, J. (new edn., Wakefield, 1976), xiii, 140-98.

Stevenson, D., *Alasdair MacColla and the Highland Problem in the 17th Century* (Edinburgh, 1980).

Stevenson, D., 'The Battle of Mauchline Moor 1648', *Ayrshire Collections*, xi (1973), 3-24.

Stevenson, D., 'The Massacre at Dunaverty, 1647', *Scot. Stud.*, xix (1975), 27-37.

Stevenson, D., *Revolution and Counter-Revolution in Scotland, 1644-1651* (London, 1977).

Stevenson, D., *Scottish Covenanters and Irish Covenanters* (Belfast, 1981).

Stevenson, D., *The Scottish Revolution 1637-1644* (Newton Abbot, 1973).

Terry, C. S., 'Free quarters in Linlithgow, 1642-47', *Scot. Hist. Rev.*, xiv (1916), 75-80.

Terry, C. S., *The Life and Campaigns of Alexander Leslie, first earl of Leven* (London, 1899).

Terry, C. S., 'The Scottish Campaigns in Northumberland . . . 1644', *Arch. Aeliana*, 2nd Ser., xxi (1899), 146-79.

Terry, C. S., 'The siege of Newcastle-upon-Tyne by the Scots in 1644', *Arch. Aeliana*, 2nd Ser., xxi (1899), 180-258.

Wedgwood, C. V., *The King's Peace 1637-1641* (paperback edn., London, 1973).

Wedgwood, C. V., *The King's War 1641-1647* (paperback edn., London, 1966).

Wenham, L. P., *The Great and Close Siege of York, 1644* (Kineton, 1970).

Wijns, J. W., 'Military forces and Warfare', *New Cambridge Modern History, iv, The Decline of Spain and the Thirty Years War (1609-1648/59)*, ed. Copper, J. P. (Cambridge, 1970), 202-25.

Willcock, J., *The Great Marquess, Life and times of Archibald 8th Earl and 1st Marquess of Argyll* (London, 1903).

Willis-Bund, J. W., *The Civil War in Worcestershire, 1642-1646; and the Scotch Invasion of 1651* (Birmingham, 1905).

Woolrych, A., *Battles of the English Civil War* (paperback edn., London, 1966).

Young, P. and Holmes, R., *The English Civil War: A Military History, The Three Civil Wars 1642-1651* (London, 1974).

Young, P., *Marston Moor 1644. The Campaign and the Battle* (Kineton, 1970).

Unpublished Secondary Sources

Bensen, R. A., 'South-West Fife and the Scottish Revolution: the presbytery of Dunfermline, 1633-52' (Edinburgh Univ., M.Litt. thesis 1978).

Boyd, H., 'The History of Coleraine from the Londoner's Plantation to the Restoration' (Queen's Univ., Belfast, M.A. thesis 1932).

Buchanan, J. N., 'Charles I and the Scots, 1637-49' (Toronto Univ., Ph.d. thesis, 1965).

Furgol, E. M., 'Religious Aspects of the Scottish Covenanting Armies, 1639-1651' (Oxford Univ., D.Phil. thesis 1983).

Makey, W., 'Ministers in Scottish parishes, 1648' (a list of the ministers with biographical data kindly loaned to me by the author).

Shepherd, W. S., 'The Politics and Society of Glasgow 1648-74' (Glasgow Univ., Ph.d. thesis 1978).

Index

437

Brymer's F AC, 302
Bryson, James, lieutenant colonel Ministers' F ASLC, 170, 171
Buccleuch, earl of, *see* Scott, Francis
Buccleuch's Retinue WR, 292-3; F AC, 293
Buchan, 30, 34-5, 67, 208, 232, 233, 234
Buchan, earl of, *see* Erskine, James
Buchan's HT EA, 269
Buchanan House, 206
Buchanan of Auchmaur, Patrick, company HA, 206
Buchanan of Buchanan, Sir George, 201; colonel F AFBW, 19; colonel F HA, 205-6; colonel F AC, 303
Buchanan's F AFBW, 19; F HA, 90, 205-6; F AC 303, 323, 385
Buchanty, Hill of, 226
Buckingham, duke of, *see*, Villiers, George
Buckingham's HT AK, 363-64
Burleigh, Lord, *see* Balfour, Robert
Burleigh's regiment ASBW, 43; F AC, 303-4
Burne, John, major Tweeddale F ASLC, 182
Burnet of Craigmill, 168
Burnet of Leys, 168, 390
Burntisland, 3, 12, 213-4, 297, 306, 311, 315, 330, 344, 349, 364, 421, 423, 424
Burntisland Defence Regiment AK, 364-65
Burton, Captain –, governor Thirwell Castle ASLC, 186
Bute, 304, 349, 385, 392, 416
Butler, James, 13th earl, 1st marquis and 1st duke of Ormond, 71, 94, 96, 369, 408
Byron, John, Lord Byron, commander English royalist army, 278
Byron, Lord, *see* Byron, John
Bywell Peter, 122, 133, 152

Caerlaverock Castle, 5, 34, 46, 154, 405
Cairnbulg House, 217
Caithness, 1; in 1640-2, 68; in 1643-7, 239, 347; in 1648-51, 249, 265, 282, 327-28, 332, 339, 350-51, 365, 393, 422, 425; Sutherland's portion, 146
Caithness' F AK, 365
Calder's retine AFBW, 19

Calderwood, William, chaplain Midlothian F ASLC, 168; same Niddrie's F ASLC, 172
Calhoun, –, routmaster Lanark's H ASLC, 154-55; cornet Dalhousie's H ASLC, 134, 139
Callander, 201; battle of, 197, 204, 230, 415
Callendar, earl of, *see*, Livingstone, James
Callendar House, 423, 424
Callendar's F ASLC, 119-22; Life Guard of H ASLC, 122; F EA, 269-71
Cambismoir Castle, 201
Cameron, Neill, chaplain Ardkinglas' Highland F NMA, 245
Cameron of Lochiel, Allan, colonel Clan Cameron ASBW, 44
Cameron of Lochiel, Sir Ewan, colonel F AK, 383
Camerons, 2, 41, 44
Campbell, Archibald, 8th earl and 1st marquis of Argyll, 1, 46, 63, 111, 112, 144, 176, 234, 257, 258, 309, 313, 323, 327, 385, 407, 425; colonel regiments AFBW, 16-17, 19, 28; colonel F regiments ASBW, 5, 40-1, 42, 44, 53, 62, 404-5; colonel F UA, 80-2; colonel regiment ASLC, 110; colonel regiments HA, 198-201; spring campaign 1644, 89, 99-100, 111, 112, 176, 195, 199, 204, 209, 212, 213, 216-20 passim, 222, 224, 225, 227, 229-30, 231, 233, 234, 238, 239, 241, 408-9; summer campaign 1644, 196, 198, 199, 220, 410; autumn campaign 1644, 100-1, 111, 112, 129, 146, 147, 178, 196, 199-200, 206, 210, 214, 217, 219, 221, 225, 228, 230, 411; Inverlochy campaign, 144, 200-1, 207, 209, 226, 235, 236, 412; at Kilsyth, 201; colonel Highland F NMA, 246-8, 292; leader WR, 6, 247, 292; ships, 16, 173, 285
Campbell, Archibald, Lord Lorne and 9th earl of Argyll, colonel His Majesty's Life Guard of F AC, 11, 317-19
Campbell, Archibald, Tutor of Craignish or Barrichbeyan, 207-8

Campbell, Archibald, provost of Kilmun, 207; co-commander Argyll's Life Guard of F ASLC, 112
Campbell, Archibald, captain Lawers' F UA, 90; routmaster Argyll's Life Guard of H ASLC, 110-11
Campbell, Colin, lieutenant colonel and major Lawers' F UA, 88, 93; colonel D AC, 304
Campbell, Colin, chaplain Perthshire (Gask's-Tullibardine's) F ASLC, 175; same Dalyell's F AK, 368
Campbell, David, chaplain Carnegie's F ASBW, 44; same Angus F ASLC, 108; same Edzell's F AC, 308; same Leven's H AC, 334
Campbell, Donald, chaplain Argyll's F ASBW, 40
Campbell, Dugald, chaplain Argyll's AFBW, 16; chaplain Argyll's F UA, 80
Campbell, Duncan, major Perthshire (Gask's-Tullibardine's F ASLC, 175
Campbell, George, tutor of Calder, 81, 112
Campbell, James, Lord Mauchline, colonel H AC, 331, 338-39, 344, 374
Campbell, James, chaplain Ministers' F ASLC, 170; same Strathearn F ASLC, 180
Campbell, Sir John, 2nd Lord and 1st earl of Loudoun, 339, 362; colonel regiment AFBW, 29; colonel F ASBW, 40, 60; colonel Loudoun-Glasgow F ASLC, 113, 162-64; commander WR, 293, 294-5; commander HT AC, 336-37
Campbell, John, captain HT UA and captain Argyll's F UA, 84; captain Argyll's Highland F HA, 202
Campbell, Matthew, captain of Skipness Castle, captain Argyll's F UA, 82, 416; major Argyll's Highland F NMA, 246
Campbell, Ninian, chaplain Loudoun-Glasgow F ASLC, 162
Campbell, Robert, chaplain Perthshire (Gask's-Tullibardine's) F ASLC, 175; same Glen-